MICROPROCESSORS
A PROGRAMMER'S VIEW

MICROPROCESSORS
A PROGRAMMER'S VIEW

Robert B. K. Dewar
Matthew Smosna

Computer Science Department
Courant Institute, New York University

McGraw-Hill Publishing Company

New York   St. Louis   San Francisco   Auckland   Bogotá   Caracas   Hamburg
Lisbon   London   Madrid   Mexico   Milan   Montreal   New Delhi
Oklahoma City   Paris   San Juan   São Paulo   Singapore   Sydney   Tokyo   Toronto

MICROPROCESSORS: A PROGRAMMER'S VIEW

1 2 3 4 5 6 7 8 9 0 DOC DOC 9 5 4 3 2 1 0

ISBN 0-07-016638-2 {SOFT}

ISBN 0-07-016639-0 {HARD}

This book was set in Adobe Garamond and Helvetica by the authors using Xerox Ventura Publisher, Adobe Illustrator, and Corel Draw.
The editor was David M. Shapiro.
R. R. Donnelley & Sons Company was printer and binder.

Library of Congress Cataloging-in-Publication Data

Dewar, Robert B. K.
    Microprocessors: A Programmer's View / Robert B. K. Dewar,
Matthew Smosna
        p.   cm.
    Includes bibliographical references.
    ISBN 0-07-016638-2.—ISBN 0-07-016639-0 (hard)
     1. Microprocessors—Programming.   I. Smosna, Matthew.
II. Title.
QA76.6.D515   1990
005.26—dc20   89-77320

To my parents,
Michael and Mary Dewar

To my father,
Stanislaw Smosna

ABOUT THE AUTHORS

Robert B. K. Dewar is a Professor of Computer Science and past chair of the department at Courant Institute of Mathematical Sciences at New York University. He has been involved with computers for over twenty-five years and has written major software systems including real-time operating systems for Honeywell on early micro-processors and a series of compilers. The SPITBOL compiler, which he originally wrote nearly twenty years ago for mainframe computers, has now been ported to most major microprocessors, including most recently the SPARC. He wrote the back end and run-time library for the Realia COBOL compiler for the IBM PC, and more recently has been involved with the Ada language, for which he was one of the language reviewers. He has also been involved in the design and implementation of the Alsys Ada compilers for the IBM PC and other microprocessors.

Matthew Smosna is a Research Scientist at the Courant Institute of Mathematical Sciences at New York University. He has worked on several implementations of the SETL system (SETL is a set theoretic language developed at NYU), and is currently involved in the implementation of a new Ada compiler for the IBM RP3 (an experimental parallel processor). His main field of research is compiler technology, with an emphasis on code generation techniques. He has taught graduate and undergraduate compiler courses at several universities, including NYU, and is currently writing a textbook on compiler design, based on the class notes, for McGraw-Hill.

CONTENTS

Chapter 4 Tasking, Virtual Memory, and Exceptions on the 80386   103

Chapter 5 Microprocessors and Floating-Point Arithmetic   135

PREFACE

The introduction of microprocessors some ten years ago was an important milestone in the use of computers. The early microcomputers had limited power, but there are many tasks which are satisfied by this limited power such as control of washing machines, automobile ignition systems, and computer games. As a result, the average house is likely to have dozens of devices that would be regarded as powerful computers by the standards of the early developers in the field.

More recently, the technology has advanced to the point where microprocessors have achieved very substantial computing power, challenging much larger systems, and this book examines and compares these powerful microprocessor architectures. What we attempt to do in writing this book is to look at these processors from a software point of view. You will find few schematic diagrams in the book, since we are not interested in the hardware level design. You will, on the other hand, find many assembly language programming examples, showing the significance of the architectural variations between the processors we examine.

The challenge of describing what a programmer needs to know about the architectural features of microprocessors has been made even more difficult, but also more entertaining, by a basic split in the architectural philosophies influencing microprocessor design. Until recently, microprocessor development has shown a trend to ever more complex hardware, including specialized features intended to support the use of high-level languages and operating systems. As VLSI techniques have allowed architects to pack more transistors on a chip, they have been able to produce microprocessors with capabilities going well beyond the mainframes of only a decade ago.

In a recent sharp reaction to this trend, a number of designers have proposed, designed and implemented a class of processors known as RISC processors, or *Reduced Instruction Set Computers*. Reduced instruction set computers are streamlined processors with a simplified instruction set. This simplified instruction set allows a hardware designer to use specialized techniques to increase the performance of a machine in a manner that is peculiar to these architectures. The RISC view is basically that more is *not* better if the efficiency cost is too high.

Mainstream architectural designs have been dubbed CISC, for *Complex Instruction Set Computers*, by RISC proponents. The implicit criticism in this acronym suggests that these processors are much too complicated. Some advocates of CISC designs have retorted that the term CISC should be taken to refer to *Complete Instruction Set Computers*. It all depends on the point of view.

In this book, we examine most of the important microprocessors, including both representative RISC and CISC processors. We certainly don't attempt to describe every feature of every processor in complete detail—the book would be too heavy to carry around if we did—but we do attempt to cover the most interesting points, and the RISC vs CISC debate is a unifying theme that runs through the book. The importance of RISC processors is well established—Wall Street is almost as familiar with the term as the computer science establishment. In this book we attempt to provide a perspective on the issues and to give a basis for looking into the future to see where this design controversy might lead.

The text is based on a "special topics" graduate course taught at New York University in the spring semester of 1989 by Robert B. K. Dewar. Matthew Smosna began taping the lectures, transcribing and typesetting them, and finally organized the notes in the first version of this book. With the help of our reviewers' comments, we then made several passes through that version, making many technical corrections and additions—the result is the book that you are now reading.

Selected chapters of the text were read by several of our friends and colleagues at New York University, including Fritz Henglein (now at Rijksuniversiteit Utrecht); Yvon Kermarrek, New York University; Cecilia Panicali, New York University and Jay Vandekopple, Marymount College. Jim Demmel, New York University, reviewed Chapter 5. Stephen P. Morse, the principle designer of the 8086, helped by telling the inside story of the design of this processor. Dan Prener, IBM Research, helped us to better understand the RIOS. Marc Auslander and Peter Oden, also of IBM Research, shared their recollections of the 801 Project. Our special thanks go to Richard Kenner and Ed Schonberg, both of New York University, who read the whole manuscript, and in some cases read some chapters several times.

We would also like to thank our official reviewers: John Hennessy, Stanford University; Kevin Kitagawa, Sun Microsystems; Daniel Tabak, George Mason University; and Safwat G. Zaky, University of Toronto.

Our proximity to McGraw-Hill in New York City led us to come in unusually close contact with several members of the McGraw-Hill staff. Our sponsoring editor, David Shapiro, provided an enormous amount of daily support. Joe Murphy, senior editing manager, assisted the authors in the art of book design, which was done entirely by the authors using desktop publishing on Compaq PC's—we don't just talk about microprocessors! Jo Satloff, our copy editor, did a wonderful job editing what was at times a very rough manuscript. Ingrid Reslmaier, editorial assistant, helped with a multitude of miscellaneous tasks and telephone calls.

Finally, in the best tradition of book authors, we wish to thank our wives Karin and Liz for putting up with us and providing invaluable support during the very busy year of 1989, during which we prepared this book.

Robert B.K. Dewar
Matthew Smosna

CHAPTER

1

MICROPROCESSORS

Microprocessors have revolutionized the use of computers at all levels of society. We are rapidly reaching the point where every kitchen appliance and every child's toy will contain a fairly sophisticated processor. In recent years, microprocessor technology has advanced to the point that performance levels rivalling those of mainframes can be achieved. This book addresses the subject of these high-end microprocessors.

Two important events led to the greatly increased usage of microprocessors. First, the introduction of the IBM PC led to the widespread use of personal computers based on the Intel series of microprocessors. Second, a number of companies, including Sun and Apollo, marketed workstations based on the Motorola microprocessors. This popularized the notion in engineering circles that it was often more effective to have a reasonably powerful workstation on your desk than a small share of a powerful mainframe.

It looked for a while as though the microprocessor products of Intel and Motorola would dominate the marketplace in high performance personal computers and workstations. However, requirements for ever increasing performance, particularly for engineering workstations, combined with continuing work in design and implementation of microprocessor architectures, has recently lead to an explosion of alternative architectures.

These alternative architectures are based on new concepts of microprocessor design, collectively referred to as *reduced instruction set computers* (RISC). In the past, large instruction sets were generally considered an advantage—manufacturers would proudly advertise "over 200 distinct instructions" in their glossy brochures. RISC advocates have turned this idea on its head by proclaiming that when it comes to microprocessor instruction design, "less is more."

The idea behind the RISC architectural philosophy is that by simplifying and reducing instruction sets by eliminating all non-essential instructions, the remaining instructions can be made to run very much faster. By non-essential instructions we mean those executed so infrequently that replacing them with sequences of simpler instructions does not have any noticeable impact on efficiency. The fundamental observation that inspired the original RISC research was that only a small part of the instruction set of most other processors were commonly executed—a large number of instructions were executed rather infrequently.

The existing philosophy, which has recently been described as *Complex Instruction Set Computers* (CISC) in a somewhat derisive fashion, is by no means dead, and indeed virtually all personal computers, including those made by IBM, Apple, Atari, Commodore and Amiga, still use CISC chips. When it comes to workstations, RISC chips are making significant inroads, although many workstations are still powered by CISC chips.

The continuing controversy between the CISC and RISC camps is a fierce one. A recent New York Times article describing a conference on the West Coast sounded more like coverage of a boxing match than a scientific meeting. The winner in the judgment of the reporter was RISC, but certainly not by a knockout.[1]

In this book we look at a number of representative CISC and RISC microprocessor designs, as well as some which do not clearly fall into either category—the line between the two philosophies is not always completely clear from a technical point of view. Our intention is to understand the strengths and weaknesses of the two approaches, and to begin to guess how the argument will eventually be settled.

WHAT IS A MICROPROCESSOR?

One of the distinguishing characteristics of the microprocessor is that it is usually implemented in VLSI. This means that, unlike minicomputers and mainframes, the complete machinery of the computer is present on a single chip, or possibly a very small number of chips. Floating-point operations, for example, are often implemented using a separate *coprocessor* chip.

As the architectural features of microprocessors have become more sophisticated, they have become less distinctive as a separate category of machine. With the most advanced microprocessors now being used in workstations, the gap between minicomputer and microcomputer has become somewhat blurred, at least from a programmer's point of view.

---

[1] "Computer Chip Starts Angry Debate," *New York Times*, September 17, 1989.

Another important characteristic of microprocessors is that they are relatively inexpensive commodity items. They can be bought off the shelf—the price range is typically $5 to $800—and computers are then built around the microprocessors by second-party manufacturers. Unlike the IBM 370, where the processor is simply one inseparable part of a complete computer system, the microprocessor is a separate chip that appears in many different hardware environments. For instance, the Intel 8088 chip is used in IBM PCs, but it also turns up as the controller chip for advanced automobile ignition systems. Very few computers using the Intel 8088 are manfactured by Intel, and indeed Intel is not really in the business of manufacturing computers.

One consequence of this approach is that there is no such thing as *the* Intel 8088 computer or *the* Motorola 68030 computer. In both cases, and in the case of most of the other microprocessors we will look at in this book, there are a great variety of computers using these chips, and two computers using the same chip may be quite incompatible in many respects. While they may share the same basic instruction set, such issues as memory access, input/output devices, and even the way floating-point computations are performed may vary from one computer to another.

The actual cost of producing a microprocessor is very small, probably just a few dollars. Of course, this figure does not take into account the fact that designing a new microprocessor may cost tens of millions of dollars, which must be recovered in the selling price. However, it does mean that in applications where sufficient numbers of chips can be sold it becomes feasible to mass produce what are in effect extremely sophisticated computers at remarkably low prices. These chips appear not only in automobile ignition systems, but in microwave ovens, washing machines, televisions, and many other items usually not thought of as requiring the power of a computer.

An interesting application for the near future is in high-definition television (HDTV). HDTV requires sophisticated real-time data compression and decompression algorithms, which need powerful processing capabilities. Within a few years, every living room will probably have more processing power available than the typical large computer center of a few years past. The microprocessor makes a commitment to such large-scale computing practical.

The User-Level View of a Microprocessor

When experienced programmers open up a manual describing a new microprocessor for the very first time, there are certain questions that they have learned to ask. What is the register structure like? What data types are supported by the machine? Are there any interesting or unusual instructions? Does it support tasking or virtual memory? How are interrupts handled? In the first chapter of this book, we will cover some of these general issues to set the scene for looking at individual designs.

Three common places to jump in and look at a new microprocessor are the register set, the instruction set, and the addressing modes. These aspects of a computer architecture are particularly important to assembly language programmers and compiler writers, who must understand this part of the processor perfectly in order to take advantage of the machine. Ideally, high-level language programmers need to know nothing about the inner workings of a processor for which their programs are compiled.

To a large extent this is true in practice—a C programmer can move C programs from one processor to another without knowing details of the different architectures. However, it is often useful to know what's going on, especially when things go wrong. It's much the same situation as driving a car—it is possible to switch from driving one car to another without being a mechanic, but if the engine suddenly conks out, it is useful to be able to look under the hood and know what is there and how it works. In that spirit, we hope to be able to provide a description of microprocessor architectures which will allow you to judge the impact of the instruction set, addressing modes, and many aspects of the hardware that influence how software is written for these machines.

The System-Level View of a Microprocessor

In addition to the user or applications view of a microprocessor, an operating system designer must understand those features of the processor that are intended for implementing system tasks, including

- Tasking and process management.
- Memory management and cache control.
- Exceptions (traps and interrupts).
- Coprocessor and floating-point unit support.

These are the basic issues we will look at as we examine several microprocessors from the point of view of someone designing a complete system.

The issues of tasking and process management have to do with the support provided in the hardware that allows two or more tasks with separate threads of control to execute on the processor as if each of them were executing simultaneously. Since a single processor can execute only one task at a time, this is achieved by allowing each task to control the processor for a few cycles, with the operating system switching between the different tasks so that they seem to be executing at the same time.

Memory management and cache control both have to do with how an operating system controls a task's use of memory. Most microprocessors have hardware support for *virtual memory*, allowing a task's addressable memory to be larger than the real memory on a machine, as well as allowing several tasks to share that memory. Caches are small (but fast) memories that hold copies of the data in the most frequently used memory locations.

Exceptions are events that cause the normal execution of a program to be interrupted. They can occur due to an internal event such as an attempt to divide by zero (a trap), or due to an external event such as a keyboard stroke (an interrupt).

Finally, floating-point support is provided by almost all microprocessors, either on the chip itself or using a separate coprocessor chip. The ability to perform floating-point computations in hardware is particularly important given the fact that microprocessors are commonly used to build workstations for scientific and engineering use.

For each microprocessor, we will describe how these features are supported and the great variety of approaches used in the design of these processors.

CISC and RISC Microprocessors

A question which is commonly asked by both applications programmers and operatings system designers is: To what extent does the processor provide specialized instructions that aid in solving the problem at hand? RISC designs generally provide only a minimal set of instructions from which more complex instructions can be constructed. On CISC processors we often find elaborate instructions intended to simplify programming of frequently occurring specialized operations.

The basic CISC philosophy is to provide an extensive set of instructions covering all sorts of special-purpose needs. In this approach, the cost of these extra instructions seems minimal—"You don't have to use them if you don't need them." The contrasting RISC attitude is that these fancy instructions are not really used often enough to justify the extra complexity in implementing the hardware and that this complexity tends to slow down the more commonly executed instructions.

In practice, the dividing line is not so clear. For example, floating-point division is an extremely complicated operation that, like other complicated operations, can be programmed using simpler instructions. However, nearly all RISC processors include a floating-point division because in this particular case it seems that the complicated instruction *is* used often enough to justify its inclusion. On the other hand, the more sophisticated system-level instructions appearing on some CISC processors, such as those that handle tasking, do not seem to be important enough to be universally included in RISC designs.

REGISTERS, ADDRESSING, AND INSTRUCTION FORMATS

Two of the major issues in the design of an architecture are the register structure of the machine and the set of addressing modes provided by the hardware. Deciding on the structure of the register set generally involves deciding how many registers a processor should have, and the degree to which any or all of the registers should have specialized functions. The latter issue is that of *register uniformity*, that is, to what extent is one register similar or identical to another register. In the design of a set of addressing modes, the designer must decide which particular addressing modes will be useful, and how they will be specified in the instruction.

Along with the design of the instruction set, both of these issues have a significant impact on the final design of the *instruction formats* of a machine, that is, the exact way in which all of the bits are laid out for each instruction in an instruction set, and their intended use. Some of the bits in an instruction must be used to define the opcode. Other bits are used to define the registers or the memory addresses or both that participate in the operation. Another set of bits must be used to specify the addressing modes. For example, when a machine allows *direct addressing*, that is, the ability to directly reference a memory location as an operand, space must be allocated so that the bit pattern that defines the memory address can be fit into the instruction format. We will begin by looking at some of the issues involved in the design of register sets and addressing modes and their impact on the final instruction format of a machine.

Register Sets

The number of registers which are to be included on a machine is a fundamental parameter that has a significant effect on the instruction formats of a processor. The trade-off is very simple: the more registers there are, the more bits are required in the instruction format to reference those registers. For example, on a machine with 32 general-purpose registers, 5 bits in an instruction will be used up each time a register appears as part of the instruction. If a designer wishes to allow register-to-register operations in which some operation is applied to two registers and the result is placed in a third register, then a 16-bit instruction format cannot be used because 15 of the 16 bits would be taken up, leaving only a single bit for the opcode—there is no hope of being able to fit three of these register operands into a 16-bit instruction format.

The issue of keeping instructions short is one that often comes up. Many of the CISC designs date from the days when memory was relatively expensive and code density (the number of bytes required to program a given function) was an important consideration. Another factor favoring compact instructions was the concern with execution speed. Instructions must be loaded from memory into the processor to be executed—the more bytes that are needed for the instructions, the more time this takes.

In RISC designs, there is much less concern over instruction density. In the first place, memory is now cheaper, and we are no longer horrified by programs that occupy several megabytes of code. Second, modern architectural techniques, including instruction lookahead and caching, have reduced the penalty for loading longer instructions, so it now is feasible to have larger numbers of registers than were previously practical.

Although keeping data in registers generally speeds up processing considerably, the point of diminishing returns is reached fairly rapidly. If one plots the speed of a program against the number of registers which are available, the curve flattens out, that is, after a while a compiler cannot make use of more registers. It seems to be generally agreed that no more than 32 registers are needed at any one point. Also, having a large number of registers is not without some cost, since at least some of them will have to be stored when the processor switches from one task to the next.

The other fundamental issue in the design of a register set is that of register uniformity. The term *general register* was first used in conjunction with the IBM 360 architecture, referring to a registers that can all be used in identical ways.

Why don't all machines have uniform register sets? The main reason is that it is tempting to design instructions in which certain registers have been designated for special purposes. By doing so, it becomes unnecessary to allocate space in the instruction for the register—the use of that register is implied in the instruction. For example, the XLAT instruction on the 386 (used for translating character sets), assumes that one particular register (EBX) points to a translation table and that another particular register (AL) contains the character to be translated. XLAT is only 1 byte long. If it had been designed so that both registers needed to be specified explicitly, it would have needed more bytes. Since code density was a major design point for the 8086, an ancestor of the 386, this lack of uniformity seems like a reasonable trade-off.

Even RISC processors occasionally break the tradition of register uniformity under the same pressures. For example, most RISC processors have a procedure call instruction that stores the return point into one specially designated register. Why choose a particular register to store the return point? In a standard RISC processor with a 32-bit instruction format and a 32-bit address space, it is desirable to have a call instruction have the largest possible range of addressability. Using a dedicated register to hold the return address frees up almost all of the 32 bits in the instruction format to hold the address—allowing different registers to be specified would reduce the range of addressability by 5 bits (for a 32-register machine).

Non-uniform registers are a particular menace to compiler writers. In writing the code generator for a compiler, you want to be able to treat the set of registers as a pool of interchangeable resources. Compilers typically are written so that there is a routine whose responsiblity is to allocate registers. It is much easier to write this routine in a compiler if the compiler does not need to deal with requests such as: "I need a register, but it has to be either special register SI or DI—none of the others will do." If every instruction has its own idiosyncratic set of register requirements, then the problem of allocating register use in an optimal manner becomes very much more complicated, and typically the result is that it simply isn't attempted.

Addressing Modes

In choosing a set of addressing modes the issues of complexity versus utility arise just as in the case of register size. As we shall see in a later section of this chapter that describes the relationship between high-level programming languages and addressing modes, the CISC tradition has been to include increasingly complex addressing modes that directly support the use of high-level languages. For example, a compiler writer will recognize one addressing mode as the one to be used for addressing variables local to a (recursively callable) procedure, and another addressing mode as the one to be used for accessing global variables.

Just as increasing the number of registers on a machine may increases the size of an instruction format, increasing the number of addressing modes may have the same effect. That trade-off has been resolved differently on different machines. In particular, we will see that the 68030 has a rich variety of addressing modes, which results in an instruction size that can vary widely, while the RISC processors all carefully restrict them to a small but important set so that they will all fit into a 32-bit instruction format.

Whether an addressing mode is important or not is quite application-dependent. The first high-level languages to be used extensively in the United States were FORTRAN and COBOL. Both languages have an essentially static view of data, which means that a smaller and simpler set of addressing modes are necessary. For example, it is not so important to provide *double indexing*, the ability to add two registers in a single instruction to form an address, since FORTRAN array accesses do not need this kind of addressing.

In Europe, on the other hand, ALGOL 60 was much more popular. ALGOL 60 has a much more complicated addressing structure, involving the use of a stack to manage recursion. Some of the early European machines had more complex addressing mechanisms reflecting this emphasis. On the home doorstep, Burroughs was a great fan of ALGOL and built machines that reflected this attraction.

These days, stack-based languages, including C, Ada, and Pascal, are in common use, and furthermore, they all support dynamic storage allocation. Modern CISC designs especially reflect anticipated use of more complicated addressing modes that arise from the use of a stack and dynamically allocated data.

Designing Instruction Formats

In designing instruction formats, there are two extreme positions. One approach is to have a very small number of formats and fit the instructions into this small set. The other approach is to design an optimal format for each instruction. Roughly speaking, RISC designers take the first approach, and CISC designers tend more to the second, although even in CISC processors there will be a degree of uniformity in that very similar instructions might as well have very similar formats.

A fundamental decision has to do with the size of the opcode, that is, the number of bits reserved for indicating the particular operation to be performed. Obviously, if more bits are used, then more distinct instructions can be supported. The cleanest approach is to use a fixed number of opcode bits for all instructions. Interestingly, although RISC processors do have uniform instruction sets, they are not quite *that* uniform, whereas there have been some CISC designs in the past (notably the IBM 360) which always used an 8-bit opcode.

In practice, a designer will recognize that certain operations are much more common than others and react by adjusting the number of opcode bits appropriately. For example, if we have determined that only 4 bits are necessary to represent the most commonly used instructions then 16 possible bit patterns are available. Fifteen of these are used for the most common 15 instructions, and the sixteenth is used to indicate all of the other instructions. Additional bits then need to be allocated elsewhere in the instruction format so that these less common instructions can be distinguished. In the CISC designs, this sort of principle is carried to extremes. For example, the number of opcode bits in 80386 instructions ranges from 5 to 19. On the other hand, RISC machines tend to have fewer instructions, so fewer opcode bits are needed.

Since various operations need different numbers and kinds of operands, space can be saved if the layout of instructions is specialized to the particular needs of the instruction. Furthermore, once this typical CISC philosophy is followed, there is no particular requirement that different instructions have similar operand structures. For example, the CAS2 instruction on the 68030 (a very complicated beast which we will dissect in detail in Chapter 6) takes six operands, but they are all registers, so the entire instruction with its operands can be fit into a specialized 48-bit format.

On the other hand, RISC designs strongly favor a small number of uniform instruction formats, preferably all of the same size. The regularity of these formats simplifies the instruction-decoding mechanism, and means that a technique known as *pipelining* can be used. One aspect of pipelining is that several instructions will typically be in the pipeline, allowing the overlapped decoding and execution of several instructions. This kind of overlapped decoding becomes much more difficult for the numerous and complex instruction formats of CISC processors.

DATA REPRESENTATION

The issue of data representation has been complicated by the variety of conventions used in different manufacturer's hardware. Machines have had different word lengths, different character sets, different ways of storing integers and floating-point values, etc. Most microprocessors, on the other hand, have a similar view of how various data types should be stored. This is one area where CISC and RISC designers have few disagreements. Since the data representations *are* so similar, we will treat them here in Chapter 1 with the understanding that they will apply with only minor modifications to all of the remaining chapters of this book.

Representation of Characters

Through the years, the methods used to represent characters have varied widely, but the basic approach has always been the same: choose a fixed number of bits and then designate a correspondence between bit patterns and characters. The number of bits chosen limits the total number of distinct characters that can be represented. For example, 6-bit codes, used on a number of earlier machines such as the CDC 6600, allow for 64 characters. This is enough to include the uppercase letters, digits, and a selection of special characters, but not the lowercase letters. One of the authors once heard a CDC salesman proclaim in the mid 1970s that "None of our customers need lowercase; it really isn't an issue." Times have certainly changed, and the use of 7- or 8-bit codes allowing lowercase letters is now universal.

Although IBM has persisted in the use of their own EBCDIC code for character representation, the rest of the computer world has standardized on the use of the ISO (International Standards Organization) code. This exists in several national variants, and the variant used in the United States is called ASCII, the American Standard Code for Information Interchange. All the microcomputers that we will look at use ASCII as the code for character representation. This fits well with the basic memory organization, which is a sequence of 8-bit bytes, each of which can be separately addressed.

The use of ASCII is usually *not* assumed in the design of the processor design. Instead, there is a set of instructions for manipulating arbitrary 8-bit quantities, including in the case of some CISC designs, fancy instructions for scanning, comparing, and moving strings of 8-bit characters. However, there is nothing in the instruction set of most processors that is concerned with what particular character 01000001 represents. In ASCII, this is the code for uppercase A, but that is not the processor's concern.

Some mainframe processors *do* have instructions that know about character codes. One example is the EDIT instruction on the IBM 370, which in a single instruction implements the kind of picture conversion that appears in COBOL programs. A single EDIT instruction, for example, can convert the integer 123456 to the character string $123,456.00, with the resulting output being represented in EBCDIC characters. None of the microprocessors we describe in this text, not even the CISC processors, have instructions of *that* level of complexity, and their instruction sets are completely neutral with respect to the choice of character sets. It would thus be quite possible to implement an EBCDIC-oriented system on a microprocessor, although not even IBM has indulged in such strange behavior.

We should note that 8 bits is not enough for representing characters sets for other languages like Japanese and Chinese. Not only do such languages require very much larger character sets, but even in English, the increased use of desktop publishing and fancy displays means that one wants not only to represent the full set of characters, but also to do it using a variety of fonts. Both requirements lead to the need for larger character sets—in the future we will probably see increasing use of 16, or even 32, bit character sets. Luckily, most microprocessors are equally at home manipulating strings of 16- or 32-bit quantities, so in this respect they are built for the future.

Japanese is the main focus of these efforts since Japan is so prominent in the computer field. The issue of character sets is perceived as an international problem that needs a smooth international solution. Japan itself is most interested in having international standards to solve such problems. At a recent meeting at which the issue of representing Japanese characters in Ada was discussed, the Japanese delegate to the relevant ISO committee explained that Japan is concerned with complaints from other countries over non-tariff barriers to imports. A Japanese standard that is not internationally accepted can be regarded as being a non-tariff barrier. It is interesting that an international political conflict can ultimately affect the representation of character codes on microprocessors!

Representation of Integers

These days, everyone agrees that storing integers in binary format is a good idea. But it hasn't always been so! Early on there was quite a constituency of decimal machines, especially in the days when tubes were used to build computers. In those days, it was cheaper to build one 10-state tube than to build four binary-state tubes.[2]

In most scientific programming, integers are stored in binary format, which allows for more efficient handling of computations. Even in commercial applications written in COBOL, the COMPUTATIONAL format allows programmers to specify the use of binary format for quantities that will be used for extensive computations.

For unsigned integers, the binary representation is obvious. Successive bits indicate powers of 2, and the most significant bit is first (at the left). For example, the decimal integer 130 is 10000010 when it is stored as an 8-bit binary value and 0000000010000010 when it is stored as a 16-bit binary value. From time to time, some mathematicians have tried to persuade the world that we should write integers the other way around (least significant digit first). Alan Turing, the famous computer scientist,

---

[2] The first author's uncle worked for Plessey's (a large computer firm in England) at one time and was involved with their very first computer. This machine (called the PEP) had registers for representing numeric quantities consisting of a row of decimal devices, followed by a binary device, a decimal device, and a 12-state device (it was called a duo-decatron). Even the British might have forgotten that that is a reasonable format for pounds, shillings (which went up to 20) and pence (which went up to 12), because the British long ago changed to a decimal money system. This is a remarkable case of hardware that *really* knew what its domain was going to be!

TABLE 1.1
The representation of signed and unsigned 4-bit values.

Bit Pattern	Unsigned Value	Signed Value
0000	0	+0
0001	1	+1
0010	2	+2
0011	3	+3
0100	4	+4
0101	5	+5
0110	6	+6
0111	7	+7
1000	8	−8
1001	9	−7
1010	10	−6
1011	11	−5
1100	12	−4
1101	13	−3
1110	14	−2
1111	15	−1

always wrote numbers the "wrong" way, but he did not manage to convince computer scientists to follow his lead! It is more a matter of convention to regard the most significant bit of a binary integer as being on the left, because, of course, left and right have no real significance on a silicon chip. Nevertheless, the convention is so universal that we always think of integers being stored this way.

There are several ways of representing signed integers, but all the microprocessors we will look at use the *two's complement* approach, so this is the only representation that we need to look at in detail. The two's complement representation can be quite confusing, even for those who know it quite well. In looking at instruction set architectures, we need to have a clear understanding to see when and why we need separate instructions for signed and unsigned numbers.

To keep our examples simple, we will for the moment assume that unsigned and signed integers are represented using four bits. In a 4-bit register, unsigned values range from 0 to 15, and signed two's complement values range from minus 8 to plus 7, as shown in the Table 1.1. Bit patterns starting with a zero bit on the left represent the same values in both the unsigned and signed case. Bit patterns starting with a one bit are interpreted as negative numbers in the signed case. The starting, or leftmost bit, is called the *sign bit*. Whether or not a bit pattern whose sign bit is set to 1 is to be regarded as negative (i.e., whether the number is to be regarded as signed or unsigned) is something that is up to the programmer—you cannot look in a register, see the sign bit set and know that a negative number is present. For example, suppose that a register contains the bit pattern 1101. This may represent either 13 or minus 3, and it is the logic of the program which determines how it is to be interpreted.

For these potentially negative numbers, the signed and unsigned interpretations always differ by 2^k, where k is the number of bits—16 in the case of 4-bit numbers. This is important to note, because it explains why the operations of addition and subtraction work for both signed and unsigned values. Consider the operation:

```
0010 + 1101 = 1111
```

If the numbers are regarded as unsigned, this is adding 2 to 13 to get 15. If the numbers are regarded as signed, this same addition is adding +2 to −3 to get −1. What is really happening is that the normal binary addition is addition mod 2^k, that is, factors of 16 are simply ignored. Since the signed and unsigned values differ by 16, the resulting bit patterns are the same in the unsigned and signed case.

In designing instruction sets, we only need one set of addition and subtraction instructions, which can then be used for signed or unsigned operands at the programmer's choice. The one difference between signed and unsigned addition arises in detecting overflow. Consider the addition:

```
0111 + 0111 = 1110
```

Considered as unsigned, this adds 7 to 7 to give a result of 14. However, if the operands are interpreted as signed, we are adding +7 to +7 and getting a result of −2, which is clearly wrong. The result has the wrong sign and is 16 different from the true mathematical result. What we have here is an addition that *from the signed point of view* causes arithmetic overflow.

A programmer will often want to be able to detect arithmetic overflow for signed values. The programming language Ada requires that these overflows be detected, since an overflow can raise an exception known as a CONSTRAINT_ERROR, which can be handled by the program. Processors take one of two possible approaches to satisfying this requirement. Either they *do* provide two sets of addition and subtraction instructions, which differ only in the detection of overflow, or they provide one set of instructions which set two separate flags, a carry flag which detects unsigned overflow, and a separate signed overflow flag for the signed case.

What about other operations? For multiplication, there are two cases. If the result is single length, then the resulting bit patterns are, like addition and subtraction, the same for the unsigned and signed cases.

```
0001 x 1111 = 1111
```

For unsigned operands, we have 1 times 15 giving a result of 15. For the signed case, we have +1 times −1 giving a result of −1. As with addition and subtraction, the overflow conditions are different, but the resulting bit patterns are the same, so only one single-length multiplication operation is required.

Many machines also provide a multiplication instruction which gives a double-length result. In this case, the signed and unsigned cases *are* different:

```
0001 x 1111 = 00001111 (unsigned case)
0001 x 1111 = 11111111 (signed case)
```

This means that if a double length result multiply instruction is provided, it should be provided in two forms, signed and unsigned. Given only one of these two possible forms, the result for the other can be obtained with only moderate effort, but it is certainly much more convenient to have both.

Division is different in the signed and unsigned cases even where all operands are single length:

```
1110 ÷ 1111 = 0000   (unsigned case)
1110 ÷ 1111 = 0010   (signed case)
```

If a machine provides divide instructions, then separate signed and unsigned forms should be provided. It is quite difficult to simulate one of these results given only the other instruction. For example, simulating unsigned division given only a signed divide instruction is unpleasant.

The final operation to be considered is comparison. Here again the situation with signed and unsigned operands is obviously different:

```
1110 > 0001   (as unsigned values)
1110 < 0001   (as signed values)
```

As with addition and subtraction, there are two approaches that can be taken. Either two sets of comparison instructions must be provided, or a single set of comparison instructions is used which sets two sets of flags, and then there are two sets of conditional branch instructions, one giving the effect of unsigned comparisons, and the other for signed comparisons.

SIGN-EXTENSION. To move an unsigned number to a larger field involves extending a value with zero bits on the left. For instance, if an 8-bit memory location contains an unsigned value in the range 0 to 255, then this value can be loaded into a 32-bit register by supplying 24 zero bits on the left.

If a *signed* value must be extended in size, then the sign bit must be copied into the extra bits on the left. This process is called sign extension. For example, if the 4-bit pattern 1100 must be extended to 8-bits, then the result is 11111110. There are various approaches to providing sign extension capabilities. Some processors have specific instructions for sign extending values. If there are no specific instructions, then sign extension is usually achieved using the arithmetic right shift instruction, which propagates sign bits, as in the following example:

```
Byte value in memory:        10101010
Load into 32-bit
   register zero extended:   00000000 00000000 00000000 10101010
Shift left 24 bits:          10101010 00000000 00000000 00000000
Shift right arithmetic 24 bits :  11111111 11111111 11111111 10101010
```

ADDRESS ARITHMETIC. One important use of unsigned arithmetic is in computing addresses. On the 32-bit microprocessors discussed in this book, address arithmetic uses 32-bit unsigned addition and subtraction.

Unsigned arithmetic has "wrap-around" semantics, which means that carries are ignored. An important consequence is that the effect of signed offsets can be achieved without signed arithmetic. For instance, if an addressing mode provides for the addition of an offset, then adding an offset of all one-bits has the effect of subtracting one. Even though the address arithmetic is unsigned, the offsets can be regarded as signed, since signed and unsigned addition gives the same results.

For the same reason, sign extension of offsets also makes sense, even though the address arithmetic is unsigned. A common arrangement is to provide short offset fields which are then sign extended before being added into the address. For example, an 8-bit offset field is first sign extended to 32 bits, and then the result is added to the address with an unsigned addition. We stress that address arithmetic is unsigned since arithmetic overflow is not relevant for address computation—we don't want any kind of overflow error conditions to be signalled as a result of computing addresses.

MULTIPLE-PRECISION ARITHMETIC. Software routines for performing arithmetic on integers that can't fit into registers can be handled naturally by the processor instructions using algorithms similar to those used by most humans to do arithmetic on long numbers. Most processors we will look at have some support for assisting in writing such routines. For addition and subtraction, a carry indication and special versions of the add and subtract operations that include the carry from a previous stage are needed, and we find such instructions even on most RISC processors. For multiplication and division, we need double-length operations, and some RISC machines don't even have single-length multiply and divide, so we don't necessarily get much help when it comes to multiple-precision multiply and divide.

Packed Decimal

With current design techniques, it is more reasonable to store decimal data as a sequence of four binary bits than in a single 10-state device. This is a very standard data format that is called *packed decimal.* If you have 4 binary bits per decimal character with the obvious binary encoding, then the decimal integer 13 looks like 00010011 in binary.

This format is important, because computer languages intended for commercial processing must be able to deal with numbers in decimal format if a program is going to do mostly I/O operations and relatively little arithmetic. The conversion of binary to decimal (and vice versa) is a rather expensive operation whether it is done in hardware or in software. Adding two packed decimal numbers, on the other hand, is less efficient that adding two's complement integers, but not terribly so. Multiplication and division of packed decimal numbers is not nearly as efficient, but since these operations may not be performed as frequently as addition and subtraction, this may not be an important concern. If all that is done is a little bit of addition and subtraction and a small amount of other arithmetic, it may be attractive to store integers in decimal format, since it will greatly improve the efficiency of input/output operations.

When arithmetic is done on integers in this packed decimal format it is nice if the hardware provides instructions that support this format. Full-scale CISC machines like the IBM 370 have instructions that add two packed decimal numbers, each with 16 digits, giving a 16-digit result. All of this is done in a single hardware instruction.

Of course, all microprocessors are capable of operating on packed decimal numbers using software. Even on some of the RISC processors that have absolutely no specialized support for packed decimal, the speeds of these software-supported operations are not much slower than the hardware instructions on the IBM mainframes. In the case of the 80386 and 68030, we do not have full-blown decimal arithmetic, but there is a small set of instructions to assist in writing software routines of this type.

Floating-Point Values

The formats used used to represent floating-point numbers have been as numerous as the variety of machines which have supported them. One unpleasant consequence of this variety is that it has created an incompatible mess of hardware where floating-point calculations have yielded slightly, or in some cases completely, different results as they were moved from one machine to another.

The IEEE P754 standard for floating-point arithmetic, approved and published in 1985, attempted to remedy this situation by specifying a uniform method for storing and operating on floating-point data. Although it has been widely recognized as specifying a highly desirable approach, it has still not been universally adopted. Too much hardware has been built using proprietary formats such as those of IBM and DEC.

However, in the microprocessor world, the IEEE standard appeared at a critical point just as Intel was designing the first commercial floating-point coprocessor chip, the 8087. This chip is not quite 100% compatible with the standard, because there were a few last-minute changes in the standard that just after the 8087 was designed. However, all subsequent microprocessor floating-point chips, including the 80287 and 80387 follow-ons to the 8087, *are* compatible with the IEEE standard.

The details of how floating-point values are stored and manipulated are quite complex. We devote the whole of Chapter 5 to this subject, reflecting the fact that floating-point calculations are extremely important in the microprocessor world. In the case of engineering workstations, floating-point performance is critical, and more mundane applications like high-definition television and top-end video games rely on efficient and accurate floating-point operations.

MEMORY ORGANIZATION

Almost all microprocessors organize memory into 32-bit words, each of which is divided into four 8-bit bytes. These bytes can be individually addressed, so for some purposes one can equally well regard the memory as being logically composed of a sequence of 8-bit bytes. The two ways in which the various processors differ are the order in which successive bytes of multiple byte quantities are stored and whether such quantities must be aligned on specific boundaries.

Big-Endian vs Little-Endian Byte Ordering

The organization of memory into bytes means that the ordering of these bytes needs to be addressed. As English speakers, we normally think of data as being arranged left to right, rather than right to left. When we think of successive bytes in memory, we think of lower-numbered bytes as being to the left of higher-numbered bytes. For example, we think of a 32-bit number in memory occupying bytes 0 to 3 laid out as

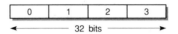

When a number is stored in a register, we think of the most significant bit being on the left and the least significant bit being on the right, because this is the way numbers are represented in English:

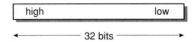

Putting these two pictures together, it is natural to assume that when a 32-bit number is loaded from memory, the high-order bit of the number is the leftmost bit of byte 0 and the low-order bit of the number is the rightmost bit of byte 3:

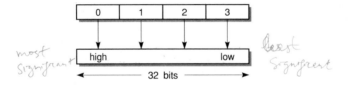

This picture corresponds to *big-endian* byte ordering, where the "big end" or the most significant byte is stored in the lowest addressed byte in memory. Many processors do indeed store multibyte quantities in memory in this manner.

However, the apparent naturalness of this ordering is, of course, simply dependent on our writing customs. Arabic is written right to left, but numbers are still written left to right.[3] Arab readers might therefore find it more natural to write the above picture in the following manner

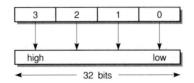

---

[3] Train schedules in the Casablanca station, for instance, have familiar times, but the departure is on the *right* of the board and the destination is on the *left*—most confusing for Western readers!

and might therefore naturally expect to find the high-order bit in the leftmost bit of byte 3 and the low-order bit in the rightmost bit of byte 0. This picture corresponds to *little-endian* byte ordering, where the "little end" of the number is stored in the lowest memory byte. The reason we mention Arabic here is to emphasize that there is nothing inherently natural in choosing one ordering over the other. You may hear people call little-endian ordering "backwards," since they are determined to think of memory as being organized left to right, and so they think of the little-endian picture as:

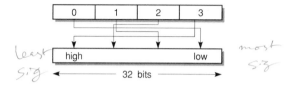

However, at the hardware level, there is no left and right, and even the convention of thinking of the register as having the most significant byte on the left is purely arbitrary. For various historical reasons, both kinds of byte ordering are found in currently available microprocessors. We will find four different approaches:

- Processors like the Intel 80386, which always use little-endian byte addressing.
- Processors like the Motorola 68030, which always use big-endian byte addressing.
- Processors like the MIPS 2000, where a signal at reset time determines whether big- or little-endian addressing is to be used, and the mode then never subsequently changed.
- Processors like the Intel i860, where there is a software instruction to change backwards and forwards between the two modes while a program is running.

From a programming point of view, it generally does not matter very much which type of addressing we have, although there are times when we certainly have to be aware of the endian mode. In particular, when binary data is passed *between* machines—for instance if we transfer a binary file from a PC, which is 386-based, to a Sun-3, which is 68030-based—we often have considerable trouble. For example, the data formats of the two processors, that is, the way integers and characters are represented, are generally identical *except* for the annoying difference in endianness. Furthermore, there is no set algorithm for the conversion—it is data dependent. Consider the case of a record containing a 4-byte field, F1, followed by two 2-byte fields, F2 and F3 (see Figure 1.1). From this picture, we can see that the pattern of byte swapping required to convert from one format to the other is dependent on a detailed knowledge of the data layout.

There are a few cases where one of the orderings is more convenient than the other. For example, if a dump of memory is displayed byte by byte left to right, big-endian ordering is more convenient (but Arabic-speaking programmers might find the situation exactly reversed). Generally, it doesn't matter which ordering is used, but unfortunately, there is no hope of agreement, since both camps are well established and each regards the other as being hopelessly backwards.

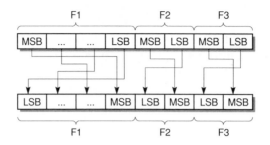

FIGURE 1.1
Converting a record from big- to little-endian.

Big-Endian vs Little-Endian Bit Ordering

When a binary value is stored in a register, we normally think of the most significant bit as being on the left just as we might think of bytes as being laid out left to right. Although this is an arbitrary convention, it is well established, and the pictures and diagrams throughout this book, and indeed throughout the reference manuals for all the processors we discuss in this book, use this convention.

However, there remains an issue of whether the bits in the register are numbered from left to right or from right to left. The left-to-right ordering means that bit 0 is on the left (the most significant bit), and bit 31 is on the right (the least significant bit):

This is called *big-endian* bit ordering. Again, this decision is arbitrary, and the opposite *little-endian* ordering is also possible, with bit 0 being the least significant bit:

For the most part, this is simply a documentation convention. One needs some way to refer to the bits in a register, and either convention may be adopted.

However, on some of the microprocessors we will look at, the bit ordering is more than simply a documentation convention, since there are a few instructions that actually use bit numberings. For instance, on the Intel 80386, the Bit Scan Forward instruction (BSF) scans for a 1 bit and gives a result which is the *little-endian* bit number of the 1 bit found. This means that the 80386 has little-endian bit ordering at the hardware level, and the small set of instructions that deal with bits are all consistent with this view, as is the documentation. On some microprocessors there is some confusion on the issue of bit ordering versus byte ordering. Usually it is most natural to make the two orderings agree, so that big-endian byte ordering goes with big-endian bit ordering, and little-endian byte ordering goes with little-endian bit ordering. However, in real life the situation is not so neat. All members of the Motorola 68000 series are documented as having little-endian bit ordering, which is strange on a machine with big-endian byte ordering. Even stranger on these processors is the fact that some bit field instructions number the bits little-endian, and others number them big-endian. The Motorola designers appear to have been confused over the issue of endianness.

Further problems arise on processors where the byte endianness can be changed. The bit ordering generally does not change in a corresponding manner (certainly the documentation does not suddenly change at run time!). Great care needs to be exercised on these processors to avoid getting confused over the ordering, particularly if a program has to be written so that it will work with either byte ordering.

The Alignment Issue

On all the processors we will examine, memory is byte-addressed, which means that a memory address is the address of a particular 8-bit byte in memory. At a hardware level, however, the memory pathways are 32 bits, or even as much as 64 bits, wide, which means that accesses to memory fetch more than a single byte whether or not that many bytes are required. The bytes in memory are arranged into words of 4 or more bytes:

When a load or store instruction fetches or stores 4 bytes in memory, it is no great surprise, given this memory organization, that the hardware designer finds it tempting to restrict an address to a multiple of 4 so the memory access will correspond to the hardware organization of memory. If we did allow unaligned accesses, for example, a 32-bit load instruction addressing byte 3

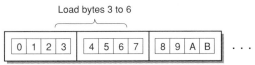

then it would be necessary to load two separate words from memory and fiddle around, shifting and merging, to assemble the required 4 bytes. This would obviously be less efficient, and would also require more complex hardware in the memory access paths, which are critical for general efficiency of operation. As we will see later, there are other issues having to do with caching and paging that also make the support of unaligned accesses embarrassing (for example, we can have a situation where part of a word is in memory and the other part must be paged in from disk).

We need to ask whether it worth complicating a processor by allowing it to reference unaligned data? From a programmer's point of view, the answer is clearly yes, even if it means that referencing unaligned data may take a little longer. From the hardware designer's point of view, the answer is no, since it does add some complexity to the hardware and may harm the efficiency of normal aligned accesses.

In the area of programming languages, a design rule called the Bauer principle advises that a price should not be paid for some feature that has been introduced into a programming language unless it is actually going to be used. A similar principle applies to hardware—if it is possible to implement unaligned access in such a manner that it does not affect the efficiency of aligned accesses, then it is a desirable feature. However, for various architectural reasons, it is quite possible that allowing unaligned access will reduce the efficiency of normal accesses, in which case the argument for providing unaligned access is more delicate. As we will see in our discussion of RISC machines in later chapters, a fundamental principle of RISC design is to avoid slowing down the machine by adding instructions whose implementation complicates the design of the machine to such a degree that all instructions are slowed down. This is why most RISC processors do not allow unaligned access.

In contrast, CISC designs generally permit unaligned access. Furthermore, the history of CISC architecture is such that the ability to access unaligned data has been added relatively late. For example, the IBM 360 required alignment, but this restriction was removed for the IBM 370. The Motorola 68000 required alignment, but the 68030 does not. The reason has to do with the implementation of high-level languages.

At first glance one would expect that the compiler for a high-level language could easily ensure that all data was appropriately aligned. This is certainly true of some languages such as Ada, for example, since almost all Ada programs can be translated with this restriction, unless they use deliberate declarations which force non-alignment. If these declarations force data to be unaligned, a slightly unpleasant sequence consisting of two load instructions and several shift and logical instructions must be used to assemble the data—exactly the sequence that would be done implicitly by the hardware if the processor supported unaligned access.

However, there are languages in which unaligned accesses occur frequently and naturally. In particular, consider how this problem might arise when compiling the following record in a COBOL program:

```
01 RECORD-AREA.
    10 STATE   PIC X(2).
    10 ZIP4    PIC X(4).
    10 TITLE   PIC X(2).
    10 YEAR    PIC X(4).
```

This defines a record named RECORD-AREA consisting of four fields, where fields STATE and TITLE are 2 bytes long and fields ZIP4 and YEAR are 4 bytes long. This corresponds to what would essentially be a record in Pascal but with one important difference. The COBOL standard requires in the absence of further declarations, that these fields be arranged in order and that they be contiguous within the record. A Pascal compiler, on the other hand, can rearrange the fields of a record any way it wishes because it is none of a programmer's business how the fields of a record are laid out within the stack frame at runtime.

The effect of this requirement in COBOL is to force a compiler to generate code that loads the field ZIP4 into a register in two pieces even though the machine is byte-addressable since there is no way all the fields can be aligned on a 32-bit boundary. In some other languages, the compiler is free to lay out records in any way it pleases and, for instance, align word components, wasting space if necessary. The reason that this is generally not permitted in COBOL is that a programmer can write

```
01  NEW-REC REDEFINES RECORD-AREA.
```

and then describe a new structure that overlays its fields on top of RECORD-AREA. For all the fields, a COBOL programmer is allowed to specify how these records are laid out and take advantage of it, so the layout of fields in a record is visible to a programmer and defined in an implementation-independent manner.

The decision to require alignment makes it more difficult to implement a COBOL compiler because it means that the compiler must be able to generate code to load one word, load another word, shift, mask, and then reassemble the field just as if the machine were not byte-addressable. Undoubtedly the COBOL situation was a major reason for the significant change made by IBM when it introduced into the hardware the extra complexity of unaligned access handling in the 370. On the other hand, few RISC processors run COBOL programs, and so this requirement is not so important.

COBOL is not the only place where the issue of alignment comes up. In FORTRAN the same issue arises because of COMMON declarations, which are mapped positionally. For instance, you might have:

```
COMMON      C, Q, R
CHARACTER  C
INTEGER     Q, R
```

There is a requirement in FORTRAN that Q immediately follow the character C, and therefore is possibly misaligned. The reason that this is significant is that in another subroutine a programmer might write

```
COMMON      C1, C2, C3, C4, C5, R
CHARACTER  C1, C2, C3, C4, C5
INTEGER     R
```

where C1 through C5 are characters and R is still an integer, expecting R to end up in the same position in both modules. Even if a compiler allocates an entire word for every one of these, even then, they will typically line up on a processor that allows misaligned data. On a processor that does not allow unaligned data, it is problematic.

Although RISC processors may not often be used for COBOL, they certainly are used for C. What is the alignment situation with respect to C? Here is one of the (many) cases where the official model of C differs from the way programmers write in C. In C, if p is a pointer to a character, then it is very easy to treat a character pointer as an integer pointer. That works on a machine that doesn't care about alignment and uses the same length pointer on characters and integers. This kind of technique works absolutely fine on the 386, but the very same program will bomb on a 68000 (with an alignment error), or simply malfunction on an IBM ROMP (which will silently produce the wrong data).

We mentioned at the start of this section that in proper "official" C, such problems could not arise. To see how such problems might arise, consider the following code written in C:

```
char p;
int i;
i = *((int *) p);
```

This is not strictly correct C, but few people write strictly correct C! That is one of the problems with C. C has two models of the world. One is the strict C definition that is presented in Kernighan and Ritchie and the ANSI definition.[4] In this case it is a strongly typed language in which you cannot play games with pointers.

The other kind of C knows that all the world is a linear address space, so that you can add 1 to a pointer or subtract 1 from it, and it is obvious how all of this should work. Unfortunately, it is not quite that obvious. Alignment is one particularly nasty fly in the ointment. The other nasty glitch occurs with a machine where integer pointers and character pointers are of different lengths, which is perfectly legitimate. This occurs in practice because there are word-based machines where an integer pointer may be just a word address but a character pointer is a combination of a word address and a character offset, and so is slightly bigger.

Most C programmers are unaware of the rule in Kernighan and Ritchie about what can be done when converting pointers from one type to another, a rule which has appeared in every edition of the book since the first edition. Section 14.4 says:

> A pointer to one type may be converted to a pointer to another type. The resulting pointer may cause addressing exceptions upon use if the subject pointer does not refer to an object suitably aligned in storage. It is guaranteed that a pointer to an object of a given size may be converted to a pointer to an object of a smaller size and back again without change.

Fans of C and Unix might ponder the fact that "malloc" exactly violates that rule and yet is a fundamental part of C. This is because "malloc" returns a character pointer that you are then expected to convert back to a word pointer (or whatever you need). But this violates the C standard. How do we get away with it? In practice, "malloc" promises to return a pointer that may be a character pointer but is aligned to the maximum extent to which alignment is needed.

Many programmers will never write assembly language programs in their jobs. But the point is, even if you never write assembly language this is a nice example of the fact that it sure pays to know what is going on at a low level because low-level concerns can show up in COBOL programs, or in C programs, or in other high-level languages.

---

[4] The original C definition is given in Kernighan and Ritchie: *The C Programming Language* (Prentice-Hall, 1978). There is now a proposed ANSI standard for C, which is still in draft form at the time of time of this writing.

PROCEDURE CALLS

In a language such as Pascal, which permits procedures to be nested and recursive procedure calls to be made, there are two issues that must be dealt with. The first issue is how a procedure will address its own local variables, since the possibility of recursion means that it is possible for more than one instance of a procedure's variables to be alive. The second is how this procedure can address variables within which it is lexically nested, that is, *non-local variables.*

The universal approach is to maintain a stack, often called the *run-time stack* (sometimes called the *activation stack*), which is used to hold the values of variables that are local to a procedure, as well as other important information. The run-time stack is organized into *stack frames* (also called *activation records*), one for each active procedure. The main purpose of a stack frame is to allocate storage for the local variables of a procedure. If a procedure has called itself recursively exactly once, then there will be two stack frames on the run-time stack, one for each instance of the procedure. On most machines the run-time stack builds down in memory, which means that it will build down to lower memory addresses.

The issue of how to manage the stack, that is, how to create and dismantle stack frames as procedures are called and returned from, forms a substantial part of what is known in textbooks as *run-time storage management.* When a procedure call occurs, a highly stylized sequence of events, called the *calling sequence*, occurs as a new stack frame can be constructed. When a called procedure completes, the stack frame must be dismantled, and the execution environment of the calling procedure must be restored, something that is done as part of the *return sequence.*

The calling and return sequences are sequences of instructions that are executed by both the calling procedure and the called procedure. This sequence of machine instructions is generated by a compiler as part of a standard set of prologues and epilogues to the procedures as well as part of the call instruction.

Before describing the structure of stack frames and how they are constructed during the calling sequence, we will begin with a short description of call instructions. Throughout this section, keep in mind that this is a simplified view of stack frames and the calling/return sequence. It ignores the differences that would arise due to either the particular machine for which a compiler is generating code or the particular programming language for which the compiler has been built.

The Call Instruction

The two basic instructions required for implementing procedure calls are the call instruction and the return instruction. A call instruction is simply a jump in which the return address is saved. A return instruction returns control to the calling procedure by restoring the saved address after the called procedure has finished executing.

Most microprocessors use one of two basic styles of call instruction. In one, the return point is placed in a register, typically a specially designated register, so that no information about which register has been used needs to be specified within the instruction format. This is desirable since call instructions require that most bits be used to specify an address and not be "wasted" on other fields that may not be particularly useful for this type of instruction. The return instruction in this case simply needs to be able to branch indirectly to a return address stored in a register.

The second style of call instruction saves the return point on a hardware stack, adjusting the value of a register that serves as a stack pointer. The corresponding return instruction pops the return point off this stack and uses it to return to the instruction just after the call. This stack-based type of call and return is particularly well suited to languages like Pascal, C, or Ada that allow recursion and depend on the use of a stack to control procedure calls.

Building a Stack Frame

In Pascal and other similar languages, a compiler must generate code so that each time a procedure is called during the execution of a program a stack frame is built for that procedure. Within that stack frame several important items are stored, each of which can generally be found at a fixed position within the frame. One of the things to be stored as a stack frame is being constructed is the return point of the procedure. In addition to the return point, space is allocated for the procedure's local variables and several other values that are both machine and language-dependent.

On return from a procedure, the corresponding stack frame must be removed from the stack. To keep track of the top position of the stack, almost all microprocessors include a stack pointer register. In addition, it is common, but not absolutely necessary, to have a separate pointer called the *frame pointer*, which points to the frame of the current stack. One of the additional items that is stored in each stack frame is the previous value of the frame pointer, so that the frames are linked together in a list.

For example, consider a procedure P in which the local variables $x1$ and $x2$ are declared. Furthermore, suppose that within P there is a procedure Q in which the local variables $y1$ and $y2$ have been declared. The actual structure of the run-time stack, as well as the actual layout of the stack frames for P and Q just after P has called Q are shown in Figure 1.2. We are assuming for this discussion that the stack builds down in memory. Although this is by far the most common approach, there are some processors that use the opposite convention and build up.[5]

In this picture, the return point for each procedure is the first item stored in each stack frame as the record is being constructed. It is either stored there automatically by the call instruction that is used to call Q, or, in the case where the call instruction puts the return point in the register, it is stored in the frame as one of the first actions of Q.

The second item that is pushed onto the stack is usually the previous value of the frame pointer, the frame pointer of the previous stack frame owned by the procedure

---

[5] A rule that seems obvious to us, but with which much of the rest of the world does not agree, is that high memory should be shown higher up on the page and low memory lower down on the page. The great advantage of this is that when one talks about high memory, one can point one's finger up, and when one talks about low memory, one can point one's finger down. Although half the world thinks this way and the other half doesn't, we hereby declare our convention, and our pictures will be drawn accordingly!

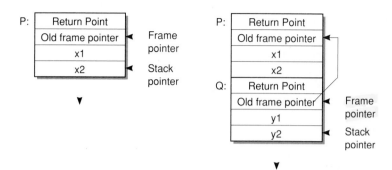

FIGURE 1.2
Stack frame grown using sample procedures P and Q.

that did the call. It is necessary to store this value so that when procedure Q returns to procedure P, the frame pointer can be restored so that it is once again pointing to the correct place. The remainder of the stack frame is used for the local variables.

While procedure Q is executing, the frame pointer will point to the location in the stack frame for Q used to store the old value of the frame pointer. Since we intend to allocate all local variables at fixed locations in this stack frame just below where the frame pointer points, we know that *y1* can be found at an offset of –4 from the frame pointer and *y2* can be found at an offset of –8 (assuming that the old frame pointer as well as *y1* and *y2* are 4-byte values).

Why a Frame Pointer Is Needed

In the description above, it might occur to the reader that there is an alternative to using the frame pointer to reference local variables in the stack frame. Why not just use the stack pointer, freeing up the register that would otherwise be dedicated as a frame pointer? After all, the stack pointer also seems to point to a fixed location in the record: the bottom location. Registers are often a scarce resource, so we might do well to free up an extra register for some other use. To understand the answer to this question, we need to look at some other uses of the stack. Suppose we have the Ada procedure

```
procedure DYNAMIC (N : INTEGER) is
        VARA, VARB : INTEGER;
        ARRA, ARRB : array (INTEGER range 1..N) of INTEGER;
begin
    ...
end DYNAMIC;
```

In this example, the lengths of the arrays ARRA and ARRB are not known at compile time, which means that they cannot be allocated at fixed locations in the stack frame. Since they are local variables, however, which logically belong somewhere in the stack frame, they must be freed on exit from the procedure.

The standard convention is to divide the stack frame into static and dynamic sections, and modify the calling sequence so that the stack frame is built in the appropriate manner. The fixed-length items, VARA and VARB in this example, are placed in the static section along with pointers to the dynamic variables, so in this case the static section will also contain pointers for ARRA and ARRB. The actual data for the arrays is allocated in the dynamic section, and now the stack pointer gets moved down to include the dynamic section (see Figure 1.3). Looking at this picture, it becomes clear that the static section of the frame could not be referenced using the stack pointer, since the offsets are not fixed at compile time.

There are some situations in which it is possible to consider avoiding the use of a dynamic section of the stack frame, and in such cases it *is* possible to get away with not having a separate frame pointer. However, the situation with dynamic arrays, and other similar situations in which data is dynamically allocated on the stack, are common, so the convention is to dedicate a register for use as the frame pointer.

Hardware Support for Stack Frames

The calling and return sequences involve use of a stack pointer, a frame pointer, and the stack, whether these are implemented in the hardware or not. For example, the typical entry code of a procedure must perform operations something like the following:

> Save the return point if not done by hardware
> Decrement stack pointer
> Store frame pointer at location referenced by stack pointer
> Copy stack pointer as new value of frame pointer
> Subtract constant from stack pointer to allocate static frame

This sequence of operations can certainly be implemented using normal move, add, and subtract instructions. However, since procedure calls are common, it is very

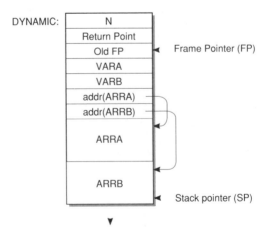

FIGURE 1.3
The activation record for the sample procedure DYNAMIC.

tempting, especially for CISC designers, to provide special instructions that assist in carrying out this sequence of operations.

The return sequence occurs on return from a procedure when a called procedure restores the stack frame of the caller. The following actions occur:

Copy frame pointer to stack pointer to remove frame
Reload frame pointer from stack
Pop stack pointer
Return to caller using stacked return point

These events have several effects: the first step reclaims the stack space allocated for the local variabls; the second step restores the frame pointer so that it points to the frame of the caller; the third step restores the stack pointer; and, the final step sets the caller executing again. We will see such instructions on both the CISC processors that we look at (the Intel 80386 and the Motorola 68030), and even some of the RISC processors have gestures in the direction of helping with these operations. After all, a procedure call is one of the most common constructions.[6]

Accessing Non-Local Variables

In the example of Figure 1.2, procedure Q can reference the variables in the outer procedure P, *x1* and *x2*. There are many ways of arranging data structures, often called displays, to allow such non-local accesses. The subject of designing these structures is fairly complex, and we will not cover it in detail here.

It is worth noting, however, that this too provides a possible target of opportunity for a CISC designer. In the past, a number of mainframe computers have had quite elaborate support for various schemes for addressing of non-local variables. Among the processors we will look at in this book, only the 80386 makes an attempt in this direction, and we will discuss the particular scheme it uses in Chapter 2. Unfortunately, as we will see in this chapter, the result is a little misguided—an interesting example of the extremes of the CISC approach.

ADDRESSING MODES

An important issue in comparing microprocessors is the manner in which they allow memory to be addressed. Typically, a processor has a variety of *addressing modes* that allow memory to be addressed in various ways. There is often a close relationship between these memory-addressing modes and the kind of memory addressing which is needed when a program written in a high-level language is compiled. These

---

[6] William Wulf has estimated that approximately one quarter of a program's execution time is spent in calling procedures, and notes that if procedure calls are very slow, programmers naturally move to a style which minimizes the use of procedures. The ultimate example of this effect happened with the original PL/1 compiler, which made a system call (which was particularly inefficient) on every procedure call. The result was that it was common practice for users of this compiler to avoid procedure calls almost completely.

addressing modes provide support for compilers that need to generate code for programs written in high-level languages. The relationship between high-level languages and the hardware that supports them has historically been something of a two-way street. On the one hand, programming languages have been influenced by the design of the hardware, and on the other hand, hardware design has been influenced by high-level languages.

In this section we will look at some of the categories of data that appear in programming languages and consider how that data can be structured in memory in such a way that the addressing modes available in the hardware can be taken advantage of. This will establish a useful perspective for understanding and evaluating the utility of the addressing mechanisms implemented in various processors. Since the issue of whether to provide elaborate and in some cases quite complex hardware addressing modes is one of the points on which CISC and RISC designers tend to diverge, it is important to understand how these modes might actually be used in practice.

Direct Memory Addressing

Most programming languages allow a programmer to define *static data*, that is, data for which one can be certain that only one instance of that data will exist in memory during the execution of a program. Examples of such data for several languages are:

- All data except parameters in FORTRAN.[7]
- All data in COBOL programs.
- Most library package data in Ada.
- Static data in C.
- Data declared in the outermost program scope of Pascal.

In these cases, the size and location of the data can be determined before the program is run—if not at compile time, then certainly at link time (see Figure 1.4(a)). This means that the actual address is known and is available in constructing instructions before execution begins.

Some, but not all processors, have a *direct addressing* mode that permits the actual address of static data to appear in the instruction. When direct addressing is not available on a processor, a commonly used technique is to have a compiler arrange the static data in a contiguous region of memory so that the offset of each variable within the region is known at compile time. Static data is then addressed by loading a register with the address of the first word in this region, and accessing the variables by adding the offset of each piece of data to the the address in this register.

---

[7] The FORTRAN standard allows local variables of subroutines to be implemented on a stack, but since FORTRAN does not allow recursion, this is not required. Almost all implementations allocate such data statically, and many programs depend, improperly, on such static allocation.

Indexed Addressing

The array appears as a data structure in almost all programming languages, and as a result, almost all hardware supports the use of array indexing. The semantics of a programming language define exactly how and where an array is allocated in memory. If an array is allocated statically, then a very simple addressing mode known as *indexed addressing* supports access to the elements of the array. If the array, on the other hand, is allocated at run time then a slightly more complex addressing mode is required.

Addressing an element in a statically allocated array requires that the base address of the array, known at either compile or link time, be added to the offset of the array element (known at run time). Indexed addressing is implemented in the hardware by having the offset (held in a register) added to a specified starting address (see Figure 1.4(b)). This diagram shows how the Nth element of the array S is accessed by adding the offset to a starting address which is known at either compile or link time.

One subtlety that is hidden in this picture commonly arises on byte-addressed machines when high-level languages are used. Consider the FORTRAN example

    DIMENSION S (100)
    S(I) = S(J)

where S is a vector of 4-byte REAL variables. The subscript values I and J are simply integers, but the corresponding array offsets must be given in bytes. This means that the subscript values in this case must be multiplied by 4 before they are used, a process known as *scaling*.

Most of the time the scaling factor will be some power of 2. In this case, a compiler will take advantage of the fact that multiplication by a power of 2 can be implemented by shifting the index value a number of times equal to the power. Since objects such as

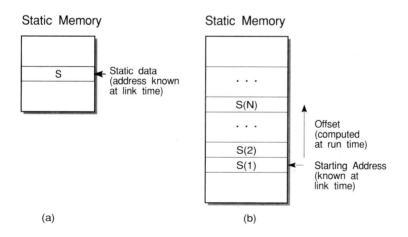

(a)   (b)

FIGURE 1.4
Addressing static scalar data and static arrays.

arrays of integers occur quite frequently in certain applications, some processors provide a feature known as *automatic scaling* to make indexing more efficient. Automatic scaling is used in conjunction with indexing so that the value added to the base address is the value in the index register automatically multiplied by a selected scaling value. These values are usually restricted to 1, 2, 4, or 8, the most common array element lengths.

Based Addressing

An addressing mode which is related to indexed addressing, but whose use is not exactly the same, is known as *based addressing*. Using based addressing, a register known as a *base register* contains the address of a block of storage.

An important case of based addressing occurs when the block of storage to which the base register is pointing is a procedure's stack frame on the run-time stack. As we discussed in the section on procedure calls, the local variables of a procedure are stored in these stack frames, and a pointer known as the frame pointer points to the stack frame of the currently executing procedure. For example, consider the C routine

```
printd
{
    int x,y,z;
    ...
}
```

Calling this procedure would establish a new stack frame containing the new instances of the local variables *x*, *y*, *z* (see Figure 1.5(a)). To access the variable *z* in the current procedure the frame pointer is used as a base register and the fixed offset (known at compile time) of the variable within the stack frame are added together to form the address. Sometimes a machine will provide an addressing mode in which that offset is added to the base register, while on other machines it may be necessary to form the address by explicitly adding the offset with a separate instruction.

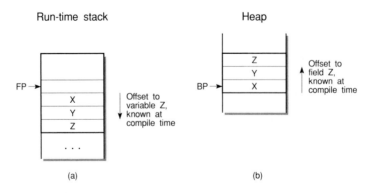

FIGURE 1.5
Based addressing of a dynamically allocated record.

Another common use of this addressing mode is to address the fields of a dynamically allocated record, as, for example in the Pascal code

```
type
  Q = record
            X : INTEGER;
            Y : INTEGER;
            Z : INTEGER;
        end;
    QA = ^Q ;        { QA points to a Q record }
var
    G : QA;
begin
    ...
    M := G^.Y;
    ...
end;
```

The reference to G^.Y would use based addressing. The compiler will generate code that loads a register with the base address in G. The base register contains the pointer G, while the offset to the field Y is statically known at compile time (see Figure 1.5(b)). Notice that these two uses of the base register to hold the address of a block of memory are quite similar. In fact, the only important difference between the two is that when the base register is used as a frame pointer the offsets of the variables in the stack frame are at a negative offset from the base register (frame pointer), and in the second case, the fields within the record are at a positive offset.

COMPARING INDEXED AND BASED ADDRESSING. Based addressing is similar to indexed addressing, but there are two important differences. First, the value in the base register is always a memory address, so it does not need scaling. Second, in the case of indexing a static variable, the static base address is a full memory address, whereas in based addressing, it is often the case that the offset within the based area of memory is small (both records and stack frames are typically small).

Many processors do not provide direct addressing, as is true, for example, of the IBM 370 and all RISC processors. When direct addressing is not possible, one method of addressing static memory is to use based addressing by first loading a register with the address of a memory location which is sufficiently close to the static data to allow base-offset addressing to be used. On the IBM 370, for example, the offset is limited to 4K bytes, so the address has to be within 4K of the required address.

Base Plus Index Addressing

When an array is dynamically allocated, or if the array is a local variable allocated in a stack frame, the addressing of an element in this array requires both based and indexed addressing. Consider the following Ada example:

```
procedure THINK is
    X, Y, Z : INTEGER;
    A : array (1..100) of INTEGER;
begin
    ...
    X := A(Y);
    ...
end
```

(frame pointer is base address)

The addressing of A(Y) involves both using the frame pointer as a base pointer and using Y as an index (see Figure 1.6). Computing the address of A(Y) involves three elements: the base address, in this case the frame pointer; the starting offset, which is known at compile time; and the index value, which may typically need scaling.

Some processors provide this type of base-index addressing, sometimes called double indexing, since, as we observed before, the functions of base registers and index registers are similar. On such processors, the fetching of A(Y) corresponds to a single load instruction. Other processors not providing this double indexing feature may require a sequence of instructions in which the necessary indexing address, that is, the sum of the frame pointer and the scaled index, must be computed and placed in an index register so that single indexing can be used.

It is also important to note that in the case if a compiler needs to generate code to access an element of an array allocated in a stack frame, there are really three

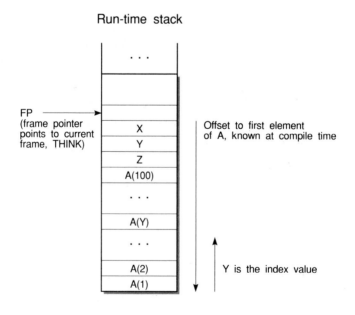

FIGURE 1.6
Use of based plus index addressing to address arrays allocated within stack frames.

components involved: the frame pointer, the starting offset of the array, and the (possibly scaled) index. As we shall see when we compare the 386 and the 68030 to the RISC chips, only the CISC processors provide an addressing mode which allows one to access such an array element in a single instruction. Some RISC chips *do* have the double indexing, but none of them allow a programmer to add two registers as well as a constant displacement to form an address. This is a consequence of the instruction formats, which are in turn a consequence of the decision to use pipelining, and is consistent with the philosophy of keeping things simple.

Indirect Addressing

When parameters are passed to procedures, the value passed and stored for use by the calling procedure is often the *address* of the actual parameter, rather than a copy of the value of the parameter. In some cases, a programming language may require the use of this method, *call by reference*, of passing parameters (e.g., the VAR parameters of Pascal). In other cases, the method of passing parameters is optional. Consider the case of the FORTRAN procedure:

```
SUBROUTINE QSIMPLE (I)
...
I = I + 1
...
END
```

Within QSIMPLE, the value stored for the parameter is not the value of I, but the address of I. This means that when I is referenced, there is an extra step of fetching the address of I and then dereferencing it (see Figure 1.7(a)). Obviously the reference to I can be achieved by first using an instruction to load the address of I into a base register and then using based addressing (with an offset of zero) to access I. However, some processors provide an addressing mode called *indirect addressing* which in a single instruction first fetches the pointer to I and then uses this pointer to fetch (or store) the actual value of I. Of course, this still takes an extra memory data reference, but an extra instruction is not required.

Indirect Addressing with Indexing

If the parameter being passed is an array, then indirect addressing and indexed addressing must be combined to access an element of the array. If in the above FORTRAN example, the parameter had been an array

```
SUBROUTINE QARRAY (D)
DIMENSION D(100)
D(I) = D(I) + 1
END
```

then accessing D(I) would involve getting the address of D and then indexing it with the subscript I (see Figure 1.7(b)).

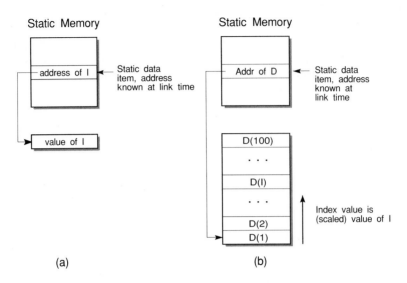

FIGURE 1.7
Indirect addressing of a simple variable, and an array.

As this gets more complicated, the issue of whether to provide a single addressing mode that handles this case becomes more contentious. Only one of the processors we look at (the Motorola 68030) has this addressing mode built in. On other processors, a sequence of two or more instructions is needed to access an indirect array element.

INDIRECT ADDRESSING WITH BASING. In our examples of indirect addressing so far, the pointer has been allocated statically. However, in a stack-based language, the pointer word itself may be allocated on the stack, and thus base addressing is required to access it. Written QSIMPLE in Pascal instead of FORTRAN,

```
procedure QSIMPLE (var I : INTEGER);
   ...
begin

   ...
   I := I + 1;
   ...
end QARRAY;
```

then the parameter passed for I would be a pointer to I and this pointer would be stored in the stack frame for QSIMPLE (see Figure 1.8). Now addressing I involves first adding an offset to a base pointer to get the pointer to I, and then using this pointer to access the value of I. Again we could do this with a sequence of instructions using simpler addressing modes, but some processors have this addressing mode built in.

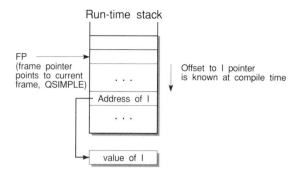

FIGURE 1.8
Using indirect addressing with based indexing.

INDIRECT ADDRESSING WITH BASING AND INDEXING. For the grand finale, consider the case where an *array* is passed as a parameter in a stack-based language. Suppose that we had written QARRAY in Ada instead of FORTRAN

```
procedure QARRAY (D : INTARRAY) is
begin           .
    ...  D(I) := D(I) + 1;  ...
end QARRAY;
```

then the parameter passed for D would be a pointer to the array, and this pointer would be stored in the stack frame for QARRAY (see Figure 1.9). Now the access to an element of D involves three steps: first we use based addressing to get the pointer to D; then we dereference this pointer; finally we used base plus index addressing, using the pointer as the base and the subscript as the index. This is getting quite complicated, and relatively few processors (just one among our examples—the Motorola 68030) have a specialized addressing mode allowing a single instruction to be used for this access. On other processors, accessing an element of D may take up to four instructions.

Even More Complicated Addressing Modes

It is possible to write structures and data accesses in high-level languages corresponding to arbitrarily complicated addressing sequences:

```
type
    A = array [1..10] of INTEGER;
    REC2 = record .... AA : A; ... end;
    REC1 = record ... Q : ^REC2; ... end record;
    X = array [1..10] of ^REC1;
var
    G : X;
    ...
    I := X(I)^.Q^.AA(J);
```

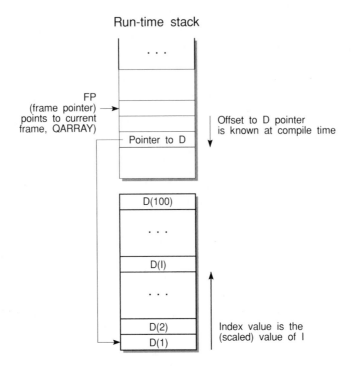

FIGURE 1.9
One use of indirect addressing with basing and indexing.

We won't even attempt to draw a picture of the memory access corresponding to this expression! You can imagine that a processor might be built with an amazing addressing mode *exactly* corresponding to the required access sequence. However, not even the most ardent CISC advocate would expect to see a processor go this far in providing specialized addressing modes!

How far is far enough? This is an important point in designing microprocessors. One of the important factors differentiating CISC and RISC designs is precisely that of addressing modes. RISC processors tend to concentrate on providing a relatively small, uniform, and highly efficient set of addressing modes from which complex addressing paths can be constructed as a sequence of instructions when needed, whereas CISC designs tend to include a complex set of addressing modes intended to take care of common high-level language situations such as those we have described here. The Motorola 68030 goes further than the examples here and includes some even more complicated modes whose use is difficult to explain in terms of programming langauge features. Whether this is an appropriate design choice is one of the questions to be answered as the CISC and RISC designers battle things out in the marketplace.

MEMORY MANAGEMENT

At the hardware level, the main memory of a microprocessor can be regarded as a vector of 8-bit bytes, where the vector subscript is the memory address. In earlier machines, and in some simple machine designs today, the logical view of memory is identical to this hardware view—when an instruction references a memory location, it corresponds to fetching or storing the data from the designated locations in physical memory.

Although this view of memory results in a very simple organization from both a sofware and hardware point of view, it is quite unsatisfactory for a number of reasons:

- If several programs are running on the same processor in a multi-programmed manner, then we have to make sure that they do not conflict in their use of memory. If programs reference physical memory directly, then this avoidance of conflicts would have to be done at the program level.

- Physical memory is limited in size. If programs address physical memory directly, then they are subject to the same limitations. Furthermore, the amount of physical memory varies from one machine to another, and we would prefer that these variations not affect the way progams are written.

- Compared to the speed of processors, memories are rather slow. If a program really has to access memory every time it executes a load or store instruction, or for that matter on every instruction, since the instruction itself has to be fetched from memory, then access to the memory would become a bottleneck that would limit the overall execution speed unacceptably.

To address these problems, the microprocessors we discuss in this book all provide for *memory management.* This phrase refers to a combination of hardware and operating system features which provide for efficient memory access by separating the notion of logical and physical memory accesses.

Memory Mapping

To solve the problem of separate programs intefering with one another, some kind of *memory mapping* facility is provided by the hardware. This automatically performs a mapping function on all addresses used by a program so that the addresses used within a program do not correspond directly to physical addresses. The simplest approach is to simply relocate all addresses by a constant, as shown in Figure 1.10. By providing a limit register, which indicates the length of the logical memory for a given program, this scheme also allows the hardware to check that a program does not reference memory outside its own logical region.

This simple base/limit approach has two limitations. First, the memory for a given program must be contiguous. It is always more difficult to allocate large, variable-sized, contiguous chunks of memory, than to allocate in small fixed-sized blocks. Secondly, there is no way that two programs can share memory. Although the general idea is to separate the logical address space of separate programs, there are cases in which we *do*

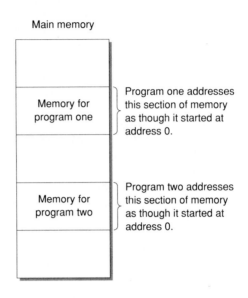

Main memory

Memory for program one

Program one addresses this section of memory as though it started at address 0.

Memory for program two

Program two addresses this section of memory as though it started at address 0.

FIGURE 1.10
Memory management through the use of relocation.

want to share memory. In particular, if two programs are using the same code, then the code itself can certainly be shared.

A more flexible scheme divides the logical address space of a program, also called its *virtual address space*, into a sequence of fixed-length chunks called *pages*. These virtual pages are individually mapped into corresponding physical pages which need not be contiguous in physical memory, allowing a simpler, more efficient allocation of physical memory.

The mechanism for mapping the pages is typically quite complex, and involves table lookup structures stored in memory. Since it would be unacceptably slow to search these structures for every memory reference, the processor has a small piece of the table stored locally in a *translation lookaside buffer* (TLB). The approach on a memory reference is to first look in the TLB, and hope that the necessary translation entry is found there. If not, the main memory tables are consulted.

The details of how these translation tables are stored and accessed, and the decision of how much of this process is in the hardware, and how much is left up to the operating system, vary considerably from one processor to another. We will see several quite different schemes as we look at the various processors.

Virtual Memory

Given that we implement a mapping scheme with fixed-size pages, it is a small step to implement the concept of *virtual memory*. This allows a program to reference a virtual memory space that is not limited by the size of physical memory.

All we have to do is to add information, typically a single bit, to the page translation tables that says "page not present." The translation process sees this bit and traps to the operating system. The operating system maintains these not-present pages on disk, and when it gets the trap, it reads the required page into memory, swapping out some other page, and fixes up the page table entries to indicate that the new page is now present. Execution of the program can then continue.

This approach is called *demand paging*, since pages are swapped in on demand, that is, when they are referenced. Obviously the execution speed becomes painfully slow if every memory reference results in a disk read, but what we hope is that in practice, the great majority of references are to pages which are present, so the overhead of page swapping is minimal.

To minimize this overhead, the operating system must make appropriate decisions as to which pages to swap out when new pages are demanded. There are many algorithms designed to optimize these decisions. Most are based on some variation of the *least recently used* (LRU) principle, which suggests that the appropriate page to discard is the one which was least recently accessed. Most paging hardware provides some limited support to assist in implementing such algorithms. In particular, we usually find two bits in the page tables, one set when a page is accessed, and the other, called the *dirty bit*, set when a page is modified. The latter information is important, since pages that have not been modified do not need to be written back to disk (the old image on disk is still valid).

Memory Caching

To avoid the problem of referencing the relatively slow main memory on every memory reference instruction, and to obtain the instructions to be executed, high-performance microprocessors use memory caches. These are small, very fast memories, either on the microprocessor chip itself, or on intimately connected separate chips. Since these memories are relatively small, it is economically feasible to use much more expensive, much faster hardware, resulting in the ability to access memory within the cache much more rapidly than main memory.

A memory reference then becomes a two-step operation. First the cache is checked to see if the desired memory location is present. If so, then it can be accessed in the cache, completely avoiding the relatively slow main memory. If not, then main memory must be accessed. As with the TLB and page table accesses, we hope that most of the time the memory we want *is* in the cache, so that the overhead of the slow main memory is minimized.

How often will we find the data in the cache? This obviously depends on both the size of the cache and the pattern of references in the program. Some cases are clearly favorable—for example, when we execute a tight loop, the instructions of the loop can generally be expected to be found in the cache, a situation we refer to as a *cache hit*. On the other hand, following a linked list which roams all around the memory space is a bad case which will result in *cache misses*.

A cache is organized into *lines* where a line is a contiguous sequence of bytes on an appropriate boundary. For example, if a cache is 4K bytes long, it might be organized as 256 lines, each containing a 16-byte chunk of memory. The choice of line size is an important design parameter. If it is too small, then the number of references to main memory is increased. If it is too large, then there are fewer lines, and we are less likely to find the memory we want in the cache. Typical choices are in the 16-byte range, although we will see caches where this parameter varies considerably.

One important design consideration is that it must be possible to search the cache very efficiently, since this search takes place on every memory reference. Going back to our example of a 4K cache divided into 256 lines of 16-bytes each, the task is to quickly determine if any of the 256 lines contains the data we are looking for.

At one extreme, a fully *associative* cache can be constructed, where the data we want can be stored in any of the 256 lines, so that at least from a logical point of view, all 256 lines have to be checked. Obviously we cannot search the lines serially, so we need some rather elaborate hardware to search all possibilities in parallel. It is possible to construct such hardware, but quite difficult to keep the performance high enough to avoid significantly slowing down memory references.

At the other extreme, a *directly addressed* cache is organized so that a given memory location can only be stored in one particular cache line. One way of doing this is to use a portion of the address to specify the cache line. For example, for 32-bit addresses cached in our 4K cache with 256 lines, the address could be divided into three fields:

20 bits	8 bits	4 bits

The 4-bit field is the byte within the cache line and the 8-bit field indicates which cache line is addressed. The issue is whether that particular cache line contains the address we want, that is whether the top 20-bits match. If not, then we immediately know that the data we want is not in the cache.

Referencing a directly addressed cache is much easier than referencing a fully associative cache. However, there is a significant disadvantage. In the directly addressed case, two memory locations that correspond to the same cache line can never be in the cache simultaneously. This considerably increases the probability of encountering unfortunate cases. In the case of our example 4K cache, a string copy from one array to another where the arrays are separated by a multiple of 2^{12} bits would result in none of the data ever being present in the cache, since we would be bounding backwards and forwards between two memory locations which needed the same cache line.

A compromise is to design a *set-associative* cache. This essentially consists of a collection of separate directly addressed caches. A given memory location can be stored in its corresponding lines in any of the separate caches. For example, we could organize our 4K cache as a 4-way set associative cache, where each section of the cache had 64 16-byte lines. The address is now interpreted as follows:

22 bits	6 bits	4 bits

The 6-bit field is the line number within any of the four parts of the cache. This means that a given memory location can be stored in any of four different cache lines. In the string copying example, the source and destination arrays can be cached in separate sections of the cache, avoiding the conflict. Searching a multiway set associative cache is much easier at the hardware level since the number of parallel searches that must be performed is much smaller.

When a cache miss occurs, a decision must be made on which data to evict from the cache. For a directly addressed cache, there *is* only one alternative, so there is no problem. For a set associative cache, or a fully associative cache, there is a choice. There is no time to execute fancy algorithms, so typical hardware makes this decision using rather simple approaches. One approach which works quite well in practice is to simply make a random choice.

TASKING

The fundamental idea behind tasking is that a machine can have two or more processes with separate threads of control that are both executing in a multiprogramming sense. Each of those tasks owns the processor and the registers when it is executing. Of course, a machine that has only one processor, one program counter, and one set of registers can execute only one program at a time. But it is possible to effectively simulate true multiprogramming by executing some instructions for one task and then, for whatever reason, switching back to the next task and executing its instructions.

In switching from one task to another, an operation known as a *context switch*, the operating system needs to save the state of the executing task, called the *machine state*. The machine state is essentially everything that is in the processor. It does not include the state of memory, because each task has its own memory. The machine state includes the instruction pointer, the flags that show the results of condition tests that might have been set, and all the registers.

Once the machine state has been saved (with the memory used by the task still preserved) the processor state is completely removed so that some other task can use the processor. Later on, the operating system will arrange to put all of the original task's machine state information back into the processor and the processor will be ready to execute the instruction that it was just about to execute when the context switch occurred. When a task is temporarily suspended, a data structure called a *task control block* (TCB) is used to store the machine state information for the inactive task.

A context switch saves the machine state for the current task in its TCB and then uses the TCB for some other task that is ready to execute to restore its machine state. With most processors, the context switch is accomplished by software, using a sequence of instructions to save the current machine state and a corresponding sequence of instructions to restore the current machine state. The TCB is an operating system data object whose structure is determined by the operating systems software.

There are situations in which the context switching time is a critical consideration. This typically arises in real-time systems, which must rapidly switch attention between input/output devices. In such situations, context switching represents yet another possible target for the eager CISC designer, always ready to implement specialized instructions to help with common operations.

Most of the processors covered in this book do not have any hardware instructions to support tasking, but there are two exceptions, the Intel 80386 and the INMOS Transputer, where the processor provides hardware support for tasking. Particularly in the case of the Transputer, this hardware support makes very rapid context switching practical.

EXCEPTIONS

An exception is an interruption of the normal flow of instruction processing. There are two situations in which this occurs. The first, which we call a trap, occurs when the processor recognizes that the execution of an instruction has caused an error of some kind. The second, which we call an interrupt, occurs when a device external to the processor signals that a certain event should be brought to its attention. The terminology in this area varies widely between processors, in a rather random manner. This is one area where we prefer to adopt a consistent terminology at the expense of not always matching every manufacturer's idiosyncratic usage.

The instructions on some processors signal an error condition (such as overflow) by setting a status flag which can be tested in a subsequent instruction. Integer overflow is handled this way on most of the processors we will look at. The alternative approach is to generate a trap, which causes a sudden transfer of control, much like a procedure call in that the calling location (i.e., the instruction causing the problem) is saved, but differing from a normal procedure call in that traps typically cause a transition into supervisor or protected state. This means that trap conditions are handled by the operating system. In some cases, this is obviously appropriate. For example, in a virtual memory environment, a trap will occur if the required page is not present. Clearly the operating system needs to handle this condition, and furthermore it certainly needs to be in supervisor state to do it. In other cases such as divide by zero, it is not so clear that the condition should be handled by the operating system. If the handling should logically be done by the application program (for instance, an Ada program needs to handle the CONSTRAINT_ERROR exception that results from a division by zero), then the operating system can transfer control back to the application program as needed.

The second situation in which the flow of instructions is suddenly modified is when an external interrupt occurs, typically signalling the completion of an input/output operation. Again, this interrupt functions similarly to a procedure call, except that it makes a transition to supervisor state. Input/output handling is clearly the province of the operating system. In the general case, it is quite likely that the task that is interrupted has nothing at all to do with the interrupt—it may well belong to some other task or some other currently running program in a multiprogramming system.

The distinction between traps and interrupts is not always precise. Traps are generally synchronous, since they occur in conjunction with the execution of particular instructions. Interrupts, on the other hand, are generally asynchronous, since they can occur at any point in time. However, there are intermediate cases. For example, some floating-point coprocessors have overlapped execution, so that a floating-point overflow—which from one point of view is a trap, since it is caused by a specific instruction on the coprocessor—behaves like an interrupt, since it occurs asynchronously on the main processor a number of instructions after the one that led to the overflow.

Hardware Support for Exceptions

All the processors we will look at have hardware support for interrupts and traps. This includes a mechanism (usually available only in supervisor state) to turn the processor interrupts on and off to control whether hardware interrupts are recognized. When an exception occurs, the machine state of the executing task must not be logically altered. This is particularly important in the case of an asynchronous interrupt—we can't have registers or flags disappearing without warning anywhere an interrupt might occur! At the very least, the hardware must save the instruction pointer, leaving the saving of registers and flags to the interrupt routine itself. Alternatively, the hardware designer may arrange to save considerably more of the machine state automatically. We will see a full variety of possibilities here as we study a range of processors.

Another respect in which processors differ is the extent to which they separate exceptions. At one extreme, every separate condition, including each interrupt from a separate device, is automatically handled by a separate exception handler. The Intel 80386 is an example of such an organization. At the other extreme, there is a single exception handler which must handle all traps and interrupts and has to check various status flags and registers to see what is going on. The i860 is arranged in this simpler manner—it is simpler for the hardware designer, but, of course, the operating systems programmer who has to write the exception routine may not see things quite the same way.

The handling of hardware interrupts poses some special problems, because several interrupts can occur at the same time and some interrupts require very rapid attention. Most processors have some kind of interrupt priority logic that assigns interrupts to various priority levels—the decision as to which device to attach to which priority is one that is made not by the designer of the processor but by the system designer who puts together a processor using a specific chip. For example, on the IBM PC, the timer has the highest priority, to ensure that no timer interrupts are lost and that the time of day stays accurate.

Other facilities often include the ability to temporarily *mask* an interrupt. The operating system uses this in organizing the handling of interrupts. One example is that generally you don't want the same device to interrupt again before you have finished handling the previous interrupt. By masking the device until the handling is complete, a second interrupt is inhibited until it is once again convenient to handle it.

Another consideration in handling device interrupts is that instructions that take a very long time to execute are problematic if interrupts occur only between instructions. There are two approaches to this problem. One is to make long instructions interruptible, so that they can be interrupted and then resume from where they left off.

The string instructions of the 80386 are designed this way. The second approach is to divide up a complex instruction into a sequence of component instructions. For example, the Transputer floating-point instructions include *Begin Square Root, Continue Square Root*, and *Finish Square Root*. To compute a square root, these three instructions are issued in sequence (they are never used separately). By using this approach, a hardware interrupt does not have to wait until the entire square root computation is complete.

CHAPTER

2

INTRODUCTION TO THE 80386

The 386 is an example, perhaps *the* example of a CISC architecture. Describing a complex instruction set is a complex operation, so we devote three chapters to it. In this chapter we look at the instruction set from an application programmer's point of view, and in later chapters describe its support for operating systems.

REGISTER STRUCTURE

A starting point for looking at any microprocessor architecture is its register structure, since this affects the instruction set to a large degree, particularly in the case of CISC processors. The 386, as we shall see, has an unusual register set whose design can be traced back to some of the earliest Intel microprocessors. Before looking at the details of the 386 register set, we will describe some of this heritage. The Intel 8080, the predecessor of the 8086, was an 8-bit machine, and its register structure, a set of eight 8-bit registers, reflected this organization. It was possible for very limited purposes to join some of these 8-bit registers to form 16-bit registers, but it was nevertheless an 8-bit machine in most other respects.

When the 8086 was designed, the issue of compatibility with the 8080 was an important one. On the one hand, Intel marketing was interested in guaranteeing total compatibility with the 8080, and the sales force gave the impression that the 8086 *would* be upwards compatible. Customers were then writing 8080 programs, and clearly had an interest in protecting their software investments. On the other hand, the redesign was seen by the engineering group as an opportunity for enhancements. At the very least, doubling the addressable memory from 64K to 128K was important. Beyond this, there seem to have been a number of conflicting desires and requirements. Some constituencies had thoughts of major surgery, and there was talk of eliminating the non-symmetrical nature of the 8080. If taken seriously, this would have meant a complete redesign. Since Intel was concerned about maintaining its customer base, which was at that time under siege from Zilog (the manufacturer of the Z80, a popular replacement for the 8080), these requirements were important to management.

The principal designer of the 8086, Stephen Morse, steered an interesting course in the middle of these conflicting requirements. On the one hand, the 8086 is quite compatible with the basic structure of the 8080. On the other hand, the design was not constrained by an absolute compatibility requirement, and in particular, the addressing was extended far beyond the 128K that had been originally envisioned, to an address space of one megabyte, which at that time seemed huge for a microprocessor. One important benefit, at least in retrospect, even if it was not a deliberately intended effect, was that the attempt to maintain a reasonable level of compatibility helped to reduce the design work required, and therefore contributed to the important goal of getting something out fast. At the same time the final result was much more than Intel management's original concept of a slightly beefed-up 8080.

To resolve the compatibility issue, a translation program was created which converted 8080 assembly language to 8086 assembly language. In practice this program generated horrible code, and no one in the engineering department at Intel ever expected it to be used. On the other hand, the sales force could now talk to customers and tell them "Don't worry, all you have to do is to feed your code through our translator program which fixes up the "minor" discrepancies between the 8080 and 8086, and you'll never know that the architecture has changed." This kind of discrepancy between what engineering thinks and what the sales force says is not uncommon—sometimes it results from confusion and wishful thinking, sometimes it is a more or less conscious deception to keep customers locked into a manufacturer's product.

Returning to the register set of the 8086, we will see that its design is strongly affected by the register structure of the 8080. With the exception of the flags register, all registers of the 8086 are 16 bits wide (see Figure 2.1). Some of the registers have curious names, which reflects their special uses. Each of the 16-bit registers AX, BX, CX, and DX is divided up into two 8-bit components that can be used as if they were individual registers. The AX register, for example, is divided into AH and AL, the former being the top 8 bits of AX and the latter being the lower 8 bits. This was done partly in an attempt to map the register structure of the 8-bit 8080 into the bottom four registers of the 16-bit 8086. If you look only at these eight registers, the register structure of the 8086 looks just like that of the 8080.

In addition to duplicating the register structure of the 8080, a full set of 8-bit instructions was also provided. In general there are two sets of instructions on the 8086.

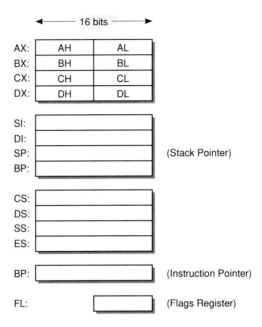

FIGURE 2.1
The register structure of the Intel 8086.

There is one bit in every opcode that determines whether an instruction is the 16-bit version of the instruction or the 8-bit version. This bit is called the W-bit, which stands for *word* bit, and it is set to 1 for the 16-bit case.

   The structure of the instruction formats of the 8086 is such that the W-bit is included as part of the opcode part of an instruction. Following the opcode in various places there are 3-bit fields that are operand/register numbers. If the W-bit is set, the register operands indicated by one of these fields will be interpreted as a 16-bit register, while if the W-bit is off it will be interpreted as an 8-bit register.

   Notice that having the W-bit in the opcode commits one from an architectural point of view to having all operands in an instruction be the same length. Looking at the kind of instructions that are available on the 8086, it is possible to write

        MOV   AL, BL   ; 8-bit register copied to 8-bit register

or

        MOV   AX, BX

but it is not possible to write

        MOV   AX, BL

What would the last instruction mean? A reasonable interpretation would be that the low order 8 bits of the BX register should be copied into the AX register, with either sign or zero extension. But neither of these reasonable interpretations is permitted since the W-bit that is part of the MOV opcode specifies that the size of all register operands is either 8 bits or 16 bits. A more general architectural design is to put designators of types and operands into the operands themselves (the VAX uses this approach). This gives a quite general mixing of operands of different types. But that, of course, takes more bits and more logic, because every operand would require such a bit.

All of this is just a matter of whether it is possible to fit into the opcode the ability to extend an 8-bit value into 16 bits. This can, of course, be programmed if necessary. It is very simple to program that operation. It is written by zero-extending BL (if that's what is required), using the sequence

```
MOV    AL, BL
MOV    AH, 0
```

Special Registers and Instructions

Each of the registers on the 8086 can be distinguished from every other register in some way. This lack of orthogonality is something for which the 8086 is well known. This architecture is thus at the opposite design extreme from machines with uniform register sets. Enumerating all the specialized uses of the registers would take too long and be too messy, so we will simply give some examples.

Multiplication on most machines involves putting a result into a register pair, since the result of an n-bit by n-bit multiplication will in general require $2n$ bits. The 8086 has a 16- by 16-bit multiply, which yields a 32-bit result. The solution on the 8086 is to require that operands and the result be placed in specific registers. This multiplication specifically requires that the multiplicand be put into AX, with the 32-bit result put into the DX:AX pair.

The register CX is another register with a special use. The 8086 has a loop instruction (LOOP) that automatically decrements the CX register and then executes a jump if CX is not equal to zero. To execute a loop 15 times, the code is

```
        MOV    CX, 15
LP:

        . . .

        LOOP   LP
```

This is very much the kind of instruction that is "mission-oriented," that is, intended for use in a very specific situation. Since the normal format of a jump instruction does not have enough room to designate a register (most conditional jump instructions test special bits within a status register such as the carry flag and the overflow flag), the operands are usually implied rather than being explicitly specified in the instruction. In this sense, the choice to use CX rather than another register as the basis of whether or not to jump is somewhat arbitrary.

The XLAT instruction makes special use of both the BX register and the AL register. The memory location whose address is formed by adding the contents of the BX and AL registers is loaded into the AL register. One obvious use of this instruction is for translating character sets—hence the name.

The index registers SI and DI have special uses in connection with string instructions that copy a sequence of bytes from one location to another. ("S" stands for source, and "D" for destination.) BP and SP have special uses in conjunction with the call stack. We will discuss the special uses of each of these registers in detail later on.

Before we go further, let us describe the register structure of the 386 and talk about the operand formats. The 386 has exactly the same structure as the 8086, except that each of the registers is 32 bits wide and each register is renamed by putting an "E" on the front (you may think of the "E" as meaning "extended"). The bottom 16 bits of each register has a name that corresponds to the old 8086 names, the right-hand half of this picture is identical in all respects to the 8086 register model (Figure 2.2).

Maintaining Compatibility with the 8086/88

The register structure of the 386 would seem rather peculiar if we did not understand its 8086 origins (see Figure 2.2). At the right, you can see a structure that looks identical to the 8086 and is completely compatible with it, but the registers are extended to 32-bits. The 16-bit CX register on the 8086, for example, becomes a 32-bit extended register called ECX on the 386.

The problem is, the instruction formats of the 386 have to be pretty much the same as the 286 because the compatibility requirement is very strong. Recall that on the 8086 and 80286 in the opcode byte (the general form of an instruction is that there is an 8-bit opcode followed by other fields) there is a W-bit that on the 286 says whether to use 8 or 16 bits. There isn't room in the 8-bit opcode field to fit an extra bit in saying, "Please use 32 bits." If the 386 were being designed from scratch, it would probably have been preferable to have three possible designators so that 8-bit, 16-bit, and 32-bit references could be freely mixed. But there just is not enough room in the existing instruction formats.

The trick that is used to solve this problem is the following. There is an overall mode for the processor that can be set to put the machine into either 16-bit mode or 32-bit mode. If W is set to 0, the processor always uses 8-bit operations, regardless of the mode, but if W is set to 1, then the processor uses either 32-bit or 16-bit operations depending on the mode. In the 32-bit mode there is a choice between 32-bit and 8-bit operands, while in the 16-bit mode there is a choice between 16-bit and 8-bit operands.

In order to write code that is compatible with the IBM PC or to run PC-compatible code, the processor will operate in 16-bit mode. In this mode, none of the code ever uses the upper half of the 32-bit registers—all the instructions work in such a way that they are blind and oblivious to the higher-order bits. To operate the 386 as a 32-bit machine, it must operate in 32-bit mode. Eight-bit operations are still available, of course, since characters are important whatever the word size.

There is one trick that gives a programmer a little more flexibility. There is an operand prefix byte (it has a special coding as 66 Hex, which is different from any opcode value) that directs the processor to change modes for the next instruction. That allows you to mix some 16-bit mode instructions into 32-bit code, or vice versa. If you have code that heavily mixes 16- and 32-bit instructions, then the code will be covered

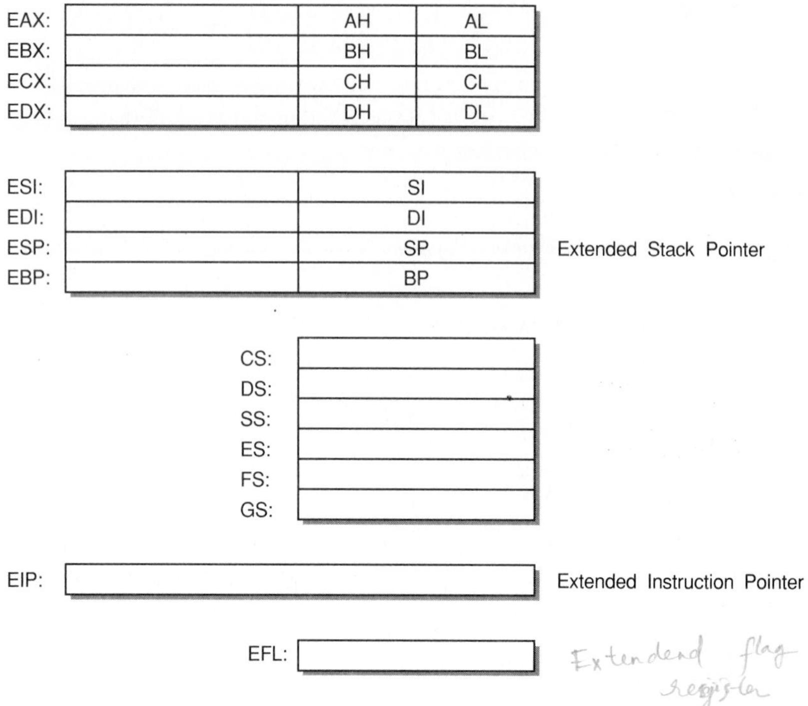

EAX:		AH	AL
EBX:		BH	BL
ECX:		CH	CL
EDX:		DH	DL

ESI:	SI
EDI:	DI
ESP:	SP	Extended Stack Pointer
EBP:	BP

CS:	
DS:	
SS:	
ES:	
FS:	
GS:	

EIP: Extended Instruction Pointer

EFL: *Extended flag register*

FIGURE 2.2
The user register set of the 80386.

with these prefixes (wasting time and space). There is no practical way to flip the current processor between 16- and 32-bit operating modes.

This mechanism is rather clumsy, probably not what would have been chosen if the design were started from scratch. If the design were not constrained by compatibility considerations, the 16-bit operations might have been omitted, or at least a more usable mechanism devised for mixing the three operand lengths.

THE USER INSTRUCTION SET

In this section, we will give a brief overview of the general design of the 386 instruction set. We will not describe every single instruction in detail—such a description can be found in the Intel 80386 Programmer's Reference Manual and in many other books on the 386. What we want to do is to get a general idea of the instructions that are available and concentrate on unusual instructions that exhibit the CISC philosophy of providing specialized instructions for common high-level programming constructs.

Basic Data Movement Instructions

The 386 move instructions allow you to move data between registers, between registers and memory, but not directly between different memory locations:

```
MOV    reg1, mem      ; load reg1 from memory
MOV    mem, reg1      ; store the value in reg1 into memory
MOV    reg1, reg2     ; copy a value from reg2 into reg1
```

The simplicity of this description of the addressing modes of the 386 hides the fact that the memory references implied by the *mem* operands actually allow a programmer to use a relatively rich set of addressing modes in defining a memory address.

Basic Arithmetic and Logical Operations

The most commonly used instructions take two operands, one of which is a register; the other can be a register or a memory location. In assembly language, one format for the addition instruction is

```
ADD    EAX, K
```

This instruction adds the contents of memory location K to the contents of the EAX register, leaving the result in EAX. The addition is a 32-bit addition that can be regarded as unsigned or two's complement. Three flags are set by the result:

- CF, the carry flag, is set if there is an unsigned overflow.
- OF, the overflow flag, is set if there is a signed overflow.
- ZF, the zero flag, is set if the result is all zero bits.

Unlike many of the other processors that we will look at, the 386 permits operations *to* memory as well as operations *from* memory:

```
ADD    K, EAX
```

computes the same sum, but the result is stored back into memory location K. The same instruction format can also be used for operations between the registers:

```
ADD    EAX, EBX
```

This instruction computes the sum of EAX and EBX, placing the sum in EAX. A large number of two-operand instructions share this basic instruction format, with the result always replacing the contents of the left operand:

```
ADC    op1, op2      ; addition including CF
SUB    op1, op2      ; subtraction
SBB    op1, op2      ; subtraction including CF
CMP    op1, op2      ; comparison (like subtraction, but no result stored)
AND    op1, op2      ; logical AND
OR     op1, op2      ; logical OR
XOR    op1, op2      ; logical exclusive OR
```

```
TEST    op1, op2          ; bit test (like AND, but no result stored)
MOV     op1, op2          ; copy operand 2 to operand 1
LEA     op1, op2          ; place address of operand 2 in operand 1
```

The ADC and SBB instructions are useful for multiple precision addition and subtraction, since they include the carry flag from the previous operation, so, for example, a typical triple-precision (96-bit) addition can be written as:

```
ADD     EAX, EDX          ; add low-order words
ADC     EBX, ESI          ; add next word with carry from previous
ADC     ECX, EDI          ; ECX:EBX:EAX = ECX:EBX:EAX + EDI:ESI:EDX
```

The comparison instruction, CMP, behaves exactly like a subtraction but does not store a result. It does, however, set the OF, CF, and ZF flags, from which a full set of both signed and unsigned comparison conditions can be deduced. A complete set of jumps is available to test these conditions:

```
JMP     lbl               ; unconditional jump
JA      lbl               ; jump above (greater than, unsigned)
JAE     lbl               ; jump above or equal (unsigned)
JB      lbl               ; jump below (less than, unsigned)
JBE     lbl               ; jump below or equal (unsigned)
JE      lbl               ; jump equal (same for signed or unsigned)
JNE     lbl               ; jump not equal (same for signed or unsigned)
JG      lbl               ; jump greater than (signed)
JGE     lbl               ; jump greater than or equal (signed)
JL      lbl               ; jump less than (signed)
JLE     lbl               ; jump less than or equal (signed)
```

Operations that take only a single operand can be used with either a register or a memory operand:

```
INC     op                ; increment operand by 1
DEC     op                ; decrement operand by 1
NEG     op                ; negate operand
NOT     op                ; invert operand bits
```

The operations described so far can operate on 8-bit operands (using one of the 8-bit registers, AL, BL, ...), 16-bit operands (using one of the 16-bit registers, AX, BX, ...), or 32-bit operands (using one of the 32-bit registers, EAX, EBX, ...). The following instructions are one of the few cases where operands of different lengths can be mixed:

```
MOVSX op1, op2            ; move with sign extension
MOVZX op1, op2            ; move with zero extension
```

The motivation behind the inclusion of these instructions in the instruction set is to allow the second operand to be shorter than the first and either sign- or zero-extended to fill the larger operand. For example, *op1* can be EAX and *op2* can be a byte in memory. In this case MOVSX loads a byte from memory, sign-extending it to fill 32 bits.

Multiplication and Division Instructions

We will complete the picture of integer arithmetic by describing the set of multiply and divide instructions. The basic multiply instruction takes only one operand:

```
MUL     op1              ; unsigned multiplication
IMUL    op1              ; signed multiplication
```
Register A

The second operand is always the accumulator (AL, AX, or EAX, depending on the length of the operand). The result always goes in the extended accumulator (AX, DX:AX, or EDX:EAX).

This specialized use of registers keeps the instructions shorter, since the instruction need not specify one of the operands. On the other hand, it complicates life for the assembler programmer and particularly for a compiler writer, because it means that multiplication must be treated in a special way compared to addition and subtraction and that EAX must be treated differently from the other registers. Division is similarly specialized:

```
DIV     op1              ; unsigned division
IDIV    op1              ; signed division
```

The dividend is always in the extended accumulator. The remainder and quotient are stored back in the two halves of the extended accumulator. For example, in the 32-bit form, EDX:EAX is divided by the 32-bit operand, with the remainder stored in EDX and the quotient stored in EAX.

On the 8086, this was the complete set of multiply and divide instructions. The 386 has some additional instructions to perform multiplication:

```
IMUL    op1, op              ; single-length multiply
IMUL    op1, op2, immediate
```

The first form performs a single-length multiplication (8-, 16-, or 32-bit), putting the result in the left operand as usual. It is interesting to note that there is no MUL in this format—none is needed, since, as in the case of addition and subtraction, the signed and unsigned results are the same if only the low-order bits are generated. This multiply instruction corresponds to the normal multiplication required in high-level languages like C or FORTRAN, so it is highly convenient for a compiler.

The second format is highly idiosyncratic. It multiplies *op2*, which can be a register or memory, by the immediate operand and places the resulting single-length product in *op1*, which must be a register. There are no other three-operand instructions of this type in the instruction set. Why on earth did this instruction get added? This is a good example of another mission-oriented CISC instruction.

Consider the case of indexing an array, where the elements of the array are 32 bytes long. The following instruction is just what is needed:

```
IMUL    EBX, I, 32
```

EBX now contains the byte offset into the array whose subscript is I. Is it worth having this special instruction? That is always the $64,000 question! On the one hand, array indexing is a common operation. On the other hand, RISC advocates would argue that a decent compiler can eliminate nearly all such multiplication instructions using a standard optimization called *strength reduction*. Consider the following loop:

```
for I in 1 .. 100 loop
    S := S + Q(I).VAL;
end loop;
```

Let us assume that Q is an array of records where each record is 32 bytes long and the VAL field is in the first 4 bytes of each record. Naive code for this loop can make nice use of the special IMUL instruction:

```
        MOV     ECX, 1          ; use ECX to hold I
LP:     IMUL    EAX, ECX, 32    ; get offset in EAX
        MOV     EBX, Q[EAX]     ; load VAL field
        ADD     S, EBX          ; add to S
        INC     ECX             ; increment I
        CMP     ECX, 100        ; test against limit
        JNE     LP              ; loop until I = 100
```

A clever compiler using strength reduction would replace I by 32*I, generating the following code:

```
        MOV     ECX, 32         ; get 32 * I in ECX
LP:     MOV     EBX, Q[ECX]     ; load VAL field
        ADD     S, EBX          ; add to S
        ADD     ECX, 32         ; add 32 to 32 * I
        CMP     ECX, 3200       ; compare against adjusted limit
        JNE     LP              ; loop until I * 32 = 100 * 32
```

This code is clearly much more efficient since it does not need to make use of the fancy multiply instruction. If it is true that compilers can always get rid of these multiplications, then the RISC advocates have a point. In practice not all of them can be eliminated, so the situation is clouded. There are also many "stupid" compilers in the world, so it can also be argued that relying on clever compilers is somewhat unrealistic.

DOUBLE-LENGTH MULTIPLY AND DIVIDE. Not all processors provide the double-length forms of multiply and divide, but as we have seen the 386 is an example of a processor that has both. Looking at high-level languages, one might wonder whether these instructions are of any use. Among all the commonly used high-level languages, *only* COBOL gives access to them. This is done using statements such as:

MULTIPLY SINGLE-ONE BY SINGLE-TWO GIVING DOUBLE-RESULT
DIVIDE DOUBLE-DIVIDEND BY SINGLE-DIVISOR GIVING SINGLE-QUOTIENT.

There are three reasons for providing these instructions. First, it tends to be more or less free in the hardware. To multiply 32 bits by 32 bits, the standard hardware algorithms require 32 steps of shifting and adding. A 64-bit result is naturally developed without any extra work. Similarly, a 32-bit division involves 32 steps and can naturally deal with a double-length dividend.

In addition, there are two programming situations in which these double-length instructions are useful. First, consider multiple-precision arithmetic. When you learn multiplication in grade school, you are taught that multiplying a single digit by a single digit can give a result of up to two digits in the form of the multiplication tables up to 10 by 10 (the 10 times table is redundant, but it is easy, and we teach it to reinforce the notion of multiplication by 10 being equivalent to moving the decimal point). When grade-school students are taught the 9 times table, they learn that nine 9s are 81—you don't learn that nine 9s are 1 and the carry doesn't matter! That's because if you want to do long multiplication by hand you need that carry-digit on multiplication.

The same principle applies to programming multiple-precision multiplications. When multiplying 10 words by 10 words, you need the one word by one word giving two words as the component instruction in the algorithm. Similarly, multiple-precision division, which is much more complicated, also requires the double-length divide.

A second situation arises in computing expressions of the form B * C / D with integer operands. With double-length operations, the result of the multiplication can temporarily overflow into double length, with the division then bringing the quotient back into single-length range. At DISC, a typesetting company in Chicago (owned by the brother of the first author), the primary application repeatedly evaluates expressions of this type for scaling graphics and type on the screen and printer. For this scaling, it is important that double-length results be permitted.

The original version of the DISC application was written in assembly language on a processor providing double-length results, so there was no problem. The most recent version of the software is written in C and runs on the 386. Although the 386 provides the double-length operations, C does not provide access to them, so there is a choice of catastrophes. The results of all arithmetic operations can either be left in single precision (in which case it is possible to get an overflow on the multiplication and hence a wrong result) *or* everything can be converted to 64 bits:

```
a = int (long(b) * long(c)) / long(d)
```

This implies a multiplication by two 64-bit values, and there certainly is not an instruction to do that. Consequently, a C compiler will generate a call to a time-consuming software multiply routine, followed by another call to an even more time-consuming 64-bit division routine, even though all of this could have been done in assembly language in two instructions.

At DISC, they finally had to resort to doing these scaling operations with a small assembler routine. Even with the extra overhead of the call, the application was speeded up by nearly 20%. That is still sort of sad, isn't it? The machine they use has the right instructions, but C does not give access to them. There isn't always perfect communication between language designers and hardware designers.

GETTING BOTH THE QUOTIENT AND REMAINDER. Another feature of the divide instruction on the 386 is that it provides both the quotient and the remainder in the same instruction. Again, this is almost free at the hardware level—think about how to do a long division. At the end of a division, the remainder is left as a consequence of doing the division. Once again, among high-level languages, only COBOL gives direct access to this instruction:

    DIVIDE A BY B GIVING C REMAINDER D.

It may be a little verbose, but at least we can do it. In Ada, we have to write

    C := A / B;
    D := A rem B;

and hope that our compiler is clever enough to notice that it only needed to do one division. We will probably be disappointed—even if the compiler recognizes and eliminates common subexpressions, it may well miss this case, because the expression is not common at the source level, only at the level of the generated code.

Decimal Arithmetic

The decimal arithmetic operations provide a nice example of the CISC design philosophy in action. Let's consider one of them, Decimal Adjust after Addition (DAA), in detail. DAA performs the following sequence of computations:

    if ((AL and 0FH) > 9) or (AF = 1) then
        AL ← AL + 6;
        AF ← 1;
    else
        AF ← 0;
    end if;
    if (AL > 9FH) or (CF = 1) then
        AL ← AL + 60H;
        CF ← 1;
    else
        CF ← 0;
    end if;

What on earth is going on here? First of all, we need to explain that AF is another status flag, which is set as the result of a normal ADD instruction. If there is a carry from bit 3 to bit 4 in the result of an addition, then AF is set (see Figure 2.3).

Even with the considerable hint given by the name of the instruction it is hard to tell what is going on. DAA is used to represent decimal numbers using packed decimal format, described in Chapter 1. With this format in mind, the DAA operation becomes a little clearer. If we get a carry (i.e., result greater than 9) in the rightmost digit, then it shows up either as the result digit being greater than 9, or by setting AF. If there is such a carry, then adding 6 is exactly the right operation to correct the result:

page 14

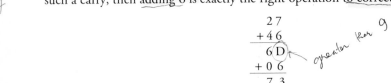

$$\begin{array}{r} 2\,7 \\ +\,4\,6 \\ \hline 6\,D \\ +\,0\,6 \\ \hline 7\,3 \end{array}$$

greater than 9

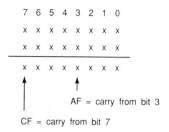

FIGURE 2.3
Setting of the AF and CF flags during decimal arithmetic.

The second test similarly corrects a carry from the left digit of an 8-bit byte. A multiple-digit packed decimal addition can thus be programmed using the normal ADC multiple-precision addition loop, with the insertion of a single DAA instruction after each addition.

This is a nice example of a complex instruction with a specific purpose. If a great deal of decimal arithmetic is required, then the DAA instruction can save a significant amount of time. COBOL compilers for the 386 make extensive use of this instruction. For general applications, especially those written in languages like C and Ada, which do not have a packed decimal datatype, the hardware for DAA is completely wasted.

It is always difficult to decide what specialized instructions to provide. A principal difference between the CISC and RISC views of the instruction set is that CISC designers are generally looking for opportunities to provide specialized instructions, whereas RISC designers eschew them completely. The 386 has an entire set of specialized instructions for decimal arithmetic, including:

DAA   Decimal Adjust after Addition
DAS   Decimal Adjust after Subtraction
AAA   ASCII Adjust after Addition
AAD   ASCII Adjust before Division
AAM   ASCII Adjust after Multiplication
AAS   ASCII Adjust after Subtraction

These instructions all perform specialized operations which are hard to understand unless their specialized use is understood. The last four cases operate on data stored in what COBOL would call DISPLAY format, one ASCII digit per 8-bit byte.

String Instructions

Another set of instructions that are intended for specialized use is the string instructions. They make special use of the registers ESI and EDI. ESI holds the address of the source string, the string from which data is used, and EDI holds the address of the destination string, the one where data is stored. In fact, the D and the S in the names of these registers come precisely from this specialized use.

With these registers loaded, the following string instructions can be used:

- MOVSB copies one character from the source string to the destination string; both pointers are incremented by 1.
- STOSB stores the contents of the AL register into the destination string, bumping the destination pointer.
- LODSB loads a character from the source string into the AL register, bumping the source pointer.
- CMPSB compares the next characters in the source and destination strings, bumping both pointers.
- SCASB compares the contents of the AL register with the next character in the destination string, bumping the destination pointer.

Although these descriptions imply that the strings are always scanned forward, it is also possible to use them to scan backward. The *direction flag* (DF) can be cleared and set using the CLD and STD instructions. If it is set, then the source and destination registers are decremented; if it is cleared they are incremented. There is also a set of instructions for loading 16- and 32-bit values, bumping the pointers by 2 or 4 bytes as appropriate.

These instructions are much more useful when they are combined with the use of the REP prefix. When any of these string instructions has a REP prefix, the instruction is repeated the number of times specified by the value stored in the ECX register. For example, to move a string, we simply execute

```
MOV    ECX, length
LEA    ESI, string1
LEA    EDI, string2
REP    MOVSB
```

and the entire string is moved by the final instruction. Of course, this instruction takes a considerable number of clocks if the string is long, but it is still much faster than programming a loop for the character move. By using REP in conjunction with CMPSB you can compare strings, stopping at the first unequal character. Similarly, using this prefix with SCASB allows scanning a string for a particular character. In both cases, the actual string operations are executed with a single instruction.

These string instructions are a good example of specialized instructions. The question to be raised for any specialized instructions is how often they are used. In the case of character strings, almost all applications use them heavily, and they are supported in all high-level programming languages—the are indeed used often.

As a programmer, you may well be disappointed by the extent to which most compilers are actually able to use these instructions. One of the continuing problems with specialized instructions is that it is relatively hard for a compiler to recognize when these instructions can be used. Suppose you write the following Ada code

```
for I in 1 .. N loop
    D(I) := S(I);
end loop;
```

or a C programmer writes

```
i = 1;
while (i < 100)
    *d++ = *s++;
```

It is not so easy for the compiler to see that a single instruction will achieve the result of the loop. Some C compilers *are* this clever, and in particular the Microsoft C compiler makes an attempt to recognize special constructs like this. In the case of Ada, the programmer should have written

```
D(1..N) := S(1..N);
```

giving the compiler a much better shot at recognizing that what is going on is a block copy. We know of no Ada compilers for the 386 that would recognize the explicit loop and compile a single REP MOVSB instruction.

Shift Instructions

The 386 has a complete set of shift and rotate instructions. Either the shift count can be implied to be 1, or put in the CL register, or given as an immediate value. The double-shift instruction, introduced in the 386, is of particular interest. The form is

```
SHRD    reg1, reg2, count
SHLD    reg1, reg2, count
```

The effect is to shift *reg1*, moving in extra bits from *reg2*. The contents of *reg2* is not affected, and the third parameter provides the count. In the Programmer's Reference Manual, Intel specifically points out, by giving detailed coding examples, that this double-shift instruction is suitable for moving arbitrarily aligned blocks of bits around in memory and for inserting arbitrary blocks of bits into memory.

Why are these operations important? Again, a very specific answer: bit-mapped graphic displays map bits in memory to display pixels on the screen. These two operations then correspond to moving and placing objects in a bit-mapped graphics display. In order to write a very fast video game on the 386, these special double-shift operations will be quite delightful. Even more delightful might be the discovery that Intel produces a specialized coprocessor with even more elaborate instructions to support graphics (this is the i860, which we will cover in a later chapter).

The Set on Condition Instructions

Comparison conditions are usually tested using conditional jumps, and this is just what is needed for most "if" statements:

```
if A = B then
    ...
end if;
```

translates directly as

```
MOV     EAX,A
CMP     EAX,B
JLE     end_if
```

However, there is another use of comparison operations in typical high-level languages, and that is the generation of Boolean values. Consider the statement:

A := (B > C) or (D = F);

If we have only conditional jump instructions, we are forced to generate something like

```
        MOV     EAX, B
        CMP     EAX, C
        MOV     BL, 0        ; 0 is false
        JLE     N1           N2
        MOV     BL, 1        ; 1 is true      yes        B > C
N1:     MOV     EAX, D
        CMP     EAX, F
        MOV     BH, 0
        JNE     N2
        MOV     BH, 1
N2:     OR      BL, BH
```

This is not a particularly attractive sequence of code, especially because jump instructions, as we will understand later, are rather inefficient.

This is another instance in which a specific set of instructions was introduced for the first time in the Intel series on the 386. The SETcc instructions check the condition code corresponding to cc and generate either a 0 or 1—which is, not at all coincidentally, *exactly* what we need. Now we can translate the assignment as

```
        MOV     EAX, B
        CMP     EAX, C
        SETG    BL           ; BL = 0/1 depending on result
        MOV     EAX, D
        CMP     EAX, F
        MOV     BH, 0
        SETE    BH
        OR      BL, BH
```

This code is, of course, much more efficient for this particular operation. As always, we need to assess whether it is likely that programs spend a substantial amount of time executing such assignment statements, and the answer in this case is probably not.

Summing Up

We certainly have not covered the entire instruction set of the 80386. For a CISC processor with well over 200 instructions, there is simply not enough room in this text. The Intel Programmer's Reference Manual devotes 174 pages to a description of the instructions that is still very terse and conveys only the bare details of what the instructions do, not how they are used.

We will cover several more instructions in other sections. In particular, the set of instructions used to call procedures and access the run-time stack is important enough that the entire following section has been devoted to them. We will also look at some of the instructions used to support the implementation of an operating system as we discuss the protection and addressing features.

The important point is to get a flavor of the design approach. The 386 is a dense chip with a large number of transistors. There is room for a large set of instructions, and the 386 designers have sat down and thought about what instructions might possibly be useful, especially from the point of view of compiler writers and high-level languages. The result is that a fair proportion of the instructions are highly specialized in that they are intended to be used in very specific situations. As we will see later, RISC designs take a very different approach, in which only general instructions usable in a large number of situations are retained.

REGISTERS AND THE RUN-TIME STACK

The 386 has fairly extensive support for the stack frame model of procedure calls. Two of the eight registers have special functions related to this use. First of all, the stack pointer ESP points to the bottom of the run-time stack, which always builds down in memory. Second, the register EBP is expected to be used as a frame pointer.[1]

The use of ESP and EBP is exactly as we described it in general terms in Chapter 1. As an example, suppose we have the Pascal procedure

```
procedure Recursive (ArgA, ArgB : Integer);
    var VarC, VarD : Integer;
begin
...
end;
```

Then when this procedure is executing, ESP and EBP are set as shown in Figure 2.4. The procedure parameters ArgA and ArgB are addressed using EBP as a base register with positive offsets, and the local variables VarA and VarB are also addressed using EBP as a based register, but with negative offsets.

Why EBP Is Needed

In Chapter 1, we discussed the need for a separate frame pointer, and in particular we pointed out that dynamic arrays are one reason for this requirement. However, Pascal does not *have* dynamic arrays, so we are once again tempted to wonder whether, at least for Pascal, we could get away with using ESP to address the stack frame. As we will see later, ESP can be used as a base register on the 386, so this is certainly a possibility. For example, VarC would be addressed as [ESP + 4] instead of [EBP − 4].

---

[1] The BP in the name stands for *base pointer*. It is true that the frame pointer is a special example of a base register, but we would have preferred the name EFP to make its function absolutely clear.

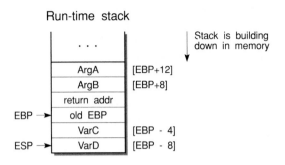

Run-time stack

Stack is building
down in memory

ArgA	[EBP+12]
ArgB	[EBP+8]
return addr	
old EBP	(EBP →)
VarC	[EBP - 4]
VarD	[EBP - 8] (ESP →)

FIGURE 2.4
The use of EBP and ESP on the 386.

It turns out that there is another pressing reason on the 386 to use a separate frame pointer. An important instruction that is likely to be executed by a procedure is the PUSH instruction. PUSH EAX, for example, takes the contents of register EAX and pushes it onto the bottom of the stack, decrementing the value of ESP in the process. If we were locating local variables at offsets from ESP rather than EBP, then this would be unfortunate, because suddenly the offset of each local variable in the frame would have changed, and continue changing as additional push instructions are executed. In the example that we have been using, the offset of VarC from ESP in the stack frame would have changed from +4 to +8.

Why not simply avoid pushing additional items onto the stack as a procedure executes? We can make that clear by showing the code that a "stupid" compiler might generate for the assignment

   A := (B + C) + (D + E);

The code generated by such a compiler for computing this expression is

```
MOV    EAX, B        ; one operand must be in a reg
ADD    EAX, C        ; add the other operand, C
PUSH   EAX           ; to compute D+E, make room in EAX
MOV    EAX, D        ; same as above
ADD    EAX, E
POP    EBX           ; pop B+C off the stack
ADD    EAX, EBX      ; add the two expressions
MOV    A, EAX        ; store to A
```

As the compiler generates code for this expression, it keeps track of which variables and expressions are contained in each register. Since the compiler may assume that all registers are empty at the start of code generation, it can emit a MOV instruction to load B followed by an ADD instruction to add the value of C to EAX. So far, so good.

Now the compiler needs to generate code to add D and E. An intelligent compiler might conclude, "Gee, I've got lots of registers. I could, for instance, use EBX for the next addition." But maybe the compiler isn't so clever and wants to use EAX for everything (lots of compilers are like that). "Oh, dear! I want to add D and E, and I need to load one of them into EAX in order to do so—but EAX has useful stuff in it. Let's save the contents of EAX on the stack using PUSH, and use EAX to add D and E."

Why would a compiler be this stupid? In compilers, simplicity and stupidity are related. A simple compiler will lack the more complex algorithms required to generate clever code. Sometimes simplicity is more important than generating good code. For example, in a compiler intended for student use, where speed of compilation is the most important issue, it is generally a poor choice to have a compiler spending a great deal of time generating more efficient code for programs that in any case are short and will be run only once or twice.

In this particular instance, the code that this hypothetical compiler generates for an addition is identical for both instances of the addition operator. That is a big simplification in the design of a compiler. It means that the compiler does not have to figure out which registers are being used and which are not since the same registers are always used for the same operations. In completing the "stupid" code sequence for our example, we need to get back the value from the stack (POP it back into EBX and do the addition, add EAX to EBX).

Even a relatively simple compiler can probably eliminate the PUSH and POP in this particular case. There will always be more complicated cases, however, where the compiler will run out of registers. In that case, the compiler will *spill* the registers to the stack, that is, the contents of the registers will be copied out to the stack to make room for a new set of values. In doing the register spill, ESP is depressed to accommodate the thing being pushed onto the stack.

Instructions That Make Use of ESP and EBP

If you did not have a clear picture in mind of how the run-time stack is used, then in browsing through a description of the 386 instruction set you would come across some special instructions that look somewhat mysterious. In this section, we will look at how these instructions make special use of ESP and EBP with this picture in mind.

THE CALL INSTRUCTION. The CALL instruction is equivalent to the pseudo-instruction sequence

```
PUSH    EIP + n
JMP     entry
```

where EIP is the *extended instruction pointer* register, and n is the length in bytes of the CALL instruction. EIP is called the extended instruction pointer because it is also 32 bits long, whereas on the 8086 it is only 16 bits long. You can't actually write such a PUSH instruction, since EIP is not one of the registers that can be referenced directly, which is why we said that the above sequence is pseudo-code.

The contents of EIP can be affected only by instructions which change the flow of control. What is a jump instruction? It is nothing but a load instruction that changes the contents of EIP. If EIP were an ordinary register, we could write

    MOV   EIP, 22

This would be equivalent to a jump instruction which branches to memory address 22 because EIP would suddenly start to take instructions from that new location. If EIP were one of the registers we could address with instructions, then we would not need a separate jump instruction since we could just use a move. However, on the 386 and many other machines where the instruction pointer is "not" a standard register, special instruction forms are needed for jump and call instructions.

A DIGRESSION ON PATENT LAW. You certainly *can* design machines so that the instruction pointer is one of the standard registers. Not only has DEC used this approach in a series of machine designs, but they hold a patent on the idea.

Looking at some of the processors in this book, we may wonder, "Wouldn't it make sense to make the instruction pointer one of the standard registers?" In some cases, at least part of the reason that this is not done is purely legal. To contest a patent you must show that the idea which has been patented is not original. But more significantly, you must be willing to commit time, effort, and a lot of resources to a legal battle you may lose. Sometimes the path of least resistance is to avoid the issue completely by avoiding conflict with the patent. Alternatively, you can license the patent if the holder is willing to do so. Again it may be easier to license the patent even if you *don't* believe that it is valid.

When Compaq agreed to pay IBM for rights to use the MCA (Micro Channel Architecture) and other features of the IBM PC and PS/2, it did not necessarily mean that Compaq agreed that the patents are all valid—it may just be that they would rather pay than fight. Of course, once one major company falls in line in this way, there is even more pressure for other companies, particularly small ones, to follow suit. Another important dynamic is that if a small company is accused of infringing on a patent owned by a larger more powerful company, even the mere threat of a lawsuit may discourage investors, and dry up resources, even *before* there is any question of going to court.

Manufacturers tend to be scared off by the DEC patent. Interestingly, DEC also has a patent on the use of a stack pointer as a general register. But nobody pays any attention to that patent. These matters have, as far as we know, never been litigated, since no one has ever challenged the patents.

Incidentally, a rule of patent law that not everyone realizes is that you can patent almost anything.[2] There are all sorts of remarkable things patented. The Dean Space

---

[2] Anything, that is, except a perpetual motion machine. There is a special exemption for perpetual motion machines, because around the turn of the last century the patent office was wasting so much time figuring out why alleged perpetual motion machines couldn't work that there is now a special clause in the patent law which says that you can patent anything except a perpetual motion machine. So, if someone does come up with a real perpetual motion machine, they won't be able to patent it!

Drive generates unidirectional motion (even though it is a violation of Newton's laws). Another remarkable machine called the Hieronymus Machine allows you to do chemical analysis with a simple amplifier circuit and nothing else. The point about patent law is that you can patent anything, but the patent has no legal validity until it is litigated. Only the patent courts that examine the patent claims can determine whether something meets the requirements of a patent, that is, if the invention is original and appropriate to be patented.

There are many cases where things have been patented and never litigated because one of the rich owners of a patent has the attitude, "Never mind if my patent is valid or not, it's going to cost you an arm and a leg (more than you've got) to litigate it." An interesting case to watch in the near future involves the patent on the basic arrangement of the fold-up lid on laptop computers. Grid took out this patent several years ago, and when Grid was acquired by Tandy, a much larger company with lots of lawyers, Tandy discovered this patent and has declared that they will try to enforce it and collect licensing fees from *all* other laptop computer manufacturers. Will they succeed? We will have to watch and see.

Another interesting development is the increasing frequency with which patents are being granted for software algorithms. Can an algorithm be patented? The answer is that almost anything can be patented. Will the software patents stand up in court? The answer to that one is not clear yet, and again, it will be interesting to watch what happens. Some observers in the software industry are concerned that the increasing use of patent protection for software will stifle innovation. On the other hand, proponents, including patent lawyers, argue that the ability to protect software research and development investments by patents will *encourage* innovation.

HOW CALL IS USED.   The purpose of the CALL instruction is to set EIP to the target address of the call and force execution to continue at the start of the procedure. Before it does that, however, it pushes the address of the instruction that follows the CALL itself onto the stack. The simplest form of the CALL is a 1-byte opcode followed by a 4-byte address that is the relative distance in bytes from the CALL to the target, so the instruction is 5 bytes long.

Why use a relative value, instead of just giving the new value of EIP? One advantage of using relative addressing for call and jump instructions is that a given section of code can be moved around in memory. Since the relative position of jumps and calls and the instructions they reference does not change, the instructions themselves do not change either. Code which can be moved around this way is called *position-independent* code. It would obviously be very hard, almost impossible, to write such code if the call and jump offsets were absolute.

Say that a compiler needs to generate code for a procedure call. As we have described in Chapter 1, making a procedure call involves setting up the stack frame for the procedure. Part of this is done before the call, part is done by the CALL instruction itself, and the last part is done by the called procedure. Similarly, upon return, the responsibility for dismantling the stack frame and returning to the calling environment is split between the caller and the called procedure.

Suppose that a procedure P is executing, and suppose that ESP is pointing to the actual bottom of the run-time stack, which is the same as the bottom of the stack frame for P (see Figure 2.5). If P makes a call to another procedure, say Q, with actual parameters *a* and *b*, and in procedure Q there are two formal parameters *x* and *y* (which are supposed to correspond to *a* and *b*), then we need to push *a* and *b* onto the run-time stack. The caller pushes *a* and *b* onto the stack using two PUSH instructions. Then a CALL is executed that causes the hardware to push the return point onto the stack, and now we continue executing at the start of the called procedure.

At this stage, the called procedure completes the setup of the stack frame by saving the old EBP and resetting EBP to point to the new frame. Finally, space for the local variables of the procedure is allocated *below* EBP, and ESP is set to point to the bottom of the stack frame (remember that the stack builds *down* on this processor). We could achieve the required adjustment of EBP and ESP by a sequence of instructions such as

```
PUSH   EBP
MOV    EBP, ESP
SUB    ESP, space_for_locals
```

The parameters that were passed to the procedure are located just above the return point (at a fixed positive offset above the new EBP) so the procedure can reference *a* and *b* using EBP as a base register with these offsets.

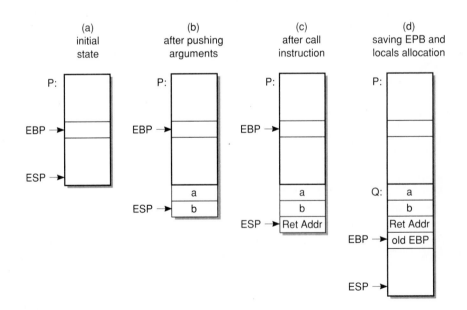

FIGURE 2.5
Stack frame construction on the 386.

On the older members of the 80x86 family (8088 and 8086), the above sequence of instructions would actually be used, but in newer members of the series, including the 286 and 386, we can use a single instruction to achieve the same result:

ENTER space_for_locals, 0

The effect of this ENTER instruction is essentially identical to the above sequence of three instructions. This is another nice example of a CISC-type instruction with a very specific purpose. If you read a description of ENTER that gave only the details of how EBP and ESP were affected without understanding the basics of stack frame construction, you would be rather mystified.

The full story of ENTER is considerably more complicated. In the above instruction, the first operand, *space_for_locals*, is simply the number of bytes to be allocated for local variables. In the last step of constructing the stack frame, EBP is decremented by this amount to create the storage needed for those locals. The second operand, on the other hand, has a use that we have not yet explained.

When the ENTER instruction is executed, if a non-zero value is used as the second operand, then the number of words specified by that operand is copied from the old EBP address to the new one. For example, for ENTER 16, 3, three words are copied from the old EBP before allocating 16 bytes of space for local variables (see Figure 2.6).

Explaining why one would want to do what seems to be a rather strange copying operation is rather complicated. To understand the motivation behind this behavior of ENTER, we need to recall the way in which local variables are referenced in languages

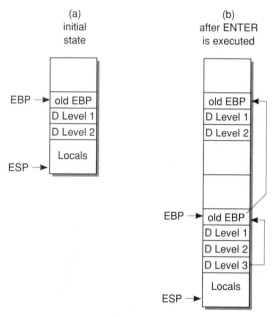

FIGURE 2.6
The use of the ENTER instruction to copy a display.

with nested procedures such as Pascal, COBOL, and Ada, but *not* C or FORTRAN, because these languages lack nested procedures. Consider the following example in Ada:

```
procedure OUTER is
    X : INTEGER;
    procedure INNER is
        Y : INTEGER;
    begin
        ... Y := X; ...
    end INNER;
end OUTER;
```

How does the procedure INNER address variables such as X in the stack frame of the procedure OUTER? There are a number of approaches to arranging for such references, and the compiler course instructor will typically spend a lecture or two considering this issue. For the ENTER instruction, we need to understand one possible approach to this problem, which historically was used in very early implementations of ALGOL-60.

Each procedure has its own stack frame. At any particular point, the variables in a procedure's own stack frame and those in the stack frames of the surrounding procedures are supposed to be available. One way to achieve this is to store a little table of stack frame pointers, called a *local display*, in the currently active stack frame. When procedure INNER is executing, it can address Y directly in its own stack frame using EBP, but to address X a sequence of two instructions is needed:

```
MOV  EBX, [EBP – 4]      ; get display pointer to OUTER frame
MOV  EAX, [EBX + ofs]    ; use it to access Y
```

Now we can see what the first parameter of ENTER is used for. When one procedure calls another, the part of the local display of the calling procedure that corresponds to stack frames visible to both the caller and called procedures must be copied to form the local display of the new procedure. It is a consequence of block structure that the called procedure can see *only* stack frames that are visible to its caller.[3] If we store the local display just below EBP, then the first parameter to ENTER is simply the number of display levels to be copied.

Why go into such programming language detail in a book that is supposed to be about architecture? Well, this is a perfect example of the CISC philosophy in action. You look at the intended applications carefully, so you can identify common complex operations. You then try to construct complex instructions that do exactly what is needed with the idea that if a stylized sequence of operations is needed, it will be more efficient to execute this sequence *within* the processor than with a sequence of instructions. There we have one of the fundamental contrasts with RISC philosophy, which takes exactly the opposite position, namely that it is actually *more* efficient to deal with such cases by using sequences of instructions.

---

[3] If you have procedure parameters, this is not quite true, and procedure parameters are indeed a bit of a nuisance to implement, but this is a subject for a book on compilers.

Is ENTER a successful application of CISC philosophy? There are two issues to be addressed in answering this question. First we have to confirm that it really does correspond to a common operation. At first glance, we can certainly agree that procedure calls are common. However, there are two flies in the ointment here. First, a great majority of procedure calls are to procedures that neither contain nested procedures nor reference variables in outer procedures. As we observed earlier, 100% of calls fall into this category in C and FORTRAN programs. Second, even if we do have nested procedures, it turns out that this method of handling non-local displays is not nearly as good as some more recently designed techniques.

What we have here is an example of an old principle of programming. It is often better to implement a good algorithm less efficiently than to implement a bad algorithm efficiently. Having an efficient implementation in the processor of what amounts to a basically bad approach is not so useful. So we have to give this round to the RISC proponents. ENTER is a good example of a powerful instruction that is not a useful one considering how it complicates the instruction set.

The other factor to consider is speed. There is no point in having a fancy instruction that replaces a sequence of instructions if it is not faster than the sequence of instructions it replaces. Later on we will address this issue in detail, but first let's finish the discussion of procedure calls and returns.

GETTING BACK—THE LEAVE AND RET INSTRUCTIONS. When a procedure returns, we have to undo the effect of the call and restore the calling environment. There are three steps. First, we must remove the frame and return to the frame of the caller. This can be accomplished with the sequence of instructions

```
MOV    ESP, EBP       ; strip the local frame
POP    EBP            ; restore the old frame pointer
```

On the older processors (8088 and 8086) we will see exactly this sequence of instructions, but on the newer processors (286 and 386), this two-instruction, three-byte sequence is replaced by a single one-byte instruction:

```
LEAVE
```

Unlike the case with ENTER, there is no question of there being a better algorithm for doing these two simple and clearly required operations, so the provision of the LEAVE instruction is a clear improvement.

The second step in completing the return process is to return control so that we resume execution with the instruction following the original CALL instruction. This is accomplished with the one-byte instruction

```
RET
```

which actually is nothing more than a POP EIP. It cannot be written that way, of course, since EIP is not an addressable register.

The third and final step is to remove the parameters from the stack, which simply involves incrementing ESP by the appropriate amount. Should this be done by the caller or by the called procedure? The answer depends on the language. In C, it is (more or less) valid to call a procedure with the "wrong" number of arguments, which means that only the caller really knows how many parameters are present, and therefore a typical call in C might appear as

```
PUSH    X              ; push parameters
PUSH    Y
CALL    P              ; call the procedure
ADD     ESP, 8         ; strip the parameters from the stack
```

For languages where the number of parameters is fixed (and typically checked by the compiler, as in Ada or Pascal), the stripping of the parameters may as well be done by the called procedure (that way there is only one instance of it, instead of a separate ADD instruction at every call). However, if we try to do the following:

```
ADD     ESP, 8
RET
```

we will be in big trouble, since RET needs ESP intact to retrieve the return point. A special form of RET solves this dilemma:

```
RET     8
```

The parameter for this form of RET is the number of bytes to be added to ESP *after* the return point has been stripped but *before* returning control to the caller.

INSTRUCTION TIMING

The 386 is currently available in versions that run up to 33 MHz, meaning that the basic clock cycle is about 33 nanoseconds. Versions running at 40 MHz are expected out soon, giving a clock cycle of 25 nsec.

As is typical of CISC machines, most instructions require more than 1 clock, so the instruction rate is considerably slower than the clock rate. How much slower? That depends on the instructions that are being executed. For operations on registers, such as register adds and subtracts, logical operations, and shifts, the typical time is 2 clocks. This might lead one to consider a 33 MHz 80386 to be approximately a 16 MIPS (million instructions per second) machine, but this would be completely misleading, since it discounts the time for memory references.

In the 80386 reference manual, the time for a typical load from memory is given as 4 clocks and for a store, as 2 clocks. Why is a store so much faster than a load? When a load is executed, the processor has to wait around for the data until it arrives. When a store is executed, on the other hand, the processor can issue the store without any concern as to when the store completes. After all, it takes much less time to post a letter to someone than to wait for a letter to arrive. This feature is called *store overlap*.

These figures, however, are optimistic in that they assume that the memory can respond immediately. In practice, this cannot always be achieved. Two memory organizations are typical. In the first, there is a single large memory that cannot run at the maximum speed required, and consequently such a memory must introduce *wait states.* For example, the IBM PS2/80 memory introduces a single wait state, meaning that we have to add a clock to the published times.

Another memory organization that is becoming increasingly more common, especially on faster machines, adds a *cache* memory between the processor and the main memory. The basic idea is to keep commonly accessed data in a faster memory to avoid the need for wait states. However, not all memory references can be satisfied from the cache memory, so, depending on the application and how many such *cache misses* occur, the load and store timings may again be misleadingly optimistic.

Calls and unconditional jumps typically take from 9 to 12 clocks. In the case of conditional jumps (which are, of course, an important component in the timing of loops), the timing is the same if the jump is taken, but only 3 clocks if the jump is not taken. This apparent discrepancy will be explained in the next section, but for the moment the important thing is to remember that jump and call instructions are quite slow. Since programs contain many jumps and calls (in some programs as many as 20% of the instructions), this is significant. As we will see later, the best of the RISC designs bend over backwards to get jumps to work in 1 clock, and this is one of the places where they score significant performance improvements over CISC architectures like the 386.

What about the timings for the complex instructions? A 32-bit divide takes 38 clocks, and a 32-bit multiply takes anywhere from 9 to 38 clocks. The varying execution times for multiplication is due to the fact that small multipliers take less time. It is possible to design multiply hardware that operates almost as fast as an add, but it takes an extravagant amount of real estate, and in designing the 386 it did not seem worthwhile to spend scarce chip space in this way. For division, there is no feasible way of doing the operation very fast. However, multiplies and divides are infrequent, so it is not so important that they take longer. As we will see later, some RISC designs react to this lower frequency by omitting multiply and divide instructions altogether!

Timing the ENTER Instruction

Finally, we promised to look at the timing of the ENTER instruction. As we noted then, it is all very nice to have complicated instructions like ENTER that do all sorts of fancy things in the hardware, but one has to wonder about the cost of executing these instructions. It is quite natural to assume that a single instruction that does many things would be cheaper than several equivalent instructions—but it is often the case that the single complicated instruction actually executes more slowly than several of the simpler ones. The simple case of ENTER,

```
ENTER  local-frame-size, 0
```

takes 10 clocks. This instruction replaces the three instruction sequence

```
PUSH   EBP
MOV    EBP, ESP
SUB    ESP, local-frame-size
```

But these three instructions take 2 clocks each, giving a total of 6 clocks. It is true that the ENTER instruction is only 4 bytes, compared to the 6 bytes of the three-instruction sequence, but it takes nearly twice as long to execute! This is, of course, the very opposite of what one would hope for. What we have here is almost a worst case of the phenomenon of providing useless complex instructions in a CISC architecture. Not only did we observe that the algorithm used for ENTER is ill-chosen, but the implementation is poor. We have a bad algorithm implemented inefficiently, the worst of both worlds.

How did the designers manage to implement ENTER so poorly? Probably what happened was that the functional specification included the requirement for ENTER but failed to note that there was no point in implementing the instruction if it couldn't be done efficiently. Everyone writing software has on occasion implemented things inefficiently, either through laziness or from expediency if space was tight—sometimes efficient algorithms take too much space. The same phenomena occur in hardware. Either the 386 designers just didn't bother hard enough with ENTER or they got crunched for space and were forced to do it inefficiently.

It is certainly not the case that all complex instructions on the 386 show this kind of behavior. For instance, the LEAVE instruction takes only 4 clocks, and replaces a sequence of two instructions taking 6 clocks, as well as saving space. However, ENTER provides a useful warning: *Do not assume that an instruction should be used just because it is there.*

If complicated instructions take too long, they are not just useless, they are insidious, because a compiler writer or an assembly language programmer will be tempted to use them when they shouldn't be used. The DEC VAX instruction set contains a good example of this phenomenon. The CALLG instruction is a very fancy procedure call instruction that does all sorts of things in setting up the stack frame and other things associated with the execution of the procedure call. Unfortunately, it is a very slow instruction, requiring as much as 200 clocks to complete on some VAX models. On the other hand, it is so convenient that the standard calling sequence on the VAX requires the use of CALLG, resulting in unnecessarily slow calls.

Pipelining and Instruction Timings

In a simple logical model of instruction execution, we would expect that each instruction would involve three steps:

    Load instruction from memory
    Interpret the instruction
    Perform the required operation

If this is how the 80386 worked, then it would be impossible for *any* instruction to take only 2 clocks, since the instruction load itself would take too long (remember that on this processor a load from memory takes 4 clocks). The explanation is that the 386 implements a very simple form of *pipelining.* This refers to the approach of overlapping separate stages of instruction execution so that the processor can work on more than one instruction at a time. As we will see later, this principle is one of the crucial parts of the RISC approach.

In the case of the 386, the only pipelining that goes on is *instruction prefetch*, which means that the loading of instructions from memory is overlapped with instruction execution. This is a very weak form of pipelining (RISC advocates might even object to using the term in this context), but even this very simple overlap is crucial to the performance of the 386.

The processor has a 16-byte instruction lookahead buffer. Whenever the path from the processor to memory is free (which happens, for example, while the processor is executing register operations), an attempt is made to load instructions into this buffer. The instruction timings in the reference manual assume that the instruction is always preloaded, so they do *not* include the time to load instructions.

Is this assumption fair? It depends on the code. If a large number of divisions are executed, it is obviously correct. On the other hand, a sequence of instructions like

```
ADD     EBX, 1000
ADD     ECX, 2000
ADD     EDX, 3000
...
```

is a much less favorable case. Supposedly these instructions take 2 clocks, but they are each 6 bytes long, so the instruction lookahead quickly gets emptied. An experiment using a 25 MHz 80386 machine with a cache memory showed that these instructions really take 4 clocks each under these conditions—twice as slow as the published timings. On a machine with wait states, the results would be even worse.

How does this effect degrade performance for real programs, that is, how unrealistic are the published timings for real programs? This is very dependent on the particular application programs. Intel publishes an estimate of 10 to 20%, but this may vary significantly depending on the particular program being run. There is insufficient information in the reference manual to work out exact instruction timings taking this effect into account. Intel recommends performing experiments on the actual executing target to answer detailed timing questions!

This instruction lookahead feature explains why calls and jumps are so slow. These are instructions for which the assumption that the look ahead is full is definitely false. When a jump is taken, the contents of the lookahead buffer have to be discarded, and the processor must start filling up the buffer from scratch. Now we can also understand why conditional jumps are so much faster if they are not taken, because, of course, in this case the instruction lookahead does *not* need to be flushed. Unfortunately, in the important case of loops, it is the jump taken that is of crucial importance, and the instruction lookahead feature does not help at all here.

CONCLUSION

This chapter is notable for what it omits. Despite the fact that we have devoted an entire chapter to the instruction set, we have still mentioned only a small fraction of the available instructions. A typical text devoted to the 386 will spend several hundred pages describing the instructions. Complicated instruction sets naturally require lengthy writeups.

From the examples we have given, the general philosophy of the instruction set design begins to be clear. The designers had a relatively luxurious amount of space available on the chip when the 386 was being laid out, and they had room for adding lots of fancy instructions. This opportunity was grabbed enthusiastically, and the 386 has many additional instructions compared to the 8086, which already had a rich instruction set. Are such rich instruction sets useful? They certainly *do* get used. The Realia COBOL compiler for the 8086 generates every single available instruction in some circumstance. On the other hand, RISC advocates would be quick to point out that what matters is not whether an instruction is used, but whether it is used sufficiently often to make it worthwhile.

It is clear that the 386 instruction set contains a significant number of instructions which fail this test. Furthermore, as we saw with the example of ENTER, there are cases where the complex instructions are clearly counter-productive. This still leaves the question of whether the presence of these instructions damages the general efficiency of the chip. If not, then you can't complain too much, no one is forcing you to use instructions you consider useless or counter-productive. On the other hand, if there is a general degradation, as RISC advocates claim, the situation is much trickier. The CISC answer to this concern is seen in the recently announced 486, which is the next member of the Intel line. This chip copies the 386 architecture, but uses RISC design techniques to optimize instruction execution throughput. We will take a closer look at this "revenge of the CISC" development in the final chapter of this book.

ADDRESSING AND MEMORY ON
THE 80386

So far we have looked at the basic instruction set of the 386, but we have not considered the issues of addressing memory. In RISC processors, this is a fairly straightforward matter since there are few instructions that address memory and they do it in a very stylized manner. For the 386, a typical CISC machine in this respect, we devote this entire chapter to the issue, since there is quite a bit of material to cover. In particular, the *segmentation* feature of the 386, which provides a means of separating the logical address space into separate logical sections, is at the same time very powerful and very complex. With an understanding of the memory addressing modes in hand, we end the chapter with a description of the instruction formats, which are inextricably bound up with these modes in a complex manner.

MEMORY ADDRESSING

Like most of the processors that we will examine, the 386 is a 32-bit machine in every respect. In particular, it is intended to be attached to a 32-bit bus: every reference to memory either reads or writes 32-bits. This contrasts with earlier versions of the Intel series: the 8088 uses an 8-bit bus, and the 8086 and 286 use a 16-bit bus.

Using 16-Bit Memory on the 386

We would expect in most cases that a processor like the 386 would be attached to a 32-bit bus. In practice, however, 386-based machines, PC-compatible machines in particular, often end up addressing memory on a 16-bit bus. How is this managed? The 386 doesn't really know what kind of memory it is attached to—it only knows that it has 32 wires coming out of it. It is perfectly possible to attach a 386 to some gizmo and then attach a 16-bit memory to the other side:

When the 386 requests the contents of some 32-bit memory location, the gizmo intervenes: "Well, wait a moment. I'm dealing with a slow memory, so I will have to throw in a few wait states." So the gizmo rushes off and asks the real memory for 16 bits and then stashes them inside itself. All this time it is saying to the processor, "Wait a moment, I'm dealing with a slow memory, so I haven't got your 32 bits yet." It then makes another request to the 16-bit real memory, gathers the completed 32 bits, and says to the processor, "Finally, your 32 bits has arrived!"

What possible advantage is there to using 16-bit memory on a 386? None whatsoever. Actually, it's a bit of a disaster from an efficiency point of view, since every reference to memory is slowed down by a factor of at least 2. However, this happens all the time in the 386 PC world. For example, if you buy a Compaq 386/25, you can plug a 16-bit memory board into one of the old-style 16-bit AT slots. The processor will use this memory, but its performance will be hobbled, not only because it has to do two memory fetches for every memory reference, but also because the bus of the Compaq runs at only one-third of the processor speed. The net result is that performance can be slowed down by a factor of 4 or 5—compatibility requirements sometimes breed strange situations!

Another advantage of using a 16-bit bus is that it is cheaper to build a system around a smaller bus. Recognizing this, Intel has produced a version of the 386, the 386SX, with this split memory access gizmo built in. On the inside, the 386SX is identical to the 386, but on the outside it looks like a 16-bit processor. The only advantage of the 386SX is that it is cheaper, the only disadvantage is that it is slower

A similar decision earlier on lead to producing the 8088, an 8-bit version of the 8086. This decision was historically crucial to Intel, since the availability of the 8-bit processor was an important component in IBM's decision to use the 8088 for the first version of the IBM PC, and compatibility considerations have resulted in follow-on PCs using later versions of the Intel architecture.

Alignment Requirements

Although the memory of the 386 is (at least logically) arranged in 32-bit words, it *does* permit non-aligned references. For example, the instruction

```
MOV     EAX, mem
```

loads 4 bytes into EAX from any four consecutive bytes in memory. If the address is aligned, that is, if the last 2 bits of the physical address are zero, then this instruction is documented to take 5 clocks. An actual experiment on a Compaq 386/25 yields a measured time of 5.28 clocks, so the documentation appears to be accurate—the slight discrepancy may result from wait states or from instruction fetch not being completely free (the timings in the manual assume that the fetch *is* free).

However, if this experiment is repeated with a non-aligned memory address, then this instruction is observed to take 10.55 clocks, meaning that it is slightly more than twice as slow. This confirms that the penalty for non-aligned references is substantial, and it is important from an efficiency point of view for programs in general, and compilers in particular, to make a real effort to align all 2-byte and 4-byte data items. On the other hand, if one really needs non-aligned data, as occurs in the case of COBOL programs, then the factor of two penalty is cheap enough, since otherwise one would be required to program a sequence of instructions something like

```
MOV     EAX, first-word
MOV     EBX, second-word
SHRD    EBX, EAX, bit-offset
```

which is more than twice as slow and requires more space besides.

All members of the Intel family of chips have allowed non-aligned data. In the case of the 8088, which uses an 8-bit bus, this is free—on this version of the processor there is no penalty for non-alignment. This was at one point an important distinction between the Intel and Motorola families, since the 68000 *did* require aligned operands. However, the 68030, a later member of the Motorola series, does not require alignment, so this is no longer a feature which distinguishes the two. Since most RISC processors *do* require aligned operands, this remains an important distinction between the CISC processors and RISC chips. Programs that extensively use non-aligned data look relatively unattractive on RISC processors.

Byte and Bit Ordering

The 386 is completely and consistently little-endian in both its byte and bit ordering. This means that multibyte values appear in memory with the least significant byte first and that values in registers are numbered with 0 being the least significant bit and 31 the most significant bit. The few bit-oriented instructions that are provided on the 386 are consistent with this little-endian bit-ordering convention.

Presumably the 386 was designed by English speakers, and as we discussed in Chapter 1, big-endian addressing seems more natural if one is used to writing memory left-to-right. Little-endian addressing gives rise to some rather curious situations. For example, consider a contiguous bit field stored in bits 6 through 12 of a register. When the contents of the register are stored in memory, this field appears to be curiously non-contiguous if the memory is viewed left to right in bytes, as shown in Figure 3.1.

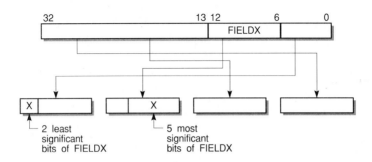

FIGURE 3.1
The effect of little-endian ordering on the position of a bit field.

Of course, if we didn't insist on writing the memory bytes left to right but would agree to write them right to left, this confusion would disappear. But since the left-to-right ordering seems natural, the question of why Intel chose little-endian ordering seems somewhat of a mystery.

THE ANCESTRAL ORIGINS OF THE 386. To answer the question of why the 386 is little-endian, we need to delve back into the origins of its design. The original Intel design started as a research experiment designed to demonstrate that an existing processor design could be duplicated on a single chip. The processor that was chosen was the controller for an intelligent terminal manufactured by Datapoint.

In those days core memory was extremely expensive—it was actually cheaper to implement memory as giant shift registers. This is done by having a whole series of gates that are flip-flops which can be set to one or zero and are joined in a big circle. There are several hundred of these flip-flops in the circle, and you can read only the bit at one particular position. To read a different bit, the clock is pulsed and the data in the circle rotates.

Some early computers used mercury delay lines (which rotated quite slowly) to provide a similar type of shift memory. Going back even further, the original IBM 360 used a physical drum for its memory. There was no electronic memory—you had to wait a long time for the next bit to come around if you just missed the drum on its revolution. The Datapoint was one of the last machines to have shift register memory. Since it was electronic shift register memory it was considerably faster than a drum, but nevertheless the issue of which bit arrived first as the memory rotated was important.

Simpleminded adders work with the LSB first (think about how you do pencil and paper addition). Very fancy adders do additions in parallel, working on all the bits at once, but the adder on the Datapoint was a simpleminded low-order bit first, serial adder. That is why on the Datapoint machine the LSB was first—so you could catch the first 8 bits from memory and be adding those bits while you were getting the next 8 bits off the shift register. This way it was not necessary to wait for an entire revolution of the shift register between bytes.

Intel decided to *exactly* duplicate this design as a test of the concept of putting a processor on a single chip. The idea was not to deviate at all from the design, because, from a research point of view, it was important not to bias the results with design decisions that were favorable to the chip approach.

Two things happened. First, Intel succeeded in duplicating the design exactly, including the shift-register-inspired little-endian byte ordering. Second, the research effort was so successful that Intel productized it in the form of their first commercial processor chip, the 4004. From that point on, there is a long history of producing ever more complex designs, but at each step compatibility considerations led Intel to retain little-endian ordering. Stephen Morse, who designed the 8086 reports that the decision to remain little-endian was touch and go when this chip was designed. On the one hand, the 8086 was supposed to be compatible with the 8080, which tended to dictate little-endian ordering, since the 8080, inspired by compatibility with the 4004, was little-endian. On the other hand, as we have already discussed, many other incompatibilities were introduced, and the decision could have gone the other way. Even if it had gone the other way, it still would not have settled the matter, since DEC also has a long history of producing little-endian machines, starting with the PDP-11, their first byte-addressed machine, and continuing with the currently popular VAX processors.

Oddly, the motivation for the little-endian choice in the DEC case involved a quite different piece of history. DEC machines preceding the PDP-11 were all word-based—the PDP-8 had 12-bit words, the PDP-9 had 18-bit words, and finally the PDP-10 had 36-bit words. The PDP-11 was initially designed basically as a 16-bit word machine. However, it seemed so attractive to be able to store two 8-bit characters in a single word and address them separately that the 16-bit address was considered to be divided into two parts. The upper 15 bits specified the word address, and the low-order bit specified which half of the word the character was located in.

If you think of the machine this way, it is essentially arbitrary whether a 1 in the low order position of the address represents the left or right half of the word. The choice was that a 1 represents the left half of the word, and the consequence of this choice is that once you regard the PDP-11 as being byte-addressed, you have little-endian addressing. The choice caused trouble from the start. For example, character strings written from memory were sent 16 bits at a time to the tape unit, which then wrote them on the tape one byte at a time, with every pair of bytes reversed.

Unluckily, DEC chose the wrong bit. At this stage DEC seems to be trapped by compatibility considerations and will undoubtedly produce little-endian machines for a long time to come. There is little or no hope of getting all machines to agree at this stage.[1]

---

[1] This is an example of a remarkable dynamic in the computer industry that allows amazing things to become standards due to compatibility considerations. Programmers still write "READ 5,10" in FORTRAN to read from the standard input file even though they have no idea what the mysterious 5 means. It happens to be the input file, and everybody knows that, since it says in your friendly FORTRAN manual that 5 is the input file. It has long since been forgotten that 30 years ago there was a tape-only machine, the IBM 7094 running the FMS system, where the fifth logical tape was the monitor input tape, which had all the programs and data on it.

ADDRESSING MODES

In addition to the extensive instruction sets implemented on many modern machines of the CISC variety, it is common to include several different ways of addressing memory. Addressing modes which seem quite useful on one machine may not even appear on other machines. We will begin by going through some of the addressing modes that appear on the 386. The 386, while it does contain a number of useful ways of addressing data, does not contain quite as many addressing modes as the 68030, although it does have many more addressing modes than the streamlined RISC chips. The addressing modes on the 386 are rich enough that when they are listed, one is tempted to ask, "Hey, what's that one for?"

Direct Addressing

Direct addressing, as the name implies, allows a programmer to directly address memory. When a programmer writes an instruction such as

```
MOV    EAX, Q
```

where Q is a 4-byteword at some fixed location of memory, the assembler for the machine will arrange to generate the appropriate code to address Q. The small fragment of 386 assembly code below shows how one could direct the assembler to define the variable Q to be a doubleword allocated at hexadecimal location 123.

```
Q      EQU     DWORD PTR DS:123H
```

Since the ability to directly address memory seems like such a natural thing to have, one might expect all machines to provide this addressing mode. In fact, very few machines have direct addressing. Of all the processors we consider in this text, only the 386 and the 68030 have direct addressing achievable in a single instruction. The reason for this is that there must be an instruction format into which one can fit a full 32-bit address. When one is designing the instruction set and the instruction formats for a machine, one must be prepared to leave enough space for these addresses.

When it is used to specify a direct address, the MOV instruction on the 386 is at least 6 bytes long. It has a format in which the first byte is the opcode, the second byte is the addressing byte (this is a byte that is encoded to say that the target of the move is EAX and the address is direct), and then finally there is a 4-byte address. Instructions such as this one are typically avoided in RISC designs where there is a premium on keeping instructions short and uniform.

Despite the length of this instruction, there are times when it is definitely useful. As an example of how the use of direct addressing might be convenient, let's first look at a simple fragment of Ada code which does *not* need direct addressing:

```
procedure Q is
    A, B : integer;
begin
    A := B;
end;
```

Here, A and B are variables that are declared local to this procedure, and in general it is not possible to know at what absolute addresses they can be found. If the procedure is called recursively, there will be several instances of both A and B located in different stack frames at each level of recursion, and these will obviously be at different addresses. These variables are allocated on the run-time stack and are always addressed at some offset relative to the frame pointer EBP. Direct addressing is not needed here, since all the variables are local to the procedure and hence are all accessible in the stack frame.

However, if we have a library package in Ada whose structure resembles the following:

```
package Q is
    A, B : integer;
begin
    ...
end;
```

then there is only one A and one B in the world, because there is only one package Q in the world. A library package is a package in which each object declared at an extreme outer level will only have one incarnation. Since there are only one A and one B, there is no reason to allocate them on the run-time stack. It is perfectly fine to allocate them at a fixed location of memory and use direct addressing to access them.

Based Addressing

Machines that do not have direct addressing will need to generate an extra instruction to locate such variables because it will first be necessary to load a pointer to the data of Q (into a register) and then use that to address those entities. What are the alternatives to giving the memory address as part of the instruction itself ? Put the memory address in a register, of course. Consider the instruction

```
MOV    EAX, [EAX]
```

This instruction directs the processor to replace the contents of register EAX with the value of the 4-byte word that EAX is pointing to.

This particular use of this addressing mode is the canonical instruction for roaring through a linked list. One common low-level implementation of a linked list (imagine code either handwritten in assembly language or generated by a clever compiler) is to chain a list of blocks together using the first word in each block as a forward pointer to the next block. If EAX is set to point to an element of the list, then each execution of this instruction will reset EAX to point to the first word of the next block in the list. In Pascal, such code is typically written as

```
a := a^.next;
```

where *a* is assumed to be a pointer to a record and *next* is a link to the next block whose *a* field is the first word of the block. To repeat, only a very clever compiler would know to put *a* into a register. If you actually write, compile, and then look at this Pascal code, you will probably see something that does not resemble the above instructions at all.

Based Addressing with Displacement

Another addressing mode available on the 386 uses a base register with a 1-byte signed offset. To move a value into a register, one can write

```
MOV    EAX, [EBX − 22]
```

This instruction is only 3-bytes long, the first byte being the opcode byte, the second the addressing byte, and the third the offset byte. This is a very important instruction form which can be used in one of several different ways, two of which we discuss below.

Consider the commonly used data structure, the linked list, in which each element of the list contains several fields, each one of which contains some data that one will occasionally need to access. If EBX is pointing to the first byte of one of these records and a procedure wishes to access an element that starts at the eighth byte of the record, then that can be done by writing

```
MOV    EAX, [EBX + 8]
```

As an addressing mode, [EBX + 8] is exactly what you want to be able to refer to that field. This is a very common style of processing in which records are linked (sometimes called *plex processing*—each record is called a *plex*). Since the individual plexes are likely to be small (fewer than 128 bytes), referencing any one of their fields will be easy by using this compact form of indexed addressing in which there is only an 8-bit offset.

The other common case where this addressing mode is useful is in addressing variables in a stack frame where the size of the stack frame is small (meaning here that all objects within the stack frame can be addressed by a 1-byte offset). For example, in the case of the first variable in the stack frame, the one closest to the frame pointer, the variable might be addressed as [EBP − *offset*], where *offset* is the offset of the variable being addressed. Note that the offset is signed—a negative offset is needed to get to the local variables of the procedure, and a positive offset is needed to get to the parameters.

A clever compiler for the 386 will do its very best to arrange the variables of a stack frame in such a way that there are as many short small variables as possible within the range addressable with the addressing mode. You want to avoid putting a big array or a big record directly under EBP (between the other local variables and the EBP). Instead, all scalars are placed under EBP so that they can be reached by these 3-byte instructions. This means that the simple Ada assignment

```
A := B;
```

should compile into two 3-byte instructions on the 386 because it's very likely that both A and B are within easy reach of EBP:

```
MOV    EAX, [EBP − 12]
MOV    [EBP − 8], EAX
```

where each of these instructions is 3 bytes in length. The entire Intel series has instruction sets which are strongly biased to producing compact programs. This special 3-byte addressing form is an example. Nearly all the other processors in the book would require a 4-byte instruction form for this purpose.

Short offsets are very common. For example, in C there is a tradition of writing very small procedures with very few local variables, so most of the time you can get away with addressing local variables using the small offset form.

MEMORY-TO-MEMORY OPERATIONS. In the above assignment, two instructions were generated, rather than a direct move. This is because there is no memory-to-memory mode. It is not possible to write:

```
MOV     [EBP – 8], [EBP – 12]
```

This results from the decision to give the addressing mode as part of the opcode sequence rather than with each operand. Looking at that format, there is an opcode (which includes a single bit saying whether data is being moved to or from memory), addressing information, and then the offset for the addressing information. This format does not allow for operands (both the left and right operand of a MOV) to both have separate addressing information. Only one memory operand can be addressed in an instruction.

The VAX, on the other hand, has an opcode and two operands, and the addressing information for each operand is in the operand itself. The VAX can do a memory-to-memory operation. The 386 way of doing things, storing the single bit in the opcode saying what the operands are, has the net effect of making the instruction stream more compact.

LONGER OFFSETS. On the 386, indexing can be done not only with a 1-byte offset but with a 4-byte offset as well.

```
MOV     EAX, [EBP + big_value_that_cannot_fit_into_a_byte]
```

Even though the ability to use such a large offset will result in a longer instruction, it gives a greater flexibility when it comes to addressing large records or large stack frames. In fact, there are many more situations in which such an ability is obviously needed. One thing about having this full 4-byte offset is that if a register is pointing at some known distance away from some variable, it does not matter how close it is. Many machines do not have this ability, which means that the compiler has to constantly worry about whether or not an offset is in range.

On the IBM 370 the offset problem becomes particularly acute. The largest offset that can be used on the 370 is the very small 4K bytes. In addition, this offset must be positive. When an object is not within the reach of a register plus this offset, a compiler must generate additional code to access it. This generally means that a register must be loaded with an address that is within 4K bytes of the data one is trying to access.

You can imagine that if you have a stack frame on the 370, and you have the equivalent of EBP (you choose one of your registers as the frame pointer, let's say R5 points to the bottom of your stack frame), you can address only 4K bytes of the frame. To address things higher up on the stack frame, you have to generate code like

```
LA      R4, 4095(,R5)       ; IBM 370 assembler
```

The effect of this will be to get R4 pointing to that portion of the stack frame that exceeds the first 4K bytes. Now you can reference up to 4K bytes using R4. Generating code for the 370 is so painful as a result of that restriction that there have even been compilers for the 370 that simply chose to limit the size of the stack frame to 4K bytes.

Double Indexing

Another indexing mode available on the 386 allows two registers to be added together with an additional 8-bit or 32-bit offset. You can write

```
MOV    EAX, [EBP– 64 + EAX]
```

Any two registers, not just EAX or EBP, can be used in this addressing mode. This example uses EBP because that is suggestive of one of the most useful applications for this mode.

Chapter 1 described an addressing mode that we called base plus index addressing which could be used to access an element of an array allocated within a stack frame. Here we see how that addressing mode has been implemented on the 386, and the code that a compiler would generate to reference an element of such an array. The base register EBP is being used in this instance as a frame pointer, and the base address of the array is given as EBP – 64. The register EAX is being used as the index register which contains the offset of the element in bytes. This picture is very similar to the one in Figure 1.8, except that we assume here that the array is an array of characters. Here we see that the ability to have two registers added together (along with the constant displacement) is just what is needed in order to address elements of an array allocated on the stack.

Double Indexing with Scaling

In the example of the previous section, suppose that the array was not an array of characters, but rather an array of integers each of which was 4 bytes long. To access the Ith element of the array A, written A(I), it is necessary to multiply I by 4, since the offset of the Ith integer is 4 * I on a byte-addressable machine. The 386 provides an address mode, an example of which is written as

```
MOV    EAX, [EAX*4 + EBP – 64]
```

which allows the index register but not the base register to be multiplied by a constant 2, 4, or 8 automatically. In the example above, the address is computed by taking 4 times the value in EAX, adding it to EBP, and then subtracting 64. This is just what is needed to reference the Ith integer in this array. The possible values that are allowed are not arbitrary, and in fact can only be 1 (which has no effect), 2, 4, or 8. These are reasonable choices. The value of 1 corresponds to the case where scaling is not required at all. The second is the case of an array in which each element is a 16-bit integer. The third choice is intended for indexing into an array of 32-bit integers. The last is for addressing double-precision floating-point values.

This set of addressing modes is quite rich, but when we get to the 68030, we will see that even more elaborate modes are possible. As an example of a situation where we do not have a 386 mode that is just right, consider a procedure call where a variable A is passed by reference (not by value). The parameter is not the value, it is a pointer to the value. Many compilers generate code to pass things by reference. In some languages, for example, COBOL, passing by reference is required. Now, if we write Q := A, the code a compiler will have to generate is:

```
MOV    EAX, A
MOV    EAX, [EAX]
MOV    Q, EAX
```

When the first instruction is executed, only the address of the variable A is loaded into EAX. The second instruction has the effect of replacing the address of A just loaded into EAX with the value of A. It would be nice to have an addressing mode that allowed this one-level indirect addressing to be done in a single instruction. The 386 does not, but the 68030 does. The decision as to how elaborate to make the addressing modes is one of the fundamental parameters of CISC machine design.

SEGMENTATION ON THE 80386

In this section we will look at segmentation, a rather controversial feature of the 386. It is the only microprocessor covered in the text that uses this rather complicated approach, and so it is worth considering in detail. The IBM RISC chips provide a form of segmentation, but it is much more limited, and accessible only at the system level.

Historical Aspects

The earlier members of the Intel family, such as the 8086, and the 286, are essentially restricted to 16-bit addresses. While 16-bit addressing will normally limit the amount of byte-addressable memory to 64K bytes, the 8086 is able to address 1 megabyte of memory, and the 286 is able to address 16 megabytes of memory. This extended addressing was accomplished through the use of a technique called *segmentation*. On the 8086 and the 286, the implementation of segmentation means that a large memory is broken down into a collection of segments, each of which is no larger than 64K bytes. An address then consists of a pair consisting of a segment and an offset, giving the segment to be referenced and the offset within the segment.

On the 8086, there were four segment registers: the code segment register (CS), the data segment register (DS), the stack segment register (SS) and the extra segment register (ES). Each of these 16-bit registers contains a segment address, which is an address pointing to some 16-byte boundary in memory, called a *paragraph*. Full addresses are 20 bits long, and the boundary requirement means that the last 4 bits of a segment address is always zero (see Figure 3.2).

Any instruction which references memory uses one of the four segment registers in determining the effective address of its operands. Usually the choice of which segment register is to be used is not explicitly specified in the instruction, but instead

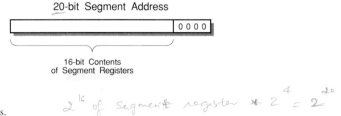

20-bit Segment Address

0 0 0 0

16-bit Contents
of Segment Registers

FIGURE 3.2
An 8086 segment address.

2^{16} of segment register $* 2^4 = 2^{20}$

is chosen by a default mechanism. For example, the jump instructions assume that the target is in the current code segment, and hence implicitly use CS as the segment register. The 16-bit offset is added to the CS register to form the physical address which is the target of the jump. Instructions such as PUSH and POP always refer to the stack segment. General data references use the DS register by default, but by preceding an instruction with a special prefix byte, data references can be forced to use one of the other three segment registers.

There are several disciplines for managing these segments, which are known as *memory models*. At one extreme, a compiler may assume that all of the code for the program itself and all of its data can fit into a single 64K byte region. In this case, all four segment registers can be set to point to the beginning of a single 64K byte area. This model, which essentially ignores segmentation, is called the *small memory model*. At the other extreme, when the *large model* is used, both the code and data can be broken up into multiple segments. In this case the compiler must generate appropriate instructions to modify the segment registers so that they point to the desired segments. In the case of jump and call instructions, there are special versions allowing transfer of control to a different code segment.

There are a number of models whose use of memory is intermediate between these extremes. In addition, there is the *huge model* which attempts to overcome the inherent limitation of segment size to 64K bytes. This model allows a single logical data object to be larger than 64K bytes. When segments are limited to 64K, a data object larger than that is normally impossible to deal with. Using the huge model, these huge objects are handled by breaking each object into several segments. When a high-level language programmer writes a reference to such an object, the generated code is a quite complicated sequence, which first has to figure out which of several segments to access. Needless to say, this is much less efficient than the corresponding code on a real 32-bit addressed machine, where huge objects can be handled with a direct reference.

Historically, the 8086, the first processor in the Intel 80x86 series, was intended as a small incremental improvement on the 8080, which was limited to 64K memory. The segmentation model of the 8086 has often been criticized for retaining some vestiges of these addressing limitations—it is indeed inconvenient compared to real 32-bit addressing. On the other hand, the restriction of offsets in instructions to 16-bits led to more compact code, which was an important consideration in the 8086 design.

The 286 was introduced because it had become clear that a 1-megabyte limit on the extent of addressable memory was unacceptable. The decision was therefore made to increase the maximum memory-addressing capability to 16 megabytes, which corresponds to 24-bit addressing. The easiest way to achieve this would have been to simply increase the number of implied 0 bits at the end of a segment address from 4 to 8. What was actually implemented was a completely different model for specifying segment addresses, something that we will consider in detail in the next section. This model still restricts an individual segment to 64K bytes but provides a much more flexible method for controlling these segments, as well as many other capabilities.

With the appearance of 32-bit addressing in the Intel series, introduced in the 386 for the first time, the original motivation for including segmentation has disappeared, since its purpose is to extend the addressing range of the processor without enlarging the basic register width. Indeed, other 32-bit processors do not have the segmentation mechanism.

Given that segmentation is not really needed in the 386, you may wonder why segmentation was retained in the design of the 386. There are two reasons. First, it was important for the 386 to be able to run 286 programs that used segmentation. For example, if this compatibility had not been maintained, then IBM's OS/2 would not be able to run on 386 machines.

The second motivation in retaining segmentation was that the "many other capabilities" referred to above are arguably important even when the addressing extension is not required. Intel certainly believes that the functionality provided by segmentation is important, but on the other hand, many other microprocessor designers consider the entire approach to be nonsense. We will try to take an objective look at these features to understand this rather fierce controversy.

The Global Descriptor Table

The segment selection mechanism introduced on the 286 (copied on the 386) involves the use of the so-called *global descriptor table* (GDT). The GDT is essentially a table kept in memory that contains the address of each segment in the system as well as other information about each segment. To locate the starting address of the GDT, the 386 uses a 32-bit register not surprisingly called the *global descriptor table register* (GDTR). The privileged instruction LGDT is used to load GDTR with the address of the GDT.

As described above, the 8086 segment registers contain the physical address of a segment. On the 286 and the 386 these registers are still 16-bits wide, but they do *not* contain the physical address of a segment. Instead, each segment register on the 286 and the 386 contain an index into the GDT, which itself contains the segment address.

To see how objects are addressed through the GDT, consider a load instruction:

```
MOV     AX, Q
```

When the processor references memory by executing such an instruction, it implicitly uses the data segment DS in determining the address of Q. But on the 386, DS contains the offset of the GDT entry, not the starting address of the segment. To compute the address of Q, the processor looks into the GDT entry to get the segment address (see Figure 3.3), and adds the offset value. Although the data segment register DS is only

16 bits wide, the number of bits in a GDT entry on the 286 is large enough that it can be used to specify an arbitrary 24-bit address, or an arbitrary 32-bit address on the 386.

The difference between the 286 and the 386 in this respect is that the individual segments on the 286 are limited to 64K bytes, while that is not the case with the 386. That restriction on the 286 makes segmentation essential. On the 386, where segments can be as large as 4 gigabytes, segmentation does not really restrict addressing at all. Most user programs on the 386 run using the "small" model, that is, the segment registers are set once and never changed. Of course, in the case of the 386, small means 4 gigabytes which is not so small, and is in any case the maximum addressing space available on the machine.

MAKING SEGMENTATION EFFICIENT. If the 386 were forced to refer to the GDT every time it needed to access some data in memory, every memory reference would effectively require two memory references. That would obviously be unacceptable, because it would slow down all memory references by a factor of 2.

To make the process of referencing data in segments more efficient, the segment registers include, in addition to the 16-bit *segment selector*, a hidden part containing complete copy of the corresponding GDT entry (see Figure 3.4). When a segment register is loaded with a selector value, the corresponding GDT entry is loaded into the hidden part of the segment register at the same time. Subsequent references using the segment register are fast, since the required GDT pointer is immediately at hand.

That is the good news. The bad news is that the instruction that loads the DS register is a very expensive 22-clock instruction. Twenty-two clocks may seem like a long time for an instruction to do nothing more than load two 32-bit values from the GDT. However, in addition to loading the segment register with those values, a great

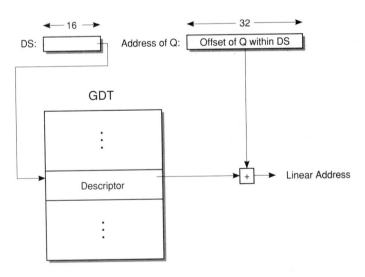

FIGURE 3.3
Translation of a 386 logical address to a linear address.

FIGURE 3.4
An 8086 segment register with the corresponding GDT entry.

deal of additional error checking is going on. In any case, the whole point of loading the DS register is to switch data segments, and this is an operation that will usually not be done very frequently.

THE STRUCTURE OF THE GDT.   So far we have described the GDT entry as containing only the address of a segment. However, the GDT entry is 64 bits wide and contains additional information related to other capabilities mentioned earlier. The structure of a GDT entry is shown in Figure 3.5.

The segment base field is the address of the segment. As shown, it is divided into three pieces in a rather odd manner. The explanation is that the 386 format is basically compatible with the 286 format *except* that the address space was expanded, so additional bits were needed for the base. To maintain compatibility, the extra base bits were stuck in a previously unused section. Once again compatibility requirements take priority over clean design!

The most important of the additional fields is the segment limit field. This controls the length of the segment, and the protection mechanism of the processor depends on the fact that the processor constantly checks references against this limit and will not allow references outside the segment. To save space the limit is only 16 bits. Since segments can be larger than 2^{16} bytes, the G (granularity) bit can be used to specify that this limit is in units of 4K bytes for large segments.

The P bit indicates whether or not the descriptor is actually in use. This is used in conjunction with virtual segmentation, which we discuss in detail in Chapter 4. The A bit, which shows whether or not a segment has been accessed is also used for control of virtual segmentation. The AVL field provides 2 bits for use by operating systems software in this connection. The DPL (descriptor privilege level) and TYPE fields are used to control access to the descriptor. We will discuss these protection mechanisms in detail in the next section.

Finally, the D bit indicates the default operation size. Normally it is set to 1 to obtain the normal 32-bit operation and addressing modes we associate with the 386. If it is set to 0, then the corresponding code in the segment uses 16-bit operations and 16-bit addressing. This is provided for compatibility with the 286. Once again it is remarkable to see how hardware acquires junk features in the name of compatibility with obsolete previous versions.

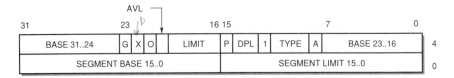

| BASE 31..24 | G | X | O | LIMIT | P | DPL | 1 | TYPE | A | BASE 23..16 | 4 |
| SEGMENT BASE 15..0 | | | | | SEGMENT LIMIT 15..0 | | | | | | 0 |

AVL   - AVAILABLE FOR PROGRAMMER USE
DPL   - DESCRIPTOR PRIVILEGE LEVEL
P   - SEGMENT PRESENT

FIGURE 3.5
The structure of a global descriptor table entry.

PROTECTION MECHANISMS

As we mentioned earlier, the introduction of the segmentation model on the 286 (and also present on the 386) provided for considerable extra functionality as well as allowing more memory to be accessed. In particular, it provides the structure on which a fully protected architecture is built. In this section we will examine the structure of these protection mechanisms.

Levels of Protection

The basic protection model on the 386 is built around four levels of protection. These levels of protection are best pictured as a series of concentric circles, where the inner circle represents the most privileged level, where all operations are permitted, and the outer circle is the least privileged level with the most restrictions. User application code will then operate at this outer level, which is protection level 3 on the 386:

In a multi-user operating system, each task running on the processor will have a certain privilege level. The main way in which the processor supports the differentiation of tasks by privilege level is by restricting access to certain instructions based on this privilege level. For example, the LGDT instruction used to load GDTR can be issued only at the highest privilege level, level 0, and input/output operations can be issued only at levels 0 or 1.

ACCESS CONTROL RIGHTS FOR SEGMENTS. The other significant difference between privilege levels involves the access control rights in the GDT. Each GDT descriptor has a privilege level called the *descriptor privilege level* (DPL). The *current* *privilege level* (CPL) is determined by the DPL of the code segment for the code that is being executed.

Data segments also have separate DPL settings, and whenever a segment register is loaded with a selector, part of the internal operations associated with the load operation checks that the DPL of the data segment being referenced is at least at the same privilege level as the CPL of the code doing the load. This means that operating system segments can reside in the GDT, and even if less privileged code knows the appropriate selector values, they will not be able to reference the segments since a trap will occur if this is ever attempted.

A length check is performed on all memory references as an integral part of this protection mechanism. This is done because it is not good enough to limit a program's access to the appropriate set of segments without also being sure that all references are confined within the segment limits.

Operating System Structure

The guiding idea in designing an operating system with multiple levels of protection is to put as little code as possible at the most privileged levels. Even operating system code should operate with as little privilege as is feasible, so that if some operating system code has a bug, the protection mechanisms are active and can control the damage that might result.

On the 386, level 0, the most privileged level, would generally be reserved for the inner kernel that manages basic system resources. In particular, the kernel would be responsible for managing the GDT, since the instructions that use the GDT can only be executed at level 0. It is interesting to note that even level 0 code cannot directly reference the GDT contents, since only memory described by segment descriptors can be referenced. In practice, the GDT will contain a descriptor that describes the GDT itself as a data segment so that the kernel can modify it as required. This descriptor will have a DPL of 0, so that only the kernel can modify the GDT. Outer-level operating system code, as well as user application code, cannot even read the contents of the GDT since only code at level zero can access this segment.

The low-level input/output control would be placed at the next level, level 1, since this is the level at which the hardware permits the IN and OUT instructions to be executed. Obviously such instructions must be privileged—we can't let an application program write directly to a disk, because it could write rubbish on someone else's data.

Level 2 would typically be used for the bulk of the operating system code. In terms of instructions which can be executed, level 2 is just as restrictive as the application level. However, the system would be designed so that various critical operating system data would reside in data segments with a DPL of 2, so that they could be referenced from this level but could not be accessed from application code.

Finally, the user application level code would operate at level 3, and since it would have a CPL of 3, it could access only segments whose DPL was 3. Naturally the operating system would take care that the only segments with this DPL were segments that properly belonged to the application program.

MAKING OPERATING SYSTEM CALLS. At various points, the application program needs to make calls to the operating system, which means that there must be some mechanism for transferring control between privilege levels (i.e., for changing the CPL). On all the other processors we will look at in this book, such a transition is accomplished simply by causing a trap or interrupt, with the handler for the trap or interrupt operating at the supervisor level (these other processors have only two levels of protection, commonly called supervisor and user modes). Since the 386 has multiple levels of protection, a more elaborate scheme is required.

First let us look at the normal method for changing the contents of the code segment register, CS. There is a special form of the CALL instruction, called a FAR CALL, which has a 7-byte format (see Figure 3.6). This instruction causes the current CS selector and EIP values to be pushed on the stack, and then CS is loaded with the specified selector, and EIP is set to the given offset. A check is made that the CPL of the target segment is greater than or equal to the current CPL. This means that this simple form of the FAR CALL cannot be used to switch to a more protected segment, which is just as well, since otherwise an application could branch into any point of a protected operating system code segment or even into the middle of an instruction in such a segment, causing chaos.

To make it possible to call an operating system routine, there is a provision for a special entry in the GDT, a call gate. A call gate contains a selector and offset value designating the entry point of a procedure in some code segment, typically an operating system code segment containing procedures for performing operating system services for user programs. To use a call gate, an application program executes a FAR CALL whose selector corresponds to the call gate (the offset is ignored in this case, since it is taken from the call gate descriptor).

For a FAR CALL using a call gate, it is permissible for the target segment to have a lower CPL value than the caller. The call gate provides sufficient protection that the higher privilege code can defend against inappropriate invasion by a lower privilege caller. First it is the operating system that controls the GDT and therefore determines what call gates are present. Second, control can be transferred only to the properly authorized entry point designated in the call gate. Third, the procedure knows that it is being called by application code, so it can indulge in whatever defensive programming and error checking is required to ensure that the call is correct and cannot cause damage.

As an example, suppose an application program wants to perform an input/output operation. The call gate has a pointer to the privileged descriptor, which points to a level 1 segment containing the I/O routine. It also has the offset that it knows is the right offset of that routine. It is neither possible to read nor to change the call gate,

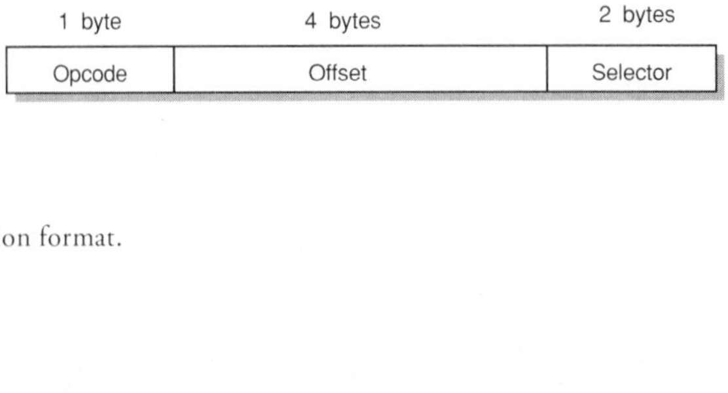

1 byte	4 bytes	2 bytes
Opcode	Offset	Selector

FIGURE 3.6
Far Call instruction format.

because all of this is privileged data in the GDT. The segment at privilege level 3 makes a call to the call gate. The call gate immediately passes control to the appropriate routine in the privileged segment. That entry point will be correct, and the entry point verifies that the appropriate parameters are being passed—for example, ensuring that a disk reference corresponds to data on the disk that properly belongs to the application program. If these checks succeed, the routine executes the corresponding IN and OUT instructions to service the user's request. Finally, the routine issues a RET instruction that returns control to the caller. Since this return involves transferring to a higher CPL value, it does not require special circuitry, because such a transition is always allowed.

An example of an operating system using this approach is OS/2. In OS/2 there are a large number of system services such as DosAlloc (to allocate memory) and DosGetMouse (to get mouse data). Every one of those OS/2 *application program interface* (API) routines corresponds to a magic selector number. The system linker knows the magic selector numbers. When a programmer writes in a C program, DosAlloc(...), with some parameters, this generates a CALL instruction with a note to the linker asking that it be filled in with the selector for the DosAlloc call gate.

Validating Parameters

We will now look at the issue of validating parameters in a little more detail. Be warned that the presence of some very complicated protection mechanisms on the 386 makes this quite difficult to understand.

Suppose we have an operating system interface that works in the following manner. The application program makes a call to open a file, and the operating system returns a selector value that corresponds to a special data segment it has installed in the GDT containing critical data on the file, including the absolute position on disk, length of the file, and other data that the user program must not be allowed to modify. This is safe, since the operating system sets the DPL of this segment to 1, making sure that the application program, running with CPL set to 3, cannot even look at the contents of this control block, let alone modify it. Subsequently the application program makes a call to read from the file with three parameters: the selector corresponding to the control block (which was returned by the open call), a buffer address, and a length. The write call works in a similar manner.

Now consider the following attempt to subvert the operating system, sometimes called a Trojan Horse—an appropriate metaphor, since what we intend to do is to smuggle in some dangerous data disguised as something harmless (the following discussion is shown in Figure 3.7). We begin by opening two files, FILEA and FILEB. We now intend to read the contents of the secret FILEA control block by making a write call with the following parameters:

Control block = FILEB   ① RPL of 3 (con next page)
Address = FILEA control block ② DPL of 1
Length = length of a control block

It is, of course, true that the DPL for the FILEA control block is 1, but by the time we get to the write, the operating system routine will be operating with CPL set to 1, so it

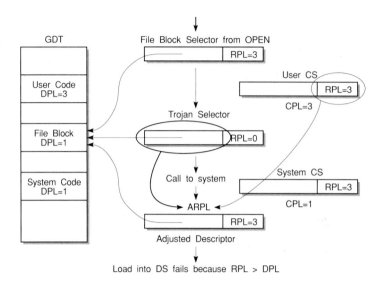

FIGURE 3.7
The Trojan Horse attack.

looks like it will be able to read the contents of the FILEA control block without noticing that this provides us with unauthorized information. Note that the read routine cannot simply check to make sure that the provided buffer address has a DPL of 3, since this routine may very well be called from all over the operating system to read sensitive data that can perfectly well have any DPL value.

Our intention, of course, is that once we have read the control block data, we can modify it and then perform the corresponding read that will modify the contents of the control block for FILEA, compromising operating system security. Of course, knowing what changes to make requires a great deal of knowledge about the operating system, but a really protected system should be safe against a deliberate assault by the author of the operating system armed with the source listings of the system, as well as against unintentional bugs in application programs.

The first line of defense against this invasion involves an extra field in selectors that we have not described yet. Selector values are actually offsets into the GDT, and since GDT entries are 8 bytes long, the lower 3 bits of every selector value are available for other uses. The lower 2 bits are used to contain a privilege level, called the *request privilege level* (RPL). When a segment register is loaded with a selector, two separate checks are made:

- The DPL of the segment must not be less than the CPL of the executing code.

- The RPL of the selector must not be greater than the DPL of the segment.

The second check provides a line of defense against the Trojan Horse. When the open routine returns, the control block selector will have a DPL of 1, but the RPL of the selector will be set to a copy of the calling routine's CPL. We are stamping the selector with a mark which says, "This selector cannot be used by high-privilege code."

Now consider the possible uses of this selector. If the FILEA selector is passed in a proper manner as the first parameter to the write routine, then the routine removes this stamp so that it can access the purported control block, carefully verifies that it really is an appropriate control block, and goes ahead and uses it. On the other hand, if the FILEA descriptor is passed as the data buffer address, the read routine simply loads it to access the data without removing the stamp. This should be fine, because only application program data segments with a DPL of 3 should be used here in any case—in the normal case, the buffer segment will have a DPL of 3, and so the routine can access the data without trouble. Our initial attempt to smuggle in the bad pointer now fails, because we supply a selector with an RPL of 3, and such a selector cannot be used to refer to a segment whose DPL is 1. An error trap will occur, and the operating system will be able to identify and arrest the guilty party.

However, a clever programmer who understands all this complicated stuff can try to get around this limitation by performing a little surgery on the selector that comes back from the open routine. By the time the applications program gets the selector it is simply 16 bits of data, and the program can certainly modify this selector. The appropriate surgery is to remove the restrictive stamp in the selector by resetting its RPL to 0. Now we use this modified descriptor in our invasion attempt.

This modified approach might succeed if the operating system is carelessly written, but the processor design has specifically considered this type of invasion by providing the special instruction Adjust Request Privilege Level (ARPL):

```
ARPL    selector1, selector2
```

This instruction checks the RPL in *selector1* against the RPL in *selector2*, and if necessary increases the *selector1* RPL so that it is not less than the *selector2* RPL. When a far call is executed, the RPL of the saved CS selector value is set to a copy of the caller's CPL. This means that the read routine should execute code similar to the following:

```
MOV     AX, callers-CS-selector
MOV     BX, supplied-data-buffer-selector
ARPL    BX, AX
MOV     DS, BX
```

The data buffer selector is not loaded until its RPL has been adjusted up to at least the caller's CPL. Our invasion attempt fails, because our fake RPL value gets reset to 3 and then the MOV to DS traps because the RPL is greater than the segment's DPL. For a proper pointer, everything would be fine, since the buffer would have a DPL of 3, and the ARPL would adjust the RPL up to 3, which causes no problems for a DPL 3 segment.

Is All This Worthwhile?

The previous section is virtually incomprehensible. You probably have to read it several times to understand it, and it is still easy to get the DPLs, CPLs and RPLs hopelessly mixed up. No other commonly used microprocessors have anything like this protection complexity, and we can legitimately raise the question of whether these features are useful and worthwhile (the Intel position) or represent design gone berserk (the position of many others).

On the plus side, the whole protection scheme is logically consistent, and it certainly is possible to create a structured operating system that is fully protected and has the important property that executing code, even in the operating system, runs at the maximum feasible protection level. This contrasts with other less capable microprocessors where often the entire operating system runs at the most privileged level.

The argument against this complexity is twofold. First there is the concern that providing all these complex structures in the hardware massively complicates the hardware design, increasing the likelihood of bugs and probably resulting in a detrimental effect on performance. Second, the complexity of the protection scheme means that the operating system itself is more complex and so is more prone to errors.

It certainly seems that operating systems have been successfully written without needing all this complicated protection support. Unix implemented on the 386 ignores most of the elaborate mechanisms and treats the 386 as though it had a much simpler structure. Operating systems are so complicated that it is very hard to make an objective judgment on the extent to which hardware features affect an operating system's reliability and performance. Other things being equal, the relative performance of Unix and OS/2 on the 386 would be interesting to measure, but of course other things are not equal, so we would be hard pressed to ascribe any reliability or performance differences to the style of using the protection hardware. There may be a case to be made for complex architectures of this style, but it is certainly not an easy case to make.

THE 80386 INSTRUCTION FORMATS

For each of the processors that we will examine in this text, there will be a section describing the instruction formats. For the RISC processors these sections will be relatively short. For the CISC processors, the 386 and the 68030, the description of the instruction formats will be a lengthy mess, even though they won't even try to be complete. While it is an explicit goal in the design of a RISC processor to keep the instruction formats regular and simple, no such statement can be made for the CISC machines. It is sometimes easy to think that CISC designers are *deliberately* complicating the instruction formats!

We will do our best to give some general impression of the organization of 386 instruction formats in this section, but the nature of CISC designs makes this very difficult to do. We have avoided presenting the instruction formats until this point, since the instruction formats are so dependent on oddities of the instruction set itself that to have any chance of understanding them it is necessary to be familiar with the instructions. Furthermore, they are tied up with the addressing formats.

Before discussing the instruction formats themselves, let us look at those components of the formats that are used to specify addressing modes. In the subsequent description of the instruction formats, we call this set of bytes as modR/M byte in the listings. The modR/M byte specifies whether an operand is in a register or in memory; if it is in memory, then fields within the byte specify the addressing mode to be used.

The modR/M byte consists of three fields, the *mod* field, the *reg* field, and the R/M field. When set to one of its four possible values, the 2-bit mod field may specify a register (in which case the register is given in the R/M field). The other three possible values of the mod field are used to select one of several possible ways of addressing memory. The *reg* field is used to specify a register operand. The address formats specified by the modR/M can range from 1 to 6 bytes in length. The set of possible formats for the addressing component of an instruction is shown in Figure 3.8.

The first format, shown in Figure 3.8(a), is used if the operand is a register, where *reg* is a 3-bit field designating one of eight registers. In this and all other instances of the modRM field, either the *rrr* field is used to designate the other operand (always a register) of a two-operand instruction or it is a 3-bit opcode extension.

The second format, shown in Figure 3.8(b), is used for the addressing form [EBX] with a single base register. The base register can be EAX, EBX, ECX, EDX, ESI, or EDI, but *not* ESP or EBP. This slight irregularity results from running out of bits (see next two formats). It is harmless in practice, since in the case of ESP, the format described

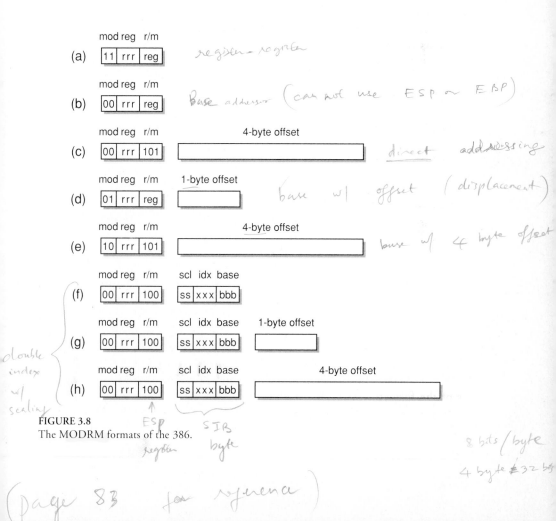

FIGURE 3.8
The MODRM formats of the 386.

just ahead, with an SIB byte can be used, and for [EBP], a 1-byte offset of 0 can be used. This fits with the typical use of EBP to point to a stack frame, so the reference to [EBP] is unusual anyway (it corresponds to the old frame pointer).

The format shown in Figure 3.8(c) is used for direct addressing with no index or base register. While a 101 code would normally designate EBP, as we noted above EBP cannot be used with *mod* equal to 00.

The fourth mode (shown in Figure 3.8(d)) uses *mod* value of 01 to designate base addressing with a 1-byte signed offset, allowing an offset of from −128 to +127. The *reg* field can designate any base register except ESP. Normally the offset would never be zero, since the form using a *mod* value of 00 can be used instead. As we noted above, the exception is for [EBP], which cannot use the *mod* 00 format.

The format shown in Figure 3.8(e) with a value of 10 for mod is used to designate base addressing with a full 4-byte offset. As with the *mod* 00 case, the *reg* field can designate any base register except ESP.

The remaining formats (Figures 3.8(f) and 3.97(g)) allow the specification of a base register and an index register to support addressing modes such as [EBX+ECX∗8]. When the modR/M byte specifies that such addressing should be used, an addition byte called the SIB byte follows it. This byte consists of a 2-bit *scale* field, a 3-bit *index* field and a 3-bit *base* field. In these formats, the *mod* field indicates the length of the offset (no offset, 1-byte signed offset, or 4-byte offset). The R/M field contains the code that would normally designate ESP. This is why ESP cannot be used as a base register in the simple 1-byte modR/M format. The *scale* field indicates the scaling of the index register:

- 00 = no scaling
- 01 = scale index register by multiplying by 2
- 10 = scale index register by multiplying by 4
- 11 = scale index register by multiplying by 8

The *index* field specifies the index register, which can be any of the eight registers *except* ESP. If *index* is set to 100 (the code normally used for ESP), then there is no index register. Finally, the *base* field specifies the base register, which can be any of the eight registers, including [ESP].

The net result of these formats is that all possible indexing modes can be represented except one in which ESP is scaled, as in [EBX + ESP ∗ 4]. However, this is not missed in practice because there would never be a situation in which it would make sense to scale ESP.

Now that we have gone through that confusing list of possible addressing forms, we can look at individual instruction formats. Remember that whenever modR/M appears, it can represent any of the eight formats described above, except that in some instructions a register operand cannot be specified. (We warned you that this would be a messy section!). Figure 3.9 shows the formats that we will consider.

The format shown in Figure 3.9(a) is the simplest of the instruction formats, 1-byte long with no operands. Examples of instructions using this format are CLC, clear the carry flag and PUSHF, push the flags.

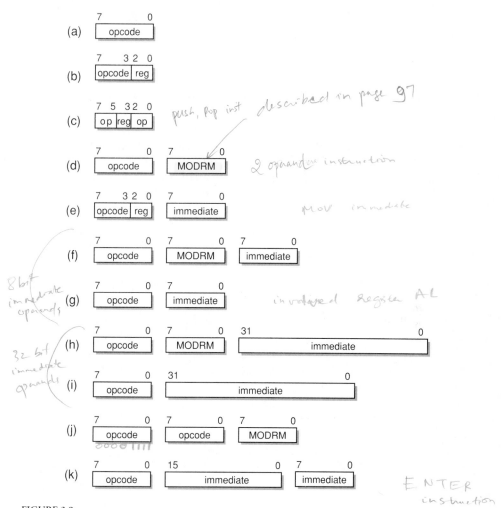

FIGURE 3.9
A sampling of the instruction formats of the Intel 80386.

The second format, shown in Figure 3.9(b), is used for a small number of instructions that take a single register operand. Examples are PUSH, POP, and INC. The idea behind having a specialized format is to keep the code as compact as possible for frequently used instructions. Actually this attempt to keep instructions as short as possible is a guiding principle behind the entire instruction set design and contributes significantly to the complexity of this section. Historically, the 8086 attempted to duplicate the very compact instruction stream of the earlier 8080, which was designed when memory was comparatively expensive. Compatibility requirements have led the 386 to share the same basic approach, although in these days of much cheaper memory it is not at all clear that it is a worthwhile approach.

The format shown in Figure 3.9(c) is an example of one of the rather strange formats with very specialized usage. It is used only for PUSH and POP applied to one of the four segment registers, DS, ES, SS, or CS.

The format shown in Figure 3.9(d) is one of the very common instruction forms, used for all two-operand instructions such as ADD and SUB, where both operands are indicated by the modRM sequence. It is also used for one-operand instructions such as NOT and NEG, in which case the *reg* field of the modR/M byte is a 3-bit opcode extension. The 2-byte format shown in Figure 3.9(e) is used only for the MOV instruction, where the first register is one of the 8-bit registers and the operand is an 8-bit immediate value.   *lower 8 bit of register A*

Formats 3.9(f) and (g) are used for 8-bit immediate instructions. The second form is a specialized format used if the register involved is AL. This favoring of AL is a historical hangover from the 8080, where the A register was the only register in which arithmetic could be performed. Again, the retention of this format reflects the concentration on keeping instruction formats short.

The formats shown in Figures 3.9(h) and (i) are the corresponding immediate formats in which a 32-bit register and a 32-bit immediate operand are involved. As in the 8-bit case, the short form is a special one used only when the register is EAX.

In the format shown in Figure 3.9(j), the first opcode byte always contains 00001111. When the 386 was designed, a large number of additional operations was added. This required a number of extra opcodes, and there was not enough room left in the normal 8-bit opcode byte. To solve this problem, one unused 286 opcode 00001111 is taken over to mean "look in the following byte to determine the operation." The particular form here is used, for example, by MOVSX (move with sign extension), which was added for the 386.

The last example is another specialized format, shown in Figure 3.9(k), used only by the ENTER instruction. The first immediate field is the stack frame size, and the second immediate field is the procedure level.

The idea of this section is not to list all the formats exhaustively, since this would be too exhausting and take too much space. To give some idea of how much more of this disorganized list would be needed, we count about 12 additional instruction formats, and that does not count the use of prefix bytes or the whole set of 16-bit addressing modes provided for back compatibility with the 286.

One purpose is precisely to point out how complex the instruction formats for a typical CISC processor are. Although there are definite patterns for some sets of instructions, there are also a number of cases where the instruction format is specially tailored. This complexity in instruction format design is one of the major distinctions between CISC and RISC architectures. RISC designers complain that CISC machines have excessively complex instruction formats, and the 386 is certainly a good example.

CONCLUSION

After looking at the addressing modes as well as the segmentation and protection mechanisms of the 386, you can begin to appreciate the C in CISC. In the CISC versus

RISC controversy, no one argues that CISC designs are not complex. The issue is whether or not this complexity is useful enough to be justified, and how much impact it has on the performance of a chip. In the case of the 386, the segmentation and protection mechanisms are highly complex, even by CISC standards. It is almost impossible to gather convincing data on whether or not these features pay off, so we probably have to settle for continued controversy of a rather subjective nature.

When it comes to the instruction formats, the CISC processors such as the 386 are affected by two factors. First there are more instructions and more addressing modes, so a certain increase in complexity is inevitable. The second issue is that, especially in the case of the 386, compact code is an important design criterion, and, just as in the case of programming, compactness and neatness conflict. If code size were not such an important consideration, the instruction formats of the 386 could be considerably cleaned up. For example, there would be no need to have offsets of different sizes, or the special addressing formats with no SIB byte present. However, there is no way to achieve the simplicity of the RISC formats—we will see later that there is simply too much information which must be encoded in the instructions for the 386 instruction set. Furthermore, a large amount of non-uniformity (things like the LOOP instruction using only the ECX register) has been inherited from the earlier Intel chips and cannot be disowned because of compatibility considerations.

CHAPTER

4

TASKING, VIRTUAL MEMORY, AND EXCEPTIONS ON THE 80386

In this third and final chapter on the 80386, we will describe the hardware support for tasking and paging, as well as the exception mechanism. If you look at the table of contents, you will notice that of all the processors covered in this text, only the 386 has three chapters devoted to it (the 68030 is described in two chapters, while all of the RISC processors are covered in a single chapter). To a certain extent, this reflects the relative complexity of the 386. Even the abbreviated description of this processor is sufficiently complex that the resulting discussion is fairly lengthy.

TASKING

As we discussed in Chapter 1, the basic facilities for supporting the notion of tasking are simple and are present on all of the microprocessors discussed in this text. What makes the 386 unusual is that, in grand CISC style, the instruction set has been enhanced with some remarkably complicated instructions and structures to support tasking.

The Local Descriptor Table

The description that has been given of segmentation so far may have led you to believe that all descriptors reside in the global descriptor table, which is not the case. There are two descriptor tables, with essentially identical formats. The second table is called the *local descriptor table* (LDT). A selector uses bit 2 to determine whether it is referencing the GDT or the LDT. The need for the LDT arises in conjunction with tasking, which is why we have not mentioned it until now. The LDTR register points to the LDT by specifying a GDT selector (the LDT itself is described as a segment in the GDT).

With only a single GDT, all tasks would be forced to share the same set of descriptors, the consequence being that all tasks would have the same set of segments. In particular, this would mean that if one application task could access a given segment, then so could another task, since each of these tasks would be operating at a privilege level of 3. This would be fine if the tasks were all part of the same program, such as several tasks that were all created by the same Ada program. It is not at all fine if the tasks are owned by a number of different programs in a multi-user environment.

One could attempt to use a single GDT for all tasks by having the operating system modify the privilege levels in the data segments in the GDT on every task switch, but this would introduce considerable overhead. Instead, the idea is to use separate LDTs to achieve this purpose. The intended organization is that the GDT will contain all the segments shared between all tasks, including operating system segments (protected by having an appropriate descriptor privilege level). Code segments for shared routines (such as math library routines), along with the call gates needed to call system services, will also use the GDT. The LDT will contain descriptors for all the data and code segments specific to a given task.

This does not mean that every task in the system must have a separate LDT. In the case of an Ada program, such as one with several tasks, it would make sense for the corresponding 386 tasks to share the same LDT since there is only one data environment for an Ada program. On the other hand, separate programs certainly *would* have different LDTs. Note that there is nothing to stop the same entry from appearing in more than one descriptor table. This means that it is possible to have two tasks, each with its own LDT, with entries duplicated in such a way that some, but not all, of the segments are shared between two tasks.

Context Switching

As we discussed in Chapter 1, context switching basically involves saving all of the registers and other machine state information associated with a task in a task control block. To start the new task executing, the machine state of the task being switched out is saved into its task control block and then the machine state of the new task is reloaded from another task control block. On most processors this is accomplished by issuing a relatively long sequence of load and store instructions.

Since this save and restore operation is expected to occur quite frequently, especially in real-time systems, where the context switch time is an important performance parameter, it is natural for a CISC designer to wonder whether special instructions can be provided to assist the context switch. This is precisely the line of reasoning that went into the 286 and 386 designs.

The context switch on these processors is accomplished by implementing a data structure in the hardware that corresponds to a task control block. On the 386, this structure is called a *task state segment* (TSS). The task state segment is organized as a normal data segment except that the descriptor in the GDT or LDT specially marks the entry as a TSS (see Figure 4.1). The TSS has enough room in it to store all the registers, including the LDT pointer. There is also space for four copies of the stack pointer, the need for which we will discuss later.

The special dedicated *task register* (TR) points to the task state segment for the current task. To effect a task switch, a special version of the FAR JMP instruction is used whose target segment corresponds to the TSS entry in the descriptor table. This single jump instruction effects the entire context switch, saving the old state in the current

31	23	15	7	0	
I/O MAP BASE		0 0 0 0 0 0 0 0 0 0 0 0 0 0 0		T	64
0 0 0 0 0 0 0 0 0 0 0 0 0 0 0 0		LDT			60
0 0 0 0 0 0 0 0 0 0 0 0 0 0 0 0		GS			5C
0 0 0 0 0 0 0 0 0 0 0 0 0 0 0 0		FS			58
0 0 0 0 0 0 0 0 0 0 0 0 0 0 0 0		DS			54
0 0 0 0 0 0 0 0 0 0 0 0 0 0 0 0		SS			50
0 0 0 0 0 0 0 0 0 0 0 0 0 0 0 0		CS			4C
0 0 0 0 0 0 0 0 0 0 0 0 0 0 0 0		ES			48
EDI					44
ESI					40
EBP					3C
ESP					38
EBX					34
EDX					30
ECX					2C
EAX					28
EFLAGS					24
INSTRUCTION POINTER (EIP)					20
CR3 (PDPR)					1C
0 0 0 0 0 0 0 0 0 0 0 0 0 0 0 0		SS2			18
ESP2					14
0 0 0 0 0 0 0 0 0 0 0 0 0 0 0 0		SS1			10
ESP1					0C
0 0 0 0 0 0 0 0 0 0 0 0 0 0 0 0		SS0			8
ESP0					4
0 0 0 0 0 0 0 0 0 0 0 0 0 0 0 0		BACK LINK TO PREVIOUS TSS			0

NOTE: 0 MEANS INTEL RESERVED. DO NOT DEFINE.

FIGURE 4.1
The 386 Task State Segment.

task as referenced by TR, switching TR to point to the new TSS, and finally restoring the machine state from this new TSS. This is certainly *not* a 1-clock instruction! The description of the JMP instruction in the 80386 Programmer's Reference Manual occupies three pages of dense 9-point type, and the particular version of the JMP that effects a task switch takes over 300 clocks.

Why does this single instruction take so many clocks? There are a large number of checks related to protection that have to be made when a call is executed. A check is made to see that the target entry is a proper TSS descriptor, that the TSS is formatted correctly, that it contains all of the appropriate information, and that the protection constraints are obeyed. If, for instance, we find that the selector is pointing to a TSS where the code segment has a privilege level of 3, and the data segment has a privilege level of 0, that is mighty suspicious. All those kinds of error checks are performed on a context switch to make sure that the target TSS is sensible and obeys all of the protection rules.

The effect of the jump is a little unusual. Since it results in saving the current CS:EIP value in the caller's TSS, it is really more like a call than a jump. When the other task executes *its* jump instruction to return control, the first task resumes with the instruction immediately following the orignal JMP.

This kind of calling linkage is called a *coroutine* linkage, since the caller and the called tasks are entirely symmetrical. It is also possible to transfer control to another task using a special version of the FAR CALL instruction, in which case there is a more conventional structure between the caller and the called task, which then terminates its thread of control by using an IRET instruction, a special form of return that in this case causes a complete context switch to return to the calling task.

Shared Memory

As we noted earlier, the typical arrangement in a 386-based operating system is for the GDT to be used for tasks that are global to the operating system—in particular, all the system segments are in the GDT, and all the call gates for the system routines that all other tasks want to see are in the GDT. All tasks share that code because they all use the same entry in the GDT. That makes sense, since for example, there only needs to be one file read routine in the system.

In addition, at least the TSS entries themselves must be in the GDT because it is necessary to switch from one task to another, that is, the GDT is used as the path from one task to another. All other data and code segments are in the local descriptor tables.

Is that what you really want? In some views of the world, that *is* what you want. For instance, in early versions of Unix, each process had a separate address space. No task could access the memory of any other task. If one task wanted to communicate with another task in these early versions of Unix, it could not do so by putting data somewhere in memory to be read—that would be useless because no other task could see the memory of another task. Instead, one task would call the system and pipe some data to the other process. The system routine would then move the data from one memory space to another (they were the only routines that could see all data at once).

For an operating system like Unix, it is perfectly fine for every task to have its own local descriptor table so that no task can access any other task's data. But that isn't *always* what the programmer wants. In a shared address space model a number of tasks can share common data structures. More recent versions of Unix provide this kind of *shared memory* access. OS/2 also has an elaborate set of facilities for such support.

How do we achieve the sharing of data segments? One possibility is to put the selector for a shared segment in the GDT where everyone can get at it. Another possibility is to duplicate the selector in the LDT of each task sharing the data. The other extreme would allow all the tasks to share exactly the same set of segments. In that case, each task does not even need its own LDT—they can all share a single LDT. This allows a designer to choose from a complete spectrum, from tasks being completely separated in address spaces, to tasks being completely merged, or something in between (where some segments are shared and some are separate).

Even in an implementation of Unix with no shared data, there will be shared segments between tasks. Which segments will be shared? Code segments are an obvious case. If one task is executing program *clunk*, and another task is executing program *clunk*, and we agree that code segments of *clunk* cannot be modified, it is evident that the code that both tasks want for *clunk* is the same. These two tasks might be executing with different data segments, but since they share the code, there can be a common code segment entry in their LDTs.

SHARING DATA. If two tasks *do* share data, then we suddenly buy into a lot of headache-causing problems. Consider the following example, in which one task executes

```
if A = 0 then
    do something sensible, assuming A is zero
end if;
```

and at exactly the same time a second task executes

```
A := 1;
```

The embarrassing situation occurs if the operating system decides to pass control from the first task to the second task just *after* the test to see if A is 0 but *before* the code which depends on the outcome of this test. Then the second task sets A to a value other than 0, and when control returns to the first task, it is in an inconsistent state.

There is no magical way to solve these problems. The programmer who is faced with accessing shared memory is forced to consider the potential conflicts at every point, and this is what makes programming of this type so difficult.

The problem might be stated this way. Suppose that there is a task consisting of 10,000 instructions. Then there are only 10,000 different instructions that the code can be executing just before a context switch occurs. In some sense this means that it is necessary to understand only 10,000 possible states.

But suppose we have 100 tasks each consisting of only 100 instructions. Any of these tasks can be executing any one of these 100 instructions, and by the same sort of crude reasoning that there are 10,000 states to consider in the first case, there are now 100^{100} states to consider, quite a large number! Unless there are tools to manage that level of complexity, the situation is likely to become diabolical. As soon as tasks interact with one another in any way, this kind of phenomenon occurs. If the tasks interact by changing variables that lie within a shared memory, it is potentially the most serious kind of interaction that could occur, because these problems can happen on an instruction-by-instruction basis.

Nevertheless, that is none of the operating system's concern, and indeed the special tasking support in the hardware of the 386 neither makes this problem easier nor harder to deal with. If you, the applications programmer, want to write programs in which an address space can be shared, it is up to you, not the operating system, to do things right. It certainly *is* helpful for the machine to provide instructions that assist in this process.

On the 386, the XCHG instruction, which exchanges the contents of a register with memory, is guaranteed to be non-interruptible. It also locks the bus, so that if two processors on the same bus issue XCHG instructions at the same time, one has to wait until the other instruction is complete. Now we can write the code with the two tasks in the following way. We have a shared variable FLAG that is normally 0. If it is set to 1, then the meaning is to place a lock, creating a so-called *critical section*, a section of code which cannot be logically interrupted and that only one task can execute to completion at a time.

In our example, the first task would execute

```
        MOV     EAX, 1
LP1:    XCHG    EAX, FLAG       ; set flag to 1, and test it
        OR      EAX, EAX
        JNZ     LP1             ; loop back if it was already set
        CMP     A,0             ; now it's safe to test A
        JNZ     DN
        ...
        {code assuming A is zero}
        ...
DN:     MOV     FLAG, 0         ; reset the flag
```

The second task protects its access to A in a similar manner:

```
        MOV     EAX, 1
LP2:    XCHG    EAX, FLAG       ; set flag to 1, and test it
        OR      EAX, EAX
        JNZ     LP2             ; loop back if it was already set
        MOV     A, 1            ; now it's safe to set A
        MOV     FLAG, 0         ; reset the flag
```

It is possible to write mutually protected code without the assistance of instructions like XCHG that allow memory to be set and tested at the same time, but it is difficult. As we will see, all the microprocessors we look at have instructions that assist with this kind of shared memory programming.

TSS: task state segment

In addition to the XCHG instruction, the 386 provides a special prefix instruction called LOCK which can be used in front of certain instructions to force them to operate with the bus locked. For instance, a repeated string move can be preceded by a LOCK prefix to ensure that the entire string is moved atomically. As one would expect, the LOCK prefix is protected, since we can't have applications programs blocking access to the bus for an extended period of time.

The System Stack

Looking back at the picture of a TSS, you will see that there is space for four separate stack pointers (SS:ESP, SS0:ESP0, SS1:ESP1, and SS2:ESP2). The four stack pointers are for use by code running at the four different privilege levels. If an application task is running and calls the system through a call gate, for example, the stack pointer is automatically switched, using the values from the current TSS.

When a task calls a system routine, there are two reasons why it is undesirable to have the system routine use the same stack that the task is using. First of all, the system routine may leave traces of itself behind, something that is generally considered to be bad policy. It may be possible to use those traces to gather information about how the operating system works and use that information to assault it. In a secure environment it should not be possible to see *any* trace of the operating system. It should not be possible to see the operating system's code, the operating system's data, or anything else that has to do with the operating system. If an operating system routine that uses the stack pushes and pops all sorts of things on the stack, that principle is violated.

A second reason to avoid having the operating system use a task's stack is that there might not be enough of the stack left for it. If an application runs out of stack space then we expect the operating system to deal with the problem. If the operating system routine itself runs out of stack space then it is not at all obvious how that should be dealt with; the fault has occurred deep within the operating system code. It is much cleaner to have the operating system supply a suitably large stack and install it in the user's TSS for subsequent use. The application program using the TSS can neither read nor write this task stack, since it will be a data segment with a privilege level making it inaccessible to the application program *until* a call to the system routine via a call gate changes the privilege level, and switches stacks.

Virtual Machine Support

An operating system is said to provide virtual machine support if it can run a task which thinks it owns the entire machine, for example, some other operating system. Basically the idea is that the task thinks it is running at protection level 0, but is really running at protection level 3. When it issues a privileged instruction, a trap to the "real" operating system occurs, and this trap routine first checks that the client task is behaving itself (and not, for example, trying to clobber memory belonging to some other task in the system), and then simulates the effect of the privileged instruction, so that the client system thinks it was able to issue the instruction, and can proceed ahead.

Neither the 286 nor the 386 was designed with the thought of full virtual machine support. There are many small examples where the attempt to implement a virtual machine concept fails. One is in the implementation of the PUSHF instruction. Consider the following sequence of instructions:

```
CLI     ; disable interrupts
...
PUSHF  ; save flags on stack
...
```

The CLI instruction turns off all interrupts and is thus, not surprisingly, privileged—we can't have one application program locking out all the others.

A virtual machine implementation would trap the CLI and pretend to lock out interrupts (for example, by not presenting any interrupts to the virtual machine until it reenabled its interrupts), but of course it would have to leave interrupts enabled so that other programs could proceed normally. Now when the PUSHF instruction is executed, it saves the flags on the stack where the program can look at them. One of these flags shows whether the "real" processor interrupts are enabled. Is PUSHF a privileged instruction? Certainly not—we cannot afford the overhead of going to the operating system for the normal use of PUSHF, which is to save user flags, like the carry flag, over a procedure call.

This means that an operating system can tell that it does not really have the full capabilities of the machine. There are many such small glitches. Will a real operating system run afoul of one of these glitches? Almost certainly yes, since operating systems are complicated and delicate pieces of software that make all kinds of assumptions about the hardware environment.

The 286 had no support for virtual machines at all. This lack of support is one of the features that prompted Bill Gates of Microsoft to refer to the 286 as a "brain-damaged" chip. Why should Microsoft be so concerned about virtual machine support—do they really want to run multiple copies of OS/2 on one machine at the same time? No, of course not, but they *desperately* want to be able to run multiple copies of old-style DOS applications, simply because there are tens of thousands of these on the market, and it would be highly desirable to be able to multiprogram and run these applications simultaneously. Since the 286 lacks the necessary hardware support, the current version of OS/2 can run only one DOS program at a time—so much for those who want to run DBase IV and Lotus 1-2-3 simultaneously!

When the 286 was designed, Intel never imagined that everyone would use it to run real-mode DOS programs to any great extent. A basic compatibility with the 8088 was provided, but it was assumed that new applications for the 286 protected mode would rapidly appear and that this would be the normal operating mode of the chip.

By the time the 386 was introduced, it had become clear that 386-based machines would be used for years to come to run old-style 8088 programs. This may make systems hardware designers weep, but occasionally the realities of the marketplace take precedence over the desire to introduce wonderful new architectures which are incompatible with the older designs. Consequently, a very important additional feature was designed into the 386 called the *virtual 8086 mode*.

Virtual 8086 mode allows the operating system to provide virtual machine capability not for the 386 itself, but for virtual 8086 machines.[1] This allows multiple copies of DOS and DOS-based applications to run at the same time.

This works as follows: There is a special form of code descriptor that can appear in the GDT or LDT that is marked as being in virtual 8086 mode. When code is operating in this mode, careful attention is paid to making sure that a full virtual machine simulation is possible. For example, the PUSHF instruction *does* trap in this mode to allow proper simulation of the behavior of the interrupt flag. Moreover, the segment addressing within a virtual 8086 mode program uses the old-style (16 * paragraph + offset) addressing instead of the GDT selector-based addressing.

At every point, careful consideration has been given to ensuring that programs running on an 8088-based PC can be properly executed in virtual 8086 mode. The success of this approach is evident; there are a number of products on the market, such as Microsoft's Windows 386, a program that allow multi-programming of existing DOS applications.

But Is It All Worth It?

A section in a previous chapter discussed this same question with respect to the ENTER instruction. The same concern applies here in even more concentrated form. A very significant chunk of processor hardware and design is devoted to this specialized support for tasking, and we need to ask if it is all worthwhile.

Obviously we could achieve the effects of context switching using ordinary instructions. Now it is probably the case that if we do absolutely *everything* that the TSS context switch does, we will end up being slower doing things in software. However, in many circumstances, we really don't need to swap that much.

For example, in most operating systems, including all versions of Unix so far implemented on the 386, a single-segment model is used, so that all of a task's data is in one segment. In writing an Ada compiler under Unix, it is typically the case that all tasks of the Ada compiler share the same segments. This means that it is *not* necessary to switch the segment registers on a context switch between Ada tasks.

What we have here is another example of a massively complicated instruction that we just might not want to use. One of the negative aspects of the 386 architecture is that tasking must be used in order to get multiple stack pointers, which are really useful. It is hard not to use some of it without buying the whole apparatus. A 300-clock context switch is not very fast—in many circumstances a software solution for context switching will be more efficient.

---

[1] Strictly speaking, it actually provides support for real-mode 386, which is subtly different from the 8086 for a few instructions, but since all marketed software runs on the 8088 as well as the 386, the distinction is not important.

On the other hand, a context switch supported in hardware does have the advantage of executing all the appropriate protection checks in the hardware. However, most systems ignore the protection on the 386 and work with only one giant segment. They don't want to know about segments, segments at different levels, or amazing logical protection. They just want to have one large logical address space and not be bothered with any of this.[2]

Additionally, the virtual 8086 mode support is widely used. Looking at the design of the 386 without a historical perspective, it would be hard to imagine what possible use there is for a special mode whose purpose is to restrict the functionality of the processor and introduce obviously inefficient execution. You might ask: "Why would anyone run anything in this silly mode?" The surprising answer is that for some time to come we can expect most 386-based PC machines to be executing in this crippled mode most of the time!

VIRTUAL MEMORY MANAGEMENT

As we discussed in the Chapter 1, the use of virtual memory allows a program to use more logical memory than there is physical memory on the machine by mapping virtual addresses into quite unrelated physical addresses and copying portions of memory to the disk when necessary. On the 386, there are two entirely separate approaches to the implementation of virtual memory—one relying on the segmentation mechanism and the other on paging.

Virtual Segmentation

In GDT

Two important bits in every segment descriptor are the *present* bit, which shows whether the entry is logically available, and the *access* bit, which is set to 1 every time the selector is loaded. If you had no idea of what it is used for, it might be a mystery as to why it should be set to 1.

Using these two bits, it is possible to implement *virtual segmentation*, a special form of memory management where a segment may reside either in memory or on the disk. A program is written with the assumption that it can access a large number of segments, but at any particular moment only a subset of these segments is resident in memory, including those referenced by the current segment register contents.

When a program loads a new segment—for example, by executing a FAR CALL to transfer control from one code segment to another—one of the checks that is made on the target segment is a check to make sure that the present bit is set. If it is *not* set, then a *segment fault* occurs, causing a trap to the operating system. The operating system trap routine recognizes that the trap has occurred because the segment just happened not to be in memory, and responds by reading the segment into memory

---

[2] One reviewer of this book penned a note saying "Does anyone use this segment junk on the 386?" The answer to his question is that it *is* used to some extent in some environments, but a great many 386 chips are being greatly underutilized if you regard full utilization as implying use of all the fancy features.

and setting up the descriptor in the GDT or LDT (including setting the *present* bit to 1). It then returns control to the application program to reexecute the FAR CALL instruction, which now succeeds.

The operating system will, of course, have to find space to load in the new segment. That may mean that another segment may have to be removed from memory to make room for the one being brought in. The segment that is removed is copied to disk, and the present bit in *its* descriptor is reset to 0, so that when the swapped out segment is referenced again, another trap will occur.

Does the operating system always have to copy the segment to disk? There are two cases in which the answer to this question is no. First of all, segments that cannot be modified—in particular this includes all code segments—need not be swapped out, since they obviously have not been changed and the old image on disk is still valid. The other case is that in which a data segment *could* be modified, but has in fact *not* been modified since the last time it was loaded. An operating system could detect this situation by initially marking the segment as read only. The first attempt to write the segment would then cause a trap, at which time the operating system could change the segment to read/write, indicating that it has been modified.

Note that if a segment is not present, the only bit tested by the hardware is the present bit. This means that the other 63 bits of the descriptor are available for operating system use. A typical use is to record the disk location of the swapped out image of the segment.

All of these operations are completely transparent to the program, which, you will remember, cannot even read the GDT, let alone change it. That is why a program cannot even tell where a segment is in memory—it must reference the GDT indirectly through the selector. This means that the operating system can move a segment around in memory without the program being aware of it. In particular, it is quite normal to swap out a segment and then, when it is swapped back in response to a later reference, to locate it at a different memory address.

Segment-Swapping Algorithms

One difficulty from the operating system's point of view is that it has to find a hole that is large enough that it can move the segment from disk to memory. Since all of the segments that are active can be anywhere in memory, the possibility of fragmentation arises. While trying to load a 22K segment back into memory from the disk, you might find that there is 2K free in one place and 20K free in another. It does not help that the total amount of memory that is available is sufficient, since a segment has to exist in a single contiguous region of memory.

That is the sort of thing the operating system must manage in an efficient manner. Notice that the operating system can move segments around. There's no problem in moving one segment down in memory as long as the operating system changes the starting address of the segment in the appropriate GDT selector. The single level of indirection allows segments to be moved around quite transparently due to the mechanism provided by the segment registers and the GDT.

On the other hand, 4 gigabytes is quite a lot of space to be moving around between memory and disk. Let's do a quick calculation as to how much time it might take to swap a segment out to disk. No one really has 4 gigabytes of memory on their machine, but they certainly may have 20 megabytes. So 20 megabytes is approximately 5 million words, and the fast MOVSD instruction can at best move 5 words per microsecond— that is roughly 5 clocks per word. The current generation of 386 chips are running at 25 MHz, and typical instructions take a few cycles—it operates at roughly 5 to 7 million instructions per second. That means that we need 10^6 microseconds. That is 1 second of the CPU grinding around to move everything in a 20 megabyte memory. If the operating system is doing *that* every 100 milliseconds, nothing at all will get done.

The operating system has to balance the need to move segments around with the need for minimizing system overhead. It might use an algorithm that shuffles things around in a simple fashion. It's the same sort of thing that you would do in a file drawer. If you're maintaining a file drawer, every time you get a new file you don't go through all the files in the office and move one file to the next drawer. Instead, you look for a file drawer nearby and shuffle things a bit to make room for the new one. That kind of algorithm is what needs adapting for this purpose.

When an operating system that uses virtual segmentation[3] finds that it has to bring in a new segment, it has to decide which old segment to get rid of, and this decision needs to be made with some intelligence. For example, the stack segment would be a very poor choice for removal—it is being used all the time, and so it would almost certainly never be swapped out.

The problem is, if there are a large number of code segments and data segments, which should you swap out? The ideal model is that you would know the future use of all segments. If somehow by divine inspiration you could tell how the segments are going to be used in the future, you would naturally swap one out that is not going to be used for a while. But you don't *really* know what the future is going to bring, that is, what the future history of the program is. The applications programmer might have a clue in some applications—but since the operating system knows nothing about the applications, virtual segmentation systems are generally designed to work blind with respect to what the future holds.

Even though the operating system cannot predict the future, it *can* learn something about what has happened in the past. The general philosophy is that if you haven't used something for a while, then you probably won't use it again for some time to come. This is an empirical observation that works pretty well in practice even though it is not perfectly reliable. The segments that may have not been used for some time may be exactly those that a program is just about to use. These strategies are not completely reliable—they just happen to be heuristics that work most of the time.

The hardware does not provide a mechanism for keeping track of which segments have been used most recently—the operating system will have to do that for itself. That

---

[3] The word *segment* is being used here in two senses. It is both the hardware segment on the 386 that is being called a segment and, in the lingo of operating systems, a logical piece of data or code (that's, of course, why Intel chose the word segment).

is where the access bit supplied in the 386 GDT entry is used. The operating system can periodically reset all of the access bits in the GDT and LDT to zero. The next time it wakes up for this purpose, it looks to see which segment has had its access bit turned on—that is how the operating system knows that those segments have been used. The operating system can record which segments were used for a certain period of time, typically several hundred milliseconds. It then resets all the access bits; a hundred milliseconds later it can ask again what new segments have been reused.

As we will see in the next section, the 386 provides an alternative mechanism for managing virtual memory, and it is likely that typical 386 systems will not make use of virtual segmentation. However, on the 286, virtual segmentation is the only mechanism for managing virtual memory, so this approach *is* used in 286-based systems. In particular OS/2 manages memory using segment swapping. OS/2 has complicated internal algorithms for determining which segments to swap out and how to move segments around in memory. How such algorithms should be designed is a major area of research in operating systems. It is not an easy problem, as can be seen from the fact that OS/2 can sometimes spend as much as 20 seconds deciding what to do—clearly Microsoft needs a little more research in this area!

Paging

On the 386, when the processor accesses the segment descriptor, it develops an address by adding the segment base address stored in this descriptor to the segment offset, developing a 32-bit *linear address*. However, this linear address is *not* necessarily a physical address in memory.

There is a bit in one of the system control registers that indicates whether paging is enabled. If paging is not enabled, then the linear address is indeed a physical address, and the base addresses and lengths in the segment descriptors are constrained by the maximum amount of physical memory. Although this can theoretically be up to 4 gigabytes, no machines yet have this much physical memory. On currently available machines, you are much more likely to get 16 or 32 megabytes at most. In any case, it's much less than the 4-gigabyte maximum.

If the paging bit is enabled, then an additional mechanism comes into play. Using tables called *page tables*, the linear address undergoes a translation to a physical address. The linear address space is broken up into 4K chunks called *pages*. Each 4K page in linear memory can be mapped into any 4K location in physical memory. The mapping is completely arbitrary. For example, a contiguous piece of linear memory may be mapped into non-contiguous pieces of physical memory (see Figure 4.2). If paging is enabled, all addresses, as we discussed in the previous chapter, are 32-bit linear addresses rather than physical addresses and get mapped by using the page tables. Even the addresses stored in the GDTR and LDTR registers, which give the locations of the GDT and LDT, are linear addresses rather than physical addresses, so the descriptor tables can also be paged.

An important point is that not all of the 4K pages have to be mapped. The page tables used to implement the mapping can indicate that a page is not present. This

Logical Pages   Physical Memory

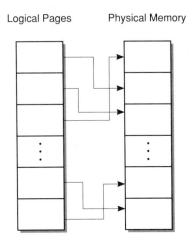

FIGURE 4.2
The mapping of logical pages into physical pages.

means that the operating system can swap pages in and out to implement *demand paging*, in a manner quite analogous to the demand segmentation discussed in the previous section. The enormous advantage of virtual paging as opposed to virtual segmentation is that pages are fixed length, so it is never possible to get memory fragmentation, and the operating system never has to move memory around to accommodate new pages.

The Format of Virtual Addresses

The mapping mechanism is implemented through a register named CR3, which contains the physical address of the *page directory.* The page directory is itself a 4K chunk (everything is divided into 4K chunks), which holds up to 1024 four-byte entries. Each of these 1024 entries can point to a page table, and each page table has 1024 entries in it, each of which finally points to a 4K chunk of real memory—finally we are pointing to a physical memory address.

This is a two-level scheme. Why have two levels? Four gigabytes is quite a lot of memory. Four gigabytes divided by the page size (which is 4K) is about 1 million pages. If we had one gigantic page table, it would have to be 4 megabytes long. That is rather large. On a machine with 8 megabytes you would have to spend half of that memory on page tables just to map the other 4 megabytes. With a two-level mechanism, entries can be missing both in the 1024-entry page directory and in individual page tables, so the page tables can be considerably compressed. It is even possible for the operating system to use demand paging for the page tables themselves, swapping in only those page tables that are actually referenced.

To get a physical address from a virtual address you take the 32-bit virtual address, and divide it into 3 pieces. The 10 high-order bits determine the page directory entry in use. The next 10 bits of linear address select which entry in the page table (which is pointed to by the root table) to use. The last 12 bits select which of the 4096 bytes you are talking about in this page (see Figure 4.3).

If you've seen paging systems before, then this sort of system is much more familiar than the virtual segmentation system discussed earlier. Everything works out very nicely when the address can be broken down into powers of 2 in this way. Two conditions must be met for this approach: first the page size must be fixed, and second it must be a power of 2.

Since all pages are on 4K boundaries, the lower 12 bits of a page address are always zero, which means that they are available for use in the page directory and page table entries. The format of these entries is as shown in Figure 4.4.

- The *present bit* (P) bit serves the same purpose as the present bit in a segment descriptor. It indicates whether or not the referenced page is present. If not, then a page fault occurs, passing control to an operating system trap handler.

- The *read/write* (R/W) bit is used for write protection. Individual pages can be protected against writing. This protection is in addition to, and quite independent from, the protection provided by the segment descriptor. One interesting possibility is to have a single segment containing both code and data. In the LDT two descriptors are built for this segment; a code segment and a data segment. The code segment is marked in the descriptor table as writable, but the page protection is used to make sure that the code is still write protected. Some Unix systems on the 386 use this memory organization, since they prefer a single-segment view.

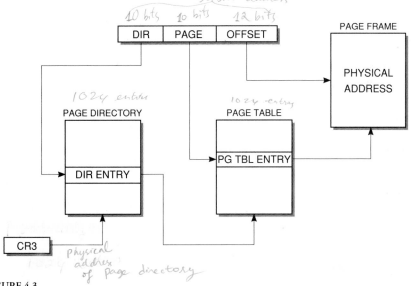

FIGURE 4.3
Page translation on the 386.

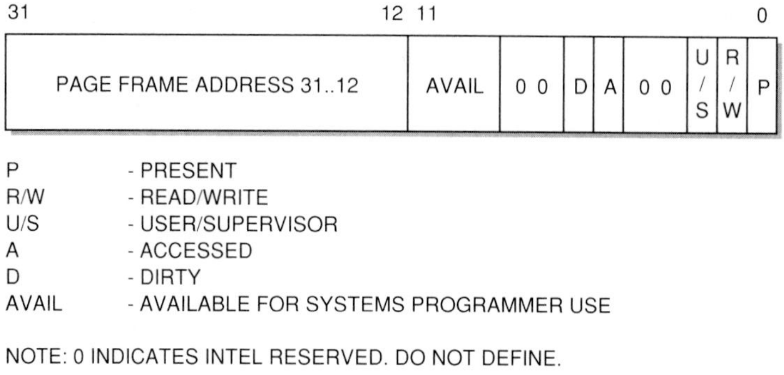

```
31                                    12 11                          0
┌──────────────────────────────────┬───────┬───┬───┬───┬───┬───┬───┬───┬───┐
│                                  │       │   │   │   │   │   │ U │ R │   │
│   PAGE FRAME ADDRESS 31..12      │ AVAIL │ 0 0 │ D │ A │ 0 0 │ / │ / │ P │
│                                  │       │   │   │   │   │   │ S │ W │   │
└──────────────────────────────────┴───────┴───┴───┴───┴───┴───┴───┴───┴───┘
```

P   - PRESENT
R/W   - READ/WRITE
U/S   - USER/SUPERVISOR
A   - ACCESSED
D   - DIRTY
AVAIL   - AVAILABLE FOR SYSTEMS PROGRAMMER USE

NOTE: 0 INDICATES INTEL RESERVED. DO NOT DEFINE.

FIGURE 4.4
The 386 Page Table Entry format.

- The *user/supervisor* (U/S) bit marks pages that are reserved to the system. If this bit is set, then the page can be accessed only if the CPL is 0, 1, or 2. Again this is a completely separate level of protection from that provided by the descriptor privilege level mechanism.

- The *access bit* (A) and the *dirty bit* (D) are used to help determine which pages should be swapped out. A is set whenever a page is accessed and can be used to gather historical data about the use of pages. D is set whenever the data of a page is modified, allowing the operating system to determine if the page needs writing out.

With this page table structure, every time memory is referenced, the processor has to follow a rather complicated sequence of steps to find the physical address:

- Get the base address of the segment from the GDT or LDT, and add this to the offset to determine the linear address.

- Locate the page directory using the value in the CR3 register, and use the first 10 bits of the linear address to select an entry in this directory.

- Load the page directory entry, and check that the P bit is set. Issue a page fault trap if it is not.

- For a write, check the R/W bit to make sure that a write is permitted. Also check the U/S bit to prevent user mode access to supervisor pages. If either check fails, issue a page fault trap.

- Set the A bit in the page directory entry and write it back to memory, since we have now accessed this entry.

- Use the address in the page directory entry to locate the page table in memory. The next 10 bits of the linear address then select the entry in this page table to be used.

- Load the page table entry and check the P, R/W, and U/S bits to ensure that we have a valid entry. Issue a page fault trap if any of these steps fails.

- Set the A bit in the page table entry, and also the D bit if the memory access is a write.

- Use the address in the page table entry to locate the referenced page, and add the low-order 12 bits of the linear address to finally determine the byte address in physical memory.

It is quite inconceivable that the 386 could actually operate that way! It would mean that every time you made one memory reference, you would actually have to make at least three memory references, which would slow the machine down by a factor of 3. How can that problem be solved?

We can't solve it in the same way as with segments, gathering all the information into the processor, because then we would need 4 megabytes in the processor to store all the possible page tables—there aren't that many transistors on the chip. There will never be enough transistors on a chip to do that, because by the time there are enough transistors to hold 4 megabytes of page tables on the processor, memories will have improved so that we need 4 terabytes of page tables.

So we seem to have a dilemma. On the one hand, we will never be able to hold page tables in an immediately accessible form—they will have to be in memory—but at the same time we cannot tolerate this two-level lookup every time we want to reference memory.

THE PAGE TRANSLATION CACHE. The solution is to use a *page translation cache*, which is also called a *translation lookaside buffer*. This is a small table in the processor with room for a small number of page table entries. In the above sequence of access steps, before going to memory to load a page directory entry or a page table entry, the processor checks to see if the entry is already stored in the page translation cache. If so, it can be retrieved instantly because the cache is on the processor and built with extremely fast memory.

Only if this search fails do we have to incur the overhead of an additional memory reference. Furthermore, when this memory reference is completed, the resulting entry is stored into the cache, replacing an older entry, so that the next time it is referenced it *will* be available. Note that when the old entry is discarded, it may be necessary to write it out if the access or dirty bits have been modified.

From the application programmer's point of view, the access to the page tables and to the page translation cache is completely transparent. The performance will depend on what fraction of the time we get a hit in the cache, and this in turn depends on the application. Most applications display a pattern of fairly localized access, meaning that at any one point they are referencing a few specific areas of memory. A worst case would be a loop following a linked list where the links are located all over a large memory space, but even in this case the code for the loop would be localized, so the memory accesses to fetch the code would be well behaved.

ACCESSING THE PAGE TRANSLATION CACHE. If you think about it for a moment, there is a problem with implementing the page translation cache exactly as we have described. It is all very well to say that this cache is implemented using very fast memory, but consider the structure of the entries in the cache.

The cache contains a number of entries which say, "Hello. I'm the entry for address 3076." Another entry says, "Well, I'm entry 144." Now you have a whole lot of these entries and you know that you want entry 3076, but how will you find it? Searching the entries one by one is much too slow, even if it is done in very fast memory at the same speed as the internal processor speed.

Instead, a technique called *associative memory* is used. The request for an address is broadcast to all entries in the cache. The cache logic checks all entries in parallel, and at most one reports a match. By performing the comparisons in parallel, the overhead of a serial search is avoided. Unfortunately, it is undesirable to build large amounts of associative memory since these searches are expensive. The success of paging depends upon the ability to build a fast page translation table with an associative memory.

How effective is this approach? Intel quotes typical hit rates in the TLB of over 90%, meaning that only one in ten times are extra memory references needed by the paging mechanism. Another measure is to observe the overall time penalty for enabling the paging, which is typically in the range of a 10% slowdown. It seems that the trade-off is about right. They could have devoted more transistors on a chip to more entries in the associative table, but on the other hand, 10% is not a disaster by any means.

Of course this discussion assumes that all the pages are in memory. If the pages are *not* in memory and page fault traps occur, then the overhead from the paging can be much greater, especially if pages are swapped to and from relatively slow disks.

Handling Page Faults

What happens if a page is not present? Turn back to the section in this chapter called "Virtual Segmentation" and reread the discussion of what happens when a segment isn't present. It is exactly the same principle. When a trap occurs as a result of a page fault, the operating system must figure out where the page is on the disk and which page to toss out of physical memory so that room can be made for the new page. The instruction that caused the page fault in the first place is then reexecuted.

The trap caused by the page fault may be due to the fact that the page containing the data may be swapped out, or, even worse, the page of the page table containing the address of the data may be swapped out (remember that page tables are themselves paged). The following describes one possible scenario where it is necessary to load both a page of the page table, and the page containing the requested data, from the disk.

When an executing program asks for the data at some address in memory, the operating system may reply (if the page containing the data is not in memory), "Oops, the page of the page table which tells me where to find the data is not present." The operating system then tosses a page out (if necessary), loads in the page table, and then sets its present bit to indicate that it is present. The processor then reexecutes the instruction, but we might get another "page not present" trap again. Once again, the operating system responds by saying, "Oh, right, the page containing the actual data (as opposed to the page containing the page table) is also on disk, so I'll go and get that and try this instruction once again." After loading in this page, the instruction will succeed. Note that in making space for the page, we had better not swap the page table entry out or we will be in big trouble, since we will trap again.

But there is a further problem. In Chapter 3, we discussed the alignment of data in memory; we noted that the 386 was able to retrieve unaligned data by getting the two words from memory and putting the appropriate bytes within the two pieces together. It may take a bit longer than getting aligned data, but it can be done.

A similar problem comes up in a paged environment. If an unaligned operand straddles a page boundary, one byte is in one page and three bytes in another page, then in order to successfully fetch the data both pages need to be present in memory at the same time. This means that the whole process of page faulting to get the necessary data can actually happen *twice* in the same instruction, or even three times if the instruction itself causes a page fault. It is an additional complication for the operating system to have to deal with the fact that you may get two page faults from the same operand.[4] For example, the operating system must be careful that the page which is swapped out in order to make way for one of the pages containing the data is not the page containing the other half of the data.

With this in mind, you can appreciate the design of the REP MOVS instruction. Since this single instruction can potentially move gigabytes of virtual memory around, it seems likely that a huge number of page faults will occur since the operating system cannot ensure that all the required pages will be in memory at the same time. However, the ESI, EDI, and ECX registers are modified as the instruction executes to indicate how far in memory the move has progressed and how much more data is left to be moved. This means that you can take a page fault in the middle of the execution of this instruction, swap in the required pages, and continue where you left off.

The operating system routine which manages page faults must determine which page to swap out. Just as in the case of segmentation, a standard approach is to periodically probe the page table, reading and resetting access bits to determine which pages are being used. When a page must be swapped out, a good choice for replacement is a page that has not been used for a while. Furthermore, if the operating system is able to find several pages that all have not been used for some time, it is more attractive to discard a "clean" page rather than a "dirty" page. This is why the D bit is so useful.

One thing that simplifies the design in the case of paging is that all the pages are the same length, something which is certainly not true of segments. There are two benefits from this. First, the operating system can discard any page and be sure to have room for the new page. Secondly, it is never advantageous to move pages around in memory. You could move them around, since they are always accessed indirectly through the page tables, but there is never any need to move them, since with fixed length pages it is not possible to get memory fragmentation.

---

[4] There were bugs in some early versions of the 386, with operands lying across page boundaries. In particular, an early version of the floating-point chip had problems if the operands lay across page boundaries, so this sort of thing causes trouble at the hardware level as well.

IMPLEMENTING A PAGING ALGORITHM. Designing efficient paging algorithms is a difficult task. There is a delicate trade-off between making good choices, which of course saves time in disk accesses, and taking too long making these good choices, which is equally problematic. The study of the performance of various paging algorithms is an important area in operating systems research, and there is a great deal of literature examining this subject. We will describe one particular scheme to give an idea of how a page fault routine can be organized. This scheme was actually used for a paging compiler system on the 386.

A table is first constructed with one entry for every physical page in memory. Each of these entries points to the page table entry that references the page, and it contains a 32-bit data word used to record segment accesses. Periodically, using a timer interrupt, the table of entries is scanned. For each entry, the 32-bit data word is shifted one bit to the right, setting its sign bit from the access bit of the page table entry. The A bit is then reset in the entry.

After a while, the 32-bit word in each entry indicates how recently the corresponding page has been accessed. If 1 bits are set on the left, it has been referenced relatively recently; if there are a lot of 0 bits on the left, it has not been referenced for a while. A word which consists of all zeros indicates that the page has not been referenced in the last 32 periods. When a page must be discarded, the one chosen is the one with the lowest integer value in its 32-bit data word.

The data gathered in this way is, of course, a little crude. We completely forget about what happened more than 32 periods ago, and we cannot tell anything about the pattern of accesses within a single time period. What should the time period be? If it is too short, then things are forgotten fast. If it is too long, then we don't get sufficiently detailed information. Furthermore, if the time period is too short, we will spend too much time updating our tables. The code for the update loop is

```
LP:    LODSD              ; load next page table pointer
       MOV EBX, [EAX]     ; load page table entry
       SHR EBX, ..        ; right position access bit
       AND [EAX], ..      ; clear access bit
       LODSD              ; load 32-bit history word
       SHRD EAX,EBX,1     ; shift in new bit
       LOOP LP
```

On a 25 MHz 386, this loop takes about 1.5 microseconds. If we have 8 megabytes of physical memory, which is 2000 pages, then the update loop would take about 3 milliseconds.

After some experimentation, the update period chosen was 100 milliseconds. This means that the page table update overhead is about 3%, and we retain information about usage over the previous 3.2-second period. In practice this seemed to be the best balance of overall behavior. Of course, different applications show considerably different patterns of memory access, and no one choice is perfect in all cases.

Virtual Segmentation and Virtual Paging

On the 386, it is possible to imagine an operating system that implements both demand paging and demand segmentation in some complicated combination. The Intel reference manual briefly describes possible organizations for such a system. There are a lot of potential complications. For example, the addressing of pages and segments is totally independent, so it is possible to have a single segment split across multiple pages, and a single page split across multiple segments.

If 4 gigabytes of virtual memory is sufficient, it is probably better to forget about virtual segmentation and depend on the paging mechanism, since it is so much easier to manage fixed-length pages than variable length segments. Most Unix systems for the 386 which have appeared so far take this approach and ignore segmentation hardware.

However, the Intel literature states that the maximum virtual memory of the 386 is measured in terabytes. Clearly this cannot be achieved by paging alone. However, if you also use virtual segmentation, it is possible to achieve the effect of considerably large virtual memories. The maximum number of segments accessible at any one time is 16K (8K in each of the LDT and GDT). Each segment can reasonably be 100 megabytes long, giving a total virtual memory of 1.6 terabytes.

So if you need really enormous virtual memories, you will have to use virtual segmentation. Furthermore, you will also need to use paging, because even one of these 100-megabyte segments cannot be held in physical memory at one time.

Of course, the complexity of the operating system is enormously increased by having both mechanisms actively used. Is it really worthwhile to consider this possibility? After all 4 gigabytes sounds like a great deal of memory—"No one could *possibly* need more than 4 gigabytes." This statement, or other statements resembling it, have been constantly repeated over the years with increasing numbers. Von Neumann thought 4K bytes was enough for anyone. IBM thought that 640K on the PC was enough for anyone.

Can we imagine a scenario under which we would want more than 4 gigabytes of virtual memory? Here is one possibility. Suppose that at some time in the future it becomes cheaper to store files in huge electronic memories, instead of magnetic disks. This is not an unreasonable possibility since memory prices have generally dropped.

If the cost of electronic memories approaches that of magnetic disks, we may very well see systems with more than 4 gigabytes of *physical* memory. There are already many computer systems with more than 4 gigabytes of disk—even some personal computers have over a gigabyte. On such a system, the idea of virtual memories larger than 4 gigabytes no longer seems so outrageous. Still, it will be a while before we see 386-based systems in which this is a serious consideration.

Another motivation for very large virtual memories occurs in managing large growing tables. In a conventional memory, it is easy to manage two such tables—you can have one array grow up and the other grow down in memory, and when they bump into each other you know that they are out of memory.

That is a very simple way of handling two arrays. But how would you handle three arrays? That is a totally different problem. There is no simple, clever way of handling three arrays that are growing to arbitrary lengths. A good example of an array that grows to an arbitrary length is a stack for a task. How do you know how long it should be? You certainly do not know in advance. Now you can start moving data around, but that gets very time-consuming since you have to deal with the whole problem of managing memory.

The other technique, if the processor has a big enough virtual memory, is to allocate more than enough space for each of the task stacks. Even if they are growing, each of them will certainly be less than 16 megabytes, so we can just allocate 16 megabytes to each of these stacks. In this logical virtual address space, the operating system will take care of the fact that there is really not that much memory.

This is a very attractive way of managing memory. Arrays and stacks are such attractive data structures that having an unlimited amount of extensible arrays is a very nice programming environment.

If you start using this technique aggressively, 4 gigabytes does not sound like so much any more—it can get carved up in a hurry. Sixteen megabytes is certainly not nearly enough if you want to play these sorts of games. The original 360s had an address space of 2^{24} bytes, with the exception of the model 360/67, which was a time-sharing machine with a 2^{31}-byte address space. IBM understood that customers need this kind of flexibility. The 360/67 was one of the first machines to provide a double-level paging scheme, although it lacked segmentation. It was introduced around 1970, but it was not very successful, because the operating system, TSS, which stood for *time sharing system*, proved too difficult even for IBM to successfully write.

An Anecdote on Paging and Protection

The point has been made several times that an operating system must manage paging in a manner that is completely transparent to an application program. The following sad experience is a reminder that this is not always as easily accomplished as one might wish.

The DEC PDP-10 was a computer that depended very much upon paging. Its first operating system, TOPS-10, generally attempted to make sure that the paging was completely transparent, with one quite deliberate exception. Page-fault data was recorded so that an application could gather information about how many page faults had occurred, and how often pages have been paged to disk. If a machine is spending all of its time swapping pages between memory and the disk, you won't get anything done and you certainly need to know about it.

Any program can be executed in a tiny physical memory when demand paging is used, but it may execute excruciatingly slowly—in the worst case, every memory reference normally taking a fraction of a microsecond becomes a disk access taking many milliseconds. In a virtual memory system, you do not ask how big a program can be executed, but rather how fast a program will run if it has a certain amount of memory.

The performance of a machine will degrade dramatically at some point when the available physical memory becomes too small. The term used to describe this behavior is *thrashing*, because the machine is spending all of its time swapping pages. Thrashing is something that obviously needs to be avoided, and so it seems reasonable to provide some instrumentation that indicates the number of page faults that have occurred, and that is why the facility was provided.

The PDP-10 was protected with passwords. It was possible to connect to a virtual terminal inside a program and try to log on. A security defense in the system would allow a user to log into the system immediately if the password was correct, whereas if the password was wrong it would wait a few seconds and then tell you it was wrong. The system seemed impregnable, because it was calculated that it would take many years of guessing a password before someone would be able to get into the system.

Someone who understood the paging mechanism also understood how to break the PDP-10's security. It was done in the following way. Imagine that there is a password whose first character happens to be positioned in memory so that the first character lies at the end of one page and the remaining characters of the password lie at the beginning of the second page. It is then possible to arrange (by doing some sequence of memory references) for the first page to be swapped in and the second page to be swapped out. That can be done by allocating variables in physical memory when only a few can fit. If one then puts an A at the end of the first page where the password starts, and then asks the operating system if AARDVARK is the correct password, it is likely that the operating system will say no, since it is unlikely that AARDVARK is the password. But the intruder can then look to see whether a page fault has occurred (since the system has purposely allowed him to do this).

Since the operating system checks the password from left to right, one character at a time, a mismatch in the first character of the intruder's guess will mean that no page fault occurs (since it was not necessary to look any further). If on the other hand, the guess of A was correct, then the routine that checks passwords will have caused a page fault and incremented a counter recording that fact.

If a page fault has not occurred, then the password does not begin with the letter A. The intruder then needs only 25 additional attempts to find out the first letter. When the first letter has been discovered, it is possible to move the whole password one character to the left and try again. Instead of 26 to the power of the number of characters in the password, it takes only 26 *times* the number of characters in the password.

With this clever trick, it was possible to write a program that broke system passwords in a reasonable amount of time. This gives some indication of how hard it is to build a system that really has impregnable security. This particular case was one where a paging system that looked completely transparent was actually the vehicle by which someone could penetrate system security. Providing the counter that gave you the number of page faults seemed to be a very reasonable bit of instrumentation but as soon as this was provided, all system security was lost.

Even if the counter had not been present, it would still probably have been possible to play the same game by watching the clock (by seeing whether or not it took that extra time to do the page fault). The solution is to check the entire password for whether or not an early character matches, but to realize this the operating system programmer would have had to be acutely aware of the paging as the code was written, and of course the whole idea, even in most of the operating system code, is to completely ignore the paging.

Paging and Virtual 8086 Mode

Now that we understand how the paging mechanism works, we can revisit an interesting detail of the virtual 8086 mode of the 386. As we described earlier, programs running in this mode insist on running in the old 8088 compatible manner, and in particular insist on computing addresses as

Address = 16 * paragraph + offset $16 * 2^{16} = 1 M$
                                                                $= 2^{20}$

where *paragraph* is the name given to the 16-bit contents of a segment register used to represent an arbitrary 16-byte boundary anywhere within the 1-megabyte addressing range of the processor. The GDT and LDT are completely bypassed when the processor is operating in this mode.

This would seem to indicate that all addresses in this mode end up being in the range 00000000 to 00010000 (i.e., the first megabyte of memory on the 386 processor). If this were the case, then obviously we could have only a single task operating in virtual 8086 mode, which would be too bad since the whole idea is to allow multiple DOS applications to run at the same time.

The paging mechanism comes to the rescue. The address that is initially developed, which is indeed in the first megabyte of the address space, is a *linear* address, not an absolute address. By turning paging on, this 1-megabyte address space can be mapped in 4K chunks to anywhere in memory (it doesn't even have to be contiguous). We can now have multiple DOS sessions by giving each of them a separate set of page tables to map their DOS region into non-overlapping available areas, so the whole physical address space of the 386 is available.

Note that the 286 does *not* have the paging mechanism, and so it would not be easy to implement anything corresponding to virtual 8086 mode on the 286. Unfortunately, IBM insisted that OS/2 must run on the 286, so that is why there is a limitation in OS/2 of running only one old-style DOS application at a time. Not only that, but the one application that is running in a completely unprotected mode—if it crashes, the whole system stops.

An application program running on the 386 in virtual 8086 mode is still completely protected and cannot damage any other running application. When a version of OS/2 finally appears for the 386, it will presumably support multiple protected DOS sessions. Indeed this feature is already implemented in a number of Unix systems, including, for example, the Sun 386i, which is a 386-based Unix machine that uses Virtual 8086 mode to support multiple virtual DOS sessions.

EXCEPTIONS ON THE 386

An exception causes the currently executing task to be interrupted. Synchronous traps correspond to error conditions detected by instructions. Integer arithmetic overflows do *not* cause traps, with the exception of division by zero. A number of other trap conditions, such as page fault and segment fault traps have been previously mentioned.

An interrupt, on the other hand, is signalled because some external event has occurred. Someone may have hit a key on the keyboard, the clock may periodically interrupt, a communications character may have come in, or the disk has finished a seek. Many external events can cause an interrupt. In contrast to traps, interrupts are asynchronous, which means that they can occur after any instruction and are in general unrelated to that instruction.

The action taken by the processor is almost identical in the trap and interrupt case. However, as we will discuss in further detail later, the action taken by the exception routine is typically quite different, since a trap relates directly to the currently executing program, whereas an interrupt need not have anything to do with the current program. For instance, in a situation where several programs are executing as separate tasks, an interrupt delivering data eventually intended for one of these programs may interrupt some other program entirely.

Each exception has a number associated with it. There are 256 separately identifiable exceptions, numbered from 0 to 255. A table called the *interrupt descriptor table* (IDT) contains up to 256 entries, one for each possible exception.[5] Some of the IDT entry numbers are permanently assigned by the processor (see Table 4.1). Almost all the entries in this table correspond to synchronous traps, which relate to either intended or accidental conditions raised by individual instructions. For example, entry 4 in the IDT is accessed if an INTO instruction is issued with the overflow set. Typically we might see the following code generated by an Ada compiler for the 386:

```
A := B + C;
. . .
MOV     EAX, B
ADD     EAX, C
INTO
MOV     A, EAX
```

If the addition overflows, then the INTO instruction will generate a trap using entry 4 in the IDT. This is an example of a case where the program definitely needs to regain control, since the required Ada action is to raise an exception. On the other hand, interrupts such as the page fault trap would typically be handled entirely by the operating system, since an executing Ada program does not need to be aware of the need to swap in pages from disk.

The one asynchronous interrupt in the reserved list is the *non-maskable interrupt* (NMI), corresponding to entry 2 in the IDT. As we will see later, most interrupts can be masked or temporarily turned off. The NMI, as its name implies, *cannot* be turned off. It is typically used for catastrophic events like hardware breakdowns, power running low, or parity errors, which *must* be handled immediately.

---

[5] One might expect this to be called the exception descriptor table. But as we warned in Chapter 1, manufacturers are inconsistent with one another in their use of terminology. In the text we follow our consistent approach of referring to traps, and interrupts collectively as exceptions. The Intel convention uses the word interrupt as the collective term, hence IDT, and what we call traps are called exceptions by Intel. Intel reserves the word trap for a special subset of synchronous exceptions corresponding to user-level error conditions.

TABLE 4.1
Interrupt Assignments on the 80386.

Interrupt Number	Description
0	Divide error
1	Debug exceptions
2	Non-maskable interrupt (NMI)
3	Breakpoint
4	Overflow (INTO instruction)
5	Bounds check (BOUND instruction)
6	Invalid opcode
7	Coprocessor not available
8	Double fault
9	(reserved)
10	Invalid TSS
11	Segment not present
12	Stack exception
13	General protection
14	Page fault
15	(reserved)
16	Coprocessor error
17 - 31	(reserved)

A Sad Story

Here's another little excursion (a sad story). The 8088, the original chip used on the IBM PC, uses some low-level interrupt numbers; there are certain IDT entries reserved by the system. For instance, entry 0 is reserved for division by zero, entry 1 is reserved for single stepping and debugging, entry 2 is reserved for unmaskable interrupts such as a parity error, entry 3 is reserved for breakpoint, and entry 4 is reserved for overflow.

Entry 5, on the other hand, is marked in the Intel manual as reserved, but it doesn't say what it is reserved for (because it doesn't do anything on the 8088). But Intel, very clearly, in all of the literature they have ever produced (which was available to everyone including IBM from the beginning of time!) says, "Reserved for use by Intel." Well, on the IBM PC, this entry is used for the (software) function print screen.

When Intel designed the 80188, it turned out to be a repackaging of the 8088 with a few extra instructions—nothing very important. The more important thing is that it drew more logic onto the chip. On the 8088 you have a separate timer chip, a separate interrupt controller chip, and a few other support chips. On the 80188, all of these are pulled onto a single chip.

That might not seem terribly significant because it is just a couple of chips, but if you're building very cheap machines the chip count is very important. Even though this timer chip seems boring compared to the 8088, it costs about the same when you are buying things in very big quantities. So the 80188 was very attractive in keeping the costs down. The IBM PC/jr was originally intended to use the 80188, but lo and behold, when the 80188 finally appeared, interrupt 5 was used for the (newly added) bounds-checking instruction, and other previously unused interrupts were now used for some of the other new functions. These were major incompatibilities with the choices that IBM had made, since IBM had used up some of those "reserved" interrupts.

It's an interesting situation. When you see "reserved" in a reference manual it really means that you should pay attention to it—it's very wrong to stomp on it. Intel made production quantities of 80188s—IBM said, "We don't want *any* of them! They're useless to us." Consequently, the 80188 has never been used in any of the mainline PC-style machines, and this entire intended market was lost. Saving a little money on the greater chip integration is attractive, but not at the expense of incompatibility in a market where compatibility is so important—if a PC can't run Microsoft Flight Simulator, then forget it!

Whose fault was it? It's hard to say. IBM was certainly at fault for not recognizing Intel's declaration of these interrupts as reserved, but at the same time, Intel knew what IBM was doing and chose to ignore it. On the other hand, Intel should have known, and should have made things compatible. When we discuss the 286 and the 386 we will see similar things. Intel sometimes paid too little attention to how the chips were being used in the real world and stuck to their "right" to use up reserved interrupts.[6]

Another instance where this sort of thing comes up is in the observance of software standards. "Correctly" written software may be compatible with new versions of hardware or operating system software, but the end user of the software will be just as irritated if incorrectly written software runs into incompatibilities.

How an Exception Is Handled

The action taken by the processor when an interrupt or trap is signalled depends on the descriptor in the corresponding entry of the IDT. Depending on the descriptor type, one of the following three general actions can occur:

- A trap can be taken at the current privilege level. This trap is handled by the currently executing program, and it is almost exactly like a procedure call except that the flags are stored on the stack as well as the current instruction location.

---

[6] A little rhyme, supposedly carved into a Scottish tombstone, has something to say about this:

Here lies the body of Angus McCay.
He died defending his right of way.
He was right, dead right, as he sped along.
But he's just as dead as if he'd been dead wrong.

Sometimes you have to consider the practical consequences of creating incompatibilities, even if these incompatibilities are strictly the user's fault.

- The IDT entry can contain a call gate, calling a system routine that can be at a different protection level and use a separate stack. This is an appropriate approach for an asynchronous interrupt handled by the system where the overhead must be kept to a minimum.

- The IDT entry can contain a task gate, causing a complete context switch to a separate task to handle the interrupt. This is conceptually the cleanest way of handling asynchronous interrupts, but it involves a substantial overhead and is not always suitable for interrupts that occur frequently.

The IDT is referenced by a special register, IDTR, which can be modified only in kernel mode. This means that an application program cannot directly affect the contents of the IDT, which is under the control of the operating system. Typically an application program makes requests to the operating system to set up the IDT in a particular manner. The operating system may or may not accede to the request. Hopefully it would allow a program to set up a simple trap gate for handling overflows, but it would probably object to a program wishing to handle page faults.

Asynchronous Interrupts

Entries 32 to 255 in the IDT are available for external interrupts. There is a convention for presenting an interrupt on the external pins of the 386 (in particular, the INTR pin is used to signal that an interrupt is present). The 386 processor checks the INTR signal after every instruction, and if it is set, an interrupt is immediately signalled.

Since there is only one INTR pin, there is no mechanism on the 386 itself for establishing multiple levels of interrupt priorities. It is usually important to introduce different priorities among the interrupts (for example, a high-priority communication line should probably have precedence over the keyboard), and a 386 system designer will achieve this effect by using separate interrupt controller chips in the system. Intel makes a chip, the 8259 which is exactly intended for this purpose. Interrupts are then signalled through the 8259 (see Figure 4.5, top half).

Up to eight devices can be attached to a single 8259. Furthermore, it is possible to attach 8259s in sequence so that even more devices can be handled. Typical 386 PC machines use two 8259s (see Figure 4.5, bottom half).

A full blown system can use 9 separate 8259 chips for a total of 72 separate interrupt levels. The 8259 accepts commands from the processor (IN and OUT instructions) that control various parameters, including the priority scheme, the mapping of the interrupts to 386 interrupt numbers, and whether individual devices are allowed to interrupt. The 8259 is a rather elaborate chip, with all sorts of specialized options, most of which are seldom used. Since the interrupt controller was on a separate chip, there is lots of chip area for doing interesting things, and clearly the designer decided it might as well be used for something useful.

The question of which devices are attached to which interrupt lines is entirely up to the system designer. In 386 PCs, the individual boards decide which device they are. This is why one occassionally runs into conflicts when PC add-on boards are installed

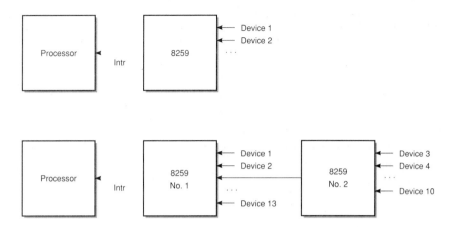

FIGURE 4.5
Possible configurations of an Intel 8259 interrupt controller.

in a PC. If two boards want to use the same interrupt number, then they interfere with one another. Since there is no central authority in charge of resolving these conflicts, there is no easy way to avoid them.

Writing Exception Handlers

When an interrupt or trap routine receives control, the flags and current instruction location (CS and EIP) are pushed on the stack. However, the other registers are unchanged. In the case of a hardware interrupt handler, the operating system trap routine must make sure that none of these registers is disturbed.

One way this can be done is to use task gates to handle interrupts. Since the task transition saves all registers, the interrupted task's status is automatically preserved. However, as we mentioned before, this introduces quite a bit of extra overhead (two task switches per interrupt at over 300 clocks apiece), so often the system will choose to use a call gate interface instead. In this case the called interrupt routine must first save any registers it uses and then service the interrupt. To return from the interrupt handler, the registers are restored, and a special form of return instruction, IRET, is used to restore the context at the point of the interrupt.

With synchronous traps, routines where the task causing the trap need to get back control, there are two options. One possibility is to put a trap descriptor in the IDT so that the running task gets control directly. However, in a system with several programs running at the same time, this would mean changing the IDT on every task switch or using a separate IDT for each task. This is often inconvenient, so many systems use call gate interfaces even for these synchronous traps, and then a single common operating system handler works out which task caused the trap and arranges for it to get control.

Fault Traps

Interrupt number 8 is reserved for *double fault*, which means that two error conditions have occurred at the same time and the processor is confused about what it should do. An example arises if the handler for a page fault attempts to switch to a stack that is currently paged out. If the processor did not detect this situation, it would get stuck in an unbreakable loop signalling page faults. So instead it signals a *double fault*, and hopefully the double fault handler will be able to recover the situation, perhaps by restarting sections of the operating system.

The situation can get even more desperate if the double fault cannot be signalled successfully, for example, if the descriptor for interrupt 8 is not present, or if it tries to swap in a non-existent stack. In this case, the processor signals a *triple fault* and closes shop. When a triple fault occurs, the processor stops executing instructions and signals an error on one of the processor pins. What happens next is up to the system designer.

In the case of the IBM AT, the triple fault error is recognized by circuitry outside the chip which causes the processor to be reset. This sequence of events is deliberately used by OS/2 when it wants to return to real mode to execute a DOS program in the compatibility box. When the 286 was designed, Intel never imagined that anyone would need to run a program in real mode, so although the processor resets initially in real mode, the assumption is that it will rapidly execute the instructions to switch into protected mode, and there is no way at all to return to real mode. Well, not quite no way at all. OS/2 first sets a flag in the memory of the clock chip indicating what is going on. It then deliberately executes a series of instructions that cause a triple fault, resulting in a reset into real mode. The reset circuit notices the special flag in the clock memory and understands that this is not a reset but rather a request for transition into real mode.

Debugging Support

The 386 has three interesting features which provide hardware support for debugging programs. First there is a 1-byte breakpoint associated with a special interrupt (interrupt 3). The idea is to replace one of the instructions in the program with a breakpoint instruction, so that a breakpoint trap will occur when this instruction is reached. This possibility exists in some form or other on nearly every processor. A special instruction is needed on the 386 because the normal trap instruction is 2 bytes long. A breakpoint has to be written over another instruction, and since there are 1 byte instructions in the instruction set, it is important to have a 1-byte breakpoint instruction.

The second feature uses another special trap (which uses entry number 1 in the IDT). There is a flag called TF (the trace flag) that can be set by the operating system to enable instruction tracing. TF can be set only in kernel mode, so an application program must request that the operating system enable instruction tracing. When TF is set, *every* instruction causes a trap. This allows a debugger to follow the execution of a program instruction by instruction. The occurrence of the trap turns off TF, which is, of course, necessary, for otherwise the processor would get stuck in a loop with the trace routine trying to trace itself.

Finally, the 386 introduces for the first time in the Intel architectures a set of special registers called the *debug registers*. These can also be set only in kernel mode, and they allow much more extensive control over debugging. The TF instruction tracing facility is very flexible, but it is not very efficient for some purposes. Suppose, for example, that the debugger has a "watch" facility that allows a programmer to watch the value of a variable, stopping if it is set to some particular value. Well, this can be done by using TF and checking the value of the variable after every instruction. The obvious drawback is that it is very slow.

The debug registers provide a much more efficient method of performing this watch function. There are four registers, which can be set to monitor four separate events, where the event consists of one of the following:

• A specified instruction is executed

• A specified memory location is modified

• A specified memory location is accessed or modified

To watch a variable, we set up one of the four debug registers with the appropriate address specifying the second option. Then the program can be run at full speed, trapping only when the specified variable is modified. At these points only, the trap routine can check for the desired value. This allows the monitoring of a variable with little or no overhead compared to the instruction trace facility.

It might seem that the first debug register option, to stop when a specified instruction is executed, is redundant, since the same feature is available using the breakpoint instruction. However, there is one important situation where the breakpoint instruction cannot be used. Suppose that the program being debugged has already been burned into ROM. Read only memory is what it says, and you can't go changing instructions in it to breakpoints. However, the debug register facility *does* allow you to stop on a specific instruction.[7]

On processors lacking this kind of hardware support, you can get somewhat the same effect by attaching an external piece of hardware to the system bus, watching the addresses placed on the bus by the processor. However, this is quite a complicated piece of hardware, and it still can't do quite as good a job, because the processor is not always perfectly synchronized with the bus activity—for example, the 386 steams on after issuing a store. By the time the debugging gizmo sees the address on the bus, the processor has already started to execute additional instructions. The signal for the trap may as a result be a little bit too late and the trap may occur one or two instructions later than the store instruction.

This is still useful, but it's much nicer to have the debugging feature built right into the processor. You might be concerned that the presence of the debug register mechanism slows down execution, but this is not the case in practice. As we have noted

---

[7] One might hope that by the time a program is burned into ROM it is already debugged, but that is not always the way things work. When the original version of the IBM PC was released, the ROM containing the BASIC interpreter had a bug that caused multiplications to give the wrong answer!

before, it is quite easy in hardware to do several things at the same time, and the comparison of the current instruction or data address with the values in the debug registers can be overlapped with other operations so that it is essentially free.

CONCLUSION

The tasking support on the 386 represents CISC tendencies at their most aggressive. Once again, it is hard to assess whether or not including such features at the hardware level has sufficient benefits in simplifying system design to be worthwhile. On a pure efficiency basis, the tasking facilities do not seem to stand up to scrutiny. One Intel document on compiler requirements had noted that hardware tasking was to be used, even though it was understood that ignoring it would be more efficient. On the other hand, the structure is very neat, particularly when it comes to handling interrupts.

The paging support is complex but relatively standard. This is one place where the CISC and RISC chips look rather alike, since the same problem has to be solved in either case, and there are no magical or simple solutions. As we will see later, there are some RISC chips which use a similar approach but, in typical RISC style, leave more up to the software. On the other hand, the support for virtual segmentation is unique to the 386. Once again, assessing its value is difficult. If everyone wrote operating systems that used full 6-byte pointers everywhere, and used virtual segmentation to achieve a very large address space, then there might be some real merit in this design. As it is, with existing operating systems, the entire segmentation feature does little more than provide compatibility with 286-based software.

One of the strengths of CISC architectures in the marketplace is precisely that they have gathered huge applications libraries, so it is not surprising to see the 386 making a big effort to be compatible with previous architectures in the series. In particular, the virtual 8086 mode is important for compatibility with old style PC applications. RISC architectures are cleaner not only because of their approach, but because they do *not* have the burden of being compatible with big libraries of existing machine language programming.

Finally, the exception handling on the 386 once again reflects the complex operating systems-oriented hardware features. The flexibility of being able to handle exceptions with a wide range of possible context switching options is obviously desirable from a systems point of view, but it does involve a considerable level of complexity.

MICROPROCESSORS AND FLOATING-POINT ARITHMETIC

Floating-point computations play an important role in the world of high-end micro-processors. Many engineering work stations are used in environments where extensive numerical calculations are performed, either programmed directly by the users, or in the form of pre-packaged applications, particularly CAD/CAM programs used for design. All the microprocessors that we examine in this book have hardware floating-point capability, and especially in the case of the RISC chips, providing efficient floating-point is an important design priority.

Relatively few systems programmers use floating-point arithmetic to any significant extent. They may occasionally divide two floating-point numbers to compute the running time of a program, but they neither know about, nor need to know about, numerical algorithms which make extensive use of floating-point. However, not needing to know about numerical algorithms is not the same thing as not needing to know about floating-point. In practice both floating-point hardware and software systems are designed by engineers and systems programmers with very little experience in numerical algorithms. In the past, floating-point systems have been designed without even consulting experts in the field, let alone having them participate in the design. It is impossible to teach in this single chapter everything there is to know about floating-point, but it should be possible to make you aware that the issues are complex and that expert advice is required to build effective floating-point systems.

One important source of expert advice is contained in the IEEE floating-point standard. This standard, which is more formally known as IEEE/ANSI Standard 754/1985, is the work of a large committee that has attempted to define how floating-point arithmetic should be implemented on all systems that intend to comply with it. The IEEE standard is of particular importance in the microprocessor world, since virtually all microprocessor implementations of floating-point at least claim compatibility with this standard. At the end of the chapter we will show how part of the IEEE standard has been implemented on the Intel 387 and the Weitek chip set, both of which provide floating-point capabilities for the Intel 386.

FLOATING-POINT IMPLEMENTATIONS

The basic idea behind floating-point implementations is a common one and has been implemented on nearly all machines for the last thirty years. The idea is to store numbers in two parts: an *exponent*, which is usually (but not always) a power of 2, and a *fraction*, also called a *mantissa* or *significand*, which is the fractional part of the result. The basic format of a Xoating-point number is thus something like

This rather unspecific picture is about as far as we can get in discussing floating-point representation and operations without referring to a particular implementation. All sorts of variations have appeared within this basic framework:

- The exponent can vary in length, with longer exponents providing greater ranges of numbers.
- The fraction can vary in length, with longer fractions providing greater precision.
- The base can be 16 instead of 2. This is the standard, and somewhat undesirable, approach of the IBM mainframes. Other bases, including 8 and 10, are in use in some systems.
- Signed numbers can be stored in either sign and magnitude form or by using a complement notation.
- The position of the implied binary point in the mantissa varies. It can be all the way to the left, so that the mantissa is a fraction, or all the way to the right, so that the mantissa is an integer.

All these decisions have subtle effects on writing floating-point software. For example, the decision to use base 16 rather than base 2 means that the number of significant bits varies with the magnitude of the number which complicates some intricate approaches to error analysis.

Floating-Point Operations: A Programmer's Nightmare

Not only do floating-point formats vary from one machine to another, but the results of floating-point operations also vary in all sorts of almost incredible ways. Historically, a lot of FORTRAN floating-point code has been written using what one might call "hope for the best" semantics. Using this model, all the programmer expects when computing A + B is that the result will be approximately equal to the real sum. No attempt is made to characterize how accurate the result is, and the programmer just hopes, often without any justification, that errors will cancel or be small enough that the final results are meaningful.

A professional numerical analyst can carry out a careful analysis of a proposed numerical algorithm to determine the maximum possible errors, but this is feasible only if the operations are reasonably well behaved and well defined. Unfortunately, hardware designers have all too often believed that "hope for the best" semantics is good enough and that it is perfectly fine to sacrifice accuracy and sensible behavior in order to squeeze as much performance as possible out of the hardware. The hardware landscape is littered with extraordinary examples of hardware designs in which this principle has been carried to absurd extremes:

- One might expect that division by 2.0 should be accurate, since in binary this is a particularly easy operation—it just corresponds to decrementing the exponent. Such expectations are thwarted on the CRAY supercomputer, which has a rather inaccurate division instruction that does not guarantee this result.[1]

- There is a Honeywell mainframe where the floating-point accumulator helpfully provides extra bits of precision for intermediate calculations. As we will see later on in this chapter, such extra precision is often useful. Unhelpfully, there is no way to save these extra bits in memory, so they are apt to disappear without warning and essentially at random if a context switch happens to occur.

- On the 1750A, a standard military architecture manufactured by a number of different companies, there is a floating-point number that can be added to itself with the result being correct and in range. However, an attempt to multiply this same number by 2.0 causes an overflow trap, even though the result is in the correct range. This behavior is not only allowed but is required by the 1750A standard.

- In a further helpful vein, the 1750A uses two's complement instead of sign and magnitude for representing negative numbers. The "extra" negative number shows up in floating-point operations by creating situations in which certain negative numbers can be effectively represented with more precision. The result is that such algebraic identities as (A − B) = − (B − A) do not always hold on the 1750A.

---

[1] One of the microprocessors we will look at, the Intel i860, has exactly the same peculiar division behavior, and we discuss this at some length in Chapter 11.

- In another "inspired" floating-point design, very small numbers could appear to be non-zero in comparisons and still appear to be zero in other operations, causing an error in divisions. In this case a statement such as

    if X <> 0.0 then R := G / X;

    can generate a division-by-zero error. To make the test work on this machine, X must be replaced by $1.0 * X$.
- Unfortunately, another devious designer has managed to create a machine on which multiplication by 1.0 can cause an overflow error, so the "fix" to the previous problem doesn't work on all machines.

What on earth is a programmer to do when confronted by this kind of chaos? Using "hope for the best" semantics seems to be an unfortunate approach, but in the face of such inconsistent designs, there often isn't much choice. Needless to say, numerical analysts find this situation extremely frustrating. It is extraordinarily difficult to write stable and accurate floating-point algorithms on all possible floating-point hardware.

The Ada Approach

Most high-level language definitions evade the issue of floating-point accuracy. Standards for typical languages such as FORTRAN and ALGOL simply contain statements requiring that the result of floating-point operations be approximations to the mathematical results, a requirement that is not much of a requirement! COBOL is even less specific—the result of evaluating an expression involving real values is said to be "implementation-dependent" and compiler writers are free to do whatever they wish.

More recently, the Ada language definition has made an attempt to be more specific. Since Ada is intended to run on all machines, it is not practical or desirable to specify floating-point accuracy and operations exactly, but the Ada definition does attempt to pin things down a little more precisely than FORTRAN.

Ada makes this attempt by defining the notion of *model numbers*, numbers that are represented exactly. Of course, all floating-point environments conform to this expectation, but Ada makes the requirement very specific and, assuming that floating-point numbers are represented in binary, also specifies the minimum acceptable set of floating-point model numbers. Given these model numbers, Ada places two requirements on floating-point computations:

- If the input values to a floating-point operation are model numbers and the result is a model number, then *exactly* this model number must be yielded as the result, not some approximation of it.
- If the result of an operation is not a model number, the result must be somewhere in the interval created by the two consecutive model numbers that bracket the true result, including both end points, and *may not* be outside this range.

These requirements, based on the *Brown model* of floating-point arithmetic, seem reasonable enough, but the Ada attempt can only be described as a limited success. On the one hand, these rules are already too restrictive for some of the badly designed architectures in common use (the CRAY, for example, does not obey the model number result rule for division by 2.0). On the other hand, the rules are not strict enough to allow numerical analysts to carry out meaningful error analysis. This last point is still being debated, but even so, it is certainly fair to say that there are eminent numerical analysts whose opinion is that Ada was trying to solve an impossible problem and that it could not, and did not, succeed.

THE IEEE FLOATING-POINT STANDARD

In an attempt to bring some order to the chaotic situation we have just described, a committee of the IEEE[2] was formed to attempt to define a standard floating-point implementation that would at the same time be practical to implement and well behaved from the point of view of both the casual user and the professional numerical analyst. Following an extended period of what at times became contentious argument, the committee finally agreed on a specification, published in 1985 as "IEEE-754 Standard for Binary Floating-Point Arithmetic."

This standard, popularly referred to simply as the IEEE floating-point standard, is of particular significance in the study of microprocessors, since virtually *all* microprocessors support this standard. The chaotic situation found on mainframe computers has been essentially eliminated in the world of microprocessors, and floating-point applications can be more easily moved from one microprocessor to another. In this section, we will examine the principal aspects of the IEEE standard, so that when we look at specific implementations of floating-point units, we will be able to understand the standard's requirements and why particular choices have been made in each case.

Basic Formats

The IEEE standard defines two basic formats in detail; each of these formats is defined down to the actual bit pattern used to represent floating-point numbers. The short format is called single format and is 32 bits long, while the long format is called the double format and is 64 bits long. These formats correspond to the usual single- and double-precision formats found in languages like FORTRAN and C. Although the IEEE standard requires the implementation of only the single format, in practice all microprocessor implementations include both—an implementation providing only 32-bit accuracy would be of limited use. These formats are shown in Figure 5.1.

In the single format, the minimum exponent value is 00000001, corresponding to 2^{-126}, and the maximum exponent value is 11111110, corresponding to 2^{+127}. This quite deliberately leaves two exponent values (00000000 and 11111111) unused—they have special uses we will describe later. The fraction is actually 24 bits long. The common trick of not actually storing the first bit of the fraction (since it is always 1 for

---

[2] IEEE stands for The Institute of Electrical and Electronics Engineers, a professional society involved with various aspects of electrical engineering, including the construction and design of computer hardware.

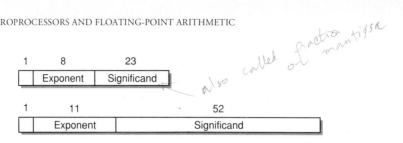

FIGURE 5.1
The single- and double-precision IEEE formats.

a normalized number) is used in IEEE basic formats. As an example of the use of this format, consider the number

$$1 \quad 10000001 \quad 10000000000000000000000$$

In this number, the sign is negative, the exponent is 129, which represents $2^{129-127}$, and the fraction is 1.10000000000000000000000 (the binary point of the fraction is considered to come after the implied initial bit). Thus the value of this floating-point number is $1.10 * 2^{+2}$, or −6.0 in decimal.

The double format is 64 bits long with the layout shown at the bottom of Figure 5.1. The exponent now has a range of −1022 to +1023, and the fraction is 53 bits (as in the single case, the initial bit of the fraction is implied). Otherwise the format is essentially identical to the single-precision format.

There is nothing particularly remarkable about these basic formats. As is the case with many standards, the important point is precisely that they *are* standardized, so that algorithms that depend on the particular precision supported can be written without worrying about differences between floating-point implementations.

Rounding Modes

Not only does the IEEE standard specify the detailed binary formats of the single and double formats, it also specifies the exact results obtained as a result of arithmetic operations. Of course, no floating-point arithmetic system can possibly give the mathematically correct results in all cases, since often the result cannot be represented exactly. However, the results obtained when using IEEE floating-point arithmetic are precisely defined, allowing accurate error analysis for numerical algorithms.

There are four *rounding modes* defined in the standard. If the result of an operation is exactly representable, then the standard requires that the result be this exactly representable result—a requirement similar to that of the Ada language. The issue of rounding arises if the result is *not* representable. In such a case, the result depends on the rounding mode currently in effect:

- Round to nearest. The result is rounded to the nearest representable number.
- Truncate. The result is rounded toward zero; in other words, the extra fractional bits that cannot be represented are simply thrown away.

- Round up. The result is always rounded up toward plus infinity.
- Round down. The result is always rounded down toward negative infinity.

Every implementation of the IEEE standard is required to support all four rounding modes. *Round to nearest* is generally the most desirable mode for most computation and is therefore typically the default mode.

UNBIASED ROUNDING. The rounding rules in IEEE standard are very strenuous. Round to nearest must be done absolutely accurately, as though the result were computed with precise mathematical accuracy, and then rounded according to this representation. As an example, suppose we have a result significand in short representation with the value:

In this case, the extra bits amount to less than 0.5 (decimal) in the last representable bit position, which means that the result must not be rounded up and the extra bits should simply be discarded. This is the proper treatment whenever the first extra bit is a zero. Consider a second example:

001 0000 0000 0000 0000 0000 10010 . . . .

first 23 bits   extra bits

In this case, the extra bits amount to more than 0.5 (decimal) in the last representable bit position, so it is appropriate to round up by adding one to the significand value, giving a rounded significand result of

001 0000 0000 0000 0000 0001

This is obviously the appropriate rounding action whenever the first non-represented bit is a 1 bit and there is at least one remaining 1 bit. The special case arises when the fraction is exactly halfway between:

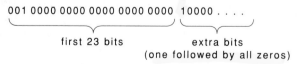

(one followed by all zeros)

Your first casual reaction might be that it doesn't matter how the result is rounded in this case. A rule which is commonly taught in high school is to round up whenever the first digit is 5 or greater. In the binary case this would correspond to rounding up if the first non-represented bit is a 1—certainly an easy rule to both state and implement.

However, choosing to always round in one direction for the halfway case introduces a small but significant bias into a sequence of computations. Somewhat surprisingly, there are algorithms that are unstable if the rounding is done in a biased manner but work fine if the rounding is unbiased. Consequently, we want to look for a way to round the halfway case in a manner that is statistically unbiased.

How might we unbias it? We could toss a coin to see whether or not to round up. From the point of view of achieving statistically unbiased results, this would be the best possible approach, but there are two arguments against tossing coins in the computer. First, it is not so easy to build devices that toss coins fairly and truly randomly, although it certainly is possible. [3] However, it seems a little unreasonable to go to all that effort just for this special rounding case, although of course if one *did* add such a device, it could also be made available in the form of an instruction that generated true random numbers. Such an instruction would be quite welcome for certain applications such as computer games and certain kinds of numerical simulation, where truly random numbers are important.

Even if such a truly random device could be built, there would still be a strong argument against using it. When a calculation is repeated, you want to get exactly the same result each time. This is particularly important during debugging to ensure that a computation path can be exactly repeated. This requirement could be met by using a pseudo-random number generator, but you don't want to be computing random numbers every time you add two floating-point numbers.

A scheme that is *nearly* correct, and on average unbiased, is called *round to nearest even*. This approach is the one required by the IEEE standard. If the result of a computation is exactly in between two representable numbers, the result is forced to be even (end with a 0 bit). In other words, the value is rounded up if the last bit is currently 1 and is left alone if the last bit is currently 0.

Another advantage of the round to even rule is that you get integer results more often, since small integer values have even fractions. This is often more pleasing to users, who prefer to see an output of 2.0000000 rather than 1.9999999, even though from a mathematical point of view, these answers have equivalent accuracy.

We should note that real hardware chips certainly do *not* compute the result of an operation to infinite precision and then apply the correct rounding function. This is simply a formal definition of the required effect. There are implementation techniques that allow this definition to be met without needing to add a lot of additional bits (a typical approach requires 3 additional bits to deal with all rounding situations).

THE OTHER ROUNDING MODES. To the casual observer, it would seem that round to nearest would be the most desirable mode—indeed, the great majority of calculations are performed in this mode. Surprisingly, most traditional floating-point

[3] One famous random number generator is Ernie, a computer that picks the winners in the premium bonds scheme in Britain. It is interesting that none of the lotteries in the United States have computerized random number generators—people wouldn't put up for it—they want to see little balls come out of a machine despite the fact that it is well known by scientists that mechanical methods of this kind are often biased.

hardware has *not* rounded properly—instead, the typical approach has been to always truncate toward zero. Truncation usually introduces very undesirable behavior, and proper rounding is one of the most important properties of IEEE arithmetic, from the point of view of both the casual user and the knowledgeable numerical analyst. There are some specialized algorithms for which truncation is more appropriate. One use of truncation is to perform a calculation twice, once in round to nearest mode and once in truncation mode. If the final results are similar, then one has greater confidence that the calculation is not excessively dependent on precision effects.

INTERVAL ARITHMETIC. The round up and round down modes can be used to implement a form of arithmetic known as *interval arithmetic.* If we compute

   A := B * C;

and we do the calculation twice, once in round up mode and once in round down mode, then the two values we get for A will bracket the true result. Now suppose that we continue the calculation,

   C := A * D;

again using round up and round down mode, with the two calculated values of A. The range of the two values of C obtained will be a little larger, and again these two values will bracket the true value.

   The idea behind interval arithmetic is that every value in the calculation is represented as a range of values with the true value somewhere within the range. By simply performing the entire calculation twice, once in each rounding mode, we will be able to look at the range of the final results and, *without* doing any elaborate analysis, we will know the possible range of the result. If this range turns out to be narrow enough, then no further analysis is needed—we have a sufficiently accurate result.

   In practice, things are not quite as simple as this. A number of special situations arise. One problem occurs when a result is close to zero and is represented by the range $x .. y$, where x is a small negative number and y is a small positive number. If we subsequently perform a division where this small number is denominator, the result could be infinite, but the interval arithmetic procedures will not reflect this possibility.

   Another problem arises with intermediate results that are intended to represent approximations in the source of a specific calculation, and are points in an interval, rather than the interval itself. For instance, in computing the square root of A, a Newton-Raphson iteration approach uses the formula:

$$G_{new} = \frac{1}{2} \left(G_{old} + \frac{A}{G_{old}} \right)$$

where G_{old} is an initial estimate of the square root and G_{new} is a new, better, estimate. If this formula is iterated using a naive interval arithmetic approach, it appears that G_{new} is getting less and less accurate, when in fact it is converging to a more and more accurate result. The trouble is that G_{new} is not an approximation of the new estimate; it is *exactly* the new estimate, and the range should be collapsed each time through the iteration.

Such details mean that in practice interval arithmetic is not the panacea for the inexperienced user that it might seem to be. Nevertheless, in the hands of an experienced numerical analyst, it is a useful tool. It is worth noting that, particularly in the case of interval analysis, it is desirable to be able to execute exactly the same code twice using different rounding modes, which implies that the most desirable implementation of the various rounding modes is to have a dynamically switchable mode.

Extended Precision Formats

In addition to the exactly specified formats for *single* and *double* reals, P754 defines optional *extended* formats. The *single extended* and *double extended* real formats have greater range and precision than the corresponding non-extended formats. The standard defines minimum requirements, as shown in Table 5.1. The standard has no more to say about the exact formats although it strongly recommends, but does not require, that the extended format corresponding to the widest implemented basic type be supported. As we have noted, all implementations covered in this book support both single and double formats, so the issue is whether or not double extended is supported.

IMPLEMENTING EXTENDED PRECISION. Some floating-point implementations *do* support double extended format, and others do not. Although the standard does not specify the exact format of double extended, all the implementations that we will describe use the format shown for double extended in Figure 5.2. For double extended, where the significand is stored completely, the trick used in the basic formats of omitting the first bit of the significand is not used .

In building floating-point hardware, it is often convenient to use 64-bit registers in any case for the significand values, and to do 64-bit arithmetic operations on these values. If this is the case, then it is almost free to provide the extended precision capability. As we will see, there are floating-point chips that perform essentially all arithmetic in this double extended format—the only point at which the basic formats come into play is in loading and storing values.

THE USE OF EXTENDED PRECISION. Since it is desirable from one point of view it is desirable to have as much precision as possible, so one can take the view that double extended is merely a third, more accurate, format to be used when maximum

TABLE 5.1
Required characteristics of the extended formats.

	Single Extended	Double Extended
Mantissa bits	≥ 32	≥ 64
Maximum exponent	$\geq +1023$	$\geq +16383$
Minimum exponent	≤ -1022	≤ -16382
Exponent width	≥ 11	≥ 15
Total width in bits	≥ 43	≥ 79

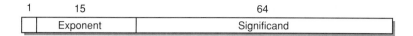

FIGURE 5.2
The double extended IEEE format.

precision is required. However, this is *not* the intention of the double extended format. Instead, the idea is that when dealing with 64-bit values (i.e., basic double format values), it is often helpful to be able to store some intermediate results in a higher precision so that the eventual 64-bit result will be accurate to a full 64 bits.

There are many examples where the use of double extended for intermediate results makes it much easier to maintain accuracy of double format calculations. As an example, suppose we want to calculate x^y, where both x and y are floating-point values. If we have a log and exponential function, we can use the identity[4]

$$x^y = 2^{\, y \log_2 x} \tag{5.1}$$

This identity is quite familiar to Pascal programmers, since Pascal has no real exponentiation but does have log and exponential functions.

However, the trouble with Eq. 5.1 is that it can be quite inaccurate, depending on the precision used to hold the intermediate values. Let's analyze the expected precision. The problem with Eq. 5.1 is that we can't really compute $\log_2 x$, instead, we compute an approximation:

$$LOG_2\, X = (log_2\ x)\ (1+\varepsilon) \tag{5.2}$$

where ε is an error term. Let's suppose that our intermediate results are computed with a precision of p binary bits. Then the error term is bounded by

$$|\varepsilon| < 2^{\,-p} \tag{5.3}$$

Here we are assuming that the intermediate values are computed accurately. Now looking back at equation (1), what we really compute is:

$$X^Y = 2^{\, y \cdot LOG_2\, X} \tag{5.4}$$

where X^Y is an approximation to x^y. How good an approximation? We can rewrite Eq. 5.4 as

$$X^Y = (x^y)\, (x^y)^{\,\varepsilon} \tag{5.5}$$

If the result needs to be accurate to s binary bits, the error term must be bounded by

$$\left| (x^y)^{\varepsilon} - 1 \right| < 2^{-s} \tag{5.6}$$

---

[4] In this discussion, logs and exponentials to any base can be used. We use base 2 because in practice these are the easiest functions to provide for floating-point numbers stored in binary.

Using the approximation $a^{\varepsilon} \sim 1 + \varepsilon \cdot \log_e a$ for small values of ε, we can rewrite Eq. 5.6 as

$$\left| \varepsilon \cdot \log_e (x^y) \right| < 2^{-s} \tag{5.7}$$

and then as

$$\left| \log_e (x^y) \right| \, | \, \varepsilon \, | < 2^{-s} \tag{5.8}$$

Plugging in the bound on ε from equation 5.3, we finally arrive at:

$$\left| \log_e (x^y) \right| < 2^{p-s} \tag{5.9}$$

Recall now that p is the precision used to carry out the calculations and s is the required final precision. In a simpleminded exponentiation programmed in Pascal using the log and exponentiation functions, p and s will be the same. Using Eq. 5.9 this means that the result will be accurate only if x^y falls into the range satisfying

$$\left| \log_e (x^y) \right| < 1 \tag{5.10}$$

This is a rather limited range, from $1/e$ to e, or approximately 0.37 to 2.7. Outside this range the result will not be accurate to the last bit *even if* the log and exponential functions are always accurate to the last bit. For large values of x^y, the result can be very far off. To get accurate results, we must have p greater than s, and the greater the difference—that is, the greater the number of extra bits used for intermediate calculations—the larger the range that we can cover. Table 5.2 shows some particular values.

The maximum and minimum exponents for IEEE double format are approximately 10^{-320} to 10^{+320}, so 10 extra bits of precision would ensure accurate results throughout the range. In practice, the extended format provides at least 11 extra bits of precision, which is more than enough (the extra bit means that the log and exponentiation do not have to be quite last-bit accurate).

This rather lengthy analysis is a good example of the kind of error analysis that can be performed if the intermediate operations have known accuracy—if you have reasonably accurate log and exponential functions for double extended format, then it *is* sufficiently accurate to compute exponentiation using the naive approach. By contrast, if extended format is not available, writing an accurate exponentiation function is an extremely tricky job—not one to be tackled by an amateur!

TABLE 5.2
Accurate result ranges for expoentiation.

Precision	Low Bound	High Bound
p = s	0.37	2.7
p = s + 8	10^{-111}	10^{+111}
p = s + 9	10^{-222}	10^{+222}
p = s + 10	10^{-444}	10^{+444}
p = s + 11	10^{-888}	10^{+888}

There are many other examples in which the availability of extended precision makes computations much more straight-forward, and this is why the IEEE standard strongly recommends that it be supported. The standard stops short of requiring this support, since in some environments the extra hardware requirement could be excessive. Still, in evaluating the relative desirability of floating-point implementations, the availability of extended precision is an important criterion.

Overflow and Infinite Values

Since the floating-point formats support a limited range of numbers an important question is: What happens when the result of a calculation is outside this range? Traditional floating-point hardware signals an *overflow* error, typically in the form of an error trap. The software then has to decide what to do in response to the overflow.

The IEEE standard requires the capability of handling overflows in this manner (with an error trap), but it also requires an interesting alternative approach in which out-of-range values are automatically replaced by one of two special values, positive or negative infinity. These infinite values are represented using an exponent of all 1 bits and a 0 significand (you will remember that this exponent value is *not* used in the representation of normalized numbers within the allowed range).

When infinite values are encountered in subsequent operations, they behave in a "reasonable" manner, for example

$$1.0 - (+\infty) = -\infty$$
$$+\infty + 1.0 = +\infty$$
$$(-\infty) \times (-\infty) = (+\infty)$$
$$1.0/(+\infty) = 0.0$$

The introduction of infinite values does not magically solve all problems associated with overflow conditions, but there are calculations in which the introduction of infinities very neatly avoids having to consider special cases. Consider the calculation of the resistance of the parallel resistance network

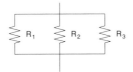

Digging out the appropriate formula from a beginning physics course, the resistance of the network is given as

$$R_n = \cfrac{1}{\cfrac{1}{R_1} + \cfrac{1}{R_2} + \cfrac{1}{R_3}}$$

Now consider the special case where one of the resistances is an open wire and has a resistance of zero. If we simply calculate the formula using infinities, the corresponding denominator term will be $+\infty$ and when we sum the three denominator terms, the sum will also be $+\infty$. Finally, when we do the division, the result will be 0.0, which is exactly the right answer. In the absence of the use of infinities, we would have had to treat this as a special case. Using infinities, the right answer falls out without any special handling.

There are many other cases in which the use of infinity simplifies dealing with special cases. Of course, an analysis is needed in each situation to ensure that the use of infinity is indeed appropriate.

Not a Number (NaNs)

Even with the introduction of infinities, there are calculations where no sensible result is possible. Examples are division of zero by zero or subtracting $+\infty$ from itself. As in the overflow case, the standard provides two possible approaches. In the first an error trap occurs, and the calculation is interrupted. In the second, a special value called an NaN (Not a Number) is generated. The exact format of NaNs is left up to the implementation—the available representations are those with a maximum exponent (all 1 bits) and a *non-zero* significand.

SIGNALLING AND NON-SIGNALLING NaNs. The IEEE standard requires the implementation of two types of NaNs—*signalling* and *non-signalling* NaNs. These differ in how they are treated when used as operands for subsequent operations. If one or both operands of an arithmetic operation are signalling NaNs, then an error trap is always generated. A typical use of signalling NaNs would be to mark uninitialized values—any attempt to use an uninitialized value would be signalled by an error trap.

If either of the operands of an arithmetic operation is a non-signalling NaN, the result is simply another NaN and no error is signalled. This silent propagation of NaNs serves to mark the subset of results that are to be considered unreliable due to some dubious calculation. One possible use of the significand bits in the NaN format is to encode an error identification that indicates the reason for the generation of the NaN.

Handling of Underflow

If numbers get out of range, then we have an overflow situation, which is in most cases an error and is handled as described in the previous section. Another special situation arises if the result of an operation has an absolute magnitude smaller than the smallest representable number. This situation is called *underflow*. Using single format as an example, the smallest normalized number is:

$$0\ \ 00000001\ \ 00000000000000000000000$$

So the question is what to do if we have a result smaller than this value. One traditional answer is called *flush* to zero, which means that all such values are simply reset to zero. Most mainframe floating-point hardware constructed prior to the issuance of the IEEE standard used this approach, and it is certainly the simplest approach from the hardware point of view.

However, there is a significant disadvantage. If we mark the real line with exactly representable numbers, flush to zero creates a hole around zero. The following picture is for the case of a 2-bit fraction field:

Negative numbers   0.0   Positive numbers

This hole has some nasty consequences. For example, if we calculate

$$(x - y) + y \tag{5.11}$$

and the calculation of $(x - y)$ underflows and is flushed to zero, the result will be y, rather than an approximation of x as expected. Normally we would analyze the accuracy of calculation of this expression as follows:

$$(X - Y) = (x - y)\ (1 + \varepsilon) \tag{5.12}$$

$$|\varepsilon| < 2^{-p} \tag{5.13}$$

where ε is the error term bounded as in equation (3) in our earlier development. However, if we have underflow and flush to zero, then $(X - Y)$ is zero and the analysis does not work. This means that in the presence of flush to zero, also called *sudden underflow*, we always have to worry about underflow as a special case.

GRADUAL UNDERFLOW AND DENORMALS. To avoid this problem, the IEEE standard requires the implementation of *gradual underflow*. The idea here is that when you get near zero, it is better to lose precision and maintain a non-zero value. The resulting numbers are not normalized and are called *denormals*. Take the single format as an example; the smallest normalized number,

0 00000001 00000000000000000000000

is the value 2^{-126}. If the result of a calculation is, for example, 2^{-128}, then instead of flushing to zero, the IEEE result is

0 00000000 01000000000000000000000

The special exponent value of all 0 bits indicates that the result is denormal, so the missing fraction bit is a 0, instead of the normal 1. This result is interpreded as having the minimum exponent (2^{-126}) and a fraction of 0.01000000000000000000000, giving the desired result of 2^{-128}. The value is accurate only to 22 bits instead of the usual 24, but it is better to have 22 bits of accuracy than *no* bits of accuracy at all, which is the flush to zero alternative. The smallest denormal value looks like

0 00000000 00000000000000000000001

which is the value 2^{-149}, and it is accurate only to one bit. Values smaller than this finally underflow to zero, but the underflow is gradual, rather than sudden. The picture of representable numbers on the real line no longer has a hole around zero:

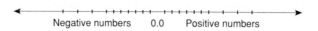

The normal error analysis approach always holds even in the case of underflow caused by cancellation. If the calculation of $(x - y)$ generates a denormal, this denormal is the *exact* representation of the result, so the error is even less than that described by the normal formula. In particular, $x - y = 0$ if and only if x is exactly equal to y, if gradual underflow is used.

To the casual numerical programmer, the distinction may seem unimportant, and indeed the issue of whether or not to require gradual underflow was argued ferociously in the literature as the standard was being developed. The argument against gradual underflow was that it was unnecessary and involved substantial additional hardware support.[5] After much argument, those numerical analysts more concerned with the ease of analysis of code and the smooth behavior of calculations involving underflow won the day and, as we have mentioned, the IEEE standard requires gradual underflow.

Specialized Operations

In addition to the standard arithmetic operations, the IEEE standard provides for a number of specialized operations including a square root and an exact remainder instruction. The square root instruction computes the (properly rounded) square root of its argument. It might seem at first that square root is rather complex to be required as a primitive operation. However, it turns out that it is possible to design hardware circuits that compute square roots very fast—as fast or even a little faster than a division.

The remainder operation subtracts an exact number of multiples of the divisor from the dividend, leaving a remainder whose absolute magnitude is less than the divisor. A typical use is to compute the remainder of an argument on dividing by a representation of 2π. This is needed for doing accurate argument reduction for trigonometric functions. The trigonometric functions themselves are *not* part of the IEEE standard, but the provision of the accurate remainder instruction considerably simplifies the writing of such functions. Using the remainder operation, it is relatively easy to write trigonometric functions which always satisfy identities like

$$\sin^2 \theta + \cos^2 \theta = 1$$

and

$$2 \sin \theta \cos \theta = \sin^2 \theta$$

for all arguments. Without the remainder, it is harder to guarantee these results—most trigonometric functions on non-IEEE machines don't have these properties.

---

[5] One consequence is that all the normal arithmetic operations have to be prepared to handled denormal inputs. One of the authors recently wrote a simulator for IEEE floating-point, and a substantial proportion, perhaps 20%, of the code is devoted to handling and generating denormal values.

Another required operation is a set of conversion operations between binary and decimal formats which are guaranteed to accurately convert integer values, and which have the property that binary $\rightarrow$ decimal $\rightarrow$ binary is the identity function.

Implementing the IEEE Standard

A very important point in implementing the IEEE standard is that it is *not* required that all, or indeed any, of the IEEE functionality be provided by hardware. A software simulator is a perfectly good implementation from the point of view of the legal requirements of the standard. Of course, users interested in high-performance floating-point may well regard a software simulation as totally useless, but it would satisfy the requirements of the standard.

More to the point in practical implementations of the standard is that not *all* the functionality needs to be provided in hardware. For instance, one might have a hardware unit that implements the basic formats and all the standard operations except square root. The combination of this hardware and a software routine to calculate the square root would constitute not only a technically legal implementation of the standard, but also a usably efficient one. Of course, we would prefer a fast, efficient square root implemented in hardware, but it is unlikely that many applications would be critically dependent on this performance difference. Furthermore the usual RISC arguments may well apply—by leaving some of the more complex operations to software, it may be possible to make the basic operations run faster, giving overall improved performance.

Even in the case of a fairly complete hardware implementation of the standard, there are aspects of the standard that have more to do with software environments than hardware implementations. For instance, there is a requirement that the application programmer be able to write trap routines for handling overflows and other exceptions. The hardware can provide the basic trap mechanism, but making this available to the application programmer requires operating system and compiler interface code. This means that a complete implementation of the standard always involves some kind of software shell, and there are actually very few complete implementations of the IEEE standard including a complete shell. The SANE (Standard Apple Numeric Environment) systems implemented on Apple computers including the Mac and the Apple II are examples of complete implementations.

IEEE-COMPATIBLE FLOATING-POINT CHIPS. As we noted in the previous section, a hardware chip alone cannot be said to implement the entire IEEE standard. The standard itself warns;

> Hardware components that require software support to conform shall not be said to conform apart from such software.

Nevertheless, manufacturers are happy to confuse the situation with claims that their floating-point chips do indeed implement the standard. For example, Intel says of the

80287 coprocessor chip in the Numeric Supplement to the iAPX 286 Programmer's Reference Manual:

> The iAPX 286/20 computing system (80286 CPU with 80287 NPX) easily supports powerful and accurate numeric applications through its implementation of the proposed IEEE 754 Standard for Binary Floating-Point Arithmetic.[6]

All such claims must be treated with a little skepticism. None of the so-called IEEE floating-point chips implements the entire standard, and one of the aspects to consider in looking at the various IEEE-compatible chips is the extent to which the standard is supported in hardware and consequently the level of software support required.

THE INTEL 387 CHIP

As we noted in the previous chapters, the Intel 386, as well as previous members of this family do not have any floating-point capability on chip. Of course, it is possible to implement floating-point using software simulation routines, and these routines could even be IEEE-compatible. There are several such sets of IEEE compatible routines available for the IBM PC, and they are typically used for numerical calculations on PCs having no attached coprocessor chip. However, performing accurate IEEE arithmetic is, as we have seen, a rather complicated proposition, and the software routines are consequently complicated and rather slow—too slow to be of much use in serious computations.

To obtain better performance for floating-point calculations, a separate *coprocessor* chip is added to the system. Intel itself manufactures a series of coprocessor chips intended to be married with corresponding processor chips (see Table 5.3).

The reason that floating-point is done on a separate chip is simply that with the technology used for building the processor chips, there was not enough room on chip for the complex logic required to support floating-point. Furthermore, the great majority of applications for the PC do not require significant floating-point capability in any case. Interestingly there will *not* be an entry in this table for the 486, because by now the technology *does* allow the floating-point logic to be on chip. Consequently there is no separate 487 chip—all the floating-point logic is included in the 486. However, the floating-point support of the 486 is functionally identical to that provided by the 387 so the description in this section also applies to the 486.

The 387 and the IEEE Standard

As we previously mentioned, Intel claims that their coprocessor chips implement the full IEEE standard. This statement is not legally accurate, but Intel has a better claim to this distinction than most manufacturers of IEEE compatible-hardware, since the implementation is quite complete. It includes

---

[6] The "proposed" here reflects that the 80287 was designed at the same time as the standard.

TABLE 5.3
Intel 80x86 Floating-Point Coprocessors.

Processor	Floating-Point Coprocessor
8086, 8088	8087
80286	80287
80386	80387

- Support for single, double, and double extended formats.
- Hardware instructions for all IEEE operations, including square root, remainder, and decimal conversions.
- Full support of denormals, infinite and NaN values, and rounding modes.

This is a good framework on which to build a full implementation of the standard, and the software shell required would be fairly small and straightforward. That the 387 implements the above features of the standard tells us a great deal about the arithmetic; for instance, we know the exact formats used for representing floating-point numbers. However, there are a lot of details left unstated by the standard, and in this section we will look at the particular set of implementation choices made by Intel in the design of the 387.

The Register Set of the 387

The standard does not have anything to say about the register structure of an IEEE-compatible implementation. There are many choices that could be made. Among the choices we see in other processors are a separate fixed set of floating-point registers, addressed in the usual manner (e.g., the SPARC and the MIPS) or a normal set of integer registers that can do double duty (as on the Motorola 88000). The Intel 387 adopts a rather different strategy, which uses a register stack (which is shown in Figure 5.3).

The registers R1 through R8 hold up to eight floating-point values, which are always stored in double extended format. The 387 supports the single and double formats in memory, but all internal computations are done using double extended format. When a single or double value is loaded from memory, it is expanded to double extended, and when a single or double value is stored into memory, the double extended value is shortened with proper rounding as appropriate.

What is unusual about the registers is that they are not addressed by using absolute register numbers. Instead they are always addressed relative to a top-of-stack (TOS) value stored in a 3-bit field in the status register. The TOS can have a value from 0 to 7. If, for example, TOS is set to 4, then the registers would be addressed as follows as shown in Table 5.4. If TOS is changed, then the addressing changes accordingly. The only way to reference registers is by using the $ST(n)$ addresses that are relative to the TOS value. We will see in the next section how this decision affects the entire approach to generating instruction sequences for the 387.

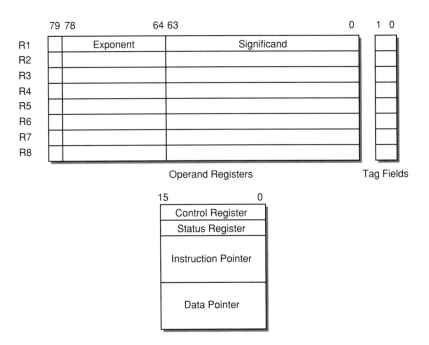

FIGURE 5.3
The register structure of the Intel 80387.

The tag fields are 2 bits long and together constitute a 16-bit register called the *tag word*. These tag values show whether the corresponding register contains a value or is empty and, if there is a value, whether it is zero or infinite.

The control register and status register contain a collection of control fields that determine rounding modes and behavior on exceptions such as overflow, as well as providing status flags to indicate which exceptions have occurred. One bit whose importance we shall examine in a later section is the *busy bit*, which shows if the coprocessor is currently executing an instruction. The instruction and data pointers have a rather subtle use, and again we will defer their discussion.

The Instruction Set of the 387

In normal use the 387 functions as a *stack machine*. Typical instructions are:

- FLD (floating load). TOS is decremented by 1, and ST(0) is loaded with the specified value.
- FADDP (floating add and pop). The values at TOS and TOS + 1 are added, the stack pointer is incremented, and the result replaces ST(0).
- FSTP (floating store and pop). The value at ST(0) is stored in memory, and the stack pointer is incremented.

TABLE 5.4
Addressing the 387 registers with TOS equal to 4.

Register	Addressed as:
R4	ST(0) (top of stack)
R5	ST(1)
R6	ST(2)
R7	ST(3)
R8	ST(4)
R1	ST(5)
R2	ST(6)
R3	ST(7)

Using instructions of this type, floating-point expressions are translated to a form reminiscent of *reverse Polish*. For example, suppose we have the following FORTRAN expression (a naive computation of the root of a quadratic)

$$X = (-B + SQRT (B * B - 4.0 * A * C)) / (2.0 * A)$$

In reverse Polish, this expression is written as:

$$B -_u B \ B * 4.0 \ A * C * -_b + \ 2.0 \ A * / \ [store \ X]$$

The corresponding 387 instruction sequence is:

```
FLD     B               ; load B
FCHS                    ; change sign (–B)
FLD     B               ; load B
FLD     B               ; load B
FMULP                   ; B * B
FLD     CON40           ; load 4.0
FLD     A               ; load A
FMULP                   ; 4.0 * A
FLD     C               ; load C
FMULP                   ; 4.0 * A * C
FSUBP                   ; B * B – 4.0 * A * C
FSQRT                   ; SQRT (B * B – 4.0 * A * C)
FADDP                   ; –B + SQRT (...)
FLD     CON20           ; 2.0
FLD     A               ; load A
FMULP                   ; 2.0 * A
FDIVP                   ; (–B + SQRT (...)) / (2.0 * A)
FSTP    X               ; store result in X
```

Note that the actual arithmetic operations have no explicit operands—none are needed because the top of stack always provides the input operands and is used to store the output operands. This type of instruction is sometimes called a *zero-address* instruction to reflect this lack of operands.

The generation of this type of code sequence is particularly easy for a compiler because it corresponds to simply walking the expression tree in a post order manner.[7] In the past, some companies, notably Burroughs, have designed complete instruction sets, including integer operations, using this stack-based approach. One of the advantages is that compilers are simplified. However, certainly for the integer case, disadvantages of the stack approach outweigh this and other considerations, and the stack approach is seldom used in current designs. The 387 is an interesting exception and is one of the few examples of zero-address instructions that we will encounter in the world of microprocessors.

CONVERSION INSTRUCTIONS. In addition to the basic arithmetic operations required by the standard, the 387 implements a full set of conversion instructions that allow floating-point values to be converted between floating formats and to and from 2-, 4-, and 8-byte integer formats.

There is also a set of instructions for converting between floating point format and packed decimal format, which consists of 18 decimal digits, stored 4 bits to a digit, two digits to a byte. This is a typical format used for commercial processing, as we previously discussed in examining instructions on the 386, such as DAS, which are specifically intended for handling this format.

It would therefore seem at first glance that the 387, although intended primarily for floating-point applications, would also be useful for commercial calculations such as those typically required by a COBOL program. Unfortunately, we have here a typical case of the standard CISC disease—a very useful instruction that is too slow to be useful. The conversion instructions take several hundred clocks, and in practice the necessary manipulations of packed decimal values can be done more efficiently using software routines written using the 386 instructions.

TRANSCENDENTAL FUNCTION INSTRUCTIONS. Many scientific calculations involve the computation of transcendental functions such as trigonometric, exponential and logarithmic functions. It is, of course, always possible to program such operations given a basic set of arithmetic operations, and it is particularly easy to write such programs using IEEE arithmetic with its accurate rounding, extended precision formats, and the special remainder instruction for doing argument reduction.

The 387, however, goes beyond the requirements of the standard and implements a complete set of trigonometric, inverse trigonometric, log, and exponential functions as basic instructions. These instructions are often quite complex and take several hundred clocks to calculate, but they are still more efficient than what could be achieved

---

[7] Owners of HP Scientific calculators will recognize this style of computation—HP has always favored the reverse Polish model in designing its calculators.

using sequences of multiplications and additions. Furthermore, they make programming on the 387 much easier for a casual user because there is no need to worry about the appropriate algorithms for calculating these functions. The experienced numerical analyst will, on the other hand, be concerned as to exactly what algorithms are being used and how accurate they are—the Intel Reference Manual is completely silent on this subject.

Executing 387 Instructions

When the 8086 and subsequent chips, including the 386, were designed, the possible presence of a coprocessor was kept in mind even though there are no floating-point facilities on chip. In particular, there is a special instruction called ESC (escape), which normally does nothing but copy the bits of the instruction to pins on the 386 chip and set a special signal indicating that an ESC instruction has been issued.

When the 387 coprocessor is attached, it watches the ESC signal, and if it is raised, the 387 acquires the ESC instruction, and treats it as a floating-point instruction. For example, the FADDP instruction has the encoding

$$11011\ 110\ \ 1100\ 0001$$

From the point of view of the 386, this is simply an ESC instruction (11011 is the opcode for ESC). However, the 387 will recognize the ESC signal being raised and acquire these instruction bits, which it will then treat as a FADDP instruction.

Normally the 386 does *not* wait for the 387 to complete processing the instruction (most of the time it operates without really even knowing whether or not the 387 is present). From the point of view of the 386, the effect is to start the FADDP calculation going and then continue executing further 386 instructions while the floating-point addition is in progress. This type of visible overlap is common in RISC architectures, but we see it for the first time in this context.

A consequence is that if the program can be arranged so that there is useful work to do during the floating-point calculations, then the cost of these calculations is almost free. Of course, in heavy floating-point calculations, there will not be enough to do, and typically another floating-point instruction will be issued by the 386 before the previous one is completed. If this happens, the 386 *does* wait for the previous instruction to be completed. This is where the busy bit of the 387 status register comes in—if the 387 is busy it sends a special signal to the 386 that causes it to wait before issuing a second floating-point instruction.

Normally the synchronization between the 386 and 387 is transparent to the programmer. The one important exception occurs after a floating-point store. A sequence of instructions such as

```
FSTP    X               ; store floating-point result
MOV     EAX, X          ; load result into EAX
```

will not work correctly because the MOV instruction will be executed immediately, before the FSTP instruction has had a chance to store the result in memory. To deal with this problem, there is a special 386 instruction FWAIT that waits for the current floating-point operation to complete (i.e., for the busy bit in the floating-point status word to go to zero). Now the above sequence of instructions is written as

```
FSTP    X            ; store floating-point result
FWAIT                ; wait for store to complete
MOV     EAX, X       ; load result into EAX
```

and the intended effect is obtained. Compilers generating code for the 386/387 combination must be sure to include FWAIT instructions wherever they are necessary to ensure consistent semantics.

COMMUNICATION BETWEEN THE 386 AND 387. The actual details of communication between the 386 and 387 are quite complex and are not fully documented by Intel. All we find is a note that programmers should avoid using I/O ports 00F8H through 00FFH since these ports are also used for communicating between the two chips. One probable use of these ports is in the calculation of memory addresses. Instructions like FLD and FSTP have a memory operand that can use all the usual addressing modes, including basing, indexing, and scaling.

Obviously we don't want to duplicate all the circuitry for calculating effective addresses and accessing memory in the 387 because the 386 contains all the necessary circuitry. Furthermore, the index and base registers used for this addressing are in the 386 and not accessible to the 387 in any case. To solve this problem, the 387 asks the 386 to carry out the necessary address calculations and memory accesses, temporarily interrupting it from its normal job of executing 386 instructions.

This is quite a tricky communication interface. Some idea of just how tricky it is can be gained from the presence of an unfortunate bug in early versions of the 386 that results in an error in this communication. The effect is for both the 386 and the 387 to hang, with a hardware reset being the only cure. Whether or not this bug shows up depends on very delicate details of the way in which the hardware designer hooks things together.[8] Hardware designs are susceptible to bugs like software programs—of course, the consequences are somewhat more alarming because it is easier to send out updates to a program than to replace millions of existing computer chips!

HANDLING EXCEPTIONS. Exceptional conditions such as overflow, underflow, or improper operands can cause exception traps, depending on the setting of appropriate flags in the control word. These traps are signalled in the normal manner, but an extra complication occurs because of the overlapped execution. The 387 may not recognize a trap condition until long after the 386 has executed the original ESC instruction, and many 386 instructions may have been executed in the meantime.

---

[8] The PS/2 model 80 is particularly susceptible to this bug, which shows up only if paging is enabled. The Compaq DP386/25, on the other hand, is immune. This bug would have caused more trouble if DOS used paging, but since it doesn't, most PS/2's are run with paging off, and the bug does not show up.

This means that the EIP value saved as a normal part of the trap processing does not point to the floating-point instruction causing the trouble. The *instruction pointer* register in the 387 is intended to deal with this problem. It records the location of the offending instruction. A trap routine will in some cases want to look at the data values involved, and the *data pointer* register of the 387 records the address of the memory data operand (if there was one) used by the offending instruction. The trap routine can read both of these registers as it determines the appropriate action to take on the trap.

The intention in the Intel 387 design is that although the trap will occur after the original instruction has been executed, it can occur only on a subsequent floating-point instruction. It is therefore more like a trap than an interrupt, although the instruction causing the trap is not the same as the instruction signalling the trap. This is quite important, since it is awkward to deal with asynchronous error traps. However, IBM, for reasons that remain unclear, decided to ignore the Intel recommendation for wiring, and on the PC and all subsequent compatible machines, including the PS/2, the floating-point exceptions are signalled as hardware interrupts through the 8259 interrupt controller, and they certainly *can* occur asynchronously.

This turns out to be an annoyance in writing operating systems, since it means that the trap can occur at a place that is logically unrelated to the code causing the trap. For example, the floating trap may occur in the middle of timer interrupt code that has nothing to do with the executing application program. This is yet another case of hardware designers failing to understand software and operating system requirements clearly. Intel got this right, but IBM got it seriously wrong. Unfortunately, hundreds of manufacturers of PC-compatible machines have carefully copied this design mistake—compatibility again proves to be more important than sensible design!

Coprocessor Emulation

If no coprocessor is present, then floating-point operations must be simulated using software. One approach would be to provide a series of routines that are called using normal CALL instructions to execute the desired operations.

A much more attractive approach is for the programmer to simply issue floating-point instructions as though the coprocessor were present and have the simulator automatically intercept these instructions and provide exactly the same results as if the coprocessor were present. The 386 provides for this possibility in a convenient manner. The EM bit in the CR0 register of the 386 controls emulation mode. If it is set, then all ESC instructions cause a trap instead of being executed in the normal manner. The trap routine for the corresponding interrupt (its interrupt number 7) then carries out the required simulation.

A typical operating system approach is to determine whether or not a coprocessor is present when the system starts up. This can be done using sequences of instructions that have different effects depending on whether or not a coprocessor is present. The EM bit in CR0 is then set appropriately. If a coprocessor is present, then ESC instructions will be executed normally with EM set to zero and the coprocessor will be used for all floating-point operations. If no coprocessor is present, then EM will be set to 1, and all coprocessor instructions will trap to the simulation routine.

You may have noticed that the title of this section uses the word emulation instead of simulation. The word *emulation* has been traditionally used in this context, but we don't know of any real distinction between the terms simulation and emulation. Historically the word *emulator* was used to describe hardware simulators (such as the IBM 1401 hardware simulator for the IBM 360). It tends to be used now to imply an absolutely accurate and complete simulation of a piece of existing hardware; it is more of an advertising issue than an actual technical distinction—"emulator" sounds a little more impressive than "simulator".

Context Switching

There is at most one coprocessor attached to a 386 and consequently only one set of coprocessor registers. In switching from one task to another, it is necessary to save and restore the machine state of the coprocessor just as it is necessary to save the registers of the 286.

There are instructions, FSAVE and FRSTOR that are precisely intended for complete saving and restoring of the coprocessor state, including the complete set of coprocessor registers. It would therefore be sufficient to simply issue these instructions on every task switch to make sure that the appropriate context for the coprocessor was established.

Unfortunately, these instructions are quite slow, and unconditionally issuing an FSAVE and FRSTOR instruction on each task switch would add 100 or 200 clocks to each task switch. This is particularly unpleasant in the common case where one or both of the tasks is not using the 387 at the time of the task switch.

To deal with this problem, the 387 task-switching mechanism incorporates a bit in CR0 called the TS or task switch bit. This bit is set whenever a task switch occurs.[9] If a floating-point instruction is issued with TS set, then a trap occurs. This trap routine deals with making sure that the appropriate context is loaded into the 387.

A typical approach is to maintain a memory word showing which task currently owns the 387 machine state. When a TS trap occurs, this word is checked. If the correct context is loaded, the TS bit is cleared and the floating-point instruction is reexecuted. If the correct context is not loaded, then and only then is an FSAVE/FRSTOR sequence used to load the required context, and then TS is cleared and execution continues. This approach ensures that context switches for the 387 occur only when they are absolutely necessary.

---

[9] If task switching is being done by software rather than by using the hardware tasking instructions, this software would have to set the TS bit itself.

THE WEITEK CHIPSET: AN ALTERNATIVE APPROACH

Although Intel clearly intends that floating-point operations be carried out using the 387 coprocessor, a consequence of having a separate floating-point chip is that it is possible for a designer to choose some other floating-point solution than the one provided by Intel. One such alternative that has appeared in the PC world is the Weitek chipset. This is another partial implementation of the IEEE floating-point standard that is about as different from the 387 as could be imagined.

First, the support for the IEEE standard is much thinner, since only the basic single and double formats are supported and there is no extended precision. As you will remember, the IEEE standard allows this choice, although it recommends that extended formats be supported. Furthermore, only the basic operations are supported—there are no trigonometric functions built in. Worse still, there is no support for denormals—underflow is sudden rather than gradual. This is a pretty serious deviation from the standard, and it means that a full implementation of the standard would require a lot of software support. In practice, most users of the Weitek chipset just live with the sudden underflow, and thus are not really operating in an IEEE compatible mode.

The second major difference is that the entire arrangement of communication between the 386 and the Weitek chip is quite different. Programs must be completely changed to take advantage of the Weitek chipset. Given this limited IEEE support, the incompatibility with the 387, and the fact that the Weitek chip is about double the price of the 387, you may wonder why anyone would use it. The answer is a single word, speed—the Weitek is 2 to 3 times faster than the 80387. In the floating-point world, performance is very often the dominating criterion, so the Weitek chipset is extensively used despite its other disadvantages.

Memory Mapped Access

The Weitek chip uses a memory mapped interface to the 386. This technique is quite commonly used for control of I/O devices. Instead of using I/O ports to communicate with a device, ordinary memory reads and writes are used. The device, in this case the Weitek chip, sits on the bus as though it were a memory board, and like a memory board it responds to certain special addresses.

The programmer writes an ordinary MOV instruction that looks like a load or store instruction, but the memory address used is one of the special addresses recognized by the Weitek chip, and the effect is to execute a floating-point instruction.

The Weitek Instruction Set

To perform a Weitek instruction, the 386 issues a MOV to a bogus 32-bit address which is specially recognized by the Weitek. A range of 64K addresses is used, corresponding to 64K different instructions. This isn't as bad as it sounds, since the Weitek has 32 registers (which we number here WR0 to WR31), so the large number of instructions corresponds to variations of a smaller set with different register numbers.

The 32-bit address presented to the Weitek is interpreted as a set of separate fields:

31	16	15	10	9	7	6	2	1	0
Weitek memory base		opcode		R high		L			R Low

The first 16 bits of the address specify a 64K section of memory which is dedicated for use by the Weitek chip. The hardware system designer selects this section, and the programmer must address the Weitek accordingly. The next 6 bits of the address select one of up to 64 opcodes (of which 51 are used). Each instruction takes two register numbers as operands. The left operand is given in bits 2-6. The right register operand is split up into two fields, with the high order in bits 7-9 and the low order in bits 0-1.

As an example of an instruction, consider a single precision add with a left operand of 4 and a right operand of 7, which causes register WR7 to be added to the contents of register WR4, with the result stored back into WR4. The opcode for this instruction is 000100 in binary. Assume that the hardware designer has specified that the area starting at address 7EEF0000 be used for the Weitek, then this subtract instruction can be triggered by referencing the address 7EEF1093.

31	16	15	10	9	7	6	2	1	0
7EEF		000100		001		00100			11

For an instruction such as this add, a MOV to memory is used, so the corresponding 386 instruction which would trigger the subtract is:

```
MOV    [7EEF1093H],AL
```

The contents of AL are not actually relevant to this instruction, since the Weitek chip is only interested in the address, and will simply ignore the contents of AL, but we have to pretend to be doing a real store for the 386's sake.

Most instructions are triggered by bogus byte stores of this kind, in which only the address is of interest, and the data is ignored. The one exception is load and store instructions. These are signalled by using the special register WR0, which tells the Weitek that it *should* pay attention to the transferred data, and in this case we will do word moves so that 32-bits can be moved between a 386 register, typically, though not necessarily, EAX and the Weitek.

AN EXAMPLE. We are now ready to write a complete example for the Weitek. We will give the Weitek code for the quadratic root calculation which we previously translated for the 387:

$$X = (-B + SQRT (B * B - 4.0 * A * C)) /(2.0 * A)$$

Assuming once again that the Weitek memory section starts at location 7EEF0000, the following sequence of code will perform this computation using the Weitek instructions:

```
MOV     EAX, B              ; EAX = b
MOV     [7EEF0404], EAX     ; WR1 = EAX (b)
MOV     [7EEF2809], AL      ; WR2 = −WR1 (−b)
MOV     [7EEF0804], AL      ; WR1 = WR1 ∗ WR1 (b²)
MOV     EAX, FOURP0         ; EAX = 4.0
MOV     [7EEF040C], EAX     ; WR3 = EAX (4.0)
MOV     EAX, A              ; EAX = a
MOV     [7EEF080C], EAX     ; WR3 = WR3 ∗ EAX (4a)
MOV     [7EEF0410], EAX     ; WR4 = EAX (a)
MOV     EAX, C              ; EAX = c
MOV     [7EEF080C], EAX     ; WR3 = WR3 ∗ EAX (4ac)
MOV     [7EEF1007], AL      ; WR1 = WR1 − WR3 (b² − 4ac)
CALL    SQRT                ; WR1 = sqrt WR1 (sqrt (b² − 4ac))
MOV     [7EEF0014], AL      ; WR4 = WR4 + WR4 (2a)
MOV     [7EEF0009], AL      ; WR2 = WR2 + WR1 (−b + sqrt (b² − 4ac))
MOV     [7EEF140C], AL      ; WR2 = WR2 / WR4 ((−b + sqrt (b² − 4ac)/2a))
MOV     EAX, [7EEF0C08]     ; EAX = WR2
MOV     X, EAX              ; store result in X
```

If we really wanted to write Weitek code in assembly language, we would certainly hope that the assembler would provide some features to hide the MOV instructions so that the Weitek operations seemed more like real instructions, something like:

```
MOV     EAX, B              ; EAX = b
WSMOV WR1, EAX              ; WR1 = EAX (b)
WSNEG WR2, WR1              ; WR2 = −WR1 (−b)
WSMUL WR1, WR1              ; WR1 = WR1 ∗ WR1 (b²)
MOV     EAX, FOURP0         ; EAX = 4.0
WSMOV WR3, EAX              ; WR3 = EAX (4.0)
MOV     EAX, A              ; EAX = a
WSMUL WR3, EAX              ; WR3 = WR3 ∗ EAX (4a)
WSMOV WR4, EAX              ; WR4 = EAX (a)
MOV     EAX, C              ; EAX = c
WSMUL WR3, EAX              ; WR3 = WR3 ∗ EAX (4ac)
WSSUB WR1, WR3              ; WR1 = WR1 − WR3 (b² − 4ac)
CALL    SQRT                ; WR1 = sqrt WR1 (sqrt (b² − 4ac))
WSADD WR4, WR4              ; WR4 = WR4 + WR4 (2a)
WSADD WR2, WR1              ; WR2 = WR2 + WR1 (−b + sqrt (b² − 4ac))
WSDIV   WR2, WR4            ; WR2 = WR2 / WR4 ((−b + sqrt (b² − 4ac)/2a))
WSMOV EAX, WR2              ; EAX = WR2
MOV     X, EAX              ; store result in X
```

The assembler would recognize the WS mnemonics as Weitek operations, and generate the required bogus MOV instructions with the appropriate memory addresses. This would certainly make life easier for the programmer, but it is important to remember that the 386 really executes these instructions as MOVs, and is quite oblivious to the fact that there is a Weitek chipset out there busily intercepting the MOV addresses and performing a sequence of floating point operations.

This sequence of code is completely different from 387 code. The difference isn't just a matter of slight variations in instructions, but the entire approach is different, since the Weitek uses a set of 32 registers organized in a conventional manner, and the 387 uses a set of 8 registers, organized as a stack.

Furthermore, the Weitek code has a significantly different effect from the corresponding 387 code. On the 387, the intermediate calculations are all done in double extended format, whereas on the Weitek they will be done only in double format. This is a particularly important distinction in this case because one of the problems in using the naive approach to computing roots of quadratic equations is that the computation of $4.0 * A * C$ can overflow even though the result is in range. On the 387, this problem is ameliorated because double extended has a much larger exponent range than double. So, not only are the code sequences for the Weitek quite different, but it may also be the case that different algorithms should be employed.

CONCLUSION

The design of floating-point hardware is a challenging problem. Floating-point operations are inherently complex, but the RISC inclination to leave complex operations to software won't work here, because floating-point applications use these instructions intensively. This means that even the most strenuous RISC designs must address the issue of providing high efficiency floating-point hardware.

In the microprocessor world, the widespread adoption of the IEEE standard brings a much greater level of uniformity and well-defined behavior than is seen in the mainframe area. Nevertheless, there are a great number of variations, and as we examine various RISC and CISC processors, we will see great variations in the extent to which the IEEE standard is supported. The 387 and Weitek chips used on the 386 give some idea of this variation—the 387 is one of the most extensive implementations, and the Weitek is by comparison much thinner.

The material in this chapter is rather complicated, and yet it has only begun to scrape the surface. The study of floating-point algorithms and the software and hardware support needed by them is a highly specialized area. If nothing else, you should learn from this chapter that you should get expert advice from numerical analysts if you are ever in the position of designing hardware or systems software that involves the handling of floating-point operations.

CHAPTER

6

THE 68030 USER PROGRAMMING MODEL

The Motorola 68030 operates in one of two states, the *user state* or the *supervisor state*. These states are similar to the protection levels of the 386 in that a subset of the instructions are privileged and can only be executed in the supervisor state. An attempt to execute privileged instructions in user state causes an error trap.

In this chapter we will discuss the user state, leaving the description of the supervisor state and all of the issues involved in utilizing that aspect of the processor until Chapter 7. In particular, we will concentrate on the addressing modes that are provided by the 68000 series.

It should be pointed out that much of what we will have to say about the user programming model of the 68030 is also true of other members in the 68000 family. Although the 68030 is identical in user mode to the 68020, earlier models of the 68000 series such as the 68000 itself are more limited than the 68030 in certain respects, particularly in the area of addressing modes. Nevertheless, much of the code running today on machines designed around the 68030 adheres to the 68000 limitations, so it will be compatible with all members of this family. This situation contrasts with the Intel family, where the 386 provides very substantial gains to user applications (notably 32-bit registers and 32-bit addressing) over the 286 and previous members of the Intel family—the 386 is essentially totally incompatible with earlier members of the series if the 32-bit capabilities are used, whereas all members of the 68000 family have provided 32-bit addressing and 32-bit operations.

THE 68030 USER REGISTER SET

From the point of view of the applications programmer, the register model of the 68030 has not changed since the introduction of the original 68000. All members of the Motorola 68000 series have sixteen 32-bit registers that are divided into eight data registers named D0 through D7 and eight address registers named A0 through A7 (see Figure 6.1). This means that the 68030 has twice as many registers as the 386, giving the 68030 a significant advantage over the 386 in this respect.

Motorola claims in both the 68030 User's Manual and their advertising that the 68030 has 16 general-purpose registers. A truly general-purpose register is a register that cannot be distinguished from any other register in the general register set. If the operand for an instruction is in a register, it can be in any of the general-purpose registers. As we shall see, that is certainly *not* true of the 68030.

The use of registers *within* the two separate sets of registers is reasonably uniform. For example, any instruction using a data register can use any of the eight data registers.

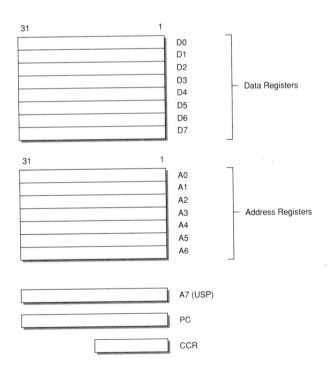

FIGURE 6.1
The 68030 user programming model register set.

Similarly, if you look at only the eight address registers, then, with the exception of address register A7, these registers are also treated uniformly in the instruction set. However, in comparing the address registers to the data registers, there are many instructions and addressing formats which do not give a programmer a choice between these two register types—either an address register or a data register is required. That is not quite the same thing as having real general purpose registers.

One user register which can clearly be distinguished from all of the other user registers is the address register A7, also known as the *user stack pointer* (USP), which is used as a stack pointer in much the same way that the register ESP is used on the 386. In particular, register A7 is used when building stack frames during procedure calls.

Do not misinterpret the statement that the 68030 register set is not truly general-purpose to mean that its register set is completely non-uniform—this is certainly not the case. That accusation can certainly be leveled against the 386, where the register set is not even close to being uniform—almost every register of the 386 is used in some special-purpose way by one of the 386 instructions. What can be said about the register set of the 68030 is that it has two distinct categories of registers, but within each set there are almost no differences. To see the differences that do occur, we need to look carefully at the instruction set and addressing modes of the 68030.

Special Purpose Registers

In addition to the address and data registers, the 68030 has a number of special-purpose registers. At the user level, just two of these are visible, the 8-bit *condition code register* (CCR) and the *program counter* (PC). There are other registers on this machine that are available only when the processor is in supervisor state, and these are covered in Chapter 7. The program counter is a 32-bit register that is separate from the address and data registers. Furthermore, PC is not one of the general registers, so it can be referenced only via special instructions such as calls and jumps.

The CCR is similar to the EFL register on the 386. CCR contains a series of bits indicating conditions set by a previous instruction (see Table 6.1). As on the 386, each instruction may or may not affect one of these flags. Conditional jump and set instructions reference the current values of these flags to perform desired tests on the outcome of a previous instruction.

TABLE 6.1
The 68030 condition code bits.

Condition Code	Purpose
X	Extend, the carry indication for multiple precision
N	Negative, indicates a negative result
Z	Zero, indicates a zero result
V	Overflow, indicates signed arithmetic overflow
C	Carry, indicates unsigned arithmetic overflow

THE 68030 LINEAR ADDRESS SPACE

The addressing model used by the 68030 is a single 4-gigabyte linear address space, addressed using 32 bits. All members of the 68000 series going back to the original 68000 were committed to this single linear address space. This 32-bit address space is byte-addressable—operands longer than a byte need *not* be aligned, even though the 68030 at the hardware level is really a 32-bit machine. As on the 386, it takes longer to retrieve data if it is unaligned, but programmers, especially COBOL programmers, would rather have these loads take a little bit longer than not be able to do them at all.

Interestingly, unaligned references were first added to the hardware of the 68000 series in the 68020. Earlier members of the family (which were really 16-bit processors at the bus level) required 16-bit alignment for word and longword (32-bit) data. In applications requiring the use of unaligned operands, the cost of using such operands on the 68000 was considerable, much higher than the cost of loading an unaligned operand on the 386. With the addition of the capability of addressing unaligned operands on the 68020, Motorola and Intel have converged to a common treatment. As we noted for the 386, it is better for a processor to allow unaligned operands and charge a time penalty for their use than not to allow them at all.

The fact that the 68000 series had such a large address space from the very beginning has been seen by many people as an important difference, making the Motorola series superior to the Intel series. Early on, when the segments of the Intel series were limited to 64K bytes, the linear address space of the 68000 was considered an important advantage, particularly in academic circles. With the introduction of the 386, however, the annoying little 64K segments of the 8086 and the 286 have grown to 4 gigabytes in size, and so they are not quite so annoying any longer.

What are the advantages and disadvantages of that large linear address space? The appeal of a large linear address space to academic circles and in the engineering workstation market, which Motorola dominates, is not entirely accidental. To some extent it has to do with the general simplicity of this approach, but it is also related to the widespread use of Unix and the C programming language in these environments.

C, Pointers, and the Linear Address Space

Unix and C have a view of addressing in which addresses are essentially the same as integers. A careful reading of the C definition will show that there is no such assumption stated anywhere. Strictly speaking, a pointer in C is a strongly typed abstract object that consists of a pair: a base address and an offset. The base address of a pointer points to the starting location of an array or possibly some piece of allocated storage. A C programmer can do pointer arithmetic only in a very limited sense—it is possible to alter the offset of a pointer, but it is not possible to alter its base.

That is the conceptual model of C. Almost no one programs with that model of C in mind, because experience has taught C programmers that the implementation of pointers in most C compilers allows one to treat an address in the same way as an integer. This is true despite the fact that the authors of *The C Programming Language* warn against this practice in a section titled "Pointers are not Integers."

Consider the following example of *address arithmetic* in C, where *p* is a pointer to an element of an array of 4-byte integers:

```
p++;
```

The official effect of this statement, assuming that *p* points to an element of a compound structure, such as an array, is to modify *p* so that it points to the next element in the structure. However, many C programs make the assumption that this statement can be interpreted as a simple addition and on a machine with a linear address space, this assumption is correct, since the appropriate machine operation *is* simply an increment. It is common knowledge that many lines of C code have been written with such technically illegal assumptions in mind.

Let us consider an example in which the code itself (unlike the small fragment above) explicitly makes certain assumptions which work just fine most of the time but are technically improper and may not work on all processors. Consider the declaration of two integers *a* and *b*, written in sequence as

```
int a, b;
```

A programmer may very well know that on the particular compiler which he is using that if *p* is set to be the address of *a*, written as

```
p = &a;
```

and *p* is then incremented, it will point to the "next" variable, *b*. If you find that this always works, you may well continue to confidently write code that depends upon it. There are many examples of C code where similar assumptions have been made. Another common assumption is that pointers and integers are freely interchangeable. C programmers sometimes convert a pointer to an integer, and then modify its value in illegal ways before converting it back to an integer, and then use this value.

On a machine that has a linear addressing model, programs such as these which violate the C standard will typically run fine. On the other hand, if the same programs are run on a segmented machine like the 8086, strange things may happen since the address space is *not* linear—instead, an address is a pair consisting of a segment and an offset within the segment. An appropriate implementation of *p++* on the 8086 is simply to increment the offset, which, assuming that a single composite object fits in a single segment, is a perfectly correct implementation of the official C rules. However, this model of simply incrementing the offset will not work in programs where the C programmer is explicitly expecting pointers to behave like integers.

Data and the Linear Address Space

Another problem that may arise in connection with segmented memory that will not arise with a single large linear address space is the problem of where to put large data objects that exceed the maximum size of a segment. Writing assembly code or compiling for a high-level language is a great deal harder when the data is large compared to the size of the segments. Writing an application intended for the 8086, for example, that needs to use an array larger than 64K bytes can be somewhat complicated.

It is, of course, possible to represent such a large array by breaking it into a set of smaller arrays. A 640K array, for example, can be divided into ten 64K pieces, with a separate array of 10 pointers used to point to each of the pieces. To access an element in this array it is first necessary to figure out which of the 10 pieces the element is in and then exactly where within that piece it is. Doing this will require a nasty sequence of 10 or 15 machine instructions, many more than would be required if the array were represented as a single large structure. It suddenly becomes more complicated and much less efficient to do something that was simple with a large linear address space.

On the advanced members of the Intel series, the issue disappears. Each segment on the 386 can be as large as 2^{32} bytes, the same as the linear address space of the 68030. In fact, if an operating system or some application committed itself to the use of the 386 segments (most software doesn't), then with the addition of virtual segmentation and demand paging it is possible to have virtual memory much bigger than 4 gigabytes.[1]

Byte Ordering

The 68030 is firmly committed to big-endian byte ordering. On all occasions where an integer, address, or other data value longer than 1 byte is stored in memory, the *most significant* byte is stored first, that is, at the lowest address. As we discussed in Chapter 1, the choice between byte-endian modes is more or less an arbitrary one. There are minor advantages to the big-endian mode, one of which arises in COBOL programs. Consider the COBOL records

```
01  REC1.
     05  FIELD1    PIC X(4).
     05  FIELD2    PIC 9(9) COMP.
02  REC1.
     05  FIELD1    PIC X(4).
     05  FIELD2    PIC 9(9) COMP.
```

The FIELD2 fields are typically represented as 32-bit unsigned binary values. If a COBOL programmer compares these two records,

```
IF REC1 IS GREATER THAN REC2 THEN ....
```

the desired result is lexicographic ordering, where the primary key is FIELD1 and the secondary key is FIELD2. The COBOL standard defines record comparison as proceeding character by character. On a big-endian machine, where the most significant byte of FIELD2 is compared first, the desired lexicographic ordering is obtained. You cannot

---

[1] There is a naughty statement in one of the Intel manuals that says, "Note. By setting all the segment registers to point to a 4 gigabyte segment, the addressing capabilities of less capable microprocessors without segmentation can be simulated." If you read between the lines, what it is saying is that if you don't have segmentation, then you have the less capable addressing of the 68000.

really justify expecting this ordering, since the representation of COMP fields is implementation-dependent, but the IBM 370 is big-endian, so COBOL programmers expect this to work.

On the 68030, a COBOL compiler will behave as expected. What we see here is yet another example of the issue of data compatibility between machines. Most COBOL programmers are used to the IBM view of the world, so it pays to agree with IBM's view of byte ordering.[2] Not only COBOL programmers suffer from these incompatibilities. It is quite easy, and unfortunately common, to write C code which depends on the byte ordering conventions, as anyone who has tried to port carelessly written PDP-11 code to the 68030 knows well!

Bit Ordering

As we noted in Chapter 1, it generally makes sense to combine big-endian byte ordering with big-endian bit ordering. This is what IBM does on the 370, and the most significant bit is thus numbered as bit 0.

However, the designers and documenters of the 68000 series seem to have been confused over this issue. The documentation of the 68000 is entirely little-endian when it comes to bit ordering. This may be the result of a bias in "hacker culture" that assumes that IBM has things "backwards" when it comes to bit ordering. In the attempt to avoid this "mistake," the 68030 documentation has got things backwards.

The numbering of bits on the 68030 is *not* simply a documentation issue. There are a number of instructions that reference bit numbers, notably the bit field extract and insert instructions. These instructions number bits in *big-endian* manner! As a result of this clash with the documentation, we get charming bits of confusion such as the following from the description of the bit field operations in the User's Manual:

> A bit operand is specified by a base address that selects one byte in memory (the base byte), and a bit number that selects the one bit in this byte. The most significant bit of the byte is bit seven. A bit field operand is specified by:
>
> 1. A base address that selects one byte in memory.
> 2. A bit field offset that indicates the leftmost (base) bit of the bit field in relation to the most significant bit of the base byte, and
> 3. A bit field width that determines how many bits to the right of the base byte are in the bit field.
>
> The most significant bit of the base byte is bit field offset 0, the least significant bit of the base byte is bit field offset 7.

Simple enough—all you have to understand is that the leftmost bit of a byte is bit 7, but has a bit field offset of 0, and the rightmost bit of a byte is bit 0, but has a bit field

---

[2] This is a significant enough point that in the Realia COBOL implementation on the Intel series there are two forms of COMP. COMP-5 is the natural (for that machine) little-endian ordering, and COMP-4 is the IBM-compatible big-endian ordering.

offset of 7, and everything is perfectly clear! Another note in the 68030 User's Manual explains that bit ordering of bit fields is the opposite of bit ordering of integers.

To further add to the confusion, the Test a Bit and Clear (BCLR) instruction, and several other similar instructions, number bits in *little-endian* style, exactly the opposite of the other bit field instructions. What a mess! It just shows how confusing the entire issue of bit- and byte-endian ordering can be.

THE 68030 USER-LEVEL INSTRUCTION SET

In this section we will summarize the user-level instruction set of the 68030. For the most part, this instruction set is straightforward. There is, however, the usual sprinkling of remarkably complex instructions, and we will look at some of these in detail.

Data Movement Instructions

The MOVE instruction can be used to move a byte, a word (2 bytes), or a longword (4 bytes) from register to memory, memory to register, or register to register. The standard assembler format has the source operand on the left, and the destination on the right:

```
MOVE.L  D3, A4
```

The effect of this instruction is to copy the longword value from register D3 to register A4. This is, of course, exactly the *opposite* of the syntactic convention used by the Intel assemblers; that is, the destination is furthest to the right in the list of operands on the 68030, whereas on the 386 the destination is placed all the way to the left.[3]

A notable restriction on the 68030 is that byte quantities cannot be moved to or from the address registers. This is a general restriction; no byte operations of any type are permitted in the address registers.

The general memory-to-memory move is interesting—among the processors covered in this book, *only* the 68030 provides this capability (the 386 has the MOVS instruction, but this has a very specialized use).

MOVE also allows an immediate operand of any size to be the source. There is a special version of the move instruction, *move quick* (MOVEQ), that takes an immediate value up to 8 bits. Another specialized move form, MOVEM, loads and stores multiple registers:

```
MOVEM.L   reglist, mem
MOVEM.L   mem, reglist
```

Here *reglist* is a 16-bit immediate value that acts as a mask to indicate which registers are to be loaded or stored. This is a useful flexibility not present on the 386 (which has only PUSHA and POPA, which always save or restore the entire register set).

---

[3] There are two quite distinct schools of thought on assembler notation: left-to-right and right-to-left. Both schools are vehement in their opinion that the other has got it all wrong. We will probably have to live with this confusion forever!

Integer Arithmetic Instructions

The basic instructions ADD, SUB, and CMP allow addition, subtraction, and comparison of byte, word and longword operands. The operands can be in memory, data registers or address registers. Both memory-to-register and register-to-memory forms are provided, as on the 386, but *not* memory-to-memory forms. A special comparison instruction, CMPM, allows memory-to-memory comparison, but in a very restricted form intended specifically for comparison of strings (much like CMPS on the 386).

Some unusual variations of the add and subtract instructions are Add Quick (ADDQ) and Subtract Quick (SUBQ). These are short (2-byte) instructions that include an immediate operand in the range of 1 to 8. These instructions are redundant in the sense that there is no reason why the standard add or subtract instructions could not be used in their place. Their presence is symptomatic of a typical CISC concern with keeping the length of common instructions as short as possible. Incrementing or decrementing by small values is so common (1 in particular is the most common, but 2, 4, and 8 also occur frequently in conjunction with addressing vectors of words, longwords, or quadwords) that a need was seen to include these in the instruction set. In the CISC view, even though an instruction already exists to add values between 1 and 8, the fact that the "quick" instructions are shorter makes it worthwhile to implement them anyway.

Multiple-precision arithmetic is supported through the use of the ADDX and SUBX. These instructions are just like the usual add and subtract instructions, except that the carry from a previous addition or subtraction, stored in the X bit of the CCR, is included as part of the operation. There is also a NEGX, which extends the value of the normal negate instruction, NEG. The 386 has the addition and subtraction forms with carry, but lacks the negation, making multiple-precision negation less convenient. Negation tends to be less common in typical high-level language programs, but nevertheless it is nice to have a complete set of operations.

The instructions EXT and EXTB are used to extend a signed value in a register, in most instances, just after it has been loaded into a register. EXT can be used to sign extend a byte to a word, or a word to a longword. EXTB can be used to extend a byte to a longword. Although these instructions have different assembler opcodes, they are actually variations of the same instruction.

The MULU and MULS instructions provide signed and unsigned multiplication. The result can be either single or double length. In the latter case, a typical assembler instruction is

```
MULS.L MEM, D3:D7
```

This instruction multiplies the contents of data register D7 by the contents of MEM. The high-order part of the double-length result is placed in D3, and the low-order part replaces D7. The 68030 instruction format is unusual in providing for a completely general specification of separate registers for the two halves of the product. Many processors use an adjacent register pair or, as on the 386, dedicated registers for the result. Compiler writers especially welcome the approach of the 68030, since it means that they do not have to complicate their register allocator to handle multiplications.

The 68030 approach obviously requires more space in the instruction (for the specification of the additional register), but CISC designers are not too concerned about adding special instruction formats for special purposes, so this is a minor concern. Note that the multiplication instructions do *not* support the address registers, so extra moves are required to multiply address values. Of course, in normal use one would not expect to need to multiply addresses, but still it would be preferable if all registers were treated identically for all operations.

The number of clocks required to execute a multiply is essentially the same as on the 386. Since the clock speeds of these machines are much the same, the speed with which multiplications can be done will be about the same.[4]

The DIVS and DIVU instructions similarly provide signed and unsigned division, again allowing for the possibility of single-length operands. This corresponds to what normally appears in high-level languages, where the dividend is both the same type and same length as the divisor. The double-length versions of the divide instructions allow separately specified registers for the two halves of the operand, as with multiplication.

Logical and Shift Instructions

The familiar basic logical operations (AND, OR, EOR and NOT) are provided. Just as in the case of multiply and divide, these work only with data registers, not address registers. As with ADD, memory-to-register, register-to-memory, and register-to-register forms are provided, but a memory-to-memory mode is not provided.

The 68030 has a complete set of shift and rotate instructions operating on byte, word, and longword quantities in data registers. Once again, we need to point out that they cannot be used on address registers. In fact, it is actually easier to say what *can* be done in address registers—basically only moves, adds, subtracts, and compares. All other operations require data registers.

A notable omission from the instruction set is any kind of double-shift instruction. As we noted in the discussion of the 386 double-shift instructions, this facility is particularly useful in doing the generalized bit moves required for manipulating bit-mapped graphic images and is also useful in dealing with unaligned bit fields. However, on the 68030, the bit field instructions are available for these purposes, which negates the need for a double shift to a considerable extent.

Bit Field Instructions

An interesting data type supported by the 68030 which does not exist on the 386 is the bit field. Suppose you need to extract a certain number of bits from a particular word in memory. The typical way of doing this is to load the required word and then use shift and mask instructions to position and isolate the field. To load bits 3 through 5

---

[4] The technology used in designing and fabricating the 386 and the 68030 chips is very similar. Differences in performance, to the extent they exist, are typically due to relative manufacturing skills or emphasis between the two companies.

of some memory location into EAX with zero extension, for example, the sequence
might be:

```
MOV    EAX, mem
SHR    EAX, 3
AND    EAX, 111B
```

How might these bit fields come up? One example occurs in Ada, which allows the
layout of a record to be specified with bit fields in words. Ada programmers can specify
the exact layout of a record down to the bit field level. Pascal gives a programmer a
similar, though less extensive, facility in the form of the packed declaration. In Pascal,
specifying that a structure be packed requests that the compiler compress the fields of
the record but does not give explicit control on a field by field basis. Data arranged in
bit fields often occurs in conjunction with specialized input/output devices which
deliver peculiarly packed data values from the outside world.

On the 68030, we can, of course, write a sequence of instructions similar to the
386 sequence, but there is also a complete set of specialized instructions for handling
unaligned bit fields of this type, including instructions for loading a signed or unsigned
bit field from a register or memory, storing a bit field, clearing a bit field, testing a bit
field, setting a bit field to all 1 or all 0 bits, and scanning for the first bit set.

Let us look at one of these instructions in a little more detail. The BFEXTU
instruction extracts a bit field and zero-extends it. This is the instruction that would be
used to replace the three-instruction sequence given above for the 386. The assembler
format is

```
BFEXTU <ea>{offset:width}, Dn
```

Here <ea> specifies the byte location of the bit field, which can be in a register or in
memory. The offset and width parameters specify the alignment and length of the bit
field and can either be immediate values or specified by data register values. The width
is in the range 1 through 32. If the offset is given as an immediate value, it is restricted
to the range 0 through 31, but if it is given in a register, it can have a full 32-bit value.
This allows a bit field to be addressed anywhere in a 256-megabyte address range by
its bit address, and importantly, the bit field can cross arbitrary byte and word
boundaries. The form of the instruction that duplicates the effect of the three instruction sequence on the 386 is:

```
BFEXTU mem{24:3}, D5
```

This is a rather typical CISC instruction that has a complicated form, but if you need
to extract arbitrary bit fields, it is, of course, exactly what you are looking for.

TIMING THE BFEXTU INSTRUCTION. Whenever you run into a complicated instruction like BFEXTU, it is worth figuring out how many clocks it takes to execute.
Computing the exact details of timing for an instruction is often tricky because of
considerations involving instruction fetch and overlap. In the case of the 386, the
timings given in the 386 Programmer's Reference Manual simply ignore instruction

fetch, which is a reasonable approximation most of the time. If you really want to know how fast an instruction runs on the Intel machines, you have to do the rather careful analysis of whether the instruction lookahead buffer is being emptied.

If the 386 executes a lot of long instructions which only require a few clocks to complete, all of the instructions in the instruction lookahead buffer may be used up. In that case, extra memory cycles will be required to fetch more instructions from memory. If, on the other hand, the processor is executing a long sequence of instructions that take a long time to execute (such as multiplications or divisions), then there is plenty of time to fill up the buffer—during the many clocks that it takes to execute these instructions, additional instructions can be prefetched. However, the 386 Programmer's Reference Manual simply does not give sufficient detailed information to accurately compute these execution times. Instead it recommends that you try it out and measure the time with a stopwatch!

The 68030 User's Manual, on the other hand, gives precise timing information about each instruction. The whole of chapter 11 of the manual is devoted to an absolutely complete and accurate description of instruction timing. It includes rather forbidding formulas like the following one used to compute the execution time for a fairly simple five-instruction sequence:

$$Execution\, Time = \begin{aligned} &CCea_1 + [CCop_1 - \min(Hop_1,\, Tea_1)] + [CCea_2 - \min(Hea_2,\, Top_1)] + \\ &[CCop_2 - \min(Hop_2,\, Tea_2)] + [CCea_3 - \min(Hea_3,\, Top_2)] + \\ &[CCop_3 - \min(Hop_3,\, Tea_3)] + [CCea_4 - \min(Hop_4,\, Top_3)] + \\ &[CCop_4 - \min(Hop_4,\, Top_3)] + [CCop_5 - \min(Hop_5,\, Top_4)] \end{aligned}$$

We do not intend to explain exactly how equations such as these are constructed—that would take far too many pages. However, we should at least note that this equation takes into account whether an instruction is found in the instruction cache or not, the cost of computing the effective address, and the time that can be saved due to instruction overlap—the minimum functions in the formula above have to do with computing the overlap between successive instructions, which is the minimum of the *tail* time for the first instruction and the *head* time for the second instruction.

Reading the timing information in this chapter of the 68030 User's Manual carefully, we can determine that the range of possible timings for BFEXTU is 21 to 22 clocks. On the 386, we have no amazing bit field extract instruction, but the sequence of three instructions that replaces it takes only 9 clocks. The BFEXTU does save space (it is only 4 bytes long, compared to the 8 bytes required for the 386 sequence), but it is not at all clear that it saves time. Even the corresponding spelled-out 68030 sequence:

```
MOV     mem, D3      ; load memory word to D reg
LSR     #5, D3       ; right position field
AND     #7, D3       ; isolate 3-bit field
```

only takes 18 to 19 clocks, so even on the 68030 itself the use of the bit field extraction instructions doesn't necessarily improve the execution speed.

An interesting question is raised by the contrast of the 18-clock 68030 three-instruction sequence vs the 9-clock 386 sequence. The 68030 definitely has a fancier instruction set than the 386 in some respects, but it seems to be basically slower for common instructions. Are these two factors related? It is entirely possible that they are. This consideration, taken to extremes, is the cornerstone of the RISC versus CISC controversy. If complex instructions are costing too much, we are not sure we want them!

Why can't the microcode be written so that the number of clocks taken up by the two different sequences of code (the BFEXTU on the one hand, and the equivalent three instruction sequence) be the same? A possible explanation is that when a machine is designed, all sorts of wonderful instructions are specified. Then the engineers find that there is no way to fit all of those wonderful intructions on the chip *and* implement them efficiently. But they may say, "Don't worry. We'll get the BFEXTU instruction on. It may not be as fast as we would like, but we'll fit it somehow. " Nowhere is it in the specifications that if you can't make BFEXTU work at least as fast as the corresponding instruction sequence, you should not even attempt to put it in.

A very good example of this phenomenon in action occurred on the IBM 360/40 which had an instruction to halve a floating point register (HER). It is supposed to be super quick, because it is supposed to simply subtract one from the exponent. It is *not* supposed to do a floating point divide. On the original 360/40 it *was* a quick instruction. However, IBM had an embarrassing experience on this machine. It originally did not implement any guard digits at all in the floating point processing. The resulting (in)accuracy was intolerable, and IBM was persuaded to upgrade the microcode in the field to include a guard digit. The IBM man arrived with the new microprogram for the 360/40 on a set of cards and plugged it in. Lo and behold, the desired guard digits appeared, but the HER now took *longer* than a division. Probably what happened was that they got desperately short of space in the microcode and to save space they removed the specialized code for HER and replaced it with a floating point divide—the whole point of providing HER had been lost!

Program Control Instructions

The branch instructions on the 68030 are generally similar to those on the 386. In particular, they always use *program counter* (PC relative) relative addressing. Two forms are available, as on the 386, one with an 8-bit displacement for the common case of conditional jumps to a location close by and one with a 32-bit displacement allowing full addressing of memory. The unconditional jump also has a general indirect form, allowing the use of jump tables and indirect links. A special conditional branch instruction, DBRA, functions just like the LOOP instruction for control of count loops, although it does not use a dedicated register—any of the data registers can be used to control a loop using DBRA.

As on the 386, it is also possible store the result of a comparison as a Boolean value using the Set According to Condition (Scc) instructions. For example, SEQ sets true on equal. One interesting little glitch in these instructions is that FALSE is all 0 bits, and TRUE is all 1 bits (255 in decimal). This can cause a compiler writer some annoyance when implementing a compiler for a language such as C or Ada, where the use of 0 as false and 1 as true is more natural.

The Branch to Subroutine (BSR) instruction functions exactly like the CALL instruction on the 386. It stores the return point on the stack (the stack builds in the same direction as the 386, that is, down in memory), and jumps to the subroutine entry point. Procedures on the 68030 are expected to be organized using frames as on the 386, with one of the address registers used as a frame pointer. The instruction LINK takes the following actions:

```
LINK     An,#
...
Sp := Sp - 4;                    ; push stack pointer
(Sp) := An;                      ; store old frame pointer on stack
An := Sp;                        ; set new frame pointer
Sp := Sp + disp;                 ; allocate stack frame (disp typically is negative)
```

The UNLINK instruction is executed after a procedure returns control to its caller and has the following effect:

```
UNLINK An
...
SP := An;                        ; strip stack frame
An := (SP)                       ; restore old frame pointer
SP := SP + 4;                    ; pop stack pointer
```

These operations are essentially identical to the ENTER and LEAVE instructions of the 386, except that there is no provision for copying local displays. However, since we concluded that this feature was misguided and incorrectly designed on the 386, we certainly don't miss it on the 68030.

The actual return from a subroutine is achieved by using the RTS instruction (identical to RET with no operand on the 386), or Return and Deallocate (RTD) which allows the stack pointer to be adjusted after the return. This is used for stripping parameters that were pushed on the stack, and is identical to the 386 RET instruction with an operand specified.

Since the arrangement and planned use of the subroutine call instructions are almost identical to those provided on the 386, we don't need to repeat our discussion of stack organization in detail. One small difference is that the 68030 instructions leave the selection of the frame pointer to the programmer, in contrast to the 386, which specifies the use of EBP. This could be used to support the use of different frame pointers for different nesting levels of procedures, but in practice the use of A6 for this purpose is firmly established, and so the difference is not that significant.

Decimal Instructions

Like the 386, the 68030 provides a specialized set of instructions to assist in handling packed decimal operands. As discussed in Chapter 1, each decimal digit of an integer is represented using 4 bits. The instructions provided by the 68030 to support this data type, however, are somewhat different from those on the 386. The 68030 includes instructions for adding, subtracting, and negating packed decimal operands 1 byte at a time (ABCD, SBCD, and NBCD). These instructions are similar to the effect of a normal add or subtract on the 386 followed by the appropriate decimal adjust instruction. There are, however, no instructions to assist in the handling of packed decimal multiplication or division.

There are also no instructions for directly handling unpacked decimal integers (for example, COBOL display data items). Instead, there are specialized instructions for packing and unpacking decimal items. Let us look at one of these in detail. The unpack instruction has the format

    UNPK   Dx, Dy, #const

It sets the last 16 bits of Dy to the value of the constant (whatever it is) plus the pattern that you get by concatenating four zeros with 4 bits from the Dx register with another four zeros and 4 more bits from Dx:

    +0000 || Dx(7..4) || 0000 || Dx(3..0)

If you know the intention behind this instruction, you will immediately recognize what it is meant for—if you *don't* recognize the intention, then it is mysterious. The intended use is that the input data for UNPK is a packed decimal byte composed of two 4-bit fields. When you unpack this byte, you want to add X'30' zones in ASCII or X'F0' zones in EBCDIC. So the constant that you use here will most frequently be X'3030' for the ASCII case. If the input is X'39', then UNPK will generate X'3339', which is the ASCII character 3 followed by the ASCII character 9, which is the proper unpacked result.

As always in the case of fancy instructions, we should check up on the timing, and we discover that UNPK with a register source operand takes 6 to 8 clocks. Let's look at the somewhat complicated sequence of instructions required on the 386 for the same unpacking function:

```
MOV     AL, BL
MOV     AH, AL
SHL     AH, 4
AND     EAX, 0F0FH
OR      EAX, 3030H
```

This takes 10 clocks, so the 68030 really is ahead with the UNPK instruction. The advantage is even more pronounced when we use the special memory-to-memory form of UNPK, which takes only 11 clocks. The comparable sequence on the 386 using LODSB and STOSB would take 17 clocks.

Code which spends much of its time doing nothing but furiously unpacking packed decimal numbers will find this instruction on the 68030 to be very useful. However, you have to wonder whether there *are* any applications that really do spend a significant amount of time on this specific function—significant enough to warrant a special instruction—and once again the answer to this kind of question lies at the core of the RISC vs CISC debate.

The CAS2 (Compare and Double Exchange) Instruction

Our summary of the instruction set is reasonably complete, but it omits a number of peculiar special-purpose instructions. We won't try to list all of these, but as an example let's look at the Compare and Double Exchange (CAS2), a perfect example of CISC philosophy in the 68030 design. CAS2 has the following format with six (!) operands:

```
CAS2    Dc1:Dc2, Du1:Du2, (Rn1):(Rn2)
```

All of the operands are required to be registers. The first four must be data registers and the last two can be either data or address registers. The meaning of this instruction is

```
if Dc1 = (Rn1) and Dc2 = (Rn2) then
    (Rn1) := Du1
    (Rn2) := Du2
else
    Dc1 := (Rn1)
    Dc2 := (Rn2)
end if;
```

Even though we have a precise description of the steps for the CAS2 instruction, it is not easy to understand from this description why CAS2 is included in the instruction set. A note in the 68030 User's Manual saying that the operation is indivisible gives a hint as to what it is used for. The question of indivisibility arises when an instruction has more than one memory reference and more than one processor can sit on the same bus. If we have two 68030s connected to the same bus, then the question to ask is whether one of the processors can go in and access memory *between* the two references of a single instruction on the other processor. If the answer is yes, then the two references may be inconsistent even though they occur within a single instruction.

This means that instructions like CAS2 have very different semantics and uses depending on the answer to the indivisibility question. If CAS2 could be interrupted by another processor referencing the bus, then in this multiprocessor environment it would have the same function as a sequence of instructions implementing the operations described above. However, given its guarantee of indivisibility, it has an important function that could not easily be duplicated by a sequence of instructions (which certainly *could* be interrupted by a reference from another processor).

The CAS2 instruction checks to see if the two comparison operands are identical, and if they are it does two corresponding assignments with the assurance that the results of the comparison are still valid. The two assignments are thus protected. The primary intended use of CAS2 occurs in dealing with a data structure where a doubly linked list is used to represent a queue, and in general, there are three kinds of things you want to do with such a list: put something on the front of the list, take something off the end, and delete an item from the middle of the list.

A typical example of this might be a queue of tasks on an Ada entry point. Normally it is just a queue where things are taken off. But occasionally, when a task is aborted, it is necessary to remove the task from the middle of the list (which is why it is doubly linked). Another use of this instruction might be for a storage allocator in which there is a doubly linked free list. Occasionally, blocks will have to be combined, in which case it will be necessary to rip something out of the middle of the queue.

The doubly linked list is a common data structure, which is usually quite simple to implement in a one processor system. In the case of a multiprocessor system, where several processors may be manipulating a common queue, or even in a system with multiple tasks that can share a single queue, it suddenly becomes difficult to guarantee that a single logical operation on the queue is free of race conditions. This might be caused by task switching or by different processors accessing the queue at crucial points.

In the absence of specialized instructions, the single-processor task switching case can be handled by locking out task switching for the duration of the operation, by either hardware or software. The operation that locks out hardware interrupts is typically a protected instruction, so it is not one that a user can issue. If this were user-level code, then a software flag would have to be used to inhibit task switching.

In either case, the approach of inhibiting task switching does not work if you have two processors on the same bus. Then you have to have a more complex protection mechanism that involves interprocessor communication. For example, some kind of semaphore lockout mechanism using shared memory could be used to create a critical section.

Instructions that guarantee indivisible access to memory avoid these problems, and in particular CAS2 is designed to allow indivisible operations on a doubly linked list. Figuring out the details of how to program these operations is not so simple. There is a very nice section in the Motorola 68030 User's Manual (Section 3.4), called "Using the CAS and CAS2 Instructions," that has actual examples (CAS is a simpler version which does only one protected comparison and assignment, and is therefore appropriate for manipulating singly linked lists.)

Let's look at one of the code examples. We have simplified it by not considering what happens in the case where the list is empty or contains only one element—we assume that there are at least two elements in the list as shown in the Figure 6.2. In this diagram, LIST_PUT points to the head of the doubly linked queue, and LIST_GET points to the its tail. Our task is to add a new element, currently pointed to by A2, at the front of the queue, adjusting LIST_PUT appropriately. Moreover, we require that the sequence of code be immune to simultaneous access to the queue from other processors. The required code, using CAS2 is:

```
        LEA     LIST_PUT, A0
        MOVE.L  A2, D2
        MOVE.L  (A0), D0
DLP:    MOVE.L  D0, (NEXT, A2)
        CLR.L   D1
        MOVE.L  D1, (PREV, A2)
        LEA     (PREV, D0), A1
        CAS2    D0:D1, D2:D2, (A0):(A1)
        BNE     DLP
```

The first instruction (load effective address) makes A0 point to LIST_PUT. Next we copy the pointer to the new block to D2 and set D0 to point to the current head of the queue.

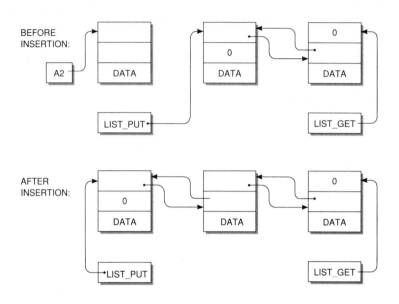

FIGURE 6.2
Adding an element to a doubly linked list using CAS2.

The loop DLP is only executed more than once if our first attempt to insert the element fails (this failure could only be caused by an unlucky simultaneous access by another task or processor). The first three instructions in this loop makes the new block point to the old head, and clears the back pointer of the new block. Finally the second LEA instruction points A1 to the previous pointer in the old first block.

We are now ready to commit to the final operations which actually modify the state of the list, namely to point LIST_PUT to the new head of the list, and to reset the back pointer of the old head block to point to the newly inserted block. However, it may be the case that the contents of LIST_PUT have been modified since we started out. Let's look at what the CAS2 instruction does:

```
if D0 = (A0) and D1 = (A1) then
    (A0) ← D2;
    (A1) ← D2;
else
    D0 ← (A0);
    D1 ← (A1);
end if;
```

The comparison is checking to make sure that LIST_PUT still points to the same head block, and that the back pointer of this head block is still zero. If so, all is well and the assignments in this section make LIST_PUT point to the new head block, and the old head block's previous pointer is set to point to this new head block.

If the CAS2 comparison fails, it means that someone else has snuck in and inserted a new block. But no matter—we have not yet done anything we regret! In this case, the statements in the else part of the CAS2 operation reset D0 to point to the new head block and we loop back to try again.

This description of CAS2 is pretty complicated, it sounds more as though we are describing a complete program than a single instruction. In a sense we *are* describing a program. CAS2 is undoubtedly implemented using internal microcode in the 68030 chip, so when the program issues a CAS2 instruction, it causes this microcoded program to be executed.

CAS2 only takes 24 clocks, so it is reasonably efficient. Certainly it is *much* faster than calling the operating system if this is the alternative to having hardware assistance of this kind. On the other hand, a relatively simple test-and-set lock would allow a program to construct a sequence equivalent to CAS2. Is it really worthwhile to implement such a complex instruction? Once again, we are touching on the kind of issue that is at the core of the RISC vs. CISC debate. CAS2 is a beautiful instruction if you need to deal with doubly linked lists avoiding race conditions, but how many programs really spend enough time doing this specific operation to justify the inclusion of such an elaborate instruction?

THE 68030 ADDRESSING MODES

One important characteristic of the Motorola series that distinguishes it from most other microprocessors is the large number of very flexible addressing modes. The 68030 User's Manual describes a total of 18 addressing modes, which are shown in Table 6.1.

Looking at a simple and very basic instruction such as MOVE, you will see that the assembler syntax is given as

```
MOVE   <ea>, <ea>
```

The symbol *<ea>* is used in the 68030 User's Manual as a general specification for an *effective address.* The effective address is implemented as part of the instruction formats as a sequence of 6 bits that is contained in many, but not all, of the instructions. The low-order 3 bits are used to specify a register, while the high-order 3 bits are used to specify a mode. Since some of the addressing modes are rather complex and may require more than a single register, one or more words called effective address extensions may follow the instruction word in which the effective address is specified.

The instruction MOVEA is a special variant of the MOVE instruction where the destination must be an address register[5]:

```
MOVEA <ea>, An
```

The description of this instruction is an example of a convention used in the 68030 User's Manual. An is used to specify any of the address registers, Dn is used to specify

---

[5] It is actually nothing but a MOVE instruction specifying address register addressing for the destination, but it is customary to make the distinction in the opcode.

TABLE 6.1
The 68030 Addressing Modes.

Addressing Mode	Syntax
Data Register Direct	Dn
Address Register Direct	An
Address Register Indirect	(An)
Address Register Indirect with Postincrement	(An)+
Address Register Indirect with Predecrement	- (An)
Address Register Indirect with Displacement	(d16, An)
Address Register Indirect with Index (8-bit Displacement)	(d8, An, Xn)
Address Register Indirect with Index (Base Displacement)	(bd, An, Xn)
Memory Indirect Post-indexed	([bd,An], Xn, od)
Memory Indirect Pre-indexed	([bd,An, Xn], od)
Program Counter Indirect with Displacement	(d16, PC)
PC Indirect with Index (8-bit Displacement)	(d8, PC, Xn)
PC Indirect with Index (Base Displacement)	(bd, PC, Xn)
PC Memory Indirect Post-indexed	([bd,PC], Xn, od)
PC Memory Indirect Pre-indexed	([bd,PC, Xn], od)
Absolute Short	(xxx).W
Absolute Long	(xxx).L
Immediate	# (data)

any of the data registers, and Xn is used to specify any of the 16 address or data registers. Some instructions can manipulate only address or data registers, while others can manipulate both. As we briefly mentioned in the discussion on register set uniformity, it would not be right to say that *any* of the addressing modes can be used since there are some exceptions.

Addressing Modes and Instruction Sizes

It is important to point out that there is a penalty to be paid for this generality in addressing modes. The PUSH EBX instruction on the 386 (for EBX and the other standard registers) is only 1 byte long. The corresponding instruction on the 68030 is 2 bytes long, because it needs the full addressing mode information as well as the register information.

The minimum instruction size on the 68030 is 2 bytes. Many instructions are longer than 2 bytes, because many of the addressing modes add 2-byte *extensions*. The longest instruction using the most complicated addressing modes can use 10 of these extensions, giving an instruction length of 22 bytes in all.

The 386 instructions are aligned on byte boundaries. There are, for example, many instructions that are 3 bytes in length. A very common instruction on the 386 loads a register with a local variable in a procedure's stack frame with a short offset, within 128 bytes of the stack frame pointer. Instructions of this type are typically 3 bytes long on the 68030. It is impossible to fit this into 2 bytes because the offset takes at least a whole byte. Instructions like this take 4 bytes on the 68000.

Why design an instruction format in this way? The design of an instruction format always involves a trade-off between more registers with more generality in terms of their use in addressing modes and the number of bits in an instruction. The 68030 has both more registers and more addressing modes than the 386, but as a consequence it also has instructions that are typically longer than those on the 386.

The other side of the coin here is that the 68030 instruction format allows for a potential gain in efficiency resulting from the simplification of the circuitry made possible by knowing that all instructions will lie on a halfword boundary. Looking at the Motorola 68000, the original member of this series, we see that the restriction that instructions be aligned on 16-bit boundaries is the due to the need to make sure that an instruction cannot be split across two hardware words. This means, for instance, that when an instruction halfword is gathered by the processor, the processor does not have to worry about getting two page faults, one for each half of the instruction. On the other hand, a single instruction composed of many instruction halfwords *can* cause multiple page faults or cache misses.

We will now describe some of the addressing modes of the 68030. The set of available addressing modes on the 68030 is more extensive than that of the 386. The 386, on the other hand, has a larger instruction set. You should be careful to avoid the conclusion that there is less that one can do with the smaller instruction set of the 68030; as we shall see, for each instruction that does exist on the 68030, there are many variations due to the flexible addressing modes.

Simple Data Movement

The MOVE instruction can be used with various addressing modes to move data from one place to another. To move some data from memory into a register, for example, we simply put the address of the data into an address register and issue the MOVE instruction

```
MOVE   (An), Dn
```

The addressing mode associated with the first operand is known in Motorola's jargon as *address register indirect*. In addition to being able to load into a register from memory, we need to be able to copy the value of one register to another.

It is also possible to directly address memory using *Absolute Long Address Mode*. This mode allows a full 32-bit address anywhere in the memory space to be specified. Typically this will simply be a variable name in assembly language:

```
MOVE   X, Dn
```

In both these examples, the right operand, Dn, uses uses what is called *register direct* mode, which simply means that we are directly referencing the contents of the register as the data. We can use this mode for both operands of the MOVE to get register-to-register moves:

```
MOVE        Dn, Dn
MOVE        Dn, An
MOVE        An, Dn
MOVE        An, An
```

Another basic addressing mode is the *immediate data* addressing mode. This addressing mode is used when an operand is some literal value. The following MOVE instruction uses this mode to store the constant value 1000 in the variable X:

```
MOVE        #1000, X
```

Postincrement and Predecrement Modes

Two very useful addressing modes that are available on the 68030 but not on the 386 are the *postincrement* and *predecrement* modes. The assembler syntax to move a value into a data register using postincrement mode is

```
MOVE.L      (An)+, Dn
```

while the syntax for moving a value into a data register using predecrement mode is

```
MOVE.L      –(An), Dn
```

The effect of postincrement mode is to retrieve the value in memory that An is pointing to and then increment An by the appropriate amount *after* the access. Predecrement mode decrements the value in An *before* accessing the value, again by an appropriate amount. What is the appropriate amount? It depends on the value that was just dereferenced. In the examples above, the .L on the opcode indicates that 4 bytes are moved, so the appropriate amount is 4. The exact number of bytes by which the address register is incremented is in general determined by the length of the data accessed.

These two addressing modes can be put to many specialized uses corresponding to common programming idioms. One simple assembly language idiom for scanning through a list of items can be written as:

```
MOVEA       (A3)+, A4
```

There is no need to explicitly increment A3. In this code, A3 is being used to point to a sequence of values, which are being successively loaded into A4.

These addressing modes may seem unfamiliar to a Pascal programmer, but they are quite familiar to a C programmer. In C, they appear as:

```
*p++;
```

and

```
* – –p;
```

These are constructs built into C that are clearly inspired by the PDP-11, the machine on which the first C compiler was built. The PDP-11 had a set of predecrement and postincrement addressing modes similar to those on the 68030. As C was being designed, it seemed natural to incorporate these useful hardware addressing modes into the language. For completeness, C adds the other two possibilities, *preincrement* and *postdecrement*, although they are not supported by the hardware. One consequence is that it is quite comfortable to write a C compiler for a machine with these addressing modes, since they map so directly into the hardware.

The fact that only the postincrement and predecrement modes are supported in the hardware has led to an informal convention that these two modes are the ones that should be used when programming in C.[6] This style of C programming in which postincrement and predecrement are preferred comes precisely from an assumption that these specific language features will be mapped directly onto the hardware.

IMPLEMENTING A STACK. Why is it so important to provide an increment that is executed *before* a fetch and a decrement that is executed *after* a fetch? If you consider the way in which stacks are manipulated then it becomes very clear why this asymmetry is desirable.

Since there is no explicit PUSH instruction on the 68000, we need some way of doing a push without it. With the aid of the postdecrement addressing mode it is easy to construct the equivalent of a PUSH instruction. If you want to push the contents of register D3 onto the stack, you would write

```
MOVE   D3, -(A7)
```

assuming that the stack is building down. The A7 register, which we have previously mentioned is actually the main user stack pointer, is decremented to make space for the new data to be stacked, and then the contents of D3 are copied to this location. To pop something off the stack we would write the instruction

```
MOVE   (A7)+, D3
```

Here the stack pointer A7 is pointing to the top element of the stack, so the data is copied from the top of the stack into D0, after which it is incremented, thus removing the data just copied from the top of the stack. If you wanted your stack to grow up instead of down, then these two instructions could be reversed. These two addressing modes go together very nicely for implementing stacks.

CONTROLLING LOOPS. As we noted previously, one standard use of these addressing modes is to control loops that manipulate large arrays by marching through their elements. Usually, we use the postincrement mode, since arrays are stored in increasing memory addresses, and we process the elements from lower subscripts toward higher subscripts. One particular case of arrays that are accessed in this

---

[6] C programmers may not know the details of assembly language, but their code is often affected by the specific machine language instructions available. This C style, acquired from copying other C programmers' style, subsequently affects hardware design. The result is that we can expect machines to copy the original PDP-11 conventions for postincrement and predecrement for ever!

manner is strings of characters. Consider the problem of copying a string from one location to another:

```
        MOVE     count, D7
        LEA      A, A0
        LEA      B, A1
L5:
        MOVE.B   (A0)+, D0
        MOVE.B   D0, (A1)+
        DBRA     D7, L5
```

This code uses A0 to hold the address of A, the string being copied, and A1 to hold the address of B, the new string being created. The use of the postincrement addressing mode here is particularly idiomatic of a machine like the 68030 that has such addressing modes.

Suppose, on the other hand, that the string was being moved to a higher location in memory and that the source and destination areas overlapped. In this case you would want to move the string backwards because otherwise the end of the string would get destroyed before the move was complete. In this case, we would run the loop backwards. Many programmers run loops backwards even when the choice is not forced, because they suspect, quite correctly on many machines, that it is more efficient to test for zero, than to test a counter for reaching some non-zero value. To run a loop backwards through an array, we use predecrement addressing:

```
        MOVE     count, D7
        LEA      A, A0
        LEA      B, A1
        ADD      D7, A0
        ADD      D7, A1
L5:
        MOVE.B   -(A0), D0
        MOVE.B   D0, -(A1)
        DBRA     D7, L5
```

It is interesting to contrast this approach with that of the 386, which does not have increment and decrement addressing modes, but which *does* have specialized instructions for string operations that can be applied to strings of 8-bit, 16-bit, or 32-bit operands. On the 386, these instructions provide for a form of automatic increment and decrement addressing using the DF flag to control the direction.

There is one very significant difference in the way the automatic increments and decrements are done. The 68030 has a postincrement and a predecrement mode, while the LODSx and STOSx instructions on the 386 do both the increment or decrement only *after* the load or store, that is they are postincrement and postdecrement forms. This is a big mistake! How does this mistake show up? Suppose you process a string from left to right that has a mixture of 1-byte and 4-byte data items. If ESI starts by pointing to the first character in the string, then moving left to right in the string works perfectly fine—you can mix LODSB and LODSD instructions in any sequence to handle data mixed in the corresponding order.

Now what about the reverse direction? It doesn't work! You start off with ESI pointing to the last character and set the direction flag backwards so that the address is decremented as LODS instructions are executed. An initial LODSB works fine to load the last character, but it leaves ESI pointing to the second from last character, which is not correct for doing a subsequent LODSD. If the backwards direction had been a predecrement, then ESI would be set to initially point *past* the end of the string and everything would go fine in the reverse direction.

As you can imagine, there are a lot of other applications of the postincrement and predecrement addressing modes in loops—it's quite a challenge for a compiler to use these effectively. It's not so much of a challenge for a C compiler to use these addressing modes, however, provided that you are content to use them only when the programmer explicitly uses the + + or − − notations.

INSTRUCTIONS VS ADDRESSING MODES. Turning through the pages of the 68030 User's Manual there seem to be fewer instructions than on the Intel series. As we have mentioned previously, this does not tell the whole story—stack manipulation provides a good example. Instructions such as PUSH and POP that appear on the Intel series are equivalent to a MOVE on the 68030, which includes the use of the postincrement and predecrement modes. But on the 68030, pushing and popping are embedded much more generally than on the 386.

On the 386, the advertisers can claim to have three instructions (MOV, PUSH and POP) to the 68030's single MOVE. However, from a functional point of view, the 68030 is actually *more* flexible than the 386. On the 386,

```
PUSH   EAX
```

works very nicely to push EAX onto the stack location specified by ESP, but that is the *only* stack for which it works. To push something onto another stack on the 386, an entirely different mechanism is needed to do your own increments and decrements. On the 68030, several different stacks can be manipulated at the same time, using a common, efficient approach.

The Register Indirect With Displacement Mode

An addressing mode which allows based addressing (as described in Chapter 1) with a 16-bit offset is what Motorola calls *Address Register Indirect with Displacement.* Typical assembler syntax is:

(d_{16}, An)

where d_{16} is a 16-bit signed offset from the single base register An. Notice that data registers cannot be used as base registers with this form of addressing mode.

One intended use of this addressing mode is to allow a compiler to generate code to access the local variables of a procedure in the stack frame, using the address (−bd, A6) (remember our discussion of based addressing in Chapter 1). The address register A6 serves as the frame pointer by convention. The displacement is then the offset of the variable measured in bytes from A6. On the 386, we would compute the same address as [EBP − bd].

This addressing mode is an example of a slightly odd 16-bit quality that one senses in the 68030. It is, of course, reasonable to provide 16-bit offsets, since this may save a few bytes on the length of an instruction (although a negative consequence is the fact that the size of a stack frame will usually be restricted to 64K bytes). Nevertheless, in general the 68030 contains more reminders of its 16-bit ancestor, the 68000, than might be expected. This is an understandable historical constraint, since it was an important requirement that the 68030 be binary compatible with the 68000. The 386 exhibited several similar 16-bit constraints as well.

It turns out that the short indexing addressing mode is redundant because there are other ways of getting that effect (as a special case of more complex addressing modes). The entire presence of this particular addressing mode is historical, and the more extensive mode *does* permit full 32-bit indexing.

The Register Indirect with Index Modes

The *address register indirect with index* mode provides a combination of based and indexed access and comes in two varieties, a more general format which allows for a 32-bit base displacement *bd*, and a short form allowing only an 8-bit displacement d_8:

```
(bd, An, Xn * scale)
(d8, An, Xn * scale)
```

This mode is very much like the general addressing format of the 386. On the 386, the same idea is expressed in assembler as, for example,

```
[EBP − 1024 + EBX*scale]
```

In the 68030 addressing mode, the base register (An) can only be an address register (this is another example, like An++, where A and D registers are *not* interchangeable). The index register can be a data register or an address register. There is a scale here; just as in the 386, the scale can be 1, 2, 4, or 8. The intention is exactly the same. If you have an array, it saves you from having to generate code to multiply the array index by the stride of the array.

One standard use of this addressing mode is in addressing array elements when the array is sitting in a stack frame. Figure 6.3 shows the a single stack frame with an array A. There is a stack frame, and an address register that points to it (the stack usually grows down). The address register thus serves the function of EBP on the 386.

If you have an array of five elements and you want to address C(J), then *bd* would be the offset to the start of the array C from the stack frame, An would be the stack

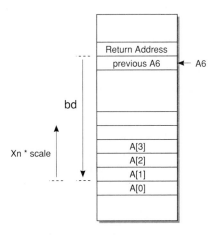

FIGURE 6.3
Addressing an array in a stack frame using one of the register indirect modes.

frame pointer, Xn would be the value of J, and the scale would be appropriate to the element size of the array.

Any one of the components of this addressing mode can be left unused. There is a bit indicating whether the component is active or not, so, for example, the field indicating the address register is 4 bits instead of the expected 3 bits, with 1 bit used to indicate whether an An component is present. Consequently, we have some more addressing modes that are simply special variations of the general scaled indexing mode:

(An, Xn * scale)
(Xn * scale)
(Xn)
(bd, Xn * scale)

The third form, in which only the index register is present and the scale is 1 is particularly important, since it allows simple indexing by a data register and also based addressing using a data register (with a scale of 1) whereas other similar modes require an address register.

SELECTING OFFSET LENGTHS. The offset in the general indexing mode can be either an 8-bit, 16-bit, or 32-bit displacement. That is a nice flexibility because the 16-bit displacement is missing from the 386, or at least it is not present in a very convenient form. It is often the case that a 16-bit displacement is enough.

One of the aggravating aspects of having multiple sizes for displacements is that there are many times when you are compiling for a high-level language and not enough information is available to select the most advantageous offset *at compile time*.

Suppose you are writing a C compiler. You may well want to gather the static data into one big chunk. That means that when several large files are compiled, the static data will be gathered into one contiguous area, and a register will point to that area. One of the reasons that this is desirable is that the value contained in this register will not need to be modified on a procedure call.

Whenever a procedure references static data, the compiler will have to decide whether to generate code that uses an 8-bit, a 16-bit or a 32-bit displacement. But whether a 16-bit displacement would do depends upon whether the *whole* program has less than 64K of static data. Now that is quite likely, since most C programs do have less than 64K of static data. But you don't know that when you are compiling separate files containing separate compilation units.

If you want the best possible code in a situation like this, it would be best not to generate any code until link time—but then linking would take forever. There is a difficult compromise to be made here.

C compilers for the 68030 typically either have an option that lets a compiler know that there is less than 64K of static data or just assume that this is the case. The compiler can then get away with using only 64K offsets. If this is something that is not known at compile time, the compiler would be forced to use 4-byte offsets everywhere. This might even make it worth having a separate area for each file to keep instructions shorter at the expense of saving and setting the register on each procedure call.

The Memory Indirect Addressing Modes

The 68030 provides addressing modes not available on the 386 that involve indirect addressing of memory. This means that a word in memory is located which contains the address to be used in completing the calculation of the final operand address, so that an extra memory reference is required. There are two of these modes on the 68030.

MEMORY INDIRECT POSTINDEXED ADDRESSING. The first of these addressing modes is called *memory indirect postindexed* mode, and it has the assembler syntax

([bd, An], Xn∗scale, od)

When an address is formed using this addressing mode, a displacement *bd* is added to an address register An, giving an address that points to some word in memory. Once the contents of that word have been loaded into some internal register, the value Xn times *scale* is added to that register. Finally, the outer displacement is added to form the final address.

Even though it is easy to write down the formula that describes how that address is computed, it is not so easy to see what it is used for. Like so many of the curious instructions on CISC machines, you often wonder what an instruction (or an addressing mode) is for. In this case, there is at least one very clear use for this addressing mode that makes it easier for a compiler to generate code for a high-level language.

Suppose we have written in Pascal a procedure Q that takes as a parameter an array C of 4-byte integers with bounds of 2 through 4, and this array is passed by reference, that is the actual value passed is the address of the first element of the array. Let's further suppose that procedure P calls procedure Q and that the array passed to Q is local to P, so that it resides in the stack frame of P.

Figure 6.4 shows the state of the run-time stack as procedure Q is executing. The stack frame for Q is shown with A6 being used as the frame pointer. In the stack frame for Q at a positive offset of 8 bytes from A6 is a pointer to the array that was passed by reference. The parameter appears at a positive offset because parameters are generally pushed onto the stack just before a procedure is called (in this case the parameter C is pushed by P just before Q is called).

Now let us consider the code that is required for accessing an element, say C(J+3) from this array. Two instructions are required. The first loads the value of J into A3, and then the second uses memory indirect postindexed addressing mode to access the required element in a single instruction:

```
MOV.L   J,A3
MOV     ([8, A2], A3*4, (3*4)-(2*4)), D4
```

The [8, A2] obtains the address of the array (this is the indirect step). This address is then added to two other components, first the value of J*4 (the 4 is because this is an array of integers), which appears as A3*4 in the instruction, and second, the outer displacement. The outer displacement has two components, the 3*4 comes from the +3 in the subscript, and the −2*4 comes from the lower bound of 2. Extracting out constants from subscripting expressions in this manner is a standard compiler optimization that is very helpful in improving the code for array addressing.

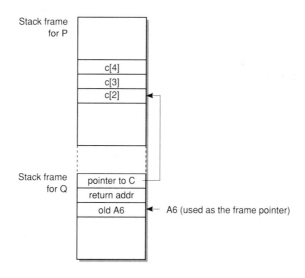

FIGURE 6.4
The use of memory indirect postindexed mode in accessing a passed by reference array.

MEMORY INDIRECT PREINDEXED ADDRESSING. Now let's look at the memory indirect preindexed addressing mode, which works in the opposite order to the indirect postindexed mode. In the memory indirect preindexed mode the indexing is applied *before* you pick up the word that is indirect. It is harder to see an immediate and obvious application for this addressing mode. The syntax is

([bd, An, Xn.SIZE * SCALE], od)

This addressing mode directs the processor to add the base displacement *bd* to the value in the address register An, and then add to this result the scaled index in register Xn to form an address. The dereferenced value of this memory address then has the outer displacement *od* added to yield the effective address.

One possible use for this addressing mode is to address a field within a record which is pointed to by one element of an array of pointers located within a stack frame. If you use this addressing mode in this way, An would function as the frame pointer, *bd* would be the offset of the array within the stack frame, and Xn would contain the scaled index into the array of pointers. Once the pointer was dereferenced, *od* is the offset of the field whose value is being accessed.

Our description of this addressing mode might make you wonder whether its inclusion into the 68030 is really useful. As we have described, it is possible to come up with reasonable examples where these addressing modes might be used, but it is an entirely different question as to whether they can be taken advantage of frequently enough, or whether a compiler will be able to take advantage of them. It is a reasonable guess to assume that this addressing mode was included simply because it was easy to implement once the other (more important) addressing modes were implemented.

TIMING THE ADDRESSING MODES. If one of the complicated addressing modes, such as memory indirect postindexed, is just what you need, then its use is certainly very neat. The cost is that you end up with a rather long instruction (8 bytes for the example we worked out in detail for accessing C(J+3)). On the 386 we don't have this sort of addressing mode, so for example, the array reference example that we worked out in the previous section requires three instructions to do the same thing:

```
MOV     EBX, J
MOV     EAX, [EBP+8]
MOV     EAX, [EAX + EBX*4 – (3*4)–(2*4)]
```

You have an extra instruction, which reflect the fact that the 386 does not have indirect addressing. However, the length of the two instructions combined is only 7 bytes. Even though more instructions are required on the 386 to accomplish the same thing as a single instruction on the 68030, the 386 is able to do the same in less space.

If you look at the timings for each of these instructions, not only is the length of these two instructions shorter, but the number of clocks required to execute the two 386 instructions is also shorter. Wading through the pages of chapter 11 of the Motorola Manual which describe the additional time required for complex addressing modes, we find that this addressing mode adds 16 clocks to the basic time of 2 clocks for the move.

But the Intel sequence, assuming memory with no wait states, and also assuming that the instructions are available in the instruction lookahead buffer, takes only 12 clocks, so it isn't even the case that the 68030 is faster. These kind of comparisons make us wonder whether having these complicated addressing modes is really worth while. At least in this particular case, it is not at all obvious that we are getting any real gain.

PC Relative Addressing Modes and Position Independent Code

In our description of the 68030, we have not covered all of the addresing modes. In particular, we have not given the details of the the so-called *PC relative* addressing modes. There is a complete collection of these modes that are related to the modes we have studied so far in that the base register, instead of being one of the address registers, is the program counter, or PC. The various possible forms allow indirect addressing with pre- or postindexing, double indexing with scaling, and various offset sizes.

What is the purpose of PC relative addressing? Consider a section of code that will be loaded into memory. If the location in memory is fixed and known at link time, then absolute addresses can be included in the code without any problem. However, suppose we want to produce *position independent code* (PIC). This term refers to code that can be loaded into memory at any location, and execute without any additional modification. One application of PIC is in the production of ROM modules containing code which can be plugged into any one of a number of available ROM slots corresponding to different memory locations.

The branch and call instructions on the 68030 always use the equivalent of PC-relative addressing, so there is no problem there. However, if the code also contains constants that are referenced by instructions in the code (a common situation when ROMs are produced, since constants are also read only data), then it is important to use the PC relative addressing modes to access these constants. This way, the resulting code and data remain position-independent.

On the 386, the call and jump instructions are also position independent, but there is no EIP relative addressing mode. The effect would have to be achieved by copying the value of EIP into another register and then using it as a base register:

```
          CALL next
next:     POP  EBX
          ...
          (code now uses EBX to access local constants)
```

This is not so bad since the register has to be set only once. PC relative addressing modes are thus a luxury rather than a necessity, but they are probably fairly inexpensive in terms of hardware, since all that needs to be done is to connect PC as the base register in existing addressing modes. Another possible advantage of the PC relative modes is that constants can be placed with the procedures that reference them and then addressed using PC relative with shorter offsets than would be necessary if absolute addressing were used. Relatively few 68030 compilers take full advantage of these modes.

Restrictions on the Use of the Addressing Modes

Wherever we see <*ea*> appear in an instruction form, for example in

    BFEXTU <ea>{offset:width}, Dn

there are all sorts of things that this instruction can do because the <*ea*> operand can be any one of the many addressing modes.

Unfortunately, it is not *really* true that wherever you see <*ea*> as an operand, any addressing mode can be substituted. Every instruction that has <*ea*> has an accompanying table showing which of the addressing modes can be used, and these tables have a lot of holes. For example, BFEXTU does not permit postincrement or predecrement addressing. Why not? Probably because it is not obvious what the increment should be—the autoincrement and autodecrement modes are only available for instructions where the length of the memory item accessed is explicitly defined in the instruction.

Of course, some of the missing addressing modes in the instruction tables make sense. For example, we can't expect to use immediate addressing with an instruction that modifies the operand, such as CLR (Clear an Operand). Compared with the 68000, the 68030 has filled in many of these holes, but there are still a number of peculiar exceptions. Consider the following random collection of examples:

- The Bit Test (BFTST) instruction tests a bit in an operand. You can use a data register as the operand, but you cannot use an A register.

- The LEA instruction takes an address as an operand. You give it an address, it computes the address and puts it in a register, just like the LEA instruction on the 386. As with BFEXTU,(An)+ or −(An) are not permitted.

- UNPK allows *only* predecrement or data register direct addressing. No other possibilities are permitted. This is because it uses a specialized instruction format.

- CMPI (Compare Immediate) does not permit the other operand to use immediate addressing (we can hear someone saying "Who could ever want to compare two immediate values?").

Irregularities of this type are particularly annoying for compiler writers, who are in the business of translating whatever rubbish is submitted and would like to treat everything in a uniform manner. The 386 may have a simpler set of addressing modes, but it does have the advantage that all instructions using memory addressing permit an absolutely identical set of possible addressing modes.

FLOATING-POINT ON THE 68030

Floating point on the 68030 is very similar to that on the 386. The role of the 387 is played by the 68881 coprocessor chip. Like the 386, the 68030 is designed to have an intimate connection with a coprocessor, so that even though the floating-point operations are performed by a separate chip, the programmer can issue floating-point instructions as though they were included in the main 68030 instruction set.

An interesting difference in approach between Motorola and Intel is evident in the respective documentation. The 386 Programmer's Reference Manual contains only five pages of information on the coprocessor, and none of the details of the hardware interface to the coprocessor. The message here is "Buy the coprocessor from us, and don't worry about the interface, we have taken care of it." The Motorola User's Manual for the 68030, on the other hand, has a 53-page chapter on the coprocessor interface, with full interface information, including schematics showing the signal connections between the two chips. This information is intended for the hardware designer who wishes to design and add new coprocessors to the system. Of course, if the standard 68881 floating-point coprocessor is used, then even a hardware designer need not know all about this interface—there is a note that the information is not relevant if the 68881 is used, since Motorola has properly implemented the interface details. In practice, the coprocessor interface has *only* been used for the floating-point coprocessor.

The 68881 itself is similar in many respects to the 387. It is a rather complete implementation of the IEEE standard, including the double extended format. It also implements a set of transcendental functions which is even more extensive than that of the 387—including, for example, a complete set of hyperbolic trigonometric functions.

The register structure of the 68881 is more conventional than that of the 387. It has a set of eight registers, each of which holds a double extended format number, but the registers are addressed in the conventional direct manner instead of the stack model of the 387. Given that the coprocessor connection allows consistent integration of the 68881 instructions, this means that the assembly language programmer sees the 68881 as a smooth extension of the 68030 instruction set and all the addressing modes of the 68030 are available for use by floating point instructions. For example, the following is a subroutine for evaluating a polynomial $c_0 x^n + c_1 x^{n-1} + \ldots + c_n$. We assume on entry that A1 points to a table consisting of the value of n-1 (one less than the last subscript) followed by a list of coefficients from c_0 to c_n in sequence. The argument x is in FP1 and the result is returned in FP0.

```
PEVAL   MOVE.W  (A1)+, D0       ; copy n to D0, point A1 to c₀
        FMOVE.X (A1)+, FP0      ; initialize result to c₀
PLOOP   FMUL.X  FP1, FP0        ; multiply result by x
        FADD.X  (A1)+, FP0      ; add next coefficient, push pointer
        DBRA    D0, PLOOP       ; loop till all done
        RTS                     ; return to caller
```

In looking at this code, note that extended values take 96 bits (12 bytes) in memory, and the auto-increment addressing mode for .X instructions understands this, so the FADD.X instruction adds 12 to A1—you can see what we mean when we say that the floating point is smoothly integrated into the instruction set.

Despite the smooth integration of the 68881, it turns out that the 68030 is also subject to the same lack of uniformity as the 386 in that there are alternate floating-point approaches. In particular the Weitek chipset exists in a form that can be used with the 68030, and is for example the processor used in Sun's Floating Point Accelerator product for the Sun Workstation. Once again, the motive is speed—the Weitek chipset has greater throughput than the 68881.

INSTRUCTION FORMATS ON THE 68030

In this section we will make an attempt to describe the instruction formats of the 68030 in a simple, coherent manner. As with the 386, this attempt will fail, since in common with other processors, the 68030 has a very complicated structure when it comes to instruction formats. The length of instructions on the 68030 ranges from 2 bytes to 22 bytes (that's not a misprint, there really is an instruction that is 22 bytes long!)

Before we begin, there is one systematic aspect of the format that we should consider. Wherever an address field is present in an instruction, it is 6 bits long and consists of a 3-bit mode field and a 3-bit register field. These 6 bits select one of 18 addressing modes, not all of which can be used with every instruction, as we have already mentioned. Some of the addressing modes (e.g., register direct mode) are complete with the 6 bits. Other addressing modes take from 1 to 5 additional 16-bit *extension* words to complete the specification of the address. The extension words have one of the forms shown in Figure 6.5.

With that preliminary out of the way, we can now look at the basic instruction formats, remembering that wherever a 6-bit effective address field occurs, we are really describing an entire family of formats, depending on the addressing mode. These basic formats range from 2 through 8 bytes in length (i.e., one through four 16-bit halfwords). A sample of some of these formats is shown in Figure 6.6.

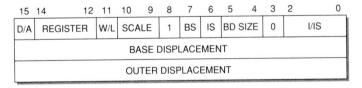

Single Effective Address Instruction Format

15	14	13	12	11	10	9	8	7	6	5 3	2 0
X	X	X	X	X	X	X	X	X	X	MODE	REG

Brief Format Extension Word

15	14 12	11	10 9	8	7 0
D/A	REGISTER	W/L	SCALE	0	DISPLACEMENT

Full Format Extension Word(s)

15	14 12	11	10 9	8	7	6	5 4	3 2	0
D/A	REGISTER	W/L	SCALE	1	BS	IS	BD SIZE	0	I/IS
BASE DISPLACEMENT										
OUTER DISPLACEMENT										

FIGURE 6.5
The effective address formats of the 68030.

Format (a) has four fields. This format is used by instructions such as MOVEA that take two operands, one of which must be a register while the other uses general addressing. Format (b) is used only by the MOVE instruction, which allows a byte, word, or longword to be moved from one generally addressed location to another. It is this form that gives rise to the longest possible instruction, since each of the effective address fields can require five extension words.

Format (c) is used by instructions that have only an effective address operand. There are relatively few instances of this format. One example is MOVE from SR, which

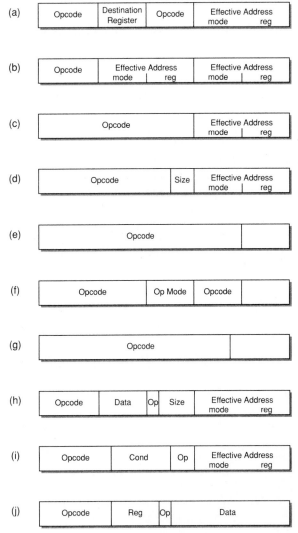

FIGURE 6.6
Some of the many 68030 instruction formats.

looks like a two-operand instruction to the assembler programmer but is really a separate instruction format with the SR operand implied. Another example is JMP, where the operand of the jump is given by using a general address.

Format (d) is related to the previous format, but contains an additional 2-bit field used to indicate whether the operand is a byte, word, or longword. For some instructions, for example, NOT, all three possibilities exist. For other instructions this is not the case. For example NBCD, the specialized instruction for negating BCD values exists only in byte form.

Format (e) is used by instructions that have a single 3-bit operand, most often a register designation. An example is the SWAP instruction, which swaps the two 16-bit halves of a 32-bit register. The BKPT (breakpoint) instruction uses a similar format, except that the *reg* field is the breakpoint number rather than a register number.

Format (f) is used *only* by the EXT instruction, with the mode field indicating which of the three possible extensions (byte to halfword, halfword to word, or byte to word) is required.

Format (g) is another specialized format used by a single instruction TRAP, where the *vector* operand is used to indicate one of 16 possible trap vector numbers.

Format (h) is used only by the ADDQ and SUBQ instructions, special add and subtract immediate instructions that can be used with data values from 1 to 8 (represented as 0 to 7 in the 3-bit *data* field). Format (i) is another format used by a single instruction, Scc (Set Condition), which uses the 4-bit condition code indicator in the *cond* field to set a boolean value corresponding to the condition in the generally addressed byte location determined by *efad*.

The specialized (j) format is used only by the MOVEQ instruction that allows an 8-bit sign-extended immediate value to be moved to a specified data register.

Had enough of this? We certainly have, and we are not yet all the way through the 1-word formats. As best as we can count, there are five 1-word formats, thirteen 2-word formats, five 3-word formats, and a single 4-word format left to go. We will spare you the gruesome excercise of going through all these formats in detail, and instead give just one example of the multiword formats.

The format in Figure 6.7 is used by the bit field instructions. The type field shows which instruction of the set of eight is involved (it is thus an opcode extension field). Do and Dw are flags indicating whether the offset and width fields are immediate bit numbers or registers containing the bit numbers. Obviously there was no way to jam

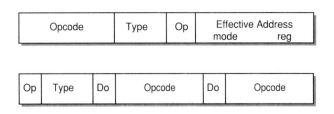

FIGURE 6.7
The instruction format used by the 68030 bit-field instructions.

all the fields in this instruction into one 16-bit word but as we can see, they *just* managed to squeeze them into two 16-bit words.

In the 68030 User's Manual, there is a section called "Instruction Format Summary" (starting on page 3-201) which doesn't even attempt to systematize the formats; it simply lists the format of each instruction separately. Well, things aren't *quite* this bad, there are *some* formats in the list above that are used by more than one instruction. However, the general design principle is clearly to jam whatever fields are needed for particular instructions into as few 16-bit words as possible, with relatively little premium on simplicity and uniformity. We will leave it to the reader to decide whether the 386 or the 68030 has the more messy and complicated set of instruction formats—it's a close call!

It is interesting to note that for all the remaining RISC processors, we will be able to do a complete job of describing the instruction formats and yet the resulting descriptions will be much simpler and more pleasant to get through than the partial presentations for the 386 and 68030. Simplicity of instruction formats is one of the important hallmarks of RISC design.

CONCLUSION

The 68030 and the 386 are the two well established CISC chips. When people talk about CISC microprocessors, they almost certainly have one or the other, or both of these chips in mind. In this chapter, we have looked at the user instruction set and addressing modes of the 68030. Even though we have not covered the whole instruction set, we have a long chapter (longer than some of the RISC chapters) which covers an entire chip.

The 68030 provides nice examples, such as CAS2, of extremely complicated instructions. Sun has claimed that in their investigation of instruction usage by C compilers, only 30% of the 68030 instruction set was used by the compiler. This seems a little low, and may partially reflect incompetence on the part of the 68030 C compiler, but it is certainly not surprising that a compiler is unable to make use of the entire instruction set. For example, it seems quite unlikely that *any* compiler would ever generate a CAS2 instruction as the translation of a sequence of high level language code which added an element to a doubly linked list.

CHAPTER

7

THE 68030 SUPERVISOR STATE

The previous chapter described the view of the 68030 that an applications programmer writing in assembly language would see. Another perspective from which to study the 68030 is to deal with the instructions, registers, and other features that can be accessed only when the processor is in supervisor mode.

This chapter will discuss the architectural features that would be of primary interest to an operating system designer. We will begin with a short section describing the special set of registers and instructions that are available only when the processor is in supervisor state. Following that we will discuss the addressing mechanisms, including the onboard instruction and data caches that are available on the chip. We shall then describe in some detail the sophisticated paging mechanism that has been implemented, a mechanism whose flexibility sets it apart from many other simpler implementations. We will end this chapter with a discussion of exceptions, interrupts, and tracing.

Keep in mind that the 68030 is really *much* simpler than the 386. The subjects of multilevel protection, segmentation, and tasking, which required considerable exposition in the case of the 386, do not arise, because there is little or no hardware support for these functions.

THE SUPERVISOR STATE REGISTERS

You will remember from the very beginning of the last chapter that the 68030 is able to operate in only one of two states, the user state and the supervisor state. This model differs from that of the 386, where there are four separate levels of protection. Having only two processor states results in a simpler system structure, at the expense of requiring a great deal of code to run at what might be an excessively high privilege level. In order for an application to get any privileges at all, it must be given the full capabilities of supervisor state. There are ways of managing this "all or nothing" way of doing things, but it does contrast significantly from the way in which an operating system might be designed for the 386 or similar machines with multiple protection levels.

A special set of registers is available to the 68030 when it is in supervisor state that are used by an operating system to control the processor (see Figure 7.1). We will see exactly how each one of those registers is used as we discuss caching, paging, interrupts, and other issues related to processor control.

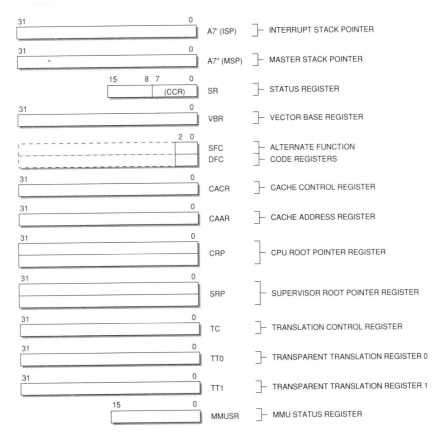

FIGURE 7.1
The 68030 supervisor programming model supplement.

THE STATUS REGISTER. The *status register* (SR) is a 16-bit register, logically divided into two parts, which contains information about the state of the processor and which can be used to control this state. The low-order 8 bits of SR constitute the *condition code register* (CCR), which is accessible from the user state, and whose use we have already described in Chapter 6. The high-order 8 bits form the *system byte*, a collection of bits that control the processor, including the single bit that determines whether the processor is in user or supervisor state. The complete structure of the status register is shown in Figure 7.2.

By modifying the bits in the system byte, an operating system can control the behavior of the processor. There are bits to control interrupts, tracing, the specification of alternate stacks on interrupts, the S-bit, which controls whether the processor is in user or supervisor state. Since an operating system for the 68030 must run in supervisor mode, it is expected that it will change the values in the status register freely. An operating system, for example, may want to give control of the processor back to some application, in which case it needs to set up the application in the environment and then change from supervisor to user state by resetting the S-bit. An application program, on the other hand, cannot change that bit to force the processor into supervisor state, since this would allow an application to take complete control of the processor. The only way in which an application running on the 68030 can move back into supervisor state is by causing an exception, something that might be done, for example, by executing a TRAP instruction.

STACK POINTERS. In Chapter 6, we described how the address register A7 had a specialized use as the user stack pointer. There are actually three separate stack pointers on the 68030. In addition to the user stack pointer, there is the *master stack pointer* (MSP) and the *interrupt stack pointer* (ISP). Even though these stack pointers are distinct registers inside the processor, they are all referenced as A7 in an instruction. No conflict results because at any one time A7 refers to only one of these—which one depends on the context. In user state A7 refers to USP, while in supervisor state it refers to either MSP or ISP.

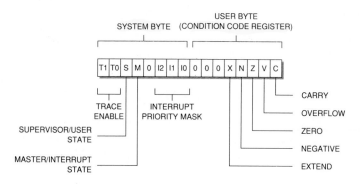

FIGURE 7.2
The 68030 Status Register.

When a trap occurs, MSP (or possibly ISP) is used as A7 in place of USP. Although USP cannot be directly referenced once the processor has switched to supervisor state, as we will see later, there is a way for the operating system to get its hands on USP if necessary. Whether MSP or ISP is used in supervisor state is controlled by the M-bit (bit 12 of the status register). If this bit is off, then the MSP is always used in the supervisor state. If M is set, then, if supervisor state is entered other than by a hardware interrupt, the stack pointer used is still MSP. However, if a hardware interrupt occurs with M set, then ISP is used as the stack pointer.

The reason for having different stack pointers for interrupts and other types of traps has to do with the structure of the operating system. A trap is always related to the user program which is currently running. For example, if the user program issues a TRAP instruction, then obviously the trap routine is servicing a request from this user program. It therefore makes sense to have separate master stacks (and separate values of MSP) for each application task. On the other hand, asynchronous interrupts do *not* belong to the task currently executing, so here it makes sense to share a single stack for all tasks in the system. This interrupt stack belongs solely to the operating system which services the interrupts and then dispatches them to the task to which they belong (which may not be the currently running task).

VECTOR BASE REGISTER. The *vector base register* (VBR) resembles the IDT register on the 386. It points to the vector of addresses that are used to handle interrupts and traps. This register can only be modified in supervisor state, since obviously control of traps and interrupts is an operating system function.

FUNCTION CODE REGISTERS. The alternate function code registers, *source function code* (SFC) and *destination function code* (DFC), are used to change the address space referenced on a memory access. We will discuss the exact use of these registers when we describe the special instruction MOVES that makes use of them.

SYSTEM CONTROL REGISTERS. The registers CACR and CAAR are used to control the on-chip caches (their use will be detailed in the section on the 68030 caches). Finally, the registers CRP, SRP, TC, TT0, and TT1 all have to do with paging which will be discussed in the section devoted to that topic—paging is one area where the 68030 is considerably *more* complex than the 386.

THE PRIVILEGED INSTRUCTION SET

The privileged instruction set of the 68030, the set of instructions that can be executed only in supervisor state, is quite small. Most of these instructions manipulate the special registers (described above) that are accessible only when the processor is in the supervisor state.

Several of the standard instructions have special variants that allow the status register to be manipulated. The MOVE instruction, for example, has the privileged forms *Move to the Status Register* (MOVE to SR) and *Move from the Status Register* (MOVE from SR) which allow the value of the status register to be read to and written from the supervisor state.

There are also special versions of the immediate OR, AND, as well as Exclusive OR instructions that will modify bits in the status register (for example, And Immediate to the Status Register (ANDI to SR)). All of these must be privileged instructions, since for one thing, the bit distinguishing the user and supervisor states is in the status register. If you want to keep things hidden away in a locked office (supervisor state), you must certainly hide the key (the supervisor bit in the status register)!

The bit modification instructions (ORI, EORI, and XORI) for the status register are obviously not critically required, since their function could be achieved by a read–modify–write sequence, but they are convenient, since, as we have seen, the status register contains a collection of bits that control essentially unrelated functions.

Another special version of the MOVE instruction can be used to move the user stack pointer to a specified register. This instruction really does not need to be privileged, but its use makes sense only in supervisor mode. A task running in user mode may, for example, trap on some instruction and force the processor into supervisor state. In order to handle the trap, the processor may need to get hold of the user's stack. This instruction copies the USP value to a specified register, where it can be used to address the user data. Obviously you don't need this instruction in *user* state, since the user stack pointer is directly available as A7.

MOVEC is the instruction that modifies one of the control registers. (Remember that many of these registers have delicate system functions.) The MOVEC instruction allows you to change the vector base register for the cache control registers, or even to modify what is going on with the memory mapping.

MOVES is a special version of MOVE, supporting all the usual addressing modes, which is available only in supervisor state and allows specification of the address space to be used for the source and destination operands. We will discuss this instruction separately in the next section.

PFLUSH, PMOVE, PLOAD, and PTEST have to do with modifying the on-chip address translation registers for the memory mapping. Again, they are appropriately protected, since the user program has no business even being aware of the paging, let alone modifying how the mapping is operating.

The Return from Exception (RTE) instruction is privileged because exceptions always run in supervisor state. It would be unfortunate if RTE were not protected, because RTE reloads the saved status register, and thus would be another way of changing the current status register and consequently "sneaking" into supervisor state. The STOP instruction is privileged because it stops the processor.

There are also privileged instructions that are intended for coprocessor save and restore (cpSAVE and cpRESTORE). It would probably be harmless to allow these instructions to be used by a program operating in user state. However, for other arbitrary coprocessors there may be critical information in the coprocessor registers which only the operating system should be allowed to modify.

That is the complete set of privileged instructions—quite a small set!

ADDRESSING ON THE 68030

The addresses generated by the 68030 include a 3-bit function code that specifies one of eight separate address spaces. This function code can be thought of as extending the addressing range of the processor from 2^{32} bytes to 2^{35} bytes. The interpretation of the values in the 3-byte function code are as follows:

000	Undefined, reserved by Motorola
001	User Data Space
010	User Program Space
011	Undefined, reserved for user
100	Undefined, reserved by Motorola
101	Supervisor Data Space
110	Supervisor Program Space
111	CPU Space

The four particularly important address spaces are the user data, user program, supervisor data, and supervisor program areas. The CPU address space is used for internal purposes within the 68030 chip. For instance, an interrupt is acknowledged by writing an interrupt acknowledge back to a specific address in the CPU space.

For the great majority of ordinary instructions, the specific address space type is an implicit part of the instruction. If, for example, the processor is in user state, it will automatically generate either a 001 or a 010 depending upon whether it is fetching an instruction or accessing some data. In other words, as a programmer, you don't have to consider the address space. Similarly, in supervisor state, either 101 or 110 is generated according to the memory reference type.

The 3-bit function code is part of the logical address which is sent to the paging translation unit and can be passed on to the external memory system. This allows the supervisor to set up the paging (or the system designer to design the external memory system) so that, for example, the address spaces for code and data are separated.

Function code 011 is marked as reserved for the "user." The user here is the system designer, who might, for example, use this function code to represent a separate address space for input/output instructions (like the IN and OUT instructions of the 386).

Although the automatically generated function code is usually the one that is appropriate, there are times when the operating system needs direct control over the address space to be accessed. The MOVES instruction allows the operating system to specify the function codes to be generated by setting up the *source function code* (SFC) and the *destination function code* (DFC) registers before issuing the MOVES instruction. Standard uses of this instruction are to treat code as data (for loading programs), to issue input/output instructions (if function code 011 is implemented this way), or to access user data from supervisor state (for example, accessing the user stack in conjunction with the MOVE USP instruction).

CACHING ON THE 68030

The 68030 has two caches on board the chip, an instruction cache and a data cache. The 256-byte instruction cache, which was also present on the earlier 68020, stores instructions which have been prefetched. The size of the data cache is also 256 bytes, a rather small size for a data cache. Still, it is 256 bytes larger than the (non-existent) data cache on the 386, and it is always possible for the system designer to add a larger external cache to be used in addition to the on-chip cache.

An important point concerning these on-chip caches is that they contain *virtual*, not *real*, addresses. What makes this significant is that processes running on the 68030 will be accessing virtual memory addresses, not physical addresses. If a cache hit occurs it means that the processor will not have to go through the paging unit at all.

Cache Organization

Both the instruction and data caches of the 68030 are *direct-mapped* caches. A direct-mapped cache is a relatively simple implementation of a cache in which each word of memory has a unique location within the cache in which a copy of its data can be stored, that is, if a memory location's data *is* in the cache, then it will always be found in the same cache location. What makes the direct-mapped cache relatively simple to implement is the manner in which memory addresses are mapped into cache addresses.

A direct-mapped cache is organized very much like main memory, except that it is much smaller. The size of the cache is typically chosen to be some power of 2. Each entry of the cache contains the following three crucial components: a tag, valid bits,

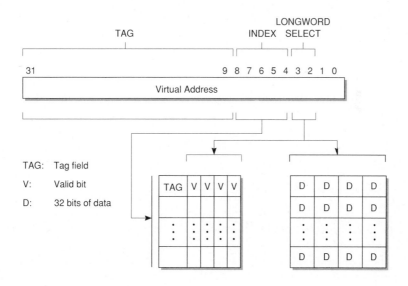

FIGURE 7.3
The on-chip instruction cache of the 68030.

and the data. The tag is used to check that the data in the cache actually corresponds to the address that is being developed (since many memory addresses map to the same location), while the valid bits determine which words within the cache are valid.

Both the instruction and the data caches of the 68030 have 16 entries, and each entry of the cache can hold a *cache line* consisting of four contiguous 32-bit words. Each of the four 32-bit entries in the cache line has a separate valid bit that indicates whether the data is valid.

When an address is developed by the 68030, that address is sent to the cache (instructions are sent to the instruction cache and data references are sent to the data cache), where it is divided into three chunks. Bits 4 through 7 are used to select a cache line, that is, those bits are used as an index into the cache. Bits 2 and 3 are used to select one of the four 32-bit entries within the cache line. Finally, bits 8 through 31 are compared against the tag field of the cache. This process is shown in Figure 7.3. Note that it is possible for an operand to be split across two cache lines if it is not aligned.

Cache Performance

The approach used on the 68030 will work reasonably well with data, although there will be some difficulty when two different pieces of data map into exactly the same cache location. For example, suppose that a program is multiplying two four-by-four matrices of 32-bit floating point numbers. The total size of the data involved is 128 bytes, and normally both matrices would fit into the cache, speeding up the matrix multiplication. However, if by bad luck the two matrices mapped into the same cache location, then they could not coexist in the cache, and the multiplication would be much slower. A user has very little control over the placement of data in a typical software environment, so this effect is hard to control.

The cache hit rate, that is, the percentage of data references that find the data present in the cache, is the crucial figure in evaluating cache performance. A 256-byte data cache is too small to be very effective, regardless of the mechanism used to determine which data to discard when a cache is full, so cache hit rates on the 68030 will not be very high. Nevertheless this is one of those situations in which every bit helps, and even a very small data cache will have a noticeable effect on performance.

For instruction caching, on the other hand, a small cache works better. At the very least, it will certainly give the effect of the 16-byte instruction lookahead on the 386, since when you fetch a single instruction byte, the cache will fetch a full 16 bytes. Much more importantly, if the instructions which form a loop are less than 256 bytes long, they will be sitting entirely in the cache after a short time. This means that further instruction fetches will not come from external memory, but from the cache. On the 386, the jump at the bottom of a loop forces the instruction lookahead to be reloaded each time around the loop.

The instruction cache is also directly addressed, and this is a limitation in some circumstances. As an example, take a small loop, say 20 bytes, that contains a call to a small subroutine, itself 20 bytes long. Most of the time there is room in the cache to hold both the code for the loop and the code for the subroutine. However, if the two sections of code were exactly 256 bytes apart, they could not coexist in the cache. This might be expected to happen about 10% of the time on average, a figure that is not so bad. You could even imagine a compiler that paid attention to this effect and attempted to avoid such unfortunate coincidences. But this would be quite a difficult optimization, and very few compilers attempt it.[1] One of the difficulties with devices like caches is that they introduce inconsistent behavior. We may find that by adding a subroutine to a program we significantly affect the performance of code elsewhere in the program, and the programmer has very little control over this effect.

Another effect of caching is to distort benchmarks. Alignment considerations and caching considerations often cause surprises in benchmarks. Peter Norton wrote a timing program called SI (System Information) whose performance indications are widely used in advertisements to claim that a manufacturer's PC-compatible has a certain performance. When a new version of this program was released in which a few extra frills had been added, the loop was misaligned. So the results from the second version were quite different from the results of the first. When he realized what had happened, he wrote an article warning that all benchmarks are dangerous!

In the case of the cache on the 68030, one can imagine a very small change to a standard benchmark program causing a 20 to 30% slowdown because of some unlucky effect with the cache. This is a big enough difference to cause a customer to choose one compiler or system over another.

Cache Control

There are two registers on the 68030 whose function is to control the precise behavior of the cache. The *cache control register* (CACR) and the *cache address register* (CAAR) can be used only in supervisor mode to control the operation of the cache.

WRITING TO THE CACHE. An important issue that arises in the presence of a data cache is whether data that is written to memory should also be written to the cache. When data is read from memory that is not already in the cache, the cache will always be loaded with the new data, assuming that caching is enabled.

When a write occurs, on the other hand, there are two possibilities. If the data *is* in the cache, then it must be modified so that the cache does not contain stale data. If the data is *not* in the cache, then it is not at all clear that the cache should be updated with the new value. Whether the cache is updated or not depends upon whether it is a good idea to assume that something a task has just written will be read in the near future.

The *write allocate* bit in the CACR register gives the operating system a choice. This bit determines whether or not a write that does not get a cache hit modifies the cache. It is an important bit that allows the operating system to tune the performance

---

[1] The "inlining" optimization, in which the body of a small routine is moved inline in place of the call, is generally useful since it saves the overhead of a call. It also incidentally avoids the particular cache problem discussed here.

of the processor. However, it is difficult to tell whether the write allocate bit should be set because it is often the case that this decision should be made based on the needs of an application, not the operating system.

The write, incidentally, is always a *write through*, which means that it writes to the real memory as well as to the cache. As long as there is only one processor in the system, this write through behavior guarantees that the main memory is always consistent with the cache.

When a system has been built with more than one processor connected to it, there is a possible problem with respect to *cache coherence*. Suppose that two processors, both with data caches, are connected to the same memory and read the value of X into a register. When the first processor loads a copy of X into one of its registers, a copy of X will be made in the first processor's data cache. Likewise, when the second processor loads X into one of its registers, a copy of X is made in its data cache. If the first processor assigns a new value to X, and a write through is done, the system will be in a situation where the first processor's cache is synchronized with memory but the second processor's cache is stale—it has an old value of X that is no longer valid.

The problem of cache coherence in a multiprocessor environment is a fundamental one which must be taken into consideration in both hardware and operating systems software design. Data that is entirely local to only one of the processors can of course be cached freely. However, shared data, like the X in our example above, must be treated carefully. In some situations, the best approach is simply to avoid caching shared data.

As an example, consider the use of the CAS2 instruction for manipulating linked lists. It would be a very bad idea to cache LIST_PUT and LIST_GET because if a system contains several separate processors it is fundamental that they must see the same value of LIST_PUT and LIST_GET or the sequence of code that uses the CAS2 instruction won't work. Not only do we need to be able to inhibit the cache, we also need ways to inhibit the caching selectively on different sets of variables—that is a considerable added complication. For the particular case of CAS2, and other instructions which are intended for synchronization, the processor assumes that you will never want to cache the data referenced, so all the instructions which lock the bus to ensure data consistency always bypass the cache. For other instructions which access shared data, the operating system must provide facilities for managing cache access. As we will see later, the paging mechanism provides facilities for disabling the cache for selected memory locations.

It is possible to design machines so that the cache (called a *snoopy* cache) watches the memory traffic on the bus. It then synchronizes its actions so that its data is always consistent with the contents of main memory. On the 68030 the cache is inside the chip, so the circuitry to achieve the snooping would have to be on the inside of the chip, and it simply isn't there!

DATA BURST. Two bits in the cache control register, the *data burst enable* (DBE) bit and the *instruction burst enable* (IBE) bit, control how data is loaded into the data and instruction caches, respectively. When a cache miss occurs, the operating system must decide whether or not to immediately load four doublewords into the appropriate cache line in what is called *bus burst mode*. In this mode the bus is locked so that 4 words are loaded into the cache in one indivisible bus cycle that takes 5 bus clocks—the bus is released only after all the data has been loaded. Alternatively, four separate requests can be made to the bus, each for one longword. This avoids locking the bus, but the total number of bus clocks required to fill the cache line is greater.

Deciding whether or not to enable bus burst mode for the caches must be determined by the characteristics of the hardware to which the 68030 is attached, that is, whether the cost of locking up the memory for 5 cycles while these caches are loaded is too high. If the system has a very ferocious I/O device, such as a disk with enormous throughput, it might not be able to tolerate the bus being locked up for five contiguous cycles. In that case, the DBE and IBE bits should be turned off.

On some buses there might be no advantage to enabling data burst, since it might not make them sufficiently faster. Often, it may be desirable to have DBE disabled while IBE is enabled, because you do want instructions read ahead in burst mode. To decide, you must consult with your friendly engineer to see whether, given the hardware to which the 68030 is attached, it is worthwhile turning these flags on. Of course the "you" here is the system programmer writing the operating system, not the applications programmer, since instructions to modify the CACR are privileged.

FREEZING AND CLEARING THE CACHE. The *clear data cache* (CD) bit in CACR is a control bit that the system needs if it changes from one task to another. The cache must be flushed on a context-switch because it contains virtual and not physical addresses. If this is not done, then the previous task's stale virtual addresses will be sitting in the cache. Normally, when the system switches from one task to another it must set the CD bit, which will clear the data cache altogether. The *clear instruction cache* (CI) bit will do the same for the instruction cache.

Clearing a cache can be done very quickly since all that needs to be done is to reset all of the valid bits. The penalty of clearing the data cache is not the time to clear the cache, but rather the time to reload it with new data. If all the separate tasks were operating in the same address space, it would not be necessary to clear the data cache. This is something that the operating system has to take care of when appropriate.

Another instance in which the instruction cache should be cleared is when instructions are read in as data. If new instructions are read, say, as part of an overlay, then the old instructions had better be cleared away from the instruction cache. The *clear entry in data cache* (CED) and the *clear entry in instruction cache* (CEI) bits allow you to clear a specific entry in the cache, allowing more precise control over the cache contents in specialized situations. This is done by loading the cache address register with the cache location and then setting one of these bits (depending, of course, on whether the entry is in the data or the instruction cache).

The data cache can be completely frozen by setting the *freeze data* (FD) bit, which means that the cache should hold onto its current data—the cache should not be updated. A situation in which that would be desirable, for example, is when a task intends to manipulate data that would be useless if it were in the cache.

In the example, where we described a 20-byte subroutine called from a 20-byte loop where the two sections of code were in the same cache line, freezing the instruction cache at the end of the loop would stop the bouncing between the two sections of code and improve the performance. Only very specialized code, for example, system code for placing font data on a display screen, might use a feature like this, not common applications.

Another specialized use of the FD bit is to freeze a null cache with no data in it. We would achieve this by setting the CD and CI bits to clear both caches and the FD bit to freeze it in this cleared state. The effect is to entirely disable the cache. This might be desirable if a hardware debugger was being used to watch memory references (you don't want to have the cache swallow up references so that you can't see them in this case) or if multiple processors were on the same bus, in which case disabling the caches would be one (rather drastic) way of solving the cache coherency problem!

The 68030 gives an operating systems designer a great deal of control over the data and instruction caches. The 386, which has no on-chip cache, obviously lacks such instructions. However, if the 386 is attached to an external cache, such as the Intel cache controller chip, then these same kinds of functions must exist, since you must have the same ability to control the external cache. The Intel cache controller chip responds to a series of IN and OUT instructions which perform the needed functions.

THE 68030 MEMORY MANAGEMENT UNIT

The 68030, like the 386, has a memory management unit on board the chip to support virtual memory. A quick look at the Motorola 68030 User's Manual makes it pretty clear that this MMU is very sophisticated, particularly in comparison with that of the 386 and even more so in comparison with many of the RISC chips we will discuss in later chapters.

Why bother putting such a complex piece of logic onto a chip when that space might have been used for some other useful functions? Part of the answer has to do with the fact that the earlier members of the 68000 series did not have any memory management circuitry on board the chip at all. Motorola did provide memory management support for the 68000, but it was provided on a separate coprocessor, called the PMMU. Since PMMU was a separate chip, there was plenty of space for an engineer to play with. Just as in the case of the interrupt controller for the 386, the designers of these chips must have looked at all of the empty real estate there and tried to decide how it could be used. It's like having a big blank book and deciding that you should write *something* in it. Since the 68030's MMU was on a separate chip and there were plenty of blank pages in that book, the designers seem to have decided to take advantage of that flexibility to add a lot of complex functionality.

In moving the logic of the separate MMU onto the 68030 itself, Motorola needed to be as compatible as possible. Not all of the functionality of the separate MMU has been incorporated, but the great majority of important functions are present. If the 68030 were designed from scratch, it might well be the case that it would seem a better choice to trade off some of this extra MMU functionality for other features, but compatibility often ends up being the most significant factor in determining a design.

The virtual memory hardware of the 68030 translates the virtual addresses that are specified in the instruction stream into the physical addresses where the data corresponding to those virtual addresses is located.[2] This information is kept in a set of page tables that we will assume for the moment are kept in main memory (remember that page tables might be paged out to the disk). The page tables contain a complete description that allows any virtual address to be translated to its physical address.

You will remember from our discussion of virtual memory and paging on the 386 that whenever a paging mechanism is used there must be some way of quickly getting to page table information without being forced each and every time to go to the page tables stored in memory. A memory reference should not always require two or more memory references, since external memory is slow enough as it is.

There are two ways on the 68030 to translate a virtual address into a physical address. The slow way of doing the translation is to use the page tables. The fast way of doing the translation is through the use of a small associative memory called the *address translation cache* (ATC). We will first discuss the structure of the ATC and then discuss the more complicated paging mechanism. It will be helpful to keep in mind that despite the difference between these two mechanisms, their goal is the same: to translate a virtual address into a physical address.

The Address Translation Cache

The address translation cache is a fully associative cache consisting of 22 entries, each of which contains the virtual address of a page, the physical address of the corresponding page, and several bits that specify the status of the entry and other important information. Since the ATC is an associative cache, one would generally expect it to be quite effective. Motorola claims a typical hit ratio of greater that 98% (as with car mileage ads, your actual hit ratio will vary, depending on the application).

Each one of the 22 ATC entries is divided into two 28-bit parts (see Figure 7.4). The virtual address along with some other information sits in the first 28-bit portion of the ATC, which is known as the *tag portion*. The physical address, also along with several status bits, resides in the second 28-bit portion, the *data portion*.

The tag portion of the ATC generally has to do with a description of the virtual address. It has the following fields:

- The *valid* (V) bit indicates whether an entry is valid. If this bit is set to 0, then the entry does not contain any useful data.
- The *function code* (FC) is a 3-bit function code that shows which one of the eight virtual address spaces is being described.
- The *logical address field* is a 24-bit field that contains the 24 most significant bits of the virtual address itself.

---

[2] Motorola uses the term *logical address* rather than virtual address in all of its documentation, and the term *translation table* instead of page table. We will adhere to the more familiar terminology.

An unusual feature of this MMU is the ability to vary the page size. More specifically, the page size can be anywhere from 256 bytes to 32K bytes. If the smallest page size is used (256 bytes), then all 24 bits must be used to define the virtual page corresponding to this entry. The designer of an operating system will probably choose to use a larger page size than 256 bytes. In that case, fewer than 24 bits are necessary to define the virtual page, and so some of the lower-order bits in the 24-bit logical address field will be ignored. For example, when pages are 1024 bytes in size they must lie on 1024-byte boundaries, which means that only the most significant 22 bits are necessary to specify the page, and the lower 2 bits are not used.

The data part of the ATC has the following fields:

- The corresponding physical address, which is also 24 bits, shows the address of the physical page that corresponds to the virtual address page. Again low-order bits are ignored if the page size is larger than 256 bytes.
- The *bus error* (B) bit indicates that the attempt to get this page failed and so the ATC entry is not usable.
- The *cache inhibit* (CI) bit allows the system to mark pages in such a way that the data in that page cannot be cached.
- The *write protect* (WP) bit indicates that no writes are to be allowed for a page. A typical use is that code pages would be marked as write protected.
- The *modified* (M) bit indicates whether or not a page has been modified. This is used to optimize page replacement strategy. A writable page that has not been modified does not need to be written back to disk if the page is abandoned.

The CI bit has some special uses that become important when several 68030 processors are combined in a multiprocessor system. As we discussed earlier, an operating system must be able to control caching of shared data in such an environment. Using the CI bit, the operating system can mark selected pages so that under no circumstances will any data on that page be cached. As an example of the use of CI, consider Ada's use of shared variables. In Ada, the pragma *shared* is a compiler directive that specifies that a variable can be asynchronously manipulated by separate tasks. An Ada compiler for this machine (especially with multiple processors) must gather variables that are declared "pragma shared" and put them into pages that are marked non-cacheable so that proper synchronous behavior would occur.

When the processor generates an address, it searches the ATC. If the entry is found in the ATC, then the corresponding physical address can be immediately accessed, and the rest of the MMU mechanism is not involved. If the ATC does *not* contain the desired page, then we have to find the page using the page tables.

The 68030 Paging Mechanism

With some luck, most memory references will result in a hit in either the data or instruction cache. In that case, since the data is right there in the appropriate cache, no further translation of any sort is needed. With a little bit less luck, the 68030 is forced

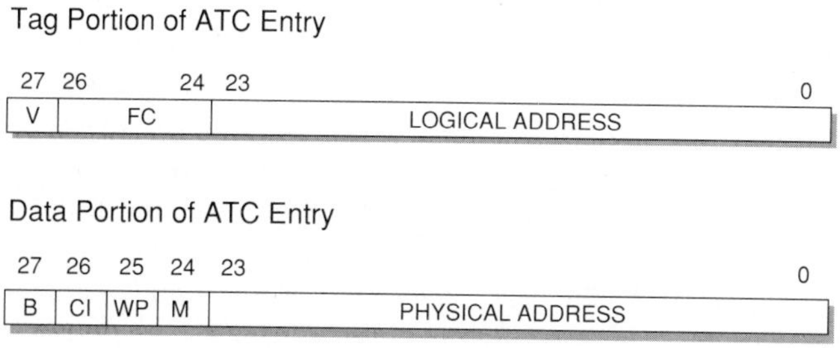

Tag Portion of ATC Entry

```
27  26        24  23                                              0
┌───┬──────────┬─────────────────────────────────────────────┐
│ V │    FC    │           LOGICAL ADDRESS                     │
└───┴──────────┴─────────────────────────────────────────────┘
```

Data Portion of ATC Entry

```
27  26  25  24  23                                              0
┌───┬───┬────┬───┬──────────────────────────────────────────┐
│ B │CI │ WP │ M │           PHYSICAL ADDRESS                 │
└───┴───┴────┴───┴──────────────────────────────────────────┘
```

FIGURE 7.4
The structure of the tag and data portions of an ATC entry.

to translate the virtual address into a real address so that it can retrieve the data from real memory, but it can at least locate the physical address of the instruction or data in the ATC. If luck runs out completely, the processor is forced to consult the page tables to figure out where in physical memory the instructions or data have been placed.

The unusual aspect of the paging mechanism on the 68030 is a very flexible page table structure organized as a multilevel tree. This page table tree can have anywhere from one to five levels, with each page table in the tree itself varying in size under operating system control.

You will remember from the description of the paging mechanism on the 386 that each 32-bit virtual address on the 386 is divided into three parts. The first 10 bits are used to index into the page directory, the second 10 bits are used to point into a page table selected by the page directory, and the remaining 12 bits are used to offset into the page. Since the size and number of the two 10-bit fields cannot vary, the whole paging mechanism is limited to two levels in which all pages are the same size. This is much simpler than what is available on the 68030.

On the 68030, the search for a physical address corresponding to a virtual address begins with one of two specialized registers, the *CPU root pointer* (CRP) or the *supervisor root pointer* (SRP), depending upon whether the processor is in user or supervisor mode. These registers point to the location where the root node of the page table structure is located. These registers are very similar to the CR3 register on the 386, which points to the 386 page table.

There are essentially two types of page tables. A *pointer table* contains pointers to other page tables. A *translation table* holds information about the translation of a virtual address to a physical address. We use the term "page table" here to refer to either type of table.

Unlike the 386, a virtual address on the 68030 is broken up into up to 5 pieces based on the settings of several fields in the *translation control* (TC) register. Instead of using a two-level page table in which all page tables have a size of 2^{10} bytes, an operating system on the 68030 can define both the depth of the page table tree and the size of the tables at each level of the tree. The translation of a virtual address to a physical address is then controlled by the setting of those fields.

A three-level page table structure, for example, could be implemented by breaking up the 32-bit virtual address into four sections. The high-order 5 bits could be used to index a level 1 pointer table that contains 2^5 entries. The next 8 bits of the virtual address just to the right of the first 5-bit field could be used to index into a second-level pointer table with 2^8 entries. The next 9 bits would then index into the final 2^9-entry translation table, which contains the physical address of the page. The remaining 10 bits contain the byte offset into the 1024-byte page. The layout of this sample set of page tables is shown in Figure 7.5.

The exact size and structure of the page tables is controlled by one of the special supervisor registers, the *translation control* (TC) register. The bits in the TC register that control the behavior of the paging mechanism are:

- The *enable* (E) bit enables the whole translation mechanism. If E is off, then paging has been disabled.

- The *supervisor root pointer enable* (SRE) bit determines which root register is used. If SRE is disabled (off), then the table is always addressed using the CPU root pointer. If SRE is enabled, then the processor uses one of the root pointers depending upon whether the processor is in supervisor or user mode.

- The *function code lookup* (FCL) bit controls whether or not the processor uses separate page tables for the eight separate address spaces available.

- The *page size* (PS) field determines the page size. It is set from 8 to 15, corresponding to page sizes from 256 to 32K bytes.

- The *initial shift* (IS) bit allows an operating system designer to limit the size of the virtual address space. It is the number of bits that should be ignored at the front of the virtual address.

- The *table index* fields TIA, TIB, TIC, and TID are the numbers of bits to be used in indexing each level of the table.

These are the fields of the TC which, taken together, give so much control over the size and shape of the page table.

Let us summarize how these fields work together to control the translation of a virtual address to a physical address. The processor first checks the E bit to see whether address translation (paging) is enabled. If it is, the processor then checks the FCL bit to see whether the separate address spaces are being used. If they are being used, then the virtual addresses are actually 35 bits in length, instead of the usual 32 bits. To decide which set of page tables is being used, the SRE bit is checked.

Assume that 32-bit addresses are being translated. The top few bits specified by the IS register are thrown away by the address translation machinery. The remaining bits are then processed as described above by the table index fields.

The flexibility of the paging system arises out of the fact that the TC register has fields that allow an operating system to select the number of levels in the page tables

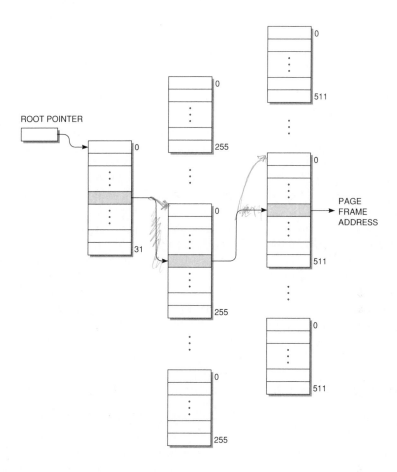

FIGURE 7.5
A sample three-level translation table tree.

and the sizes of the tables. For the example shown in Figure 7.5 we would have the following settings:

FCL = 0	No initial function code table	
IS = 0	No initial shift, all 32 bits used	
TIA = 5	5 bits to index first level of table	
TIB = 8	8 bits to index second level of table	
TIC = 9	9 bits to index third level of table	
TID = 0	No fourth level	
PS = 10	Page size = 1024 (2^{10})	

Note that the sum of IS + TIA + TIB + TIC + TID + PS must always equal 32, so that we specify the use of all 32 bits in the virtual address.

To model the paging system of the 386, IS would be set to 0, TIA and TIB would be set to 10, with the page size set to 4K, and TIC and TID would be set to 0. The operating system has total flexibility as to the total number of levels in the table and how many bits are being used for each level.

The Structure of a 68030 Page Table

Each entry in the page tables, called a *descriptor,* has a specific structure depending upon exactly what kind of page entry it describes. An entry may either contain the translation of a virtual-to-physical address or specify another page table where a further search must be performed to find the needed information.

Using the Motorola nomenclature, the tables constituting the virtual memory system are known as either *pointer tables* or *page tables.* A pointer table is part of the paging system (we have to be careful here about the more generic use of the term "page tables") whose entries point to other tables, rather than containing information about virtual to physical translation. What do these page table entries look like? They have somewhat similar formats whether they are page table entries, page descriptors, or table entries. There are actually two formats.

The *descriptor type* (DT) field indicates whether the entry is an actual page descriptor (at the bottom level of the translation tree) or whether it is a descriptor higher up in the tree which points to another page table entry.

Given the description so far, it would seem that the height of the tree is fixed, and that therefore the DT fixeld is redundant, since you know where leaf nodes are by the depth of the tree. However, there is a special mechanism which makes use of the DT field to provide *early termination page entries.* If a contiguous series of virtual pages can be mapped into a corresponding contiguous series of physical pages, then DT can be set higher up in the tree, saying "Stop the search! This is a special case, and you are already where you need to be." The remainder of the address then functions as a (longer than usual) offset into the set of contiguous pages. This mechanism improves efficiency in special cases where contiguous arrangement is possible by reducing the number of search levels in the tree. This is an interesting mechanism, but it is probably more trouble than it is worth to consider using it in most operating systems. Unix typically uses a simple two-level page structure with no early termination page entries at all. As is often the case on CISC machines, it is not always the case that a feature is useful just because it is present.

The U bit in the descriptor, like the access bit, shows whether the entry has been used. It is used by the operating system to help determine which pages, or even page tables, should be swapped out if new pages must be loaded. The M bit similarly indicates whether a referenced page has been modified and is also used in this determination.

The *write protect* (WP) and *cache inhibit* (CI) bits determine whether the page is to be write protected and/or cached. These bits are copied into the ATC entry if the page is accessed. The *limit field* (LIMIT) and the L/U bit that indicates whether it is to be treated as a lower or upper limit. These can be used to limit the size of page tables or the intermediate page directory levels, so that not all the entries need to be present.

The S bit, which can appear anywhere in the tree, specifies the entry can only be accessed in supervisor state—you cannot go further down the translation tree in user mode.

Finally, there is a 28-bit table address, used either as the page address, or as a table address. Motorola makes a point that having a full 28-bit address means that page tables do not have to be on a page boundary, which saves space compared to other systems ("other systems" in the Motorola manual presumably refers to the 386, which *does* require page tables to be on page boundaries and consequently takes more space, since the minimum size for a page table is 4K bytes).

Page indirection, and its multiple levels, are controlled by the *indirect bit* in a descriptor. It indicates that the entry is not actually there but rather that the entry points to a table at the next level that may contain the actual page translation information.

Why is an extra level of indirection with page tables useful? Say you have a separate search tree for each task, which is a common arrangement (for example, in Unix each process has a separate logical address space). The context switch will change the CPU base register, but you may still have some pages shared between tasks (for example, code may be shared even if data is separate). If tasks share pages, it's nice for them to share individual page table entries so that you have only one modified bit and one accessed bit. That can be accomplished by using indirect pointers. They allow you to determine on a page-by-page basis whether tables are shared, which is an attractive possibility.

This entire elaborate search mechanism occurs only in the case where there is neither a cache hit nor an ATC match. With a five-level table, the overhead of searching the paging tables might be worrisome, so cache and ATC hit ratios become relatively more important.

Transparent Translation

The transparent translation registers TT0 and TT1, which are among the system control registers, allow certain addresses to bypass the memory management unit completely. Each of these registers specifies a range of virtual addresses that are mapped into identical physical addresses. Each register contains an address range (specified by giving the upper 8 bits of the address to be treated specially), together with a function code to select which address space or spaces are to be treated specially.

The TT0 and TT1 registers are checked at the same time that the ATC is being checked for an address translation entry, so this checking is done in parallel and does not take additional time. If either TT0 or TT1 indicates that an address fetch is to be done without translation, the result of searching the ATC is abandoned, and we immediately have the physical address, without any paging overhead. That is a facility that doesn't exist on the 386.

A good application would be to put system hardware interrupt handlers in a non-translated area of memory because there is no possibility of those being swapped out. They are time-critical; you don't want any overhead from the paging. With a little bit of careful planning you can reduce the paging system overhead by putting things under the transparent region of memory that you know are going to be resident all the time and that you are willing to address all the time.

CONTEXT SWITCHING

Unlike the treatment of context switching for the 386, this section will be quite short. Why? There is essentially no hardware support for context switching on the 68030. However, before we get too worried about such lack of support, we should remember that in many situations, switching contexts on the 386 was faster in software than using the built-in hardware instructions.

The 68030 does have some basic mechanisms that help in the programming of a context switch. The MOVEM instruction, for example, allows the entire register set, or any subset of it, to be loaded or stored using a single instruction. In addition, there are instructions that will modify certain system registers. For example, the CRP (the CPU root register) holds the address map—and we may also want to swap the user stack pointer and the master stack pointer. Finally, some fiddling with the cache and ATC may be needed to ensure that the translation is valid for the new task.

Even if *all* of these functions are performed by software on a context switch, it will probably be faster than if the context switch was done in hardware on the 386. The one weak point occurs in the handling of the coprocessor. If a floating-point coprocessor is in use, we probably have little choice but to save and restore it on every context switch, whereas on the 386 the TS bit, which caused a trap if the coprocessor was being used by a different task, allowed us to optimize the handling of the coprocessor.

TRACE CONTROL

Trace control on the 68030 is somewhat more sophisticated than on the 386. There are three states controlled by the setting of the two trace bits in the status register. In normal execution mode, both these bits are set to zero, so that no trace trapping occurs.

The *trace all* mode (when the trace bits are set to 10) is exactly like the trace status flag on the 386. When this bit is set, a trap occurs before each instruction is executed. A software debugger can watch the progress of a program instruction by instruction and see exactly where in the sequence of instructions the program is.

If the trace bits are set to 01, *flow change tracing* is enabled. Flow change is really quite a clever feature. It traces only jumps, calls, and returns, that is, instructions that change the flow of control. From an efficiency point of view, that is a reasonable compromise since it allows a debugger to interrupt only when there is a change in program flow. In the absence of a breakpoint (which would be a change of flow), you're happy to have the instructions between two such points executed without interference. If you want to watch where your program is going, all you really need to know is where the flow changes. It's just like following a car—the critical thing is figuring out when it will turn and where; when it's on a straight road you know where it's going.

Flow tracing is a useful feature that is not present on the 386, allowing tracing of a program in a more efficient manner than is possible on the 386. However, this is the whole story of the on-chip capabilities on the 68030. There are no debug registers, and so there is no data trapping or anything like that. However, critical addressing lines are brought out on the external pins, and it is possible to disable the caching. An auxiliary hardware device can thus be built that watches what is happening on the bus and provides the kind of data and instruction trapping that is on the 386. The need for more sophisticated debugging can be handled in this manner if it is needed.

Once again the issue of whether to do things on-chip or off-chip is raised. The considerations in this case are the usual ones. Putting debugging capabilities on-chip means that they are always present, and so standard software systems can assume their use. From the hardware designer's point of view, the number of components is reduced, which reduces the cost. On the other hand, if the debugging capabilities are placed off-chip, then they can be much more sophisticated and extensive—for instance, an off-chip debugger could have it's own memory for holding symbolic address information, or a trace buffer which would keep track of the last 1000 instructions executed.

EXCEPTIONS

The 68030 has an exception mechanism that supports exceptions generated both internally and externally, just as most microprocessors do. Externally generated exceptions can occur due to interrupts or bus errors, or for several other reasons associated with hardware external to the processor. Internally generated errors are generally caused by instructions such as a division by zero, instructions that are the result of logical errors within the instruction stream.

We will see that the exception mechanism of the 68030 is not nearly as complicated as that of the 386. There are no call gates, task gates, or any of the fancier things that are found on the 386. Exceptions on the 68030 are similar to trap gates on the 386, except that the stack pointer of the user state is replaced with the system stack pointer. There is no way for an application to handle a trap in user state on the 68030.

All exceptions on the 68030, whether due to internal or external causes, are handled through the use of what is called by Motorola an *exception vector table*, a contiguous table in memory that contains 256 32-bit addresses known as *exception vectors*. Each exception vector contains the address of a routine that handles the exception if it happens to occur.

Since this table can be located at any address in memory that the designer of an operating system wants, there must be some way to locate it. One of the special system registers, the *vector base register* (VBR), must be set to point to the starting address of the exception table. Motorola has reserved the first 64 addresses for its own use with the remaining addresses being left to the engineer to use as needed.

Trap Processing

What happens when a trap (as opposed to an interrupt, something like a zero divide or a trace trap) occurs is that the old status register is saved and the trace bits are set to zero so that you don't trace the trap. If desired the debugger can notice the trap occurring and force the trace trap bits back on to trace the trap routine, but normally a user is not interested in tracing operating system trap routines. The S bit is set to 1 causing a switch to supervisor state, and the master stack pointer is established as the current stack pointer (A7 value). Finally the instruction pointer is set to the start of the trap routine.

At the end of an interrupt, a return from interrupt (RTE) instruction is issued. The old status register as well as the T1, T0, and S bits and the instruction pointer, are restored.

This is a much simpler model than the 386 with its task gates, call gates, and trap gates. On the other hand, these synchronous traps are sometimes user-level functions, but on the 68030 we unconditionally enter supervisor state to handle them. That is too bad, because it means, for example, that zero divide has to be handled by the operating system.

On a Unix system, for example, it means that you are committed to a very long delay in handling division by zero, because what happens in a typical system is that the trap is signalled and then goes through some layers of exception handlers which finally figures out that control should be given back to the task at some location. The system then laboriously unwinds through its layers of trap handling to return control. Therefore, a disadvantage of this design is that even simple synchronous traps on errors such as a divide by zero force the processor into supervisor mode.

For many programming environments, letting the operating system handle errors like zero divide is not an impediment. For instance, C programmers are happy to have their programs aborted on a zero divide. On the other hand, languages like Ada require that the user program be able to handle divide by zero (as a CONSTRAINT_ERROR exception). A compiled Ada program for the 68030 could always test to avoid dividing by zero by emitting instructions, but this seems undesirable, given that the hardware performs the check automatically in any case. Furthermore, the idea in Ada is that you should not pay a price for exceptions unless they happen. This ideal can be achieved only by letting the hardware check.

Interrupt Processing

Interrupt processing is somewhat different from trap processing. One of the differences is that the stack may have to be changed from the user stack to the interrupt stack if the M bit is set in the status register (remember the difference between the two stack pointers).

Also, I2, I1, and I0, which forms the interrupt mask, are automatically set to the interrupt level. If you get a level 4 interrupt, part of the processing for the interrupt automatically locks out interrupts of that level or any equal or lower interrupt level.

When you return from the interrupt, you will restore the old interrupt mask. This gives you classical, nested priority interrupts. An interrupt routine can be interrupted by an interrupt routine of higher priority but not by one of lower priority. Interrupt routines naturally nest. If you have multiple devices at the same level, when you execute the RTE, waiting interrupts can be resignalled. During the execution of the interrupt routine you are masking off (refusing) any interrupts that occur at that same level. As soon as you do the RTE, the old interrupt mask will be restored. If some other device is still asserting that same level, you will get another interrupt right there (allowing multiple devices to be served at the same level).

If multiple devices are attached to the same level, then the interrupt routine says something like, "Hello. I'm interrupt level 4. I wonder what is going on. Let's see. I've got a communications line on level 4, and I've got an oblong robot on level 4." So the routine sends out a command to the oblong robot asking, "Is it you, oblong robot, that is interrupting at level 4?" The oblong robot replies, "No. It isn't me. I haven't got anything to do with it." The processor then asks, "Is it you, the communications line?," eliciting the response, "It's about time, I've got urgent data for you!" The processor replies, "All right, I'll take your data now." Then the interrupt routine issues an RTE, by which time the oblong robot may be asserting an interrupt, at which point the processor might have to go through the interrogation again. That is how you put multiple devices on the same interrupt level. Obviously this requires careful coordination at both the hardware and operating systems level.

Another approach that can be followed if there are more devices than interrupt levels is to introduce interrupt control circuitry off-chip. Such a device can handle several separate interrupts and be attached to a single interrupt level on the 68030. On the 386, this approach is always used, since there *is* only one interrupt level on the 386 itself, and the controlling of multiple levels is always done off-chip using an 8259 interrupt controller chip.

Reserved Exceptions

To get a sense of the sort of exceptions someone using the 68030 expects to encounter, we will look at some of these reserved exceptions. For the most part, these exceptions deal with how the hardware will behave if something goes wrong.

Locations 0 and 1 in the interrupt vector are used to specify the initial values of the program counter and the stack pointer when the processor is reset (or the power just happens to be turned on). These are dummy entries which do not correspond to exceptions. The processor needs some standard location to obtain this data, and uses the interrupt vector for this purpose.

- An *address error* (exception 3) is signalled if an attempt is made to fetch an instruction from an odd address. By "odd address" we don't mean to suggest an unusual address, but an address with its last bit set. Even though instructions on the 68030 must be aligned along 2-byte boundaries in memory, it is possible that a flaw in a compiler might generate executable code where some of the instructions are not correctly aligned. Occasionally, clever compiler designers can find a use for deliberately branching to an odd address so that the attempt can be trapped by the hardware.

- An *illegal instruction error* (exception 4) is signalled if the processor detects an instruction whose opcode has not been defined. As in the case of an address error, clever programmers might sometimes find uses for deliberately issuing illegal instructions. Recognizing this possibility, Motorola provides a special instruction

(ILLEGAL) that is guaranteed to be illegal on all future versions of the chip. Using any other illegal instruction is treading on Motorola's toes, since they may introduce additional legal instructions in some later version of the processor.

- Zero divide (exception 5) is signalled on a divide by zero.

- Exception 6 is used by the CHK and CHK2 instructions, which are used for generating checks (for example, checking to make sure that an array subscript is in bounds).

- Exception 7 is used for the trap on condition instructions (cpTRAPcc, TRAPcc, and TRAPV). All these traps are typically used for quick detection of user level errors in application programs. For example, the exceptions of the Ada language would often be detected using one of these traps.

- A *privilege violation* (exception 8) is signalled if a user-level program issues a protected instruction. The operating system would normally respond by terminating the program, which has either gone berserk or is attempting to behave in a sinister manner!

- The *trace* trap (exception 9) is taken on every instruction or every jump (depending upon how the trace bits in the system status register are set) if tracing is enabled.

- Exceptions 13 and 14 have to do with the coprocessor communicating incorrectly with the processor.

- Exceptions 25 to 31 correspond to hardware interrupts for level 1 to 7.

- Interrupts 32 to 47 are the trap interrupt vector elements, which are used by a program running in user mode to deliberately switch to supervisor state. For those who know MS-DOS, their use is similar to the use of INT 21 on the PC to make operating system requests.

- Vector addresses 48 through 55 are for reserved coprocessor interrupts. Although these are reserved by Motorola, there is an entertaining phrase in the 68030 User's Manual which says, "The reserved vectors may be used for other purposes at the discretion of the hardware designer."

Exceptions 13 and 14, which signal errors in communicating with the coprocessor are an example of "defensive programming" at the hardware level. It is a reasonable thing for the processor to do error checking at the coprocessor communication level, since the processor opens itself up considerably to the coprocessor. If the coprocessor is designed by someone else, you can imagine problems of the worst kind appearing , and you will want to protect against those.

CONCLUSION

The 68030 takes a less aggressive CISC view at the supervisor level, which is why we only needed one chapter for the 68030, where two were needed for the 386. Missing from the 68030 is any support for hardware tasking, segmentation, or elaborate protection mechanisms.

The only note of complexity in the 68030 supervisor state is in the paging mechanism, a remarkably elaborate MMU design that gives the operating system very elaborate control over the structure of the page tables. Other than this, the 68030 supervisor state is similar in many respects to what we will see in RISC chips.

The 68030 has been widely used in engineering workstations, and this is precisely the area where RISC chips have made their biggest inroads. Motorola has announced the forthcoming release of a new member of this series, the 68040. While no technical details are available at the time of this writing, it is clear from what Motorola has said that this will be an advanced design using RISC techniques, and will bear much the same relationship with the 68030 as the 486 does with the 386. It remains to be seen whether this attempt at maintaining and improving the 68030 CISC technology will be sufficiently effective to ward off the RISC chips.

CHAPTER 8

AN INTRODUCTION TO RISC ARCHITECTURES

Von Neumann, who is generally considered to be the inventor of the stored-program, sequential execution model that is the basis of all the microprocessor architectures considered in this text, had the following to say about choosing instruction sets:

> The really decisive considerations from the present point of view, in selecting a code, are more of a practical nature: the simplicity of the equipment demanded by the code, and the clarity of its application to the actually important problems together with the speed of its handling of those problems.[1]

In some sense, how can anyone disagree with that? Everyone would agree that useless instructions should not be put into an instruction set. Everyone would also agree, in principle at least, that when one reaches the point at which the addition of a complex instruction to an instruction set has an impact on the efficiency of the processor as a whole, it is important to consider whether it is worth having the instruction at all. This

---

[1] Burks, A.W., Goldstine, H.H., and von Neumann, J. Preliminary discussion of the logical design of an electronic computing instrument. Rep. to U.S. Army Ordinance Dept., 1946.

quote, sometimes cited by designers as one of the basic ideas behind the RISC approach, involves taking a long hard look at "the actually important problems" and the "speed of handling these problems."

This sentiment, on the other hand, which seems reasonable from a purely hardware point of view, is not necessarily an absolute principle. A different point of view, which at one time represented an important trend in architectural design, was that machines should be built to cater to the needs of high-level languages. With the so-called software crisis desperately demanding a solution, and hardware getting cheaper and cheaper, the important point was to improve the efficiency of high-level languages by providing specialized instructions precisely suited to translating high-level languages. Furthermore, there was the expectation that including such instructions would simplify compiler writing. An extreme point of view was expressed in one paper published in the early 1970s in which someone suggested the possibility of a machine which would directly execute FORTRAN *source* code.

As we shall see, the issue of which instructions to include in an instruction set and which instructions to exclude is one of the main points differentiating the design philosophy of RISC from that of CISC. This single aspect of RISC architectures is what gives RISC its name—Reduced Instruction Set Computer.

We will begin by looking at some of the characteristics of the CISC machines of the 1960s and 1970s so we can later put into perspective some of the architectural features of RISC. We will then enumerate several of the major characteristics of RISC machines before describing in some detail some of the most popular RISC chips.

INSTRUCTION SET DESIGN: A BRIEF HISTORY

Ever since high-level languages started to appear, the idea of tailoring computer architectures so that they would be "suitable" has influenced instruction set design. For example, one of the instructions on the IBM7040, a machine in use in the late 1960s, was CAS, Compare Accumulator With Storage. This instruction executed a comparison and skipped zero, one, or two instructions depending on whether the result was less than, equal, or greater than. This was clearly influenced by the three-way IF of FORTRAN 2,

    IF (A – B) 10, 20, 30

which would jump to label 10, 20, or 30, depending on whether the result of the expression was less than zero, zero, or greater than zero. Somewhat ironically, no FORTRAN compiler ever made use of this instruction in compiling IF statements. This is probably one of the first examples of an increasingly common phenomenon— interesting-sounding high-level instructions that turn out to be less useful than the designer imagined.

Other manufacturers went much further along the path of tailoring architectures to high-level languages. Burroughs was a very important supplier of computers to the banking industry in the early days of computing. They had a strong commitment to machines that were heavily oriented to the implementation of ALGOL 60, and indeed the B5500, a machine popular in the late 1960s, was delivered *without* any assembler—you were expected to do all your programming in ALGOL 60.

Central to the design of this machine was a hardware evaluation stack, somewhat similar to that of the 387 math coprocessor but used for all calculations including address and integer computations. Given a statement such as

A := B + (C * D)

the B5500 ALGOL 60 compiler would generate code similar to the following:

```
LOAD   B
LOAD   C
LOAD   D
MUL
ADD
STORE  A
```

There were no registers, and all the operations worked in conjunction with the stack. One idea in taking this approach was that it should simplify compilers to generate code of this type (conversion from infix form to postfix Polish, which is essentially what this code represents, is a relatively trivial transformation).

The Burroughs 6700 went even further than this. For an array reference such as A(J, I) the hardware had built-in array descriptor formats as well as an instruction that took advantage of those formats. To generate code for such an array reference, a descriptor would be built in memory that contained both the upper and lower bounds for both the first and second subscripts, as well as the address of the array. The assembly code for the indexing would resemble something like this:

```
PUSHAD    DESCR
PUSH      I
PUSH      J
SUBSCRIPT
```

Once all the information for computing the subscript was present in the descriptor, the subscript instruction would do the rest. Again, one of the ideas behind implementing this type of operation was that it should simplify the writing of a compiler. The enthusiasm for high-level architectures of this type was quite widespread. One designer expressed the opinion that anyone proposing the design of a machine which included the use of registers should have the soundness of their judgment questioned.

Unfortunately, the basic premise here is misleading. It is certainly not easy to write high-quality optimizing compilers. But working out the details of how to generate code for simple expressions and subscript references is certainly *not* the main source of the difficulty. This was true long before the 6700 was designed. One of the difficulties was that the 6700 performed rather poorly, even compared to naive code running on more conventional register-oriented processors.

What *do* compiler writers have trouble doing? The most difficult problems involve clever optimizations. Consider the following FORTRAN example:

```
            DIMENSION A(23, ...)
            DO I = 1,N
            A(J,I) = A(J,I) + 1
    1       CONTINUE
```

In generating code for the Burroughs machine, where array references use a descriptor, we would simply generate literal code for the loop, where each reference to A(J,I) corresponds to an application of the amazing subscript operation. The code would be easy to generate but would probably be slightly less efficient than naive code for a register machine. More important, it would be *much* less efficient than carefully optimized code.

Naive code for this loop would compute the double-subscripted reference to A(J,I) once each time through the loop.[2] However, if we examine this loop carefully, we see that the subscript being varied is the one that moves less rapidly in terms of the storage layout. This means that successive addresses of A(J, I) on iterations of the loop are 23 * 4 bytes apart, because the first subscript is 23 and the stride of the array is 4.

A clever compiler (the kind that is a bit more difficult to write) would do the following kind of analysis. The compiler would first recognize that the value of I itself is not of any interest (it is not used after the loop), so the compiler doesn't need to maintain I as a variable that goes from 1 to N. Instead it would be much more useful to have a variable that increments in units of 23 * 4 and compare it with N * 23 * 4. This optimization, called *strength reduction*, is documented in almost all compiler texts and implemented in many production quality compilers (these optimizations are not recent inventions).

The result of such an analysis on the 386, combined with an effort to use registers as much as possible and avoid memory references, might result in the following code:

```
            EAX ← 23 * 4 * N + address(A(J,I))
            EBX ← address(A(J,1))
    LP:
            INC     DWORD PTR [EBX]
            ADD     EBX, 23 * 4
            CMP     EBX;EAX
            JB      LP
```

The result is a very simple loop of only four instructions. For such a small loop, the compiler may even replicate the first two instructions (called *unrolling* the loop).

The use of FORTRAN here is deliberate. FORTRAN compilers have matured to the point that they are able to perform extensive optimizations, so we can in fact expect code pretty similar to the optimized example given here.

Going back to the Burroughs machine, the lack of registers makes it much harder to use these techniques. This means that the attempt to make things simpler by providing just the instructions we need backfires if execution efficiency is important.

---

[2] A really silly compiler would compute it twice each time through the loop, but it is no problem to eliminate that level of incompetence.

Not all of the older machines were committed to fancy instructions, and indeed machines have been built with all sorts of variations on the general theme. The PDP-8 is an example of a rather early machine with a limited set of only registers, and only eight instructions. Although that may sound pretty reduced, the PDP-8 lacked many other characteristics of a modern RISC architecture.

A more important example of early simplified approaches was found in the early CDC machines designed by Seymour Cray, who has always said that he could never understand anything complicated. The CDC6600 not only had a very simple instruction set with few instruction formats but also embodied other RISC principles such as overlapped execution and limiting memory accesses to loads and stores. Even the more modern Cray has a relatively simple instruction set. Seymour Cray is sometimes given credit for being one of the first RISC designers, although of course the term did not exist when the CDC 6600 was designed.

The IBM 360 Series

IBM led the march in a new direction with the IBM 360 series. The 360 has sometimes been given credit as defining the first computer architecture. What is meant by that is that the 360 architecture was designed independently of the hardware used to build the machine itself. It was designed as an abstract architecture from which one could build machines that embody that architecture.[3]

The initial set of machines implementing this architecture ranged from the 360/30 to the 360/91, with many models in between. These machines came with complicated instruction sets. For example, instructions were included to do full decimal arithmetic aimed that were aimed at commercial users. An editing instruction supported features of COBOL that did exactly what a COBOL programmer would want when, for example, a field was edited using a "picture" (putting in check protection and commas, asterisks, leading zeros, dollar signs, etc.)—all of this could be done with one very complicated instruction. Various string and bit manipulation instructions were also included.

As a particular example of a fancy instruction, consider the Translate and Test (TRT) instruction on the 360. This instruction scans a string in memory, examining each character in turn. The character is examined by using a 256-character lookup table specified as one of the operands in the instruction. A non-zero entry in the lookup table terminates the translate and test scan.

Suppose that you need to find the first character that is not a letter in a string. This can be done with a single TRT instruction on the 360 by defining a table that contains non-zero entries for all characters other than letters. For a compiler writer who needs to scan out identifiers, this is certainly a very convenient instruction. However, as always, when confronted by such a complex instruction, we must wonder whether

---

[3] The ICL 1900 series, developed by ICL in England a little later on, had a similar approach and covered an even more extensive range of machines than the original 360 series, from very small minicomputers to very large and powerful mainframes.

there are any programs whose performance is significantly affected by the presence of this instruction. This concern is especially relevant for the TRT instruction, since it is very unlikely that compilers for conventional languages can manage to make use of this instruction in translating user code.

One problem with a very rich instruction set like this is that at the low end of the series the hardware to execute such a wide range of instructions is unaffordable. IBM addressed this problem by implementing 360s using several techniques.

The first technique, *microcoding*, means that you are not really buying a 360 at all—you are buying a 360 simulator. The simulator is fast enough because it is hardware assisted by an efficient microprogram controller—this is really a processor with an instruction set quite distinct from the 360 instruction set. Since this simulation is done with a relatively fast processor, the resulting performance is good enough for the low end of the range. Machines at the low end using this approach included the 360/30 and 360/40, which both relied on microprogramming for what essentially amounts to the entire 360 instruction set.[4]

Another technique for implementing the entire instruction set of the 360 architecture is *trap and emulate*. For example, the 360/44, which was primarily intended as a scientific machine, had a fairly fast hardware implementation of many of the instructions but did not implement decimal arithmetic at all. Instead the processor recognized such instructions and generated a trap to a software routine that would emulate the missing instructions slowly. The entire instruction set was available from the point of view of the user, although certain instructions were much less efficient.

Higher up in the range, the machines used a combination of real hardware and microprogramming. For example, on the 360/65, such instructions as load and store and integer arithmetic were implemented in direct hardware logic, but more complicated instructions were handled by microprogramming. The entire instruction set was available from the point of view of the programmer, even though the more complex instructions were microprogrammed rather than being implemented directly in hardware.

At the extreme top end of the range, where it was necessary to achieve maximum speed, the instructions that were implemented were implemented only in hardware. Not all of the complex instructions could feasibly be implemented in hardware, so again the trap and emulate approach was used for some of them—microcode was avoided entirely. As in the case of the 360/44, these high-end machines, for example, the 360/91, were intended primarily for scientific processing, so the fact that some of the complex instructions were emulated was not so important. Also, the fact that the basic instruction set executed very fast on these high-end machines meant that even the emulated instructions were reasonably efficient. As we will see later on, the philosophy of these high-end 360 machines involved exactly the same considerations as the RISC machines, although they were not so visible.

---

[4] The inner machine of the 360/40 was a 16-bit machine not unlike the PDP-11. Perhaps IBM could have marketed this machine directly with Unix and been even more successful in selling it!

The philosophy of the 360 architecture was thus to provide, one way or another, a rich set of instructions throughout the entire range of machines. There is no question that having fancy instructions around that do exactly what you want is handy when you are coding in assembly language. Furthermore, you tend to get much more use than you might expect out of the fancy instructions, because once they are there an assembly language programmer will try to use them. The questionable TRT instruction, for instance, was employed very aggressively in the SPITBOL compiler for the IBM 360, resulting in a compiler that was able to compile 50,000 to 100,000 lines a minute on machines that are much slower than current mainframes. Nevertheless, this aspect of the machine's performance is an isolated one, and much more significant is the fact that the thousands of COBOL programs running on 360s made absolutely no use of this instruction.

It is probably fair to say that IBM solidified the trend to complicated instruction sets. IBM considered both stack and register architectures for the 360, and the decision was in the balance until quite late. The final decision, in favor of a register model, was influenced by efficiency considerations, and this single decision probably spared us from an even more aggressive excursion into the land of "high-level" architectures.

The VAX is another notable example of a CISC machine, and it is also an example of a major architecture—it is now *the* major DEC architecture. Perhaps the most extreme commitment to complicated instruction set architectures was the Intel 432, a stack-based microprocessor with no registers and no status flags based on the high-level notion of typed pointers and run-time checking of pointer access. The 432 was a complete failure, mostly because its performance was appallingly slow compared to that of competitive chips, such as Intel's own 80286, which used a conventional register structure.

The idea that high-level languages should dictate the design of instruction sets is by no means dead and buried. When Ada was designed, a number of Department of Defense agencies expressed an interest in building processors specialized for execution of Ada code. This work never went anywhere, and it is just as well, because Ada was designed to work well on conventional existing architectures, and indeed the RISC architectures are quite friendly to Ada. The proper answer to the DoD officials looking to add special instructions to help Ada execution was very probably that they should be looking to *remove* little-used instructions rather than adding new ones!

We may be entering a relatively stable stage in the development of CISC architectures. The IBM 370 and subsequent mainframes were substantially compatible with the architecture of the 360. The Intel 486 is binary-compatible with the 386; that is, the architecture from a programmer's point of view is identical. Similarly, the Motorola 68040 will be binary-compatible with the 68030. The CISC architectures of the major mainframes and widely used microprocessors are also relatively stable at this point. Whether these architectures will survive the onslaught of the RISC attack is one of the fascinating things to be observed over the next few years.

WHAT IS RISC?

As we have seen, during the 1970s, computer architects designed machines in which the instruction sets grew larger and in which many of the instructions became increasingly complex. Advances in VLSI technology, and, more specifically, the number of transistors that could be packed onto a single chip made this possible. As we outlined in the previous section, the general mind set of most designers favored supporting instructions that mirrored the high-level operations and addressing modes of high-level programming languages.

These complicated instructions and addressing modes were provided in the belief that if they could be utilized by either clever compilers or assembly language programmers, substantial gains in the performance of such machines would result. One of the basic assumptions underlying this belief was that anything implemented in hardware would be faster than if it were implemented in software. One example of such an instruction is the VAX CASE instruction, which directly mirrors the semantics of the case statements of many programming languages. This particular instruction not only implements a jump based on a case index, but also checks to see that the index is within the legitimate bounds of the range of possible cases.

Some of these design principles began to be questioned in the mid-1970s and early 1980s by early RISC researchers. The justification for the RISC design philosophy is based on two important observations. First of all, some of the instructions provided by CISC processors are so esoteric that many compilers simply do not attempt to use them. Looking back at the CAS2 instruction on the 68030, it is hard to imagine how the data structures implemented in hardware by that instruction could be easily mapped onto data structures constructed in a program written in a high-level language. It is more likely that such instructions will be used only in carefully hand written assembly language code used by an operating system or some other specialized application. Second, even if such specialized instructions could be used by compilers, it is hard to imagine that they would be used very frequently.

These observations are of great importance to those who implement hardware, because complex instructions contribute in many ways to reducing the efficiency of a chip as a whole. In the minds of RISC designers, the only complex instructions worth including are those whose benefit is clearly established in terms of performance. Not only can complex instructions require many cycles to execute, but the extra logic required to implement even a single instruction may lengthen the basic cycle time. One of the main motivations behind the idea of RISC is to simplify all of the architectural aspects of the design of a machine so that its implementation can be made more efficient. George Radin, the head of the IBM 801 research effort, described this effect as follows:

> Complex, high-function instructions, which require several cycles to execute, are conventionally realized by some combination of random logic and microcode ... We have no objection to this strategy, provided the frequency of use justifies the cost, and more importantly, provided these complex functions in no way slow down the primitive instructions.

But it is just this pernicious effect on the primitive instructions that has made us suspicious. Most instruction frequency studies show a sharp skew in favor of high usage of primitive instructions (such as LOAD, STORE, BRANCH, COMPARE, ADD). If the presence of a more complex set adds just one logic level to a ten-level basic machine cycle (e.g., to fetch a microinstruction from ROS), the CPU has been slowed down by 10%. The frequency and performance improvement of the complex functions must first overcome this 10% degradation and then justify the additional cost.

We should point out that the term Reduced Instruction Set Computer really refers to a set of reduced instructions, not a reduced set of instructions. The goal of RISC is not simply to reduce the number of instructions, but rather to simplify the instructions that are included in the instruction set of a machine. Each individual instruction needs to be simplified to the extent that some significant advantage in performance can be obtained when the instruction set is implemented. RISC machines do, in general, have a smaller total number of instructions than many CISC processors, but this is a consequence of the fact that careful study of instruction frequencies fails to justify larger numbers of instructions.

We will now look at some of the fundamental characteristics of RISC and some of the arguments in their support. We won't be able to establish an absolutely hard and fast criterion for determining whether a processor qualifies as a genuine RISC machine, but we will list a set of typical characteristics. Some machines will clearly be classified as RISC machines, and others will equally clearly fall into the CISC classification. However, the line is not well defined, and we will encounter a number of machines that incorporate some, but not all, of the RISC design techniques.[5] Not all of these characteristics are present in all RISC designs, but taken together they represent a general philosophy of instruction set and architectural design that stands in definite contrast to the CISC tradition of providing as many useful instructions as possible.

One Instruction per Clock Cycle

A goal to which the designers of all RISC processors aspire is the ability to sustain an execution rate of one instruction per cycle, or even possibly more than one instruction per cycle. It is important to understand that in a literal sense a processor cannot really execute an instruction in one cycle. It is difficult to imagine a processor that could take an instruction and, *boom,* cause everything required by the instruction to happen at once. That is simply not the way processors are designed. The only way in which it is possible to effectively execute an instruction in a single cycle is through the use of a *pipeline* in which several instructions are being executed at once, or through the use of

---

[5] Defining anything by listing a set of characteristics is something that one must be careful about. Remember back to high school biology class, where one unit attempts to define life by listing a set of characteristics. Once you've written these down, you often find that there are certain anomalies. A wound up rubber band, for example, might be described as being alive because it moves autonomously. Once you have added intelligence to the list, you might conclude that an amoeba is not alive because it is not intelligent, and so on. We face a similar problem in trying to define RISC.

instruction lookahead or parallel execution units. The general idea is to do more than one thing at a time and to execute instructions in parallel to the greatest extent possible.

In practice, most RISC processors currently do not quite achieve the one instruction per clock goal, but they do come much closer than CISC chips. Figures of 1.5 clocks per instruction can be achieved on a number of current RISC chips, compared with something more like 3 to 4 clocks per instruction on the 386.

Pipelining

Pipelining is a general term used to describe the design approach in which a complex operation is broken down into stages so that the stages can be executed in parallel. In RISC processors the application of this technique to the basic instruction interpretation and execution is a key to achieving the high throughput. Furthermore, many of the other characteristics of RISC, such as simplified instruction sets, are consequences of the decision to pipeline instruction execution.

To pipeline instruction execution, the execution of an individual instruction is broken down into a sequence of separate phases. The exact division of work between the phases varies between processors, but the following is a common description:

- *Instruction Fetch* (IF). This phase is the actual loading of the instruction from memory into the processor.

- *Instruction Decode* (ID). During this phase, the instruction is decoded. The decoding phase on a RISC processor is *much* simpler than the decoding that is required by CISC processors.

- *Operand Fetch* (OF). During the operand fetch phase, operands (typically operands in registers) are read from the registers into an appropriate place on the chip where the operation is performed.

- *Operate* (OP). The operation is actually executed during this phase.

- *Write Back* (WB). The result of an operation is written back into a register (or into a memory location).

These phases are the *logical phases* of instruction execution. They are not necessarily distinct in the sense that they must be executed sequentially, each in its own separate cycle. It is possible, for example, to overlap the instruction decode and operand fetch phases if the format of the instructions and the chip's logic allow it, resulting in a pipeline with four stages as shown in Figure 8.1.

If we look at these phases, and consider that they are supposed to be executed independently, we can immediately see why it would be quite difficult to pipeline a typical CISC machine. Consider an ADD instruction on the 68030. The first problem is that the instruction can vary in length from 2 to 14 bytes, depending on the addressing mode. The instruction fetch phase needs to know the length in order to fetch the bytes of the instruction. In the non-pipelined implementation used by the 68030, this is not

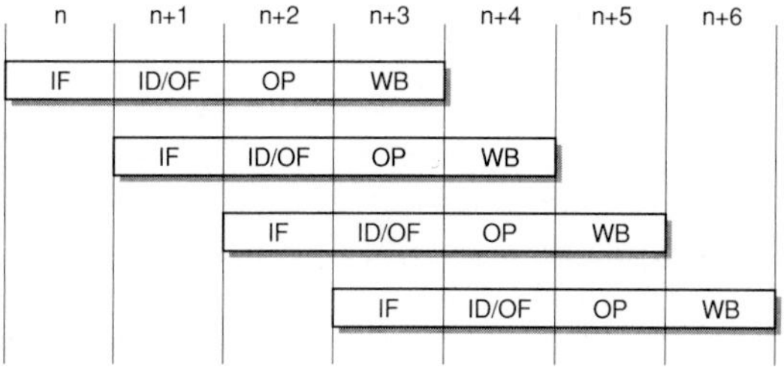

FIGURE 8.1
A simple 4-stage instruction pipeline.

a problem, since the necessary words are loaded from the instruction stream as they are needed. In a pipelined approach, however, we are deliberately trying to avoid this kind of intermixed processing.

Another problem on the 68030 arises during the instruction decode and operand fetch phases. Even if these phases are not combined, we are in big trouble. Recall the sections describing the rather messy operand formats and addressing modes of the 68030. The instruction decode phase has to work its way through a great variety of instruction formats and addressing modes to find out what the operands are. Needless to say, accomplishing this in a single clock is not easy. Moving on into the operand fetch phase, we have further problems in that one of the operands may be in memory. Not only that, but in the case of the memory indirect addressing modes, we have to fetch indirect address links from memory as well. As we will see later, memory loads are a real problem because memory is quite slow and the progress of the pipeline may be interrupted. On a CISC processor, almost any instruction can reference memory, so the problem of memory loads has to be addressed at all points in the instruction set.

All these problems add up to make it impossible or at least extremely difficult to fully pipeline a CISC instruction set like that found on the 80386 or 68030.[6] A RISC processor, on the other hand, is specially designed to facilitate the pipelined approach.

Both fetching an instruction and decoding an instruction on most RISC processors is simplified. When fetching an instruction, the processor is able to assume on most machines that the instruction length is 32 bits. This means that the instruction fetch phase simply loads a word from memory, without needing to examine any of the initial bits of the instruction to determine the number of bytes in the instruction. Instruction decoding is simplified because there are very few instruction formats. The few formats which do exist place the fields such as the opcode and operand fields in consistent positions. This means that the instruction decoding and the process of identifying the operands are much simplified.

---

[6] The recently announced 486 and 68040 chips *do* make a not completely successful, but quite impressive, attempt at pipelining these instruction sets—we will discuss these attempts in further detail in the closing chapter.

When it comes to fetching the operands, an important simplification is that only load and store instructions can reference memory. As we will see later, loads in particular raise some special problems, which we will deal with separately. By requiring all operands to be in registers for other instructions, such as arithmetic and logical operations, the process of fetching operands is reduced to referencing the necessary registers. Again, this is a much simpler process than interpreting the complex addressing modes of the CISC processors.

With these kinds of simplifications, it is not only practical but also relatively straightforward to pipeline the execution of the successive phases. Suppose we have the following sequence of operations:

```
ADD     R1, R2, R3      ; instruction 1 (result into R1)
ADD     R4, R5, R6      ; instruction 2
ADD     R7, R8, R9      ; instruction 3
ADD     R10, R11, R12   ; instruction 4
```

The state of the pipeline just as the fourth instruction is being fetched, and with the first three instructions in various stages of execution, is as follows:

- The IF phase is loading instruction 4.

- The ID/OF phase is interpreting instruction 3 and fetching its operands (R8 and R9).

- The OP phase is executing instruction 2 (adding the contents of the R5 and R6).

- The WB phase is writing back the result from instruction 1 (the sum of R2 and R3 to be stored in R1).

Although each instruction takes 4 clocks to execute, the throughput is one instruction per clock, since a new instruction can enter the IF phase on each clock. As long as the pipeline is not disturbed, this throughput can be maintained, and the RISC goal of executing one instruction per clock is achieved.

KEEPING THE PIPELINE FLOWING. In the example just above, the four ADD instructions were completely independent. This is not always the case, since simple-minded code frequently uses values just computed in subsequent instructions. A more typical example of a sequence of instructions would be

```
ADD     R1, R2, R3      ; instruction 1      (sets R1)
ADD     R5, R1, R4      ; instruction 2      (uses R1, sets R5)
ADD     R7, R5, R6      ; instruction 3      (uses R5, sets R7)
ADD     R8, R7, R8      ; instruction 4      (uses R7, sets R8)
```

In this sequence, each instruction needs results from the previous instruction. Looking again at Figure 8.1 it seems that this would hold up the pipeline, because the operand fetch phase of each instruction execution seems to need the result stored by the write back phase of the previous instruction, and the result isn't there soon enough.

This problem is solved by using a technique called *forwarding* in which the result from one operation is immediately fed into the next operation in the special case where the output register of one operation is the same as one of the input registers of the next operation. Since the instruction formats are simple, this case can be detected early on, and arrangements can be made to forward the necessary result so that it does not become necessary to hold up the pipeline. Logically what we have is an extra connection between pipeline stages:

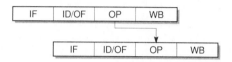

By forwarding results in this manner, the pipeline can be kept flowing at maximum speed, so such "conflicts" in the use of registers do not reduce the instruction throughput.

LOADS AND THE PIPELINE. Load instructions are different from other instructions in one important respect—the data may not be immediately available in a register when it is requested since there may be a delay of several cycles before the data arrives. It is certainly not economically practical to build large memories that will yield data fast enough to keep a pipeline supplied if the data is needed immediately. As time goes on the technology for memories improves—faster memory has become cheaper. However, it is a good guess that processor technology will always march along as fast or even faster than memory technology so that the discrepancy will always exist. Consider the following sequence of instructions:

```
L       R2, CLUNK
L       R3, JUNK
ADD     R4, R2, R3
```

A key part of the RISC approach is to make heavy use of fast caches to reduce effective memory access time, but even if JUNK is in the cache it is still quite difficult to make the data immediately available on the following instruction. If we could guarantee that there would always be a sufficient number of intervening instructions between the load and the use of the data to allow the data to arrive, then the pipelined execution could proceed without delay.

One approach would be to require that compilers (and humans writing in assembly language) ensure that a sufficient number of instructions *do* intervene, inserting NOP (no operation) instructions if necessary. The trouble with this approach is that we would be forced to consider the worst case—a cache miss with the slowest possible memory—all the time. Such assumptions are much too pessimistic because most data references will result in cache hits and the data will be available much earlier. If compilers were forced to assume the worst case all the time, the code generated would be severely and unnecessarily degraded.

The most common approach, used on almost all RISC processors, is to implement an interlock scheme. Whenever a value is loaded from memory, a *scoreboard* is used to keep track of the register into which the value is being loaded so that it cannot be used until the data arrives. If the register is referenced *before* the data arrives, the pipeline is held up until the data is available. If, on the other hand, the data arrives before it is needed, the register is unmarked in the scoreboard, and the pipeline can proceed.

This extra step of checking that the data is available is just the sort of complication that we prefer to avoid in a pipelined design, where we want to keep the complexity of the hardware at a minimum. Nevertheless, we do need some solution to the problem of data arriving late.

Among the microprocessors that we examine in detail, one, the MIPS R2000, takes a slightly different approach. It represents a partial attempt to implement the method of having the compiler insert sufficient instructions to guarantee that the data is available. On the MIPS, if the data is in the cache, then it is guaranteed to appear in the appropriate register one instruction later. Consider the following piece of code with no NOPs inserted.

```
L       R3, GUNK        ; load GUNK into R3
ADD     R4, R3, 1
```

The ADD instruction in this sequence appears too early, since even if there is a cache hit, GUNK will not arrive in time. The first instruction requests that GUNK be loaded into R3, but even if the variable GUNK happens to be in the data cache, it will require one additional cycle to be loaded. However, if one NOP is inserted:

```
L       R3, GUNK
NOP
ADD     R4, R3, 1
```

then as long as GUNK is in the cache, the data is guaranteed to be available in time for the ADD *without* the need to have the hardware check. This position in the instruction sequence is known as a *load delay slot.*

Of course, we have to ask what happens if GUNK is *not* in the cache. In this case the pipeline is held up right away, at the point of the load, so that the data is definitely available on time. Note that this contrasts with the interlock method in that the pipeline is unconditionally held up on a cache miss. We will discuss the consequences of this design approach in the Chapter 9.

STORE INSTRUCTIONS. Store instructions do not pose the same difficulties as loads in that the processor does not need to wait around for the result of a store before subsequent computations can complete. However, consider the sequence

```
ST      R1, A           ; store R1 to AL
L       R2, A           ; reload A into R2
```

We *do* have to be careful that the value of A loaded into R2 is the value just stored from R1 and not some previous value of A.

To maintain the 1 clock per instruction performance, this will require some special logic in the load/store circuits that detect this case and handle it properly. It is not always easy to provide this extra logic, so an alternative approach is to hold things up until the store completes. In particular, some early versions of the SPARC take this approach and suffer as a result from a rather lengthy 3-clock store instruction.

INSTRUCTION SCHEDULING. In the case of the MIPS approach, we have to put at least one instruction between the load and the use of the loaded data. In the previous example, we showed a NOP as the inserted instruction, but of course it is much better to do something useful that to waste time doing nothing!

Often it is possible for the compiler to rearrange instructions so that the requirement that there be an intervening instruction is met without needing to insert a NOP. For example, suppose that the initial code is something like

```
L     R2, JUNK
L     R3, GUNK
ADD   R4, R2, R3
L     R5, XYZ
L     R6, DEF
ADD   R7, R5, R6
```

Instead of inserting a NOP after the instructions which loads GUNK and DEF, it is possible to rearrange the instructions as follows[7]:

```
L     R2, JUNK
L     R3, GUNK
L     R5, XYZ
L     R6, DEF
ADD   R4, R2, R3
ADD   R7, R5, R6
```

With the instructions rearranged, NOP instructions are not needed, since the new sequence, which is functionally equivalent to the initial sequence, meets the requirements of not using data immediately after it is loaded. Of course, the compiler must be sure that any rearrangement does not affect the meaning of the program—this is the sort of condition that compilers are used to dealing with in other kinds of optimization.

Using the MIPS approach, minimal scheduling (insertion of no-ops) is required. With the interlock approach, scheduling is *not* required to keep the program correct, but *is* desirable from an efficiency point of view. Using interlocking, scheduling is more important. In the MIPS case, there is no point in moving the reference further than one instruction from the load, but in the interlock approach, if a cache miss occurs, it pays to have as much separation as possible between the load and the reference.

---

[7] We assume for this example that the processor allows multiple loads to proceed simultaneously. This is not true on all RISC processors. Instruction scheduling is often quite processor-dependent and will be governed by a detailed set of rules indicating what overlaps and delays apply to a particular processor.

Looking at our rearranged code in the previous example, the MIPS conditions were met, and for the MIPS there is no point in doing anything more. However, for an interlock approach, the instruction ADD R7, R5, R6 occurs rather soon after the load for R6. If DEF is in the cache, there is no problem, but if we get a cache miss in loading DEF, then this ADD will interlock. So in the interlock case, the compiler should look for additional instructions to insert before the ADD. Of course, there is no point in inserting NOP instructions, but if some useful instructions can be found to insert, then the performance in the case of a cache miss will be improved.

BRANCH DELAYS. Another important problem associated with the use of an instruction pipeline occurs when a branch is encountered in an executing program. There are two aspects to this problem. First, the instruction following the branch has already entered the pipeline by the time the processor realizes it has a branch on its hands. Second, the instruction that *is* needed next will not have been loaded by the instruction fetch phase in time to keep the pipeline running at full speed.

Real programs contain a surprisingly high proportion of jump and call instructions; as many as 20% of the executing instructions are branches in many programs. This means that execution efficiency of branches is important and must be addressed as part of the RISC design if the goal of one instruction per clock is to be approached.

Even on CISC machines without pipelining, branches are a headache in trying to achieve efficient execution. For example, the 386 maintains an instruction prefetch queue that has to be flushed whenever a branch instruction is encountered. A jump or call on the 386 takes between 8 and 12 clocks, depending on the size of the target instruction. This is quite slow considering that a register-to-register instruction will take only 2 clocks and a memory load only 5 clocks.

The most common technique used on RISC machines for dealing with the branch problem is called a *delayed branch* (or a *delayed jump*). When a branch is taken, since the instruction immediately following the branch is already in the pipeline, rather than sending a message along saying "Hey, send that instruction back, it shouldn't have been put on the conveyer belt," it is allowed to proceed and be fully executed.

The instruction fetch phase realizes that the flow of control has been changed by the *second* instruction after the branch and can load the target instruction in time for it to enter the pipeline one instruction later. To see how this works, consider the following sequence of instructions.

```
        L       R9, 4              R9 = 4
        JMP     LBL
        ADD     R9, 1              R9 + 1 = 5
        ADD     R9, 1
        ...

LBL:
        L       R3, R9             R3 = 5
```

When the JMP instruction is interpreted, the first ADD is already in the pipeline and is allowed to proceed. The next instruction to enter the pipeline is the load instruction just after the label LBL, and so the final result stored in R3 is 5.

Reading programs that execute in this manner may be somewhat confusing to humans expecting instructions to execute in sequence. But since the rules are clear and consistent, a compiler can generate code with this understanding of the instruction execution sequence without having to hold up the pipeline. A throughput of one instruction per clock can be maintained even when a conditional jump is taken.[8]

USING THE BRANCH DELAY SLOT. When generating code for a machine that uses the approach of delayed branches, the compiler or human assembly language programmer must make sure that an appropriate instruction follows each branch, in what is called the *branch delay slot*, remembering that it is going to be logically executed *before* the branch. This requirement can be met simply by placing a NOP instruction after each jump, but in that case the whole advantage of the delay slot approach is negated. The problem, therefore, is to find a useful instruction to use in the delay slot, called *filling* a delay slot.

There are several cases to be considered, of which unconditional jumps are the easiest type. Usually such a jump is within a single module (few programming languages permit jumps from one module to another), so the target instruction is known to the back end of the compiler. For example, if the initial code (ignoring the delay slot requirement) is

```
        JMP     LBL
        ...
LBL:
        ADD     R2, R1, 1
        L       R3, R9
```

then all we have do is to move the target instruction into the delay slot:

```
        JMP     LBLX
        ADD     R2, R1, 1
        ...
LBL:
        ADD     R2, R1, 1
LBLX:
        L       R3, R9
```

The ADD is now executed *before* the jump, and the jump transfers control to the instruction at LDX. The original instruction at LBL is retained in case control flows into this code from above; if the compiler can determine that this cannot happen, then the second ADD instruction can be removed.

---

[8] We should note that the description in this chapter is a little idealized. Not *all* RISC processors can guarantee 1-clock execution of jumps, but this goal certainly can be achieved and *is* achieved by at least some of the processors that we consider in this book.

Call instructions can be handled the same way if the first instruction of the procedure is known. A problem can arise if the procedure is separately compiled and the first instruction is unknown.[9] In this case we don't know what instruction to move back into the delay slot. Often we can instead move an instruction *forward* into the delay slot, particularly if the procedure has parameters passed in registers, a common case. Suppose that the initial code (not considering delay slots) is

```
        L       R1, 5           ; first parameter set to 5
        L       R2, 10          ; second parameter set to 10
        CALL    PROC            ; call the procedure
```

All we have to do is move the second parameter load instruction into the delay slot:

```
        L       R1, 5           ; first parameter set to 5
        CALL    PROC            ; call the procedure
        L       R2, 10          ; second parameter set to 10
```

and we have properly sequenced code with the delay slot filled. If the procedure has no parameters and there is no instruction that can be moved to the delay slot, then we may have to put a NOP after the CALL. Not all delay slots can be filled in practice. The goal is to fill as many as possible, so that the throughput remains close to 1 clock per instruction.

The worst problem arises in the case of conditional jumps. These are, of course, very important, since loops in particular, involve a conditional jump on each iteration. Suppose we have the following Pascal loop:

```
S := 0;
for I := 1 to 100 do
    S := S − I;
```

Generating code for this loop and ignoring the delay slot issue would result in an instruction sequence like

```
        L       R1, 0           ; keep value of S in R1
        L       R2, 1           ; keep value of I in R2
LP:     SUB     R1, R1, R2      ; S := S − I
        BEQ     R2, 100, EXIT   ; done if I = 100
        ADD     R2, R2, 1       ; else increment I
        JMP     LP              ; back to start of loop
```

The JMP is easy enough to deal with, because the SUB instruction is always the target. The problem is the conditional BEQ instruction. We can't move the ADD instruction into the BEQ delay slot, because it will get executed one too many times (since the delay slot instruction is executed whether or not the jump is taken), resulting in the wrong value in S. A very clever compiler may be able to reorganize the loop and its surrounding instructions to eliminate the problem, but the final code is more likely to be

---

[9] Even if procedures are separately compiled, there may be some situations in which the first instruction is known anyway, in the case where the procedure prologue is stylized and always starts with the same instruction.

```
          L       R1, 0              ; keep value of S in R1
          L       R2, 1              ; keep value of I in R2
LP:       SUB     R1, R1, R2         ; S := S – I
LP1:      BEQ     R2, 100, EXIT      ; done if I = 100
          NOP                        ; fill BEQ delay slot
          ADD     R2, R2, 1          ; else increment I
          JMP     LP1                ; back to start of loop
          SUB     R1, R1, R2         ; execute SUB in JMP delay slot
```

Some of the processors we will look at, notably the SPARC, provide a feature to deal with this problem, and we will look at this solution in Chapter 10. In the case of other processors such as the MIPS where the behavior is exactly as we describe it here, the problem of filling branch delay slots can be tricky.

Simplified Memory Addressing

One of the common simplifications in the design of a RISC processor, whose intention is to simplify the design while maintaining maximum throughput, is that all memory references must be aligned. A load instruction that loads a 32-bit value into a register will typically require that the memory address be aligned on a 4-byte boundary, corresponding to the hardware organization of the memory. This has two advantages. First, a single load instruction in the program corresponds to a single load on the memory bus. It is bad enough having to arrange for dealing with one load interfering with the pipeline, without having to handle the special case of a single instruction generating two bus loads.

The second important advantage is that the handling of caches and virtual memory paging is simplified. These structures are designed to work with groups of words. This means that a word is either in the cache or it isn't, and it is either in a swapped-in page or it isn't. If we allowed a single 32-bit memory reference to span two hardware words, then we could have a situation where half the word is in the cache and the other half causes a cache miss or, in the paging case, half the word could be in main memory and the other half still on disk. Dealing with these nasty hybrid cases considerably complicates design of both the hardware and software, and it certainly is attractive to eliminate these difficulties by requiring alignment.

In the case of double-word loads, which arise in the context of double-precision floating-point operations if not elsewhere, RISC processors usually require that the operand be aligned on a double-word boundary. Here it is only the second point that is a consideration, since a double word load requires two loads on a 32-bit bus, and this cannot be avoided. The cache and paging simplification is still possible, by making sure that the caching and paging structures work with collections of double-words and requiring double-word alignment.

Despite the problems caused in software by requiring alignment, most RISC designers have made the judgment that the extra complexity required for handling unaligned operands does not justify the cost. This is the usual complexity–cost trade-off that is fundamental to the RISC position.

PARTIAL WORD ACCESS. Since typical RISC memory units work at the 32-bit level, one would expect a RISC machine to provide only 32-bit loads and to avoid the extra complexity of dealing with memory references to smaller quantities such as 8-bit bytes and 16-bit halfwords. There are indeed RISC processors that take the approach of providing only 32-bit memory accesses, notably the AMD 29000. On this machine, if bytes are to be loaded and stored, the effect must be achieved with a sequence of instructions involving fullword memory accesses.

On the other hand, many programs, particularly those written in C, spend much time accessing and manipulating characters and other 8-bit quantities. An analysis of the efficiency trade-offs here has convinced most RISC designers that it *is* worthwhile to provide 8-bit and 16-bit load and store instructions. The 16-bit instructions require halfword alignment to avoid crossing a word boundary, but, of course, the 8-bit instructions require no alignment.

BIG-ENDIAN VS LITTLE-ENDIAN ADDRESSING. RISC processors have generally continued the CISC tradition of failing to standardize in this area—both little-endian and big-endian byte addressing are encountered. One feature seen in a number of RISC processors is the ability to switch between big- and little-endian byte addressing. There is no particular reason why such an option should be confined to RISC designs. It represents a pragmatic reaction to the fact that the two major CISC processors have conflicting views on addressing, not to mention the two major computer vendors, IBM and DEC.

When it comes to bit ordering, the great majority of RISC processors do not provide any bit instructions, so the issue does not affect the hardware design—it is merely a matter of documentation. Most RISC machines are documented as using little-endian bit addressing (least significant bit is bit zero), even when the byte addressing is big-endian. They thus copy the confusion inaugurated by the 68000.

Avoiding Microcoding

Most CISC processors use *microcoding* to implement complex instructions. The approach is to write a program to implement the complex instruction, typically using an inner instruction set (or a subset) on the chip. This program is then coded into a small read only memory that is part of the basic processor chip. The instruction execution circuit then recognizes the instructions that are implemented in this manner and transfers control to the internal microprogram to execute the instruction.

It is usually difficult to know exactly which instructions are microcoded, or even whether this approach is being used at all, because manufacturers do not publish details of the internal arrangements of their chips. However, it is certainly the case that both the 386 and the 68030 do use microcoding for some of the complex instructions.

At first glance, the microcoding approach seems to offer a compromise between the CISC and RISC approaches. An ideal situation would be to implement the simple instructions using the RISC pipelining approach and then transfer control to microcode for the complicated instructions, giving the best of both worlds.

From a RISC point of view, the problem with this approach is that it is difficult to implement a microcoded approach at all without slowing down the basic instruction processing. Constructing the pipeline so that it deals with the special case of recognizing microcoded instructions and holds up the pipeline while they are executed is not impossible, but it is certainly difficult, and it is likely to reduce the maximum speed at which the pipeline can operate. This would violate the fundamental RISC rule that the fast useful instructions are not supposed to incur any burden from the slow, less used instructions.

Furthermore, since microcode is nothing but a program in which simple instructions are run at a high speed, RISC architects ask whether there is any remaining advantage to microcoding if they can make the main instruction set run at a comparable speed. The answer is often no. In this book, we encounter many situations where a CISC instruction, presumably implemented with microcode, is actually slower than the corresponding sequence of RISC instructions for the same function.

For this reason, a general characteristic of RISC architectures is that microcode is eliminated.[10] This simplifies the design of the pipeline and, of course, means that chip space does not have to be wasted on the read only memory otherwise required to store the microprogram instructions.

Register-to-Register Operations

As we have already mentioned, RISC processors generally restrict the instructions that can reference memory to loads and stores. All other instructions have their input operands in registers, and the output results are also stored in registers. There are a number of reasons for this decision.

- Keeping the pipeline simple. The pipeline is disrupted by memory references, particularly loads, and it is difficult to design a pipeline so that memory references can occur in any instruction.

- Keeping memory references simple. Since memory references need to be handled in a special manner, it is important to be able to recognize and interpret them as fast as possible, so that the memory request can be issued as early as possible. By having only a few instructions that can reference memory, it is easier for the earlier stages of the pipeline to recognize a memory reference.

- Keeping instructions simple. An architecture in which there are basically two instruction formats, one for memory references and one for operations on values in registers, allows for a simpler instruction set design, especially if all instructions must be fit into 32 bits.

---

[10]The Clipper RISC chip takes advantage of this by providing on-chip trap and emulate processing for some of the more complex instructions. These instructions trap to sequences of RISC instructions which are stored in read-only memory on the main processor chip of the Clipper.

For all these reasons, the restriction of memory references to load and store instructions is a standard feature of RISC processors. One might at first think that this would result in a considerable number of extra instructions—something we always have to be concerned about since it is not much use getting down to 1 clock per instruction if you need lots more instructions! Consider the following statement:

A := A + B + C;

On the 386, the most efficient code is

```
MOV     EAX, B
ADD     EAX, C
ADD     A, EAX
```

Naive code for a RISC machine, where the ADD instruction cannot reference memory might be

```
L       R1, A           ; load A into R1
L       R2, B
L       R3, C
ADD     R1, R1, R2      ; store result of addition into R1
ADD     R1, R1, R3
ST      R1, A
```

This is twice as many instructions, and the advertised advantage of the RISC approach is not going to be achieved if this kind of expansion is typical. However, we can use compilers that solve this problem by attempting to keep variables in registers wherever possible. In practice, most references are to local procedure variables, which often can be kept in registers. If in this example A, B, and C are all in registers (say, R1, R2, and R3), then the required code is

```
ADD     R1, R1, R2
ADD     R1, R1, R3
```

which is actually *fewer* instructions than in the CISC case. Of course, a compiler for a CISC machine can also attempt to keep variables in registers, but this is often less successful because CISC machines typically have fewer registers.

Simple Instruction Formats

RISC machines generally have regular instruction formats, usually with a fixed instruction length. This regularity allows simplification of the pipeline by allowing different fields within an instruction to be processed in parallel by logic on board the chip.

An important example of how this is accomplished is the opcode itself. On most RISC processors, the opcode field is generally fixed in both length and location within a 32-bit instruction format (several RISC processors have a secondary opcode field, but even this field can usually be found at a fixed location). This allows the opcode to be decoded at the same time as other fields within the instruction are being processed.

An extremely simple view of instruction formats is that there is an opcode field and everything else. "Everything else" may refer to register specifications, memory addresses, offsets, or any other way of specifying any of the required operands. RISC instruction formats are clearly designed to allow for the fastest possible decoding of both instructions and operands.

All six of the SPARC instruction formats, for example, fall into only three groups. Each major instruction format group can be determined by having the hardware look at the two most significant bits of each 32-bit instruction. The first of these general formats, the CALL format, will have the 2 most significant bits set to zero, with the remaining 30 bits set to the address of the CALL. The other two instruction formats have additional fields allocated in fixed locations to further specify the instruction, since 2 bits is obviously not enough for a useful range of operations!

Register Sets in RISC Machines

As we have seen, because of the pipelining difficulties caused by memory references, typical RISC architectures confine memory references to load and store instructions. This means that other instructions, such as arithmetic or logical instructions, must have all their operands in registers. A consequence of this approach is that it is very important to keep variables and other temporary values in registers rather than in memory wherever possible.

To facilitate keeping variables and intermediate values in registers, RISC processors are usually designed with relatively large numbers of registers—a typical minimum is 32 registers. Furthermore, an effort is made to keep these registers uniform, so that they can be treated in a simple manner by the compiler. This makes it easier for the compiler to succeed in keeping variables in registers, since the assignment of variables to registers is not encumbered by concerns about special-purpose instructions reference special-purpose registers (i.e., registers whose allocation cannot be freely chosen). In that case, a compiler is forced to *spill* the contents of some of the registers to memory and then load them back in again when they are needed.

Increasing the number of registers will have the effect of reducing the number of loads and stores, since temporary data can be kept in these registers rather than in memory. Fewer loads and stores, in turn, means that the average number of cycles required to execute an instruction will be lower—no load from real memory is needed if the data is in a register.

HOW MANY REGISTERS? From one point of view, it might be thought that the more registers the better, since a larger number of registers increases the possibilities for storing variables in registers and avoiding memory references that disrupt the pipeline. However, there are three reasons for not making the number of registers arbitrarily high. First, there is the hardware cost—increasing the number of registers obviously increases the number of transistors on the chip and ultimately makes the chip harder to fabricate. Second, if we have too many registers, then saving and restoring them on a context switch becomes burdensome. Finally, one of the advantages of using registers is that they can be referenced compactly. If we have 32 registers, then we can easily fit three register references into a single 32-bit instruction. On the other hand, with 1024 registers, we would need 10 bits to specify a register number, and we clearly could *not* fit three register references into a typical 32-bit instruction and still have enough room left for the opcode.

It is this last factor that proves most significant. The RISC designs we will look at all use 32-bit instruction words and the three-address format, with one destination register and two source registers. A 5-bit width for the register field allows a sufficient number of bits to be left over in the instruction word for opcode and other control bits, and at the same time, 32 registers seems in practice to be sufficient to allow compilers to keep the most important variables in registers. Studies have shown diminishing returns when the number of registers is increased past 32. However, the jump from 16 to 32 registers *does* prove significant. From this point of view CISC chips seem to have an insufficient number of registers, although, as we have previously noted, CISC chips are not so sensitive to whether data is kept in memory or not because of the large number of instructions that can reference memory.

ALLOCATING REGISTERS. One of the important jobs for a compiler is *register allocation*, which is the process of deciding what should be in registers and which registers to use. A typical approach in RISC compilers is to initially generate code assuming an infinite number of *symbolic* registers. The compiler then maps these symbolic registers into machine registers. If there is an insufficient number of real machine registers, then the compiler must generate the necessary load and store instructions to spill the extra symbolic registers to memory.

Most high-level languages allow procedures to be compiled separately. Normally we would expect that the compiler would generate the code for each procedure at the time that procedure is compiled. If this model is followed, then it is important for the compiler to minimize the number of registers used in each procedure; otherwise what is gained by keeping variables in registers can be partially lost by the extra work of saving and restoring registers on procedure calls. The question of how to allocate registers efficiently has been quite thoroughly studied. One approach, proposed by Gregory Chaitin of IBM, uses *register coloring*, where registers are represented as nodes in the graph, and register conflicts are represented as arcs. The register coloring algorithm then colors the graph with the minimum number of colors so that no two connected nodes have the same color.[11] Finally, a separate hardware register is assigned for each unique color found by this algorithm. Other, simpler algorithms have been studied that are not quite as efficient but whose basic purpose is the same—minimize the total number of registers used.

---

[11] Computer scientists will be quick to note that register coloring is an NP-complete problem, meaning that there are no known solutions that take less than exponential time. It is indeed the fact that Chaitin's experimental compiler could on occasion take an exponential amount of time in coloring a program. Consequently, it had a special switch called noNP for programs who did not feel like waiting all night for 100 line program to compiler.

More efficient register allocation can be achieved if register allocation is deferred until link time, when the code of all procedures is known. This deferral can considerably improve the overall performance of the program by minimizing the number of register saves and loads required. However, it is likely to add a considerable burden to the time required to link object modules and may simply not be feasible for large programs.

REGISTER WINDOWS: ANOTHER APPROACH. Another approach to dealing with the problem of allocating registers effectively is to help out at the hardware level with the concept of *register windows*. Here, the idea is to provide a very large number of registers divided up into separate sets, or windows. Each procedure has its own set of registers, so there is no need to save and restore registers on a procedure call.

This certainly simplifies life for the compiler, but at the expense of complicating the hardware, both by increasing the total number of registers (and hence the transistor count) and by complicating register references (since there is now a level of indirection needed to determine which register set is currently being referenced).

The issue of whether the register window approach is advantageous is a controversial one, which we will look at in more detail in the MIPS and SPARC chapters, since these two chips champion opposite approaches in this respect. The register window advocates essentially argue that the costs of increasing the basic cycle time of a chip are negligible compared to the benefits and that the number of register saves and restores is significantly decreased. The advocates of a single register set claim that optimizing compilers can bridge the gap, especially if register allocation is deferred to link time.

REGISTER ASSIGNMENT AND INSTRUCTION SCHEDULING. We have seen that a typical RISC compiler is required to perform instruction scheduling (to minimize pipeline delays resulting from register conflicts) and to assign registers (mapping the symbolic registers to real hardware registers). An interesting question arises as to whether instruction scheduling should be done *before* register assignment (using symbolic registers) or *after* register assignment (using real registers).

As is often the case in optimization issues in compilers, we can find cases where both orderings make sense, and in this particular case, the examples are sufficiently convincing that a common strategy is to do instruction scheduling twice, once before register assignment and once after. To see this, consider the code sequence

```
L       SR1, A
L       SR2, B
ADD     SR3, SR1, SR2
L       SR4, C
L       SR5, D
ADD     SR6, SR4, SR5
```

Here SR is used to emphasize that these are symbolic registers. Now if we assign registers before scheduling, we will get

```
L      MR1, A
L      MR2, B
ADD    MR1, MR1, MR2
L      MR2, C
L      MR3, D
ADD    MR2, MR2, MR3
```

A total of three machine registers are used, but now that the two additions use the same register we no longer have the opportunity to interleave the calculations for scheduling purposes. If we had first scheduled the code, we would have obtained

```
L      SR1, A
L      SR2, B
L      SR4, C
L      SR5, D
ADD    SR3, SR1, SR2
ADD    SR6, SR4, SR5
```

This avoids the pipeline conflicts caused by immediately referencing loaded data. Now if we do register assignment on this modified sequence, we get

```
L      MR1, A
L      MR2, B
L      MR3, C
L      MR4, D
ADD    MR5, MR1, MR2
ADD    MR1, MR3, MR4
```

Five machine registers are used instead of three, but the scheduling is much better.

On the other hand, we certainly have to schedule after register assignment, to be sure that the final scheduling is based on the actual machine registers. One case in which the need for final scheduling arises is when the register assignment phase eliminates dead code. Suppose that in the example above, the addition of C and D is eliminated as dead code. Now the output sequence from register assignment would be

```
L      MR1, A
L      MR2, B
ADD    MR5, MR1, MR2
```

We must now resolve the clear scheduling conflict before final code generation.

CISC, RISC AND PROGRAMMING LANGUAGES

What is the main inspiration behind the RISC philosophy? The statement by George Radin quoted near the beginning of the previous section may possibly make the most important point. If one were to look at the instruction set of a CISC machine and empirically measure how often a typical instruction was used, the result would be somewhat surprising (although certainly not to the proponents of RISC technology, who have used this sort of empirical data to justify their architectural point of view).

Sun notes in their literature on the SPARC chip that the Sun C compiler for the 68020 uses only 30% of the instructions that are available. Since almost all of the software for these machines is written in C, that means that 70% of the instructions are not just being infrequently used—they are *never* being used. They could grow rusty or not work and no one would notice!

C, a simple language that one might regard as a reduced instruction set computer language, is an extreme case for this kind of observation. It has a very simple set of operations and a very simple set of data types as well as a very simple view of aggregate structures and control flow. Consequently, it is a bit tricky to translate C to high-level CISC machines and use the instructions effectively. The semantic level of C is even lower than the semantic level of the 386. The battle in compiling C for the 386 is to go from compiling low-level C into a high-level assembly language such as 386 assembler. Let's look at an idiom in C that copies an n-character string:

```
while (n– –) *c++ = *d++;
```

This statement says: Take the pointer *d,* increment it, and get the contents of the cell that it points to. Then assign that value to pointer *c,* and increment that pointer as well. This operation is repeated *n* times. A straightforward C compiler might generate:

```
LP:     MOV     ECX, N
        DEC     N
        JECXZ   DN
        MOV     EAX, D
        MOV     BL, [EAX]
        INC     D
        MOV     EAX, C
        MOV     [EAX], BL
        INC     C
        JMP     LP
```

This is fairly naive code. A somewhat clever optimizer might be able to avoid repeatedly loading N, D, and C. It wouldn't be surprising if an optimizer tried to move these loads out of the loop, resulting in the following considerably improved sequence

```
        MOV     ECX, N
        JECXZ   EXIT        ; skip loop if N = 0
        MOV     EBX, C      ; preload C for loop
        MOV     EDX, D      ; preload D for loop
LP:     MOV     AL, [EBX]
        INC     EBX
        MOV     [EDX], AL
        INC     EDX
        LOOP    LP
EXIT:
        MOV     C, EBX      ; store updated value of C back
        MOV     D, EDX      ; store updated value of D back
```

This is certainly a considerable improvement since we have only five instructions in the inner loop instead of ten. However, writing in assembly language, the main work in the loop can be done in a single instruction on the 386 using the even more efficient code sequence

```
MOV    ECX, N
MOV    ESI, D
ADD    D, ECX
MOV    EDI, C
ADD    C, ECX
REP    MOVSB
```

The important work in the loop is done by the last instruction. It is pretty hard work for a compiler to take this C code and generate efficient code using REP MOVSB. The Microsoft C compiler manages to do this optimization in some limited situations, but it is probably not the consequence of some general method of performing amazing optimizations. It's probably the result of looking for that specific case and saying, "Ah!— I've found the standard C string copy loop—I know how to generate code for that!"

With a less clever compiler, the MOVSB instruction is not used. You can imagine RISC architects looking at the code generated by a C compiler and saying "Ah-hah, MOVSB is a junk instruction that is never used, get rid of it." The use of low level dictions in C has biased things a bit. If one is committed to writing programs at the semantic level of C, the RISC machines are even more attractive. The code generated by C compilers is likely to use a smaller part of the instruction set than many other languages.[12]

Of course, the argument that a clever assembly language programmer might find an important use for an instruction is not necessarily a strong one. Almost all code written today is written in a high-level language. If compiler technology is not good enough to make use of the amazingly efficient instructions in an instruction set, then there is not much point in having this instruction even if theoretically it could be put to good use. This balance between what instructions should be implemented and which instructions can be used by compilers needs to be constantly reevaluated because compiler technology is always improving. Certainly, with the current state of technology, it is often difficult to make effective use of complex instructions.

One more point is that many of the ingredients that go into RISC designs—simpler instruction formats, fewer instructions, lots of registers, uniform treatment of registers, etc.—contribute to making compilers simpler, in much the same way that the hardware itself is simplified. In the hardware case, this simplification allowed a more efficient implementation of these simpler instructions. Exactly the same phenomenon occurs in compilers. If the basic structures that the compiler deals with are simpler, then it is much easier to implement aggressive optimization algorithms. Many CISC compilers are so burdened by attempts to make use of complicated instructions and addressing modes that some optimizations become prohibitively complex.

---

[12] For example, the Realia COBOL compiler uses every single instruction on the 286, and MOVSB is heavily used.

THE FIRST RISC PROCESSORS

The first RISC processors were all started as research projects. They include the IBM 801, which was developed at IBM T. J. Watson Research Labs; the Berkeley RISC I and RISC II, developed at the University of California at Berkeley; and the Stanford MIPS, designed at Stanford University. Before giving some of the historical background, we will begin with a short description of the CDC 6600, a machine which is sometimes credited as being the first machine to introduce RISC principles into an architecture.

The CDC 6600

The CDC 6600, which was introduced in the early 1960s, is sometimes given credit as being the first RISC architecture. This machine was designed by Seymour Cray with a single goal in mind—to attain the maximum speed possible for scientific applications.

The CDC 6600 was a large mainframe, costing several million dollars at the time. Although the 6600 was very different from the inexpensive processors described in this book, Cray was motivated by some of the same considerations that influence modern RISC design. In particular, because the pattern of instruction use by scientific programs is very stylized, Cray discovered that he could implement a very small instruction set and still build FORTRAN compilers that were able to generate efficient code. Long before the term RISC had been coined, Cray discovered that by making simplifications in the instruction set, significant improvements in instruction throughput were possible. Among the RISC-like characteristics of the 6600 are the following:

- Only load and store instructions reference memory (these are rather peculiar—an address register is set to the address of the memory location involved, and as a side effect the operand is loaded into, or stored, from the matching data register).

- Operations in registers are in three-address form, with two input registers and a separate output register.

- The instruction formats are very simple and uniform.

- There are multiple functional units, and instruction execution is pipelined, with a scoreboard used to mark busy registers to create the necessary interlocks.

Despite these similarities with current RISC processors, there are a number of respects in which the 6600 departs significantly from the general RISC model. In particular, there is a rather small number of registers, and they are not uniform. There is also no visible concurrency—from the programmer's point of view, execution is strictly sequential. Most important, the hardware used to implement the 6600 is completely different, since the CDC 6600 predated the development of integrated circuits. The CDC 6600 was a marvel of hand-wired separate components. On opening up the main processor cabinet, one was confronted with a daunting tangle of wires. Hardware problems with the 6600 often had to be solved by slightly lengthening or shortening one of these wires to control signal propagation times.

The IBM 801 Project

The IBM 801 Project was the first attempt to develop an architecture whose design could be intentionally described as RISC. Almost all modern RISC ideas are present in the original 801 design. Although we have noted in the previous section that the 6600 has sometimes been called the first RISC processor due to its similarities with current RISC architectures, the 801 can certainly be credited with being the first machine designed with these goals explicitly in mind.

The project started in 1974, when IBM was investigating the possibility of building an all-digital telephone exchange capable of handling approximately 1 million calls per hour. Certainly a general-purpose machine was not the best choice for this task, since, for example, there were stringent real-time requirements.

A decision was made to investigate the development of a special-purpose architecture suitable for this application. The first 801 design was significantly influenced by these requirements. In particular, there was no requirement for floating-point, so the first 801 did not provide any hardware floating-point capability. The primary requirements were extremely fast execution and low cost. As is often the case with development projects in computer science, the original application was eventually forgotten. Even though the idea of telephone exchanges was abandoned, the processor concepts were evidently important and powerful, and so work proceeded with the goal of producing an extremely fast computer suitable for use with high-level languages.

Researchers at IBM had been thinking of how to design fast machines for a long time. With these ideas in mind, a group (led by George Radin for much of its lifetime), with John Cocke as a consultant, was formed.[13] One of the decisions that was immediately made was that the machine that they were about to design would be programmed in a high-level language—for a long time the machine was thought of as a one-language system. Although this did not influence the design of the hardware, the architecture would not be driven exclusively by issues of primitive speed, but also by how well a compiler could compile for that architecture.

THE HARDWARE. From the inception of the 801 Project, it was decided that a pipelined design in which all instructions would take the same time to execute would be used. The design constraints were that instructions had to execute in one cycle and that the length of the cycle should not be increased unless it was absolutely necessary. Those were day-in and day-out constraint that affected which instructions were implemented and which instructions were excluded.

With the decision to use pipelining, several other issues needed to be resolved. Pretty quickly, the researchers came to the conclusion that they would not expose the pipeline. In other words, from the programmer's point of view, the semantics of instruction execution would be strictly sequential. The alternative approach exposes the pipeline and requires the compiler to ensure that instructions are not issued before

---

[13] John Cocke, who received the Turing Award in 1987 for his work in both compiler design and RISC architecture development, is often regarded as the "father of RISC."

their operands are available. A compiler can deal with an exposed pipeline in straight line code, but handling an exposed pipeline across branches is much harder. Writing in assembly language, humans have an even harder time. The conclusion was that the cost of using interlocking was so small that it was unnecessary to expose the pipeline (As we shall see, the MIPS, which makes the pipeline partly visible to the programmer, was designed with a different point of view). The one exception was that jumps would have delay slots (i.e., the instruction after the jump would always be executed). This idea was introduced in the 801 design and, as we will see, has been adopted by nearly all subsequent RISC designs.

Briefly put, the IBM view in the design of the original 801 was that reordering of instructions might be needed for maximum efficiency of code. Although the compiler was expected to schedule instructions with this goal in mind, it was seen as undesirable for a compiler to be forced to reorder instructions in order to ensure correct code. This philosophy has been a central characteristic of all the IBM RISC designs.

When it was designed, the first version of the 801 was a 24-bit machine with 16 registers. The initial work on the design was done using software simulation. Using the traditional approach of instruction set simulators, namely, writing a program which reads and interprets the instructions of the target architecture one by one, a simulator runs much more slowly than the real target machine. The 801 simulator was one of the first to use a now-familiar technique in which the target instructions are translated on the fly to corresponding instruction sequences for the simulated machine. In the 801 simulator, each 801 instruction could be mapped to a block of eight 370 instructions, the blocks being filled as execution proceeded. Using this approach, the 801 simulator was fast enough to allow large-scale simulations to be performed at a reasonable rate.[14]

All of the research on the 801's instruction set was done using this simulator. Long before the hardware ever got built, several versions of the architecture had been designed and simulated and a compiler had been built that generated code for the architecture. A prototype of the 801 was finally built in 1980, by which time interest in this implementation had considerably diminished. Nevertheless, the research carried out between 1975 and 1980 had an important influence on the development of RISC architecture both inside and outside IBM.

THE INFLUENCE OF PAGING. One of the important problems in maintaining the single-cycle property is dealing with storage references and stores, particularly loads that cannot take a single cycle. Part of the problem of loads is what to do about page faults. The 801 viewpoint was that a load instruction had completed when it had requested the storage access. It takes one cycle to compute an effective address and put it into an independent parallel memory unit that can do the fetch and return the value. The target register is then interlocked on that load so that the software can

---

[14] This technique, which one company has more recently dubbed *software coprocessing*, allows simulators to perform with remarkable efficiency. In particular, 68030 simulators for the 386 have become commercially viable and permit simulation of IBM PC applications on 68030 machines such as the Mac II.

try (but doesn't have to) schedule other instructions while the value is required. The expectation was that a machine could be designed in which the value of a load would only become available two instructions past the load, that is, the instruction immediately following the load could not use the result of the load instruction.

The problem was page faults. It is difficult to determine quickly enough whether or not a load instruction can succeed. The first 801 did not address this issue and did not provide virtual memory mapping. This decision simplified the implementation of the load instruction, since the issue of how to back out subsequent instructions on a page fault did not arise. In retrospect, this decision was inappropriate. Virtual memory implementations are required on modern computer systems, not only to deal with programs with very large memory requirements, but also to accommodate the needs of modern operating systems for multiprogramming, and address space management. Even at the expense of complicating the design and slowing down instruction throughput, it is necessary to provide page fault traps that can recover and continue execution.

INSTRUCTION SETS. Reducing the size of the instruction set was never an explicit goal of the IBM RISC effort. However, the IBM researchers had access to extensive libraries of trace tapes that had been gathered at customer sites. These tapes were used by IBM to plan future performance enhancements to the 370 line, but, of course, they also contained exactly the critical information needed for the design of RISC architectures—namely, the instruction execution frequency figures that can be used to decide which instructions are needed and which may be omitted.

These trace tapes were probably biased in favor of commercial applications, since this is typical of the environment of IBM mainframe customers. The 801 design reflects this bias in not having floating-point, and in providing an assist for packed decimal instructions (similar to the instructions on the 386). The 801 is the only RISC architecture to provide for decimal arithmetic—even IBM abandons this feature in its latest RISC designs. Another feature of commercial applications is that they tend to be rather rich semantically, and to use a larger instruction set. Most of the other RISC designs have been biased by systems-type applications written in C, which tend to be much more spartan in their use of instructions.

THE PROGRAMMING LANGUAGE PL.8. At the same time that both the 801 simulator and the hardware were being built, a compiler for the machine was being developed. This compiler was intended for the initial architecture, but both the compiler and the architecture evolved as new things were learned.

The programming language first used to generate code for the 801 was PL.8, a language derived from PL/1. Since PL/1 presented some unique optimization problems that the IBM researchers wanted to avoid, they decided to write in a subset of the language. While writing in this subset, enhancements to the subset not contained in PL/1 were added,—the language eventually became incompatible with PL/1.

That language, which became known as PL.8—the .8 reflected the initial intent that the important 80% of the language should be included—continued to evolve during the course of the project. Eventually, the project broke free from the PL/1 compiler and bootstrapped the PL.8 compiler. From then on, the language was changed as needed. Several of the features that were added to it were motivated by its intended use as the systems programming language for the 801 itself, not unlike the way C is used in Unix systems. Several aspects of this new language were the result of the design philosophy that said that the compiler and the hardware should be interrelated. This interrelationship is an important theme in RISC design and strongly influenced both the 801 design and the language design.

PROTECTION ISSUES. One issue that shows how the decisions about hardware and software were made together involved the issue of protection. Originally the architecture had no hardware protection mechanism, since that protection was guaranteed by the compiler. One of the research issues that was being explored was to see if such errors as attempts to reference an arrays out of bounds could be efficiently caught by compiler-generated software checks, thus avoiding the need to relying on hardware memory protection. One of the reasons for choosing PL/1 as the systems language for the 801 was that the semantic model of PL/1 was easier to push into the model of a protected language than C.

One of the results of this was that software checking, that is, checking that array indices were in bounds and pointers were valid, was very important. Every pointer dereference, for example, was checked to see that it was legal. The programming style that PL.8 adopted was to use offsets rather than pointers, offsets being relative pointers within some region of memory. The generated code then checked all offset uses to verify that they were in the correct region of memory. Similarly, all array and string references were checked to see that they were in bounds.

The architecture of the 801 included trap instructions to make this type of checking efficient. Traps are basically compares that fault or trap if the compare fails or succeeds (whichever way you want to think about it), but whose fall-through path is single-cycle. If conditional branches are used for checking, the control-flow impact is more severe—traps are known not to return, whereas branches look like you are going somewhere, that is, the compiler does not have to deal with the trap taken fault.

All of this led to an interesting result: the measured cost for complete checking added only 5 percent to the execution time, because the optimization was so effective in removing unnecessary checks. That is a good example of the synergy which developed between the architecture and the language design. The machine had to have trap instructions, or this would not have been nearly as workable and the compiler had to deal with them properly to make it worthwhile.

This 5 percent figure is impressively low. What it means is that it is not worth implementing protection in the hardware unless it can be done at a smaller cost than 5 percent. However, although the result is convincing from a technical point of view, it turns out that it is impractical to design systems for the real world using this approach. In practice people do not trust compilers to generate all the required checks, and more significantly, programmers will not put up with single language systems—they want to be able to use a wide range of existing languages, including languages like C where software checking is much more difficult.

CONDITION CODES. Another one of the things that was learned from building the 801 compiler was the value of uniformity in handling condition codes or flag settings. It is difficult for a compiler to deal with condition code setting side effects that are different for each instruction. It is much easier to deal with them if the condition code setting side effects characterize something about the result rather than something about the operations that led to the result. That way it becomes a piece of information whose meaning is independent of how you compute it.

The 801 condition codes are significantly different from those on the 370, reflecting this observation. For example, the 370 condition code for an add instruction can indicate "overflow," which is not a characterization of the result. The 801 style is what you would have gotten if you compared to zero. A compiler can use this result to eliminate comparisons of the result to zero. The fact than overflow occurred during this integer operation turns out to be uninteresting.

OPERATING SYSTEM ISSUES. By the end of the 1970s, IBM had developed a compiler and a toy operating system and was compiling code for this system. At that point it was decided to compile for the the 370 as well, and so a back end was completed. The operating system was viewed as the third component of an integrated system (besides the architecture itself and the compiler).

An important architectural issue is whether to include elaborate features intended for use by the operating system. In particular, there is the question of whether or not to implement a massive hardware state change for first-level interrupt handling. IBM concluded pretty early that it would be a mistake. A look at the implementation of such schemes that had existed show that none of them had performed very well. Here we see consideration of the important principle that it is not worth implementing fancy features if they cannot be implemented efficiently. As we have seen, on the 386, it is quicker to program task switches using software than to use the hardware tasking feature. The feeling was that all attempts to implement multiple register set machines with the constraint of not expanding the basic cycle had been failures because no one knew how to manage a fixed number of register sets for a general-purpose operating system, and so they wound up doing software management for one of their register sets for almost all the processes anyway.

As a result of these design considerations, the 801 was designed to do a program state save very quickly, minimizing the time for the interrupt path itself. The interrupt changes the privilege state of the machine and branches to a fixed location. Everything else is up to the software. One advantage of this approach is that if you have one particular interrupt that occurs very frequently, and servicing the interrupt is trivial, then you do not need to save the entire machine state to service the interrupt.

Similarly, for system SVCs (supervisor calls for privileged operations), system calls that have very short path lengths and high traffic can be special-cased to again not do a complete state save but just program what they have to very quickly and get back. In a later IBM architecture, there was an example of a system call taking only 30 cycles to complete.

THE SECOND 801 ARCHITECTURE. By the late 1970s, the IBM researchers were already designing another architecture. Once the simulator and the compiler were done and IBM had enough experience in programming the 801, they concluded that they had made a number of mistakes. The most important change was in the register structure—the second architecture used thirty-two 32-bit registers rather than the sixteen 24-bit registers of the first 801. From experiments with the simulator, IBM concluded that 32 registers was the best choice. With the 16 registers of the earlier design, there were many programs for which the compiler ran out of registers. With 32 registers, this occurred much less frequently, and experimentation with various numbers showed that going beyond 32 registers encountered diminishing returns.

In conjunction with the new 32-register architecture, there was extensive work on the question of how to allocate these registers efficiently at compile time. One area that was focused upon was that of procedure linkage. Although all procedure linkage was important, one focus of the work was to optimize procedure calls to *leaf* procedures (procedures that have no procedure declared within them and do make calls to other procedures.) IBM concluded, from both measurements and intuition, that such procedures constituted most of the procedure call traffic, and also argued that the linkage that it is most important to optimize is the linkage to these small leaf procedures. If a procedure is large, then the amortized cost of the linkage to it is small. Linkage costs become important when the subroutines you are calling are very small procedures.

It was decided that it would be adequate to optimize calls to leaf procedures and the strategy was to do it by register conventions—to establish a linkage convention in which the calling program expects that some of its registers will not survive the call. The called program attempts to compute only in the registers that it is not required to preserve across the call, and small leaf procedures can normally do that and thus can operate without any explicit register save cost.

Now, there is no magic. The cost is someplace. It comes from the register allocator having to to work its way around those registers that were not going to survive a call. It did not require that any values that are in them which are alive be saved. But with 32 registers the global register allocator was found to meet this requirement without introducing an excessive number of register spills.

In some sense the whole cost of calling leaf procedures disappeared in register allocation for 32 registers using this approach. IBM was, and remains, convinced that this is a better approach than the register window approach. The IBM compiler at that time did not attempt any cross-procedure optimization of register allocation—the implementation of more aggressive optimizations of this type would presumably push the balance even further away from the register window approach.

INSTRUCTION SIZE. Another important change for the second 801 architecture was that all instructions were uniform length (32 bits). In the earlier 801, there were 16-bit and 32-bit instructions. The 16-bit instructions were introduced because of concerns with code size. With the development of faster and cheaper memories, it became clear that the extra complexity of a non-uniform instruction size was not worth the saving in code size.

Going to 32-bit instructions was also dictated by the increase in the number of registers. Since 5 bits were now needed to designate a register, there simply was not room in a 16-bit instruction for the necessary operands. Another constraint that had been caused by the 16-bit instruction formats, namely destructive operations in which the destination register is the same register as one of the source operands (as on the 386), was also removed for the 32-register version, and the familiar three-register form of the instruction appears throughout the instruction set of the second 801.

The Berkeley RISC and Stanford MIPS Projects

Two chips which are somewhat better known than the 801 are the Stanford MIPS and the Berkeley RISC I and RISC II. Both of these chips were developed in the first few years of the 1980s, some time after the 801 had been simulated and designed. However, possibly due to the proprietary nature of the 801, very little information was available about the details of the architecture. As a result, as the Stanford and Berkeley implementations were done, the academic nature of these projects resulted in exactly the opposite attitude—many papers were written describing their experiments.

The Berkeley RISC I and RISC II processors were designed and implemented from 1980 through 1983, by a team of graduate students led by David Patterson. [15] One of its most unique features was the use of overlapping register windows, which was carried over into the design of the SPARC. The two designs are, in fact, very similar in many, but not all, respects.

The other major early RISC chips was designed and built at Stanford by a group led by John Hennessy. The design of the MIPS was distinguished by the lack of interlocks—MIPS is an acronym for Multiprocessor without Interlocking Pipeline Stages. Again, the modern MIPS chips discussed in Chapter 9 have retained some, but not all, of the characteristics of the original research chips.

CONCLUSION

The history of CISC designs showed an increasing complexity in the instructions included on these machines. The motivation behind the inclusion of these instructions was the belief that they would help support the increasingly used high-level languages.

RISC designs can be viewed as a reaction to the complexity of CISC processors. The main empirical data used to justify the approach is the observation that most of the complex instructions on a CISC machine, precisely those that complicate its implementation the most, are the instructions that are used least, and their presence does not justify their cost.

---

[15] A thorough description of the history of these chips is given in *Reduced Instruction Set Computer Architectures for VLSI*, a doctoral dissertation written by Manolis Katevenis, and so we do not repeat it here. The MIPS is not quite as well documented, although several papers can be found in the literature (see the Bibliography).

THE MIPS PROCESSORS

The MIPS R3000, which is designed and manufactured by MIPS Computer Systems, is based on one of the earliest RISC designs, the Stanford MIPS chip. One factor which makes the MIPS chip commercially interesting is that it has been chosen by DEC for use in a recent line of workstations, despite the fact that DEC has the resources to design and fabricate chips of its own. DEC designed a number of workstations in the mid-1980s around the VAX architecture. Although these workstations had the advantage of running all of the software that had already been written for the VAX, they were slow compared with many other workstations and failed in the marketplace. Possibly as a result of this failure, DEC made the decision to build the DEC 3100 DECstations around the MIPS chip.

We will describe the general structure of the MIPS processor and its standard coprocessor, and then describe its instruction pipeline, in which the use of software to control data dependencies is a major distinguishing characteristic. We will also discuss the instruction set, memory management for this machine, and several other issues related to the implementation of operating systems on this processor.

The MIPS architecture is currently represented by two chips, the MIPS R2000 and the MIPS R3000. Other than the faster speed of the R3000, these two implementations are architecturally identical. We will refer to both as the "MIPS chip."

THE MIPS CHIP

The MIPS chip is composed of two logically independent processors, a main processor known simply as the CPU, and an internal coprocessor known as CP0. The CPU is a 32-bit RISC processor that incorporates a standard set of arithmetic and logical instructions. Memory management facilities, as well as exception management and other operating system functions, are all under the control of the coprocessor CP0. The general structure of the MIPS chip is shown in Figure 9.1. In addition to CP0, the MIPS is able to support up to three additional coprocessors, CP1 through CP3, of which CP1 is conventionally used for floating-point calculations and the other two are free for special-purpose use.

The instruction set of the MIPS includes special instructions that allow the main processor to communicate with any of the coprocessors that happen to be attached to it. Coprocessor instructions allow the CPU to read from and write to the registers of a coprocessor. Instructions on the coprocessors are triggered by sending a pattern of bits whose interpretation is up to the designer of the coprocessor. The special coprocessor CP0 has exactly the same interface, but because it is on board the main chip, and because its structure is defined, it has some additional predefined and specialized instructions that deal with some of the memory and interrupt management functions. MIPS Inc. also produces a floating-point chip called the R2010 FPA, which is intended to be attached to the MIPS as CP1.

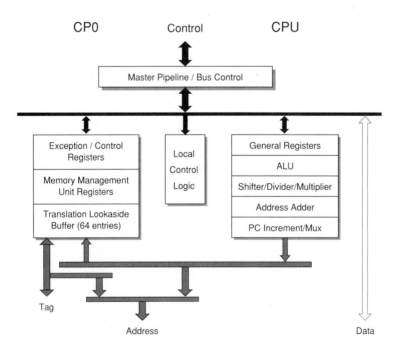

FIGURE 9.1
A block functional diagram of the MIPS.

Register Structure of the CPU

In keeping with RISC principles, the register structure of the CPU is far simpler than those of either the 386 or the 68030. There are thirty-two 32-bit registers which, with two exceptions, are treated in a uniform way by the instruction set. The sole exceptions are that register 0 always contains the value 0, while the *link register*, register 31, is used for procedure linkage. The only other CPU registers on the machine are the program counter (PC) and two registers, HI and LO, that are used in multiplication and division. The coprocessor CP0 has a separate set of registers whose use is related to memory management and exception handling; they are described in a later section.

Even though all the registers are identical in terms of the hardware (other than the two exceptions noted above), the MIPS User's Manual does suggest some software conventions as to how they should be used. Register R29, for example, is used by convention as the stack pointer. Registers R8 through R15 are used by a compiler to store temporary results whose values are not preserved across procedure calls. These conventions, which all compilers are expected to observe, are shown in Table 9.1.

Without such clearly stated conventions, one possible disadvantage of having completely indistinguishable registers is that there is a potential for software anarchy. If the implementers of a C compiler and a Pascal compiler, for example, choose to use different registers as the stack pointer, someone implementing software using more than one language will have trouble, for example, in calling procedures written in C from Pascal. By establishing appropriate software conventions as an adjunct to the hardware design, these kind of incompatibilities are avoided. Software conventions such as these often appear in hardware reference manuals even though, from a purely formal point of view, they have nothing to do with the hardware.

TABLE 9.1

MIPS Conventions for Register Use by Software.

Register Name	Use and Linkage
R0	Always has the value 0.
Rat or R1	Reserved for the assembler.
R2 .. R3	Used for expression evaluation and to hold integer function results. Also used to pass the static link when calling nested procedures.
R4 .. R7	Used to pass the first 4 words of integer type actual arguments; their values are not preserved across procedure calls.
R8 .. R15	Temporary registers used for expression evaluations; their values are not preserved across procedure calls.
R16 .. R23	Saved registers; their values must be preserved across procedure calls.
R24 .. R25	Temporary registers used for expression evaluations; their values are not preserved across procedure calls.
R26 .. R27 or Rkt0 .. Rkt 1	Reserved for the operating system kernel.
R28 or Rgp	Contains the global pointer.
R29 or Rsp	Contains the stack pointer.
r30	A saved register.
r31	Contains the return address; used for expression evaluation.

Even though this flexibility exists in the hardware, such conventions will nevertheless become embedded in operating systems and other software in such a way that from a programmer's view they have almost the same status as a hardware convention. For example, the IBM 370 has registers that are largely indistinguishable from each other. Very early on, however, IBM committed itself to a badly designed, but standard, calling sequence. The fact that compilers designed for the 370 have had to meet these conventions has resulted in a higher procedure call overhead than necessary. Programmers have been forced to live with this design for a very long time.

THE INSTRUCTION PIPELINE

The acronym MIPS was originally derived from the phrase *Microprocessor without Interlocked Pipeline Stages*. This acronym was used by the Stanford MIPS project but has been officially abandoned by MIPS Computer Systems, Inc. Nevertheless, we shall see that one of the features that distinguishes the MIPS from the other RISC processors described in this text *is* a reliance on software conventions rather than hardware interlocks in handling load delay slots.

The MIPS uses a five-stage pipeline (shown in Figure 9.2). This pipeline consists of the following stages (we assume in this description that no stalls occur):

- During the *instruction fetch stage* (IF), the instruction address is calculated and then loaded from the instruction cache.

- During the *read stage* (RD), any *register* operands required by the instruction are read from the CPU registers; instruction decoding is overlapped with this phase.

- During the *ALU* phase, one of two different operations can occur. In the case of a general computational instruction, the operation is actually performed on the operands, which must be in registers. In the case of load and store instructions, the effective address calculation is performed.

- During the *memory* (MEM) phase, any operands that are in memory are accessed if they are required by the instruction.

- The *writeback* (WB) phase writes back the ALU result or the result of a load to the appropriate register.

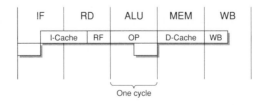

FIGURE 9.2
The MIPS instruction execution sequence.

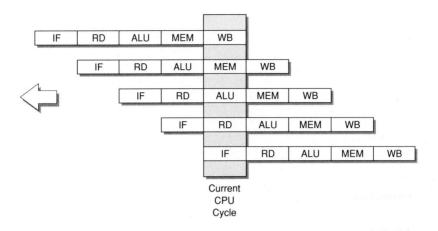

FIGURE 9.3
The five-stage pipeline of the MIPS R2000.

As we described in Chapter 8, an instruction does not really take a single cycle, but rather several overlapped cycles (see Figure 9.3), five in the case of the MIPS; that is, the latency of an instruction is 5 cycles, but the throughput can approach one instruction per cycle.

Remember that two things could potentially affect the instruction pipeline: instructions that change the flow of the program (jumps and branches) and data dependencies between instructions when values are being loaded into registers. The data dependency disruptions in the pipeline are solved in most RISC machines by having the hardware interlock the instructions, that is, a scoreboard is used to record which registers are busy, and a subsequent instruction requiring a busy register is delayed until the data arrives.

The feature that distinguishes the MIPS from other RISC processors is that it avoids the need for implementing hardware interlock by shifting the responsibility from the hardware to the software. Compilers and assemblers for the MIPS must be sure to fill a load delay slot either with a useful instruction or, in the worst case, with a no-op since there is no hardware interlock. In addition, compilers and assemblers must make sure that all instructions placed after a branch can be executed whether the branch is taken or not.

A typical instruction to load a word from memory into a register is written as[1]:

    LW   R2, A

---

[1] The MIPS assembler expects a programmer to refer to register 2 as $2, rather than R2. We use the notation R2 throughout this chapter to be more consistent with usage elsewhere.

A rule in the MIPS reference manual states:

> All load operations have a latency of one instruction. That is, the instruction immediately following a load cannot use the contents of the register which will be loaded with the data being fetched from storage. An exception is that the target register for the load word left and load word right instructions may be specified as the same register used as the destination of a load instruction that immediately precedes it.

It is hard to tell whether this simply gives advice or states a definite rule. Such a warning should probably read that the effect of referencing R2 in the next instruction is undefined. Perhaps you get the old value, or some rubbish value, or some other strange behavior. The behavior may be predictable, but the hardware designer does not care to tell you what happens, so you must avoid the problem.[2]

The idea here is that as long as the data desired is currently located in the data cache, which we hope is most of the time, it is guaranteed to arrive from the cache one instruction later than the load. In other words, the second instruction after the load can be sure that the data is available, without needing to check that it has actually arrived.

The Stall Cycle

It is all very well to say that the data cache guarantees that the data will arrive in time for the second instruction after the load, but what if the data is *not* currently in the cache. In this case, a load from real memory is required, a process that will certainly take more than 2 cycles. Given a sequence of instructions such as:

```
LW      R2, A
some instruction not referencing R2
LW      R3, 10(R2)
```

The data loaded into R2 is not referenced until the second instruction after the LW, so this sequence of code meets the rules. What will happen if the contents of A are not in the cache? It is generally too expensive to build an external memory that can return data in 2 clocks. In practice, access times of 4 or 5 clocks are more typical.

This is a fact of life that has to do with the differences between the clock speeds of processors and the access times of memory. While a 30-MHz processor has a clock speed of approximately 33 nanoseconds per clock, the best RAM access times are only about 80 nanoseconds, almost three times slower. It is possible to build much faster *static* RAM memories, but these are much more expensive, and it is usually not feasible to build large memories using static RAM. Caches *are* typically built from static RAM, which is why they can be significantly faster than main memory.

---

[2] The hardware designer cannot take the attitude that absolutely anything could happen. For instance, if the effect of doing something that you "may not" do is to put the processor in supervisor state, then a terrible hole in the protection has been created. Furthermore, the documentation invites discovery of the hole—one of the first approaches of an intruding hacker is to systematically try every variation of things that you are not supposed to do!

If it takes 1 or 2 clocks just to put a request for data onto the address bus, and 3 cycles to get the result back, then this explains why 4 or 5 cycles is the minimum number of cycles required to load data from real memory. This discrepancy between processor and memory times is *not* improving as technology advances. If anything, the situation is getting worse. The original IBM PC ran at 4.77 MHz and used 150- or 200-nanosecond memory chips. Current PC compatibles running at 25 MHz are more than five times faster and yet use memory with cycle times of 90 nanoseconds, only twice as fast. As memory chips are built with larger capacities, it becomes harder to build them so that they are both larger and faster at the same time.

Given this discrepancy between processor speed and memory speed, we are now in a bit of a bind. The MIPS requires data to appear 2 clocks after a load (a 1-cycle delay) and has no interlock mechanism to hold up references if the data is not yet available. If the cache does not deliver, that is, if it does *not* contain the data being referenced, then external memory has no hope of meeting the 2 clock requirement.

On most RISC processors, the interlock mechanism would cause the processor to wait for the data to arrive from memory *if* it were required before it was available. On the MIPS, an alternative approach is used. If the cache cannot deliver the data, then stall cycles are added to the pipeline so that the entire pipeline is frozen until the data appears. This is like a guy on an assembly line dropping his hammer and yelling for the belt to be turned off while he picks it up. Of course, when the belt stops, everyone is held up (every instruction in the pipeline is held up until the data appears).

A stall cycle can occur not only when there is a miss in the data cache, but also when there is an instruction cache miss or a busy write buffer is unable to deal with a flurry of write commands quickly enough.

There are cases where the use of the stall cycle is inferior to interlocking. Consider the following sequence of instructions:

```
LW    R9, MEM
ADD   R2, R2, R2
ADD   R3, R3, R3
ADD   R4, R4, R4
ADD   R5, R5, R5
ADD   R6, R6, R6
ADD   R7, R7, R7
SUB   R8, R8, R9
```

The sequence of add instructions gives plenty of time for the value of MEM to arrive, even on a cache miss, before it is needed for the subtract instruction. On a RISC design with interlocking, this program could run at full speed without holding up the pipeline. On the MIPS, a cache miss would cause the pipeline to stall unnecessarily, waiting for MEM to arrive from memory, before executing the second ADD instruction.

The issue of which approach is better (interlocking or stalling) is one of the hot arguments in the RISC field. The MIPS approach results in simpler hardware design, which should ultimately pay off in greater throughput. On the other hand, it can introduce inefficiencies, as shown in this example. The question is: How often do such situations arise?

In practice, benchmarks and other measurements indicate that the penalty from pipeline stalls is small, so the cost of the MIPS approach is not a significant issue. On the other hand, it is unclear that the MIPS approach really *does* result in faster implementations. Probably the best judgment observing this argument from outside is that this is *not* such a crucial issue, and in practice the two approaches result in rather similar performance characteristics.[3]

If the pipeline *does* have to stall for a moment, there is an external signal that tells the outside world the pipeline is closed down so that all coprocessors, interrupt controllers, caches, and any other external chips connected will know that the processor is out of business for a moment. If this signal is not asserted, then the "outside world" can depend on the fact that the MIPS pipeline is marching along unimpeded.

THE INSTRUCTION SET

The MIPS, in keeping both the number of instructions and the number of instruction formats to a minimum, is quintessentially RISC. This should not come as much of a surprise since the MIPS is, after all, the descendant of the original Stanford MIPS, one of the machines that in some sense defines what it means to be RISC.

The Instruction Formats

There are only three basic instruction formats, each of which is 32 bits wide. All three of the instruction formats use the high-order 6 bits for the opcode but divide up the remaining bits into fields in a variety of ways based on the requirements of the specific format (see Figure 9.4). Fields that are common to more than one format, such as the *rt* field described below, appear in exactly the same location in all of these formats.

The *register-type* (abbreviated R-type) format contains the standard 6-bit opcode field, followed by three 5-bit register fields, *rs*, *rt*, and *rd*. The last two fields of the address format, *shamt* (for Shift Amount) and *funct* (for Function), have specialized uses in connection with certain instructions. The Shift Left Logical (SLL) instruction, for example, uses the *shamt* field to specify the number of bits by which to shift.

The *immediate-type* (I-type) instruction format has four fields and may be thought of as a variant of the R-type format that is used when an immediate operand is needed. This format consists of a 6-bit opcode field, a 5-bit target register field *rt*, a 5-bit source register field *rs*, and a 16-bit immediate field.

The opcode determines how these fields are used. As an example, consider the load and store instructions, all of which fall into this format. To load a value from memory into the target register *rt*, the register specified by *rs* is used as a base address into memory, and the offset field is used as an offset into memory. The Add Immediate instruction, on the other hand, uses the offset field to hold a 16-bit signed constant

---

[3] When this book was reviewed, discussions like this often provoked very different responses from reviewers from MIPS and Sun. One thing to remember is that many of these arguments come down to rather small performance differences, which are soon overshadowed by increasing chip clock speeds and other factors.

I-Type Format (Immediate)

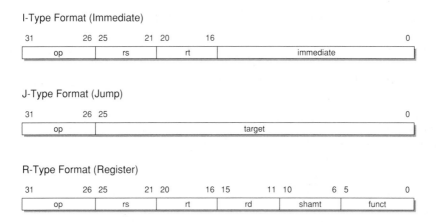

FIGURE 9.4
The instruction formats of the MIPS R2000.

that is then added to the contents of the source register, with the results placed in the target register. The branch instructions use the offset field as a branch displacement from the current program counter location.

The *jump-type* (J-type) instruction format also uses a 6-bit opcode field, which is followed by a 26-bit target field that specifies the address to which to jump. Because instructions are all 32 bits long, this format uses the somewhat standard trick of extending the range of a jump by adding two zeros to the end of the target field. This can be done because all instructions are required to be aligned on a 4-byte boundary, and therefore the two low-order bits of an instruction address are always 0. This means that the effective range of addressing is plus or minus 2^{27} bytes. Even though the only instructions that use this format are the call instructions and the unconditional jumps, those are the two crucial instances where this kind of full addressing capability is needed.

The Load and Store Instructions

In our introduction to RISC architectures, the restriction that only load and store instructions could access memory was presented as one of several RISC characteristics. While that section warned that not all of the characteristics listed could be found on all RISC chips, the use of only load and store instructions to reference memory *is* certainly a universal feature of RISC processors. On the MIPS, we see this for the first time. The basic load instructions are

LB	Load Byte (signed)
LBU	Load Byte Unsigned
LH	Load Halfword (signed)

LHU	Load Halfword Unsigned
LW	Load Word
LWL	Load Word Left
LWR	Load Word Right

It is a fairly minor design point whether both the signed and unsigned forms of partial word loads, LBU and LHU, are available. By the end of this text we will have seen processors that provide one or the other or, as in the case of the MIPS, both. From a programmer's point of view, however, the flexibility of both is very welcome.

The store instructions are exactly parallel to the load instructions:

STB	Store Byte
SH	Store Halfword
SW	Store Word
SWL	Store Word Left
SWR	Store Word Right

Both the load and the store instructions require alignment, with the exception of the special "left" and "right" variants described below. Addressing an unaligned operand will result in an address exception error, forcing the processor into supervisor state to handle the exception. Note that the load and store instructions are not symmetrical since there is no point in including signed and unsigned variants of the partial word store instructions.

UNALIGNED DATA. An interesting set of instructions found on the MIPS allows an unaligned word to be loaded from and stored to memory. These instructions are Load Word Left and Load Word Right and their counterparts, Store Word Left and Store Word Right. To understand the idea behind the use of these instructions, we need to understand exactly how the standard load and store instructions work.

The effective address specified in the standard multibyte load instructions, LW or LH, is required to be aligned. In the case of the LW instruction, this requirement means that the two low-order bits of the effective address must be zero, while in the case of the LH instruction it means that the low-order bit of the effective address must be zero. If one of these load instructions is executed and the requirement is not met, an addressing exception will occur.

To load a word (i.e., a 4-byte quantity) that straddles across a natural word boundary, the two instructions, LWL and LWR, are used in sequence. These load the unaligned data in two parts. The address specified in the LWL instruction is a byte address, that can point at any one of the bytes in a word. The bytes that are copied into the register include the byte at the specified byte address and all of the bytes in the direction of higher addresses up to the word boundary. These bytes are copied into the high-order bytes of the register, leaving the low-order bytes untouched. The LWL instruction is similar, except that the bytes that are copied from memory start at the specified byte address and move toward low memory until a word boundary is reached. These bytes are placed in the low-order bytes of the specified register, leaving the high-order bytes untouched.

For example, if you issue the instruction

LWL   R10, 1(R0)

the effect of this instruction is to load bytes 1, 2, and 3 into the top leftmost 3 bytes of register 10, leaving the rightmost byte untouched. If you then issue the instruction

LWR   R10, 4(R0)

the effect is to load the single byte at absolute address 4 into register 10, leaving the left part of register 10 untouched. In this way, the contiguous bytes at locations 1 through 4 are loaded into register 10 (see Figure 9.5).

This is the second approach that we have seen in treating unaligned data. The first approach, used on both the 386 and the 68030, was to have the hardware automatically load unaligned data in pieces and automatically reassemble the unaligned word. Although this may cost a few extra clocks, no extra instructions are required. The approach taken on the MIPS is to use two instructions, but the cost is minimal provided that we know in advance whether or not the word is aligned (this is not always true, for instance, when parameters are passed by reference to a procedure). A third approach, used on the SPARC, is simply to forbid unaligned data.

As we discussed in Chapter 1, the alignment issue comes up in the case of several languages, including COBOL and FORTRAN. One important case arises in conjunction with COBOL records, which are generally required to be compact. A COBOL compiler is not permitted to reorder the fields in a record, since this would change the semantics of dealing with items at the group level and with overlaying field definitions. A knowledgeable programmer who knew what processor a program was intended to run on could deliberately arrange records so that the fields were aligned, but one cannot expect typical programs to be written with that much attention to this detail.

The consequence is that if you are compiling COBOL programs on a chip like the SPARC, which lacks any facility for handling unaligned data, you are in hot water. Executing a load is not too difficult. The two words in which the unaligned data is found must be loaded, and then with some shifting and masking (helped significantly by the presence of a double shift if it is available), the data word can be assembled. The

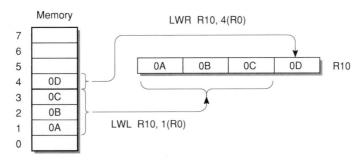

FIGURE 9.5
Loading a word which causes a page boundary using LWL and LWR.

length of this sequence will be somewhere between four and six instructions. The store, on the other hand, is considerably more troublesome, because here you have to load the two words, clear out the old contents of the field (one piece in each word), stick in the new value (one piece in each word), and then store the words back in memory. This is perhaps as many as 10 instructions in all, leading to a potential explosion in code size and a considerable performance penalty.

Given all these problems, the compromise in the MIPS chip seems well chosen. By having two instructions for the load or store, the problem of multiple TLB misses or multiple cache misses is avoided, since the operand of each instruction lies entirely in a single word. Executing only two instructions to do an unaligned access is quite efficient. It should be noted that one might be concerned that the sequence LWL LWR violates the rule on consecutive load instructions using the same register. However, there is a special exception for this pair of instructions and for the corresponding SWL SWR sequence. After all, by definition, the two instructions deal with quite separate sections of the register, so they can be executed independently.

BIG-ENDIAN AND LITTLE-ENDIAN BYTE ORDERING.

An option that is present on the MIPS, that we have not seen on any CISC processors, is the ability to put the processor into either big- or little-endian mode. On the MIPS, either of these addressing modes is selected when the processor is reset and remains in effect until the next reset. The i860, covered in a later chapter, is also able to operate in either of these modes, although it can change from one mode to the other dynamically.

One must be careful to understand exactly what this means. The effect of changing modes is to renumber the memory locations—it does *not* change which bytes go into which memory locations. The question is: How are these bytes numbered? Are they numbered 0, 1, 2, 3 or 3, 2, 1, 0? That is all that the little- or big-endian selection does on the MIPS.

The effect of this renumbering of bytes can be seen in instructions that load and store *part* of a word. As an example, take the Load Byte Unsigned (LBU) instruction, which loads a byte from memory into the low-order 8 bits of a register and fills the high-order 24 bits of the register with 0s.

The description of this instruction is given in the MIPS reference manual using a so-called *register transfer language* as:

$$mem \leftarrow LoadMemory(...)$$
$$byte \leftarrow VirtualAddress_{1..0}$$
$$\text{if BigEndian then}$$
$$\quad GPR[rt] \leftarrow 0^{24} \mathbin{||} mem_{31 - 8 * byte .. 24 - 8 * byte}$$
$$\text{else}$$
$$\quad GPR[rt] \leftarrow 0^{24} \mathbin{||} mem_{7 + 8 * byte .. 8 * byte}$$
$$\text{end if}$$

where *byte* refers to the two low-order bits of the effective address and *mem* refers to the value loaded from memory. In the big-endian case, this description says to concatenate 24 zeros to the byte that can be found in the bits specified by the formula.

For example, if one wants to load a byte at an address whose last two bits are zero, the 32-bit word containing the byte is first loaded into the processor in big-endian fashion. If the processor is in big-endian mode, the first alternative in the "if" statement specifies that bits 31 through 24 of the value loaded in from memory, with 24 zero concatenated at the front, should be put into the general-purpose register *rt*. In little-endian mode, bits 7 through 0 are loaded. As one reads through the instruction set, many load and store instructions contain similar descriptions.

Note that the effect of the LW and STW instructions is *not* dependent on the endian mode. LW and STW always load and store physical words in memory. This means that even if it were possible to change modes dynamically it would not be possible to reference mixed little- and big-endian data by this mechanism.

One consequence of these two different modes is that it is almost like having two different machines. In particular, compilers must be able to handle generation of code for either case. This is not always taken into account. For example, one manufacturer's Ada compiler for the MIPS expects big-endian ordering. This compiler absolutely cannot run on the DEC workstation that uses the MIPS chip, since DEC chooses to always run in little-endian mode.[4]

The Computational Instructions

Just as the load and store instructions of the MIPS are characteristically RISC , the instructions that perform arithmetic and logical operations also conform to one of the related "pure" RISC principles: All computational instructions restrict their operands to registers and immediate constants. The actual set of arithmetic and logical instructions contains no surprises. The usual set of addition and subtraction instructions, as well as logical operations, are provided, but there is one unusual thing about them, as we shall see.

ADDITION AND SUBTRACTION. The add and subtract instructions come in several varieties. First of all, the most general form for addition and subtraction are the instructions Add (ADD) and Subtract (SUB). These instructions, which fall into the R-Type format, allow two registers to be added, and store the result in a third register.

In addition to these register-to-register add and subtract instructions, there is an Add Immediate (ADDI) instruction and Subtract Immediate (SUBI) instruction which fall in the I-Type format. These instructions add the sign-extended value of the 16-bit immediate field to a register and place the result in another register.

When executing any of the above add or subtract instructions, an exception will be raised if an integer overflow occurs. All of these instructions have unsigned variants, ADDU, ADDIU, SUBU, and SUBIU, which are identical to the other instructions except that the overflow exception does *not* occur.

---

[4] Hardly a surprising decision, since DEC has been a champion of little-endian design and is responsible for marketing the first such machine (the PDP-11). All subsequent DEC machines, including the VAX, are little-endian.

This selection of instructions is quite unusual. It is one of the few chips in which such an exception will occur. If you are in an environment where this exception is desirable, then of course it is attractive that no extra instruction is needed. On the other hand, there is no way to test overflow *except* by getting an exception trap. There are situations in which this represents a somewhat unfortunate design choice. Even on the 370, where a system trap occurs, a programmer is given the choice of masking it or not. The result of this decision is that, for instance, the C compiler for the MIPS chip will generate unsigned additions in all cases because a C programmer does not expect to be knocked out of the water by an overflow. The following example shows a situation in which the forced trap is unfortunate.

```
begin
    A := B + C;
exception
    when CONSTRAINT_ERROR =>
      OVFLOW := TRUE;
end;
```

For this particular example of an exception handler, the appealing code is to generate an addition for B and C followed by a conditional jump based on whether an overflow occurred. If it does not cause an overflow then the result is assigned to A; if it does cause an overflow, then true is assigned to OVFLOW and the assignment to A is skipped.

On the MIPS, we have no way of doing the addition and determining whether it overflows without taking a system trap. In a typical Unix system, the expense paid for *any* trap is considerable, so we cannot easily generate efficient code for this Ada example. On the other hand, for the general situation in Ada it *is* attractive to have an automatic trap on overflow, because this corresponds to the normal Ada semantics. In the case where the exception is handled in a higher scope, the generalized exception manager has to be called in any case, and the overhead of the trap is not so significant.

MULTIPLICATION AND DIVISION. The MIPS chip has a complete set of multiply and divide instructions with an interesting design. Having looked at the 386 and the 68030, this may not come as much of a surprise. From the CISC point of view, it seems obvious that all four of the major arithmetic operators should be included in an instruction set. But this is far from being true of all RISC processors. Several RISC processors, including the SPARC, which is described in the next chapter, do not include a division instruction or special hardware support of any kind for division.

The MIPS, on the other hand, provides complete multiplication and division instructions in both signed and unsigned variants. The multiply instruction has two operands, *rs* and *rt*, which are the source and target registers, respectively. The result goes into the special registers HI and LO, which are used only for multiplication and division. The division instruction will divide only a 32-bit number by a 32-bit number—the hardware does not support 64-bit by 32-bit division. Since this is what most programming languages provide, the omission is not serious, although it would complicate multiple precision division.

In order to manipulate the special registers HI and LO, the MIPS provides special instructions that move data to and from these registers (MFHI, MFLO, MTHI, MTLO). To perform a multiplication, the two operands are placed in two general-purpose registers. After the multiplication has completed, the low-order 32 bits of the result will be left in LO. To perform a division, the dividend and divisor are placed in two general purpose registers. After the division is complete, the quotient is left in HI and the remainder in LO.

How many clocks does it take to perform a multiplication or division? In one sense, these instructions take only 1 clock, since they do not hold up the pipeline. A separate multiplication/division unit within the MIPS carries on the operation in parallel with other instructions already in the pipeline, allowing the rest of the pipeline to keep moving. On the other hand, on one implementation of the MIPS the multiplication takes 12 cycles to complete while the division takes 35 clocks. If another instruction following the multiply or divide tries to reference the result of the operation before it has completed, then the processor will cause the pipeline to stop. The pipeline will be restarted only after the result of the operation is complete.

Note that this is an instance in which the MIPS chip, despite the heritage of its name *is* using an interlocking mechanism. The pipeline stall occurs if and when the result of a multiplication or division is referenced before the operation is complete. This is similar to the normal register reference logic on RISC machines which use interlocking as the basic approach for data synchronization. Of course in the MIPS case, only the special registers LO and HI are affected, so the only instructions that have to deal with interlocking are the special instructions MFLO and MFHI, and the multiply and divide instructions themselves (which must wait for the previous operation to complete before continuing).

LOGICAL INSTRUCTIONS. The usual logical instructions AND, OR, and XOR are available on the MIPS. These instructions take two register operands and place the result in a third, not necessarily distinct, register. The instructions also come in immediate variants (ANDI, ORI, and XORI) in which the logical operation is applied to a register and a 16-bit immediate constant.

There is also a fourth logical instruction Not Or (NOR). While most machines include the first three logical operations, the choice of a fourth logical opcode varies from machine to machine. This has to do with the fact that only the first three logical operations are really required, but in representing these three opcodes, if the instruction format contains 2 bits for the logical operations, a fourth operation is free.

The OR instruction has a special significance, when it is used with the special register R0, due to the fact that the MIPS does not have a register-to-register move instruction. No special instruction is needed, since the assembler pseudo-instruction

```
MOVE   R2, R4
```

can be translated very easily into

```
OR      R2, R4, R0
```

This example shows how R0 can be used to extend the function of other instructions. As you will see later, there are many examples of this, and it is also the case that the use of R0 in addressing modes can be used to extend their effective functions.

SHIFT INSTRUCTIONS. The MIPS includes three types of shift instructions that each come in two flavors. The basic shift instructions are Shift Left Logical (SLL), Shift Right Logical (SRL), and Shift Right Arithmetic (SRA). The shift count in each of these instructions is present as part of the instruction format itself in the *shamt*, or *shift amount*, field. If the shift amount is variable, then there is a corresponding set of instructions: SLLV, SRLV, and SRAV, where the shift count is in a register, rather than in the instruction itself.

The variable shift count forms are useful in a number of situations. Consider how one might represent a bit string in Ada:

```
declare
    type BIT_STRING is array (0..31) of BOOLEAN;
    pragma PACK (BIT_STRING);
    B : BIT_STRING;
    J : INTEGER;
    Q : BOOLEAN; begin
begin
    ...
    Q := B(J);
    ...
end;
```

This fragment of Ada code shows how pragma PACK can force the representation of an array of booleans as a bit string. The reference B(J) would translate into a sequence such as

```
L      R4, B
NOP
L      R2, J
NOP
SHRV   R3, R4, R2
AND    R3, R3, 1
```

This leaves bit B(J) in register 3. We assume here that the bits of the bit string are arranged in little-endian order, so that B(0) is the rightmost bit. Interestingly, this is one of the very few cases where the code sequences for the little-endian and big-endian bit orderings are not equivalent. For big-endian ordering we would need an extra instruction:

```
L      R4, B
NOP
L      R2, J
NOP
```

```
SHLV    R3, R4, R2
SHR     R3, 31
AND     R3, R3, 1
```

since even in the big-endian case we want the extracted bit to end up at the least significant end of the word.

Immediate Instructions

There is a complete set of immediate instructions on the MIPS: ADDI, ADDIU (the unsigned add), ANDI, ORI, and XORI. All these instructions have the format:

```
xxxl    rt, rs, immediate
```

where *rs* provides a source operand, and the immediate value is 16 bits and is either zero-extended (for the logical instructions), or sign-extended (for the add immediate instructions). The required operation is performed between the contents of *rs* and this extended immediate value, and the result is stored in *rt*. By using R0 (which always contains zero), the utility of these instructions can be extended: ADDI using R0 for *rs* provides a sign-extended 16-bit load, and ORI with R0 provides a 16-bit unsigned (i.e., zero-extended) load. Furthermore, there is no need to have subtract immediate instructions, since the required effect can be achieved with add immediate instructions by using the negative of the required value.

Even with these uses of R0, this set of instructions is incomplete because of the limitation that the immediate value can be only 16 bits. To address this problem, MIPS uses an approach that is typical of 32-bit RISC machines, providing an instruction LUI (Load Upper Immediate). LUI has the format

```
LUI     rt, immediate
```

The immediate value is shifted left 16 bits, and the result placed in register *rt* is zero. Using this instruction we can place an arbitrary 32-bit constant in a register. For instance, to set register *rt* to contain X'12345678', we can execute the sequence of instructions:

```
LUI  rt, X'1234'
ORI  rt, R0, X'5678'
```

Although this takes two instructions, the resulting instruction sequence is still only 8 bytes long. The corresponding 386 sequence to load a register with a 32-bit constant is only one instruction, but it is 6 bytes long. The difference in code size between the two processors is not that significant, and the timing on the MIPS (2 clocks) also compares favorably with that of the 386, where the MOV immediate instruction is a 2-clock instruction.

Given this method of placing arbitrary 32-bit constants in a register, we can obtain the effect of any immediate instruction with a large operand by simply building the required constant in a register and then performing the required operation, something that will require three instructions.

The Jump and Branch Instructions

There are no flags of any kind on the MIPS, something that is quite novel. Instead, there are Branch on Equal (BEQ) and a Branch on Not Equal (BNE) instructions that take two registers specified by the *rs* and *rt* fields of the I-Type instruction format. It is only possible to jump to an address that is within a signed 16-bit displacement because the I-Type format has only a 16 bit data field. You will remember that since register R0 is always wired to 0, this provides branches based on a comparison to 0 (i.e., branch on zero, or branch on non-zero) without requiring special instructions.

Because jumps are restricted to a 2^{16} offset, it may be necessary to use an unconditional jump to jump to the appropriate location, since it has a much wider range (the jump instruction J has a 26-bit offset). All jumps have an unconditional delay slot. Whether they are taken or not, the delay slot instruction is executed.

There are a few more variations of the branch and jump instructions. There are instructions to jump if a register is greater than (or greater than or equal to) 0 or a jump can be made if a register is greater than zero (BGTZ), greater than or equal to zero (BGEZ), less than zero (BLTZ), or less than or equal to zero (BLEZ).

While there is no jump that allows you to compare two registers and jump on the basis of a non-equal comparison condition, there is a Set on Less Than (SLT) instruction that can be used for this purpose. It is a three-register format instruction, that is, you specify a destination register, and two source registers, and it sets a value of 1 or 0 depending upon whether that is true or false in the target register:

```
SLT     rd, rs, rt          ; rd := rs < rt
```

These instructions are also present on the 386 and the 68000 series. They are used by a C code generator for a statement like

```
a = b < c;
```

for which the above instruction is exactly what you need.

You do not normally think of using these instructions for conditional jumps, but on the MIPS they also play that role. A conditional jump after the SLT can test whether the result register is zero or non-zero, thus achieving the effect of a jump on less than. Note that it is no accident that the values set by SLT are just what C requires.

What do you gain by removing the condition flags? The condition flags on processors like the 386 and the 68030 are a dedicated facility that act essentially like a single register, which must be taken into account in pipelining and instruction scheduling. Having only one output register for the result of a compare is a little like having only one output register for the result of an addition: It introduces an irregularity into the architecture. On the MIPS chip, one can do separate comparison instructions in separate registers, overlapping the store of the results. This approach is also more amenable from the compiler's point of view, in that results of conditionals are in registers like other results and can be tracked and allocated using the same mechanism, rather than having to be handled specially, as is the case on processors with flags.

The final jump instruction is (JR) which jumps to address contained in a general purpose register. This can be used for implementing branch tables.

Procedure Call Instructions

The instruction JAL is similar to J except that the return address (which is the address of the JAL + 8, i.e., the address of the instruction following the delay slot) is stored in register R31. Specifying a fixed register for the return point seems to violate the RISC principle of general registers. The explanation for this deviation is that the call needs all the addressing bits that it can get since the call in general may reference any location in a large program.

A typical approach in compiling code for this situation is to distinguish the case of leaf procedures that do not have calls to other procedures inside them. Such a procedure can leave the return point in R31 throughout its execution and then simply return by doing JR specifying R31. For other procedures, those that do contain calls to further procedures, the contents of R31 will be save on entry and then restored on exit to effect the return.

A variation is the JALR instruction, in which the procedure address is stored in a general purpose register. This can be used for calling functions in C where the programmer specifies the address of the function. Finally, there are the instructions BGEZAL and BLTZAL, which are variants of the conditional jumps that set the return point in R31 and thus acts as conditional call instructions.

The Coprocessor Instructions

The coprocessor instructions fall into four classes: load a coprocessor register, store a coprocessor register, issue a 20-bit coprocessor instruction, and, finally, conditionally branch on the contents of a coprocessor condition.

These are the instructions that would be used for a floating-point unit, a floating-point vector unit, an I/O unit, or any other kind of coprocessor that might be attached to the main processor. This is the most flexible of the chips we will see from the point of view of coprocessor interfacing.

We will look later at the standard floating-point coprocessor that is usually attached to the MIPS CPU. About other coprocessors, we have little to say, since whether they are included, and what they do is entirely up to the designer of an individual MIPS-based system.

Special Instructions

There are only two special instructions, System Call (SYSCALL) and Break (BREAK). The SYSCALL instruction causes a trap to occur, giving control to the exception handler. The BREAK instruction causes a breakpoint exception.

SYSCALL, as its name implies, is used to call the operating system. As we will see later, all exception routines operate in supervisor state, so SYSCALL is a protected method for making a transition to supervisor state. The BREAK instruction is intended for debugging purposes, although this is only a software convention—there is no kind of debugging hardware on the MIPS.

ADDRESSING MODES

The only memory addressing mode available on the MIPS is base plus offset, with a 16-bit signed offset. Notably missing (compared to CISC processors like the 386 and 68030) are indexing modes with scaling, index plus base modes and direct addressing. In addition, since the offset is limited to 16 bits, we also miss the base/offset mode where the offset is a full 32 bits.

The general RISC philosophy is to keep things simple and then deal with more complicated cases by using a sequence of instructions. Let's see how some of the "missing" addressing modes would be handled on the MIPS.

Direct Addressing

Suppose we want to load a word from an absolute location in memory, say location X'12345678'. One approach would be to place this constant in a register and then use the register as a base register with an offset of zero. This would take three instructions, but we can do better than this using the two-instruction sequence

```
LUI    R4, X'1234'
LW     R4, X'5678' (R4)
```

The LUI instruction sets the upper bits of the base register appropriately, and then the lower bits are provided by the offset of the load instruction itself. Since the offset is signed, we have to be a little careful in the case where the offset looks negative—in this case the upper 16 bits need appropriate adjustment so that the final result will be correct.

For example, suppose we are loading from address X'1234ABCD'. The proper sequence is then

```
LUI    R4, X'1234'
LW     R4, X'ABCD' (R4)
```

The upper 16 bits are fudged up by 1 to cancel the effect of the sign extension, which will add X'FFFF' (i.e., subtract 1) from the upper 16 bits.

This two-instruction sequence for direct addressing compares reasonably favorably with the single instruction on the 386, which is 6 bytes long (but takes considerably more clocks). A friendly assembler will hide these details from an assembly language programmer by allowing this sequence to be generated automatically in response to an assembly instruction such as

```
LW     R4, VARIABLE
```

The MIPS assembler is friendly in this respect and allows such LW instructions to be written. It is important to note that if the address of VARIABLE is not known until link time (the typical case with direct addressing), then the linker must be prepared to handle some rather peculiar relocation types, which separately relocate the upper and lower 16 bits, knowing how to fudge the upper 16 bits if the lower 16 bits are negative. The failure of a linker to provide this relocation severely restricts the code that can be written.[5] The store word can be done in a similar manner, though of course in this case we need an extra scratch register to temporarily hold the address.

If a similar store instruction is written:

```
STW     R4, variable
```

a similar approach can be used, but an extra register is required for the address:

```
LUI     R1, variable.hi
STW     R4, variable.lo(R1)
```

Now we can understand the rule that R1 is reserved for the assembler and understand its alternative name, Rat—*at* stands for *address temporary*.

It is possible to avoid direct addressing using base plus offset addressing instead. In this approach, a register is set to point to a region of static storage, and then this static storage can be addressed using offsets from this base register. The MIPS has a 16-bit offset, which is fairly generous, at least compared with some other RISC architectures. A single base register used in this way could reach 64K bytes of static storage, which will often be enough. For example, all the static scalar variables in a C program, or in library packages of an Ada program, will likely fit in this limit.

Indexed and Base/Index Addressing

The MIPS lacks base plus index addressing, a decision that allows the offset to be larger than it would otherwise be, which, as we saw in the previous section, is definitely advantageous. A CISC designer might be perfectly happy to have two formats, one with a big offset and one base register and another with a smaller offset and an index register, but this sort of complication is unwelcome in a RISC design.

To get the effect of base plus index addressing, extra instructions have to be generated to add the components of the address first. For the 386 instruction:

```
MOV     EAX, [EBX + ECX*4 + 1000]
```

this same effect can be obtained on the MIPS with R2, R3, R4 playing the role of EAX, EBX, ECX by using two extra instructions:

```
SLL     R1, R4, 2
ADD     R1, R1, R3
LW      R2, 1000 (R1)
```

Although this three-instruction sequence (12 bytes) is longer than the MOV instruction (6 bytes), it will execute in 3 or 4 clocks and the 386 MOV instruction takes 5 clocks.

---

[5] The AIX linker for the IBM RT cannot handle this type of relocation, probably because AIX adopted the standard Unix COFF format, which does not provide for this possibility. Consequently, direct addressing cannot be used in this environment. The AOS system for the RT allows for this special relocation but insists that the two instructions be adjacent, which is an unfortunate restriction because it means that the two instructions cannot be separated for scheduling purposes.

Furthermore, a clever compiler can often eliminate the need for this type of addressing mode in the first place. Suppose we have the Pascal loop

```
S := 0;
for I := 1 to 100 do
    S := S + ARR(I);
```

On the 386, we can generate the following sequence of code:

```
        SUB     ECX, ECX         ; use ECX to hold value of S (zero it)
        MOV     EBX, 1           ; use EBX to hold value of I
LP:     ADD     ECX, ARR[EBX*4]  ; perform addition
        INC     EBX              ; bump I
        CMP     EBX,100          ; loop till 100 loops completed
        JLE     LP
```

Here we assume that ARR is an array on the current stack frame, so it is addressed using EBP as a base register. Obviously we could use the same approach on the MIPS, replacing the ADD instruction with a four-instruction sequence (three instructions to load the value and one for the ADD). However, a clever compiler can do much better using standard optimization techniques and generate

```
        ORI     R4, R0, 0        ; use R4 to hold value of S (zero it)
        LA      R2, ARR          ; point R2 to first element of ARR
LP:     LW      R3, 0 (R2)       ; load next word
        ADD     R4, R3           ; add into sum
        ADDU    R2, R0, 4        ; bump R2 to point to next word
        SLTI    R3, R2, 4*100    ; R3 is true (non-zero) till end of loop
        BNE     R3, R0, LP
```

Using this approach we have eliminated the need for the base plus index addressing mode altogether. In practice it is well within current compiler technology to eliminate such complex addressing modes in most cases.

Base Plus Offset Addressing

The basic addressing mode provides base plus offset mode where the offset is limited to 16 bits. If the offset is greater than 16 bits, then base plus offset addressing requires a sequence of instructions. The assembler automatically generates these sequences. For example, if an assembly language programmer writes

```
LW      R3, X'12345678' (R4)
```

Then the assembler generates the following two-instruction sequence:

```
LUI     R3, X'1234'
LW      R3, X'5678' (R4)
```

Once again, the sequence is not unreasonable, although it is certainly longer than the corresponding 6-byte single instruction on the 386. Base plus offset mode is typically used for addressing stack frames and record fields, and relatively few stack frames or records are greater than 64K.

One problem arises if the compiler does not know *at compile time* whether the offset is limited to 64K. If not, then there are two slightly unpleasant choices. Either an arbitrary limit must be applied or the worst-case two-instruction code must be unconditionally generated. This situation arises with package subunits in Ada:

```
procedure X is
     Y : INTEGER;
     Z : INTEGER;

     package G is
        procedure Q;
     end G;

     package G is separate;

     M : INTEGER;
```

The body of G is compiled separately, and its variables are part of the stack frame of procedure X. Since you don't know how many variables G has when you compile procedure X, you have to either limit stack frames to 64K bytes unconditionally or assume the worst when generating references to variables in the stack.

MEMORY MANAGEMENT ON THE MIPS

The MIPS implements virtual memory with the hardware support of the on-chip coprocessor CP0. This hardware support is provided by a translation lookaside buffer (TLB) and several other registers located within CP0. In keeping with the RISC philosophy of keeping things simple, memory management on the MIPS is far simpler than either the segmented and paged memory of the 386 or that of the multilevel page tables of the 68030.

The Address Space

Addresses on the MIPS are 32 bits wide, corresponding to a 4-gigabyte memory, but this address space is carved up into a small number of separate sections called *segments* (see Figure 9.6) although the term should not be confused with the logical segments of the 386 or the segments of other machines. The format of a virtual address on the MIPS is divided into three major pieces (see Figure 9.7). The 3 high-order bits are used to select a segment. Bits 12 through 28 select a virtual page number, and the 12 low-order bits are used to specify a byte offset within a page.

The user address space is always mapped. Both in kernel mode and user mode it is possible to reference and load 2 gigabytes. That gives the kernel the same virtual address view of user memory that the user has.

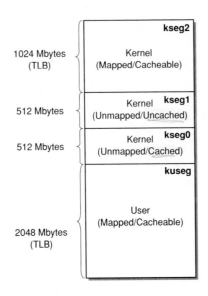

1024 Mbytes (TLB)

kseg2

Kernel
(Mapped/Cacheable)

512 Mbytes

Kernel **kseg1**
(Unmapped/Uncached)

512 Mbytes

Kernel **kseg0**
(Unmapped/Cached)

kuseg

2048 Mbytes (TLB)

User
(Mapped/Cacheable)

FIGURE 9.6
The layout of virtual memory on the MIPS R2000.

The supervisor region is mapped through the virtual memory mechanism in the usual manner, but it is accessible only in supervisor state. If the processor is in user state and an instruction tries to make a reference to something in the supervisor's address space, then an *invalid address exception* will occur. The reason this is distinguished from other TLB reference errors is that checking for this possibility does not slow down the normal TLB replacement logic.

The remaining two segments map into the low one-half gigabyte of physical memory. Existing machines do not have more than half a gigabyte of real memory, so the intention behind this design is that *all* of physical memory can be mapped into these segments. In supervisor state only, absolute memory references can be made, bypassing the virtual memory mechanism. Of the two segments of memory that work this way, one segment gives cached access to this area and the other gives uncached access, so just by modifying the address used, a load or store can determine whether or not the reference should be cached. One use of this mechanism is in referencing instructions in the page fault routine—it can get a little embarrassing if instruction accesses within the page fault routine can themselves cause page faults.

The provision of a separate segment which bypasses the cache is useful in situations where caching is undesirable. One example of undesirable uncached accesses is a memory-mapped I/O device. If some memory on a machine is a direct-mapped graphics screen, it is not terribly exciting to be able to quickly write the graphics data into a cache since it wouldn't show up on the screen! There are places, Such references to memory-mapped devices would typically occur in supervisor mode in any case. There

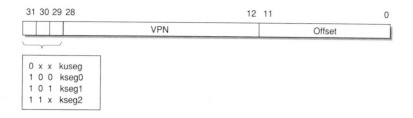

FIGURE 9.7
The virtual address format of the MIPS R2000.

are other cases in which one might want non-cacheable references from user mode programs, but this can be achieved by using the bit in the virtual memory page tables that inhibits the use of the cache.

A slight disadvantage of this design is that it gives uncomfortably easy access to all of memory. One accidental misuse of an instruction in supervisor state can, if its address ends up in this unmapped area of memory, destroy absolutely anything, including page tables or other critical data. So the supervisor had better not contain any incorrect code! This contrasts with the philosophy of the multiple levels of protection on the 386, where the idea is that only very small parts of the operating system kernel can do unlimited damage. Of course, the supervisor doesn't really need to protect itself against its own maliciousness. But it is of some value for the supervisor to protect itself against its own easily foreseeable accidents. Anyone who has done any programming with pointers knows that coming up with an incorrect pointer address is a frequent accident.

The Instruction and Data Caches

As we mentioned previously, the use of caches on a RISC processor is important in reducing the number of loads required from the main memory, since the pipeline may have to be halted while data is loaded unless it is in the cache. In the MIPS design, there is no cache on board the chip itself, although there is on-chip support for an external cache.[6]

An alternate arrangement for a microprocessor is one in which the cache is on the chip and connected to memory. After the processor has developed the address of the data it wants, it looks to the cache to see whether the data is there. If the processor gets a cache hit, it then makes the data available to the processor directly from the cache, and if not, the processor will be forced to make a request to real memory. If data needs to be stored rather than read, the processor will arrange for the data to be written to both the cache and to memory.

---

[6] This is the current design of the MIPS processor. There is nothing, of course, to prevent both caches from being placed onto the chip.

Although the MIPS does not have an on board cache, there are very well defined interfaces provided to cache both data and instructions. The idea behind this part of the design is to produce an interface that is fast enough so that a large cache can be built from commercial static RAM rather than trying to bring the cache onto the chip.

The issue of whether to put a cache on board the chip or not involves a trade-off between hit rate and access time. The advantage of having the cache off the chip is that it is easy to make it larger, with a potential improvement in the cache hit rate. In the high-end PC market, for example, where machines run at 25 MHz or more, there is a noticeable gain in the performance of a machine in moving from a 32K byte cache to a 64K byte cache, while moving beyond 64K does not make much of a difference.

The down side of taking the cache off the chip is that the time required to access data in the cache may be longer than if the cache were on the chip, since chip-to-chip communications may introduce delays. These potential inefficiencies are mitigated somewhat in the MIPS chip by having special attachments to the cache rather than simple transparent connections.

CACHE SPEED REQUIREMENTS. One important issue with respect to the cache on the MIPS is that the cache is *absolutely committed* to returning data in time for the second instruction after the load to reference it. On a machine with interlocks, failing to meet such a specification would degrade the efficiency, since there would be extra holdups from the interlocks, but the program would still work. On the MIPS, failure of data to report from the cache on time will cause the program to malfunction.

A concern is whether the cache can keep up if the processor speed is increased. Reportedly, there have been some initial problems with making the cache run fast enough to keep up with a 33MHz R3000 which may well stem from this fundamental consideration. Of course there is nothing to stop one from redesigning the MIPS chip to use interlocks, but all the MIPS compilers assume that all they need to do is to insert one instruction between a load and a reference, and they would have to be changed to do more aggressive register scheduling if the MIPS design were changed in this manner.

Whether or not this requirement on cache speed is a problem in the future depends on the relative development of processor and cache technologies. It will be interesting to see if any difficulties develop as the MIPS design is moved to more advanced technlogies. MIPS is committed to the position that the interlock-free approach is superior, so one can expect a maximum effort to maintain this approach in the future.

The Translation Lookaside Buffer

The onboard coprocessor CP0 has a fully associative translation lookaside buffer (TLB) that contains 64 entries. The TLBs on most microprocessors are often multiway associative rather than fully associative. A fully associative TLB of this size is really quite large and represents an impressive piece of hardware for a microprocessor. The translation lookaside buffer of the 68030, which you will remember is called the ATC, is also fully associative, although it has only 22 entries.

The precise structure of the TLB in the MIPS is similar to that of many other processors. Since the whole point of the TLB is to store information mapping virtual pages into physical pages, several fields are commonly present. Each entry in the TLB consists of the following fields:

- The 20-bit *virtual page number* (VPN) contains the virtual page number for which this entry is providing translation information. Bits 12 through 28 of a virtual address are compared against this field to determine whether an entry is in the TLB to perform the virtual-to-physical translation.

- The 20-bit *page frame number* (PFN) contains the physical address of the page frame in which the virtual page has been placed.

- The *valid* (V) bit specifies whether the entry is valid.

- The 6-bit *process id* (PID) field identifies the process which "owns" the page, allowing separate processes to have separate page table entries.

- The *non-cacheable* (N) bit. If set, any data references to this page are not placed in the cache.

- The *dirty* (D) bit. This is a write protect bit. We will explain later how it can also function as a dirty bit, giving its is name.

- The *global* (G) bit. If this bit is set, then no checking of the PID field is done by the memory management.

Most processors have page table entries that look similar to the entries in the TLB of the MIPS (a comparison of the fields in the translation lookaside buffers for the MIPS and the 68030 is shown in Table 9.2).

THE TRANSLATION MECHANISM. The translation of a virtual address to a physical address occurs in several steps. At any point during this translation, an exception

TABLE 9.2
The MIPS and 68030 Translation Lookaside Buffer Structure.

MIPS	68030	Comparison
Virtual page number	Logical address	MIPS has a 20-bit logical address; 68030 has a 24-bit logical address
Page frame number	Physical address	MIPS has 20-bit page frame descriptor; 68030 has 24-bit page frame descriptor
Valid bit	Valid bit	Essentially the same
Process ID	function code	Similar function, but different notions of address space
Non-cacheable	Cache inhibit	Similar
Dirty bit	Modified bit	See text
Global	—	
—	Bus error	
Dirty bit	Write protect	Essentially the same

may occur. The virtual address must first be checked to see that a user level process is not attempting to reference the address space of a kernel mode process. This is simply done by checking that the most significant bit of the virtual address is 0, since such addresses are guaranteed to be in the user address space rather than the kernel's address space. Once this hurdle has been passed, a check is made to see if the TLB contains the physical page number corresponding to the virtual page number whose translation is needed. Even if the entry has been found, however, several other events may cause an exception.

If the TLB entry maps a page which is *not* global, that is, it is not available to all processes, then the PID field must be checked against the ID of the current process. If everything has gone well up to this point, the hardware must still check to see if the entry is valid (the entry in the TLB contains valid data). Finally, the hardware must still determine whether the page can be either read or written to.

If a read being done, the checking is complete. For a write, the dirty bit is checked. If it is not set, then a trap occurs. We discuss later on how the D bit can be used to serve both as a write protect bit and as a dirty bit.

All of this is quite standard. The difference in the MIPS approach, compared to other microprocessors having memory management, is what happens if an entry is *not* found in the TLB. Most other chips implement some form of data structure in the hardware to support paging on the chip itself. In earlier chapters we have seen that the 386 has a two-level page table. The 68030 implements an even more flexible scheme in hardware that allows an operating system designer to choose the number of levels in the page tables. The logic for accessing the page table is part of the hardware circuitry of the processor on most chips. Only if the relevant page table entry is marked as not present is an exception presented to the processor for handling by an appropriate software exception routine.

On the MIPS processor, no logic of this kind is built in. After a TLB miss, an exception is signalled and the processor traps to a kernel mode routine. The operating system is forced to deal with a miss in the TLB simply because the hardware does not exist to support paging to any further extent. The TLB is just part of the coprocessor CP0, so there are instructions that the processor can issue to the coprocessor to load entries in the TLB. The job of the exception routine is to consult its internal data structures to determine what should be done.

These internal structures might well be page tables in some format very similar to that of the 68030, although this need not be so. Whether a two-level page table is used or a multilevel page table is used, the manner in which a virtual address is broken up into separate fields defining separate page table levels is entirely up to the software.

The supervisor trap routine will look at the virtual address, consult its page tables (but remember that they are just software and not hardware data structures), and figure out which entry needs to be in the TLB. This may involve swapping in or swapping out a page of memory, or it may not. Remember that a trap may occur if the page is currently in memory and the TLB does not contain the entry for this page. This is unlike the page fault traps of the 386 or 68030, which occurs only if the page is not in memory.

This design approach is called *software* TLB reload. This means that the software must determine which TLB entry should be replaced by the new TLB entry required for the access that caused the trap. From the processor's point of view, this has nothing specifically to do with paging. The fact that you might want to use it for paging (and, of course, you are expected to use it that way) is a software convention.

The decision as to which of the 64 entries in the TLB to remove can be made in different ways. For example, one might decide to use an elaborate algorithm similar to the kind used in deciding which page in a virtual memory system to swap out.

The only trouble is that traps caused by a TLB entry not being present occur much more frequently than those that occur when a real page fault occurs. Since the page size on the MIPS is 4K bytes, it is only possible to describe a total of 256K bytes of memory in the TLB. On a 30 MHz processor, you can move through a great deal of data very fast. If you are dealing with large arrays, TLB misses may occur frequently.

In designing the exception routine that handles TLB misses, it is probably not worth going through some elaborate scheme to find out which of the TLB entries to replace. Instead some simpler, cruder algorithm is needed. One perfectly plausible scheme is to just replace a random entry in the TLB. To make that particular approach viable, there is a register in the CP0 coprocessor called the *random register* (a rather amusing name), which we describe next.

THE RANDOM REGISTER. When a TLB miss occurs, a new page table entry must be loaded into the TLB, and the question is which entry to replace. Ideally we would like to replace the entry for the page least likely to be used in the future, but of course there is no way of knowing which page that is. An approximation is to replace the least recently used page, but doing this accurately requires too much bookkeeping, and even an approximate LRU algorithm can require quite a bit of overhead. Another approach is to simply replace a random entry in the TLB. This may result in an inappropriate choice, but the average performance resulting from random replacement is quite good and has the advantage of being easy to implement.

To assist in the use of this random replacement approach, MIPS provides a special register called the *random register*. This is a 32-bit register that always holds a value between 8 and 63. The value is not truly random; it is actually a counter that is decremented on every reference to the TLB. However, given the large number of TLB references, the value at any particular time has the effect of being random. The random register is used to determine which entry in the TLB to replace.

When the value in the random register reaches 8, the value wraps around to 63, so values in the range 0 through 7 are never generated—in this way the first eight TLB entries are protected. Replacing an entirely random entry in the TLB would be a bad idea in some circumstances. The routine that handles exceptions, for example, will be reading instructions, page tables, and other structures important to the operating system. Since these structures may be mapped through the TLB, it is not desirable to replace the entries that refer to these structures. In general, there may be a set of TLB entries that it is important never to replace or, at the very least, to replace only under controlled circumstances. By restricting the values in the random register, the first eight entries of the TLB are reserved, but the other 56 entries can be replaced at random.

There are three instructions that are used to access the TLB. It is possible to read or write an entry indexed by the TLB index register, and it is possible to write an entry indexed by the random register. The latter instruction is what is used for a rapid procedure that avoids executing any clever algorithm for determining which TLB entry to replace.

SOFTWARE VS HARDWARE TLB RELOAD. It may seem somewhat worrisome to call an exception routine every time there is a TLB miss, but the total number of instructions for a straightforward TLB replacement can be as small as 12 on the MIPS. This translates to perhaps 15 or 18 clocks, which is not significantly worse than the time for a segment register load on the 386. It *is* worse than the overhead on some other MMUs with hardware TLB reload, but in practice the number of TLB reloads, especially with the big, fully associative TLB, is not that great.

The difference between having the processor do something and doing it in software is not so critical in a RISC processor. After all, if you are going to reference memory, the processor can't do it any faster than you can. A TLB miss in either case involves a number of real memory references, which are going to take time no matter who is dealing with it. In fact, the MIPS approach is a purer version of the RISC philosophy. The built-in logic for searching the page tables, potentially executed on any memory reference, smacks of CISC complexity!

THE DIRTY BIT. At the hardware level the dirty bit is nothing more nor less than a write protect bit. On a write, a trap occurs if the dirty bit is not set. However, due to the software reload used in the TLB, it is possible for the operating system software to use this bit both as a write protect bit and a dirty bit in the following way.

All entries initially loaded into the TLB have their dirty bits set off. In the case of a read-only page, any attempt to write that page will cause a trap, and the trap routine will realize the page involved is read-only (by consulting its own data structures) and reflect the fact in considering the trap to be an erroneous attempt to write on a read-only page.

If, on the other hand, the trap routine determines that the page is writable, then it can note in its own data structures that the page has been written and is now dirty, set the dirty bit in the TLB entry, and reexecute the instruction, which will now succeed since the dirty bit will now be set.

FLOATING-POINT ON THE MIPS

Floating-point operations on the MIPS are provided by the R2010 or R3010 floating-point accelerator (FPA) chips. These are similar in function to the 387 coprocessor used for the Intel 386. Unlike the 387, the MIPS coprocessor chips have a conventional register structure consisting of 32 registers numbered F0 to F31. These registers are used in even odd pairs, and each register pair can hold either a 32-bit single-precision or a 64-bit double-precision operand value. All floating-point instructions specify even register numbers that refer to one of the 16 register pairs. MIPS calls the individual 32-bit registers *floating-point general-purpose registers* (FGR), and the register pairs are called *floating-point registers* (FPR). From a computational point of view there are only 16 registers. Load and store instructions, however, have only a 32-bit data path, so to load and store values, the individual FGRs must be addressed. Note that register F0 is a normal register—the trick of making register 0 be permanently zero is not used here.

The 32-bit single-precision and 64-bit double-precision formats are compatible with the IEEE standard, as are all of the arithmetic operations that are provided. The extended format, however, is not supported. In addition to the 16 operand registers, there is a small set of *floating-point control registers* (FCR) that contain the flags and control bits for implementing the IEEE rounding, precision control, and exception control modes. There is also an FCR that contains implementation and revision information identifying the version of the coprocessor chip in use.

The floating-point registers (see Figure 9.8) are loaded and stored using the LWC1 and SWC1 instructions, which move data between memory and a specified FGR, or the MFC1 and MTC1 instructions, which move data between the integer registers and the FGRs. In both cases only 32 bits can be moved at a time, so handling double-precision values involves two operations that address the two FGRs making up a single FPR. The format and addressing modes of the load and store instructions are identical to those provided for integer operands. The instructions CFC1 and CTC1 are used to move data between the FCRs and the integer registers—there is no provision for loading or storing these values directly in memory.

The arithmetic operations are always performed on register values—following the usual RISC philosophy of restricting memory reference instructions to loads and

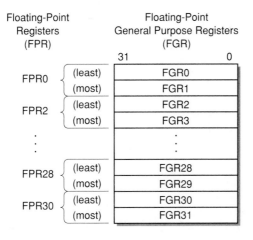
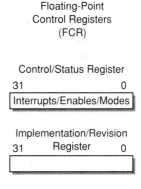

FIGURE 9.8
The register structure of the MIPS chip.

stores. The typical format has two source registers and one destination register. For example, a typical instruction has the format

    ADD.D   F4, F6, F8

This instruction sums the contents of F6 and F8 and places the result in F4. The .D suffix indicates double-precision format. The corresponding single-precision format has a .S suffix. A full set of basic arithmetic operations is provided, including addition, subtraction, multiplication, division, absolute value, and negation. However, there is no hardware support for other required IEEE operations such as square root or remainder. These operations must be provided in software.

In addition to the basic operations, there is a set of instructions which convert between the two floating-point formats, and convert to and from binary integer formats (the suffix .w is used to indicate integer format for these instructions). There are no instructions to support conversion between floating-point and decimal formats.

Finally, there is a floating-point compare instruction that sets a flag that can be tested using the BC1F and BC1T instructions, which branch on false or true, respectively. The comparison instruction indicates which condition (less than, equal, or unordered) is to be tested.

The implementation of the IEEE standard is thus considerably thinner than that of the 387. On the other hand, the speed of the basic arithmetic operations of the FPA is considerably greater than that of the corresponding operations on the 387. Remember that the IEEE standard is a combined hardware–software standard. It is perfectly reasonable to perform functions like remainder in software, since they are relatively much less frequent than the basic arithmetic operations. Even though more operations are performed in software, the overall performance of the FPA is still superior to that of the 387. What we are seeing here is another instance of the RISC philosophy that it is better to support a smaller set of basic instructions efficiently than a large set of instructions at the expense of slower execution time for the important instructions.

Instruction Scheduling

The FPA requires that instruction scheduling be done in much the same way as it is done for integer instructions. In particular, the result of a load instruction cannot be referenced in the next instruction following the load. In a sequence such as

    MTC1   F4, FPTLO
    MTC1   F5, FPTHI
    ADD.D   F2, F2, F4

an instruction must be placed between the second MTC1 instruction and the ADD. As usual, a compiler for the MIPS will try to find a useful instruction to place into this slot; if no instruction can be found, a NOP instruction will be inserted. Similarly, following a floating-point comparison instruction, one instruction must intervene before the corresponding conditional branch instruction can be executed.

Trap Handling and Overlapped Execution

An important design feature of the FPA is that it appears to the program to be completely synchronous; that is, it behaves as though each floating-point instruction is completely executed before the following instruction is executed. Even exception traps are guaranteed to be synchronized so that the trap routine receives control, with the program counter identifying the floating-point instruction that caused the trap, so that no additional instructions (floating-point or integer) have been executed. This contrasts with the 387, where the overlapped execution is visible when an exception occurs (additional 386 instructions may have been executed following the instruction causing the exception) and after stores (the store does not complete immediately, so the value is not immediately available in memory).

High floating-point performance would be impossible to achieve if the FPA really operated in a completely synchronous manner, because floating-point operations are inherently complex—they typically take several clocks to complete. To achieve high floating-point throughput, the FPA not only overlaps floating-point operations with integer operations, as on the 387, but also uses a six-stage pipeline of its own to overlap successive floating-point operations. Unlike the integer pipeline, the floating-point pipeline cannot quite achieve a 1 clock per instruction throughput. Floating point operations take from 1 to 19 clocks, as shown in Figure 9.9.

On other processors, including the SPARC, where overlapped floating-point operations are possible, a floating-point trap routine must deal with the problem of having several outstanding floating-point instructions in various stages of completion. The MIPS FPA provides overlapped floating-point operations, but guarantees synchronized traps. How is this achieved? A rather clever scheme is used in which the operands

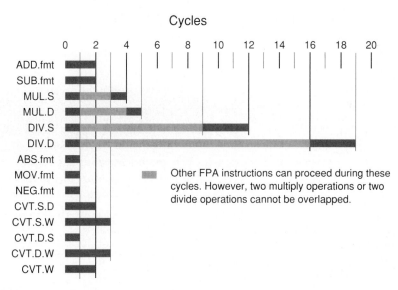

FIGURE 9.9
Instruction tmings of the MIPS floating-point instructions.

are preexamined. As soon as a floating-point operation is first encountered, the exponent fields are checked to see whether an overflow could possibly occur. If it could, then the pipeline is held up; all previous operations are completed, and the current operation is executed in non-overlapped mode to see if it really does cause an exception. Most of the time, the operands pass this exponent check, so no holdup is needed.

This technique works well for overflow and underflow traps, as well as for invalid operation traps. However, the IEEE inexact trap is much more troublesome, since it is impossible to tell whether a given floating-point operation will give an exact result. The consequence is that if the inexact trap is enabled, the floating-point pipeline is completely disabled. This is a heavy penalty, but in practice the inexact trap is very rarely used, so performance of normal applications will not be affected.

EXCEPTION HANDLING ON THE MIPS

Exceptions are handled on the MIPS by CP0, the coprocessor which is implemented on the same chip as the main processor CPU. Several standard exceptions can occur:

- An *address error exception* occurs when an attempt is made to fetch an inappropriately aligned operand. The trap routine that handles this exception can either consider it to be an error or simulate the intended effect of a non-aligned reference.

- A *breakpoint exception* is caused by a BREAK instruction used for debugging purposes. The instruction format of the BREAK instruction has 20 unused bits that can be used to pass information to a debugger.

- A *bus error exception* occurs in response to an external bus error signal. It is up to the designer of a hardware system to determine appropriate uses for this signal. One use would be to signal a parity error on a reference to external memory.

- A *coprocessor unusable exception* occurs if an instruction references a non-existent coprocessor. A trap routine could be used to simulate the required operation.

- An *interrupt exception* is signalled by one of eight interrupt conditions, two of which can be generated by software; the other six correspond to external hardware interrupts.

- An *overflow* exception occurs when a signed add or subtract instruction signals an arithmetic overflow.

- A *reserved instruction exception* occurs when an undefined instruction is executed. One possible use of this instruction is to provide additional instructions, which are provided by simulation in the corresponding trap routine.

- A *reset exception* occurs when the external RESET signal is asserted. In particular, this exception occurs when the chip is first powered up.

- A *system call exception* occurs in response to a SYSCALL exception. Its intended use is to request services from the operating system.

- There are several TLB exceptions, each caused by misses in the TLB. These are signalled by exceptions, since the MIPS relies on software for maintaining the TLB.

There are three distinct exception handlers, each with its own exception vector at a specific address, which contains the starting address of the code for the handler:

- The RESET exception handler, whose vector is located at address X'BFC00000', has control passed to it when a reset exception occurs at power-up time, or in response to an external reset signal. The handler for this exception is used to perform the required startup code.

- The UTLB exception handler, whose vector is at address X'80000000', is passed control *only* on a TLB miss for user space. It is specially distinguished from other traps so that TLB miss processing can be as efficient as possible.

- The *general* exception routine, whose vector is at address X'80000080' is passed control on all other exceptions. The exception routine uses the *cause* and *status* registers to determine which exception occurred.

Five registers in CP0 are used for exception handling:

- The *cause* register is used to determine which of several exceptions occurred.

- The *exception program counter* (EPC) register. This contains the program counter at the time of an exception.

- The *status* register. This provides additional information about the exception as well as some control flags, such as the interrupt mask that indicates which hardware interrupts are permitted to occur.

- The *bad virtual address* register records the virtual address that caused an addressing trap.

- The *context* register, which contains additional information needed to recover from an addressing trap.

All exceptions are handled in kernel mode, so the exception causes an automatic transition to kernel mode. The status register contains a 3-bit stack that records previous settings of the user/kernel mode bits, allowing the previous mode to be restored on exit from the trap routine. The Return From Exception (RFE) instruction is used to perform the necessary reverse operations to restore the original mode. RFE usually occurs in the delay slot of a Jump Register (JR) instruction used to restore the program counter.

The EPC register records the exception address. Normally this is the address of the instruction that caused the exception. The one situation in which this is not the case is when this instruction occurs in the delay slot following a jump. The problem is that the exception handler will typically return to the instruction causing the exception. Consider the following sequence of instructions:

```
JAL    subroutine
LW     R3, param
```

Suppose the LW instruction causes a TLB miss. If EPC pointed to the LW, then on return we would execute the LW and continue by executing the instruction immediately after the LW, in effect "forgetting" that we were about to call the subroutine.

exception

To deal with this problem, the EPC in this situation always points to the jump instruction, so that on return from the trap, both the jump and the instruction in the delay slot are reexecuted. This means that the exception routine may need to be aware that when an exception apparently occurs on a jump instruction, it may be the following instruction in the delay slot that is actually the source of trouble.

Hardware Interrupts

Hardware interrupts are handled like any other exception, by branching to the general exception vector. There are six hardware interrupt lines, which can be individually masked and unmasked by setting and resetting bits in the *status* register. The *cause* register contains a code indicating that a hardware interrupt has occurred, and the trap routine reacts by processing the hardware interrupt, communicating with the corresponding device as needed.

CONCLUSION

The MIPS architecture is a true RISC architecture whose design is based on the Stanford MIPS chip. Its name originally came from the fact that there is no hardware interlocking, that is to say, the software (compilers and assemblers) must fill delay slots either with useful instructions or, in the worst case, with no-ops.

A unique characteristic (among the processors discussed in this book) is that there is no hardware support for paging apart from the TLB. Misses in the TLB must be handled by the software, which maintains pages tables whose structure is determined by the operating system and not by the hardware.

The MIPS design incorporates essentially all the RISC characteristics that we discussed in Chapter 8. We chose the MIPS as the first RISC processor to examine because it is the simplest and most uncluttered of the RISC designs, and from now on we will use it as a comparison point for other RISC architectures.

CHAPTER 10

THE SPARC ARCHITECTURE

The SPARC is a computer architecture developed by Sun Microsystems. SPARC's heritage can be traced to the original Berkeley RISC chips. The feature that distinguishes the SPARC from all of the other RISC machines described in this book are the register windows first introduced in the Berkeley RISC designs.

THE SPARC ARCHITECTURE

The first thing we should point out is that SPARC, an acronym for *Scalable Processor Architecture*, is the name of an architecture and not of a specific chip. That is an important distinction from Sun Microsystems' point of view. The individual chips that have been built around the SPARC architecture are highly proprietary; the architecture, on the other hand, is open. Sun encourages other companies to license the SPARC trademark and build their own implementations in the hope it will become a standard.[1]

---

[1] As this book was being written, Sun had just signed an agreement with Toshiba for the production of SPARC-based machines. Perhaps by the time you read this, you will be able to buy SPARC-based laptops.

In attempting to establish a standard when introducing new products and technologies into the marketplace, there are generally two strategies that a manufacturer can adopt. One approach is to keep them highly proprietary in an effort to dominate the market. The other approach is to open them up in the hope that other manufacturers will copy them, thus establishing a de facto standard. IBM successfully took the second approach with the original IBM PC, whereas Apple took the first approach with the Macintosh. In the world of microprocessor design, we see the same two choices. Intel takes the proprietary approach with the 386 design in an effort to maintain a position as sole supplier. The decision by Sun to use the open approach is presumably based on the hope that it will result in their having a non-exclusive share of a large market, rather than an exclusive share of a much smaller market.

General Organization

A SPARC implementation consists of up to three logical units:

- The instruction unit (IU)
- The floating-point unit (FPU)
- The coprocessor (CP)

An implementation is only required to include the integer unit, although in practice all implementations will include the floating-point unit as well. The optional coprocessor is intended to support an additional set of functions tailored to the needs of a specific system. The logical organization of these units is shown in Figure 10.1.

The IU executes the basic arithmetic, logical, and shift operations, as well as other user and supervisor instructions. In addition, the IU has a set of load, store, and operate instructions that control the floating-point unit and the coprocessor if either is part of an implementation. For example, when a floating-point load instruction is issued by the IU, the contents of a given memory location are loaded into the appropriate register of the FPU. Since they are issued by the IU, these instructions are considered to be IU instructions. In this respect, the floating-point registers might be viewed as if they were an extension of the IU.

The floating-point unit is an IEEE-compatible design supporting all single-, double- and, optionally, extended precision formats. Floating-point operate instructions are issued by the IU, and cause the appropriate operation to be executed by the floating-point unit.

The SPARC definition has very little to say about the coprocessor other than that it can have up to thirty-two 32-bit registers that are visible to the user and up to 1024 different instructions. The coprocessor (CP) is also controlled by the IU through the use of load, store, and operate instructions. Unlike the FPU, the CP has no predefined operations in the sense that a meaning can be be attached to the bit pattern in the opcode field of an operate instruction only if one is describing a specific CP implementation. It is up to an engineer to define those instructions, or some subset of them, as the coprocessor is designed. As in the case of the FPU, there are load and store instructions to put values into and get values from registers.

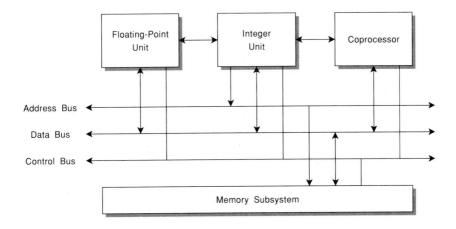

FIGURE 10.1
The logical organization of the SPARC function units.

What are some examples of coprocessors that would be useful? A floating point vector processor is one good example. A coprocessor could also be used to implement a commercial instruction set with decimal arithmetic, since, as we shall see, the SPARC instruction set is weak in supporting applications related to commercial processing. Yet another possibility would be a very simple coprocessor that had only a divide instruction, because the SPARC defines no divide instruction in its basic instruction set. If some useful function *can* be found for the coprocessor, a coprocessor chip can be built that implements what is needed, and then it can be put under the control of the IU.

The SPARC architecture does not specify whether each of these units is implemented as an individual chip, whether they should all be implemented on a single chip, or anything else of that nature. These decisions are made on the basis of available technology and other design considerations. The first implementation of SPARC, for example, used an IU implemented on a single chip and an FPU consisting of three chips.

The SPARC Signals

In defining a computer architecture at the abstract level, one would generally not expect to specify any of the signals required in a real implementation. However, there are a few exceptions in the SPARC case, reflecting the existence of signals that are logically important from an architectural point of view. This is the only place in the SPARC Architecture Manual where something having to do with the hardware is mentioned. Before describing the structure of the IU and the FPU, we will describe the function of these signals. The names used here are those described in the SPARC Architecture

Manual. The same set of signals described here is present on the CYPRESS implementation of SPARC, but they have different names.

SPARC requires that there be four interrupt input lines called BP_IRL by which external interrupts can be signalled. In addition, the pin BP_RESET_IN causes the processor to reset. There is a well-defined action that occurs when the processor receives that signal.

The error pin, BP_ERROR, signals that the processor has been put into a sufficiently inconsistent state (similar to the triple fault on the 386) that recovery from this situation is difficult. For example, if a synchronous trap is issued and traps have been inhibited, the processor will be forced to go into an error state, setting the error pin. In some implementations the pins might be wired so that it would cause a reset, but that is not required by the specification.

A pin called BP_RETAIN_BUS is used to lock the bus. The locked exchange instruction, used for synchronization purposes, is executed with the bus locked, as is required when multiple SPARC chips share memory on a common bus.

The BP_FPU_PRESENT bit signals that an implementation includes floating-point hardware, rather than emulating floating-point operations. Although current SPARC implementations do include hardware floating-point, the definition of this signal allows a SPARC implementation where floating-point is provided in software only. There is a corresponding signal called BP_CP_PRESENT that signals whether the CP is present. The BP_MEMORY_ACCESS_EXCEPTION signal is set if an attempt is made to access memory and something goes wrong. Specifically, the pin is set on an access error and causes the IU to be interrupted.

The SPARC architecture itself does not specifically define a memory management interface, although an interface known as the SPARC Reference MMU has been suggested as a standard by Sun. The memory management is a multilevel paging system, similar to that of the 386 or 68030. In particular, it uses a three-level page map, and unlike the MIPS it specifies that TLB misses are to be handled by hardware.

That is all that the SPARC specification has to say about the hardware interface to the outside world. It does have something to say about the memory from a logical point of view, but that issue will be discussed a later section.

THE IU REGISTER SET

The register set of the integer unit has an organization quite different from those of the 386 and the 68030, as well as all of the other RISC processors described in this book. More specifically, the register model is based on the concept of overlapping register windows, an idea pioneered in the Berkeley RISC I processor.

The User Register Set

An executing procedure on the SPARC has access to a total of 32 registers, the same number as the MIPS. But unlike the MIPS, the SPARC architecture divides these registers into several classes because of the influence of the register window model. From the point of view of a single user procedure executing on the SPARC, all of these registers can be treated in the same way. However, a set of conventions specifies that registers are to be used in specific ways as part of the procedure call convention. For example, some registers are used to pass parameters, and other registers are used to hold the results of intermediate computations.

The view that a single procedure has of the standard register set is completely independent of the register window mechanism, but if these conventions are followed, the interface between procedures can use the register window mechanism in an effective manner. In other words, the conventions for which registers to use for parameter passing are *not* simply software conventions, as on the MIPS—they are dictated by, or at least suggested by, the register window mechanism.

One register that behaves differently whether register windows are used or not is register 0. Register 0 behaves in a similar fashion to register 0 on the MIPS—it always contains the value 0. While the general intention of this hardware convention is similar to that of the MIPS, the uses of this register are somewhat different.

REGISTER ZERO. The "trick" of wiring register 0 so that it always contains the value 0 is used on the SPARC just as on the MIPS. In both cases, this use of register 0 allows for some interesting applications. Remember that if R0 is used as a source operand, the value 0 is automatically provided. If R0 is used as a destination operand, then the value will vanish into a black hole.

One use of this register on the SPARC involves the use of logical instructions that test condition code bits. First, consider the corresponding situation on the 386. The AND instruction on the 386 takes the logical AND of two registers and puts the result into the destination register:

```
AND  EAX, EBX
```

In this case, EAX will contain the result of ANDing EAX and EBX. The TEST instruction

```
TEST EAX, EBX
```

is exactly the same thing as the AND instruction except that it does not put the result back into EAX. Why use a TEST instead of an AND? A programmer may just want to see if there are any non-zero bits in the result without regard to exactly what that pattern of bits is.

On the SPARC, the effect of both the AND and the TEST instructions of the 386 can be achieved with only a *single* instruction. On the SPARC, the standard AND instruction would be

```
ANDcc   %1, %2, %3
```

which logically means

```
R1 ← R2 and R3
```

All instructions of this type are three address operations in SPARC, so the destination register can be different from the two source registers. The *cc* in the instruction means that the instruction will set the condition code. To get the effect of the TEST instruction above, you would write

    ANDcc   %0, %2, %3

which gives the logical effect:

    R0 ← R2 and R3

Since the target register of the SPARC's ANDcc instruction is register 0, the effect is that the result is thrown away. The use of register 0 on the SPARC means that one instruction suffices where two are required on the 386.

Another use of register 0 is to remove the need for special simplified addressing modes. On a machine with double indexing like the SPARC, two registers are added to form an address. In some cases, only one register is needed to form the address. Instead of providing two separate addressing modes, one for single indexing and the other for double indexing, single indexing can be implemented as double indexing by using R0 as one of the two registers. Similarly, an absolute reference to low memory can be achieved using register R0 as the base register and the memory address as the offset.

The System Register Set

SPARC defines several registers in addition to the general purpose registers. There are registers to control the register windows, a register to control traps, two program counters, a register to aid in multiplication, and a register defining the processor's state. Some of these registers are reserved for use in supervisor state, while others may be modified or tested by user programs.

The *processor state register* (PSR) has a number of fields that describe the current state of the processor (see Figure 10.2). The VER and IMPL fields indicate the version and implementation identification for the particular SPARC chip in use. ICC holds the four standard condition code bits: the negative bit, the zero bit, the overflow bit, and the carry bit can all be found in the PSR.

The PSR also includes bits that allow software to test which coprocessors, if any, are attached to a specific SPARC implementation. If the corresponding bit is not set, a

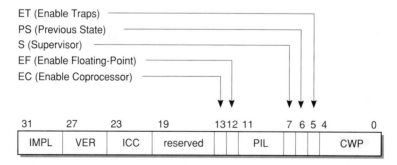

FIGURE 10.2
The processor state register of the SPARC.

trap will occur if one tries to issue a floating-point or coprocessor instruction. The S-bit determines whether the processor is in a supervisor or user state. Finally, there is a 5-bit field that is the *current window pointer* (CWP).

A few of the other 16 system registers are also used for system status information. The *window invalid register* is used with the register windows and will be discussed in a later section. Some of the bits are set to indicate how many windows are implemented on this machine. Obviously, the operating system needs to know this number, for example, to know how much space to save for the registers on a context switch.

Register Windows

The term *register window* is intended to suggest that a procedure's view of its available registers represents only a small portion of a larger panorama of registers known as a *register file.* We first mentioned this in Chapter 8 as one solution to the problem of register allocation in connection with procedure calls.

The fundamental idea behind the use of register windows is to reduce the overhead of procedure calls. Procedure call overhead is a well-known source of irritation to hardware implementers and compiler writers.[2] One cause of this overhead is the need to save registers containing live values in memory when a procedure call is made, and then restore those registers on procedure return. Another source of procedure call overhead comes from the need to pass parameters in both directions between procedure calls. The register window design of the Berkeley RISC chips and the SPARC provide an imaginative solution that reduces the overhead associated with these problems.

At any moment during execution, a procedure can refer to any one of 32 registers. The first eight registers are global registers that can always be referenced by any procedure. The remaining 24 registers constitute the register window. These 24 registers are divided into three groups: *in registers*, *out registers*, and *local registers.* The *out* registers are numbered 8 through 15, the *local* registers are numbered 16 thorough 23, and the *in* registers are numbered 24 through 31 (see Figure 10.3).

When the currently executing procedure calls another procedure, the usual convention is that the called procedure executes the special instruction SAVE. The effect of this instruction is to decrement the CWP, a 5-bit field within the PSR, moving the current register window down by 16 registers in the register file. Even though each register window contains 24 registers, the current window is moved only 16 registers down in the register file. This makes the *out* registers of the calling procedure the *in* registers of the called procedure, in effect passing parameters without having to copy them from one set of registers to another. The local registers are not shared between the caller and the called procedures and are used for storage of local variables or

---

[2] William Wulf, the author of the BLISS-11 programming language and an important contributor to compiler technology, has observed that programmers tend to gravitate toward a style in which approximately 25% of the execution time is spent on procedure call overhead. If this overhead is very high, procedures will be used much less often.

temporary results computed by the called procedure. From the point of view of the called procedure, the *in* region of its window contains the required parameter values.

One important case where a procedure may decide not to decrement CWP is when that procedure does not call any other procedures. These procedures, known as *leaf procedures*, need not change CWP because they are certain not to require additional register windows. The idea is for leaf procedures to perform all their computations using the set of *out* registers. If the leaf procedure needs more registers, then it can get a new window in the usual way, but if it can live entirely in the *out* registers, then the overhead of manipulating the window can be avoided.

In practice, programs dynamically call a significant number of small leaf procedures that can be optimized in this way. This is why the save and restore instructions are separate from the call and return instructions.

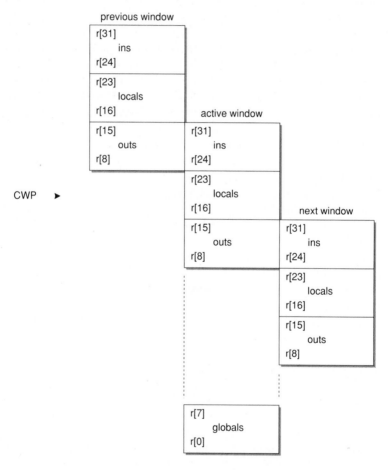

FIGURE 10.3
The register window scheme of the SPARC.

THE STACK AND FRAME POINTERS. In preparation for a procedure call, a compiler must generate code that places the parameters in what the calling procedure refers to as %o0 through %o7, its eight *out* registers (R8 through R15). *After* the CALL instruction has been executed, the called procedure executes a SAVE instruction that bumps the register window. In the new window these same registers are now referred to as %i0 through %i7, the eight *in* registers of the called procedure (R24 through R31). The need to explicitly save and restore registers is eliminated by this mechanism.

A key point of the register window approach is that it is expected that most parameters will be passed in registers in this way rather than on a stack. On other machines, the choice of passing parameters in registers or on the stack is one of the decisions that must be made by a compiler writer. On the SPARC it is more or less assumed that it will not be necessary to save and restore registers on procedure call and return because this windowing mechanism obviates any need to do this. However, we still need the usual arrangement of stack and frame pointers to manage local variables of procedures.

The suggested convention on the SPARC is to use only six of the eight *out* registers for passing parameters. Register 14 (%o6) is used as a stack pointer, and register 15 is reserved as a temporary register, leaving only six registers for parameters. Consider the normal requirement for manipulating the stack and frame pointers on entry to a procedure. The following three steps need to be performed:

- Save the old frame pointer.
- Set the new frame pointer to the stack pointer.
- Adjust the stack pointer for the new local frame.

The SAVE instruction automatically performs the first two steps. We use register 30 (%i6) as the frame pointer. When the register window is decremented, the old frame pointer (i.e., the old %i6) is safely saved away in the previous window, and the old stack pointer (i.e., the old %o6) is copied into the frame pointer (the new %i6)—of course, it isn't really copied, it happens to be there already due to the overlapping of the windows. What about the third step? So far in our description of SAVE, no operands were needed. However, this instruction is 32 bits like all others, so there is plenty of room, and we find that SAVE has the capability of performing the operation

Rd ← Rs + constant

as well as performing the register window manipulations. Now we can see how to use this addition operation. We set Rd to %o6 (the new stack pointer) and Rs to %i6 (which is a copy of the old stack pointer). The constant is set to the size of the procedure frame (either plus or minus depending on which way the stack grows).

The RESTORE instruction undoes the effect of the SAVE, restoring the original frame and stack pointers. Thus we see that the entire job of building nested stack frames, as well as that of saving and restoring registers, is handled by a single instruction on entry and exit to the procedure, and these instructions require only a single clock.

THE NUMBER OF REGISTERS AND WINDOWS. The SPARC architectural specification allows an implementation to have anywhere from 2 to 32 register windows. There must be at least two register windows available because, as we shall discuss in more detail later, when a trap occurs there will definitely be a change of windows. Two register windows, on the other hand, is not a practical number, as the discussion of this section will show.

Each register window is actually 16 registers long, since there is an overlap between adjacent sets. Furthermore, the *out* registers of the last window overlap the *in* registers of the first window. In other words, the register windows are arranged in a circle. The total number of registers available on a machine would therefore be 40 in the case of a two-window implementation, or 520 in the case of a 32-window implementation. The initial Fujitsu implementation of the SPARC used seven register windows, for a total of 120 registers. These figures are computed using the formula

Total number of registers = 8 + (16 × Number of register windows)

The 8 in this formula reflects the eight global registers that are always available. The total number of register windows is hidden from software. The program is written as though an infinite number of windows are available, and it is the job of the operating system to manage the register windows so that this view is transparent.

Managing the Register File

Because of the dynamic manner in which procedures call each other, and in particular the possibility of recursion in many common programming languages, procedure call depth cannot be predicted. Since the SPARC architecture requires that the number of register windows on any implementation be limited to between 2 and 32, it is to be expected that a typical large program will "run out" of available register windows.

At least two important questions arise from the fact that the number of register windows is limited. First, when the procedure call depth exceeds the maximum number of register windows, what mechanism is used to allocate the required windows? Second, what is the cost of dealing with such a register overflow, and does it occur so infrequently that this cost does not become a major consideration?

To understand the answer to the first question, consider an implementation with eight register windows, as shown in Figure 10.4. The CWP (current window pointer) register is initialized to 7. As successive procedures are called, CWP is decremented so that the next window is used. Let's look at the situation when CWP is set to 1 and we call one more procedure that does a SAVE operation. We would expect CWP to be decremented to zero, but we can't actually use window 0. Why not? Because it overlaps with window 7, which is in use at the highest level. If CWP is decremented to zero without doing something, the newly called procedure will destroy registers belonging to the procedure seven levels up on the call chain, which certainly will not do.

The required mechanism is provided by the *window invalid mask* (WIM), one of the supervisor registers. One bit exists in the WIM register for each possible register window. For implementations where the maximum number of registers are not available, the bits for unimplemented windows are wired to 1 and cannot be changed.

The bits for the windows that are present can be modified, but only in supervisor mode. When a SAVE instruction is executed, it first decrements the CWP register, and then checks the corresponding bit in the WIM register to make sure that the resulting window is valid. If not, a *window overflow* trap occurs.

Like other traps and interrupts, the window overflow trap routine operates in supervisor mode and is thus able to manipulate the CWP and WIM registers. This routine has the job of saving some of the registers in memory, adjusting WIM accordingly, and then returning control to the routine that caused the window overflow trap. A typical strategy is to save some number of previously used register windows in memory and then reset the appropriate bits in the WIM register. The best choice of how many windows to save and restore depends upon the pattern of calls in a program and the number of register windows.

For our example, WIM would be set to indicate that *w0* was invalid, thus causing an overflow trap on the SAVE instruction that tries to use this window. A typical approach in the overflow trap routine is as follows:

- Save the contents of windows *w6* and *w7.* →can execute 2 more windows in place of these windows
- Set *w6* as invalid in the WIM.
- Set *w0* as now being valid in the WIM.
- Re-execute the SAVE instruction that caused the trap.

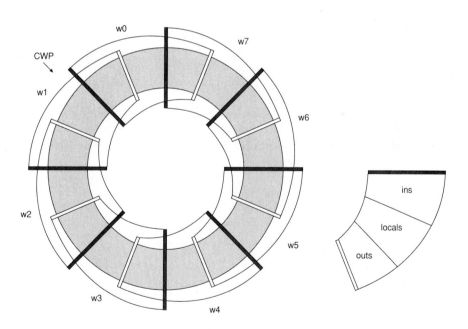

FIGURE 10.4
The circular organization of the register file with overlapping register windows.

The SAVE now succeeds, and the procedure can use w0. On the next call, CWP is decremented—it wraps from w0 to w7, and one more procedure can be executed before another window invalid trap occurs. On the way back up, as the corresponding RESTORE instructions are executed, another window invalid trap will occur when we increment from w5 to w6, due to the new setting of WIM. The window invalid trap routine will then restore the contents of w7 and w6 and reset WIM to its original state.

A perceptive reader will notice that in Figure 10.4 there is one set of eight registers that never gets used, namely, the locals of the window marked invalid. These registers actually do serve an important function. When a window invalid trap, or any other exception, occurs, the CWP is decremented *without* checking WIM. The exception routine is always free to use the locals of the current window for its own use, without the overhead of saving and restoring user program registers, and without interfering with the live registers of any active procedure.

The cyclical nature of the register window set is important to the operating efficiency of this approach. If the register windows were laid out in a vector with a fixed maximum and minimum value for CWP, then the window invalid trap would have to move the entire register set up and down, which would be unpleasantly inefficient. With the cyclical arrangement of the SPARC, only the registers that actually need to be saved must be moved.

The issue of how many windows to save on the window invalid trap is a matter for careful consideration. If too few windows are saved, then we will get too many traps. On the other hand, if too many windows are saved, we will waste time saving and restoring registers. The issue of how to manage register windows, and more specifically how to handle overflows and underflows, was an important component of the research conducted as part of the original Berkeley RISC effort. One study concluded that when the number of register windows was greater than eight, an effective number of windows to save and restore would be two. With fewer than eight register windows, saving and restoring one window was best.

An important question to ask is how often do overflows and underflows occur? Any reasonably large application will of course exceed seven dynamic levels of nesting, so overflow will certainly occur. The critical question is how frequently overflows and the corresponding underflows occurs. The issue is not the depth of the call chain, but its variance—how often the depth changes by enough to cause a window overflow. Most typically, a plot of the dynamic behavior of the call depth is relatively stable for extended periods, even at points where calls are deeply nested. There are exceptions to this pattern—for example, heavy use of deep recursion is a worst case. If the operating system saves one window on an overflow, then a window overflow trap will be generated on each recursive call. Literature cited by the designers of the RISC I claims that with a set of 8 register windows, only one percent of the total calls in a "typical" sample of programs resulted in window overflow.

THE USE OF REGISTER WINDOWS. The intention behind the provision of register windows is that a SAVE instruction should be issued on entry to a procedure, and a corresponding RESTORE on exit. However, there is no rule that demands that this procedure always be followed, and one of the arguments used by advocates of the register window approach is that there is complete flexibility in the way the register window facility is used. Sun has a printed form called "SPARC Register Window Scheme." The blanks in this form can be filled in to specify a particular use of the register window mechanism.

Register Window Scheme #1B (Modified SunOS Scheme), for example, splits the register file into two pieces, one for user processes and the other for supervisor processes. The intention behind this scheme is to ensure that the operating system has some windows reserved for its own use, so that it does not need to worry about the possibility of window overflow during execution of system routines.

A second register window scheme suggests that each task, including the kernel, should get a fixed number of register windows. The idea here is that no saving or restoring of windows is required on a context switch. This scheme is intended to be used in real-time systems where there are a small fixed number of tasks.

Although it is true that the window mechanism can be used in many different ways, a typical operating system and software environment makes a specific choice among the schemes. Since any application program will call the operating system to perform system services, including task management, the application program will find itself forced to use a particular approach. This means that the flexibility implied by the various schemes for using register windows is something that a systems designer can take advantage of, but not the programmer using a specific system.

ADVANTAGES AND DISADVANTAGES. The use of register windows can be contrasted to the register models of other RISC machines such as the MIPS which have quite a large number of registers compared to more traditional machines but lack register windowing support for procedure calls.

The advantage of register windows is that it is almost never necessary to explicitly save and restore registers for a procedure call, because a new set of registers will be provided in the newly allocated register window. Since each procedure has its own register set, the compiler simply has to worry about allocating the registers *within* each procedure in an efficient manner and can ignore the issue of register allocation between procedures.

Using the MIPS approach in the most effective manner requires that the compiler pay attention to efficient use of the register set. Each procedure should use as few registers as possible, since using many registers will result in wasting time saving and restoring registers. Deciding on the best balance between the number of registers used and code efficiency is not always easy. For the best possible utilization of the register set, register allocation should be deferred till link time, when all the code of all the procedures is available. Not only does this up the ante in compiler and linker complexity; but it can also cause the link step to become unmanageably slow.

The SPARC approach clearly simplifies the process of register allocation for the compiler. It is always desirable to simplify system software. For one thing, there tends to be a direct relation between the complexity of the compiler and its reliability. Another effect is that, given a fixed amount of effort on the compiler, time saved in implementing complex register management can be put to use in improving other optimizations. Although there is general agreement that windows simplify the compiler, the significance of this simplification is hotly contested. The MIPS view is that register allocation is a fairly standard technology, so that the actual magnitude of the effect is small.

The second issue to be addressed is performance. When window overflow and underflow traps occur, we have the overhead of the traps themselves as well as the overhead of saving and restoring register windows. How does this compare with the time spent on saving and restoring registers explicitly in the MIPS approach? The comparison between register windows and careful allocation of a large fixed set of registers is a tricky one. Papers have been written in support of both points of view, and, as with benchmarks, it is easy to present theoretical arguments and empirical observations that support either position.

A fair judgment is that for typical applications there is not a lot to choose between the two approaches and that the overhead from register saving and restoring can be reduced to a low level in both cases. This is probably regarded as a controversial statement in some quarters, and we may need more time and more data to make the final judgment. In particular, most of the current data comes from a rather restricted domain of engineering and systems applications running under Unix, and it is not clear that this data is representative of a wider range of typical applications programs.

Another potential disadvantage of the register window approach is that, especially with a large number of register windows, switching from one task to another may require that a large number of registers be spilled to memory. The extent to which the register file is filled with live values will vary dynamically. But if an implementation provides a reasonable number of register windows, as in the first Fujitsu implementation, where there are 120 registers, it is possible that all of them will have to be saved, increasing the worst-case context switching time by a considerable margin. This may be a critical point in real-time systems, where high-priority tasks require immediate response to external events.

One consideration in the register window approach is that it creates a certain degree of non-uniform behavior. A given procedure call may take much longer if it just happens to run out of register windows. In particular, recursive procedures are very likely to run out of window space. Consider, for example, the following programming gem in C for outputting an unsigned integer as ASCII characters left to right:

```
out (u)
unsigned u;
{
    if (u >= 10) out (u / 10);
        putchar ('0' + (u % 10));
}
```

This is a particularly happy use of recursion to deal with the problem of not knowing in advance how many digits will be output. It should be highly efficient, since only u need be saved recursively. However, unless the SPARC C compiler is extraordinarily clever, it will generate a window push for this routine, and almost certainly the result will be window spill, which will make this approach significantly inefficient. To the extent that such non-uniform behavior distorts programming style, it is quite undesirable. This possibility is worrisome, and leads us to slightly prefer the MIPS approach.

It is important to remember that no one is forcing a compiler writer or other programmer to use the register window mechanism—this is a decision to be made on the basis of performance considerations. A standard part of the rhetoric used to support the register window approach notes that providing register windows cannot be any worse than not providing them, since you don't have to use them, so they are cost-free. This isn't quite true, because implementing register windows is liable to cause a small but measurable increase in the basic cycle time of the hardware. Furthermore, as we have pointed out, a given application written in a high-level language using a compiler committed to the use of register windows is not free to take advantage of the possibility of ignoring their use.

The majority of chips take the approach in which a single set of registers is used rather than the register window approach. Nevertheless, we may have to wait to see which approach proves to be better. David Patterson, the leader of the Berkeley RISC effort, described trade-offs between the use of register windows and better register allocation in the following way:

> What is the best way to keep operands in registers? The disadvantages of register windows are that they use more chip area and slow the basic clock cycle. This is due to the capacitive loading of the longer bus, and although context switches rarely occur—about 100 to 1000 procedure calls for every context switch—they require that about two to three times as many registers be saved, on average. The only drawbacks of the optimizing compiler are that it is about half the speed of a simple compiler and ignores the register saving penalty of procedure calls. ... If compiler technology can reduce the number of LOADs and STOREs to the extent that register windows can, the optimizing compiler will stand in clear superiority.

Of course, if register windows turn out *not* to have a significant advantage, we would just as soon not have them, because it takes a lot of real estate on the chip to support so many fast registers. On the other hand, if chips get so dense that we have more space than we know what to do with, the limit of 32 register windows may prove to be too conservative.

SPARC ADDRESSING MODES

As in the case of the MIPS, the SPARC has a small number of addressing modes, although it is slightly more flexible than the MIPS. Not only is the number of addressing modes limited, but their use is restricted to the various types of load and store instructions described in the next section. This way of doing things is consistent with RISC constraints, and the SPARC addressing modes are faithful to the RISC philosophy. First of all, as with all RISC machines, there is no direct addressing of data. It is simply impossible to fit a 32-bit address into one of these instruction formats. The SPARC does include an addressing form that allows a programmer to access the lower 2^{13} bytes of memory, but this is of limited use.

The instruction formats of the load and store instructions come in two versions. In the first form, the source operand address is specified by giving a register and a 13-bit offset. In the second form, the source address is specified by two registers whose values are added to form the address. Let us see how these addressing modes support the addressing model described in Chapter 1.

The first of these modes allows a 13-bit immediate value to be added to a register to form an address. This can be used to implement what we have called based addressing. For static data, a register can point to the base address of the data, using the 13-bit offset to address some item within the area. For data allocated on the stack, the register might be used as a frame pointer, with the 13-bit offset used to select an item within the stack frame. Finally, for dynamic data, we might use the register as a pointer to a dynamically allocated record, the offset once again being used to locate a particular field.

The second of these formats, where two registers are added together, also maps nicely into some of the addressing modes described in Chapter 1. The based addressing plus index mode requires two registers, one for the base address of the array and the other for the scaled index value. Indexed addressing of static data could be accomplished by using one register to point to the start of the static array and the other register to hold the scaled index.

From this discussion we can see that many of the addressing modes described in Chapter 1 are available even with the limited addressing hardware of the SPARC. There are, however, some situations where the SPARC lacks a required addressing mode. For example, consider the case of an array allocated within a stack frame. To access an element of such an array, one needs two registers, one to serve as a frame pointer and one to hold the index, as well as an immediate value for the offset of the starting location of the array. But the SPARC addressing modes allow the first source register to be added *either* to another register *or* to the 13-bit immediate, not both. So this type of addressing would require an extra instruction on the SPARC. Like most RISC processors, the SPARC does not cover the basic set of addressing modes of the 386, let alone the more elaborate modes of the 68030.

THE SHORT OFFSET. The SPARC offset is painfully short—only 13 bits compared with the 16-bit offsets of the MIPS. This is a noticeable limitation for some uses. For instance, stack frames can be up to 32K bytes on the MIPS before addressing them begins to require multiple instructions, but on the SPARC the corresponding limit is 4K bytes.

The difference between the offset sizes of these machines is partially accounted for by the availability of double indexing on the SPARC, a feature that is omitted from the MIPS. How important is this omission? There are obviously cases where it is simpler to address an array if two registers can be used. In many cases, a compiler can reorganize the addressing using strength reduction to avoid the need for double indexing, another example of the MIPS design relying on more sophisticated compiler technology.

However, it is not always possible for the compiler to fix things up. Consider the following artificial C program:

```
main()
{
    char c[100];
    int i, j;
    for (i = 0; I  100; i++) c[i] = 5;

    i = 5;
    for (j = 0; j  1000000; j++)
    {
        i = c[i];
        ...               /* the same statement repeated several times. */
        i = c[i];
    }
}
```

The reference to c[i] here naturally requires double indexing (the frame pointer is one index, and the subscript *i* is the other). On the SPARC, the compiler can generate a single instruction:

```
ldsb      [%o0 + %fp], %o0
```

for this statement. However, this is a bad case for the MIPS—the compiler can't strength reduce the reference, because the subscript is always computed by the previous statement. As a result, two intructions are needed for each statement on the MIPS. Not surprisingly, this program runs faster (by about 25%) on the SPARC than on the MIPS. However, it is admittedly a "cooked-up" example, chosen to favor the double indexing on the SPARC. How often do such situations appear in real programs? Probably *not* very often, so it may well be the case that the MIPS decision to give up double indexing in return for a larger offset makes sense.

THE SPARC INSTRUCTION SET

Each instruction in the SPARC's instruction set falls into one of three formats. Since two of the formats have variants, one might say that there are actually a total of six subclasses of instruction formats. The *call* format is used only for procedure call instructions. The second format is used by the arithmetic and logical instructions. The SETHI format is used for one special instruction known as SETHI. The *branch* format is used for both conditional and unconditional branches. Figure 10.5 shows the layout of the fields in each of these formats.

All the instruction formats are 32 bits long and are distinguished by their two high-order bits. Once again, as on the MIPS, we see that the instruction formats have their fields laid out in a regular and relatively simple way. This is another instance of a RISC machine in which the need to decode instructions quickly in the pipeline has a clear effect on the instruction formats. Instructions themselves are required to be aligned on a 4-byte boundary, just as on the MIPS. As we have pointed out, this

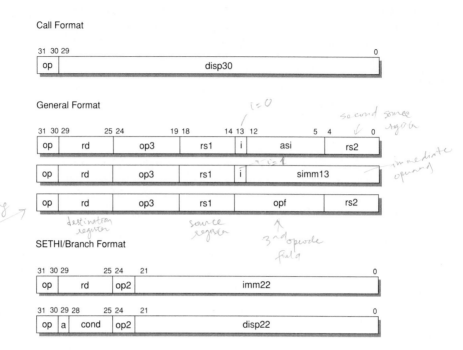

Call Format

General Format

i = 0

second source
reg 0 [a]

destination
register

source
register

3rd opcode
field

immediate
operand

For floating
point and
coprocessor
instr

SETHI/Branch Format

FIGURE 10.5
The SPARC instruction formats.

requirement simplifies the hardware, since a page fault cannot be caused by an instruction that lies across two pages, one of which has been paged out to the disk.

The Call Instruction Format

The call instruction format is the simplest of the three formats with only two fields: a 2-bit opcode field and a 30-bit address field. Since all instructions are required to be aligned on a 4-byte boundary, the 30-bit address field is large enough to cover the full 32-bit logical address space (two zero bits are appended at the right end of the 30-bit address given in the instruction).

The General Instruction Format

The general instruction format comes in three variants, all shown in Figure 10.5. The first two of these formats should really be thought of as a pair, in which the interpretation of the low-order bits is controlled by bit 13, the *i bit*. The last of the three versions of the general format is used for the floating-point and coprocessor instructions.

The first two forms of the general format consist of a 2-bit opcode field that identifies the instruction as a general format instruction, followed by a 5-bit field specifying a destination register. This is followed by a secondary 6-bit operation field that specifies which instruction in this format is to be executed, and then a 5-bit field specifying the first of the source registers involved in the computation.

The interpretation of the remaining fields of the opcode is then controlled by the *i* bit. If the *i* bit is clear, then of the remaining 13 bits in the instruction format, the low-order 5 bits specify a second source register, such as might be required in doing a register-to-register addition. Eight bits are completely ignored in this case. If the *i* bit is set, then the remaining 13 bits are interpreted as an immediate operand.

The third general format variant is used for floating-point operations and coprocessor instructions. The first four fields are identical to those described above. Instead of the *i* bit controlling the interpretation of the lower-order fields, this instruction format has three fields of fixed length: a 5-bit source register field, a third opcode field 9 bits wide, and another 5-bit source register field for the second operand of a two-operand instruction.

THE LOAD INSTRUCTIONS. We will begin our description of the general format with the load instructions. As in most RISC processors, the load and store instructions are the only ones that can access data in memory. The assembler format for the load instructions is

ld{s,u}{b,h}{a}   [rs1 + rs2], rd

or

ld{d}{a}   [rs1 + rs2],rd

where S stands for signed, U stands for unsigned, B for byte, H for halfword, and D for doubleword. The optional character A can be appended to any one of the basic load instructions, to indicate an alternate address space access, as described below. To load a single word, for example, the instruction LD is used. To load a single byte without sign extension, LDUB is used, while to load a byte with sign extension, LDSB is used.

The load instructions specify the data type to be loaded, either a byte, halfword, word, or doubleword. In the case of a byte or halfword, a programmer can specify either sign extension or zero extension to handle signed or unsigned data. The load doubleword instruction requires the operand to be doubleword aligned. This avoids the possibility of a page fault being caused by a single instruction. In fact, all data types must be aligned on their respective boundaries. Since the load and store instructions are the only instructions that can reference memory, it also means that the only addressing modes are those provided for this format.

All the load instructions use a common format, in which *rs1* and *rs2* are used to form the effective address. The third format allows the effective address to be formed by adding *rs1* to *rs2*, i.e., double indexing but without a constant offset. The second format does allow a signed 13-bit displacement which is added to *rs1*, yielding an addressing mode which allows displacements of plus or minus 4K bytes without automatic scaling.

That is a very narrow window of addressability—just 1 bit better than the IBM 370 and lacking the nasty asymmetry of the 370, where it is only possible to have a positive index. On the 370, this means it is not possible to use an addressing mode to compute an address relative to the frame pointer when the address is at a negative offset. The standard model of local variables at negative offsets and parameters at positive offsets must be modified on this machine. On the SPARC, even though the general model, which uses positive and negative offsets, can be used, the 13-bit offset is restrictive enough that in compiling code for this machine one will quite often have to play many of the same games used on the 370—for example, keeping base registers pointing near the data that needs to be addressed. If a register is not pointing within that range, then you cannot easily get at the data. That is a substantial restriction compared to an architecture with full blown addressability such as the 386 or the 68030. It is for example much more restrictive than the MIPS, which allows a 16-bit offset. On the other hand, the MIPS does not permit double indexing. Basically one has a choice in designing the instructions to allow single indexing, leaving more space for the offset, or double indexing, in which case there is less room left for the offset.

THE ASI INSTRUCTIONS. Each of the IU load instructions has a variant whose assembly language syntax is indicated by appending an A and whose effect is to enable an alternate address space. When one of these special load and store instructions is issued, an 8-bit field within the instruction holds an *alternate address space identifier* (ASI). In the resulting memory access, this 8-bit ASI is appended to the front of the standard 32 bits. The 40-bit extended address is then presented to the "outside" world. Of the possible 256 ASIs, four standard values are defined:

8	User instruction space
9	Supervisor instruction space
10	User data space
11	Supervisor data space

When instructions are being fetched from memory, the ASI is set to 8 or 9 depending upon whether the processor is operating in user or supervisor state. For load and store instructions, the ASI is set to 10 or 11. For example, when an ordinary load is done, one that is executed in user state, an ASI value of 10 is used.

There is no requirement that the memory management pay any attention to the ASI values, but if it does, and if it separates the address spaces for instructions from those for data, then a user program will not be able to load instructions, because the ASI value will be different for data and instruction fetches. On the other hand, in supervisor mode, the ASI value can be specified, so the supervisor can load and store instructions into the instruction space, as indeed it must be able to do to load user programs.

Since not all of the 256 ASI values are reserved for a specific use, they can be used in different ways by different hardware implementations. If no MMU is attached, and logical addresses are identical to physical addresses, then the ASI values might well be ignored. With an MMU in place, quite different paging maps might be used for instructions and data, or for user and supervisor state memory accesses, with the ASI values used to select the paging map. In supervisor state they could be used to extend the addressing range of the SPARC by 8 bits.

One possible use for alternate ASI values is to have one of them specify a separate I/O address space. Just as the 386 has in/out instructions that have a completely different address space from memory references, an engineer can decide that in his particular computer system one of the unused ASI values will indicate an I/O space. The other address spaces can be defined for any other purposes required, although they will be accessible only from the supervisor state.

The SPARC MMU reference document suggests using one of the additional ASI values (the particular one is left up to the implementation) for specifying flushing of the translation look aside buffer (called the Page Descriptor Cache, PDC). The address used in the alternate address space reference specifies the entry to be flushed (the actual data of the associated store operation being ignored).

THE STORE INSTRUCTIONS. The store instructions are written in SPARC assembly language as

```
ST{B,H,D}{A}              [rs1 + rs2], rd
```

with the optional A denoting an alternative address space just as in the case of the load instructions. This instruction allows one to store a byte, halfword, word, or doubleword into memory using either double indexing or indexing with a 13-bit signed offset. On a store, there is, of course, no issue of sign or zero extension, so we do not need multiple forms of these instructions of the sort that were required for the load instruction.

FLOATING-POINT LOADS AND STORES. There are instructions to load and store floating-point registers, for both the single- and double-precision cases, and also for the floating-point status register:

```
LDF/STF
LDDF/STDF
LDFSR/STFSR
```

The floating-point specification is IEEE 754 compatible. The status register contains condition codes and fields such as the rounding mode that can be set in the IEEE standard to force rounding to the nearest even, or truncation. It has all the control functions that the IEEE standard requires, such as whether the processor will trap on an overflow, how you deal with infinities, and so on.

There is a special instruction whose mnemonic is

```
STDFQ
```

that is used to store an instruction/address pair in a floating-point queue (described in a later section in this chapter on SPARC floating-point). There is an exactly parallel set of instructions where the F in each instruction above is replaced by C which refers to the coprocessor registers and status register.

SYNCHRONIZATION INSTRUCTIONS. There are two special load and store instructions, Load and Store Unsigned Byte (LDSTUB) and the ASI variant Load and Store Unsigned Byte into Alternate Address Space (LDSTUBA). These instructions load a byte into a register and then set the bits of that byte *in memory* to 1, all in a single indivisible unit. They allow a process to retrieve a byte from memory and then set or reset all the bits with the certainty that no other process has managed to change it. It is clear that these instructions are intended to provide hardware support for providing exclusive access to some resource that can be shared by many processes.

If the value of the byte in memory is 0, this means that no process has obtained access to the resource that is being guarded by that byte. If one process wants access to the resource, by issuing this instruction it can be sure that if a 0 is loaded into the register by this instruction, the resource was free *and* the byte has been set to signal that it is no longer free. If, on the other hand, the result of issuing one of these instructions is to cause all 1s to appear in the register, then the process concludes that the resource is not free. The fact that the byte has been set to 1s by this instruction does not matter, since it was set that way in any case. The process can just spin, waiting for the resource to be available, or, it can wait for the operating system or simply give up waiting.

The intention of these load and store instructions is to enable a task to gain access to some resource without having to go through what may amount to an expensive operating system call. If the resource that is being requested is not free, an operating system call may actually be required, but if the resource is free, then the use of this faster instruction may suffice. The only time you need to contact the operating system is if a "policeman" is needed because two processes want the resource at the same time.

Similarly, the Swap (SWAP and SWAPA) instructions swap the entire contents of a register with a word in memory in an interlocked manner. Their intended use is similar to that of the above two instructions, but they allow a full word as the operand, and thus allow more flexible usage.

ADDITION AND SUBTRACTION. The add instruction on the SPARC comes in several versions. In addition to the standard Add (ADD) instruction, there is an Add Extended (ADDX) instruction that can be used to extend precision by adding the carry bit from the previous addition.

Each of these instructions has another variant (written as ADDcc and ADDXcc) that gives a programmer the option of setting or not setting the condition code bits. The ability to specify which instructions affect the condition codes is quite valuable, since it is often necessary to do an addition in order to compute an address— an operation that should not set the condition codes.

Another situation in which having this control is useful when, for example, generating code for a loop that adds 2000 numbers. As the loop executes, you may want to add the carry from one iteration of the loop to the next using the ADDX instruction. But the loop will also need an add to bump the index register. You don't want the add that bumps the index register to affect the condition codes because you will need the carry for the sum that you are computing. Having both versions of the add makes it very convenient to generate such code.

The 386 addresses the same issue, although in a less general way. The INC instruction does not change the carry flag, while the ADD instruction does. The mechanism here on the SPARC is a cleaner, much more general mechanism, since all instructions for which it is relevant have the option of setting or not setting the condition codes. The subtract instructions (the assembler mnemonics being SUB and SUBX with an option *cc* appended) are similar to the add instructions.

TAGGED ADDITION AND SUBTRACTION. A rather peculiar (for a RISC processor) additional set of instructions provides *tagged* addition and subtraction operations, where the tag is a value specified in bits 0 and 1 of each of the operands:

TADDcc
TADDccTV
TSUBcc
TSUBccTV

These instructions function in a manner similar to the corresponding ADDcc and SUBcc instructions except that the overflow bit V in the program state register is set if either of the operands has a non-zero tag or if a normal arithmetic overflow occurs. In the case of the TV variants, a trap is generated as well.

In a manner reminiscent of several instructions we encountered on the CISC processors, it is natural to ask: What is the intention behind these peculiar instructions? Consider an implementation of LISP, where objects are either list cells or atoms, and the atoms can be either integers or strings. The intended use of the tagged add and subtract involves using the tag of every value to indicate its type, for instance, 00 for integer, 01 for string, and 11 for pointer.

Now suppose we are generating code for the LISP expression (+ X Y), which is valid only if X and Y are integers. The tagged add instruction is just what we need. We unconditionally generate a TADDccTV instruction to add X and Y. If the LISP program is incorrect and either X or Y is *not* an integer, then an error trap is generated. All of this happens in a single cycle, thus eliminating the need for an explicit sequence of instructions to mask out and check the tag.

Instructions such as these are actually much more reminiscent of the sort of design we find in CISC processors. Is it really the case, even for a LISP compiler, that the frequency of use of this instruction justifies its inclusion? Although some studies suggest that the use of tagged instructions does significantly increase performance for some specialized applications, choosing to put in the tagged add and subtract in preference to many other specialized instructions is a little odd, and probably reflects some peculiar interests of the designers.

MULTIPLICATION AND DIVISION. The SPARC, like some other RISC designs, does not have a full multiple-clock multiply instruction, but instead implements multiplication by executing a sequence of Multiply Step (MULScc) instructions, which do a 1-bit step of a multiplication.

A 32-bit multiply takes approximately 40 clocks, including the prologue and epilogue code required to set up and complete the multiplication, as well as the 32 1-clock multiply step instructions themselves. There is a standard routine at the back of the architecture manual that shows how to implement a multiply by issuing an appropriate number of multiply step instructions.

Note that in the common case—which arises, for example, in computing array addresses, and where the multiplier is a small constant known at compile time—it is possible to complete the multiplication using only the appropriate number of multiply steps. For example, to multiply by 9, only four multiply steps are required, and then the total time required to do a multiplication becomes very competitive with the performance available on CISC processors, which *do* provide the full multiply capability. Furthermore, for multiplications by small constants known at compile time, it is often more efficient, even on CISC processors, to replace multiplications by sequences of adds and shifts.

When it comes to division, it is a little surprising to find that not only does the SPARC have no divide instruction, it doesn't even have a divide step instruction. Implementing a division algorithm in software efficiently is not a trivial task. What the SPARC architecture offers in its place is a section at the back of the reference manual that shows how to implement a division algorithm with the instructions that are available. This includes a three-page C routine that implements division with various optimizations. The manual does not say how many instructions it will take, but it is a fair guess to say that it may take as long as 120 clocks.

The decision to leave out a divide instruction completely is motivated by a desire to save chip area and is justified by the belief that divisions occur relatively infrequently. Hardware divide and multiply instructions take up a great deal of chip area, and Sun has decided to use the available area in a different manner. In particular, the use of register windows (which requires a very large number of registers) commits much of the available chip area to the register file. As for the belief that divisions do not occur frequently in practice, perhaps that is true, but there are several important situations where it is not.

Remember our previous discussion of typesetting software, where the scaling of fonts requires division operations? That code certainly would not look good on a SPARC. Another example where division plays an important role is in the addressing of an array of 6-bit elements packed so that there are five elements per word (such packing must be supported in an Ada implementation). Accessing elements of the array involves dividing by 5 to determine which word is being referenced.

LOGICAL INSTRUCTIONS. The logical instructions include And and And Not instructions (AND and ANDN), Or, and Or Not instructions (OR and ORN) as well as Exclusive Or and Exclusive Or Not instructions. As with several other instructions, the condition codes can either be set or not set, as a programmer wishes.

Using the AND instruction, you normally put a 1 in the bit mask for bits you want to keep, and 0 for bits you want to clear. In using the ANDN, things are exactly the other way around, that is, you place a 1 in the bit mask for the bits you want to clear and 0 for the bits you want to keep. There are a whole range of DEC machines that don't have the AND. Instead, they have the Bit Clear (which is the And Not). On the SPARC there is a full set of logical operations.

Notice that by using register 0, which you will remember is permanently wired to 0, you can synthesize some additional operations. In particular, the one's complement or logical NOT, can be written as

R3 ← R0 ANDN R4

which inverts the bits in R4 and puts the result in R3.

As for shift instructions, the SPARC contains the usual ones, including Shift Right Logical (SHR), Shift Left Logical (SLL), and a Shift Right Arithmetic (SRA) which is sign extended. There are no rotate instructions, and more importantly, there is no shift double instruction, which complicates the code for extracting arbitrarily positioned bit fields. One might imagine that code intended to run on RISC processors should generally avoid bit fields that can be positioned over a word boundary, but it is not always possible to avoid them. For example, Ada has a feature that allows programmers to force bit fields to lie across word boundaries.

SPECIAL PURPOSE INSTRUCTIONS. The instructions SAVE and RESTORE push and pop the register frames and have already been discussed in connection with the register window mechanism.

There are a number of instructions that are used to read or write the state registers of the SPARC. There are special read and write instructions to read the program state register, the Y register (which is used in connection with the multiply step instruction), the WIM register, and the trap base register. All of these are protected instructions that give access to the system registers.

There is a guaranteed unimplemented instruction that can be assumed to remain unimplemented on future versions of the architecture. We saw a similar device in the 68030. The idea is that if you need a trick that depends on the trap from an unimplemented instruction, use this one, and you won't run into trouble on future versions of SPARC.

The Instruction Cache Flush (IFLUSH) instruction flushes an instruction from the instruction cache. If there is no instruction cache, then this instruction does not do anything. If there is an instruction cache then this instruction flushes the cache through some implementation mechanism.

The Jump and Link (JMPL) instruction has a format that allows the processor to jump to an arbitrary location computed in one of two standard ways, *rs1* plus *rs2* or *rs1* plus a 13-bit offset. This instruction is generally used to return from a called procedure. When a call is executed, the processor puts the return address (actually the address of the call instruction itself) into R15. The registers then slide, and R15 becomes R31, which is the return register. You don't need to worry about saving and restoring the return register—this comes from saving and restoring windows. JMPL allows you to get back, and you need to jump a little bit past the CALL instruction, so the 13-bit immediate format is usually used to specify an offset of 8 bytes, which allows for the CALL and the instruction in the delay slot.[3]

The SETHI Instruction Format

The instruction Set High (SETHI) has its own instruction format and a special use similar to that of the LUI instruction on the MIPS. On a 32-bit RISC machine such as the SPARC, there must be some way of loading a 32-bit constant into a register. This is important because 32-bit values may have to be generated both as constant values and as addresses.

On CISC machines, where the width of an instruction format is allowed to vary so that it can be extended beyond 32 bits, it is very likely that some instruction format will be large enough to allow the specification of full 32-bit values. But on most RISC machines, where the instruction format is limited to 32 bits, there is simply not enough room for both an opcode and the literal value itself. The solution chosen on most RISC processors is to provide instructions that allow a programmer to construct a 32-bit literal value in two parts, the upper set of bits and the lower set of bits. This is exactly what SETHI is intended for.

The instruction SETHI sets the 22 high-order bits of a register, leaving the remaining low bits as 0. If one is constructing a 32-bit value in a register, this can be done by first issuing a SETHI instruction with the appropriate high-order value and then filling in the low-order 10 bits with one of the regular instructions. A quick look at the general instruction format shows that the largest literal that can be specified directly in an instruction is 13 bits wide, more than enough to fill in the low-order 10 bits not set by SETHI.

USING SETHI FOR DIRECT ADDRESSING. The most frequent use of the SETHI instruction arises in instructions to load or store a fixed static location in memory. We saw this for this first time on the MIPS, where a load instruction requires that the upper half of an address has to be loaded first, and then the lower half of the address is supplied as the offset of the load instruction.

On the SPARC, a similar sequence of instructions is used, although a 32-bit address is not divided into equal 16-bit parts but rather into a high-order 22-bit field and a low-order 10-bit field. To load a value from location i in memory, we would use a sequence such as:

```
sethi    %hi(i), %o0
ld       [%o0 + %lo(i)], %o0
```

---

[3] It is usually easy to fill in the delay slot on a CALL, because you can just put the last instruction before the call in the slot—for example, an instruction to load the last parameter. Generally it does *not* work to take the approach of putting the first instruction of the procedure there, because the procedure would often be compiled separately. Of course, the linker could have a mechanism for doing this, but it is not worth it, since we usually have no problem filling this delay slot in any case.

Here the SETHI instruction first sets the 22 high-order bits of the address of i in register %o0—the macros "%hi" and "%lo" are used to reference the appropriate number of high- and low-order bits. The LD instruction then uses this value as an index, with a displacement consisting of the low-order 10 bits of the address of i, so that the effective address of the instruction is the address of i.

Although this variant of "direct addressing" takes two instructions, the comparison with the 386 is still reasonably favorable. The load takes 3 clocks [4] and only 8 bytes (assuming no interlock), compared with 5 clocks and 6 bytes on the 386.

The other approach for addressing memory is to make sure that an index register is pointing close by (within 4K bytes), and then index with this register. This would, for example, be used for accessing most variables off the frame pointer. However, given this small offset range, this approach is not so useful for global data. For example, it certainly would not be acceptable to limit the static data of each file in a C program or each package in an Ada program to 8K bytes.

This approach to addressing is very similar to that used on the MIPS. An important practical difference is that, because of the short offset of the SPARC, trying to address global static data using base registers is much less attractive. Consequently, the use of the direct addressing idiom is relatively more important in the SPARC architecture. It is also interesting to note that in the MIPS case, the instructions for dealing with the upper half of the register needed only 16 bits and hence fit into the normal instruction formats. Because of the small offset on the SPARC, the SETHI instruction needs a large operand, and this is why it has a special instruction format all to itself.

The Conditional Branch Instructions

The Branch instruction format supports the conditional branch instructions, which include a 4-bit condition code that matches against the four standard condition code bits so that it is possible to test any combination of conditions. Two limiting cases are Never Jump and Always Jump.

Other forms of the conditional branch allow branch decisions to be based on floating-point condition codes. The interpretations of these codes are similar, although not identical, to those of the integer unit. These instructions check against a 4-bit condition code pattern. In the case of the coprocessor, a similar set of conditional branches is available, but since the interpretation of these bits is completely up to the designer of the coprocessor, no predefined meaning can be attached to them.

After all other bits have been allocated in the instruction format, 22 bits are left over for the displacement. These 22 bits really amount to 24 bits of addressing, since the address specified in the 22 bits is shifted left 2 bits by the hardware, as in the case of the call instruction format. The effect of this format is to give a signed 8-megabyte

---

[4] Given the fact that we expect RISC machines to take 1 clock per instruction, you might expect the load to take only 2 clocks, but the current implementations of the SPARC do not achieve these 1-clock loads, and load instructions take 2 clocks.

range for conditional jumps, which is certainly sufficient for most applications. One usually expects conditional jumps to occur *within* a single procedure, and programs are not expected to contain single procedures with more than 8 megabytes of code!

THE ANNUL BIT. The *annul bit* (A-bit), which is present in all conditional jump instructions, is one of the more interesting and unusual features of the SPARC architecture. This bit makes it simpler for a compiler to fill a branch delay slot.

As we discussed in Chapter 8, in many RISC machines, notably the MIPS, the instruction placed in the delay slot is executed whether or not the conditional jump is executed. This means that on such a machine the instruction that is used to fill the delay slot must be an instruction that needs to be executed regardless of whether or not the branch is taken. If such an instruction cannot be found, the delay slot must be filled with a no-op.

A useful optimization in the instruction set of the SPARC is to provide two variations for each conditional branch. If the annul bit is set and the branch is *not* taken, then the instruction right after the branch is skipped. The processor will suppress the effects of that instruction even though it is already in the pipeline.

This feature is useful because it makes it easier for a compiler to fill the delay slot. Since the instruction in the delay slot can be annulled, there is one instruction that can always be put after the conditional branch: the instruction that is the target of the branch. For example, if the target of a branch is at location L, there must be an instruction at L. Putting that instruction into the delay slot with the annul bit set and then branching to L + 4, is a simple systematic way of filling the delay slot. On the MIPS you might not be able to find an instruction that you need in both cases and end up putting a no-op into the delay slot.

Without any specific knowledge about how the branch was being used, you might conclude that filling the delay slot with the annul bit set would be useful only half the time on average. In practice, however, the instruction in the delay slot will usually *not* be annulled since in the case where the conditional branch is used to control a loop, jumps are taken much more often than not.

This has an interesting effect on compilers, since it means that it is very desirable to have the conditional test (that controls whether or not the loop is executed again) at the end of the loop. A "while" loop is naively translated by generating a test and conditional branch at the top of the loop (which controls when the loop is exited), followed by the body of the loop, and ending with an unconditional branch to the top of the loop. On any machine, performance is improved by testing the condition once on entry to the loop, and then putting the test at the bottom of the loop. This optimization is even more important on the SPARC, given the way the annul bit works.

To see how a compiler might generate code that uses the annul bit, consider the following simple "if" statement.

```
if i < 10 then
    j := i + 1
else
    j := i - 1;
```

A straightforward translation of this statement into SPARC assembler might take the following form:

```
          sethi   %hi(i), %o0
          ld      [%o0 + %lo(i)], %o0
          cmp     %o0, 10
          ble     L1
          nop
          sethi   %hi(i), %o1
          ld      [%o1 + %lo(i)], %o1
          inc     %o1
          sethi   %hi(j), %o2
          st      %o1, [%o2 + %lo(j)]
          b       L2
          nop
l1:
          sethi   %hi(i), %o3
          ld      [%o3 + %lo(i)], %o4
          dec     %o4
          sethi   %hi(j), %o5
          st      %o1, [%o2 + %lo(j)]
l2:
                  %o4
```

Standard compiler optimizations that have nothing to do with RISC machines are generally effective in being able to perform these two transformations on the above code. First, notice that the last two loads of *i* do not have to be redone because the value of *i* that is loaded into %o0 will always be the same as the values loaded in statements further below. Second, the code contains two stores to *j* which can be merged and moved to the end of the loop, since the value to be stored in *j* will be put into %o0 whichever branch is taken.

```
          sethi   %hi(i), %o0
          ld      [%o0 + %lo(i)], %o0
          cmp     %o0, 10
          ble     L1
          nop
          inc     %o0
          b       L2
          nop
l1:
          dec     %o0
l2:
          sethi   %hi(j), %o2
          st      %o0, [%o2 + %lo(j)]
```

It is now possible to perform some optimizations peculiar to SPARC. In this case, the decrement instruction after L2 can be moved into the delay slot after the conditional branch, replacing the no-op in that location. The annul bit is set on this branch so that the decrement is performed only when the jump is taken.

```
            sethi   %hi(i), %o0
            ld      [%o0 + %lo(i)], %o0
            cmp     %o0, 10
            ble.a   L1
            dec     %o0
            inc     %o0
            b       L2
            nop
    l1:
    l2:
            sethi   %hi(j), %o2
            st      %o0, [%o2 + %lo(j)]
```

With this transformation, the branch to L2 is no longer required and can be completely removed along with the following *nop* and the label L2.

```
            sethi   %hi(i), %o0
            ld      [%o0 + %lo(i)], %o0
            cmp     %o0, 10
            ble.a   L1
            dec     %o0
            inc     %o0
    l1:
            sethi   %hi(j), %o2
            st      %o0, [%o2 + %lo(j)]
```

Although this code is quite an improvement over the original code from which it was derived, there is still a potential problem in the second and third lines. Because the second instruction is loading the value *i* from memory, the comparison in the next instruction may have to be held off until the data arrives. In terms of scheduling, it would be better to have an instruction after the load that did not use register %o0. The SETHI instruction that prepares for the store to *j* can be moved into that position, with the resulting code:

```
            sethi   %hi(i), %o0
            ld      [%o0 + %lo(i)], %o0
            sethi   %hi(j), %o2
            cmp     %o0, 10
            ble.a   L1
            dec     %o0
            inc     %o0
    l1:
            st      %o0, [%o2 + %lo(j)]
```

The actual code generated by the SPARC compiler includes all these optimizations except the final move of the SETHI back after the load. This is a rather tricky move, since it involves moving an instruction across a conditionally executed section of code. As usual, the compiler is sometimes the limiting factor in the overall performance of compiled code on the machine, and this should always be borne in mind when comparing different architectures.

EXCEPTIONS

An exception can occur either because of an external interrupt or because an instruction has issued a trap. Traps may occur either as part of the operation of the IU or because of the floating-point processor or the coprocessor. Traps will only occur if the *enable trap* bit (ET) bit in the PSR is set.

There is a set of 16 trap instructions that tests any requested combination of bits in the integer condition code field of the PSR. There is, for example, a Trap Always (TA) instruction, and a Trap on Greater Than (TGT) instruction, to name just two.

Note that integer overflow can only be checked with an explicit trap or branch instruction—there is no facility for generating an automatic trap. As we discussed for the MIPS (which has only the automatic trap facility), this is both an advantage and disadvantage depending on whether the program needs to get control on an overflow.

When an exception occurs, the steps taken to handle the exception are as follows:

- The ET bit in the PSR is set to 0, disabling exceptions for the moment.

- The PS bit in the PSR is set so that it indicates whether the processor was in supervisor or user state when the exception occurred, that is, it is set to a copy of the S bit of the PSR.

- The S bit is set to 1, since exceptions are always handled in supervisor state.

- The current window pointer is decremented so that a new register window is allocated. The WIM register is *not* checked for validity.

- The PC and nPC registers are copied into registers 17 and 18. This is done so that the exception routine knows which instruction caused the exception and which instruction would have been executed next if the exception had not occurred.

- The exception number is written by the hardware into the *trap type* field of the *trap base register* (TBR). The address of the specific exception handler is formed by concatenating these high-order bits, which specify the starting address of the table with the specific trap type. The trap type is thus an index into the trap table.

- The program counter, PC, is set to the contents of the trap vector entry, and nPC is set to the contents of that entry plus 4. Control then passes to the exception routine.[5] Note that the exception routine does *not* store anything in memory. Many CISC designs, such as the 386, save old state information in memory on an exception, which does lead to a slightly simpler description of exception semantics. However, memory references are potentially slow, so avoiding them ensures fast handling of exceptions and is a technique often seen in RISC designs. Rather than saving and restoring the program state register, we do a little reversible surgery on it. Of course, if the exception routine wants to enable exceptions while it is executing, it must save the old state in memory before setting ET.

---

[5] Once again, there is a conflict between our standard terminology and the particular choice made by SPARC, which uses trap as the generic term to describe all exceptions.

We noted that the WIM is not checked for validity. The exception routine uses the new window without checking whether it overlaps a window that is already in use. As long as the exception routine modifies only the temporary registers of this window, all is well. Of course, additional registers can be used if they are saved and restored—the exception routine can even execute a SAVE instruction if it wants to. However, eight registers is enough for many exception routines, and, more importantly, we avoid the possibility of a window overflow trap, which might delay handling of a time-critical interrupt.

In order for the exception handler to return control of the processor to the task that caused the exception, it is necessary to restore both the PC and the nPC. This requires some special effort, because normally PC and nPC cannot be set to arbitrary values. The Return From Trap (RETT) instruction is set up to do exactly the required fiddling. It is placed immediately after a JMPL instruction, and it interferes with the effect of the JMPL precisely in not setting nPC in the normal manner. RETT can occur *only* in the delay slot of a JMPL with this very special meaning.

While many processors require only a single program counter, the SPARC has two program counters, PC and nPC. The register PC contains the instruction being executed, while nPC contains the next instruction to be executed. Normally nPC is simply PC + 4, so it may seem redundant to have two program counters. However, this relation does not hold when an instruction in the branch delay slot is being executed.

Suppose we have a jump to label X, and we are executing the instruction after the jump (before jumping off to X). PC then points to the instruction after the jump, and nPC points to X. If the processor then receives a trap or interrupt, we have both program counters and can return to the same "split location" situation that held at the time of the trap.

This shows why it is convenient to have two program counters. Some RISC processors with jump delay slots, as we saw on the MIPS, have only a single program counter. To deal with the problem of an exception occurring as the processor is about to execute an instruction in the delay slot, the program counter is backed up to the point of the jump. This is done so that when a procedure returns from the point at which an exception occurred, both the jump instruction and the instruction after it will be executed again. The disadvantage of this approach is that the exception routine becomes more complicated, so it is not always possible to know whether the exception was caused by the jump or by the following instruction. On the SPARC, the exception routine is simplified at the cost of an extra system register.

Once the exception has been handled, the processor must be returned to the appropriate state. The PS bit contains the previous state of the supervisor bit so that on return from an exception the processor can be set into the appropriate mode. RETT undoes the effect of the exception. It increments the current pointer, it sets the supervisor state to what PS was, and it sets ET back to 1.[6]

---

[6] With the description of RETT, we have now gone through the entire IU instruction set without skipping a single instruction. Here we see that RISC design means RIWL (Reduced Instruction Writeup Length)!

FLOATING-POINT ON THE SPARC

One of the factors that has made RISC chips successful in the marketplace is that almost all of them provide substantial floating-point capabilities. Floating-point instructions are by their nature rather complex, so they do not easily fit into the "keep instructions simple so that we can pipeline them and execute one instruction per clock" model. However, in numerical code it is clear that floating-point instructions *must* be provided, because they are executed with high frequency, and decomposing them into a sequence of simple instructions would not be acceptably efficient.

The SPARC architecture includes an IEEE 754 compatible floating-point specification, which you will remember means that even though not all of the standard has been implemented, there is enough support in the hardware that the full standard can be implemented without great difficulty.

The first implementations of the SPARC architecture have depended on the use of a separate IEEE-compatible floating-point coprocessor. If the floating-point hardware is *not* integrated onto the chip itself, it is possible that different implementations of the processor may have different floating-point characteristics. SPARC cures this problem by including the specification of the floating-point behavior as part of the architecture. It is possible, for example, to use either the Weitek or 387 chips to provide the floating-point capability in a SPARC environment, but it would have to be done with some "glue" between the SPARC processor and the floating-point chip that ensured that, from a programmer's point of view, the behavior would be identical. This contrasts with the situation on the 386, where these two coprocessor environments look totally different to a programmer.

As we briefly mentioned earlier, the floating-point load and store operations are issued by the IU rather than the floating-point unit. This is important because of the way the load and store instructions behave. In a typical implementation of the SPARC architecture, floating-point operations are overlapped with IU operations.

However, the idea is that this overlap should be completely transparent to the program, which should be able to think of the floating-point instructions as being executed sequentially in a strictly synchronized manner. This is easily enough achieved with operations like addition, using techniques similar to those used to interlock integer load instructions. The result register of the addition is marked busy, and any attempt to use it before the addition is complete will hold things up.

A special case arises with stores. If the store instruction is allowed to overlap other integer operations, then the overlap may become visible. We have encountered this situation in conjunction with the Intel 387 coprocessor which also uses the approach of overlapping floating-point operations. On the 387, we generally have to follow an FST (floating store) operation by an FWAIT to make sure that the store is complete. Otherwise a subsequent reference to the stored value might occur too early, *before* the store is complete.

On the SPARC the floating-point store is handled by the IU, which guarantees it is synchronized in the same sense that ordinary stores are synchronized. A subsequent load of the memory location, by either a floating-point or an integer load, is guaranteed to always get the new value, obviating the need for any explicit synchronization.

This approach means that the overlap of floating-point operations is completely transparent to the applications program. The only point at which the overlap has to be taken into account is in handling exceptions, and that is the domain of the operating system. There is no experiment, other than measuring timing performance, that an applications program can carry out to determine whether or not, and to what extent, floating-point operations are overlapped.

Floating-Point Registers

The floating-point register set includes thirty-two 32-bit registers, which are organized in such a way that they can be used as 32-bit, 64-bit, and 128-bit operands with only 80 bits used for the extended precision format (although the extended precision is optional and not currently provided by SPARC chips). The floating-point register model of the SPARC does not include register windows or any of the complications that arise with the IU register set. A compiler for the SPARC will have to treat these registers in the same way as a compiler treats the general registers on a processor with no register windows. Even though the presence of register windows simplifies register allocation as far as the integer unit is concerned, the compiler writer is still required to manage floating-point registers in the standard manner, that is, without register windows.

This somewhat undermines the argument that register windows simplify the job of writing the compiler. For example, in the case of floating-point registers, it is no longer the case that allocation of registers in separate procedures is completely independent, and optimal register allocation can be done only at link time.[7]

Compared to other floating-point implementations, the SPARC specification of floating-point is somewhat richer than that of some other RISC chips, because it includes the square root function and remainder functions. On the other hand, it does not have as complete a floating-point implementation as the Intel 387, which also includes the transcendental functions such as sine and cosine.

Overlapped Multiplication and Addition

A specific implementation of the SPARC's floating-point unit may be realized by separate functional units. The first implementation of SPARC, for example, consisted of a floating-point controller, a floating-point multiplier, and an ALU that included the logic to perform addition and subtraction (we will refer to this as the *adder*).

A floating-point unit in which the addition and multiplication logic are on separate chips is capable of performing two operations in parallel. The dispatch logic can keep issuing floating-point instructions as long as there is a free unit to handle them.

---

[7] This chapter was reviewed by representatives associated with Sun and MIPS, and this particular sentence drew rather different reactions. The MIPS reviewer noted: "Important point, don't forget it!" in large letters, while the Sun reviewer noted that this is not such an important point, since in practice the use of floating-point registers is not nearly so intensive as is the case for integer registers, which are also used for addressing.

The processor could, for example, dispatch a multiplication out to the multiplication unit and then subsequently dispatch a subtract instruction out to the adder unit, without waiting for the multiply to complete. A third floating-point operation would have to wait for one of the previous ones to complete. The amount of overlap is an architectural decision—there is nothing to prevent an implementation from having lots of multipliers and lots of adders, allowing a significant overlap of instructions.

TAKING ADVANTAGE OF OVERLAPPED OPERATIONS. To see the usefulness of having separate add and multiply units, consider the standard problem of computing the product of two matrices. The inner loop involves computing a dot product:

$$P(I,J) = A(I,1)*B(1,J) + A(I,2)*B(2,J) + A(I,3)*B(3,J) + ...$$

If you think about the way data flows in that computation, you can do a multiply, and then when you get a result, you can start adding that result to the sum and meanwhile start on the next multiply. If you program a matrix multiply in the obvious naive way, this scheme of overlap will mean that you are always overlapping multiplication and addition. It may be possible to double the floating-point throughput if there are separate multiplication and addition units.

The SPARC architecture allows any number of functional units, so the maximum number of simultaneous floating-point operations is not specified. In the matrix multiplication example, we could take advantage of separate multiply and add units without special programming. However, there are other cases where the style of programming is affected by the number of functional units. Consider the polynomial:

$$R = ax^4 + bx^3 + cx^2 + dx + e$$

The familiar efficient scheme for evaluating this polynomial uses Horner's rule, which reduces the number of multiplications by factoring as follows:

```
R := a * x;
R := R + b;
R := R * x;
R := R + c;
R := R * x;
R := R + d;
R := R * x;
R := R + e;
```

This approach minimizes the number of operations (a total of eight operations are required). However, it is not suitable for taking advantage of parallel execution units, since each computation involves the previous result. Consider the following alternative computation scheme:

```
T1 := d * x;    X2 := x * x;
T2 := c * X2;   T3 := T1 + e;   X3 := X2 * x;
T4 := T2 + T3;  T5 := b * X3;   X4 := X3 * x;
T6 := T4 + T5;  T7 := a * X4;   R := T6 + T7;
```

If we have two multiplication units and two addition units, all of which can operate in parallel, then the set of operations on each line can be executed in parallel. This means that in such circumstances, this computation scheme is faster than Horner's rule (five operation times instead of eight), even though the total number of operations is greater (11 instead of 8).

HANDLING TRAPS IN OVERLAPPED OPERATIONS. One difficulty with this kind of overlapped approach is that one of these instructions may cause a trap, due to the requirements of the IEEE standard. The traps are purely synchronous. You cannot get a trap occurring on one of these instructions between the two floating-point operations (The Intel 387 design for the overlapped architecture is also synchronous, but as we discussed previously, IBM's wiring of the 387 results in asynchronous traps).

Even synchronous traps can be a problem if they occur other than on the instruction causing the trap condition. The floating-point unit on the MIPS pre-examines the the operand exponents to insure that this never occurs, but on the SPARC, the expectation is that it will be the case that a trap caused by one operation may be signalled on a subsequent operation. Consider the following pattern of operations:

```
FPOP   * (instruction A)
...
FPOP   + (instruction B)
...
FPOP   * (instruction C)
```

If a trap occurs during execution of instruction C in this example, it might be instruction A that actually caused the trouble. Meanwhile instruction B may be completed, waiting to get started, or at some intermediate stage of execution. The trap routine at this stage has to have some way of knowing what is going on.

What sort of things must be done by a trap routine? It might be necessary to abandon the computation completely and go on to the next one. In that case it is sufficient to have a scheme for flushing out the operations that have not completed. But you may also want to substitute some sort of value in the computation and then carry on with the computations. Again the IEEE standard requires this capability. A typical example is that if you get an underflow trap, you may want to record the fact that you have an underflow trap on some sort of log file and then replace the result with 0 or some other small value. There are different numerical reasons for proceeding in different ways. If you get a divide overflow, you may want to register this fact and then replace it with a positive infinity value.

In this case, the operating system must simulate things as though the trap had occurred at the appropriate instruction, with the proper value substituted. But it can't just jump back to the second instruction, because all sorts of IU instructions may have executed in between and obviously cannot be reexecuted. There must be a way for the floating point unit to tell the processor what has happened in some detail.

That is what the privileged Store Double Floating-Point Queue (MSTDFQ) instruction is. The idea is that it be used in standard code supplied by the operating system and would be executed only as part of an exception routine operating in supervisor state. STDFQ stores a double word. The first word is the address of the floating-point instruction that caused the trap (which in this case would be instruction A). The second word is a copy of the floating-point instruction that caused the trap.[8]

When the processor executes an STDFQ instruction, the first element that it gives you is the one corresponding to the instruction that caused the trap (instruction A in this example). At this stage you can examine the instruction and decode it. You can also interrogate the status flags in the floating-point unit to see what kind of interrupt occurred and what the situation was when the interrupt occurred. You can then either reexecute the instruction, having fixed up some of the operands, or you can just simulate the instruction and provide an appropriate substitute result.

Now we have dealt with the instruction that caused the trap (instruction A). But what about instructions B and C? They have to be simulated, since control will finally return from the trap routine just past instruction C. To solve this problem, we issue another STDFQ. It gives us another double-word pair, which references the first undone, uncompleted floating-point instruction (in this case instruction B). The exception routine now reexecutes instruction B. If this instruction causes a trap as well, then we need some software convention to decide what should happen if a number of instructions cause traps. How will you signal that to the application program in a clear manner? That has to be addressed. Finally, the third SDFQ yields the final instruction, the one where the trap was actually signalled (instruction C in this example).

There is a status bit in the floating-point register that shows whether the queue is empty, so the exception routine issues SDFQ instructions until this status is set. The maximum number of queue entries is one of the implementation parameters of the architecture. It depends on the maximum number of floating-point instructions that can be executing simultaneously. In general, the exception routine will be written to handle any number of elements in the queue, and then this routine will work regardless of the overlap provided by the implementation.

This level of complication in the floating-point exception routines can often be avoided in some situations. For example, it may be the case that when there is a floating-point overflow, it simply means that something has gone wrong and that the program has been terminated—a typical approach for FORTRAN programs. However, some applications require more precise control.

An example of such a requirement occurs in Ada programs, where an exception handler can be defined that gets control on a floating-point overflow. One would expect a language like Ada to be defined in terms of sequential execution, so that exceptions

---

[8] This copy of the floating-point instruction is often not really needed, since it could be loaded from the program, but it helps not to have to worry about accessing the instructions from the trap routine with attendant paging problems. Furthermore, in a memory mapped environment with separate data and instruction spaces, it may not be straightforward to load instructions as data. Since the floating-point unit has obviously picked up the instruction, it can easily give it back.

are raised as statements are executed. Ada is indeed generally defined in this manner, and the overlapped execution raises some concerns. Are we allowed to carry on IU instructions after starting the floating-point instruction if it might raise an exception? The Ada design specifically addresses this issue. Section 11.6 of the Ada Reference Manual allows an implementation to perform certain optimizations, one of which exactly corresponds to the kind of overlapped execution, delayed trap semantics that is provided on the SPARC.

THE SPARC IMPLEMENTATIONS

The SPARC architecture was defined in 1985, with the first implementation appearing in 1987. That implementation, used for the first time in the Sun-4 workstation series, was the result of an arrangement between Sun Microsystems and the Japanese company Fujitsu. The Fujitsu implementation of the SPARC was based on CMOS *gate array* technology, a technique that might be described as a "chip kit."

A gate array provides a way of bypassing much of the layout cost associated with traditional VLSI design, allowing a chip to be brought to the market very rapidly. As initially manufactured, the gate array consists of a set of logic gates *without* the top layer containing the connecting wires. To complete the implementation of a new chip, all that needs to be done is to etch in the top layer containing the desired set of wires. The advantage of gate arrays is that they are a fast way of producing a chip. The disadvantage of this technology is that the resulting chips are somewhat slower than custom-designed chips, and cannot be packed so densely.[9]

The technology used on the Fujitsu SPARC implementation is a little fat (1.5 microns) and the clock speed a little slow (16.6 MHz) by current standards. On the other hand, when one considers that in 1986 the fastest of the Intel 386 implementations was 16 MHz, the Fujitsu implementation was reasonably competitive for its time.

In general, it seems that manufacturers are able to produce both RISC and CISC chips at roughly the same clock speeds, leaving the performance gain to result from the reduction in the number of clocks per instruction. The Fujitsu chip does not fully achieve the 1 clock per instruction goal; loads, for example, take 2 clocks and stores 3 clocks. However, the performance was still well above that of comparable contemporary CISC chips. The published performance figures for the Fujitsu SPARC implementation are 10 MIPS and 1.8 MFLOPS for floating-point performance.

A more recent implementation, the CYPRESS chip, used in the new series of Sun workstations, is a CMOS custom chip that is designed from scratch. It uses sub-micron technology that is close to the reasonable limit of VLSI designs available at the time of the writing of this book. It will be a 33 MHz processor, advertised to be 20 MIPS with

---

[9] Although the gate-array approach to chip design may not allow use of the most current technology, the time to bring something into the marketplace may sometimes be more important than clock speed!

a floating point speed of 3.8 MFLOPS. It comes closer to the 1 clock per instruction goal—with estimated throughput for typical implementations in the range of 1.5 instructions per clock.[10]

You will remember that the number of register windows provided can vary from implementation to implementation but that the number must be somewhere between 2 and 32. The Fujitsu implementation provided seven register windows, for a total of 120 registers. The CYPRESS implementation provides eight register windows, with 136 registers in the register file. The increase in number of windows gives a small but measurable advantage. Studies seem to indicate that using more than eight windows reaches the point of diminishing returns.

Now for some science fiction. There is a plan for a high-density VLSI chip by BIT that is 40 MIPS. This is supposed to be near production stage, but it has not yet appeared in workstations on the market. Metaflow is working on 100 MIPS SPARC using ECL technology. Finally, PRISMA is working on a 250 MIPS gallium arsenide chip.

A fundamental argument that is made with RISC is that since the designs are much simpler you should be able to more easily adapt to state-of-the-art technology. We might expect, for example, that a SPARC in GaAs would be considerably easier to manufacture than an 386 in GaAs—time will tell! The Cray-3 is built making extensive use of GaAs, but it costs many millions of dollars. How interesting the GaAs SPARC is depends, of course, on its cost.

CONCLUSION

SPARC is an important entry in the RISC scene from a commercial point of view, since it represents a major commitment to RISC by the leading workstation vendor. SPARC and MIPS represent rival designs of architectures that are designed with very similar goals and general design criteria. Nevertheless, there are a number of crucial technical differences, including the use of register windows and double indexing in the SPARC and the larger addressing offsets and different pipeline approach of the MIPS.

All these design differences are the subject of fierce technical arguments, and the literature is unusually full of advocacy documents that argue strongly for one or the other approach, often backed up by benchmarks of the usual questionable nature.

Which of the two architectures really is better? This isn't an easy question to answer. For one thing, it is hard to separate the architecture from its implementations. Current implementations of the MIPS seem to be somewhat more efficient that those of the SPARC—the CYPRESS, for example, is still burdened by a three-clock store. However, this does not seem to be a necessary consequence of the architectural differences.

Just as a programmer can make a theoretically less efficient algorithm run faster by clever coding, a hardware designer can often overcome architectural difficulties with

---

[10]Remember that cache misses, particularly instruction cache misses, hold up the pipeline, so even if all the instructions take 1 clock under ideal conditions, we cannot expect to see the overall throughput achieve this peak performance.

clever implementation. A reasonable conclusion is that the two approaches are roughly equivalent in performance. Both architectures clearly demonstrate the viability of the fundamental RISC notion that simplifying the instruction set design can lead to significantly improved performance.

CHAPTER

11

THE INTEL i860

Regardless of its ultimate success, the Intel i860 is a chip that is certain to get a great deal of attention.[1] Although it was designed primarily to be a graphics coprocessor, Intel has more recently presented it as a processor with a potentially much wider range of uses. The i860 includes many of the characteristics of RISC machines and is certainly considered by Intel to be a RISC chip.

It is interesting that as the i860 was being developed, there was a lively rivalry between the division designing the i860 and the division working on the 486. The division of Intel involved in the development of the 486 had been pooh-poohing the idea of RISC chips, and yet all the time another large division in Intel was furiously working at producing a 1 million transistor RISC chip!

Some evidence of this internal feuding was in evidence when the announcement of the Intel 80486 was made. The press release might be summarized as saying that the division of Intel that was producing the 486 had concluded that the performance of the 486 had shown that the whole RISC idea was rubbish—they had, after all, been able to accomplish all of the same things with the unabashedly-CISC 486.

---

[1] The i860 was originally known as the N10. It has been officially christened the i860, and so we will refer to it by that name.

A SUMMARY OF THE i860

Unlike some other RISC processors in which the number of transistors is kept deliberately small, the i860 chip contains over a million transistors. Some RISC processors purposely attempt to keep the transistor count low so that, among other reasons, the hardware can be laid out easily and without error. But, despite the fact that Intel has chosen to characterize it as a RISC chip, the Intel i860 is not a simple chip!

Intel expects to introduce the i860 in 25 MHz, 33 MHz, 40 MHz and 50 MHz versions. The 33 MHz version appears to be the fastest available as of July 1989, since the published benchmarks are for a 33 MHz chip.[2] The 33 MHz clock speed of the i860 is the same maximum speed available in mid-1989 for the 386, and so it seems reasonable to assume that the technology of the two chips is comparable. Intel hopes to be able to produce versions of the i860 that run at 50 MHz in the near future. Presumably, it will be possible for Intel to manufacture 50 MHz 386 or 486 chips by that time as well.

While the clock speed of the i860 is not particularly surprising (whether one assumes that it operates at a rate of 33 MHz or 50 MHz), the claimed figures for instruction throughput certainly are. Intel claims that a 50 MHz i860 will operate at 150 *million operations per second* (MOPS).

There is a difference between a MIP and a MOP. A MIP is a measure of instructions, and a MOP is a measure of operations. As we will see later, the i860 has instructions which perform multiple operations, so the two measures are not the same. Floating-point operations on the 50 MHz i860 can reach a peak of 100 MFLOPS, 100 *million floating-point operations per second.*

These are pretty staggering figures. They can be interpreted as claiming that the i860 can achieve three operations per clock, two of which can be floating-point operations. It is not easy to see how it is possible to issue that many instructions, let alone keep executing them at that speed. As we shall see, the unusual architectural features of the i860 explain these apparent discrepancies.

Basic Structure of the i860

The basic structure of the i860 is similar to that of other RISC chips in many respects. The i860 has thirty-two 32-bit registers (see Figure 11.1), *without* the register windows that we have seen on the SPARC. The i860 also has thirty-two 32-bit floating-point registers, which can also be used as sixteen 64-bit double-precision floating-point registers. The floating-point formats generally adhere to the IEEE 754 floating-point standard. The memory management unit and the floating-point unit are on board the

---

[2] The benchmark figures are presented as though they were measured using a 40 MHz chip. The figures seem to have been obtained by scaling the actual results of runs on a 33 MHz chip. The conclusions reached by benchmarks have to be watched very carefully—they are subject to all kinds of trickery! The 50 MHz chip certainly seems to exist, at least for advertising purposes, but no one has ever seen one.

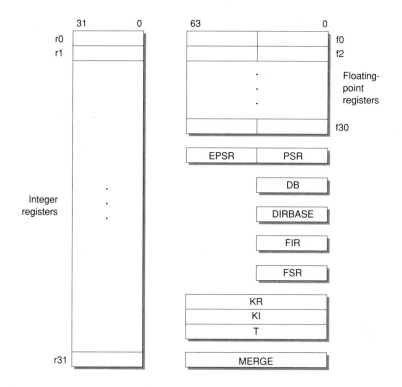

FIGURE 11.1
The register structure of the i860.

chip, which helps to explain why so many transistors are being used in a chip that Intel has described as being based on RISC principles.

The i860 also has an 8K data cache and a 4K instruction cache built into the chip. Both of these are two-way set-associative caches. The implementation of memory management is absolutely identical to that of the 386 (and the 486). This is quite deliberate—it means that it is possible to have a system with both a 386 or 486 *and* an i860 on the same bus sharing the same memory *and* the same page tables.

It is also probable that this has been done so that parts of the hardware design can be reused between the 486 and the i860. Presumably, since both teams work for the same company, the rivalry between the groups does not extend so far as to exclude cooperation of this type. Major portions of a particular chip can indeed be reused on other chips, much in the same way as software components can be reused.

HARDWARE COMPONENTS. The i860 is built from three separate units: the *integer core unit* (usually referred to simply as the *core unit*), the *floating-point unit* and the *graphics unit*. Looking only at the core unit of the i860, what you have is a typical RISC machine with a small set of instructions that execute very quickly.

Benchmarks published by Intel compare integer performance with the MIPS and SPARC chips. Not surprisingly, Intel's benchmarks show that the i860 significantly outperforms these two processors. However, if all the figures are normalized by clock speed (which is certainly legitimate, since, as we mentioned before, Intel scales its own figures from 33 MHz to 40 MHz) then, to a first approximation, all three chips have roughly the same integer mode performance. A fair conclusion that can be drawn is that if the only point of interest is the speed of the core unit, and the design of an i860-based system does not plan to take advantage of the floating-point or graphics units, the i860 is more or less just another RISC chip. In fact, its instruction set is in some respects even smaller and thinner than those of some of its competitors. The most unusual aspects of the i860 have to do with floating-point and graphics support.

The floating-point unit and the graphics unit are very closely related, even though they are described as being logically separate. The graphics unit implements a very specialized set of graphics instructions. We will consider the floating-point and graphics units and their related instructions later on.

Instruction Formats

The core instructions come in two general formats, the REG format and the CTRL format. The CTRL format is used for branch and call instructions while the REG format is used for most other instructions. There are four variants of the REG format.

The *general format* consists of a 6-bit opcode field in the most significant bits of the instruction, followed by three 5-bit opcode fields. These fields are the *src2* field, the *dest* field, and, in the least significant position, the *src1* field. The general format is shown in Figure 11.2, along with the other REG formats. There are 11 bits left over that are used in some instructions but not in others. A variation of this format called the *16-bit immediate variant* is used to extend the range of the null/immediate/offset field from 11 bits to 16 bits.

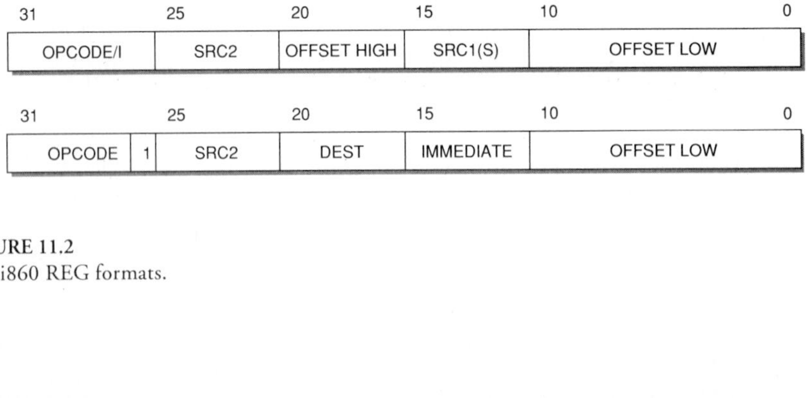

FIGURE 11.2
The i860 REG formats.

The Processor Status Registers

The i860 has a register file consisting of several system registers. The architecture allows some registers to be available only in supervisor mode and some registers to be available in both supervisor mode and user mode (called the *problem state* on the i860). There is even one register in which some bits can be changed only in supervisor mode but other bits can be changed in user mode. That happens to be the *program state register* (PSR), which has three fields of particular interest, discussed in a later section.

All the system registers, including the protected ones, can be *read* in problem state. At first glance, this seems perfectly reasonable, since after all, reading a register, even one that has to do with control of the processor, should not cause any trouble. This approach, however, has at least one significant disadvantage. In many operating systems, it is desirable to implement the notion of *virtual machines*, where a program thinks it has the entire machine at its disposal, including the protected instructions and supervisor mode. The operating system provides this virtual machine mode by trapping protected instructions and then simulating them to give the program the result it would have obtained if it were running by itself on the physical machine. Clearly, it is important for this purpose to trap both reads and writes to the system registers, since the operating system has to give as the result of a read the value corresponding to the virtual machine. This value may be different from the actual physical values. Thus the i860 is not a convenient processor to implement a virtual machine operating system.

OTHER PSR FIELDS. Another system field in the PSR that is accessible in problem state is the *Shift Count* field. The shift count is used by only one instruction, the Shift Right Double (SHRD) instruction. The trouble with a double shift is that the instruction formats are not large enough to handle this number of registers, since two registers are needed to participate as the source of the shift, and a third register is needed for the result. As a consequence, the shift count is forced into the program state register.

The rest of the PSR contains supervisor state information—most of it quite conventional. There is a bit that says whether the processor is in user state, a bit that specifies whether interrupts are enabled, and so on. Figure 11.3 shows the complete layout of the PSR.

DUAL INSTRUCTION MODE. An important bit in the PSR register is the *dual instruction mode* bit. This status flag provides one of the keys to the mystery of how the i860 can perform operations at a greater throughput than the basic clock speed.

The i860 can operate in either of two modes. In *single instruction mode,* one new instruction enters the execution pipeline on each clock cycle in the conventional manner. To the extent that the RISC principle of 1 clock per instruction is achieved, this gives a peak throughput of 50 MIPS on a 50 MHz machine. In *dual instruction mode,* the processor picks up two instructions on each clock. This is possible because the i860 is basically a 64-bit machine, with data paths that accommodate accesses of this width.

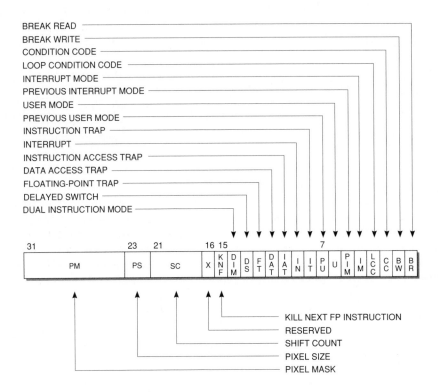

FIGURE 11.3
The i860 processor status register.

The instructions being picked up, however, must include one integer core unit instruction and one floating-point unit instruction. If the compiler can successfully find some useful set of computations that include one integer and one floating-point instruction, then the two instructions are executed in parallel. On a 50 MHz machine, this will result in 100 MIPS throughput. This figure is still short of the 150 MOPS performance claim made by Intel, but we will defer discussion of how that throughput is achieved until the section on the floating-point unit.

The *kill next floating-point flag* in the PSR is also unusual, and is needed in connection with the dual instruction mode. When two instructions are being executed at the same time, either one of them may cause a trap. If this happens, the trap routine may need to reexecute the integer operation but skip the floating-point operation when it restarts. This is done by setting this flag in the PSR.

Returning from a trap on the i860 is usually rather complicated. The reference manual contains half a page of highly opaque code explaining how to set everything up on return from the trap.

Extended Processor Status Register

The *extended processor status register* (EPSR) is a 32-bit register with several fields that add to the functionality of the PSR (see Figure 11.4). The low-order bits of the EPSR specify the processor type, which is set equal to 1 for the i860. Presumably the intention of this field is to distinguish different future versions of the i860. Software should be able to adapt to future versions of the chip by checking the value in this field.

WHY HAVE VERSION INFORMATION? Two fields in particular are of interest. There is a 4-bit implementation field and a 4-bit version number field that identify which implementation it is and what version of that chip it is. Even though a programmer would hope to be able to write code that is independent of a particular chip's implementation, experience has taught some manufacturers that this information certainly can be useful.

In Intel's case, this experience may have been hard earned. The version field would certainly be most welcome in the Intel 80x86 chips. There is a 386 A-mask, a B-mask, etc., up to the E-mask, each of which has had various bugs fixed. The 286 also has several versions. The B-step, which is the version of the 286 which is used on most of the IBM ATs that were bought early on, has a serious bug. When a general protection trap occurs, a trap which happens when a program accesses memory that does not exist or attempts to access memory beyond the bounds of a segment, the CX register gets destroyed in a random manner. Even though this happens only occasionally, it is a horrible bug because it means that the general protection trap is not reliable.

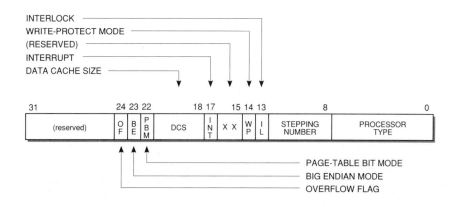

FIGURE 11.4
The i860 extended processor status register.

The design of the 286 processor is based on the idea that segments can grow down if a small stack has to be allocated. If you happen to run into the end of it, a general protection trap occurs. That means that a task needs more space, and so the operating system allocates a bigger segment, shuffles the segments around, sets up the GDT, goes back, and executes the same instruction. But this is inoperable on the B-step chip.

This particular bug must certainly have caused Microsoft a big headache. They were forced to implement OS/2 so that it would work on machines that had the B-step 80286. It was not only a brain-damaged architecture, but a brain-damaged implementation of a brain-damaged architecture, from Bill Gates' point of view.

How do you find out what step of the chip you have? It is almost impossible, because the bug shows itself only rarely. So if you do write software that depends upon the C-step chip (which is true, for example, of Digital Research's Flex-OS), there is no way that that software can be sure it is on the C-step chip. It just issues the instructions and hopes for the best.[3]

Thus the explicit identification at the hardware level of the hardware revision is a welcome feature. That these fields are needed on the i860 is certainly evident—the first released version of the i860 contains a significant bug. This bug has not been documented yet, but the published benchmarks give two columns of figures—one is the actual measured results, and the other, slightly faster, is the computed values of what could be achieved in the absence of this bug!

INTERLOCK BIT. The *interlock bit* (IL) in the EPSR register is used in conjunction with two of the instructions, LOCK and UNLOCK. The LOCK instruction locks the bus so that no other device can use the bus until the UNLOCK instruction is issued. Since the processor cannot keep the bus locked indefinitely, sooner or later a trap will occur.

A couple of instructions can be fit in between the lock and unlock implementing functions such as Test and Set, a locked swap, and similar specialized functions. The processor simply issues the lock, then issues the exchange sequence, and then issues the unlock. This interlock bit shows whether the processor is in the interlock state.

There must be some way of providing such locked accesses, because it is too expensive to go into supervisor state each time something needs to be done that requires communication between a process and the operating system. Consider a binary semaphore that is protecting some resource. If another process has the resource, it will be necessary to request that the operating system queue the current process. If the resource is not being used by another process, then it is important to be able to obtain access to the resource quickly, that is, without operating system intervention.

---

[3] We once purchased a 186 accelerator board that worked perfectly fine with one minor exception. We discovered that under certain circumstances the multiply didn't work. The Intel errata sheet admitted that a version of the 186 chip messed up on the multiply under certain circumstances. We called up the company that made the board and told them that they were using B-step chips. They said, "What! We thought we had C-step chips." If a manufacturer didn't know which version of a chip was on a board, how can an average user know?

All the machines we have seen so far have specialized instructions to do this, while the i860 provides this more general mechanism via the lock and unlock instructions. The 386 has the simple Test and Set, while the 68030 has the powerful CAS2. Notice that CAS2 is composed of a sequence of instructions that could be put between LOCK and UNLOCK. CAS2 is a very specialized instruction that works very nicely for doubly linked lists—a very particular situation. The lock and unlock allow the equivalent of CAS2 to be programmed as well as many variations on this theme.

Although the LOCK instruction locks the bus, it does not prevent interrupts or traps. It is quite possible for a trap to occur between the time the bus is locked and when it is unlocked. When the trap occurs, the hardware will see that the IL bit is set, and will presumably react by not performing a context switch. The lock does not inhibit interrupts from occurring; it just locks the bus. Interrupts can come in from a mechanism completely independent of the data lines of the bus, for example, from within the processor itself. The lock is strictly for a configuration in which several processors share the bus.

Another configuration field in the EPSR is the *data cache size* (DCS) field. On the initial model of the i860, it is absolutely fixed at 8K bytes. That this field is present presumably indicates the intention to make different models of the i860 in which the cache size may be larger. Depending upon the size of the data cache, it is possible to adopt totally different programming techniques in certain situations to achieve maximum performance. As we will see when we discuss the floating-point instructions, the size of the cache has a very significant effect on floating-point algorithms.

BIG-ENDIAN VS LITTLE-ENDIAN. The *big-endian* bit (BE) in the EPSR specifies whether big-endian mode is enabled or not. Like the MIPS, the i860 can run in either big-endian or little-endian mode. Unlike the MIPS, this mode can be switched dynamically, that is, while the processor is running. This would, for instance, allow an operating system to run multiple programs, some little-endian and some big-endian, at the same time. However, this is probably only a theoretical possibility—the added complexity at the operating system level would be considerable.

As on the MIPS, the endian control does not affect the order of bytes in memory (which is always little-endian at the physical level). If the big-endian mode is set, then the number of bytes is changed so that the program perceives them to be switched around into big-endian order. For example, if a load byte instruction is issued, the low 3 bits of the address are complemented so that the sequence of logical addresses 0 through 7 corresponds to the actual addresses 7 through 0.

This feature allows the i860 to be used in different hardware environments. Remember that the i860 is intended to be used as a graphics coprocessor. Even though it is powerful enough to be used as a main processor, one of its principal uses will certainly be as a graphics coprocessor. In that case, this flexibility is important since it may be desirable to attach the i860 to a 68030 (in which case one will expect big-endian integers) or the 386 (in which case one will expect little-endian integers).

Debugging Support

Another system register that is of interest is the *data break point register* (DB). This register contains a 32-bit virtual address to which every data address developed by the processor is compared. If the current data address matches the contents of the DB register, a trap will occur immediately.

The 386 has a more elaborate debugging mechanism than the i860, which also allows one to set hardware instruction breakpoints. It is the data breakpoint, however, that is the crucial feature needed for what is called *watchpoint* debugging, where a programmer is able to monitor how a variable is being manipulated without slowing down the processor. Except in a ROM-based system, it is always possible to get the effect of instruction breakpoints by including breakpoint instructions directly in the code that is being debugged.

Although this is an approach we have seen on the 386, it is the first time we have seen such a mechanism on a RISC chip. The fact that the i860 depends upon pipelining in the tradition of the RISC design philosophy means that a trap that is the result of a breakpoint will not be precise—it will be possible to know within a few instructions where the trouble is, but not exactly! Providing that one is willing to tolerate the imprecision of the trap, there is no reason why a data breakpoint should slow things down, since the comparison can be done in parallel with other aspects of the memory reference.

MEMORY MANAGEMENT

The memory management unit for the i860 has been implemented so that it is entirely on board the chip. One might expect that this would force us into a fairly long and involved description giving all the peculiarities of paging and addressing on the i860, just as we needed to do for several other processors. That is not the case, for one very simple reason. The memory management scheme of the i860 is identical in all respects to that of the 386.

Choosing to make the paging mechanism of the i860 identical to that of the 386 (and the 486) makes the i860 very attractive for use as a coprocessor in a system containing either of those two processors. In such a system the i860 can be used as either a floating-point vector coprocessor or a graphics coprocessor. Since the main method of communication between the two processors in such a system is via main memory, having the same virtual addresses is highly advantageous. The communication of data can be done using virtual addresses rather than physical addresses.

Instead of maintaining separate sets of page tables, only one copy of the relevant page directory and the page tables needs to be stored in the common memory. On the 386 or 486, the CR3 register will point to the page directory. On the i860, a system register known as the *directory base register* (DIRBASE), whose function is exactly the same, will point to the page directory. This means that the maintenance of the page tables can be done by just one processor and the addressing comes free on the other processor.

If the i860 is used as a coprocessor for some other system (e.g., a system where the main processor is a Motorola 680x0), then this nice correspondence will not hold. Two separate sets of page tables must be maintained in this case, and communication via memory will involve translating virtual addresses to physical addresses or trying to match the mapping of virtual addresses as closely as possible and then keeping the two sets of page tables coordinated. Notice, however, that there is a slight glitch if the i860 is operating in big-endian mode. The i860 access to the page tables is not affected by the endian mode. The result is that the page tables seem to be in a strange order (with pairs of words reversed) if the processor is operating in big-endian mode. Anyone using the i860 as a coprocessor will quickly wish that the main processor were a 386, or 486, which presumably does not distress Intel at all!

The i860 Cache

The i860 has both an 8K data cache and a 4K instruction cache, a configuration similar to the 486. The data cache is *not* write allocate, which means that the cache will be completely bypassed when a store to memory is done and the corresponding address is not already cached.

Whether a cache is designed to be write allocate or not depends upon what is being done with the data. When some piece of code sets all the elements of a gigantic array to 0s, it is useless to put those 0s in the cache because it will wipe out data that is much more likely to be used. When working with a much smaller data structure, on the other hand, it may be desirable to have that data in the cache. In working with a small data structure it is likely that data will be loaded and then stored back in the same place. In that case, everything will be in the cache anyway.

Cache management on the i860 is not totally transparent. A write, for instance, will update the data cache if the location is already cached, but it never updates the instruction cache, meaning that attempts to write self-modifying code will result in surprises. In the i860 Programmer's Reference Manual, we read that "Under certain circumstances, such as I/O references, self-modifying code, page-table updates, or shared data in a multiprocessing system, it is necessary to bypass or to flush the caches."

There are two mechanisms for the operating system to deal with such situations. First of all, the page tables have a bit to indicate that caching should be disabled (and this signal is fed to the outside world via a pin, so that it can be noted by an external secondary cache). Second, there is a flush instruction that can be used to deliberately flush the cache. This is a rather involved process. The reference manual gives the exact, though rather tricky sequence for using the flush instruction and warns: "Note. The flush instruction must only be used as in Example 5-2." Half a page of complicated code follows this remark, ending with the statement, "Any other use of flush is undefined." It is a delicate operation that must be used carefully in order for the cache to maintain its integrity.

One minor problem occurs in systems with a 386 or a 486 and an i860 sharing the same memory. Even though both the 486 and the i860 have onboard caches with the same configuration, the cache on the 486 is a snoopy cache while the i860's is not.

Since snoopy caches are always watching the bus to see if data has been modified, when the i860 modifies data the 486 will detect that. The two processors would join more smoothly if they were watching each other. As a result, the operating system designer needs to worry about cache coherence.

THE INTEGER CORE INSTRUCTION SET

The integer core instruction set of the i860 is quite small, numbering only about 4 dozen. The i860 Programmer's Manual divides these instructions into several categories, including load and store of integers and floating-point values, and pixel stores. There are add and subtract instructions, shift instructions, and logical instructions. There are several more exotic instruction types as well.

Integer Load and Store

The *load integer* (LD) instruction comes in three forms, depending upon whether one wants to load a byte, a 2-byte short integer, or a 4-byte long integer:[4]

```
LD.B    src1(src2), rdest
LD.S    src1(src2), rdest
LD.L    src1(src2), rdest
```

The first two instructions are always sign-extended. To get the effect of zero extension, it is necessary to issue a sequence such as

```
LD.S    0(R2), R3
AND     0x0000FFFF, R3, R3
```

This sequence of instructions will strip out any of the unwanted 1s that might appear in the higher-order bits. The lack of an unsigned load for bytes and words is notable, resulting in less desirable code for small unsigned integers compared to the MIPS or the SPARC.

All the instructions are automatically interlocked, as on all the other RISC chips in this text, with the exception of the MIPS. The i860 Programmer's Reference Manual contains a section called "Programming Notes" following several of the instruction descriptions. This section occasionally mentions that an instruction should not be used in some particular way. That does not mean that something terrible will happen if a programmer happens to do something that the manual suggests should not be done—it just means that the code may execute more slowly.

One of the rules mentioned, for instance, in the section of the i860 Programmer's Reference Manual on the integer loads is, "A load instruction should not directly follow a store that is expected to hit in the data cache." It is, of course, generally not possible

---

[4] As we can see from this example, the i860 assembly language is left to right (with the destination on the right) as opposed to the 386, which is right to left. What a state of confusion—we can't even get people within a single company to see eye to eye on this issue!

to know in advance what will or will not be in the cache, and so there is no guarantee that this rule can always be followed. If the above advice is not taken, the load will be delayed by an additional clock cycle. There are many other rules like this one. This is certainly one of the hardest microprocessors to program by hand if one attempts to take these rules into account.

There is a corresponding set of store instructions:

```
ST.B    src1(src2), rdest
ST.S    src1(src2), rdest
ST.L    src1(src2), rdest
```

As is usual in RISC processors, only load and store instructions can reference memory. All operands must be aligned on an appropriate boundary.

Integer Addition and Subtraction

There are two sets of add and subtract instructions, signed and unsigned, which give exactly the same results. The only way in which they differ is the way in which they set the overflow flag and the condition flag. The condition flag is just a single bit, that is, the single Boolean result of some test.

Some other machines have two separate bits, the carry flag and the overflow flag. The consequence of having these two flags is that a wider range of instructions is needed that can branch on some combination of their settings.

Since the i860 has only a single condition code, there are only two types of branches (four if the effects of the delay slot are included), Branch on Condition and Branch on Not Condition with or without a delay slot. On the other hand, it is necessary to double the number of add and subtract instructions.

Comparisons can be done with either an add or a subtract. To do a comparison using an add, the complement of a number is added, setting the condition flag in the opposite sense than if a subtraction were executed. This works out rather nicely for constants; for example, a comparison of A with +3, can be done either by subtracting 3 from A or by adding −3 to A. The condition flags are set in such a way that a full set of comparisons are available.

On the other hand, it is not as convenient to compare two variables, A and B. The i860 does not really have a full set of comparisons—two of them are missing. It is first necessary to complement B, and then there is a problem with the largest negative number. The code for doing general comparisons of two variables is thus somewhat inefficient.

The i860 Programmer's Reference Manual mentions in passing that the ADDU instruction can be used to perform multiple-precision additions. But the instruction that you want for that, the extended add, which takes the carry flag from the last add and adds it to the sum of the two operands, is not in the set of addition operations. To get the effect of the extended add, it is necessary to add the carry flag explicitly with additional instructions, consequently complicating multiple-precision arithmetic.

Multiplication and Division on the i860

The i860 does not have any integer instructions to do multiplication or division. It does not even have a multiply step or divide step instruction to help in constructing a multiplication or division routine. In the case of multiplication, at least, there is a simple reason for that. The floating-point unit on the i860 is so blazingly fast that it can be used to perform the integer multiplication efficiently. The case of division is an altogether different matter.

The instruction sequence for performing an integer multiplication consists of converting the two integer operands to floating-point, doing the floating-point multiplication, and then converting the result back to an integer value, an operation that will take four instructions. If these four instructions are issued and the result is needed right away, because a compiler cannot think of how to use the processor in the meantime, then it takes 9 clocks to complete the integer multiply. That is a very respectable number of clocks for a multiplication, and is, in fact, faster than most processors that *do* have an integer multiply instruction. If a compiler *can* figure out something to do while the multiply is going on, then the performance of this machine is even better, because the floating-point multiply is overlapped, leaving five slots free out of a total of nine for other instructions. That is a very fast integer multiplication, much faster than that of any of the other machines we have seen, including the CISC machines.

Division, on the other hand, comes nowhere near as close in terms of speed as the multiply instruction. Why? There is no floating-point divide. How can one manage without a floating-point divide instruction? Not easily—we will see how this is handled later on. If one regards the i860 simply as a RISC chip, then leaving out integer division is not so terrible, since after all the SPARC also has neither an integer divide instruction nor a divide step.

The Shift Instructions

There are several basic single-length shift instructions, Shift Left (SHL), Shift Right (SHR), and Shift Right Arithmetic (SHRA). In addition to these relatively standard shift instructions, there is the Shift Right Double instruction that allows one to perform shifts of 64-bit quantities that are in two registers. This instruction shifts the double register content to the right, and the low-order 32 bits go into the destination.

The absence of a double shift is often significant, since the double shift is the key to dealing with misaligned data. In addition, with a little bit of imagination a rotate instruction can be simulated. If the same register is used as both register arguments to this instruction, the Shift Right Double instruction becomes a rotate.

Shifts are also the preferred method of moving one register to another, using a shift count of zero. This is another case where an assembler is expected to provide some pseudo-ops that hide the fact that a register-to-register move is actually implemented through the use of the shift instructions. The assembler mnemonic MOV is actually a shift that uses register R0 (which, if you remember, is always set to 0) so that

```
MOV     src2, rdest
```

is actually equivalent to

```
SHL      R0, src2, rdest
```

The introduction of pseudo-instructions into the assembly language is a common technique for simplifying the reading of such material. A consequence is that at the assembly language level, there appear to be more instructions than there really are.

The Logical Instructions

The logical instructions include the usual set, AND, OR, and XOR. There is also an ANDNOT, which can be used as a simple NOT by using R0. All these instructions exist in variants that operate on the upper 16 bits of the value, for use when the operand is a constant. As on the RIOS, 32-bit constants can be built in two instructions using the ORH (or high) instruction to set the upper 16 bits of the constant value.

To load a constant into a register, the special register R0 must once again be made use of. Just as the register-to-register move described in the previous section was implemented with shift instructions using R0, the Load Immediate instruction can be simulated using OR. Register 0 is ORed with a 16-bit immediate operand, and the result is placed into some other register. That instruction at least gives one a 16-bit load. By then executing an *or high* it is possible to set the high-order 16 bits of the 32-bit value, in that way completing the construction of the value needed. With the help of several pseudo-ops, the fact that it takes two instructions to put a literal value into a register on the i860 is effectively hidden.

Another use of the logical instructions to remove another standard CISC-style instruction from the instruction set involves tests for equality. An exclusive OR can be used to create a test for equality by issuing the instruction with the two values being compared in two registers and the result going into R0. Despite the fact that the difference of the two values is lost by storing the result into R0, the condition code is set to indicate whether the result of the operation was zero or non-zero. Once again, there is an assembler pseudo-op, so it appears to the assembly language programmer of this machine that there is a conventional equality test.

Control Transfer (Branch and Jump) Instructions

Another set of instructions available on the i860 that will be familiar by now are the unconditional branch instructions with a delay slot afterward. There are two forms that that branch can take. The Branch and Branch on Not CC do not have a delay slot, and then there are versions with a conditional delay slot (which is just like the annul bit being set on the SPARC). These execute the delay instruction only if the branch is taken. Note that there are no conditional branch instructions which unconditionally execute the instruction in the delay slot.

One more very specialized instruction is Branch on LCC and Add. It is a specialized loop instruction for executing a number of instructions a certain number of times. One operand is the loop counter, and the other operand is the loop increment, generally set to −1, which keeps branching until the appropriate number of loops have been taken. It uses a special condition bit called the *loop condition code.*

The programming note in the i860 Programmer's Reference Manual associated with this instruction directs a programmer not to call subroutines in the middle of a BLA loop because the subroutine might want to use the same bit. The only time you can use it is for very stylized small loops, such as building the sequence for a character string move. FORTRAN DO loops are not translated as a matter of course to BLAs.

The call instruction, used to pass control to procedures, has an unconditional delay slot. CALL specifically sets general register R1 to the return address. It has a 6-bit opcode field and a 26-bit offset. The 26-bit offset is shifted left two bits to form the branch offset, so the branch has a range of plus or minus 128 megabytes. This is large, but does not cover the theoretical maximum possible range. Nevertheless, it is probably enough to keep the guys at the Pentagon happy for a little while. In practice you can afford to use the direct call instruction with this format all the time.

There is also a call indirect instruction which removes the limitation and allows a programmer to put a full 32-bit target address into a register. This CALLI instruction is also used for calling procedure variables in a language like C.

A Digression on Ada - Access Before Elaboration

The call indirect instruction has an important use in connection with an Ada compiler. You would normally expect that there would be no use for the call indirect except for calling procedure variables—since Ada has no procedure variables, you wouldn't expect to see it at all. However, if you look at the code generated by an Ada compiler for an i860, you may well find that procedures are almost always called using CALLI instead of CALL. Why is this? If you give a *procedure specification* in Ada as

    procedure X;

and quite separately you define the body of the procedure as

    procedure X is ...

then as soon as you have given the specification, procedure X is potentially visible so that the appropriate code to which X is visible may call X. But when you are compiling things separately, you can construct situations in which a program attempts to call X before it has elaborated the package that contains the procedure body.

The model in Ada is that if you have not elaborated the procedure body then the procedure body does not exist. Executing the call to X before the procedure body has been elaborated causes a user-detectable exception. The situation is called "access before elaboration."

One implementation of this check is to perform an indirect call to X, where the address initially points to a trap routine. When the body is elaborated the address is fixed up to point to the genuine procedure. You don't want to do a test every time procedure X is called to see whether it has been elaborated. So the call indirect instruction is of significant value in reducing the overhead which would be associated with an explicit test.

Some variation of this instruction is liable to be present on any machine, because languages like C permit the use of procedure variables that are addresses. During the design of Ada, there was a discussion of whether the error of access before elaboration should lead to an exception (and thus whether the check should be required), or whether it should simply lead to undefined execution (called *erroneous execution* in Ada). The observation that the indirect call was relatively cheap and existed on virtually all processors won the day for a required check—an interesting example of hardware specifications affecting language design.

FLOATING-POINT OPERATIONS ON THE i860

The floating-point unit of the i860 is built into the chip itself and is far more elaborate than any of the CISC or RISC floating-point coprocessors we have seen so far, whether they were implemented on-chip or on a separate chip.

There are 32 floating-point registers, each of which can hold a 32-bit floating-point value in IEEE-compatible singl format, or two adjacent registers (an even–odd pair) that can hold a 64-bit floating-point value in IEEE double format. No extended formats are available, and registers F0 and F1 always contain zero.

Floating-Point Load and Store

We will begin by looking at the floating-point load instructions. In some sense, it is difficult to decide which part of this chapter these instructions should appear in. From a logical point of view, they are certainly floating-point instructions, but in terms of the organization of the chip they are considered to be operations of the integer core unit. As we will see later, this is a very important distinction. There are three load instructions,

```
FLD.L    src1(src2), freg
FLD.D    src1(src2), freg
FLD.Q    src1(src2), freg
```

The L form of the floating-point load instruction loads one single value. The D form can be used to load two single values or one double value, and the Q form can be used to load four single values or two double values.

The existence of the Q form is quite important because the ability to reach peak speed in floating-point often depends on the ability to funnel data into the processor fast enough. Although the i860 generally has 64-bit data paths, the internal data path to the cache is 128 bits, so the FLD.Q still takes only 1 clock if the data is in the cache. As is typical in pipelined RISC architectures, the data from a FLD instruction is not immediately available, and if you access it in the following instruction you get an extra delay from the scoreboard. FLD.Q requires that its operand is aligned on a 16-byte boundary. As usual the motivation is to avoid the problem of an operand which crosses a cache line boundary.

The FLD instructions are quite conventional, but in addition to these, the i860 has what it calls a *pipelined* version of the floating-point load. All loads are pipelined in the normal instruction processor sense, but in the pipelined floating-point load, a quite separate pipeline from the instruction pipeline is used, and it is visible to the programmer. The format is:

```
PFLD.L  src1(src2), freg
PFLD.D  src1(src2), freg
```

The format of these instructions is quite conventional, but the effect is most unusual. The floating-point load pipeline has three stages, which means that at any one moment it contains three values. The effect of the PFLD is to feed in its source value to the first stage, shift the values in the pipeline one to the right, and store the value shifted out of the right end in the destination register of the PFLD instruction:

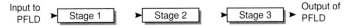

This means that the value obtained by a PFLD is the value which was accessed by the third previous PFLD instruction:

```
PFLD.L  DATA1, F0      ; load data1, throw away output
PFLD.L  DATA2, F0      ; load data2, throw away output
PFLD.L  DATA3, F0      ; load data3, throw away output
PFLD.L  DATA4, F2      ; load data4, data1 finally arrives
PFLD.L  DATA5, F3      ; load data5, data2 arrives
PFLD.L  JUNK, F4       ; load junk to force out data3
PFLD.L  JUNK, F5       ; load junk to force out data4
PFLD.L  JUNK, F6       ; load junk to force out data5
```

The pipeline moves only if a PFLD instruction is issued, so there can be other instructions between the PFLDs in the sequence above and the effect will be the same. When programming using the PFLD, you have to keep in mind that there are three values in the pipeline at all times. As in the above sequence, it is typical for the code using the pipeline to be arranged into three phases. First you prime the pipeline by loading the initial values, throwing away the junk output. Then you go into a production phase (which typically would be a loop running for some time), when good data is loaded in and good data comes out on each pipeline operation. Finally there is a cleanup phase where you load junk values to force out the remaining good data.[5]

Who would have thought that a "simple" load could get so complicated, and what on earth is all this for? To answer this question, we first note an important difference between the pipelined and non-pipelined versions of the floating-point loads. The standard floating-point load uses the cache, while the pipelined version bypasses the cache. The idea behind this approach is that if you are streaming in a lot of data

---

[5] Economical cooks know the trick of putting cheap breadcrumbs into a meat grinder to force out the last of the expensive meat. This is much the same situation!

from memory then it may be pointless to put that data in the cache, and it is certainly pointless to expect it to be in the cache.

Suppose, for example, you want to compute the dot product of a 10,000-element vector. It is certain that this data will not all be in the cache; it simply would not fit. Furthermore, there is no point in putting it in the cache, since the space for each element is needed only once, so the useful data may as well be left undisturbed in the cache.

The conventional approach used in integer code is to issue simple loads and hope that cache hits occur with some frequency. Remember that the performance of a typical pipelined RISC processor very much depends on finding most of its data in the cache. The dot product, for example, which is quite typical of floating-point calculations, is a situation in which the "hope for a cache hit" approach is not going to work if the vectors are long. Instead we have to expect that loads will take a while. The PFLD instruction allows up to three loads to be outstanding on the bus at a time, allowing maximum overlap for fetching data from external memory.

This means that you can arrange your program to stream data through at maximum speed even when there are no cache hits. This also explains why there is no PFLD.Q—the data path to external memory is only 64 bits, so there would be no point in a PFLD.Q since it would have to do two loads anyway. Only the internal path to the cache is 128 bits.

The general approach on the i860 is to analyze your problem and decide whether or not it is reasonable to expect the data to be in cache. If so, use FLD instructions to fetch the data. If not, PFLD should be used. This is why the size of the data cache is so important on the i860 (and is a parameter that can be read from the system registers). It affects not only the performance but the whole style of programming.

In a matrix multiply, for example, if both matrices fit in the cache, then FLDs can be used and the program is relatively conventional, at least as far as the loads go. For larger matrices, we may have a case where we can fit at least one row of one matrix in the cache, and we use FLD for this row and PFLD to load elements of the other matrix directly from memory. A general matrix multiply that wants to work efficiently on future versions of the i860 should look at the size of the matrices and read the DCS (data cache size) from the EPSR register, and then decide which of two or more separate algorithms will be most efficient.

In addition to the FLD and PFLD, there is an instruction Transfer Integer to F-P Register (IXFR), which does exactly what it says: an integer-to-floating-point conversion. Again this instruction is categorized as an integer core instruction rather than a floating-point instruction. One use of IXFR is in performing an integer multiplication, which, as we noted, must be performed by converting the integers to floating-point, doing a floating-point multiply, and converting the result back to an integer.

The *store floating-point* instructions exist only in standard forms:

```
FST.L    src1(src2), freg
FST.D    src1(src2), freg
FST.Q    src1(src2), freg
```

There is no need for pipelined floating-point stores, since stores can be overlapped in any case, and no one is waiting around for the data to appear. Remember that on the i860 stores are never write allocate, which means that the data cache is affected only if the value is already in the cache. Again this makes sense when dealing with large data arrays. For example, if we are multiplying all elements of a 1000-element floating-point array by a constant, there is no point in flooding the cache with all the results.

Floating-Point Addition

There are two approaches to floating-point addition on the i860. The first is similar to instructions we have encountered on other RISC chips:

```
FADD.SS FR2, FR4, FR6      ; single-precision addition
FADD.DD FR2, FR4, FR6      ; double precision-addition
FSUB.SS FR2, FR4, FR6      ; single precision-subtraction
FSUB.DD FR2, FR4, FR6      ; double precision-subtraction
```

These instructions compute the value FR2 + FR4 or FR2 − FR4 and place the result in FR6 using IEEE 754 semantics, including proper rounding (there is a control register to specify the rounding mode). Like similar instructions on the 387 or the SPARC floating-point coprocessor, these instructions are scoreboard interlocked, so if a subsequent instruction attempts to use FR6 before the result is ready or if another FADD operation is attempted, then the pipeline is held up.

It takes approximately three instructions for the result to be ready, so using FADD, the maximum throughput of floating-point additions is about one every 3 clocks, or about 17 MFLOPS on the 50 MHz processor. This is a far cry from the claimed peak throughput of 100 MFLOPS, so we certainly need some additional mechanisms to explain these claims.

THE FLOATING-POINT ADDITION PIPELINE. In a manner reminiscent of the pipelined floating-point load, there is a second set of floating-point addition instructions:

```
PFADD.SS  FR2, FR4, FR6    ; single-precision addition
PFADD.DD FR2, FR4, FR6     ; double-precision addition
PFSUB.SS  FR2, FR4, FR6    ; single-precision subtraction
PFSUB.DD FR2, FR4, FR6     ; double-precision subtraction
```

The pipelined add and subtract make use of another visible three-stage pipeline. The addition takes place in three stages. When a PFADD instruction is issued, the source inputs (FR2 and FR4 in the above examples) are fed as input operands to the first stage of the pipeline, the pipeline is then advanced, and the result from the third stage of the pipeline, corresponding to the PFADD or PFSUB issued three operations back, is placed in the result register. The pipeline moves only when PFADD or PFSUB operations are given, so it is possible to intersperse other instructions. However, the pipeline is capable of operating at full clock speed, so a PFADD can be issued every clock, obtaining one addition result per clock once the pipeline is started up. This brings us up to 50 MFLOPS, so we are getting closer to the claimed peak performance!

These visible pipelines are a characteristic peculiar to the i860. Although this text has discussed pipelining in the context of several microprocessors, understanding the precise mechanism used to implement the pipeline was not necessary to program those processors. The SPARC, for example, can be thought of for the most part as a synchronous machine. Only if performance and its analysis were of some concern would a programmer have to worry about their concurrency, with the exception of the jump, which is a special case that is not too difficult to deal with. The fact that these machines are executing three or more instructions at a time is generally not observable. Remember that one case in which this concurrency is observable on the SPARC is when an interrupt occurs: Two program counters are necessary to figure out what is going on. But generally, you do not need to know the details of how the pipeline works.

On the i860 the pipelines are very visible and the programmer must keep track of the operations going on. In the case of PFADD, the programmer must be aware that at any one time three additions may be in various stages of completion. The advantage is that, as we saw above, much greater throughput of floating-point operations can be achieved. On the other hand, the additional programming complexity is a little frightening! As with the floating-point load pipeline, typical code has three phases. During the first phase, the pipeline is being loaded up, and the outputs are rubbish. Then the production phase follows, during which operands are loaded and useful results are extracted at the same time. Finally there is a cleanup phase in which the final three results are forced out by feeding in junk input values.

Floating-Point Multiplication

There are two styles of floating-point multiplication, exactly analogous to the addition/subtraction situation. The first set is conventional:

```
FMUL.SS   FR2, FR4, FR6    ; single-precision multiplication
FMUL.DD   FR2, FR4, FR6    ; double-precision multiplication
```

These instructions compute the product FR2 * FR2 and place the result in FR6 using normal IEEE 754 semantics. As with the addition and subtraction case, the result is interlocked in the normal manner. The multiplier and adder units are separate, so a FADD issued between two FMULs is perfectly fine, but an FMUL will wait for completion of a previous FMUL.

THE FLOATING-POINT MULTIPLICATION PIPELINE. In addition to the FMUL instructions, there is a set of floating-point multiply operations that are visibly pipelined as for addition:

```
FMUL.SS   FR2, FR4, FR6    ; single-precision multiplication
FMUL.DD   FR2, FR4, FR6    ; double-precision multiplication
```

The pipelined multiply makes use of yet another visible pipeline (separate from the adder pipeline and the load pipeline). The multiplication takes place in either three stages (for single precision) or two stages (for double precision). Mixing precisions in the pipeline can be hazardous to one's mental health, but Intel does give a complicated set of rules describing what happens (preceded by a header saying "For the adventuresome, the rules for mixing precisions are as follows").

It may seem strange that the double-precision operation takes fewer stages. What is happening here is that the single-precision case can operate at full clock speed, so that products can be pumped out every clock. The double-precision pipeline takes 2 clocks for each move, so the throughput is actually less than in the single-precision case.

Adding and Multiplying at the Same Time

Now, finally, we come to the secret that reveals how Intel can claim a maximum throughput of 100 MFLOPS and 150 MOPS. As we have noted, the addition and multiplication pipelines are quite independent and can potentially advance at the same time. However, they advance only if a PFMUL or PFADD is issued, so using these instructions we cannot operate the two pipelines in parallel.

A separate and extravagantly complex set of instructions comes to the rescue, the so-called *dual operation* instructions. There are four of them:

```
PFAM.P     FR2, FR4, FR6    ; add and multiply
PFSM.P     FR2, FR4, FR6    ; subtract and multiply
PFMAM.P    FR2, FR4, FR6    ; multiply with add
PFMSM.P    FR2, FR4, FR6    ; multiply with subtract
```

The .P in these instructions is either .SS for single-precision, or .DD for double-precision operation. All instructions cause both the addition and multiplication pipelines to be advanced, with the FR6 result being taken from the last stage of the addition pipeline for PFAM and PFSM, and from the last stage of the multiplication pipeline for PFMAM and PFMSM.

This still leaves a bit of a mystery, since the instructions have only two inputs (FR2 and FR4 in the above examples), and obviously to advance two pipelines at once, we need four inputs. Moreover, what happens to the result of the other pipeline? To answer this question, we need a diagram of the connections between the multiplication and addition pipelines (see Figure 11.5).

As we can see from this figure, the output of the adder can be fed in as the *op2* input of the multiplier, and the output of the multiplier can either be fed in as the *op2* input of the adder, or it can be fed into a special register called the T register (for transfer). Furthermore, the T register can serve as the *op1* input for the adder, and either of two special registers KI or KR (the "Konstant" registers) can serve as the *op1* input of the multiplier.

The first source operand of the dual operation instruction (FR2 in the above examples) can either be fed into the KI or KR registers or serve as the *op1* input for either the adder or the multiplier. The second source operand of the dual operation instruction (FR4 in the above examples) can serve as the *op2* input for either the adder or the multiplier.

What a mess! There seem to be endless possibilities for arranging the inputs and outputs of the two pipelines. How on earth does a programmer specify how things are

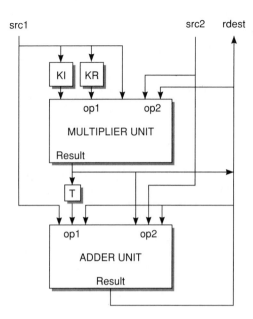

FIGURE 11.5
Data paths connecting the multiply and add pipelines.

to be connected? The answer is that each dual operation instruction contains a field called the DPC (data path control) field that specifies which wires are to be connected. There are 16 (!) separate possibilities, so, taking into account the four instruction types and two precisions, we have 64 different dual operation instructions. The i860 Programmer's Reference Manual contains eight pages of diagrams, four to a page, showing how the connections between the units are hooked up for all DPC settings.

Finally we see how the 100 MFLOPS figure is achieved. Providing that we issue a dual operation instruction on every clock (using single precision—remember that the double-precision multiplication slows down to half speed), we can indeed perform 100 million floating-point operations a second on a 50 MHz processor. However, we should ask whether we can actually find a useful example where such peak speed could be reached. Let's look at just one of the possible dual mode instructions: the PFAM with DPC set to 0011.

The assembly mnemonic for this particular instruction is R2APT.[6] From the appropriate diagram, the data paths for this particular case are as shown in Figure 11.6. The first input to the multiply unit is whatever is in the special KR register. The second operand for the multiply unit is *src2*. The add unit has two operands, one from the T register and the second from the add result. So the add result feeds back into the add

---

[6] Intel has designed a complicated system for relating the data paths to a set of pretty mysterious mnemonics. We won't even *attempt* to describe this system, because it seems diabolically complicated.

input. Does that make sense? When you want the add result to feed back into the add input you must be adding a sequence of numbers. You pump one number into the adder and then three accumulating results go around and around. Now let's try to find a *useful* calculation that can be performed using R2APT. To see that R2APT does have at least one interesting use, consider the problem of computing the dot product of two vectors. Here we are computing

$$\sum_{i=0}^{n} a_i * b_i$$

At each point we want to take two input values, a_i and b_i, multiply them together, and add the result into the accumulating sum. That is exactly the effect of the R2APT instruction, as shown in the preceding diagram. The two operands *src1* and *src2* feed into the multiplier (the source 1 input is delayed one operation because it first goes through the KR register, so you have to stagger the two inputs one off, providing the *src2* operand one operation earlier than its corresponding *src1* operand, adding to the fun). The result of the product feeds into the adder, which circulates the sums around and around. Only at the end of the operation is the output of the adder of interest. Actually, things are a little more complex. Because we have three separate sums cycling around in the adder pipeline, the initialization has to load three zeros to start with, and the cleanup will have to add the three separately accumulated sums to get the final result.

The program to calculate a dot product is too complicated to write out in full here, and in general any code using the dual operation instructions is extremely complicated and should not be attempted by the faint of heart.

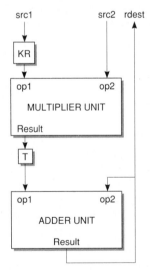

FIGURE 11.6
The data paths for the R2APT instruction.

One question that immediately arises is: How on earth is a compiler expected to generate such complicated code and take advantage of these instructions? There are three possible styles of compilers for this chip. The first is to simply ignore the pipelined floating-point instructions altogether. With this approach, the performance will still be quite reasonable compared with that of other microprocessors with more conventional floating-point instruction sets, but the special capabilities of the i860 would be ignored. Some of these capabilities could be provided by allowing the programmer to make explicit calls on hand-coded routines such as matrix multiplication, but this would require changes to source programs.

In the second approach, conventional vectorizing technology is applied. The compiler analyzes loops to discover standard operations such as dot product and other simple vector operations and then makes calls to a library of carefully coded assembly language routines to perform these operations, using efficient sequences of dual operation instructions where appropriate. On more conventional vector processors, such operations correspond to single vector instructions, and a lot of work has been done in understanding how to analyze programs to extract these vector operations. This approach still does not take full advantage of the processor, since, given that the different dual operation instructions can be mixed together in various sequences, there are literally thousands of possible operations.

The third approach is have a compiler analyze the source program in terms of the available dual operation instructions and generates an optimal sequence for the particular loop coded in the source program. This is an extraordinarily difficult task. It will be interesting to see whether anyone manages to achieve this goal anytime soon.

By exposing the pipelines, the i860 provides an extraordinarily flexible and powerful environment. Really what we have here is a kit for building your own set of vector and matrix instructions, rather than being provided with a limited set of fixed operations as on other typical vector machines. Whether software can manage to take full advantage of this flexibility remains to be seen.

Using Dual Instruction Mode

Returning to the example of the dot product, there is an important additional issue that needs to be addressed. As long as the operands are all in registers, then it is indeed possible to issue a series of R2APT instructions and (for a short moment) compute at the full 100 MFLOP rate. A more realistic example, however, involves vectors that are in memory. This means that loads must be interspersed, and one would expect this to slow down operation.

This is where the dual instruction mode plays an important role. By setting the D bit of the EPSR, the processor is placed in dual instruction mode. As one might expect on a pipelined machine, the effect of setting the D bit is delayed, so turning it on causes the dual instruction mode to be entered 1 clock later, and turning it off similarly causes the single instruction mode to be resumed 1 clock later.

In dual instruction mode, the i860 picks up 64 bits from the instruction stream at a time (remember that the data paths are all 64 bits in this processor). The 32 low-order bits must contain an integer core instruction, and the 32 high-order bits must contain a floating-point instruction. Both of these instructions are executed in the *same* clock cycle. This means that the processor is executing two instructions on each clock, allowing peak performance of 100 MIPS, and given that the floating-point instruction can be a dual operation instruction, we can do *three* operations on each clock. Finally we see how Intel is able to claim 150 MOPS peak throughput.

Now we can also understand why it is so important that a floating-point load should be regarded as an integer core operation rather than a floating-point operation. This classification means that we can execute floating-point load operations in parallel with floating-point calculations. Well, of course, this is exactly what we need for coputations like the dot product. If both vectors are in the cache, then we can issue FLD.D instructions to load two values at a time (enough for the dot product case) or FLD.Q instructions to load four single-precision values at a time (or two double-precision values). If the vectors are too long to be in the cache, then it will be better to issue PFL.D instructions and use the floating-point load pipeline. In the single-precision case, we can still load the necessary two values on each cycle using PFLD.D.

Taking advantage of the dual instruction mode in conjunction with dual operation modes thus allows certain calculations to reach the peak performance claimed, although the corresponding code is enormously complicated. How often can we expect to reach peak performance? This is very application-dependent. For certain applications, the calculations are repetitive and stylized and correspond exactly to "lucky" cases that can operate close to peak performance. Other applications may not easily be able to take advantage of the remarkable parallelism and may show performance no better than a more conventional machine.

The same kind of range of performance is common with vector processing machines such as the Cray. As time goes on, continued research into better compiling techniques and better algorithms improves the situation. Sometimes you prefer to use an algorithm that seems less efficient in that it executes more operations but is in practice faster because it can better take advantage of the parallel operation. Undoubtedly, full utilization of the i860 will require the development of algorithms specialized to the available instruction set on this processor.

It is fascinating to compare the performance of the i860 processor with big, expensive vector machines such as the Cray and the ETA. Assuming that peak performance can be reached in both cases, it seems hard to believe that the big machines are worth paying $20 million or so for, given that a single i860 chip, which probably will cost on the order of $500, can execute at a significant fraction of the mainframe's capability. It remains to be seen if hardware and software systems can be put together that realize this potential. Certainly, makers of the big machines must be watching these developments with interest.[7]

---

[7] ETA, one of the two remaining supercomputer manufacturers in the United States, suddenly closed their doors in May of 1989 without warning, firing everyone. It is certainly not the case that the i860 specifically caused this closedown, but the general phenomenon of the desktop computers with ever more powerful floating-point performance has had a significant effect on the market for supercomputers.

Floating-Point Division

An unusual aspect of the i860 is that there is no floating-point division instruction. On some of the high-end IBM 370s there is no divide for some of the higher-precision formats, but since you have a 64-bit precision divide you can do double-precision division by multiple applications of the single-precision division. On the i860 there is no floating-point divide at all.

There is, however, an instruction called *floating-point reciprocal* (FRCP.P). The instructions

```
FRCP.SS    FR2, FR4          ; single-precision
FRCP.DD    FR2, FR4          ; double-precision
```

set FR4 to approximately 1/FR2. How approximately? Only 8 bits of the mantissa can be relied on to be correct. So it is an extremely crude instruction, but it delivers its result in 1 clock. Why is this helpful for division? Well, if we had an *accurate* reciprocal, we could do a division by multiplying by this reciprocal:

$$\frac{a}{b} = a \times \frac{1}{b}$$

Let's look at how we can use this idea to do a division on the i860. We have available an extremely inaccurate reciprocal, and we want a very accurate reciprocal. Generally the Newton-Raphson algorithm allows us to compute a function by successive approximations if the inverse of the function is very fast to compute. Since the inverse of division is multiplication, Newton-Raphson is appropriate. The formula looks like this:

$$G_{new} = G_{old} \, (2 - G_{old} * Y)$$

where G_{old} is a starting approximation to the reciprocal of Y and G_{new} is a better approximation. For example, suppose we are computing the reciprocal of 10 and our intial estimate is 0.11,

$$G_{old} = 0.11$$
$$G_{new} = 0.11 \, (2 - 0.11 * 10) = 0.099$$
$$G_{new} = 0.099 \, (2 - 0.099 * 10) = 0.09999$$

At each stage, the number of bits of accuracy doubles. We are starting with an approximation that is 8 bits accurate. For the 32-bit case, two iterations will give us (approximately) 32-bit accuracy. An iteration involves two multiplies and a subtract, which are all operations that can be done quickly. So it really takes seven operations to do a divide. We need one reciprocal, and each iteration takes two multiplies and one subtract.

If you need the result and have nothing else to do meanwhile, this approach takes 22 clocks to do a floating-point divide, but you can generally do better than that because the number of instructions is only 8, so 22–8 delay slots are available for doing something else while you are doing the divide. That is still very fast compared to other floating-point processors. For the 64-bit case, three iterations are required.

This approach seems complex, but if speed is important it is much faster than doing a divide directly. It is interesting to note that the Cray supercomputers use a similar approach. However, there is a black lining to this silver cloud.

Even if a completely accurate reciprocal is available, the value obtained in this manner can be 1 bit off in certain cases. This is true even if the multiplication rounds properly. The error is not simply a matter of not obeying the requirements of IEEE 754 rounding; you can get a wrong result even when proper rounding is used at each step. Characterizing exactly what error can occur is tricky, and numerical analysts are not amused by this transformation. Basically this approach is fine if your attitude toward floating-point is *hope for the best*. But it is very annoying to a numerical analyst who depends upon an exact understanding of the rounding semantics. The i860 thus has only a very thin claim to actually supporting the IEEE floating-point standard.

What we have here is an interesting conflict between two points of view. The casual "hope for the best" numerical coders are quite happy with approximate results, especially when using 64-bit precision, and are delighted by the high speed. The numerical analysts regard getting wrong answers fast as a terrible way to do business. By providing the fast reciprocal and leaving out divide, the i860 puts itself into the same camp as Cray, probably figuring that most numerical types would love to have a Cray on their desks, and what is good enough for a $7 million Cray should be good enough for a superchip costing a few hundred dollars! After all, Crays seem to sell very well considering their cost, and many useful calculations are done on them, so why pay too much attention in this case to the IEEE floating-point standard?

How difficult is it to do an absolutely accurate IEEE divide if it is not in the hardware? There are cases in which it can be shown that double precision is really required. That means that computing the single-precision divide is no problem, because it is possible to use double-precision operations but getting the double-precision 64-bit result will require 128-bit arithmetic, which is not there and which therefore needs to be concocted in software. Conclusion: It is difficult and the resulting code would be miserably slow.

Intel will undoubtedly provide fully compatible IEEE division routines in their libraries of code for the i860 and can therefore claim that they conform to the standard. However, using these software routines would be painful from an efficiency point of view, especially in the double-precision case.

On the other hand, division is not that common in floating-point code compared to addition, subtraction, and multiplication, so the effect of a slow floating-point divide is not as severe as one might expect. For example, computation of elementary functions typically involves several additions and multiplications to evaluate a power series, but at most one division is involved when the result is expressed as the quotient of two power series, and often such calculations can be done using no divisions at all.

Floating-Point Square Root

There is no square root instruction, but there is a set of *floating-point reciprocal square root* (FRSQR.P) instructions:

```
FRSQR.SS FR2, FR4          ; single-precision
FRSQR.DD FR2, FR4          ; double-precision
```

These instructions compute the very approximate value $1/\sqrt{src2}$, accurate only to 8 bits as with the floating-point reciprocal. You use that to kick off a Newton-Raphson iteration for the square root.

When using Newton-Raphson to compute a square root, you can, of course, start off with any value. If you want the square root of 4 you can start with 1, but the Newton-Raphson algorithm is slow in approaching its result until you get pretty close. The FRSQR instruction provides you with a starting point that allows you to get a 32-bit result with only two iterations and a 64-bit result with three iterations. This means that the time to compute a square root is just about the same as the divide, because the Newton-Raphson algorithm for square root is no more complicated than that for division.

IEEE 754 Compatibility

As we have seen, the basic addition, subtraction, and multiplication operations, as well as the basic floating-point formats, conform to the IEEE standard and thus provide a base for a full implementation of IEEE 754. The division is an embarrassment, but it certainly is possible to write software routines that provide IEEE division.

One other area to consider is the handling of denormals. Denormals, if you recall from Chapter 5, result when there is a minimum exponent and several leading 0s in the mantissa. It is a less accurate result, but it avoids the sudden underflow near zero. The IEEE standard requires that denormal values be handled in this manner.

The i860 will neither generate denormals nor handle them on input. But it gives a handle for implementing the IEEE standard properly. There are two modes for handling underflow. One is flush to zero, which is totally incompatible with IEEE (but if it is good enough for the Cray, it must be good enough for the i860!) The other mode traps on an underflow without changing the operand values. You get a trap indicating the instruction that could not compute the value. You can have a software routine at that point that looks at the value and says, "Oh yes. This should really be a denormal." You then generate in software the appropriate denormal value and give that as the result. Finally control returns from the trap routine to continue execution (this is one of the cases in which you would use the *kill next floating-point bit* to avoid reexecuting the troublesome instruction).

When you do further computations with that denormal value, the other thing that the floating-point unit of the i860 does is to trap when it sees a denormal. That trap routine can access the operands and conclude that the operands are denormals and then do in software what the IEEE standard requires. Generating the result might yield a normalized result and move the processor back into fast execution mode, or the result might continue to be a denormal and keep the processor in this slow mode.

How often do denormals occur in computations and how acceptable is this? Generally denormals are rare. The one disadvantage of this approach is that you get some nasty discontinuities in timing. You might have one run of a program in which no denormals are generated, and then in the next run with only slightly different input data the program will generate many denormals and slow down substantially.

The i860 compromises in order to maintain its very fast speed. To handle denormals usually requires an extra clock because you have to normalize things in advance using an extended exponent. That is what the Intel 387 does. If a load is made of a denormal from memory, it prenormalizes it using an extended exponent. That would add an extra stage to the floating-point pipeline.

It is bad enough that the floating-point add pipeline is three stages (it could conceivably be only two). The third stage of the floating-point add pipeline is there to deal with the second rounding that can occur in floating-point after a renormalization, so we are already paying a price for proper rounding, and that is a sufficient concession to the IEEE standard.[8]

THE i860 GRAPHICS UNIT

If you already feel overwhelmed by the complexity of the i860, we are afraid there is no rest for the weary! We still have not visited the graphics instructions. Remember that the chip was first designed as a graphics coprocessor, so it is not surprising that there are specialized graphics operations, and given what we have already seen on the i860, it is no surprise that these operations are at the same time extraordinarily powerful and extremely complex.

First we note that there are (relatively simple) instructions that do 32- and 64-bit integer adds in the floating-point registers. They are floating-point instructions, so they can be combined with core instructions. That means that you can be doing a pipelined floating-point load together with these 32- and 64-bit additions. These instructions do not have to be used in conjunction with graphics, but they are particularly intended to be used in that way. They do not set the condition codes; they are just straight adds. They do give you a 64-bit add that can, of course, be used for any purpose.

Graphics Pixel Data Type

An unusual data type that is supported on the i860 is the pixel. There are three different formats for pixel data, controlled by the *pixel size* (PS) field in thr PSR, which specifies a pixel size of 8, 16, or 32 bits.

We can assume that this kind of processor is going to be used only on high-end graphics devices where there are, at the very least, 8 bits per pixel. In fact, 8 bits is a very small format and is probably not very useful on this machine. A more reasonable pixel format for a machine of this power would be a 32-bit pixel, with an 8-bit intensity for each of the three primary colors. That gives a total of 2^{24} colors, since each color can be at any of 256 intensities. The 8 bits that are left over can be used for such special effects as blinking, texture, and other effects that can be used to modify an image.

---

[8] The CRAY does not round properly, so it is even worse than the i860 from a numerical analyst's point of view.

A 16-bit pixel format is much more crowded. The 16-bit format allocates 6 bits for red, 6 bits for green, and 4 bits for blue—no extra bits are available. The 8-bit pixel format simply selects the intensity and possibly some color information. In 8-bit format, the processor does not specify the division of the fields, which is up to the implementor of the graphics system. You might, for instance, use 4 bits for the color and 4 bits for the intensity.

The field in the program state register that controls pixel size can be set in either supervisor state or problem state. This field selects one of three possible pixel formats to be used. All the instructions that are specifically intended to be used for graphics behave differently depending upon how PS is set. The pixel mask, another graphics-related field in the PSR, is also accessible in problem state and has a special use in some of the graphics instructions.

Graphics Instructions

Among the more complex instructions are graphics operations for handling Z-Buffer Checks. To understand these instructions, we need to know a little about a standard approach to solving what is known as the *hidden line* problem. Imagine a screen composed of pixels, and for each pixel, we have the x, y and z coordinates of the point in 3-space, where x and y correspond to the position on the screen of the two-dimensional representation, and the z value is the depth, so that a small value for z means that the point is closer to the viwer.

Suppose that a new feature is painted on the scene at some distance. For each of the related pixels, the computation we want to do is: Is the new pixel that was just computed nearer to the viewer than the current pixel on the screen, i.e. is its z coordinate less than that of the currently visible point? If it is, then we want to replace the pixel and then change the entry in the array of z coordinate values to contain the new, nearer, value. This is a very simple calculation which simply involves comparing the new z coordinate with the current value, and replacing it with the minimum of the two values. However, this very simple calculation needs to be repeated an enormous number of

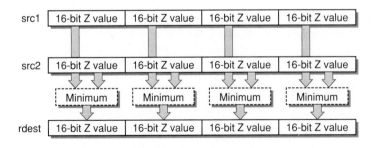

FIGURE 11.7
The effect of the FZCHK instruction.

times, given that a graphics screen can easily contain millions of pixels. What the FZCHK instruction does is to do this very fast. The form of the instruction is

FZCHKS *src1, src2, rdest*

where each of the operands is a 64-bit word consisting of four separate 16-bit values. The instruction compares those four separate values and generates as output a 64-bit value where each 16-bit component contains the minimum of the two corresponding input values (see Figure 11.7).

In addition to the output of the minimum values, the pixel mask in the system registers records whether or not a new minimum value replaced the original value in each case. The pixel mask is treated in the following way: It is first shifted left 4 bits. The 4 bits at the right are then set to indicate whether the new distance updated the current distance. So a 0 means that the old distance is good enough, and a 1 means that the new distance should be made the current distance.

There is a related instruction called *pixel store* (PST) in the set of core instructions that takes however many pixels fit into 64 bits (either 2 or 4) and updates a target 64 bits depending upon how the bits in the pixel mask were set by a previous FZCHKS instruction. FZCHKS is categorized as a floating-point instruction for the purpose of dual instruction mode, and PST is categorized as a core integer instruction. This means that in dual instruction mode, one can approach a peak performance in which 4 pixels are processed on every clock cycle, giving a maximum throughput of 200 million pixels per second on a 50 MHz processor. Of course, as with floating-point, it is rarely possible to achieve this peak performance.

To add to the fun, there is an instruction PFZCHKS. As you can probably guess by now, the initial P means that the instruction operates with a visible pipeline, so that the output corresponds to the inputs from a previous instruction. Sure enough, PFZCHKS operates using yet another pipeline, the graphics pipeline, and without going into gory details we can just say that the principles for manipulating this pipeline are similar to those for the floating-point pipelines.

There are a number of other complex graphics instructions, but this chapter is getting long enough, so we will not try to describe them in detail. The FZCHKL and PFZCHKL instructions are 32-bit versions of the Z-buffer check, where Z values are kept in 32 bits, allowing greater precision at the expense of slower throughput. The FADDP instruction allows interpolation of pixel intensity values—useful if you want to compute a smooth shading of an area from one intensity to another. As usual for these types of instructions, there is a pipelined version, PFADDP. Finally, there are two instructions, FADDZ and PFADDZ that are used to interpolate z values for use in the Z-buffer check instructions.

The graphics instructions are, of course, highly specialized. They are in a sense ultimate examples of complex instructions. Are such complex instructions justified? The answer is yes only if there are applications that spend a significant amount of time performing these operations, and graphics applications do precisely that.

For many other applications, these instructions will *never* be used. On the other hand, if you are in the graphics business, then the special capabilities of the i860 here are quite remarkable. In terms of operations per second, it is fair to consider that a PFZCHK combined with a PST performs up to eight operations per clock (four minimum operations, together with four conditional pixel store operations), giving a peak throughput of 400 million operations per second, or nearly half a GigaMOP—incredibly high performance for a single chip! In comparing this performance with typical RISC and CISC chips we have seen, each of these operations actually corresponds to a sequence of several instructions, so to get comparable performance one would need clock speeds approaching 1000 MHz on chips such as the 386 or the SPARC, clearly way beyond currently imaginable technology.

One caution is that complex operations are appropriate only if they are the *right* operations. Apparently Intel feels that some standard algorithms, such as the Z-Buffer approach, are sufficiently well established that they can be put into silicon. The computational intensity that is required for high-end CAD/CAM displays is extremely high. Even at the PACMAN end of things, some arcade games have enormous processing power. One arcade game requires 100 MFLOPS of graphics power on board because it is doing elaborate three-dimensional graphics. The only way to achieve this kind of throughput is with highly specialized hardware.

EXCEPTIONS

Describing the basic approach to exception handling on the i860 is very simple. On most machines there is some sort of interrupt priorities. On the i860, all traps and all interrupts branch to a fixed location in memory. There is only a pin to signal an external interrupt. The idea behind this is that there will be some other support chip external to the i860 that will implement multiple levels of priority or whatever an engineer wants. On this chip there is nothing more than a trap that causes control to go to location FFFFFF00. Of course, with paging, that address could be mapped anywhere. There is one trap routine that has to figure out what is going on when the trap occurs.

There are bits scattered around in the system registers that will give a clue as to what kind of trap has occurred. For instance, if there is a hardware interrupt, there is a bit specifying that the hardware interrupt has occurred. You can imagine that when the trap routine gets control, it asks, "What's going on? Was that a hardware interrupt?" Yes. So it branches to part of the code that handles hardware interrupts.

The part that handles the hardware interrupt interrogates the interrupt controlling device on the bus and asks, "Hey. What's going on with this interrupt?" The interrupt chip replies, "I just received a level 3 interrupt from the XYZ device, and you need to handle that interrupt appropriately." If, on the other hand, it was not a hardware interrupt, then the processor needs to decide if it was an overflow trap or a floating-point underflow trap. Gradually it can disambiguate all possible trap conditions.

One special case of a trap is caused by executing a TRAP instruction. This is the conventional way for a program in problem state to pass control to the operating system. Like any other trap, this passes control in supervisor state to the common exception routine, which must sort this case out from all the other possibilities.

Context Switching

Suppose that the exception routine decides that a context switch should be performed (perhaps, for example, the processor is time slicing, and a timer interrupt is expected to cause switch to another task). The task of context switching is made much more difficult on the i860 by the presence of the visible pipelines. Saving and restoring the registers is no big deal, but the pipelines are another matter, because we need to know the contents of each stage of the pipeline There may be three partial results from additions, multiplications as well as three floating-point loads, as well as some graphics operations going on.

All of this has to be saved when the task is removed, and restored again when the task is made active again, so that the executing program sees the pipelines in exactly the state they were left at the point of the exception.

To do this, the exception routine has to "fake out" the pipelines so that they appear to contain the same data. For example, to save the multiply pipeline you do a few bogus multiplies to cough out the result remembering whether they caused exceptions. When you come back to restore the context you feed some bogus multiplications in (multiplying by 1.0) so that the results will come out again in the order the program expects. If exceptions occurred in the original multiplications, then the bogus multiplications fed in must duplicate these exceptions. The code for flushing out the pipelines and then reassembling them for the other process is very unpleasant. That is one of the places that shows that the i860 was intended to be a specialized processor. Presumably context switches are not a crucial factor in the context of specialized graphics processing, where the processor is clearly dedicated to a single graphics display, but in general real-time environments, the complexity of the context switch would be a significant liability.

PROGRAMMING MODEL

There is an interesting section at the end of the i860 Programmer's Reference Manual called "Programming Model". It is a little unusual to find this in a programming reference manual because nothing said in this section has anything at all to do with the hardware. What it does is specify a set of software conventions and request that programmers adhere to these conventions if they want their programs to be compatible with Intel compilers.

Quite often architectures come with that kind of understanding. Anyone who has worked on an IBM 370, for instance, knows that there is nothing in the hardware that says you do BALR 14,15 to get to a subroutine, but the entire software world of the 370 depends upon that software convention. Sometimes the success of an architecture depends upon whether you can come up with uniformly followed software standards.

This is an interesting attempt by Intel to immediately establish the software standards. The sort of thing it specifies is that registers 16 through 27 are supposed to be used for parameters, that the stack pointer is always register 2, and that the frame pointer is always register 3.

That whole section is completely devoted to software standards. Every now and then, however, it says something like, "The dividing point between locals and parameters is not yet firm. For the purposes of this diagram it has been chosen to be 8. Note that this convention remains tentative and may be changed." So Intel hasn't quite got everything worked out yet!

CONCLUSION

The i860 is a powerful chip with a novel design. For specialized operations for which it is specifically intended, in particular for graphics algorithms corresponding to its built-in graphics instructions, it has no equal in terms of performance, although the graphics instructions are complex and their effective use is not a trivial task.

When it comes to floating-point, the potential peak throughput is very impressive. However, here again the exposed pipelines of the instructions which are used to achieve this throughput introduce an unusual level of complexity into the code. It is doubtful whether a standard general purpose compiler could even begin to take advantage of these features, so for some time to come, the full advantage of the architecture will only be available to hand-written assembly language routines.

The i860 takes RISC architectures to a new level of complexity. No one would describe the i860 instruction set as simple or reduced. Is it fair to call the i860 a RISC architecture? This question gets harder to answer as chips like the i860 blur the distinction. On the one hand, the broad instruction set with its highly specialized graphics instructions seems to be the antithesis of RISC design philosophy. On the other hand, may other aspects of the design such as large number of registers, uniform instruction sets and pipelined implementation are reminiscent of RISC design principles. Another of these principles is visible concurrency, and this is a feature which the i860 has to an almost overwhelming extent—no other processor we look at reveals the inner workings of its overlapped pipelines to the extent that the i860 does.

Depending on its availability and price, the i860 should be an attractive component in many high performance systems. One early use of this chip is in building very high performance laser printers, where of course the graphics capabilities are useful in constructing the bit maps for laser output. Machines have also been announced, though not shipped in quantity as of the end of 1989, in which an i860 is paired with a 486. Such dual processor machines seem attractive for a wide range of applications, and as we have noted, the two processors are happy to live together and share page tables. The i860 in such a configuration can be used for high performance floating-point and graphics tasks, and the 486 provides compatibility with existing PC applications.

CHAPTER

12

THE IBM RISC CHIPS

This chapter describes the IBM RISC chips. As we discussed in Chapter 8, the IBM 801 project was one of the first research efforts whose explicit goal was to design an architecture that could be described as being RISC. Although the 801 has not been of much commercial significance—the only product in which it is used is the input/output channel of the 3090 mainframe—the research work has had a significant influence on the design of other RISC chips, including the subsequent IBM RISC processors. In particular, rumors of its design contributed to the beginnings of both the Stanford MIPS and Berkeley RISC projects.

There are two other IBM RISC architectures that have made their way into products. The first, called the ROMP, is an adaptation of the earlier version of the 801. It was used in the IBM RT, which was IBM's first entry into the scientific workstation market. This architecture was somewhat of a disappointment from both a technical and a marketing point of view. However, the appearance of the RT had a significant impact on the marketplace since it helped to establish and legitimize the RISC approach. As is often the case in the computer field, when IBM follows a certain design approach, the industry generally follows its lead. When a small company introduces a new design approach that has *not* been given the IBM stamp of approval, both users and investors are more nervous about making commitments.

Just about the time this book is scheduled to appear, IBM is expected to release a new series of scientific workstations based on a completely new RISC architecture. The basic elements of this architecture were first made public in October 1989 at the IEEE International Conference on Computer Design in Boston. The official designation given to this architecture is "IBM Second Generation RISC." Since this is a rather awkward phrase, we will instead use what has been reported in the trade press as the code name for this architecture, namely, RIOS. It is impossible to know if this is the final name that will be used—it may not even *be* the official IBM code name. In any case, IBM has a history of changing code names frequently.[1]

The RIOS design is so completely new that it bears only superficial resemblance to its 801 ancestors. As we will see, it combines features of a number of the other chips we have previously looked at, including the i860, but it is quite distinct in its design approach from any of these chips and is in many respects the most unusual RISC design. Unlike the ROMP, it seems probable that the RIOS *will* play an important technical role in the developing RISC marketplace—if RIOS chips can be developed with reasonably high clock speeds their performance should be very impressive.

THE IBM ROMP

The first commercial IBM RISC processor appeared in the RT work station. There is an interesting history behind this development, which we will trace in this section.

Originally, IBM was interested in producing a fancy word processor which would be a follow-on to the Display Writer product, which was IBM's main product in the dedicated word processing market—before the advent of personal computers, this was an important office automation market. For various reasons, possibly including the desire to make sure that the design was non-clonable, IBM decided to use a proprietary architecture for this purpose. Since the 801 designs were available, the approach taken was to modify the 801 design for use in this dedicated word processing station. As we have discussed in chapter 8, there were two versions of the 801, the original 16-register design with 16- and 32-bit instructions, and the newer 32-register design with only 32-bit instructions. Because of the timing of the decision, and possibly because memory was still expensive, so that the relatively more compact code of the earlier design was desirable, this earlier design was chosen as the basis for the new product.

The only significant modification made to the design was to change the register size from 24 to 32 bits. No attempt was made to implement floating-point, since word processing certainly does not require this. However, a fairly sophisticated virtual memory system was added. As we discussed in chapter 8, the early 801 did not address the issue of implementing virtual memory page faults efficiently in the pipeline, so one of the consequences of this decision was that the pipeline was significantly slowed down by the addition of virtual memory, resulting in slow performance by RISC standards.

---

[1] The original code name for the ROMP chip was ALAMO. The trade press reports that the original code name for the RIOS chip was SAN JACINTO, which is where the American forces regrouped for the counterattack after the disaster of El Alamo.

More significantly, the attempt to implement the early 801 in ECL had run into considerable difficulties, and in any case speed was not a significant consideration in the word processing product. Consequently the initial implementation of the ROMP employed a conventional CISC approach, including the heavy use of micro-code, in a very slow (6MHz) CMOS implementation. By the standards of other RISC chips we have looked at, the resulting performance is disappointing—the original ROMP did not even compare well with contemporary CISC chips. Nevertheless, for the intended purpose of word processing, this slow performance was not a matter for concern.

Some months before the new word processor was to be released, IBM suddenly had a change of viewpoint, and decided that it was urgent to release a scientific work station to compete with Sun and other work station vendors, who were making significant gains in what was perceived to be an important marketplace.

Rather than design a new product from scratch, someone at IBM came up with the idea of converting the ROMP-based word processor into a scientific work station. After all, it was a 32-bit based system with a large virtual memory, and most of the details had already been worked out, allowing a much reduced to-market time.

One small detail which had *not* been worked out was the need for floating-point capabilities. There was no time to redesign the processor to properly integrate floating-point, so instead a floating-point processor was glued on, using memory mapped input/output for its control, in a manner similar to what we described in chapter 5 for the Weitek chipset on the 386. The registers of the floating point coprocessor are simply addressed as special memory locations, and the floating-point operations are triggered by issuing memory accesses to special addresses—the bits of the address actually function as the opcode for the desired floating-point operation.

The trouble with this approach is that, as we have seen in RISC designs, absolute memory references are not very convenient. In particular, it is not possible to address one of these floating-point pseudo-memory locations using a single ROMP instruction. Consequently, typical ROMP floating-point operations require two instructions. In an environment where floating-point performance is critical, this is a significant liability. Furthermore, the generally poor performance of the ROMP for non floating-point operations, resulting from the microcoded implementation and the slow clock speed, was not corrected.

The result was a machine which was marketed as a high-performance, RISC-based scientific workstation, but its performance did not live up to these claims. Although the architecture had some RISCy flavor, including the delay slots on the jumps, the ROMP really cannot be said to be a RISC implementation in any real sense of the word.

The RT was by any reasonable judgment a commercial failure. Although subsequent implementations of the ROMP improved the performance by a significant factor (there was a long way to go!), the fundamental problems, including the small register set, the unfortunate instruction format, and the failure to properly integrate floating-point, were incurable, and the successive versions of the RT have never competed successfully against workstations from Sun based on the 68020, let alone the new RISC based workstations from other vendors.

The IBM strategy of using the ROMP to get a foot in the door in the workstation market was unsuccessful since the price performance of the RT was never sufficiently attractive. There were some interesting architectural features in the design—in particular, the virtual memory management and locking features were novel. This particular aspect of the ROMP has been adopted and extended in the new IBM RISC architecture, so we will look at it in detail in that connection.

As we have noted before, the primary effect of the ROMP was to help legitimize the RISC approach. Not till the introduction of the second generation RISC architecture has IBM produced a product which matches up to the expectations of RISC technology.

THE IBM RIOS ARCHITECTURE

The IBM RIOS is a completely new design. There is clear input from the second 801 design in terms of instruction formats, and the instruction set for integer and logical operations, but, as we will see, the overall structure is completely different from the 801, and from any of the other RISC chips we have looked at. The general structure of the RIOS architecture is shown in Figure 12.1. The shaded boxes indicate the separate chips of this multichip system. As shown, the main processing elements require four separate chips: the branch unit, the arithmetic-logical unit, the floating-point unit, and the I/O processor. In addition, there is a data cache composed of four separate chips.

In a multichip implementation of a microprocessor, it often makes sense to regard one of the chips as the main processor, and the other chips (such as the MMU and floating-point coprocessor) as auxiliary support chips. In the RIOS architecture, the logical control is distributed, so we cannot identify any single chip as *the* processor chip. Although there is no requirement that the RIOS be implemented on several chips, the architecture has been designed with the understanding that the chip-to-chip communication will be slow. By heavy use of buffering and queueing of data flowing from chip to chip, the effect of these slow communication paths is minimized.

Each of the chips is quite complex. The total number of transistors not including the data cache and the I/O support chips is over 1.7 million, almost half again as many as the i860 (and the i860 count *includes* its data cache). The four chips of the data cache add another 4.5 million transistors to this count. This is by no means a stripped down design that is restricted to simple functionality. Like the i860, it is a complex design with a complex instruction set. Whether it deserves to be called a RISC processor is an interesting debate that we shall return to later. The IBM designers have sometimes referred to this architecture as "Post-RISC" to emphasize the difference in approach between the RIOS and more conventional RISC chips.

The Branch Unit

The branch unit is part of the same chip as the instruction cache and is thus intimately connected to this cache. The path between the cache and the branch unit is 128 bits wide, which means that four instructions can be fetched from the cache in a single clock. Also on this same chip is a small register set consisting of six 32-bit registers:

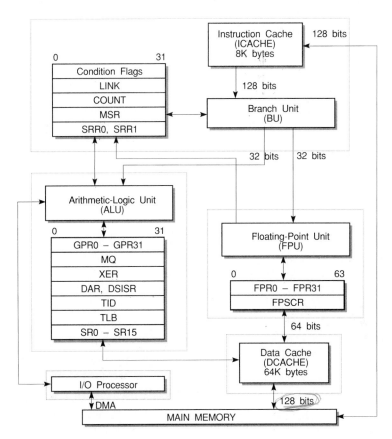

FIGURE 12.1
The RIOS architecture.

- The *condition flags* register is a 32-bit register divided into eight fields of 4 bits each. Each field can be used to store the result of a comparison.
- The LINK register is a 32-bit register used to hold a procedure's return address.
- The COUNT register is a 32-bit register used to control loops.
- The *machine state register* (MSR) contains the system status flags, including a bit that indicates whether the processor is running in supervisor or problem state.
- The SRR0 and SRR1 registers are used to save the machine state on an interrupt. As we have seen on other RISC processors, saving the machine state using on-chip registers rather than main memory improves interrupt response time.

These registers are the ones that are most directly concerned with branch instructions, which is why they are located in the branch unit. As we can see from the diagram, there is also a path from the ALU to these registers (to read or write their contents), and one from the FPU (to set condition codes).

The branch unit acts as a scheduler and coordinator for the entire system. It loads instructions as fast as possible and divides them into four categories for processing:

- Branch Instructions. These are processed entirely within the branch unit. In the case of unconditional branches, the branch address is interpreted by the BU to determine where subsequent instructions should be fetched from. Note that there are no delay slots, so instructions following an unconditional branch, or the instructions for a conditional branch path not taken, are simply discarded. Conditional branches test a specified bit in the condition flags register or use the COUNT register for loop control.

- Condition Flags Instructions. A complete set of logical instructions is provided for operating on condition flags. For example, a given flag bit can be set to the exclusive OR of two other specified flag bits. These instructions are also handled entirely within the branch unit.

- Arithmetic and Logical Instructions. These include all the usual load, store, arithmetic, and logical instructions for operating on integer or fixed-point values (the ALU is also called the fixed-point unit). These instructions are queued for processing by the ALU. The branch unit feeds the ALU with a continuous stream of instructions that can be executed at full (1 clock per instruction) speed. Note that the stream never contains any branch instructions, since all branch instructions have been filtered out and processed by the branch unit.

- Floating-Point Instructions. These include a complete set of floating-point operations that use the floating-point register set. They are queued up for processing by the FPU. Again, no branch instructions appear in this stream.

Under ideal conditions, four instructions can be processed on each clock cycle, one in each category, giving a peak instruction rate of four times the clock rate. This can only be achieved if there are no interlocks, if the distribution of instructions in the instruction stream is reasonable, and if all instructions and data can be accessed without cache misses. Note that the distribution only needs to be reasonably even—it is not necessary to carefully partition the stream so that the four types of instructions alternate, since both the ALU and the FPU have a 12-instruction queue to smooth out the supply rate.

This approach presents an interesting contrast with that of the Intel i860, which also allows for peak instruction execution rates exceeding 1 clock per instruction. The i860 achieves these high rates by requiring the programmer to arrange instructions in pairs. The i860 essentially switches into a *very long instruction word* (VLIW) mode, where instructions are 64 bits long. On the RIOS, the branch unit provides the same kind of functionality, but does it on the fly, without requiring any special arrangement of instructions in the input stream.

If the instructions are arranged poorly—for example, 100 floating-point instructions followed by 100 fixed-point instructions—the peak instruction rate will be reduced to 1 clock per instruction. If the branch unit is given a more favorable mix, it can keep the ALU and FPU busy, while processing branch instructions and condition flag instructions in parallel.

The degree of parallelism is thus flexible and depends solely on the pattern of instructions in the input stream. This approach has been called *variable-length* VLIW, and its great advantage is that the correctness of the instruction stream can be determined independently of scheduling instructions. Naive code, which would work in a simple single-thread non-pipelined processor, will have exactly the same functional effect on the RIOS architecture. The view that the scheduling done by a compiler should be relied on for efficiency and throughput, but *not* for correctness, is implemented in its purest form in this chip—we do not even have to worry about filling branch slots.

The Arithmetic-Logic Unit.

The ALU handles all computational instructions except for floating-point operations. A full set of arithmetic and logical instructions is provided, with the commonly used RISC three-address format, where there are usually two input registers and one output register. The following registers are on the same chip as the ALU (they are effectively part of this unit):

- GPR0 through GPR31 are thirty-two 32-bit general-purpose registers, used for all arithmetic, addressing, and logical operations. Unlike many other RISC processors, GPR0 is not wired to zero and can be used to hold values in computations. However, GPR0 cannot be used as a base or index register. Specifying GPR0 in a base of index field is how you specify that there is no base or index contribution to the address, a scheme common to many IBM designs including the 360 and 370.
- The *multiplier-quotient* (MQ) register is used for double-length multiply and divide and extended shift instructions.
- XER is a status register used to contain overflow and carry flags. It also provides data for some specialized instructions.
- The *data address register* (DAR) and *data storage interrupt status register* (DSISR) record information following a memory reference interrupt (e.g., a page fault) which allows the trap routine to recover and retry the instruction causing the problem.
- The TLB is a 128-entry translation lookahead buffer used in conjunction with memory management and paging.
- TID is a task identifier used in the hardware locking mechanism, discussed later.
- Finally, the 16 segment registers, SR0–SR15, are used in forming virtual addresses.

An important part of the design is that, as on the i860, floating-point load and store instructions are handled by the ALU rather than by the FPU. Although there is no direct connection between the ALU and the FPU, there are connections between the cache and both sets of registers. This means that the ALU can request loading or storing of either set of registers, and can properly synchronize these operations.

The Floating-Point Unit

The FPU handles floating-point computations. As noted in the previous section, all these operations use source operands in registers and place results in registers, since the ALU is responsible for managing floating-point loads and stores.

The arithmetic is IEEE-compatible, supporting both the 32-bit single and 64-bit double formats (there is no general support for double extended format). Floating-point numbers in registers are always stored in the 64-bit format, and the register set can therefore hold 32 double format numbers. This contrasts with other RISC architectures we have looked at, which can hold only 16 double numbers in registers.

The usual argument for providing only 16 floating-point registers is that their use is not as intensive as the fixed-point registers, since the latter are used for addressing as well as for integer computations. It is not clear that there is a significant gain in the quality of code resulting from the additional number of registers—this remains to be seen from further experience in comparing these two approaches. However, there certainly *is* a gain in terms of the simplicity of the architectural design. With 32 registers, the structure of the fixed-point and floating-point instructions can be similar.

From the compiler writer's point of view, the RIOS floating-point register structure is much more convenient than that of other RISC chips. In some other architectures, such as the SPARC and Motorola 88000, single-precision floating-point values occupy one register, and double-precision values occupy a register pair. This complicates the allocation of registers for programs in which single and double floating-point values are intermixed.

The throughput of the FPU approaches one operation per clock, and of course this can only be achieved by pipelining. The length of the pipelines and their configuration are generally *not* a matter of concern to a programmer or even a compiler writer. The scheduling of floating-point instructions is essentially similar to the normal situation with fixed-point instructions—the idea is to insert instructions between a load and the use of the loaded operand to avoid interlocks. In addition a computed result should not be immediately used in a subsequent operation, because it must be given time to emerge from the pipeline.

The i860 also achieves a throughput approaching one operation per clock for floating-point operations, but only if the complex pipelined forms of the instructions are used. These instructions require a compiler to be very aware of the structure of the pipelines. Without such information, compilers will not be able to make full use of the potential computational power of this chip. One would therefore expect that in practice the RIOS would achieve considerably greater floating-point throughput, even though on paper the two processors have similar peak computing power.

As we noted in the previous section, floating-point loads and stores are handled by the ALU rather than the FPU. This decision simplifies the design since the FPU does not need to contain the logic for loads and stores and does not require any connection with the cache. In particular, it means that all memory management functions can be handled on the ALU chip. Furthermore, if the FPU handled its own loads, it would have to access the GPR values in the ALU for addressing purposes, which is clearly impractical given the delay on off-chip references.

Handling floating-point loads as fixed-point instructions means that an instruction stream consisting of intermixed floating-point operations and floating-point loads and stores can run at higher throughput, since the loads and stores are placed in the ALU stream, and the floating-point operations are placed in the FPU stream. The result is that the memory operations can overlap the computations.

As on the i860, this overlap is crucial in approaching peak performance for floating-point algorithms. There is no point in being able to carry out fast floating-point operations if the data cannot be made available to keep the floating-point unit busy. The important contrast with the i860 is that this overlap is automatic. If floating-point operations and loads are interspersed, which is typical even of naive code, then the overlap occurs without any special programming. On the i860, the overlap can only be achieved in dual instruction mode, which requires careful layout of the instructions.

Register Renaming

In addition to the 32 visible registers, the FPU has six *rename registers*. These are used in a transparent manner to eliminate conflicts from reuse of registers. Consider the following sequence of instructions:[2]

```
FLD      FR1, MEM1
FADD     FR2, FR1, FR1
FADD     FR3, FR2, FR2
FLD      FR2, MEM2
```

At the point when the ALU is interpreting the second FLD instruction, FR2 will be in use, since the FADD instructions will still be in the pipeline. Rather than holding up the load (and subsequent operations that use the new value of FR2), the processor remaps the old FR2 to one of the six rename registers. This means that FR2 is no longer in use and the second load can proceed.

As we will see later, register renaming plays an important role in improving the performance of loops. IBM has a lot of experience in implementing this approach, since it is the only way to get anything like decent performance from the IBM 370 architecture, where there are only four visible floating-point registers.

Data Cache

The data cache of the RIOS is organized into 512 cache lines of 128 bytes each, a total of 64K bytes. Compared to other cache organizations we have looked at, this is a very large line size. A consequence is that a cache miss involves reading a considerable amount of data. Although the path to memory is very wide, the read still requires eight memory accesses (128 bits on each read).

---

[2] We have no idea what the assembly language will look like for this machine. In this chapter, we will use a convention similar to that followed with the SPARC or the MIPS, where the destination register is written first, followed by the source operands.

This raises concerns over the efficiency of accessing data in a cache miss situation. Suppose that the last byte of a 128-byte block is referenced and that this particular block is not currently cached. Will the processor have to wait till the full 128 bytes is read into the cache before proceeding?

The answer is no. The data cache has a specialized mechanism that uses a separate 128-byte buffer to read a new block from memory. This buffer is filled by first reading the data that is immediately needed. (In our example, the last 128 bits of the cache line would be read first.) As soon as this data is read, it is provided to the requester, and meanwhile the remainder of the buffer is filled. When the buffer is full, the data is transferred into one of the cache lines. This rather elaborate logic allows the use of large cache lines, which is more efficient in terms of memory access, without the penalty that would normally be associated with large lines.

THE RIOS INSTRUCTION SET

The basic instruction formats of the RIOS are similar to those of the 801 and those of the MIPS. Arithmetic and logical instructions generally take three operands:

        ADD   R1, R2, R3

This instruction computes the sum of R2 and R3 and places the result in R1. All instructions in this format have a bit that indicates whether condition flags should be set to indicate the status of the result. Setting this bit causes the four flags of CC0 to be set to indicate an overflow, a zero result, a negative result, and a positive result. The add and subtract operations exist in only one form, which is used for both signed and unsigned addition. A carry flag is stored in the integer status register and can be subsequently referenced by special extended add and subtract instructions, thus providing multiprecision integer arithmetic. The arithmetic set is unusually rich for a RISC design and includes support for maximum, minimum, and absolute value operations.

The comparison instructions (both fixed- and floating-point) have an extra 3-bit field that indicates which of the eight condition code sets is to receive the result of the comparison. This means that comparisons can be treated like any other operations by the compiler: They take two input registers and place their result in a specified output register. A typical RIOS compiler will allocate these condition codes using normal register allocation techniques to minimize conflicts and maximize overlap. Since the eight condition code sets are independent, the potential overlap is considerably better than that of architectures into which all comparisons set a single condition code. The MIPS addresses this same problem in a slightly different manner, by placing the result of a comparison in one of the general registers. [3]

---

[3] In the first version of the RIOS chips, there are only four independent condition codes—since they are linked in pairs. This is a relatively minor compromise. Compilers do need to be aware of this limitation and allocate condition code registers appropriately.

The integer comparison instructions *do* exist in two separate forms for signed and unsigned (called logical) comparison forms. In both cases, the flags of the specified condition code register are set to indicate an equal, greater than, or less than result.

Bit Field Instructions

The RIOS has a full set of shift and logical instructions, and bit fields can be manipulated using these sequences. For instance, to isolate a field in a register, a typical sequence is two instructions, a shift, followed by an AND to isolate the bits of the field. However, there is also a complete set of specialized instructions for manipulating bit fields directly. These include instructions for inserting and extracting bit fields and positioning masks for subsequent logical operations. The bit extract instruction only appears in an unsigned form—there is no provision for extracting and sign-extending a specified field. It is relatively unusual to pack signed values, so this is a reasonable choice.

These bit field instructions only work within a single register. However, fields that lie across word boundaries can be handled using the double shift instructions to first position the field within a single register, and then the bit field instructions can be used to extract the field.

Complex Instructions

The IBM approach to RISC design has never included reducing the size of the instruction set as an explicit goal.[4] The idea is that it is important to streamline and simplify the instruction formats, but there is no intrinsic merit in reducing the number of instructions. The RIOS design exhibits this philosophy, and, as on the i860, the instruction set includes a significant number of fairly complex instructions that one might not expect to see on a RISC machine.

One advantage of the multichip design is that the real estate on any particular chip is not nearly so scarce. Since the ALU chip has to deal *only* with integer and logical operations, there is plenty of room to add some relatively complicated instructions, including separate integer multiply and divide instructions, and the instruction set of the RIOS does provide them. These instructions provide the traditional double-length operations, making use of an auxiliary register called the *multiplier quotient* register (MQ), also used for double-length shift instructions.

Since there is a very efficient floating-point processor close by (which is always required to be present), one might think that the RIOS would take the same approach as the i860, and assume that integer multiplication can be handled using the floating-point multiply unit. However, looking carefully at the block diagram of the RIOS, you will see that there is *no* means of direct connection between the ALU and the FPU.

---

[4] Dan Prener, of IBM Research, has noted that RISC should be taken as referring to a set of reduced instructions rather than a reduced set of instructions. This view is particularly relevant to the RIOS design, which has a very large, but very uniform, set of instructions.

The only way to get information from the fixed-point registers to the floating-point registers is via memory. This means that the overhead of using the floating-point multiplication instruction to achieve a fixed-point multiply would be considerably worse than on the i860. There are other cases in which it is necessary to convert between floating-point and integer values, and such conversions must be done via memory.

The decision to avoid any direct connection between the floating-point and fixed-point registers is quite deliberate. It is one of the consequences of committing to a multichip design. Any connection between the processors introduces relatively long delays, and such delays are not merely an efficiency consideration but must also be taken into account in the pipeline. A direct (register-to-register) integer to floating-point conversion would not only be a slow instruction in any case, but it would also considerably complicate the design of the ALU and FPU.

Another set of instructions implemented by the ALU allows multiple registers to be loaded and stored in a single instruction. These load and store multiple instructions do not save processor cycles directly, since loading two registers takes two cycles in any case. However, an important consequence is that code size is decreased for procedure entry and exit sequences. Although RISC designs often pay relatively little attention to code density, claiming that memory is cheap, there is an important effect on efficiency.

Instruction caches are typically quite limited in size. When we speak of instructions taking 1 clock, we are always assuming that the instructions are present in the instruction cache. If an instruction cache miss occurs, the pipeline has no choice but to stall till the needed instruction is available. This stall occurs even on processors like the SPARC that do not normally need stall cycles for data accesses. The frequency of such stalls has a significant effect on processor throughput, and thus code density *can* affect execution efficiency.

A variant of the load multiple instruction searches for a specified byte value in the stream of words being loaded and terminates the load operation, indicating the position of the byte, if a match is found. This is not quite as convenient as the SCAS instruction of the 80386, but it performs the same function and can be used for all sorts of high-level operations, such as scanning for a blank in a string. One particularly important application is in searching for a null (zero) byte that terminates a string. C strings are always null terminated, and C programs can spend a significant amount of time in such scans.

As always, we question whether implementation of specialized complex instructions has a significant effect on overall performance. IBM has access to extremely large databases of instruction execution frequencies, gathered from instrumenting customer mainframe sites. One can therefore assume that decisions on such questions are very well informed.

Floating-Point Instructions

The floating-point unit implements the basic set of arithmetic operations on single and double format numbers and also contains the full set of controls over rounding modes and exceptions required by the IEEE standard. Only the basic operations, including square root and remainder, are implemented, and the other specialized operations, such as decimal to floating-point conversion, must all be implemented in software.

Although single format (32-bit) arithmetic is supported, all arithmetic is done in 64-bit mode. Explicit instructions are needed to convert results to 32 bits, and these take additional execution time, because an extra rounding step is required. We therefore have the rather anomalous situation of a machine where double-precision floating-point operations are faster than single precision floating-point, and the general expectation is that most floating-point calculations will be done in double precision. Unlike the Intel i860, where single-precision multiplication is twice as fast as double-precision multiplication, the floating-point pipeline on the RIOS provides maximum throughput for double-precision calculations, and floating-point multiplications can be pipelined with a throughput of one product per clock.

As for fixed-point instructions, there is a bit in every floating-point operation that specifies whether condition codes should be set to reflect the result of the operation. If this bit is set, then CC1 will contain flags indicating whether the operation overflowed or resulted in some other exception.

It is possible to set a mode in which exceptions result in precise traps. However, this mode essentially disables the floating-point pipeline, so it is only intended to be used as a debugging aid. It is also possible to selectively cause precise traps by following an instruction with an explicit trap instruction. The IEEE standard requires that the capability of providing user trap routines be provided, but it also provides for the possibility of replacing results on exceptions, and this option is also available on the RIOS and does not hold up the pipeline.

An important addition to the floating-point instruction set is a combined add and multiply instruction, called Accumulate:

```
ACCUM FR1, FR2, FR3, FR4
```

As we see, the instruction has a unique format with three inputs and one output. There is plenty of room in the 32-bit instruction for four 5-bit register fields, although having a special format for a single instruction is reminiscent of CISC philosophy.

As always with complex instructions, we wonder whether they are worthwhile—in this particular case, it certainly *is* true that the addition of this single instruction has a significant effect on throughput of certain floating-point algorithms. The operation multiplies the contents of FR3 and FR4 and then adds the product to FR2 and places the result in FR1. A typical use of this operation is in computing a dot product:

$$\sum_{i=1}^{n} a_i \, b_i$$

Each step of this computation requires exactly the combined multiply/add operation provided by ACCUM. Since computation of dot products is the central operation in matrix multiplication, we can expect that this operation will be heavily used.

An interesting aspect of this instruction is that the result is exact with respect to the current rounding mode. The intermediate product is *not* rounded; it is held in full double-precision. There is just one rounding step at the end of the addition. In some cases, the improved accuracy compared with doing two separate operations can be significant. The product has a double-length (106-bit) fraction. It is possible for the addition to completely cancel the first half of this double length product. If two separate steps were performed, then the result would underflow to zero. However, because the double-length product is retained, the rounding step will yield the lower 53 bits of the product fraction, so the result retains full precision.

Informally, it seems clearly advantageous to provide *more* accuracy in floating-point computations. However, the IEEE standard, strictly interpreted, does not permit this extra accuracy, unless it is achieved by implementing the double extended format. If this format is provided, then the standard requires that *all* operations be available. The provision of extra precision in one specialized operation does not fit into the IEEE model. However, the extra precision is clearly in the spirit of the IEEE design and is certainly of value in implementing certain algorithms. In practice it would be desirable to provide a compiler option that avoids the use of this instruction so that algorithms can be checked out in a standard IEEE environment where portability is important.[5]

The provision of this double instruction potentially doubles the floating-point throughput, though, as always, achieving peak performance is not always easy. The i860 also provided this kind of overlapped multiply and add capability (using dual operation mode), but only by using the exposed add and multiply pipelines with rather complicated interconnections. Using these instructions on the i860 represents a significant challenge for a compiler. On the RIOS it is a relatively simple matter for a code generator to check for the special case of an add and multiply appearing in a fixed relation in an expression tree. On detecting this pattern, the ACCUM instruction can be generated, and no heroic optimization algorithms need be present. This kind of pattern matching is standard in any code generator, and one could expect quite simpleminded compilers to be able to take advantage of this instruction.

Branch Instructions

All of the instruction formats of the RIOS begin with a 6-bit opcode field. In the case of an unconditional jump, this leaves 26 bits free to hold the target address of the jump, although only 24 bits are used. These 24 bits, shifted left 2 bits since all instructions are on 32-bit boundaries, provide a signed relative offset from the current location, giving an unconditional branch a range of plus or minus 32 megabytes. Since even the Department of Defense does not get into the business of generating single programs approaching this size, this offset is essentially unlimited.

How are the two mysterious missing bits used? One of them can be used to turn a jump instruction into a procedure call. The branch unit has an internal register called the LINK register. The effect of setting the call bit is to save the return point (i.e., the updated instruction counter) in the LINK register. There is an return corresponding instruction which branches to the contents of the LINK register.

---

[5] Apparently, Kahan, considered the father of the IEEE standard, has discussed this specific point and issued a "papal dispensation" allowing this deviation from the standard.

The LINK register can be transferred to and from the ALU if necessary, allowing the return point to be saved and restored. A typical approach would be to identify leaf procedures that contain no other calls. Leaf procedures can keep their return point in the LINK register. Other procedures will have to save and restore the return point to make the LINK register available for nested calls.

The second "missing" bit can be set to make the branch *absolute*. In this case, the 26-bit shifted value is taken as an absolute signed memory address, allowing any address in the first or last 32 megabytes to be addressed directly. One possible use of this feature is to provide a standard set of service routines or shared library routines that are at a fixed address—an address that is the same in the memory map of all programs. Another use is in internal transfers within the operating system.

The conditional jump instructions contain two additional fields. First there is a 5-bit field specifying one of the 32 bits in the conditional flags register to be tested. As we previously noted, comparison instructions can specify which of eight 4-bit condition code registers are to be set, and the corresponding conditional jump specifies which flag is to be tested.

The second field is a 5-bit opcode extension, which has various settings. Using this field, the following types of conditional jumps can be specified:

- Jump if specified condition flag bit is set (true).
- Jump if specified condition flag bit is reset (false).
- Decrement the COUNT register, and branch if the result is zero.
- Decrement the COUNT register, and branch if the result is non-zero.
- Test both the COUNT register and a specified condition code bit.

A comparison instruction sets one of three flag bits to indicate an equal, less than, or greater than condition. Since we can branch on true or false, all possible conditions can be handled with a single jump. For instance, to jump on greater than or equal, we jump on the *less than* flag being false.

The conditional jump instructions that use the COUNT register are analogous to the LOOP instruction on the 386, including their use of a distinguished special register. This is another respect in which the multichip nature of the RIOS design affects the instruction set. Having this special instruction is not simply a matter of avoiding the explicit decrement that would otherwise be used. In addition to removing an instruction, it also avoids the relatively slow ALU-to-BU communication needed for comparison instructions.

The need to add extra fields to the instruction formats of the conditional branch instructions leaves fewer bits available for the offset operand. More precisely, there are 16 bits left over that allow a branch range of plus or minus 128K bytes—considerably smaller than the range available for the unconditional branch. This is usually enough for typical conditional branches within a single procedure. If a jump is out of range, then it can always be transformed into a two-instruction sequence using an unconditional jump with a conditional jump of the opposite sense, and this sequence has an essentially unlimited range.

The call and absolute addressing bits are also present in conditional jumps. The call bit turns conditional jumps into conditional procedure calls, such as "call on equal." These are often quite useful—the Intel 8080 contains a full set of instructions like this, but they have disappeared from subsequent Intel architectures. Among the other processors discussed in this book, only the MIPS has such instructions, and then only in a limited form.

As with the floating-point add and multiply, it is fairly easy for a compiler to recognize a conditional jump and a call occurring in combination, and replace them with the appropriate conditional call. Of course, these conditional calls are usable only if the procedure being called is nearby, so generally they will only be of use for calling internal procedures within the current code module.

The final category of branches is a complete set of trap instructions that specifies which condition flag is to be tested for the trap. An important consequence of the separate branch unit architecture is that these traps are synchronous, since the BU can simply avoid dispatching any instructions following the trap. On other RISC architectures, trap instructions often hold up the pipeline or are not fully synchronized (i.e., by the time the trap is taken, an extra instruction may have executed).

Of course, to get the full benefit of these synchronized trap instructions, the trap must be scheduled to be separated from the instruction that sets the flag to be tested by a sufficient distance to avoid holding up the branch unit. In the case of arithmetic operations, 3 clocks are required for the condition flag to be set. For floating-point operations, the required separation may be considerably greater, since the result must emerge from the floating-point pipeline.

Condition Flag Instructions

A special category of instructions allows logical operations on specified condition code bits. For example:

```
ORF      13, 12, 15
```

This instruction does a logical OR on the contents of bits 12 and 15 of the condition flags register and places the result in bit 13. There are several important uses of these instructions. First, Boolean variables appearing in a program can be allocated bit positions in the condition flags register, just as integer variables might be allocated to fixed-point registers. Boolean operations in the source program then result in single-condition flag instructions.

A second use for these instructions is in compiling code for complex conditional tests. Consider the Ada statement

```
if J < 0 and C(J) > 0 then
    ...
end if;
```

Ada semantics require that both conditions be evaluated when the AND operator is used. To generate RIOS code for this test, we could perform the two comparisons using separate condition code registers. Then an ANDF instruction would be used to AND the results, and a single conditional branch would test the resulting bit.

This code is efficient enough that it compares favorably with "short-circuited" evaluation, where the first comparison is followed by a conditional branch. The Ada statement:

```
if J < 0 and then C(J) > 0 then
    ...
end if;
```

requires such short-circuited evaluation, so the ANDF instruction could not be used in this case. However, in Pascal, the corresponding statements:

```
if (J < 0) and (C(J) > 0) then
    ...;
```

specifically leaves it up to the compiler writer whether evaluation is to be short-circuited or not. Compilers for most processors would choose to short-circuit, but in the case of the RIOS, the efficient handling of the condition codes may make it preferable to carry out the full evaluation in some cases.

This is true because these special condition flag instructions are processed by the branch unit and can be overlapped with other operations. Since we would not generally expect to have one in every four instructions be a condition flag instruction, the unit that handles these instructions is usually underused. As a consequence, introducing additional condition flag instructions will in practice have no additional cost.

MEMORY ADDRESSING

Like the other microprocessors discussed in this book, the RIOS has 32-bit addresses. The memory management unit provides a much wider virtual address space using a segmented approach similar in some respects to that of the 386. We will discuss this later, but for now we will look at addressing from the application point of view, where addresses are only 32 bits.

Addressing Modes

Memory reference instructions have two addressing modes. The first is base plus displacement, with a signed 16-bit displacement. The second is base plus index without scaling (which must be done by separate instructions). This addressing scheme might be described as a combination of the MIPS and SPARC addressing modes. Like the MIPS, it provides reasonably large 16-bit offsets, but like the SPARC, there is a base plus index form where two registers are added in forming the address.

The load and store instructions can specify auto-increment mode, where the offset (or index register) acts as both the addressing offset and the increment. As on the i860, this provides a flexible mechanism for addressing vectors, both in the case where the elements are contiguous and when they are non-contiguous, separated by a non-zero stride. Generally we expect to see some provision made for auto-increment addressing on machines with very fast floating-point pipelines, because explicit increment instructions would slow down the pipeline.

On the 68030, the auto-increment form has a fixed value corresponding to the size of the element, so it is only useful in addressing contiguous elements. The RIOS approach, which is copied from the original 801 design, and is also used on the i860, has two advantages.

First, the increment can be any value, allowing the processing of non-contiguous arrays. This is important in numerical processing, since non-contiguous vectors arise in processing multi-dimensional arrays.

Second, the increment operation is easy to implement. The sum of the offset and the index register, which is the updated value that gets written back to the index register, is the sum which has to be computed anyway to get the effective address.

Direct Addressing

An interesting difference between the RIOS and both the MIPS and the SPARC is in their approach to direct addressing. The latter two processors use the "trick" of directly addressing memory using the following two-instruction sequence:

```
LUI     R1, address-upper
LW      R1, address-lower (R1)
```

The RIOS has a complete set of instructions for setting the upper 16 bits of a register. These instructions take the form of logical immediate instructions with the output being set in the upper 16 bits, and in particular there is an instruction Logical Or Upper that can be used to load a constant into the upper 16 bits in a manner similar to the LUI instruction of the MIPS.

The *hardware* of the RIOS thus perfectly well supports the MIPS direct addressing approach, where an arbitrary location in memory can be addressed by using two instructions, only one of which is a memory reference. However, the *software* environment of the RIOS not only discourages this usage, but also essentially makes it impossible by failing to provide the special "half address" relocation possibilities in the linker.

This means that direct addressing is not possible, and all static global memory must be addressed via a register. The standard IBM approach is to permanently allocate a *table of contents* or TOC register that points to a list of address constants. These address constants in turn point to the global objects to be addressed. This means that to address a global object, two instructions are required:

```
L     R1, address-con (TOC)    ; load address con from TOC
L     R2, offset (R1)          ; access required location
```

As long as these instructions can be scheduled sufficiently far apart that no interlock occurs on the second reference, the speed is equivalent to the direct addressing sequence. The IBM design view is that this scheduling is generally possible, so there is no need to provide for direct addressing.

This approach is undoubtedly influenced by other architectures, notably the IBM 360 and 370, where a similar approach is always used because direct addressing is simply not possible—there is no reasonable way to set a full address width constant on these machines without referencing memory. An important point used to support the IBM approach is that the resulting code is completely position-independent and reentrant, in the sense that the same code can be shared with different instances of global data simply by setting the TOC register to point to different sets of address constants. A MIPS program using the LUI approach contains hard-coded addresses in the program and thus cannot be shared for separate instances of data at separate addresses. There is still a possibility of sharing such code by using separate page tables, but this is considerably more complex at the operating system level.

We reemphasize that this is *not* a hardware difference between the RIOS and the MIPS. It is merely a case of taking two different views in designing system software. Nevertheless it has just as much influence on compiler writers as if it were a hardware difference, since you can't generate instructions if they aren't supported by the software. It is not unusual to find cases in which the hardware can do something, but the system software, in particular the linker, does not provide the necessary support.

Operand Alignment

Uniquely among the RISC processors we are looking at, the RIOS does *not* require that operands be aligned in all cases. If the operand for a fixed-point 2- or 4-byte load instruction is not aligned, then there are two cases:

- The operand lies entirely within a single cache line. In this case the unaligned operand is delivered to the target register without any pipeline penalty.
- The operand crosses two cache lines. In this case a trap is generated. The intention is that the trap routine will correctly simulate the loading of the unaligned operand and continue execution.

You will recall that there were two motivations for avoiding unaligned operands. First, if the operand lies across a hardware memory boundary, it complicates things to turn one logical reference into two physical references. Second, if the operand lies across cache or page boundaries, we have to deal with half-cached and half-swapped-in values, which is an additional complication.

The RIOS approach avoids both of these difficulties by trapping in the embarrassing cases. Of course, it would be possible on any processor that traps on unaligned operands to have the trap routine fix things up, but what makes the RIOS approach viable is that the cache lines are very large (128 bytes). This means that there is a high probability that the operand *will* lie within a cache line. For a 4-byte operand, we have a 125/128 chance that there will be no trap. For the slightly less than 3% of the time that we do get a trap, we probably need execute about 20 instructions to simulate the unaligned load. This gives an effective performance penalty on average for unaligned loads of less than 1 clock—certainly a small and acceptable slowdown, much smaller than on the Intel and Motorola CISC processors.

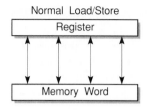
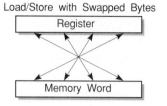

FIGURE 12.2
Byte-swapping on the RIOS on loads and stores.

Recalling that IBM has large databases of actual instruction execution frequencies, it is reasonable to speculate that they also know a lot about the frequency of unaligned operand references. Their data will tend to be more influenced by commercial applications than data collected in a Unix/C environment, and, as we have pointed out, it is in commercial applications that unaligned references are most likely to occur. In any case, the RIOS approach certainly seems to give us the best of both worlds—unaligned references when we need them with a very small penalty, and aligned references with no penalty at all.

The permission for operands to be unaligned is not universally available. In particular, floating-point operands must be aligned. This is probably reasonable. There is no good reason why floating-point operands should not be aligned. In particular, COBOL, which is a major perpetrator of unaligned references, does not provide floating-point formats at all.[6]

Big-Endian Ordering

IBM machines have traditionally used big-endian ordering for both bits and bytes. In particular, the 360 and 370 mainframe architectures have been exclusively big-endian. It is thus no surprise to find that the RIOS follows this approach. The addressing of bytes for multibyte quantities is big-endian, and the bit numbering, which shows up in the bit field instructions, is also big-endian.

Unlike the MIPS and the i860, there is no provision on the RIOS for switching the processor between big- and little-endian modes. There is, however, a useful set of load and store instructions that swap the 4 bytes of the memory operand on the way to and from the memory word (see Figure 12.2). These instructions allow little-endian data to be processed in an efficient manner. For certain purposes, these instructions are more powerful than the mode switching of the other processors, which only renumber the bytes in memory, and do *not* provide for this kind of byte swapping. Consider, for instance, the problem of processing data from external sources that contain a mixture

---

[6] Earlier versions of the IBM COBOL compiler did provide floating-point, but this facility was non-standard and not often used, and it has been removed from the most recent COBOL versions.

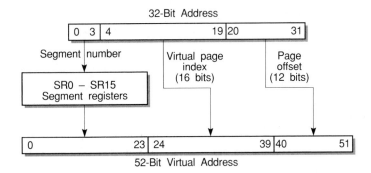

FIGURE 12.3
Virtual address translation on the RIOS.

of big- and little-endian data. The byte-swapping load and store are just what is needed for efficient processing of such data.

We mentioned earlier that COBOL compilers for the PC allow programmers to specify and mix little-endian and big-endian data. It is even possible at the COBOL source level to describe a single data word as being both little-endian and big-endian, and access it in two different manners. The RIOS is the only processor we have looked at which provides efficient support for such programs.

Memory Management

From a program's point of view, addresses are 32 bits long. This 32-bit address is divided into three fields. The first 4 bits select one of the 16 segment registers, which contain the first 24 bits of a 52-bit virtual address. The next 16 bits of the 32-bit address, called the *virtual page index*, provide the next 16 bits of the 52-bit virtual address. Finally, the last 12 bits of the 32-bit address, called the *page off*set, provides the last 12 bits of the 52-bit virtual address (see Figure 12.3). Fifty-two bits allows for a huge virtual address space, (i.e., 2^{52} bytes, or 4 petabytes) much larger than the address space on any of the other processors we have looked at.

Why would IBM decided to use such a large virtual address space? It is certainly a deliberate choice, since the size of the segment registers has been increased compared to the first-generation ROMP chips, which first introduced this segmentation model. One motivation behind this choice is a specific view of virtual memory in which all data in the system, *including all file data*, is regarded as addressable.[7] Using this architectural approach, reading or writing a file involves asking the operating system

---

[7] This is somewhat similar to the view of memory taken by MULTICS. MULTICS was an operating system designed by GE, MIT, and Bell Labs for the GE645. Unix was originally derived as a substantial simplification of MULTICS.

to provide an address for the file data, and then normal load and store instructions can be used to read and write the file. 2^{52} bytes sounds like a ridiculous amount of memory, but not if it includes all files, including those on "dusty tapes." There are already commercial installations with terabyte (2^{40}) secondary memories installed, so virtual address spaces limited to 2^{32} bytes are quite inadequate for supporting this approach.

Of course, the operating system must provide a mechanism for using this large virtual address space. At any one time, only 16 segment values can be loaded into the segment registers. Each of these registers can address 256 megabytes, which is a reasonable limit for one element of a file system. However, a limit of 16 files is clearly unacceptable. This means that the operating system must maintain a much larger logical segment table and provide efficient means for moving these values into physical segment registers. This move has to be performed by the system, since the segment registers can be manipulated only in supervisor mode.

It is quite possible to design specialized supervisor call instructions that perform the required segment register loads very rapidly. An experimental operating system developed by IBM for the ROMP chip (which had a similar segmented architecture) could achieve this processing, including validating the request, in less than 30 instructions. This is comparable to the speed of reloading a TLB entry on a machine like the MIPS with software TLB reload, or executing a segment register load instruction on the 386, so it is quite acceptable.

While the segmentation approach makes this kind of operating system interface possible, we may wait a while to see a system that makes use of the segmentation. Initial implementations of RIOS will be Unix-based, and Unix has no mechanism for handling segmentation—it will simply use a flat 32-bit memory model. New features for implementing virtual file systems are beginning to appear in some versions of Unix, but they are not specifically oriented to the hardware approach of the RIOS, which is what is needed for best utilization of the segmentation feature. It will be interesting to see if someone makes an attempt to utilize the segmented architecture by writing an operating system around the idea of addressing all data via full-length virtual addresses.

Paging Mechanisms

As usual, the purpose of paging is to translate virtual addresses to their corresponding physical addresses. The TLB is used to cache entries describing virtual-to-physical addresses in the usual manner. The large virtual address size is not a problem for the TLB mechanism—the TLB entries simply have to be long enough to fit them.

The huge virtual address space *does* cause a problem in the case of a TLB miss. The RIOS page size is 4K bytes, so the number of pages in the virtual address space is 2^{40} bytes. If we use the familiar approach of multilevel page tables accessed by using pieces of the virtual address, we have to make a rather uncomfortable trade-off between number of page table levels and page table size. For example, if we follow the 386 approach of using 4K byte page tables, then we need four levels of page tables, which will certainly slow down processing of TLB misses.

Furthermore, arranging page tables in this manner may require a great deal of space even if we use several levels in the page table, especially if we implement an operating system that maps large files into the virtual address space. If a large file is mapped in, the page tables necessary to support random access to this file begin to take up a large amount of space.

To address this problem, RIOS uses a completely different approach, which was first implemented in the ROMP. A table known as the *page frame table* (PFT) contains one entry for each *physical* page in memory. This table has been called an *inverted page table* in previous IBM architectures, since it is constructed the opposite way around from more familiar page tables. Instead of being a table of physical page addresses that are indexed by the virtual address, the PFT is a table of virtual page addresses indexed by the physical address.

Figure 12.4 shows the format of a PFT entry. It contains familiar page table entry bits, such as the modified and referenced bits and the protection bits, and also contains a number of unfamiliar fields that we will examine later. First we address the problem of finding the PFT entry. Given a virtual page number, the task is to find the PFT that contains a matching virtual page number. The corresponding physical page address can then be determined from the PFT entry itself, since the PFT is arranged in order by physical page number.

How can we find the PFT entry with a matching address? One correct approach would be to search the PFT sequentially. The entry would be found if it existed, but of course, it is infeasibly slow. There are many algorithms which could be used to speed up the search and since we are interested in average case performance rather than the

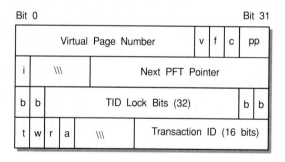

Symbol	Description
v	Set if page is valid
f	Set if page is referenced
c	Set if page is modified
pp	Page protect bits
i	Set if PFT pointer invalid
t	Read/write indication for locks
w	Set if write locks to be granted
r	Set if read locks to be granted
a	Set if reads to locked memory allowed

FIGURE 12.4
The structure of a page frame table entry.

theoretical worst case, hashing algorithms are particularly appropriate. The RIOS memory management uses a familiar hashing algorithm for locating the PFT entry.

First, the virtual page number is hashed using some sequence of logical operations. This hashed value is used to index into the *hash anchor table* (HAT), which contains pointers to corresponding PFT entries. As in any hashing scheme, it is possible for multiple distinct virtual page numbers to generate the same hash index. This is handled by chaining PFT entries with the same hash index, using the next PFT field. The invalid pointer bit is set to indicate the end of the hash chain, as shown in Figure 12.5.[8]

The hashing and searching of the corresponding hash chain is all performed by hardware logic in the ALU. The HAT is the same length as the number of physical pages, so the average length of hash chains is at most one, and if there is a matching PFT entry, it can on average be located quickly. IBM argues that conducting this search with hardware, rather than relying on software TLB reload as on the MIPS, is an important advantage, but this is a controversial issue, and it is not easy to judge whether this is true without detailed timing figures.

If the hash search runs into an entry with the invalid pointer bit set, then there is no matching PFT entry, and a page fault trap is taken. The system software then swaps in a new page, updating the hash chains in the PFT appropriately.

The attractive feature of this approach is that it is generally better in both time and space performance than the multilevel page table approach. On average only a little more than two memory references are required, since there will be relatively few clashes in the hashing. The space required is always proportional to the number of *physical* pages, rather than the number of virtual pages, and is thus minimal. As with any hashing algorithm, there *are* worst cases which are pretty horrible, but these are very unlikely to occur. The one place where consideration of worst cases might be significant is in real time applications, with extremely fine and severe deadline requirements.

Hardware Locking

The hardware locking feature provides an efficient mechanism for signalling that small (128-byte) chunks of memory are currently locked by a single task. The lock will prevent other tasks from writing (and optionally from reading) the chunk of memory. These locks would typically be used in database implementations for locking records in shared transaction systems. In most cases, locks are granted and checked by the hardware, allowing for very efficient processing of locks.

The PFT entry contains a number of fields that are used to implement this locking scheme. Segments can be marked as *special* by using a bit in the segment register. Pages within a special segment are each divided into thirty-two 128-byte lines. For each line,

---

[8] One detail that a sharp reader may spot is that the virtual page number in the PFT entry is only 27 bits, whereas a full virtual page number is 40 bits. The explanation for this discrepancy is that the hash index guarantees that the low-order 13 bits of the page number are uniquely represented in the hash index (i.e., if two virtual addresses are different in their low-order 13 bits, then the hash indexes are never the same). This means that only the upper 27 bits need to be checked.

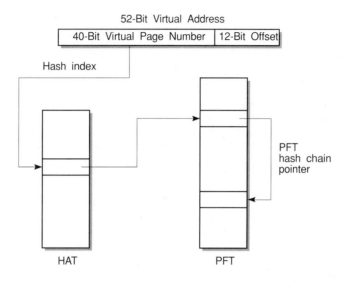

FIGURE 12.5
Page translation on the RIOS

there is a corresponding lock bit in the PFT entry. The transaction ID field in the PFT entry indicates the task that owns the locks. Recall that the TID register in the ALU indicates the current task, so the hardware can check that the current task owns the corresponding lock.

As long as the locks in a given page are owned by a single task, they can be managed (set, released and checked) entirely by the hardware. In the relatively rare case where two separate tasks are actively sharing a single page, a lock violation exception is generated, so that the situation can be resolved by operating system software routines.

This rather elaborate mechanism is another unique feature of the RIOS. A similar mechanism, in slightly less elaborate form, was incorporated into the original 801 design and is present in the ROMP. It is interesting that IBM clearly considers this an important feature, and yet other RISC designers have ignored locking completely. The probable explanation is that for commercial processing and database applications this kind of locking approach is important; most other RISC chips have been developed in the context of engineering workstations running Unix, where such considerations are less important. Earlier versions of Unix provided no facility for locking records, even at the operating system level, whereas management of transaction locks is a major design issue in commercial operating systems.

PERFORMANCE CONSIDERATIONS

Intel claims that a 50 MHz i860 chip has a peak throughput of 100 megaflops and 150 MOPS (million *operations* per second). IBM can make corresponding claims that a 50 MHz RIOS chip has a peak performance of the same 100 megaflops, and 250 MOPS. This figure of 250 MOPS can be reached by keeping all four parallel instruction streams busy, which means that the code has to have the appropriate mix of fixed-point, floating-point, branch, and condition code instructions, and furthermore that all the floating-point instructions are combined add/multiply operations.[9]

Peak performances are, of course, deceptive. It is certainly possible to cook up examples that reach this peak performance, and consequently manufacturer's benchmarks for machines of this type should be looked at with a great deal of skepticism. The two questions to be asked are:

- Are there useful algorithms for important problems where the peak performance can be approached?

- Can compilers for high-level languages make use of the high performance for "normal" application code?

The answer to the first question is a qualified yes. For an ideal problem like matrix multiplication of floating-point matrices, we probably can't easily reach the peak, but by using specialized assembly language routines we can approach this level of performance, and we can certainly expect to cross the 1 clock per instruction barrier by a comfortable margin.

This means that we can expect desktop machines in the near future with floating-point performance that is a substantial portion of the computing power provided by top-end computers. These machines will have a significant impact in many areas. Typical engineers would prefer to have a workstation running at 10% the speed of a Cray all to themselves than to have a small share of the Cray.

The second question is more problematic. Can compilers make use of the high performance? Much more experience is required to answer this question, but we can certainly be sure that the RIOS approach, where the instruction stream is relatively conventional and depends on instruction scheduling only for performance purposes, is *much* easier to deal with than the specialized instruction formats and arrangements of the i860.

In compiling code for the RIOS, we essentially need only conventional RISC instruction scheduling techniques. The constraints on the scheduling are more severe, in that the mix of the four types of instructions has to be considered, but it is not necessary to analyze the structure of the code and significantly transform it to achieve efficient throughput.

---

[9] At the time of writing this book, the clock rates of the RIOS chip have not been published. However, given the technology, it is reasonable to assume that speeds in the range of 50 MHz are achievable. Probably the initial chips will be slower, but since Intel quotes non-existent 50 MHz chips as the basis of their performance figures, it seems only fair to use the same figure for the RIOS.

An Example: Matrix Multiplication

There are some special considerations in generating code for the RIOS due to the arrangement of the separate branch processor. Conditional jumps are potentially slow if the instruction setting the condition flag bit cannot be separated from the jump. These jumps take 0 to 3 clocks, depending on this separation—at least clocks separation between the compare and the test are necessary to make the jump free. Note that this is 3 *clocks*, not three *instructions*. If the intervening instructions can themselves be overlapped with one another, then considerably more than three separating instructions may be needed. This relatively long delay results from the interchip communication cost—the compare is done in the ALU or FPU, and the condition flag bit is in the BU.

This is why the branch unit implements the special COUNT register for controlling jumps. The jump controlling a count loop is not subject to these delays, since the COUNT register is in the BU. This means that there is a premium on converting while loops and for loops into count loops where possible. For example, consider:

```
I := 1;
S := 0;
while I <= N loop
    S := S + B(J,I) * C(I,K);
    I := I + 1;
end loop;
```

Naive code would simply use the variable I to control the loop, checking against the value of N at the end of the loop. Even if I and N are held in fixed-point registers, the conditional jump is likely to be costly. In this example, it pays to do the analysis that determines that I is a simple induction variable (incremented by 1 each time through the loop) and that N is not modified in the loop, so the number of loops can be determined in advance, allowing the COUNT register to be used to control the loop. If the code were written in FORTRAN as a DO loop, this determination would be trivial, since these two characteristics are true of *all* DO loops in FORTRAN.

This fragment of code is the inner loop of a matrix multiplication routine, so it is interesting to continue in some detail the analysis of what code can easily be generated. The next observation we can make is that the array addressing calculations can be strength reduced so that the subscript multiplications are eliminated. Compiling code based on these two assumptions results in

```
            R1 = address of B(J,1) – B.stride
            R2 = address of C(1,K) – C.stride
            FR1 (S) = 0.0
            COUNT = N
LP:     FLD.I    FR2, B.stride(R1)    ; load next element of B, increment
        FLD.I    FR3, C.stride(R2)    ; load next element of C, increment
        ACCUM FR1, FR1, FR2, FR3 ; accumulate dot product
        BRN.C    LP                   ; loop back using COUNT register
```

This loop contains two fixed-point operations, one floating-point operation, and one branch. Let us analyze the performance of this loop assuming that all data and instructions are in the cache (certainly a reasonable assumption for the instructions, and a reasonable assumption for data if the matrices are small).

Using the same kind of thinking that is applicable to other RISC architectures, we might worry about the fact that the ACCUM instruction uses a register loaded by the previous instruction. While it is true that this may hold things up the *first* time through the loop, it is *not* a problem on subsequent loops, because after a while the branch unit has queued up a series of FLD instructions for the ALU and a series of ACCUM instructions for the FPU, so both units always have something to work on.

The next concern might be that the FLD from the following loop gets held up until the previous ACCUM instruction has finished with FR2 and FR3. This is precisely what the register renaming facility for. As soon as the new FLD instructions come in, FR2 and FR3 are renamed so that the previous ACCUM instruction can still get the values it needs but is no longer blocking the load of FR2 and FR3 with new data.

Since each loop contains two ALU instructions, the maximum throughput is one loop every 2 clocks. However, this can't quite be achieved because we do have one conflict—each ACCUM instruction relies on the result of the previous ACCUM. The floating-point pipeline introduces a delay so that ACCUM instructions in a sequence of this type can execute at the rate of only one every 3 clocks. That is still very respectable performance, corresponding on a 50 MHz processor to 33 MFLOPS, 66 MIPS, 83 MOPS (the ACCUM counts as two operations), and 0.75 clocks per instruction, thus breaking the 1 clock per instruction barrier.

How can the performance of this loop be improved? An approach that is often helpful in improving loop performance is to *unroll* the loop, so that several elements are accumulated each time through the loop:

```
        R1 ← address of B(J,1) − B.stride
        R2 ← address of C(1,K) − C.stride
        FR1(S) ← 0.0
        COUNT ← N / 3

LP:     FLD.I    FR2, B.stride(R1)    ; load next element of B, increment
        FLD.I    FR3, C.stride(R2)    ; load next element of C, increment
        ACCUM    FR1, FR1, FR2, FR3   ; accumulate dot product
        FLD.I    FR4, B.stride(R1)    ; load next element of B, increment
        FLD.I    FR5, C.stride(R2)    ; load next element of C, increment
        ACCUM    FR1, FR1, FR4, FR5   ; accumulate dot product
        FLD.I    FR6, B.stride(R1)    ; load next element of B, increment
        FLD.I    FR7, C.stride(R2)    ; load next element of C, increment
        ACCUM    FR1, FR1, FR6, FR7   ; accumulate dot product
        BRN.C    LP                   ; loop back using COUNT register
```

On most machines, this unrolling would improve efficiency. We have eliminated the possible conflicts on the loading of registers, and we execute a branch one-third as often.

Surprisingly, this unrolling has *no advantage whatsoever* on the RIOS. The register conflicts were resolved in the "rolled-up" case by register renaming, and the branch instruction was free because it was executed by the branch unit. An ACCUM-to-ACCUM conflict exists, with the same result—one ACCUM is executed every 3 clocks.

Once again we see that the RIOS design is kinder to compilers, since it automatically performs optimizations that would otherwise add complexity to compilers. In assessing this simplification, note that our unrolling of the loop illustrated above is simplified since it does not include dealing with the odd loops left over when the number of loops is not a multiple of three.

Something to note about the unrolled loop is that although the matrix multiplication will take exactly the same amount of time, the performance in terms of MIPS has got worse. It is now 55 MIPS instead of 66. This is because we have eliminated "useless" branch instructions. MIPS figures are often criticized as misleading, and this example certainly shows why we need to be careful in comparing such figures across different architectures. We could improve the MIPS ratings of RIOS programs by having the compiler stick in useless branch and condition flag instructions, but this wouldn't be any help to the programmer.

Although unrolling the loop does not help, it does suggest an approach to improving the throughput. If we accumulate the result in three separate registers and then sum them at the end, we can avoid the ACCUM conflicts. This approach is reminiscent of what would be required on the i860 using the explicit pipeline instructions. Is such a transformation within reach of a compiler? With the current state of the art, the answer is probably no. Even if it *were* possible for a compiler to do this kind of optimization, it would be quite improper for it to do so. This is because we would end up adding the elements in a different order, which in general leads to a different result because of floating-point rounding.

It happens to be generally acceptable to reorder the additions of the dot product accumulation in the case of matrix multiplication. However, there is no way for the compiler to know that this is the case. Compiler writers in the past have occasionally made the assumption that (A + B) + C is "near enough" equal to A + (B + C) and that a compiler is consequently free to make the substitution. Numerical analysts realize that these two expressions can have quite different values, and dealing with compilers that mangle expressions in this manner is an unpleasant occupation.

The programmer can, however, restructure the loop at the source program level to allow the three separate accumulating sums:

```
I := 1;
S1 := 0;
S2 := 0;
S3 := 0;
while I <= N / 3 loop
    S1 := S1 + B(J,I) * C(I,K);
    I := I + 1;
    S2 := S2 + B(J,I) * C(I,K);
    I := I + 1;
    S3 := S3 + B(J,I) * C(I,K);
    I := I + 1;
end loop;
S := S1 + S2 + S3;
```

For simplicity, we ignore the detail of dealing with odd elements left over after the division by 3. The interesting thing about this program is that if we translate it using our reasonably clever compiler, we will get something like:

```
R1 ← address of B(J,1) − B.stride
R2 ← address of C(1,K) − C.stride
FR1 (S1) ← 0.0
FR2 (S2) ← 0.0
FR3 (S3) ← 0.0
COUNT ← N / 3
```

```
LP:     FLD.I    FR4, B.stride(R1)       ; load next element of B, increment
        FLD.I    FR5, C.stride(R2)       ; load next element of C, increment
        ACCUM    FR1, FR1, FR4, FR5      ; accumulate S1 partial product
        FLD.I    FR4, B.stride(R1)       ; load next element of B, increment
        FLD.I    FR5, C.stride(R2)       ; load next element of C, increment
        ACCUM    FR2, FR2, FR4, FR5      ; accumulate S2 partial product
        FLD.I    FR4, B.stride(R1)       ; load next element of B, increment
        FLD.I    FR5, C.stride(R2)       ; load next element of C, increment
        ACCUM    FR3, FR3, FR4, FR5      ; accumulate S3 partial product
        BRN.C    LP                      ; loop back using COUNT register
        FADD     FR1, FR1, FR2           ; S := S1 + S2
        FADD     FR1, FR1, FR3           ; S := S1 + S2 + S3
```

This has much better overlap characteristics, because now the successive ACCUM instructions do not conflict, and we can execute the ACCUM instructions as fast as they are presented. The result is that we can now do one accumulation every 2 clocks, resulting in a performance on a 50 MHz RIOS of 50 MFLOPS and 0.6 clocks per instruction.

Consider compiling the same code for the i860. There is an efficient translation using the pipelined add and multiply, since the three stages of the add pipeline can be used to accumulate the three partial results. However, it takes a great deal of sophisticated pattern matching for the compiler to transform this loop into code that uses the pipeline of the i860 in this manner (complete with the required priming and flushing of results at the end). It is certainly possible to build an i860 compiler that recognizes *this particular* case, but implementing general optimizations that can handle transformations of this type is extremely difficult.

The i860 code for the dot product calculation is sufficiently complex that we decided *not* to present it in chapter 12. This example is worked out in detail in the Intel Programmer's Reference Manual for the i860, and it is extremely hard to understand, let alone to believe that a compiler could generate this type of code automatically.

The RIOS thus has the considerable advantage that with just a little knowledge of what is going on—basically little more than the rule that you should not use results you just computed—the programmer can write code that compiles in a highly efficient manner, without needing a sophisticated optimizing compiler.

An optimal matrix multiplication routine will approach the peak rate still closer by reordering the operations to minimize load instructions and reuse data. An optimal matrix multiplication routine will also have to worry about the use of the cache. If the two matrices fit in the cache, then locality of reference is not a problem. If on the other hand, the matrices are too large to fit in the cache, it is necessary to completely reorganize the approach and work with blocks of the matrix one at a time. Although we cannot expect compilers to generate elaborate code of this type from naive matrix multiplication source code, it is quite reasonable to restructure the source code so that the required efficient code is generated—the need for very careful assembly coding should be considerably reduced on the RIOS as compared to the i860.

Scheduling Comparison Instructions

The weakest point of the RIOS design is the potential 3-clock delay on conditional jumps that test a condition set by a comparison instruction. This long delay results from the situation in which the condition is set on one chip (the ALU) and tested on another (the BU)—it is the one case where the separate chip approach has a significant cost. Minimizing these delays is helped by aggressive scheduling of comparison instructions, but it is not always possible to separate the comparison from the test by a sufficient margin to avoid the penalty. For example, consider the following loop in C, which searches a list for the null pointer (zero) at the end of the list:

```
while (*p != 0) p = *p;
```

The loop here is only one instruction long, and there is no opportunity for moving the test away, since we can't go on to the next loop before completing the test. Another similar embarrassment occurs in Ada programs with constraint checking turned on. Suppose we have a series of assignments:

```
A := B + 1;
C := A + 2;
D := C + 3;
```

Ada semantics does not permit the stores to be carried out until the range test on the result of the addition is completed. Since every arithmetic operation potentially involves such a test, we may easily run out of scheduling room in trying to separate the checks from the corresponding arithmetic routines. Floating-point checks are particularly painful, since in this case we have to wait for the floating-point pipeline as well as the off-chip delay in setting the condition register flags. IBM has done extensive research on implementing optimization approaches that minimize the need for such checks, and it appears that such technology will be particularly valuable on the RIOS.

Hand-Coded Routines

To get the absolute maximum performance out of a specialized architecture like the RIOS, it is probably necessary to resort to very carefully hand-coded sequences that are written with a full knowledge of the pipeline delays. Such code is very difficult to write, but standard algorithms, particularly numerical algorithms found in typical linear algebra packages, are used sufficiently intensively to justify this special effort.

Worrying about such details as the length of the floating-point pipeline and the delays for off-chip communications complicates things enormously. The RIOS loses some of its advantage over the i860 in this context, although it is still much easier to write efficient assembly language for the RIOS than for the i860.

The performance of the two processors for such hand-coded routines is also similar in the single-precision case. The i860 has somewhat more flexibility in handling the cache and in combining multiply and add operations, which may result in slightly better performance in some cases. It can also load data faster, since it can load two or four values in each load instruction. On the other hand, the free branches on the RIOS make up for at least some of this difference.

For double-precision, the RIOS has a clear advantage, since it has much better throughput for floating-point multiply operations—one result every clock, instead of one result every 2 clocks. Since many numerical computations involve loops containing multiplications, this is a significant difference.

SUMMARY

The IBM research into RISC design approaches has played a fundamental role in the development of RISC technology. Up to this point, IBM has not succeeded in taking commercial advantage of this technology The main effect of the RT introduction seems to have been to confer legitimacy on other manufacturers' more successful use of RISC chips in engineering workstations. The ROMP helped to legitimize RISC technology, but the RT which was based on this chip was never successful, primarily because both the design and implementation of the ROMP were inherently inefficient.

The RIOS architecture not only represents the culmination of the IBM RISC research effort to date, but it also has a very good chance of playing an important commercial role. Machines built around this chip should perform very competitively with workstations built around less advanced RISC technologies. The RIOS represents the most elaborate RISC architecture to date, and under favorable circumstances appears to have significantly greater potential performance, especially in floating-point, than chips like the MIPS or the SPARC.

Of course, to be fair, the IBM chip has only *just* been released. Comparisons of one manufacturer's just-announced product with another product that has been on the market for a while can be misleading. We certainly don't know what is being cooked up in the design cellars at MIPS, but we can be sure that they are not standing still! The same is true of the further development of the SPARC architecture. Nevertheless, the successful design and fabrication of the RIOS architecture is an important milestone in the continuing development of RISC technology. In particular, the design indicates that very high multiple instructions per clock throughput can be achieved without the complexity of the i860 approach.

CHAPTER

13

THE INMOS TRANSPUTER

The Transputer was developed by the INMOS Corporation, a company supported by the British government as both a social project and an engineering project. INMOS is located in Wales, where the industrial economy was severely depressed at the time. INMOS was intended to give Britain some presence in the computer chip business at the same time that it created high-tech jobs.

At first, INMOS did rather poorly and lost barrels of the British taxpayers' money. However, they started to manufacture memory chips at a time when that was highly profitable. In a lucky stroke of timing, the Thatcher government managed to sell the company just as they were at top value, getting the British government out of the chip business just in time. Since then, INMOS, like other companies whose only business is manufacturing chips, has not done so well.

Despite this rather lackluster commercial performance, INMOS has one very interesting product, the Transputer, which is a novel microprocessor architecture for which they have constructed a series of chips. The Transputer was developed in the early 1980s and thus predates the current enthusiasm for RISC technology. However, as we will see, there are a number of interesting parallels between the Transputer and current RISC design techniques, although INMOS is rather careful *not* to describe the Transputer as a RISC chip.

The particular Transputer chip described in this chapter is the T800, which is the top-of-the-line 32-bit chip with an integral floating-point unit. There are models of the Transputer that omit floating-point, and there are also 16-bit versions.

THE TRANSPUTER AND OCCAM

The architecture of the Transputer has been heavily influenced by the high-level language OCCAM. As a result, before looking into the details of the Transputer, we will have a brief look at this language.

OCCAM was inspired by the programming language CSP, which stands for Communicating Sequential Processes. CSP is a very simple language whose central feature is a primitive notion of communication between processes and was originally designed as a formal description language. OCCAM might be viewed as the result of an attempt to define and implement CSP so that it could be used for real programming tasks.

OCCAM has copied CSP's notion of process communication, a notion that makes OCCAM unusual. Apart from this, OCCAM is a fairly conventional and relatively simple language.[1] The communication in OCCAM uses the concept of a *channel*. A channel is an abstract data structure that supports two operations: An item can be read from a channel, and an item can be written to a channel. In OCCAM, these operations are written as:

```
c ? x      Read from channel c into variable x
c ! exp    Write contents of the expression to channel c
```

One process performs the read, and another process performs the write. The process performing the earlier operation is held up until the corresponding operation is performed by the other process. Then, with the two processes synchronized at the send and receive, the data is transferred, and then both processes proceed. This communication is reminiscent of the rendezvous in Ada, except that the channel is a data structure rather than a control structure, so any process can write to a channel and any process can read from a channel. This simple form of channel communication can be modelled in Ada by the following server task:

```
task CHANNEL is
    entry READ_CHANNEL (READ_DATA : out DATA_TYPE);
    entry WRITE_CHANNEL (WRITE_DATA : in DATA_TYPE);
end CHANNEL

task body CHANNEL is
```

---

[1] Occam was an Irish monk and philosopher living in the middle ages whose best-known contribution is *Occam's razor*—the principle that unnecessary complication should be avoided and that the simpler solution is always preferable, other things being equal. This philosophical principle is the basis for the design of the OCCAM language, and it is, of course, related to the idea of keeping design simple, which is one of the cornerstones of the RISC philosophy.

```
      begin
        loop
          accept READ_CHANNEL do
            accept WRITE_CHANNEL do
              READ_DATA := WRITE_DATA;
            end;
          end;
        end loop;
      end;
```

An important point is that the task CHANNEL does *not* need a buffer to hold the data, since the data is transferred only when both the reader and writer are ready. This contrasts with a mailbox approach, represented by the following Ada task definition:

```
      task MAIL_BOX is
        entry READ_MAIL_BOX (READ_DATA : out DATA_TYPE);
        entry WRITE_MAIL_BOX (WRITE_DATA : in DATA_TYPE);
      end MAIL_BOX

      task body MAIL_BOX is
        INTERNAL_BUFFER : DATA_TYPE;
      begin
        loop
          accept WRITE_MAIL_BOX do
            INTERNAL_BUFFER := WRITE_DATA;
          end;
          accept READ_MAIL_BOX do
            READ_DATA := INTERNAL_BUFFER;
          end;
        end loop;
      end;
```

In this mailbox model, the writer can proceed to execute without waiting for the reader, but the consequence is that an internal buffer is needed. As we will see in the Transputer implementation of OCCAM channels, this difference is important. To carry the mail analogy a little further; a channel is like registered mail, the mailman insists on passing the data from his hand to yours, and the mailbox is not used.

Although this model of communication between processes is extremely simple, a programmer can build up arbitrarily complicated models of communication using these primitives. The literature contains numerous instances where researchers have shown how other synchronization disciplines can be modeled in CSP. Simple semaphores as well as the more complex Ada rendezvous can be modelled in CSP and hence in OCCAM. The channel input/output in OCCAM differs from that of CSP in that neither a sender nor a receiver needs to name the other process, whereas in CSP the communication is between two processes that name one another. The Transputer follows the model of OCCAM, which is more general than the CSP model, so anything that can be expressed in CSP can certainly be programmed in OCCAM.

THE STRUCTURE OF THE TRANSPUTER

The most important distinguishing characteristic of the Transputer design is the high level of integration on the chip. Not only is the floating-point unit on the chip (as on the i860), but, much more important, there is an elaborate implementation of chip-to-chip communications, with all the circuitry for managing this communication integrated as part of the Transputer.

Almost any microprocessor can be used to assemble a parallel machine in which many processors are connected together. The simplest arrangement for such parallel machines is a bus-oriented design:

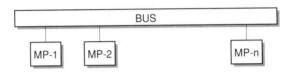

Since all the microprocessors we have looked at are intended to be connected to memory via a bus, this kind of arrangement is compatible with any of the processors. However, the maximum number of processors that can be attached this way is rather small, perhaps in the range of 16 to 32. In order to connect a very large number of processors together, this approach would not work since they would saturate the bus. The more common approach is to connect the processors together in some kind of network, where each processor is connected to a small number of other processors.

The Transputer is specifically designed to facilitate this kind of loosely coupled connection. Each Transputer can be connected to as many as four other Transputers, and all the circuitry for implementing very high bandwidth communication is on-chip, so no extra chips are needed in the design. As we might expect, the implementation model for these chip-to-chip communication channels is based on the OCCAM notion of a channel. This communication capability is unique among the microprocessors we have looked at. Although the Transputer has a number of interesting features when looked at as a single processor, it becomes much more interesting when we consider building a parallel machine with multiple Transputers.

Instruction Format

In looking at a processor, the structure of the instruction formats is not where we usually start. But in the case of the Transputer, the instruction format is so remarkable that it should be mentioned up front—there *is* only one instruction format:

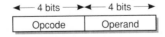

There are no other instruction formats and there are no variations on this single format—*every* instruction has this 8-bit format.

The fact that all instructions fit into this single format is remarkable achievement, even by RISC standards. Indeed, it is hard to imagine how one can manage with such a limited instruction format. Even if 16 instructions are considered to be sufficient, the restriction to a 4-bit operand seems to present an intolerable limitation. We will discuss the instruction set and how these instruction formats are used later on in this chapter.

Register Structure

The register set of the Transputer has only six registers (so in this respect the organization is quite different from what we expect in a RISC design). The registers are called A, B, and C, the *workspace pointer* (WP), *next instruction* (N), and the operand register (see Figure 13.1). The A, B, and C registers are work registers for intermediate evaluation results, and they work like a very small stack. When a load is done into A, A is copied into B, B is copied into C, and C falls into the bit bucket. The loss of the old value in C is not considered an error and is not signalled in any way.

One might think that this is a rather small stack (with only three elements), and indeed this is true. A compiler writer must struggle to make expressions fit in three stack elements wherever possible. If this is not possible, extra code must be generated to rescue the contents of C if they are important. In practice, most expressions in programs are rather short, so this is less of a problem than might be expected. The A, B, and C registers are also used by some of the more complicated instructions to supply additional operands.

The workspace pointer points to a location in memory and can be roughly thought of as being a frame pointer or a stack pointer. Remember that distinct frame and stack pointers are not necessary when the size of a stack frame is fixed. A single register can serve as both the stack pointer, and the frame pointer since the same pointer can be used to point to the last element of the stack and all data is at a fixed distance from this pointer. The workspace pointer is exactly that. It is the frame pointer and the stack pointer with the assumption that all stack frames are fixed size. The stack builds down in the Transputer, so new stack frames are allocated by subtracting a constant from the workspace pointer.

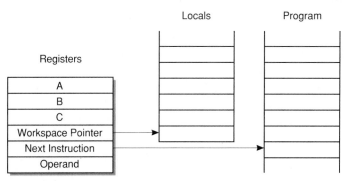

FIGURE 13.1
The register set of the Transputer.

The next instruction register is simply the instruction pointer. The Transputer has a design that completely omits pipelining, so there are no special considerations of multiple instruction pointers, or imprecise interrupts that have to be addressed. As we look further at the architecture, we will see that there is no reason why it should not be pipelined, and in fact, the engineers at INMOS agree. We see no reason why it should not be pipelined, and indeed, conversations with INMOS engineers make it clear that we can expect to future versions of the Transputer that advantage of pipelining techniques.

Finally, the *operand register* is used to build operand values. We will discuss how this is done in detail in a later section.

Memory Structure

The memory of the Transputer is physically divided into two sections. One section is very fast, on chip, and quite large (4K bytes). The remainder of the memory is off chip and so can be managed by a cache or controlled by an MMU (there is no on-chip cache or MMU). It is important to note that this fast local memory is quite different from the on-chip caches that we have encountered in some other microprocessors. The on-chip memory on the Transputer, is, from a programmer's point of view, normal memory, that is, certain memory addresses correspond to the on-chip memory, and other addresses correspond to off-chip memory.

To make effective use of the fast on-chip memory of the Transputer, it is expected that the stack frames of procedures will be kept very small and that these stack frames will be kept in the on-chip memory as the procedures are executing. This means that for best performance, the workspace pointer should be pointing to a frame stored in the on-chip memory.

In terms of performance, one can compare the fast on-chip memory of the Transputer to the register windows of the SPARC. From this point of view, the workspace pointer acts as a means of implementing a register window base pointer. Furthermore, this is a flexibly sized window because procedures are not limited to having a fixed number of "registers."[2]

There is no differentiation from a functional point of view between the fast and slow memory. It is simply a matter of a certain range of memory being implemented with faster hardware, and all instructions that reference memory can equally well reference fast or slow memory. For example, the workspace pointer can equally well point to fast or slow memory. For efficiency, it is obviously desirable that stack frames be in fast memory, but this is not a requirement. One approach taken in an Ada implementation for the Transputer is to allow the programmer to specify on a task-by-task basis whether the stack frames should be in fast or slow memory.

---

[2] If the public relations department at INMOS wanted to generate glossy brochures making the Transputer sound more RISC-like, they could claim that they had 1000 registers on chip with flexible register windowing!

OCCAM has no recursion, which means that the maximum depth of the run-time stack can be computed at compile time because the call graph (a directed graph whose nodes are procedures, and whose edges are procedure calls) has no loops, it is just a call tree. This makes it straightforward to take an OCCAM program and compute its maximum stack depth, allowing the operating system to know how much workspace to set aside for that OCCAM process. It can be allocated statically in the fast memory area, and no checks will ever have to be made for stack overflow. Furthermore, the number of processes is fixed and known at compile time in OCCAM, so you can further partition the fast memory statically among processes. This is a case of a programming language being modeled to be kind to a machine (they were very much developed in parallel).

Historically, the intention behind this design was that *only* fast memory be used. When the Transputer was developed, memory was quite expensive, and the idea was to add memory to a system by adding more processors, each with its fast on chip memory. However, in the first place, this kind of highly distributed memory is hard to manage (it would mean, for example, that a single 10,000-element array would have to be split across many processors), and second, the trend to cheaper prices makes it economically reasonable to put a lot of memory on each processor.

Interestingly, the latest versions of the Transputer chip have an external signal that can completely disable the fast internal memory, so that all memory references are to the externally attached memory. The reason for this rather strange capability is that in some military applications there are both security and radiation concerns over having CMOS memory on board the chip. One of the appeals of the Transputer is that the technology it uses is radiation resistant except for the fast memory on board the chip.[3]

Loading Values From Memory

Since the opcode field of an instruction is 4 bits wide, there are 16 possible basic instructions. The remaining 4 bits are used to specify an operand. Although 4 bits does not seem like very much for either the opcode or the operand fields, we will see that the range of the opcodes and operands can be extended, so things are not quite as limited as they seem.

One of the 16 basic instructions is called Load Local (LDL). This instruction is used to load a value from the stack frame of the current procedure into the A register (with A being copied to B, B being copied to C, and C being lost). The single 4-bit operand of this instruction is interpreted as a word offset from the workspace pointer. Using Load Local in its 8-bit form allows one to load into the A register any one of 16

---

[3] Designers of military hardware worry about a phenomenon known as EMP (electromagnetic pulse), which arises when radiation is generated by exploding a nuclear device high up in the atmosphere. No one is quite sure how fierce this effect is—no one has performed the necessary experiment! In the worst scenario, many chips die instantly. According to press rumors, when a Soviet fighter pilot defected to Japan about ten years ago, U.S. intelligence examined the aircraft and were surprised to find that tubes were used instead of transistors. It was not clear whether this represented backward technology or an exhibition of concern over the EMP effect—tubes are *not* affected!

words on the front of the workspace (i.e., the 16 words starting at the location referenced by the workspace pointer). This means that for procedures with small stack frames, all access to local variables can be performed using 1-byte instructions. Since most procedures meet this criterion, typical Transputer programs can use the LDL instruction for most data references, resulting in very compact code.

Extending Operand Values

Obviously restricting procedures to 16 words of local storage would be intolerable, so there must be some mechanism for addressing locations higher up in the workspace. Here we see one of the really clever ideas in the Transputer. Two of the 16 basic instructions, Prefix (PFIX) and Negative Prefix (NFIX), are used to extend the operand range.

To understand how these prefix instructions work, let us look at the exact mechanism used for executing instructions and obtaining operand values. For all instructions *except* the prefix instructions, including LDL, the actual steps that are performed in decoding an instruction are the following:

- The contents of the operand register is shifted 4 bits to the left.
- The 4-bit operand in the instruction is ORed into 4 low-order bits of the operand register.
- The instruction is executed, using the value in the operand register as the operand of the instruction.
- The operand register is cleared to all zero bits.

All the instructions except Prefix and Negative Prefix work this way. If we execute nothing but these instructions, the upper 28 bits of the operand register would always be zero, because of the last step which zeros this register. This means that the effect of the steps described above is simply to use the 4-bit operand field of the current instruction as the operand value.

However, the prefix instructions operate in a slightly different manner:

- For the NFIX case only, invert all the bits in the operand register.
- Shift the operand register 4 bits to the left.
- OR in the 4-bit operand from the PFIX or NFIX instruction into the 4 low-order bits of the operand register.

Note that the operand register is *not* cleared to zeros at the end of a prefix instruction. The prefix instructions are the only instructions which can leave the operand register containing a non-zero value. The result of this arrangement is that we can get the effect of arbitrarily large operand values by preceding one of the normal format instructions with a series of prefix instructions. This means for example, that to perform a Load Local instruction where the offset of the word in the stack frame was at offset 312 decimal (= 148 hexadecimal), we would write the three-instruction sequence:

```
PFIX    1
PFIX    4
LDL     8
```

The two prefix instructions set the operand register to contain 00000014 (hexadecimal), and the Load Local instruction shifts this value to the left to get 00000140, ORs in its operand to get 00000148, and then loads word 148.

Any number of prefix and negative prefix instructions may precede one of the other 14 instructions to provide it with an arbitrary 32-bit operand. It is, of course, possible to build an arbitrary 32-bit operand, including negative numbers, using only the PFIX instruction, but the NFIX instruction allows small negative numbers to be built with far fewer instructions. For example, to perform a LDL instruction where the offset is -136, which is FFFFFF78 in hexadecimal, the following sequence of instructions can be used:

```
NFIX    7
LDL     8
```

An arbitrary 32-bit operand can often be built up in fewer than than 7 bytes using a non-obvious combination of NFIX and PFIX instructions. There is an algorithm in the Transputer Reference Manual[4] that shows how to determine the optimal sequence of NFIX and PFIX instructions for any particular operand.

For some operand values, as many as seven prefix instructions might be needed, but in most cases far fewer prefixes will suffice, since most operands are small. For example, any word in a 256-word stack frame can be accessed using a single prefix. We never need more than 7 prefix bytes, since the longest operand is 32 bits, and the last 4 bits are supplied by the final instruction. INMOS claims that about 70% of the instructions in most programs do not require any prefixes and are thus only 1-byte long. This means that Transputer programs are very compact in comparison to the other instruction sets we have looked at. Even in the worst case of a full 7 prefix bytes, the effective overall instruction length is only 8 bytes, which is not so shocking by CISC standards (both the 386 and 68030 have instructions much longer than 8 bytes).

The Remaining Basic Instructions

We have now looked at three out of the possible 16 basic instructions, so there are 13 more to go (the opcode field is only 4 bits long).

LOAD CONSTANT. The Load Constant (LDC) instruction loads the A register with the operand value. As with all the other load instructions, the evaluation stack is pushed down so, as part of the execution of LDC, A is copied to B, B is copied to C, and the contents of C is lost. Prefix instructions can as usual precede the LDC

---

[4] The algorithm is stated in OCCAM, but is recursive. The authors of the manual must have conveniently forgotten the restriction that OCCAM does not permit recursion!

instruction so arbitrary 32-bit constant values can be loaded. Once again, most constants in typical programs are small, so most of the time few or no prefix bytes are required.

STORE LOCAL. The Store Local (STL) instruction stores the A register into a local word, addressed by the sum of the operand values and the workspace pointer, just like LDL. Like other store instructions, STL also copies B to A and C to B, effectively popping the evaluation stack. As with LDL, the 1-byte form of STL is sufficient for accessing small local stack frames (up to 16 words), and then prefix instructions can be used to extend the addressability as needed.

ADD CONSTANT. Add Constant (ADC) adds its operand value to the value in the A register. The contents of B and C are not affected. This addition is a signed addition. If overflow occurs, then an error condition is signalled. We will discuss later how error conditions are handled. Typical code for incrementing a variable, A := A + 1, would be the sequence

```
LDL    A
ADC    1
STL    A
```

With so few registers, there is, of course, no possibility of keeping variables in registers, but usually this instruction sequence is only 3 bytes long, so it actually takes less space than the corresponding addition instruction for a RISC chip where A is stored in a register. Even the 386, with its specialized INC instruction, does not beat the Transputer here—INC for a local variable on the 386 also takes three bytes.

LOAD NON-LOCAL. The Load Non-Local (LDNL) instruction is a memory load that uses the A register as the base address instead of the workspace pointer. This allows the program to access memory outside the local stack frame. First the A register is loaded with the required base pointer, and then LDNL is used to address the required word, with the operand being an offset from the base address in A. The result replaces the value in the A register, and the stack is *not* pushed down, although typically the instructions used to load the pointer into A would have pushed the stack down, so the combined effect of the sequence acts as a normal stack load.

A typical implementation would use static links for accessing more global scopes in the stack. Using this approach, each stack frame for a nested procedure contains a pointer to the stack frame of the procedure in which it is statically nested.

Accessing a series of static links means loading the link from each successively higher scope and using the link to access the higher-level frame. Assuming that the link is always in the bottom 16 words of each frame, which is a reasonable assumption since the link is accessed with relatively high frequency and thus can be deliberately allocated in this region of the frame, the access to a variable in an outer scope can be achieved with a series of 1-byte instructions:

```
LDL      link1
LDNL     link2
...
LDNL     variable
```

This is an attractive implementation of static links, given that it is unusual to have more than a few static levels. The code size for a non-local reference using static links on a Transputer will often be smaller than conventional processors using displays.

STORE NON-LOCAL. Store Non-Local (STNL) is the store instruction corresponding to LDNL. It stores the contents of the B register in memory, using the A register as the base address. The stack is then popped twice, so the original contents of C end up in the A register.

JUMP. The Jump (J) instruction interprets its operand as a displacement from the instruction following the jump Short forward jumps, up to 16 bytes past the J instruction, do not require prefix bytes. Any other jumps, including all backward jumps, need prefix bytes to extend the operand in the usual manner.

When a single prefix instruction is used to extend the range of a jump, the effect is a 2-byte instruction with an 8-bit signed jump (using PFIX or NFIX). This is even more compact than the jump on the 386, which is considered to have a very compact instruction stream. The conditional jump on the 386 is a 2-byte instruction, but the maximum jump range is only 7 bits.

The jump instruction takes its operand from the operand register, as usual, and the appropriate number of prefix instructions depends on how far away the jump is. In the case of a forward jump, determining the number of prefixes is in principle no more difficult than the familiar task of selecting long or short jumps on a processor like the 386, except that it is a little more painful to take the easy way out on the Transputer—it would mean that all forward jumps had seven prefix bytes! In any case, the programmer writing in assembly language never has to worry about generating prefix instructions, since this is taken care of by the assembler. In general we would expect the assembler to take care of prefix sequences, allowing us, for example, to write ADC 299, generating two prefix instructions and an ADC.

One important note is that the jump instruction destroys the contents of the A, B, and C registers—or at least the programmer must program as though it destroyed these registers—their contents cannot be counted on at the target of the jump. This seems highly peculiar, but later we will see that it is all part of the scheme of making process control efficient.

LOAD LOCAL POINTER. The Load Local Pointer (LDLP) instruction is similar to LDL except that instead of loading the addressed word, it places the *address* of the word in the A register. In other words, LDLP computes the sum of the workspace pointer and the operand value shifted left 2 bits. A typical use of LDLP is to compute the address of a parameter that is to be passed by reference to a procedure.

LOAD NON-LOCAL POINTER. Similarly, the Load Non-Local Pointer (LDNLP) instruction is like LDNL except that it loads the address of the variable instead of the contents. The effect is thus simply to add the operand value to the value in the A register. LDNLP is thus very similar to the ADC instruction. The difference is that LDNLP never signals an error condition, allowing wraparound addressing, and its operand, a word offset, is shifted left 2 bits.

CONDITIONAL JUMP. The Conditional Jump instruction (CJ) tests the A register to determine if it contains true (non-zero) or false (zero). In either case the A register is popped off the stack. If the value was true, then the jump is taken, using the operand to determine the jump address just like the J instruction. Otherwise, the next instruction is executed.

EQUALS CONSTANT. The Equals Constant (EQC) instruction compares the A register with the constant value (which is the operand) and replaces A by either 1 or 0 (true or false) depending on whether the value is equal or not. Typically EQC is followed by a CJ instruction that tests the outcome of the comparison.

ADJUST WORKSPACE. The Adjust Workspace (AJW) instruction adds its operand value to the workspace pointer. Since the operand is signed, this can be used to either allocate or deallocate stack frames. There is no provision for checking for stack overflow. As we noted previously, in OCCAM it is possible to determine the maximum stack depth at compile time, and apparently what is good enough for OCCAM is expected to be good enough for everybody else. In practice, languages like C or Ada that allow recursion will have to add an explicit stack overflow check.

CALL PROCEDURE (CALL). The Call Procedure (CALL) instruction uses its operand to address the procedure, exactly as for the jump instruction, but in addition it stores the return point and also allows for passing parameters. As part of the execution of CALL, the workspace pointer is decremented by 16 (4 words), and these 4 words are set to contain the old contents of the A, B, and C registers and the return point.

The called procedure then uses AJW to allocate additional workspace for local variables, resulting in the stack frame shown in Figure 13.2. Typically the A, B, and C registers are used to pass parameters, and are thus stored in the frame of the called procedure, where they can be referenced via the workspace pointer in the usual manner.

The Extended Instruction Set (Operate)

If you have been counting, you will have noticed that only 15 basic instructions have been described so far. Since the opcode field is only 4 bits long, there are 16 possible opcode patterns, which might lead you to think that only one instruction is left. Although this is true from a formal point of view, it is quite misleading, since the Transputer has a large and quite complicated instruction set. The remaining instruction

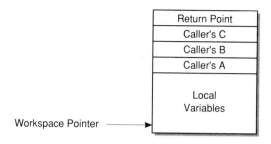

| Return Point |
| Caller's C |
| Caller's B |
| Caller's A |
| Local
Variables |

Workspace Pointer ⟶

FIGURE 13.2
A Tranputer stack frame.

is called Operate (OPR). The OPR instruction actually corresponds to a whole set of possible operations.

On a stack machine, the actual operations such as arithmetic and logical operations do not require any explicit operands, since both the input operands and the output result are placed on top of the stack (we have seen this kind of code before in Chapter 5, since the Intel floating-point coprocessors also use a stack approach). For example, the statement:

A := (B + 3) + D;

would generate the following sequence of instructions:

```
LDL    B
ADC    3
LDL    D
ADD
STL    A
```

The ADD instruction adds the contents of A and B, popping them off the evaluation stack (which moves C up to A), and then pushes the result back onto the stack (so that the original value of C ends up in B, and the result ends up in A).

The ADD instruction does not need any operands, and it is actually a shorthand notation for one of the operate instructions. The operand of OPR is used to indicate which of several possible operations are to be performed. ADD is an OPR instruction with an operand value of 5 and could thus have been written:

```
OPR    5
```

Since OPR takes a 4-bit operand, there are 15 other 1-byte OPR instructions, but this still isn't the end of the story. OPR works like all other instructions on the Transputer, so its operand can be extended with prefix instructions. Theoretically, this means that by adding more prefix codes the Transputer has an essentially unlimited supply of opcodes. In practice, a single PFIX instruction allows more than enough expansion of the range, and the T800 reference manual lists 146 operate instructions, all of which can be coded in either 1 or 2 bytes. By using NFIX as well, up to 512 opcodes can be represented in 2 bytes, but 146 is a large number of instructions even by CISC standards, so it is unlikely that the Transputer will ever need to take advantage of this observation. In any case, as an example of the use of PFIX in conjunction with OPR, the logical AND instruction (AND) has an operate code of hexadecimal 46. It could be coded as

```
PFIX    4
OPR     6
```

although in practice any reasonable assembler for the Transputer would recognize the opcode AND and generate these two instructions.

So the Transputer is *not* a reduced instruction set computer after all. If anything, its available set of operations is even more extensive than those of CISC processors we have studied. The following is a brief summary of the available operations:

- A set of integer arithmetic operations, including multiply and divide, with overflow checking.
- A set of unsigned (modular) arithmetic operations.
- A set of logical and shift operations.
- A set of integer arithmetic operations specially intended for efficient implementation of multiple-precision integer arithmetic.
- A set of instructions for moving sections of two-dimensional byte arrays around in memory. These are intended for graphics applications, where pixel maps are implemented in memory. These operations then correspond to moving patterns around on a display screen.
- A set of bit manipulation instructions.
- A set of array subscripting operations, suitable for indexing into either byte or word arrays.
- A set of operations for handling the onboard timers. Two timers are integrated into the Transputer rather than being implemented by a separate input/output device as on other chips like the Intel 386.
- A set of input/output operations for sending and receiving messages via the four built-in communication channels.
- A set of operations for controlling process operations. We have not mentioned it explicitly yet, but the Transputer contains a hardware tasking implementation, similar to, but more elaborate than, the Intel 386 implementation of tasking. This should not be too surprising, since we observed that the Transputer was based on OCCAM, and processes are a very important feature of this language.
- A full set of floating-point operations. These are implemented on chip, not by a separate coprocessor.

Even this brief summary of the T800 instruction set is rather lengthy, and we certainly do not intend to go into great detail on all of these instructions. Interestingly, the

Transputer Databook, the main source of technical information for the Transputer, does not go into the details of the instructions either. Instead one has to look to the Compiler Writer's Guide for instruction details. This reflects the INMOS attitude that all programs should be written in high-level languages (preferably OCCAM) and that therefore only compiler writers need to know how the instruction set works.

Even in the Compiler Writer's Guide, many of the operating system functions such as process control are not fully described. Apparently INMOS assumes that only the writer of the operating system (i.e., INMOS themselves) needs to know about such things. Another way in which the Transputer is unique among the chips described in this book in that it is hard to get a full description of the architecture. Some of the details described in this chapter have been obtained by looking at a Transputer chip and its OCCAM compiler and seeing what they do. This, of course, is not a desirable approach, since it is not clear what is an intended part of the architectural design and what simply reflects specialized implementation choices. Still, in the absence of full documentation, this is the best we can do.

Although we will not describe all the operations in detail, we will describe a few of the more complicated instructions to give some of the flavor of the unusual aspects of the Transputer.

FRACTIONAL MULTIPLY. There are conventional division and multiplication instructions for use with integer operands. In addition, there is an unusual multiplication instruction called Fractional Multiply (FMUL) that is used with fixed-point fractions. Suppose that in Ada we declare

```
type FRAC is delta 2.0**(-31) range -1.0 .. +1.0;
X, Y, Z : FRAC;
```

This corresponds to a binary fraction, where the binary point is at the start of the 32-bit word, right after the sign bit. Now if we multiply two such words:

```
X := FRAC (Y * Z);
```

the result is the *high order* of the double-length product, not the low order that we want in the integer case. Furthermore, it makes sense to round the result in this case, since we may as well have the result represented as accurately as possible (although Ada does not require this rounding). The FMUL instruction is exactly the operation that is needed in this case, including a rounding step using IEEE-like round to nearest even. Although this should make Ada compiler writers happy,[5] it is a little surprising to find such a specialized instruction, since binary fractions are not often used.

A possible explanation is that early versions of the Transputer did not have hardware floating-point, so fixed-point fractional form was likely to be used more often, and, in particular, the fractional multiply is useful in writing floating-point simulators in software.

---

[5] In fact, it probably makes Ada compiler writers *unhappy*, since taking advantage of specialized instructions of this type always adds complexity to a compiler.

MULTIPLE-PRECISION ARITHMETIC. We noted that the Transputer has a full set of operations for performing multiple-precision integer arithmetic. As an example, let's consider just one of these: the Long Multiply (LMUL) instruction. LMUL takes three operands, which are loaded into the A, B, and C registers, and performs the following computations:

A = Low order (A ∗ B + C)
B = High order (A ∗ B + C)
C = C (unchanged)

Here the register names on the right side of the equal sign are the old values, and the register names on the left side of the equal sign are the new values. This is another one of those instructions that seems a little peculiar unless you see exactly what it is intended to be used for. Consider the problem of multiplying a long binary number, one consisting of a series of 32-bit words, by a single word.

At each stage in the inner loop of this multiplication, we multiply the current word of the multiplicand by the current word of the multiplier, adding in the high-order carry from the previous multiplication. The low-order word of this product is the next word of the result, and the high order is the carry word for the next multiplication. Now we can see that the long multiply is *exactly* what the doctor ordered for this inner loop—at each stage, C is the carry from the previous LMUL operation and A and B are loaded with the next words from the multiplier and multiplicand. After the LMUL, A is the next result word, and B is the carry, ready for the following LMUL.

As usual, we have a complex instruction that is exactly right for a very specific task. If this task is the one at hand, then, of course, having the specially tailored instruction is very convenient and very efficient—considerably more efficient than constructing the same effect with a sequence of instructions. However, the RISC point of view asks us whether it is really the case that programs spend enough of their time doing this particular operation to warrant the expense (in design complexity, and possibly in general speed of the chip) of putting in the specialized instruction. In the case of multiple-precision multiplication, the answer is almost surely no—it is very unlikely that a program will spend most of its time doing multiple-precision multiplications.

THE CRC INSTRUCTIONS. Two unusual instructions are CRCBYTE and CRCWORD, which are used to calculate a cyclic redundancy check for either a byte or word quantity. These instructions perform what seem to be very peculiar bit-oriented operations. There are two inputs, the current cyclic check and the input byte. The single output is an updated cyclic check value, obtained by a seemingly random sequence of shifts and rearrangement of bits.

CRC is certainly an instruction whose purpose is completely incomprehensible without some rather specialized knowledge about its intended domain, which is in the area of communications. When a communications message is sent down a potentially noisy channel, a checksum is usually sent along with it. This is done in the hope that any error in the channel will result in the received message having an incorrect checksum, thus leading to detection and subsequent correction of the message (typically by requesting its retransmission).

The cyclic redundancy check, which is actually a polynomial multiplication where the input values are considered to be polynomials over the two-element ring whose values correspond to the bit settings 0 and 1, is a particularly effective form of such a checksum. It is a little hard to compute, but it has very desirable mathematical characteristics. For instance, it is very effective in detecting *burst* errors that destroy a sequence of adjacent bits, whereas simple parity checks are not so effective in this situation.

So—very nice if what you want to do is to send messages around on noisy channels, but what on earth is such a specialized instruction doing in a general instruction set? The explanation is rather obvious. As we mentioned previously, one of the important points of the Transputer design is that it has four communication channels integrated onto the chip. These communication channels happen to use a CRC to guarantee error-free communication. Since this means that the CRC logic is present in any case, why not make it available to the programmer? Here is a case where we cannot make the usual complaint about unnecessary complex instructions!

THE SQUARE ROOT INSTRUCTIONS.   The floating-point instruction set is a fairly complete implementation of the IEEE standard. It handles both the 32-bit and 64-bit basic formats, but not the extended format.

The operation set includes both remainder and square root instructions, but these instructions take considerably longer than other instructions to complete. Since the Transputer is intended for use in real time applications, it is important to avoid holding up interrupts for even the few microseconds that would be required to complete a square root operation. To avoid this problem, there are three separate square root instructions:

```
FPUSQRTFIRST          ; square root first step
FPUSQRTSTEP           ; square root step
FPUSQRTLAST           ; square root end
```

A single-precision square root requires a FIRST instruction, followed by two STEP instructions, followed by a LAST instruction. Interrupts can occur between any two of these instructions in the sequence, avoiding the problem of increasing interrupt latency to an unacceptable degree. Presumably, the FIRST instruction computes an initial approximation, and the STEP instruction does a Newton-Raphson iteration step, although this is not documented. The result is a computation scheme for square root not unlike what is found on the Intel i860 but encoded in special instructions, so that the instruction sequence is considerably more compact.

Using the Evaluation Stack

An interesting challenge for a Transputer compiler is to fit the evaluation of expressions in the 3 register stack whenever possible. Consider the following expression:

    (a + b) / (c - (d * e))

A naive translation of this expression yields the instruction sequence:

    ldl a; ldl b; add;
    ldl c; ldl d; ldl e; mul; sub;
    div;

but this evaluation sequence would require four stack locations. Making use of the REV (reverse) instruction which interchanges the top two stack locations, an alternative sequence is:

    ldl c; ldl d; ldl e; mul; sub;
    ldl a; ldl b; add;
    rev; div;

This sequence requires only three stack locations, and thus fits in the A, B, C, registers. The Transputer Compiler Writer's Guide contains an extensive discussion of techniques for determining efficient evaluation sequences for expressions.

COMMUNICATION BETWEEN PROCESSES

In this section, we will look at the communications channels and process management on the Transputer, the two features that are the most distinctive and characteristic aspects of this processor.

The Transputer is a hardware mapping of OCCAM, and OCCAM has the notion of communication by channels. In OCCAM, we have the primitive statement forms that read and write a channel, and it is no great surprise to find that the Transputer instruction set contains corresponding instructions. There are three instructions that can be used to output data on a channel:

    OUTBYTE   ; output a single byte
    OUTWORD   ; output a single word
    OUT   ; output an arbitrary length message

There is only one input instruction:

    IN   ; Input message

There are no separate instructions to input a byte or word, but the IN instruction supplies the length as one of the parameters, so the case of 1 or 4 bytes can be handled by supplying the appropriate length. The length given for the IN and OUT instructions should be the same, or unexpected memory destruction can occur. Similarly, it is up to the program to make sure that one process issues an OUT instruction and the other issues an IN instruction. The result of issuing two OUT instructions to the same channel is undefined. In fact, what actually happens is that when the second process executes the OUT instruction, it just assumes that the first process must have executed an IN instruction, and the first process will be surprised to find data *arriving* instead of being sent out. The OCCAM language includes structuring rules to make this sort of occurrence impossible, but of course there is no such protection for an assembly language programmer.

In looking at these instructions, it is important to remember that the transfer takes place only when both receiver and sender are ready. This is why a message can be of arbitrary length. Once the sender and receiver are both "locked on" to the channel, the data is transmitted in a stream directly from the memory of the sender to the memory of the receiver, and no intermediate buffer is required. If the communication channel had mailbox semantics, then a buffer would have to be allocated somewhere and the length of messages would have to be restricted.

Internal and External Channels

Channel input/output is controlled by a channel control word that contains data indicating the status of the channel. A channel is in one of three states:

- Inactive. The channel is not currently being used.
- Ready. A process has issued an IN or OUT instruction, but the corresponding operation has not yet been performed. In this case the channel control word points to the workspace of the process that issued the operation, and the length and address of the data are stored in this workspace.
- Active. Data is being transferred from the sender to the receiver, using the address and length previously stored.

There are both internal and external channels. The four external links can support eight external channels (a channel is a one-way communication device, and the links are each bi-directional, allowing two channels on each link, one for input and one for output). Messages using the external channels are transferred to other processes residing on other Transputer chips using the chip-to-chip communication links. The internal channels merely cause data to be transferred from one process to another on the same Transputer.

There can be any number of internal channels. Since all processes on a single Transputer can potentially share memory, it would be possible for processes running on the same Transputer to transfer data directly using this shared memory without using channels. However, this would undermine a very important part of the OCCAM and Transputer design, namely the principle that any process can run on any processor, and, apart from efficiency considerations, a program should be completely unaware of whether it is operating on one or many Transputers. By keeping the address spaces of processes separate and communicating between processes only by using channels, the program is completely independent of how the processes are mapped to processors.

Process Control

A Transputer program consists of a set of independent processes (a process is the INMOS and OCCAM term for a task). The Transputer instruction set contains instructions for manipulating these processes, including:

STARTP   Start Process
ENDP   End Process
RUNP   Run Process
STOPP   Stop Process

All these operations are quite rapid, taking about 12 clocks on the T800. This means that process control, including process creation and destruction, on the Transputer is comparably efficient to procedure call and return. This contrasts with the other processors we have looked at where context switches are much more expensive than procedure calls. Here we see one of the advantages of the very small register set of the Transputer. A context switch can be performed much more rapidly if there is no need to save and restore a large set of registers.

Once a set of processes has been created, individual processes can issue IN and OUT instructions. When one of these instructions is executed, the data cannot be transferred until the corresponding sender or receiver is ready. In OCCAM, this would cause the issuing process to be blocked until the other process was ready. The Transputer models exactly the same behavior. The hardware contains a complete implementation of multitasking. This implementation is quite similar to the multitasking in the 386 in that the hardware keeps track of multiple processes and can automatically perform context switches from one process to another under suitable circumstances.

One of these circumstances occurs precisely when a process issues a channel operation and no other process has issued the corresponding operation to complete the link. When this happens, the current process is suspended and some other ready process is run. The suspended process is automatically made ready again when the channel link is completed and the data is transferred.

PROCESS SCHEDULING. The Transputer processor maintains a ready queue of processes, which are linked through their workspaces. When a process is descheduled, two words at the bottom of the workspace are used to hold the saved instruction pointer and a link pointer for the ready queue. Two special processor registers point to the front and back of this linked list (see Figure 13.3). In this example, process W is currently active, so the registers of the processor reference this process. Processes X, Y, and Z are ready to run but are not currently running, with X at the head of the list and Z at the end. If process W issues an IN instruction on a previously inactive channel, then it will be descheduled and process X will be scheduled. In this case, process W is *not* added to the end of the list. Instead, a pointer to W is stored in the relevant channel control word, and then when the message is completed, W will be rescheduled by adding it to the ready process list.

This picture is a simplified one in that there are actually two ready queues, one for high-priority processes and one for low-priority processes. A high-priority process is always scheduled in preference to a low-priority process if possible. Low-priority processes will run only if no high-priority process is being run.

DESCHEDULING PROCESSES. There are two other ways (besides being suspended by a channel operation) that processes can be descheduled. First, an external interrupt

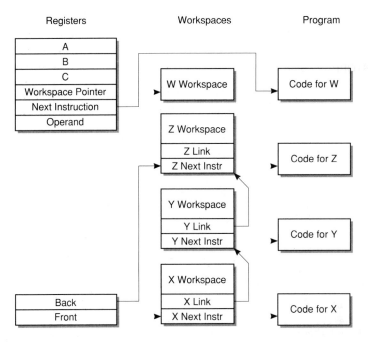

FIGURE 13.3
The process scheduling queue on the Transputer.

can arrive. If a high-priority process is waiting for this interrupt, or if a high-priority process completes the transmission of a message, then a currently running low-priority process can be preempted so the high-priority process can be run immediately. All the registers of the low-priority process are saved in this case, so it can resume running from the point of preemption when it is scheduled at some later time.

The other way that a process can be descheduled occurs as a result of the time-slicing feature. The Transputer time-slices low-priority processes, giving each process a slice of time and then transferring control to the next process. This time slicing is an important feature, because you will remember that the intention is that a program should have the same behavior regardless of whether its processes are running on the same processor or on separate Transputers in a network. If each process were running on a separate processor, then the processes would certainly be running in parallel. If they are running on a single processor, then we need time slicing to approximate the parallel running behavior.

Furthermore, to make this approximation effective, we want a very rapid time-slice period. In most operating systems, the time-slice period cannot be made too short, since there would be too much context switching overhead—values of 50 to 100 milliseconds are typical. The Transputer, on the other hand, implements a time-slice period of 1 millisecond. To avoid the problem of excessive overhead, the context switch is implemented as efficiently as possible and ends up taking only slightly longer than a procedure call.

This very fast context switch is achieved partly by *not* bothering to save the contents of the A, B, C, and Operand registers. This is rather surprising, because any program on the Transputer depends heavily on the contents of these registers, and one cannot have them disappearing without warning.[6] It is all very well to decide to improve the context switch by not bothering to save registers, but it clearly seems unreasonable that the A, B, C, and operand registers can disappear at any moment. The answer is that they can't disappear at *any* moment but only at what are known as *descheduling* points.

The possible descheduling points are unconditional jump instructions, channel operations and process control operations. For any other instructions, it is impossible to get a time slice. This means that the programmer must be aware in issuing any of these instructions that the A, B, and C registers may disappear. For example, in a loop with an unconditional jump at the bottom, it is not permissible to hold values in the A, B, or C registers across this jump. The operand stack is *very* temporary. This helps to explain why it is so small. A larger stack is not so useful when you cannot keep the values around. One interesting effect of the notion of descheduling points is that the compiler had better be sure to generate them periodically, or the resulting process will grab the processor and lock out other low-priority processes.

This requirement has some interesting effects on code generation. For example, consider a while loop. The straightforward code is:

```
test condition
jump if false to end of loop
body of loop
unconditional jump back to test
```

Clever compilers like to avoid the unconditional jump by transforming this to:

```
jump to test
body of loop
test condition
jump if true to start of loop
```

This clever transformation would *not* be a good idea on the Transputer, since the resulting loop, though it has fewer instructions on each loop, has no descheduling points, and hence the process could not be time sliced to allow some other low-priority task to run. It can of course still be preempted by a high-priority task in response to an interrupt.

Recursive procedure calls are another situation in which a long sequence of code may be executed that contains no unconditional jump instructions. Of course, the OCCAM compiler does not have to worry about this, but a compiler for another language should consider inserting a jump instruction between two successive call instructions if it does not otherwise generate one.

---

[6] The disappearing floating-point guard bits on the Honeywell machine were bad enough, but having all the integer registers disappear is going *too* far!

In the preemption case, when a low-priority process is suspended to execute a high priority, it is, of course, necessary to save all the registers. This is done using a special reserved area in the fast memory. There is only one such area because at most one low-priority process can be in preempted state. When the processor finishes executing, the interrupting high-priority process (and any other high-priority processes that become ready), it always returns to the preempted low-priority task if there is one, so there can never be more than one preempted task, and only one register save area is required.

THE ALTERNATE INSTRUCTION. OCCAM has a special construction allowing a single process to wait for data from multiple channels, or for multiple interrupt conditions, such as timer interrupts. For example, in OCCAM, we can write:

```
ALT
    allowcount & count ? signal
        counter := counter + 1

    allowtotal & total ? signal
        SEQ
            out ! counter
            counter := 0
```

This causes the process to wait for input from either the *count* channel or the *total* channel, whichever appears first. The guards *allowcount* and *allowtotal* are Boolean expressions that allow input from the corresponding channel only if the expression evaluates to true. Any or all of the alternatives can be guarded, but there must be at least one open (i.e., true or unguarded) alternative or the process will wait forever. When data is received from one of the channels, the corresponding sequence of code is executed (the SEQ in OCCAM is like begin-end in Pascal; it marks a series of statements to be executed in sequence as a single statement).

Since OCCAM has this construct, we would expect to find instructions to implement ALT on the Transputer, and indeed we do—there are actually a whole collection of constructs and a rather complicated protocol for implementing the ALT construct. First of all we issue an Alt Start (ALT) instruction, which initializes the execution of an ALT structure and in particular clears an internal flag, *guard OK*, to false. For each of the alternatives, we then issue an *enable channel* (ENBC) instruction that takes as parameters the guard value and the channel value. ENBC checks for the case of an open guard with a channel ready to send data. If it finds such a case, then the internal register *guard OK* is set true; otherwise, if the guard is true but the channel is not ready to send data, then the channel word is set to point to the current process to indicate that it is ready to receive data.

After all the ENBC instructions have been issued, an Alt Wait (ALTWT) instruction is issued. If *guard OK* is true, indicating that there is a channel ready to send data, or that some other relevant event has occurred, then ALTWT allows the process to proceed (note that the message has *not* been transmitted yet). If no channel is ready, then the process is descheduled.

Following the ALTWT instruction, a series of Disable Channel (DISC) instructions are issued, one for each of the alternatives. The DISC instruction will receive data from the channel if it is ready, executing the associated code. Finally, the entire structure is terminated by executing an Alt End (ALTEND) instruction.

The algorithms for handling this alternation structure are quite complex and certainly not fully documented. It appears that race conditions are eliminated during the period of issuing ENBC instructions, probably by disabling interrupts, which certainly simplifies things.

If the process is scheduled, then we have to worry about how to handle the case of multiple processes sending data to separate channels at the same time. The trick that is used in this case is for the sender to recognize the special case of a waiting receiver who is executing an ALT structure. Instead of trying to send the data right away, the sender is descheduled and is then woken up only when the corresponding DISC instruction is executed. If several processes send messages, only the first will be woken up for transmission, the remainder will remain descheduled, waiting for some other process to read their channel.

In addition to the instructions described, it is also possible in OCCAM to specify an alternative that waits for a certain amount of time using the timer (similar to the delay alternative in an Ada select statement). A parallel set of instructions (Timer Alt Start, Timer Enable, Timer Alt Wait, Disable Timer) are provided to implement this possibility.

This description is unavoidably complicated. We have gone into some detail to emphasize the remarkable complexity of the Transputer design and the degree to which it is specialized for communication and multiprocessing functions. Once again we observe that although the Transputer may have RISC-like characteristics, avoidance of complex instructions is not among them!

Interrupt Handling

In addition to the four wires coming into the chip from other Transputers, there is one more wire, which is another specialized channel for external events (interrupts). Interrupts are handled using channel read instructions; a high-priority process issues an in word or in byte operation to this interrupt channel and is blocked. When the interrupt comes in, it is as though the external device has written to this channel, causing the high-priority process to wake up and preempt the currently running low-priority process. This high-priority process can then handle the interrupt. Another source of interrupts comes from the built-in timers on the Transputer chip.

This handling of interrupts is the primary reason for needing two levels of priority. Normal application processes run at low-priority and are expected to issue descheduling instructions with sufficient frequency to permit effective time slicing. A process which needs to service an interrupt with minimum latency is run at high priority. When the interrupt comes in, it is immediately scheduled, preempting the current low-priority task.

In more conventional architectures, we might be concerned about causing a process switch on every interrupt. For example, the use of task gates for interrupt handling on the 386 is very neat from a functional point of view, but many interrupt handlers will not be prepared to accept the 600-clock overhead of this approach, which is why Intel provides other alternatives for interrupt handling. In the Transputer case, the process switch is so efficient that it makes perfect sense to switch processes—the Transputer process switch is faster than a trap gate, which is the fastest possible 386 interrupt mechanism.

Error Handling.

If we tried to be consistent with our standard terminology, this section might be called "Trap Handling", since it discusses how conditions like overflow are handled. However, the Transputer doesn't really have traps in the conventional sense, so we will follow the INMOS terminology.

There is a status flag called *error*, which can be set by any of the following events:

- Integer overflow, signalled by ADD, SUB, MUL or DIV instructions.

- Subscript out of range, signalled by the CSUB0 (check subscript from zero) instruction.

- Message length is incorrect, signalled by the CCNT1 (check count from one) instruction.

- SETERR instruction, which unconditionally sets the error flag.

A program can handle errors in one of two ways. It can either test for the error, using the TESTERR instruction with a conditional jump, or it can issue a STOPERR instruction which causes the current process to be descheduled if the error flag is set.

An approach used in an Ada compiler for the Transputer for exception handling is to have the Ada process issue a STOPERR instruction to raise an exception. A run-time monitoring process wakes up every millisecond and checks to see if the Ada process has stopped as a result of an exception.

TRANSPUTER NETWORKS

A system that is built from a single Transputer is not very interesting. What *is* interesting is an array of Transputers connected together in a way that gives a very rapid communication channel because all the communication hardware is on the chip. The four connections available for each Transputer are enough to build almost any inter-connected arrangement. If more connections are needed, then you can glue more than one Transputer together to form a single node.

Possible Network Arrangements

There are many possible arrangements for connecting processors together to form a network. The properties of the network depend on the pattern of connections, and the most desirable arrangement is partially application dependent. In this section we give some examples of possible network topologies.

TWO-DIMENSIONAL GRID. Many problems require calculations over a two-dimensional grid, where information is passed between adjacent elements of the grid. A Transputer network could model such a grid directly, by using the four connections to link to the neighboring points in the grid in both directions. Examples where this kind of arrangement is appropriate include pattern recognition (where each node is a point in a picture) and weather forecasting (where each node is a point in the mapping grid for the region being modeled).

PERFECT SHUFFLE NETWORK. In the perfect shuffle network, each node is joined to its immediate neighbors and to what its neighbors would be if the "deck" of processors were subjected to what a conjurer would call a perfect riffle shuffle.

This network topology has been studied in some detail and has some interesting theoretical characteristics. For instance, an arbitrary permutation of data among the nodes of this network can always be achieved in $\log N$ time, where N is the number of processors.

HYPERCUBE NETWORK. A hypercube is an array of processors arranged as though they were the points at the corners of an N-dimensional hypercube, and the connections are the edges of the cube. The four connections of the Transputer allow direct construction of a four-dimensional hypercube containing 16 processors. Higher-order hypercubes can be constructed by putting more than one Transputer at each node. For instance, if we connect two Transputers together at each node, there are six remaining connections, which allows the construction of an order 6 hypercube containing 64 processors.

Other Network Arrangements

As illustrated by the examples in the previous section, the Transputer functions rather like a child's construction toy, and an almost endless variety of network topologies are possible. Of course, any processors can be linked together into a network, but with processors other than the Transputer a considerable amount of additional hardware is required to control the interprocessor communication. The beauty of the Transputer is that all the necessary circuitry is contained in a single chip, so it is particularly practical and economical to construct network machines with various designs using the Transputer.

There is even a machine on the market where the connections between the Transputers can be reprogrammed by software instructions. This is perhaps the ultimately flexible network computer. A programmer first designs the hardware arrangement it wants to run on and then executes on what is essentially a custom constructed network computer.

CONCLUSION

The Transputer is a novel architecture, quite different from any other processor we have looked at. Both its instruction set and its register set are idiosyncratic, and heavily influenced by its intended use in a parallel network of linked Transputers.

This book is arranged to treat CISC architectures first, and then RISC architectures. The Transputer really doesn't fit comfortably in either category. It certainly exhibits some important RISC characteristics, notably in its extremely simple instruction format, and in that many simple instructions take a single clock. However, it has a large complicated instruction set, and lacks the large register set of RISC machines.

The Transputer is most interesting when it is used to construct networks of parallel microprocessors. It is unique among the processors we have looked at, in that the issue of processor-to-processor communications is directly addressed, both at the architecture level (with special communication instructions), and at the hardware level (where the interchip communications channels are integrated into the processor chip). Given that parallel processing is becoming more and more important, it may well be that the Transputer will play a more important role as time passes, especially if future implementations narrow the performance gap between the Transputer and typical RISC chips.

CHAPTER

14

THE FUTURE OF MICROPROCESSOR DESIGN

DEVELOPMENTS IN INSTRUCTION SET DESIGNS

There was a period in the middle and late 1970s when it appeared that instruction set designs would stabilize. The IBM 360 architecture was enormously successful, and its instruction set was copied by many other manufacturers, including Honeywell, Univac, Amdahl, Fujitsu, and NEC. It was not ususual to hear people claim that assembly language was a good approximation to writing portable code, since virtually all machines used this instruction set, and the others didn't matter.

The appearance of microprocessors in the early 1980s changed this picture almost overnight. The Intel and Motorola designs were quickly established as the architectures of choice for personal computers and workstations. It is now undoubtedly the case that there are more machines based on these architectures than there are IBM-compatible mainframes.

More recently, the introduction of RISC designs has led to an even greater proliferation of quite incompatible architectures. An important element in this that has made this proliferation of instruction set designs practical is the emergence of Unix as an important force in the marketplace. A wide range of engineering applications are written in C to run under Unix, and are easily moved from one machine to another. The users of such a program don't care which particular chip is used in their workstation—all that is important to them is performance.

RISC designs have been particularly effective in meeting the needs of high-performance Unix-based workstations. Modern VLSI design and fabrication techniques have developed to the point where designing and implementing a new RISC architecture is well within reach of quite a large number of companies.

We have examined a number of RISC architectures in this book and have discussed many important design variations, but our treatment has by no means been comprehensive. There are a number of important RISC designs that we have not covered that exhibit all sorts of interesting variations on the RISC theme.

The Motorola 88000, for example, is interesting from a commercial point of view as Motorola's entry into the RISC field—it competes with Motorola's successful 68030 CISC microprocessor. The 88000 distinguishes itself from the other microprocessors covered in this book by using only a single set of registers for both integer and floating-point values. This approach has the advantage of greater uniformity—these are *true* general-purpose registers. On the other hand, this design complicates the kind of separation of functional units that we have seen in the RIOS.

The AMD 29000 is another example of a processor whose architecture is based on the RISC philosophy. Like the SPARC, this chip implements register windows, but unlike the SPARC, the size of a register window can change—instructions similar to the SPARC's SAVE and RESTORE specify the size of the window. This means that procedures using only a small number of registers use fewer registers in the register file. The result is that less time is spent on register saves and restores at the expense of greater complexity in accessing registers. Another interesting feature of this chip is that load and store instructions can only reference 4-byte words—there are no partial word loads or stores. This is more faithful to the pure RISC philosophy of keeping memory accesses simple, but it does result in more complex code for partial word accesses.

There are many other examples of interesting RISC processors, and it is likely that more designs will appear. The factors contributing to diversity in instruction set design will continue to favor experimentation in architectures—less code will be written in assembly language, so making use of these new architectures will be easier and easier.

THE CISC CHIPS FIGHT BACK

The main criticism leveled against CISC processors such as the 80386 and the 68030 is that they are too slow and that this poor performance is an inevitable consequence of their complex instruction sets.

Certainly no one can contest that the currently available RISC chips can run circles around these CISC chips in many common uses. It may be possible to construct benchmarks that take direct advantage of the fancy instructions on the CISC chips and narrow or even close the performance gap, but for a wide range of general applications, the RISC chips seem to have a clear advantage.

In the RIOS chapter we noted that it is often misleading to compare the performance of a newly released product with the performance of an established product that was released considerably earlier. In comparing the latest MIPS and SPARC chips with the 386, we are doing exactly that, since the 386 has been available for a considerable length of time.

As this book is going to press, both Intel and Motorola have announced successor chips to the 386 and the 68030— the 486 and the 68040, respectively. The 486 began to appear in products in the fall of 1989, and as we write this book, full technical details of the 486 have just been made available. Chapters 2 through 4 could have been written using the 486 rather than the 386, but we chose not to for two reasons:

- First, since the 386 and the 486 are essentially identical insofar as the instruction set and general architecture are concerned, the great majority of material would have remained unchanged.

- Second, presenting the 486 as a representative CISC architecture would have been confusing, because the 486 differs from the 386 precisely in that it uses a number of RISC design techniques to improve performance.

From a programmer's point of view, the main differences between the 386 and the 486 are the difference in instruction timings and the inclusion of floating-point instructions on the processor chip. There are a few additional instructions, including a byte swap instruction (for conversion between little-endian and big-endian formats) and a few synchronization instructions that Microsoft felt would be helpful in the implementation of the OS/2 operating system,[1] but these additions are rather minor.

The instruction timings of the 486 are interesting. All MOV instructions between general registers and memory are listed as taking 1 clock in the case where the data is in the cache. As we know from our study of RISC architectures, this kind of performance can be achieved only if pipelining techniques are used—it is clear that the 80486 is extensively pipelined.

An implicit part of the RISC design philosophy is the assumption that it is impractical to pipeline instruction sets unless they have clean and simple instruction formats. No one pretends that the implementation of a pipelined architecture on a machine with an instruction set as complex as the 386 or the 486 is simple; indeed, the designers of the 486 noted at a recent conference that the effort had been difficult. What is important is that the successful production of the 486 shows that this pipelining *can* be achieved.

The results of this effort are not perfect. Most register-to-register operations take 1 clock as is usual in RISC style, but there are certain peculiar exceptions. For example, register shifts take 2 clocks. Another area in which the 486 falls short of RISC performance expectations is that jumps and calls take 3 clocks. If the instruction set of

---

[1] It is hard to believe that these synchronization instructions could have a significant effect. Including these instructions is probably another instance of the CISC disease of providing special purpose instructions without convincing evidence that their use will significantly improve overall performance.

the 386 were being designed from scratch, it would be quite reasonable to implement jumps with delay slots so that these delays would be eliminated. However, market practicalities militate against any changes in the instruction set, since the important advantage of the 486 as compared with other RISC chips is precisely that it can execute existing 386 object code.

There are many other instructions that take more than 1 clock. For example, the instruction

```
ADD     MEM, 3
```

takes 3 clocks. However, it wouldn't be fair to complain that this instruction takes more than 1 clock, since a RISC processor following the principle of only allowing loads and stores to reference memory would also take three clocks for this operation and would also require three instructions, increasing the code size. There are a number of other cases where complex 486 instructions take several clocks but are still as fast as or faster than the corresponding sequence of RISC instructions.

An interesting consequence of the requirement for executing existing code is seen in the aggressive nature of the pipelining. Consider the following instruction sequence

```
MOV     EAX, MEM
ADD     EAX, EBX
```

Normally, we would expect the immediate use of a loaded value to involve a delay, even if the MOV resulted in a cache hit. This delay, which is typically 1 clock, is not particularly disturbing in a RISC design, because we certainly expect the compiler to eliminate most of these through instruction scheduling. However, on the 486, there is *no* pipeline delay for this sequence, which implies a rather complex implementation of forwarding.

Why would the 486 go to the trouble of eliminating delays of this nature? There are two reasons. First, the 486 is very short of registers by RISC standards. This means that instruction scheduling is less effective, since it is not so easy to keep values in registers. Second, and more important, it is inevitable that the 486 machines that are sold will spend most of their time executing existing 386 code that is *not* scheduled with pipelining in mind—we cannot expect manufacturers to rewrite all their code for the 486, and even if they do, there will be lots of users with old 386 code on their machines who are not about to go out and purchase updated versions.

There are still some cases where the pipelining cannot eliminate dependencies between instructions. For example, in the sequence:

```
MOV     EBX, MEM1
MOV     EAX, MEM2 [EBX]
```

there is a 1-clock delay resulting from using EBX in the addressing of the subsequent instruction. This is not surprising; the pipeline needs the address for a load pretty early so that the memory reference can be initiated. A compiler generating code specifically for the 486 will therefore still need to include instruction scheduling to eliminate such delays to achieve maximum performance.

The performance of the 486 approaches that of competitive RISC chips without any sacrifice in the complexity of the instruction set. The floating-point performance is also competitive with that of low-end RISC machines. The technical details of the 68040 design are not yet available, but from preliminary press releases, it seems likely that Motorola has achieved a similar result in improving the performance of the 68030 instruction set.

Once again, we are making the potentially misleading mistake of comparing brand new products with established ones, and it is quite likely that the latest RISC chips, including the RIOS and new MIPS and SPARC chips will once again chalk up a clear performance win against the 486 and the 68040. However, no one is standing still—Intel is hard at work on the 80586, and we can expect that this chip will again achieve significant performance gains.[2]

CISC VS RISC

The theme of CISC versus RISC has been a continuing one in our discussions of various representative microprocessors from the two design camps. It seems appropriate to end this book by trying to address the question of which approach is superior in light of these discussions.

The problem is that it has become increasingly difficult to agree on the exact definitions of RISC and CISC. The popular press and Wall Street seem quite convinced that there is a clear distinction. A recent article on the front page of PC Week carried the headline "Olivetti Announces 80486 Server with Socket for RISC Chip." We had to read nearly the whole article before we found a little note near the end that the RISC chip involved is the Intel i860. It is clear that the author of this article, like many other observers, considers the fact that the socket holds a RISC chip to be more important than the particular chip involved. RISC is used here as a kind of code word for "high performance microprocessor."

What is a RISC chip really? In Chapter 8, we listed a number of characteristics and warned that such a list must be suspect. The distinction between the two is becoming more and more clouded. On the one hand, the 486 and 68040 show how RISC design techniques can be employed in efficient implementations of CISC architectures. Are the resulting chips to be considered CISC or RISC? The answer is unclear—they certainly embody some of the important characteristics of RISC design.

On the other hand, the most elaborate of the RISC chips, such as the Intel i860 and the IBM RIOS, exhibit rather complex instruction sets that we normally associate with CISC designs. In the case of the RIOS, we see no trace of explicit parallelism, a characteristic that seemed to clearly distinguish RISC chips from CISC chips. In the case of the RIOS, even the delay slots after jumps have disappeared.

We can imagine an architecture that would be even more ambiguous. Suppose we designed an instruction set very similar to the 386 except that the instructions were

---

[2] Bill Gates has claimed that the 586 will perform at a level significantly better than one clock per instruction, implying a RIOS-like commitment to multiple-instruction units.

more uniform, there were lots of registers, and there were delay slots after the jumps and calls. This would be an easier processor to implement than the 486. It would have all the RISC characteristics listed in Chapter 8 but still have the complex instruction set of a CISC machine. Would this chip be more accurately described as being a RISC chip or a CISC chip? The question would not be very meaningful when applied to an architecture like this.

In short, Wall Street and the publicity departments of major manufacturers may feel that the distinction is clear, but we aren't so sure. Rather than thinking of RISC as a clearly defined characteristic of microprocessors, it is better to think of RISC as being a term for a collection of design techniques used to improve performance.

There are some important lessons to be learned from the devlopment of these RISC techniques. In particular, it seems clear that a large register set is desirable in any instruction set. It is also clear that instruction sets should be designed in as uniform a manner as possible—previous concerns with code size and consequent attempts to make instruction sequences as compact as possible are no longer important. We can also probably agree that the excess complexity of the addressing modes as implemented on the 68030 may well not be justified.

These lessons will almost certainly be incorporated in any future instruction set designs. Furthermore, RISC implementation techniques, such as pipelining, forwarding, and register renaming, are likely to appear in any implementations of these architectures. The sharp distinction that exists in the minds of many observers in the computer field between CISC and RISC is rather artificial now and will seem more so as time progresses. In retrospect, we believe that RISC as an issue will disappear and will be seen historically as referring to the development of a collection of useful design and implementation techniques that are commonly accepted.

GLOSSARY

Activation record. See *Stack frame.*

Activation stack. A term sometimes used for the stack associated with a task in a block-structured environment because it contains the *activation records*, or *stack frames*, of the task.

Ada. A recently designed programming language whose development was sponsored by the U.S. Department of Defense. Ada features real-time facilities, including tasking, extensive run-time checking, and separate compilation facilities.

Address arithmetic. In computing addresses of array elements and other components of complex objects, arithmetic must be performed on addresses. This address arithmetic differs from normal integer arithmetic in that signed overflow is not significant.

ALU. Arithmetic and Logic Unit. The section of logic in a processor that implements the standard arithmetic and logical functions.

Annul bit. A single bit in the branch instructions of the SPARC that signals that an instruction in the delay slot after a branch should be annulled. It can be viewed as an optimization that allows the branch delay slot to be more easily filled.

ASCII. American Standard Code for Information Interchange. A standard for the representation of data. It is best known for its definition of how characters are mapped into integers so that they can be represented in computer systems. ASCII is the U.S. version of the international ISO code.

Associative memory. A memory in which an entry is located by its contents rather than by its address. Associative memories are often used for TLB access. In a fully associative cache, a given address can be assigned to any cache line.

Asynchronous. Events that happen at random or at not exactly predictable times with respect to one another. For example, hardware interrupts are asynchronous, since they can occur at any point in time, regardless of what instruction has just been executed.

Base register. A register that points to a block of contiguous storage. Based addressing uses this base register to refer to a particular location in this block.

Basic programming model. The Intel phrase for an application programmer's view of a microprocessor. Motorola uses the term *user programming model.*

Big-endian. Microprocessors differ in whether multibyte quantities are stored least significant byte (LSB) first, or most significant byte (MSB) first. *Big-endian* refers to the scheme where the MSB is always stored first. Similarly, for bit ordering, big-endian refers to the scheme where the leftmost, or most significant, bit of a word is numbered bit zero.

Breakpoint. A trap intended to be used for debugging purposes. Some processors have a unique trap instruction for this purpose.

Brown model. A model of floating-point arithmetic based on the notion of a well-defined subset of model intervals that can be represented exactly. See also *Model number.*

Burst mode. A mode that allows a sequence of words to be obtained from memory without releasing the bus. It increases throughput at the expense of locking up the bus for a longer period.

Byte. An 8-bit unit of data. In all microprocessors, memory is byte-addressed, which means that each byte has a unique address.

C. A relatively low-level language intended for systems programming as well as general-purpose use. It is associated with the Unix operating system, which is written entirely in C.

Cache. A small, but particularly fast, type of memory which holds a duplicate copy of the contents of the most frequently used memory addresses. Some microprocessors contain a separate data cache (used only to hold data) and instruction cache (used to hold the most frequently executed instructions).

Cache line. An indivisible unit of data stored in a cache. The size of the cache line affects performance and is one of the important design parameters of a cache. Cache line sizes of processors discussed in this book range from 4 to 128 bytes.

Channel. A path of communication. In the Transputer, a channel is a hardware entity used for communicating between two processors, either on the same Transputer or across the links that join Transputers.

CISC. Complex Instruction Set Computer. The term CISC is most commonly used to contrast a computer architecture with the RISC philosophy. It is sometimes used in a derogatory manner by RISC advocates.

Clock. A unit of time by which a processor is driven, typically 16 to 40 MHz. Processor speed is characterized by the number of clocks, also called cycles, taken by each instruction. One stated goal of RISC processors is to reduce the instruction throughput to 1 clock per instruction.

CMOS. Complementary Metal Oxide Semiconductor. A technology used for building chips whose main characteristic is their low power consumption.

Context switch. The sequence of steps required to swap the *machine state* in order to switch from one task to another.

Coprocessor. An accessory chip, with some specialized supporting function, that is connected to the main microprocessor in an implementation of a computer system. Coprocessors are most commonly floating-point processors.

CRC. Cyclic Redundancy Check. A checksum generated by using binary polynomial arithmetic that provides effective error detection and error correction for transmitted messages.

Cycle. See *Clock*.

Data bus. The set of paths on a computer system by which a processor communicates with memory and other system components such as input/output devices.

Data cache. See *Cache*.

Delayed branch. A common technique on RISC processors, first proposed by John Cocke for the IBM 801, in which a jump is not immediately effective, but instead one additional instruction following the jump is executed before the jump takes place.

Delay slot. A position within a sequence of executable instructions on a RISC processor to which an instruction can be moved to improve the execution of the program. The fact that performance is improved by moving an instruction into a delay slot is a consequence of pipelining.

Denormal. In the IEEE floating-point standard, a number that is smaller than the smallest normalized number. See also *Gradual underflow*.

Descriptor. A general term used to refer to a data structure that describes characteristics of a data object elsewhere in memory. Typically a descriptor is a small record with fixed fields containing the required information. Descriptors are used both by the hardware (for example, in describing memory segments on the 386) and by software (for example, in describing the allocation of a dynamic array).

Direct addressing. Addressing a specific location anywhere in memory without using index or base registers. On CISC machines, it is usually possible to specify direct addressing in a single instruction, whereas RISC processors require a sequence of two instructions because the necessary 32-bit address cannot fit in a 32-bit instruction.

Directly addressed cache. A cache in which a given address can be assigned to only one possible cache line, so the lookup is greatly simplified.

Dirty bit. A bit in a page table that indicates whether or not a page has been modified. This bit is inspected by the operating system to decide whether or not a page needs to be written back to the disk (untouched pages are not written back, since the image of the page in memory is the same as that on the disk).

Dual instruction mode. A mode on the i860 that allows the processor to execute two instructions at a time in parallel. See also *VLIW*.

Dual operation mode. On the i860, the mode in which the processor operates that allows a floating-point multiply and add to be issued at the same time. The RIOS has a similar facility, but IBM does not use this term.

EBCDIC. A code for the representation of characters, used by IBM instead of ASCII.

ECC. Error Correcting Code. A checksum that allows errors to be corrected as well as detected. It not only indicates that there is an error, but also determines which bit is in error. A common application is in building memory units that automatically correct single-bit errors.

ECL. Emitter Coupled Logic. A technology for chip construction that promises considerable speed improvements over current CMOS technology. ECL versions of microprocessors are just starting to be commercially viable.

Exception. A condition that causes the current flow of execution to be temporarily suspended and control passed to an exception routine. Exceptions are divided into asynchronous interrupts (typically from hardware devices) and synchronous traps caused by individual instructions, such as divide by zero or a page fault.

Exponent. One of two components of a floating-point number. The *fraction*, or *mantissa*, is the magnitude of the value. The *exponent* is a power of 2, or some other base (also called the radix), by which the fraction must be multiplied to obtain the complete value of the floating-point number.

FORTRAN. An acronym for FORmula TRANslator. One of the earliest high-level languages, FORTRAN emphasizes facilities for scientific computation, including efficient processing of multidimensional arrays.

Fraction. See *Exponent*.

Frame pointer. A pointer to a specific location in a stack frame that is used as a base by which objects in the stack frame can be addressed. Microprocessors such as the 386 have specialized registers whose intended use is as a frame pointer, while most others use some software convention to specify a particular register for this use.

GaAs. Gallium Arsenide. A metallic compound used in a new technology for producing faster chips. GaAs is potentially much faster than CMOS or ECL, but fabrication problems have so far prevented its use in microprocessor chips.

Gate array. A chip in which the gates are in place, but the wires joining them are not. A particular customization of a gate array is achieved by providing the required wires.

GDT. Global Descriptor Table. A special data structure used on the 386, stored in memory and supported by the hardware, that supports the segmentation mechanism of the 386. The GDT is composed of descriptors, each of which contains information that describes such characteristics of a segment as its location, size, and protection level.

Gradual underflow. The approach that, in the IEEE floating-point standard, requires that if the result of a floating-point operation is smaller than the smallest normalized number, the result can be a small denormal rather than zero. Gradual underflow is required by the IEEE floating-point standard.

Guard bit. In floating-point operations, an extra bit retained at the low-order end of intermediate results to improve the precision of the final result.

IEEE standard. The IEEE floating-point standard, more formally known as IEEE/ANSI Standard 754/1985. This standard specifies standard formats for representation of floating-point values as well as the exact results of floating-point operations using these formats.

Immediate addressing. An addressing mode that allows the fixed constant operand of an instruction to appear as one of the fields of the instruction itself, rather than being fetched from a designated register or memory location.

Index register. A register used to hold the offset of an array element. Indexed addressing specifies an index register to access the element and thus corresponds to subscripting in high-level languages.

Indirect addressing mode. A mode in which the address specifies not the data

to be addressed, but the location of a pointer that references the required data.

Instruction cache. See *Cache.*

Instruction format. A small record with fields designating the operation code and its operands. Typical microprocessors have several different possible instruction formats, depending on the number and type of operands required.

Instruction lookahead. A method of fetching future instructions so that after one instruction has been executed the CPU does not have to execute a fetch to memory for the next instruction. The lookahead unit may need to be flushed when a jump is executed because the instructions in the lookahead unit are no longer valid.

Instruction pointer. A register that points to the next instruction to be executed. This is also called a *program counter* on some processors.

Interrupt. An asynchronous interruption of an executing program, typically caused by an external event such as an input/output operation completing. See also *Exception.*

Inverted page table. On the IBM RISC chips, a page table used to record virtual to physical page mapping. Unlike the normal page tables used on other processors, the inverted page table is indexed by physical, rather than virtual, addresses.

ISO. International Standards Organization. An organization responsible for the generation of a series of standards covering all aspects of computing, as well as other fields. In particular, the ISO code for information interchange, often referred to simply as ISO, is the international version of ASCII.

IU. Integer Unit. A generic term used to refer to the part of a RISC processor that contains the standard integer arithmetic and logic functions. Also explicitly used by some manufacturers in their technical documentation (e.g., Sun). See also *ALU*.

Kernel. The central part of an operating system that controls the processor. Application processes must make requests to the kernel through well-defined interfaces for "system services." In operating systems that are layered, the kernel is the inner layer and typically controls functions such as process management and memory allocation.

LDT. Local Descriptor Table. On the 386, segments can be either global to all tasks or local to a specific task. The LDT is used to describe the local segments. Its structure is similar to that of the GDT.

Linker. A system software component used to combine the output of modules that have been separately compiled or assembled into a single program. It typically has facilities for resolving external references and relocating operands whose final address depends on knowing the complete layout of a program.

Little-endian. Microprocessors differ in whether multibyte quantities are stored LSB first or MSB first. Little-endian refers to the scheme where the LSB is always stored first. Similarly, for bit ordering, little-endian refers to the scheme

where the rightmost or least significant bit of a word is numbered as zero.

Local variable. An object allocated each time a procedure is called. Local variables are usually stored in the stack frame of a procedure when it is called.

Leaf procedure. A procedure that has no calls to other procedures. Leaf procedures can be treated specially since the registers they use cannot be used by the other procedures they call.

Loop unrolling. An optimization in which the body of a loop is repeated two or more times, thus reducing the number of tests and branches that need to be executed, but at the cost of expanding the code size.

LSB. An acronym for the least significant byte of a multibyte quantity. In the context of bit addressing, LSB may also stand for Least Significant Bit. See also *Little-endian*.

Machine state. The set of register values and other processor state information associated with the currently running task.

Mantissa. See *Exponent*.

MFLOPS. Millions of FLoating point Operations Per Second. A common measure of floating-point performance. Typical microprocessors have performances in the range of 1 to 50 MFLOPS. Large supercomputers can achieve rates up to the gigaflop range).

Microcode. A technique used for implementing complex instructions by providing a small on-chip program that simulates the effect of the instruction using other simpler instructions. Microcode is a cheap, but relatively inefficient, method of implementing operations whose cost would be prohibitive in direct logic.

MIPS. A commonly used acronym for Million Instructions Per Second, a metric used to evaluate processor performance. MIPS also refers to the RISC chip based on the Stanford MIPS chip that is produced by MIPS Computer Systems, Inc. MIPS in this usage originally stood for Multiprocessor without Interlocking Pipeline Stages, but is now simply the name of the company.

MMU. Memory Management Unit. A unit used to translate virtual addresses into physical addresses. The specific mechanism used on various microprocessors to perform this function varies widely.

Model number. In Ada, a real number that can be represented exactly by using the available hardware floating-point representation. For instance, on a binary machine, 0.5 is a model number, but 0.1 is not, since 0.1 cannot be represented exactly.

MSB. An acronym for the most significant byte of a multibyte quantity. In the context of bit addressing, MSB may also stand for Most Significant Bit. See also *Big-endian*.

Multiply step. Some RISC machines do not provide a full multiply instruction. Instead, a *multiply step* operation does the adds and shifts required for 1 or 2 bits of a multiply. A full multiply is achieved by issuing a series of multiply step operations.

NaN. Not A Number. In the IEEE floating-point standard, NaNs are used to represent indeterminate results such as the result of dividing zero by zero.

Non-local variables. In a block-structured language, such as Pascal or Ada, a variable that does not lie in the stack frame of the currently executing procedure and that cannot be addressed from the current frame pointer.

OCCAM. A programming language designed by Tony Hoare emphasizing interprocess communication. OCCAM is therefore a good match for multiprocessor systems with no shared memory, and in particular has been adopted as the standard language for the Transputer.

Packed decimal. A method for storing decimal data, in which each digit is represented by 4 bits, so that each byte holds two decimal digits.

Page fault. A trap that occurs if a reference is made to a page that either is not in memory or, in the case of some processors, is not in the translation lookaside buffer. The operating system responds by making the desired page available and restarting the failed instruction.

Paging. The division of the virtual address space into chunks called pages, which are individually mapped into physical memory. A combination of hardware and operating systems software manages this mapping.

Paragraph. On the 8086, a 16-byte chunk of memory on a 16-byte boundary. Segment addressing on the early Intel processors was paragraph-based.

Pipeline. A sequence of logic units arranged to work on different stages of an instruction simultaneously so that the instruction must be "fed through" the pipeline to be completely executed. Using this approach, several instructions can be decoded at the same time, increasing system throughput.

Pixel. Picture element; a single point in a graphics display. A pixel has X and Y coordinates, representing its position on the screen, and color information.

Plex. A (typically small) record allocated in the dynamic heap that contains pointers to other plexes. Plex processing is another term for *list processing*, in which the data structures used consist of linked trees or graphs represented by plex structures.

Position-independent code. C o d e that can be moved around during execution. Most processors provide relative branch instructions, making this possible.

Postincrement addressing. An addressing mode in which an index register is incremented after a memory reference.

Pragma. A pragma is a compiler directive. The term is most often associated with the programming language Ada.

Predecrement Addressing. An addressing mode in which an index register is decremented before a memory reference.

Prefix. An instruction prefix is a special instruction which affects the operation of the following instruction. Examples are the REP prefix of the 386, used to repeat string operations, and the PFIX and NFIX operations of the transputer, used to extend the operand of the following instruction.

Preincrement. Preincrement addressing refers to an addressing mode in which an index register is incremented before the reference.

Process. See *Task*.

Program counter. Another name for the *Instruction pointer*.

Race condition. A situation in which two events can happen asynchronously at about the same time. If one of them occurs first, everything is all right, but if the other one occurs first, then an error results. A race condition will occur, for instance, when a word is accessed just as it is being updated by another task. Race conditions must be avoided in tasking programs and operating systems.

Radix. The base used for expressing floating-point numbers. See *Exponent*.

Register allocation. The phase of a compiler that allocates registers for a user program. The standard problem encountered by a compiler doing register allocation is that not enough registers may be available as a procedure is being compiled, so that some registers may have to be *spilled* to memory.

Register coloring. A compiler technique for allocating registers that is based on the notion of graph coloring. Each variable is assigned a color. If two variables are live at the same time, they must have different colors. Registers are then assigned to unique colors.

Register renaming. A technique in which the hardware remaps busy registers to other registers so that the pipeline is not held up. See also *Scoreboard*.

Register window. A collection of registers accessed by the hardware as sets. One of the first implementations of register windows was done on the Berkeley RISC I and RISC II processors. More recently, the SPARC has also used this scheme.

RISC. Reduced Instruction Set Computer. An architectural point of view that seeks to speed the general throughput of a processor by reducing the complexity of the instruction set.

ROMP. The name for the processor used in the IBM RT-PC workstations.

Run-time stack. The area of run-time memory that is used to allocate space for, among other things, the local variables of a procedure. See *Stack frame*.

Scaling. When an *index register* is used to access an element in the array, it must be scaled by the size of the array element. Some processors provide this scaling as part of the addressing mode.

Scoreboard. A technique used in RISC machines to allow multiple instructions to operate at the same time. The scoreboard keeps track of registers that are targets for operations not yet completed, and holds up references to the contents

of these registers until the corresponding operation is complete.

Segment. A segment is a logically contiguous section of bytes of memory. In this book we usually use the term when the hardware implements segments, as in the case of the 386, where memory is divided into segments using the descriptor tables. See also *GDT*.

Set associative. A technique for organizing caches in which a given address can be assigned to any one of a small number, typically 2 or 4, of cache lines. See also *directly addressed cache* and *associative memory*.

Significand. The term is used by the IEEE floating-point standard to refer to the *mantissa* of a floating-point value.

Snoopy cache. A cache that watches memory transactions on the bus so that it can guarantee that its data is consistent with main memory.

SPARC. Scalable Processor ARChitecture. The RISC architecture defined by Sun Microsystems, Inc. that defines an extendable architecture (whose most distinguishing feature is register windows).

Spill. If a compiler runs out of registers while generating code, it must generate extra code to copy the values held in some of the registers into memory so that some registers are freed up. This is called a *register spill*, and the code that stores the register values is called *spill code*.

Stack frame. A contiguous region of memory (also known as an *activation record*) allocated on the run-time stack where the local variables for a procedure, as well as other information used for connecting various stack frames and saving registers, is stored.

Stack pointer. A pointer that points to the top of some region of memory that is being used as a stack. Some microprocessors (such as the 386 and the 68030) implement the stack pointer as a special register with special instructions to manipulate it. On other microprocessors, one of the general registers can be used as a stack pointer, but there is no hardware dedicated register.

Strength reduction. An optimization technique in which a complex operation in a loop can be replaced by a simpler one. The most common example is the replacement of a multiplication by successive additions.

Sudden underflow. Processors not providing a *gradual underflow* capability merely reset the result of a floating-point operation to zero if the result is smaller than the smallest normalized number. This is called *sudden underflow.*

Synchronous. Events that occur in strict sequence. For example, a divide by zero causes a synchronous trap on most processors—the trap occurs on the divide instruction.

Task. An executing thread of control with its own *machine state.* A tasking program is composed of a set of tasks. The term *task* and *process* are used interchangeably in this book, although Ada terminology uses the term *task.*

TCB. Task Control Block. A block of memory used to save information about the status of an executing process when it has been suspended by an operating system. The task control block includes information about the machine state as well as other information.

Thrashing. A phenomenon which occurs when an operating system is forced to spend most of its time bringing in new pages from secondary storage instead of executing a program itself. It usually occurs when the amount of physical storage is insuffient to handle the *working set* of one or several executing programs.

TLB. Translation Lookaside Buffer. A cache which is specially designed for use in a paging mechanism. When a virtual address is translated into a physical address, the TLB is consulted to see if it contains the translation. If not, the paging tables in memory must be consulted.

Trace. For debugging purposes, it is often desirable to trace the execution of the program by following the instructions one by one at the machine level. Several processors contain hardware support for assisting in this process by generating a trap after each instruction.

Trap. An error condition such as divide by zero which causes the flow of procesing to be interrupted. See also *Exception.*

Two's complement. A representation for integers that is commonly used by most hardware. It is essentially equivalent to unsigned arithmetic, except that bit patterns starting with a one bit are interpreted as negative.

VHLL. Very High Level Language. Although many definitions are possible,

semantic level which is much higher than that of typical hardware.

Virtual address. An address that is generated by a processor and is then modified to a different physical address in a manner that is dependent upon whether a segmentation or paging mechanism is present on the processor. This translation is performed by an *MMU.*

Virtual segmentation. A hardware technique in which segments can either reside in memory or be copied off to the disk. Segments can be managed similarly to pages and swapped in as needed.

VLIW. Very Long Instruction Word. An architectural design approach in

the same time and executed in parallel.

Wait states. Wasted cycles inserted by some memory units when a memory cannot respond to a memory request by a processor.

Working set. The set of pages which are in active use by a task in a virtual memory system.

Workspace. On the Transputer, the term used to refer to the stack of a process. The *workspace register* points to the current stack frame in this stack.

Write allocate cache. A cache in which store-to-memory operations also write

there.

Write through. A cache in which all writes to the cache are also immediately written to main memory, helping to ensure that main memory is consistent at all times with the cache contents.

BIBLIOGRAPHY

American National Standards Institute, *American National Standard Programming Language COBOL* X3.23, American National Standards Institute, 1985.

American National Standards Institute, *American National Standard Programming Language FORTRAN* X3.9, American National Standards Insitute, 1977.

Auslander, M., and Hopkins, M. E., "An Overview of the PL.8 Compiler," *Proceedings of the SIGPLAN '82 Symposium on Compiler Construction*, Boston, MA, June 23–25, 1982.

Bell, C. G., "RISC: Back to the Future?," *Datamation*, June 1, 1986, pp. 96-108.

Bakoglu, H. B., et. al., "IBM Second Generation RISC Organization," *Proceedings of the International Conference on Computer Design*, Cambridge, MA, 1989.

Chaitin, G. J., "Register Allocation and Spilling via Graph Coloring," *Proceedings of the SIGPLAN '82 Symposium on Compiler Construction*, SIGPLAN Notices, Vol. 17, No. 6, June 1982, pp. 98–105.

Chow, F., and Hennessy, J., "Register Allocation by Priority-Based Coloring," *Proceedings of the SIGPLAN '84 Symposium on Compiler Construction*, SIGPLAN Notices, Vol. 19, No. 6, June 1984, pp. 95–105.

Chow, F., Himelstein, M., Weber, L., "Engineering a RISC Compiler System," Proceedings, COMPCON, Spring 1986, March 1986.

Clark, D. W., and Strecker, W. D., "Comments on the Case for the Reduced Instruction Set Computer," *Computer Architecture News*, August 1980, pp. 34–38.

El-Ayat, K. A., and Agarwal, R. K., "The Intel 80386—Architecture and Implementation," *IEEE Micro*, December 1985, pp. 4–22.

Groves, R. D., and Oehler, R., "An IBM Second Generation RISC Architecture," *Proceedings of the International Conference on Computer Design*, Spring 1989.

Hennessy, J., Jouppi, N., Przybylski, S., Rowen, C., Gross, T., Baskett, F., and Gill, J., "MIPS: A Microprocessor Architecture," *Proceedings of the Sigma Micro 15th Annual Microprogramming Workshop*, 1982.

Hennessy, J. L., "VLSI Processor Architecture," *IEEE Transactions on Computers*, Vol. C-33, No. 12, 1984, pp. 1221–1246.

Institute of Electrical and Electronic Engineers, "IEEE Standard for Floating-Point Arithmetic," ANSI/IEEE Standard 754–1985, IEEE Inc., 1985.

Intel, *80386 Programmer's Reference Manual,* Intel Corporation, Santa Clara, CA, 1988.

Intel, *i860 64-Bit Microprocessor Programmer's Reference Manual,* Intel Corporation, Santa Clara, CA, 1989.

Jensen, K., and Wirth, N., *Pascal User Manual and Report,* 3rd ed., revised by Mickel, A. B., and Miner, J.F., Springer-Verlag, 1985.

Kane, G., *MIPS R2000 RISC Architecture*, Prentice-Hall, Englewood Cliffs, NJ, 1987.

Katevenis, M., *Reduced Instruction Set Computers for VLSI*, MIT Press, 1985.

Kernighan, B. W., and Ritchie, D. M., *The C Programming Language*, Prentice-Hall, 1978.

Markoff, J., "RISC Chips," BYTE, November 1984.

Motorola, *Enhanced 32-Bit Microprocessor User's Manual* (2nd ed.), Prentice-Hall, Englewood Cliffs, NJ, 1989.

Neff, L. "Clipper Microprocessor Architecture," *Proceedings, COMPCON*, Spring 1986, March 1986.

Patterson, D. A., and Ditzel, D. R., "The Case for the Reduced Instruction Set Computer," *Computer Architecture News*, Vol. 8, No. 6, 1980, pp. 25–33.

Patterson, D. A., and Piepho, R. S., "Assessing RISCs in High-Level Language Support," *IEEE Micro*, November 1982, pp. 9–18.

Patterson, D. A., "RISC Watch," *Computer Architecture News*, March 1984.

Patterson, D. A., and Sequin, C. H., "RISC-I: A Reduced Instruction Set Computer," *Proceedings of the Eighth Annual Symposium on Computer Architectures*, May 1981, pp. 443–458.

Patterson, D. A., and Sequin. C. H., "A VLSI RISC," *Computer*, Vol. 15, No. 9, 1982, pp. 8–21.

Patterson, D. A., "Reduced Instruction Set Computers," *Communications of the ACM*, Vol. 28, No. 1, 1985.

Radin, G., "The 801 Minicomputer," *Proceedings of the Symposium on Architectural Support for Programming Languages and Operating Systems*, March 1982, pp. 39–47.

United States Department of Defense, *Reference Manual for the Ada Programming Language,* United States Department of Defense, 1983.

Yuval, T., and Sequin, C. H., "Strategies for Managing the Register File in RISC," IEEE Transactions on Computers, Vol. C-32, No. 11, 1983, pp. 977–989.

Wulf, W. A., "Compilers and Computer Architecture," *Computer*, Vol. 14, No. 7, 1981, pp. 41–47.

INDEX